MW01127532

From Texts to Text

Mastering Academic Discourse

George H. Jensen
Southwest Missouri State University

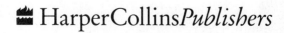

HarperCollins*Publishers*

Sponsoring Editor: Constance Rajala/Patricia Rossi
Development Editor: Marisa L'Heureux
Art Direction: Jaye Zimet
Text Design: Merlin Communications, Inc.
Cover Design: Jaye Zimet
Cover Illustration: *L'Arlesienne: Madame Joseph-Michel Ginoux*—Vincent Van Gogh
  The Metropolitan Museum of Art, Bequest of Sam A. Lewisohn, 1951. (51.112.3)
Production Administrator: Beth Maglione
Compositor: BookMasters, Inc.
Printer and Binder: R. R. Donnelley & Sons Company
Cover Printer: New England Book Components, Inc.

From Texts to Text: Mastering Academic Discourse

Copyright © 1991 by George H. Jensen

All rights reserved. Printed in the United States of America. No part of this book may
be used or reproduced in any manner whatsoever without written permission, except in
the case of brief quotations embodied in critical articles and reviews. For information
address HarperCollins Publishers Inc., 10 East 53rd Street, New York, NY 10022.

Library of Congress Cataloging-in-Publication Data

Jensen, George H.
    From texts to text / George H. Jensen.
      p.   cm.
    Includes index.
    ISBN 0-673-38563-9 (Student Edition)—ISBN 0-673-53580-0 (Teacher Edition)
    1. College readers.   2. English language—Rhetoric.   I. Title.
PE1417.J46   1991
808'.0427—dc20   90-47240
                                                                 CIP

90 91 92 93 9 8 7 6 5 4   3 2 1

To Louise Jensen

During the Great Depression, her mother and father made sacrifices to send her and her sister to college. Her family did not eat well and she had to borrow textbooks from her classmates, but she finished her degree. She then raised two sons by herself on her teacher's salary, working two jobs, earning a master's in educational counseling, and making sacrifices to send the next generation of her family to college. In her last years as a counselor in junior high school, she saved money to send her grandchildren to college. This textbook is part of her legacy.

Contents

Preface ix

Preview 1
  "A Writing Lesson," Claude Lévi-Strauss 2

Chapter 1 Anthropology: Culture and Power 15
  Studying Culture Through Texts 15
  "The Human Scapegoat in Ancient Greece," Sir James George Frazer 16
  The Difficulties and Rewards of Fieldwork 22
  "Doing Fieldwork Among the Yąnomamö," Napoleon A. Chagnon 24
  Understanding Rituals 36
  "The Growth and Initiation of an Arapesh Boy," Margaret Mead 38
  Interpreting Dreams 53
  "Dark Dreams About the White Man," Thomas Gregor 53
  Fieldwork as the Interaction of Cultures 63
  "Women and Men," Marjorie Shostak 64
  "Men and Women," Nisa's Text 72
  Synthesis 86

Chapter 2 Science: The Quest for Objectivity 87
  From Myth to Reason 88
  "The Origin of Science," Karl Popper 89
  The Move Toward Experimentation 94
  "Aphorisms Concerning the Interpretation of Nature
    and the Kingdom of Man," Francis Bacon 95
  Experimentation Gone Awry 107
  "Samuel George Morton—Empiricist of Polygeny,"
    Stephen Jay Gould 108
  Science and Myth 130
  "Some Biomythology," Lewis Thomas 131
  Science and Gender 137
  "A World of Difference," Evelyn Fox Keller 138
  Synthesis 155

Chapter 3 Psychology: Developing the Talking Cure   157
  The Origin of the Talking Cure   158
    "The Case of Anna O.," Peter Gay   159
  Freud and the Case Study   168
    "Katharina ———," Sigmund Freud   169
  The Talking Cure and Hypnosis   180
    "Ann," Milton H. Erickson   182
  The Talking Cure and Logic   187
    "Martha," Albert Ellis   189
  The Talking Cure and Communication   201
    "Patterns of Communication," Virginia Satir   202
  Synthesis   217

Chapter 4 Rhetoric and Philosophy: The Ethics of Persuasion   219
  Classical Rhetoric and Ethics   219
    Excerpt from *Gorgias*, Plato   221
  A Critique of Advertising   231
    "The Psycho-Seduction of Children," Vance Packard   232
  An Apology for Advertising   241
    "The Social and Economic Context of Advertising," John Hobson   242
  Propaganda and Ethics   255
    "War Propaganda," Adolf Hitler   255
  Synthesis   273

Chapter 5 Criticism: Literature and Its Context   283
  Tragedy and Society   284
    Medea, Euripides   285
  Tragedy: Ancient and Modern   318
    Excerpt from *Poetics*, Aristotle   319
  Fiction and Community   327
    "The Abortion," Alice Walker   328
  Poetry and Politics   338
    "To Whom It May Concern," Sipho Sepamla   343
    "The Ballot and the Bullet," Chris van Wyk   348
    "*Kodwa Nkosana* . . . (And Yet, Master . . .), M. T. Mazibuko   348
    "Small Passing," Ingrid de Kok   349
    "Exit Visa," Arthur Nortje   351
    "Steve Biko's Anthem," Mazisi Kunene   353
    "The Tyrant," Mazisi Kunene   354
    "Cowardice," Mazisi Kunene   354
    "The Body Is a Country of Joy and of Pain," Douglas Reid Skinner   355
  Synthesis

Chapter 6 History: Facts and Narration   361
  The Writing of History   362
    "History by the Ounce," Barbara Tuchman   364

Contents

Learning from History 375
  Excerpt from *Giving Up the Gun*, Noel Perrin 379
  Excerpt from *Hagakure: The Book of the Samurai*, Yamamoto Tsunetomo 384
  Excerpts from "The Fire Book," Miyamoto Musashi 390
  "The Japanese at War," Ruth Benedict 394
  "Technology, War, and Government," Arnold J. Toynbee 407
Another Look at the Fact 416
  " 'Fictio,' or the Purposes of Historical Statements," John Lukacs 417
Synthesis

Appendix A: Reading Like a Writer 423
  Rereading in Order to Write 423
  Writing Responses to Texts 424
  Writing Summaries and Isolating Facts 427
  Arguing with Texts 430
  Empathizing with Texts 435
  Reading from a Perspective 437
  Switching Perspectives 439

Appendix B: Exploring Your Writing Process 443
  Exploring Your Writing Process 443
  Victor: The Active Writer 444
  Darel: The Reflective Writer 447
  Sean: The Factual Writer 449
  Scott: The Abstract Writer 452
  Mitzie: The Objective Writer 454
  Maria: The Personal Writer 457
  Douna: The Focused Writer 460
  Monique: The Inclusive Writer 462

Appendix C: Exploring Texts 467
  Four Approaches to Writing Narratives 467
  Gender Differences 473

Appendix D: Working with Quotations 479

Appendix E: Reading Like an Editor 483
  Editing Techniques 483
  Editing Sentences 484
  Editing for Clarity 486
  Editing for Formality 487
  Editing for Punctuation 489
  Editing for Agreement 492

Index 495

Preface

When I began to write *From Texts to Text*, I knew that I did not want to produce the kind of textbook that leads both instructor and student down a clearly marked and predictable path. I wanted instead to create a textbook, an intellectual landscape, that could be explored from several directions. This is not to say that I did not have clear goals in mind.

I wanted to leave the readings in this textbook open to shaping and reshaping by students and instructor, yet I also wanted to present an organic whole. The first part of *From Texts to Text* is divided into six chapters that can be covered in any order. Although most instructors will begin with the Preview section, which explains the organization and apparatus of the text, they alternatively could move through the six chapters of readings in any order. Each chapter acts as a self-contained unit, drawing readings from a specific discipline, such as anthropology, psychology, literature, or history. The readings within each chapter also move historically through the development of a theme important to that discipline and a form of epistemology characteristic of that discipline. For example, the anthropology chapter, which focuses on the theme of culture and power, begins with a reading by Sir George Frazer, an armchair anthropologist who did not understand the power relations implicit in his secondhand data. The chapter then moves into the work of ethnographers such as Napoleon Chagnon, who discusses the difficulties of doing fieldwork and the rewards of understanding a culture—its power relations as well as its rituals and myths—by living it.

The appendixes at the end of the textbook—"handouts" on reading skills, writing processes, analyzing texts, using quotations, and editing that can be used to generate class discussion—are also designed to allow the instructor and the student more flexibility. Although the "handouts" follow a general movement from reading to writing to revising to editing, they can be used in any order or sequence that will fit the needs of distinct classes or individual students.

I wanted challenging readings, yet I also wanted to provide the kind of apparatus that makes students feel that interpretations are within

their reach. In *From Texts to Text*, students will encounter the works of Aristotle, Freud, Lévi-Strauss, Mead, Keller, Gould, and others. These texts will bear serious reading and rereading, and the apparatus and writing assignments encourage and reward repeated encounters with each text.

Before they read, students are provided with background on the author and a discussion of the context of the reading. They also work through a prereading activity that helps them develop an advanced organizer. Once they have finished a first reading, students write a response, an initial opportunity to construct an interpretation as they explore their thoughts in writing. With their instructor, students work through questions that help them further refine their initial interpretations and understand the rhetorical structure of the readings. Even with this support, students will, no doubt, find the readings challenging, but they will also find them to be rich sources from which to write.

With related texts, I wanted to illustrate the intertextuality of academic writing, while also acknowledging that the self is an important source of knowing. The chapters are organized by themes; for example, the anthropology chapter deals with the theme of culture and power. Students build knowledge on that theme as they work through the chapter, as they better understand how writers draw upon the texts that they have read to write texts and how readers draw upon texts to interpret texts. In addition, excerpts from texts are sometimes used in the prereading activity to provide needed background for the reading or as part of interpretation questions to provide direct commentary on the reading.

In the writing assignments, students are encouraged to draw from what they have read to construct their own text, but they are also frequently asked to draw from personal experience, to write texts from the self that transform the self. For example, in the psychology chapter, students are asked to write about and *revise* a personal myth. They are asked, in effect, to re-see their sense of self.

Finally, I wanted to illustrate the importance of a discipline to the formation of academic writing, yet I also wanted to show that disciplines are protean and disciplinary boundaries are fluid. In designing this textbook, I attempted to show, especially when presenting epistemologies, that the practitioners of one discipline think differently than those of another. They also, I want to suggest, write differently. In the rhetorical analysis sections that follow each reading, I have drawn heavily from the rhetoric of inquiry, the newly emerging body of research into the forms of rhetoric that are specific to particular disciplines. In the writing assignments, students are often asked to write not only about a discipline but also in the mode of that discipline. For example, in a writing assignment for the anthropology chapter, students are asked to write fieldnotes as they observe an unfamiliar cultural setting.

As I have already stated, the readings in this textbook are organized around a theme from a particular discipline. Instructors and students will find, however, that they revisit these themes again and again as they read through other chapters. For example, many of the readings in the anthropology chapter deal with male–female relations and social roles. This theme is picked up in the science chapter when Keller launches her feminist critique of science. It is picked up again in the psychology chapter when Freud discusses his case study of Katharina, a victim of incest. I believe that instructors will find that the intellectual landscape of this textbook changes as one alters his or her path. Moving from the anthropology chapter to the psychology chapter will not be the same as moving from the psychology chapter to the anthropology chapter.

When instructors first use this text, they will probably work through the readings of one chapter and then move on to another chapter. After they have used it for a few semesters, they will probably begin with one chapter, say anthropology, and then take detours to readings in psychology or history that will shed light on the themes—the lines of inquiry— that develop within the discourse of that unique group of students. I hope that both instructors and students will enjoy discovering connections within and across chapters and disciplines.

If I came close to achieving the above goals, it was because I had a great deal of support. I began writing this textbook with a fairly cynical attitude: I doubted that it was possible to begin with a vision and have it even remotely fulfilled at the end of the process. I felt that reviewers and editors would send such contradictory messages that the entire project would fall apart. Such was not the case. I was either incredibly lucky, or I need to thank a number of very insightful and helpful people.

My special thanks to Marti Singer and Sheryl Gowen, two former colleagues at Georgia State University, who helped me to pilot early versions. I gained a great deal of insight from these two exceptional teachers and generous friends.

If there is a richness and diversity in the readings of this text, it is due in large part to Chip Sills of the United States Naval Academy; he brought a number of the readings incorporated into this text to my attention as we talked in lieu of collaborating on another project.

To the many reviewers who offered valuable reactions and encouragement to a work in progress, my thanks: David Bartholomae, University of Pittsburgh; LTC John A. Calabro, United States Military Academy; Joseph Comprone, Michigan Technological University; William Covino, University of Illinois; Michael Kleine, University of Arkansas at Little Rock; Barry M. Maid, University of Arkansas at Little Rock; Christina Murphy, Texas Christian University; Karen Rodis, Dartmouth College; Jeff Schiff, Columbia College, Chicago; Charles I. Schuster, University of Wisconsin–Milwaukee; Josephine K. Tarvers, Rutgers University.

To Marisa L'Heureux, Constance Rajala, Anne Smith, Patricia Rossi, Thomas R. Farrell, and David Munger of HarperCollins, my thanks for their faith, encouragement, rationality, and intelligence. Special thanks to Marisa, who helped me to find the underlying thread of meaning among reviews.

To my wife, Donna, and two sons, Jay and Jeffrey, my thanks for their patience and support. Special thanks for Jeffrey, who often sat in my lap as I composed the rough draft and who finally began to sleep a little so that I could work toward a final version.

GEORGE H. JENSEN

Preview

From Texts to Text re-creates one of the more important movements in academic writing: the movement from reading the texts of other writers to creating your own text. This preview section illustrates the format of the textbook and how the book will help in your movement from texts to text.

Each reading assignment will begin with some background information on the author and his or her text. The purpose of the background information is to place the reading in a meaningful context.

The reading presented in this preview section is from Claude Lévi-Strauss's *Tristes Tropiques*. Lévi-Strauss (born 1908) is a French anthropologist who, shortly after becoming a professor at the University of São Paulo in 1934, began to study the Indians of Brazil. His book *Tristes Tropiques* (or *Sad Tropics*) tells the story of his journey to Brazil and his first attempts to do the work of an anthropologist.

In "A Writing Lesson," a chapter from *Tristes Tropiques*, Lévi-Strauss tells of a trip that he made into the jungle to estimate the size of the Nambikwara tribe, which would, he realized, be no easy task. The Nambikwara are nomads who were scattered across a primitive area then unknown to civilized people. No white person had even traveled into the area since 1925, when seven telegraph workers were murdered there.

Undaunted, Lévi-Strauss decided to visit one Nambikwara village, count its population, and then use that count to estimate the population of the entire Nambikwara tribe. He asked the chief of the friendly Utiarity tribe, who were kin to the Nambikwara, to act as guide and intermediary.

_____ **Prereading**

Each reading will be preceded by a Prereading section, which will further prepare you for the reading. The section will ask you to think about some specific topic that will be covered in the reading assignment. Your instructor may use the topic raised in the Prereading section as the basis for a class discussion before you read the assignment, or may ask you to explore your thoughts on the topic by writing a few paragraphs.

The title of this reading, "A Writing Lesson," can be taken in two senses. As described in the reading, Lévi-Strauss gave a writing lesson to his guide, the chief of the Utiarity tribe—at least, he taught the chief how to mimic the act of writing. In another sense, the chief gave Lévi-Strauss a writing lesson because the chief taught him something about the use of writing, or literacy.

Before reading "A Writing Lesson," think about how writing or literacy is discussed in our society. Is literacy something that we value? How do we use writing or literacy? How do we react to people who do not know how to read or write? How do we react to people who do not speak "correct" English?

A Writing Lesson

Claude Lévi-Strauss

In retrospect, this journey, which was an extremely hazardous one,   1
seems to me now to have been like some grotesque interlude. We had hardly left Juruena when my Brazilian companion noticed that the women and children were not with us: we were accompanied only by the men, armed with bows and arrows. In travel books, such circumstances mean that an attack is imminent. So we moved ahead with mixed feelings, checking the position of our Smith-and-Wesson revolvers (our men pronounced the name as "Cemite Vechetone") and our rifles from time to time. Our fears proved groundless: about midday we caught up with the rest of the group, whom the chief had taken the precaution of sending off the previous evening, knowing that our mules would advance more quickly than the basket-carrying women, whose pace was further slowed down by the children.

A little later, however, the Indians lost their way: the new route was   2
not as straightforward as they had imagined. Towards evening we had to stop in the bush; we had been told that there would be game to shoot; the natives were relying on our rifles and had brought nothing with them; we only had emergency provisions, which could not possibly be shared out among everybody. A herd of deer grazing around a water-hole fled at our approach. The next morning, there was widespread discontent, openly directed against the chief who was held responsible for a plan he and I had devised together. Instead of setting out on a hunting or collecting expedition, all the natives decided to lie

Source: "A Writing Lesson" from *Tristes Tropiques* by Claude Lévi-Strauss, pp. 332–339. Translated from the French by John and Doreen Wrightman. Copyright © 1955 Librarie Plon; English translation copyright © 1973 by Jonathan Cape, Ltd. Reprinted with permission of Atheneum Publishers, an imprint of Macmillan Publishing Company.

down under the shelters, leaving the chief to discover the solution to the problem. He disappeared along with one of his wives; towards evening we saw them both return, their heavy baskets full of the grasshoppers they had spent the entire day collecting. Although crushed grasshopper is considered rather poor fare, the natives all ate heartily and recovered their spirits. We set off again the following morning.

At last we reached the appointed meeting-place. It was a sandy terrace overlooking a stream lined with trees, between which lay half-hidden native gardens. Groups arrived intermittently. Towards evening, there were seventy-five persons representing seventeen families, all grouped together under thirteen shelters hardly more substantial than those to be found in native camps. It was explained to me that, during the rainy season, all these people would be housed in five round huts built to last for some months. Several of the natives appeard never to have seen a white man before and their surly attitude and the chief's edginess suggested that he had persuaded them to come rather against their will. We did not feel safe, nor did the Indians. The night promised to be cold, and as there were no trees on the terrace, we had to lie down like the Nambikwara on the bare earth. Nobody slept: the hours were spent keeping a close but polite watch on each other.

It would have been unwise to prolong such a dangerous situation, so I urged the chief to proceed without further delay to the exchange of gifts. It was at this point that there occurred an extraordinary incident that I can only explain by going back a little. It is unnecessary to point out that the Nambikwara have no written language, but they do not know how to draw either, apart from making a few dotted lines or zigzags on their gourds. Nevertheless, as I had done among the Caduveo, I handed out sheets of paper and pencils. At first they did nothing with them, then one day I saw that they were all busy drawing wavy, horizontal lines. I wondered what they were trying to do, then it was suddenly borne upon me that they were writing or, to be more accurate, were trying to use their pencils in the same way as I did mine, which was the only way they could conceive of, because I had not yet tried to amuse them with my drawings. The majority did this and no more, but the chief had further ambitions. No doubt he was the only one who had grasped the purpose of writing. So he asked me for a writing-pad, and when we both had one, and were working together, if I asked for information on a given point, he did not supply it verbally but drew wavy lines on his paper and presented them to me, as if I could read his reply. He was half taken in by his own make-believe; each time he completed a line, he examined it anxiously as if expecting the meaning to leap from the page, and the same look of disappointment came over his face. But he never admitted this, and there was a tacit understanding between us to the effect that his unintelligible scribbling had a meaning which I pretended to decipher; his verbal commentary followed almost at once, relieving me of the need to ask for explanations.

As soon as he had got the company together, he took from a basket a 5
piece of paper covered with wavy lines and made a show of reading it,
pretending to hesitate as he checked on it the list of objects I was to
give in exchange for the presents offered me: so-and-so was to have a
chopper in exchange for a bow and arrows, someone else beads in exchange for his necklaces . . . This farce went on for two hours. Was he
perhaps hoping to delude himself? More probably he wanted to aston-
ish his companions, to convince them that he was acting as an intermediary agent for the exchange of the goods, that he was in alliance
with the white man and shared his secrets. We were eager to be off,
since the most dangerous point would obviously be reached when all
the marvels I had brought had been transferred to native hands. So I
did not try to explore the matter further, and we began the return journey with the Indians still acting as our guides.

The abortive meeting and the piece of humbug of which I had unwit- 6
tingly been the cause had created an atmosphere of irritation; to make
matters worse, my mule had ulcers in its mouth which were causing it
pain. It either rushed impatiently ahead or came to a sudden stop; the
two of us fell out. Suddenly, before I realized what was happening, I
found myself alone in the bush, with no idea which way to go.

Travel books tell us that the thing to do is attract the attention of the 7
main party by firing a shot. I got down from my mount and fired. No
response. At the second shot I seemed to hear a reply. I fired a third,
the only effect of which was to frighten the mule; it trotted off and
stopped some distance away.

I systematically divested myself of my weapons and photographic 8
equipment and laid them all at the foot of a tree, carefully noting its
position. Then I ran off to recapture my mule, which I had glimpsed
in the distance, seemingly in docile mood. It waited till I got near,
then fled just as I was about to seize the reins, repeating this little
game several times and leading me further and further on. In despair
I took a leap and hung on to its tail with both hands. Surprised at
this unwonted procedure, it made no further attempt to escape from
me. I climbed back into the saddle and tried to return to collect my
equipment, but we had wandered round so much that I was unable to
find it.

Disheartened by the loss, I then decided to try and rejoin the cara- 9
van. Neither the mule nor I knew which way it had gone. Either I
would decide on one direction which the mule was reluctant to follow,
or I would let it have its head, and it would start going round in circles. The sun was sinking towards the horizon, I had lost my weapons
and at any moment I expected to be pierced by a shower of arrows.
I might not be the first person to have entered that hostile area, but
my predecessors had not returned, and, irrespective of myself, my
mule would be a most desirable prey for people whose food supplies
were scanty. While turning these sombre thoughts over and over in my

mind, I waited for the sun to set, my plan being to start a bush fire, since at least I had some matches. Just when I was about to do this, I heard voices: two Nambikwara had turned back as soon as my absence was noticed and had been following my trail since midday; for them, finding my equipment was child's play. They led me back through the darkness to the encampment, where the others were waiting.

Being still perturbed by this stupid incident, I slept badly and whiled **10** away the sleepless hours by thinking over the episode of the exchange of gifts. Writing had, on that occasion, made its appearance among the Nambikwara but not, as one might have imagined, as a result of long and laborious training. It had been borrowed as a symbol, and for a sociological rather than an intellectual purpose, while its reality remained unknown. It had not been a question of acquiring knowledge, of remembering or understanding, but rather of increasing the authority and prestige of one individual—or function—at the expense of others. A native still living in the Stone Age had guessed that this great means towards understanding, even if he was unable to understand it, could be made to serve other purposes. After all, for thousands of years, writing has existed as an institution—and such is still the case today in a large part of the world—in societies the majority of whose members have never learnt to handle it. The inhabitants of the villages I stayed in the Chittagong hills in eastern Pakistan were illiterate, but each village had its scribe who acted on behalf of individuals or of the community as a whole. All the villagers know about writing, and make use of it if the need arises, but they do so from the outside, as if it were a foreign mediatory agent that they communicate with by oral methods. The scribe is rarely a functionary or employee of the group: his knowledge is accompanied by power, with the result that the same individual is often both scribe and money-lender; not just because he needs to be able to read and write to carry on his business, but because he thus happens to be, on two different counts, someone who *has a hold* over others.

Writing is a strange invention. One might suppose that its emergence **11** could not fail to bring about profound changes in the conditions of human existence, and that these transformations must of necessity be of an intellectual nature. The possession of writing vastly increases man's ability to preserve knowledge. It can be thought of as an artificial memory, the development of which ought to lead to a clearer awareness of the past, and hence to a greater ability to organize both the present and the future. After eliminating all other criteria which have been put forward to distinguish between barbarism and civilization, it is tempting to retain this one at least: there are peoples with, or without, writing; the former are able to store up their past achievements and to move with ever-increasing rapidity towards the goal they have set themselves, whereas the latter, being incapable of remembering the past beyond the narrow margin of individual memory, seem bound to remain imprisoned in a fluctuating history which will always lack both a beginning and any lasting awareness of an aim.

Yet nothing we know about writing and the part it has played in   **12**
man's evolution justifies this view. One of the most creative periods
in the history of mankind occurred during the early stages of the neolithic age, which was responsible for agriculture, the domestication of
animals and various arts and crafts. This stage could only have been
reached if, for thousands of years, small communities had been observing, experimenting and handing on their findings. This great development was carried out with an accuracy and a continuity which are
proved by its success, although writing was still unknown at the time.
If writing was invented between 4000 and 3000 B.C., it must be looked
upon as an already remote (and no doubt indirect) result of the neolithic revolution, but certainly not as the necessary precondition for
it. If we ask ourselves what great innovation writing was linked to,
there is little we can suggest on the technical level, apart from architecture. But Egyptian and Sumerian architecture was not superior to the
achievements of certain American peoples who knew nothing of writing
in the pre-Columbian period. Conversely, from the invention of writing
right up to the birth of modern science, the world lived through some
five thousand years when knowledge fluctuated more than it increased.
It has often been pointed out that the way of life of a Greek or Roman
citizen was not so very different from that of an eighteenth-century
middle-class European. During the neolithic age, mankind made gigan-
tic strides without the help of writing; with writing, the historic civilizations of the West stagnated for a long time. It would no doubt be
difficult to imagine the expansion of science in the nineteenth and
twentieth centuries without writing. But, although a necessary precondition, it is certainly not enough to explain the expansion.

To establish a correlation between the emergence of writing and cer-   **13**
tain characteristic features of civilization, we must look in a quite different direction. The only phenomenon with which writing has always
been concomitant is the creation of cities and empires, that is the integration of large numbers of individuals into a political system, and their
grading into castes or classes. Such, at any rate, is the typical pattern of
development to be observed from Egypt to China, at the time when
writing first emerged: it seems to have favoured the exploitation of human beings rather than their enlightenment. This exploitation, which
made it possible to assemble thousands of workers and force them to
carry out exhausting tasks, is a much more likely explanation of the
birth of architecture than the direct link referred to above. My hypothesis, if correct, would oblige us to recognize the fact that the primary
function of written communication is to facilitate slavery. The use of
writing for disinterested purposes, and as a souce of intellectual and
aesthetic pleasure, is a secondary result, and more often than not it
may even be turned into a means of strengthening, justifying or concealing the other.

There are, nevertheless, exceptions to the rule: there were native em- **14**
pires in Africa which grouped together several hundreds of thousands
of subjects; millions lived under the Inca empire in pre-Columbian
America. But in both continents such attempts at empire building did
not produce lasting results. We know that the Inca empire was established around the twelfth century: Pizarro's soldiers would not have
conquered it so easily, three centuries later, had they not found it in a
state of advanced decay. Although we know little about ancient African
history, we can sense that the situation must have been similar: great
political groupings came into being and then vanished again within
the space of a few decades. It is possible, then, that these examples
confirm the hypothesis, instead of contradicting it. Although writing
may not have been enough to consolidate knowledge, it was perhaps
indispensable for the strengthening of dominion. If we look at the
situation nearer home, we see that the systematic development of
compulsory education in the European countries goes hand in hand
with the extension of military service and proletarianization. The fight
against illiteracy is therefore connected with an increase in governmental authority over the citizens. Everyone must be able to read, so that
the government can say: Ignorance of the law is no excuse.

The process has moved from the national to the international level, **15**
thanks to a kind of complicity that has grown up between newly created states—which find themselves facing problems which we had to
cope with a hundred or two hundred years ago—and an international
society of privileged countries worried by the possibility of its stability
being threatened by the reactions of peoples insufficiently trained in
the use of the written word to think in slogans that can be modified at
will or to be an easy prey to suggestion. Through gaining access to the
knowledge stored in libraries, these peoples have also become vulnerable to the still greater proportion of lies propagated in printed documents. No doubt, there can be no turning back now. But in my Nambikwara village, the insubordinate characters were the most sensible.
The villagers who withdrew their allegiance to their chief after he had
tried to exploit a feature of civilization (after my visit he was abandoned
by most of his people) felt in some obscure way that writing and deceit
had penetrated simultaneously into their midst. They went off into a
more remote area of the bush to allow themselves a period of respite.
Yet at the same time I could not help admiring their chief's genius in
instantly recognizing that writing could increase his authority, thus
grasping the basis of the institution without knowing how to use it.

_____ **Written Response**

After each reading assignment, you will be asked to write a response. The re-
sponse is intended to provide an opportunity for you to explore your thoughts
about some aspect of the reading assignment. When you write your response,
remember that it is more important to explore your reactions to what you have

just read than it is to produce polished prose about well-considered and firm positions. Your response may even raise more questions than it answers. In order to allow you the freedom to explore a wide range of thoughts, the response questions have intentionally been worded so that they are open-ended and broad. If you fully explore the issue raised in the question, your written response will often serve as a starting point for class discussion and can sometimes even be reworked into a rough draft.

Some examples of written responses can be found in "Writing Responses to Texts" (see pages 424–427).

In "A Writing Lesson," Lévi-Strauss states that writing is used to gain and maintain power over others. What are your reactions to this idea? Do you agree with Lévi-Strauss? Can you think of any examples from your own experience that would support or refute Lévi-Strauss's claim?

_____ **Rhetorical Analysis**

The Rhetorical Analysis section that follows each reading will draw your attention to some stylistic or organizational aspect of the reading. This information should help you to analyze the reading from the perspective of how it is written, or it might suggest a rhetorical strategy for your next essay. These questions can be discussed in small groups or with your entire class. Your instructor might also choose to have different members of the class (or different groups) take the responsibility of leading the class discussion on specific questions.

1. The basic structure or organization of "A Writing Lesson" is what is typically called "induction," which means moving from the specific to the general. In what way does "A Writing Lesson" move from the specific to the general?

2. Once Lévi-Strauss begins to discuss his ideas about the nature of writing, his discourse moves from a narration of an episode to a theoretical exploration of its importance. He does not just state clear conclusions; he seems to think on paper, much as you did when you wrote a response to "A Writing Lesson." At one point, Lévi-Strauss writes: "Writing is a strange invention. One might suppose that its emergence could not fail to bring about profound changes in the conditions of human existence, and that these transformations must of necessity be of an intellectual nature." Lévi-Strauss then goes on to explore this basic idea. Can you find other portions of the text where Lévi-Strauss explores ideas rather than states conclusions?

_____ **Interpretation**

The Interpretation section that follows each reading will raise issues that can be discussed in small groups or as an entire class. Your discussion of the questions in this section will be more focused than was your written response. In your written response, you used the reading as a point of departure to trigger a wide range of ideas and reactions. You moved from the text to an exploration of ideas outside of

*the text. Here, you will deal more directly with the ideas in the text that you have
just read and that you will now reread and analyze.*

*Some of the interpretation questions will ask you to read a brief quotation that
is a direct or indirect commentary on the reading selection. Your instructor might
wish to lead the class in a close reading of these commentaries, reading and discussing them sentence by sentence, and then move from the commentary back to
the reading selection. One of the ways that writers, including professional writers,
come to terms with texts is by reading other texts that directly comment on them
or that touch upon the same basic topic. By doing a close reading of the commentary texts and then applying what you have learned to the reading selection, you
will begin to understand how this process works.*

*As with the Rhetorical Analysis section, your instructor might choose to have
different members of the class (or different groups) take the responsibility of leading the class discussion on specific questions.*

1. Some writers, such as Lévi-Strauss, seek universal truth; that is, they
seek to find what is true of all humans rather than just some. For example, Lévi-Strauss argues that writing is *always* used to dominate others.
When Lévi-Strauss makes a universal statement (or claim) like this, he is
particularly vulnerable to criticism. Another scholar can cite counter-
examples (examples that refute the universal statement); these authors
argue that truth varies from context to context, and that universal claims
can never apply to all situations. This is the approach that Robert
Pattison takes as he criticizes Lévi-Strauss in *On Literacy* (New York: Oxford, 1982):

> Claude Lévi-Strauss asserts that the introduction of writing is invariably
> followed by a consolidation of power in the hands of an authoritarian
> elite. . . . Ancient history provides numerous examples that refute him. In
> parts of Greece knowledge of reading and writing combined with existing
> economies to produce democratic revolutions. It seems probable that the
> first elements of the Athenian population that learned reading and writing
> were the businessmen and traders. The commercial advantage they gained
> by the new technology made them more prosperous, then more politically
> assertive. In the century before Pericles the wealth of Athens, assisted by
> the technology of writing, facilitated the enfranchisement first of the mid-
> dle classes and then of all free men. Aristocrats like Plato were ambivalent
> about the new technology. In Athens it is probable that the appearance of
> writing meant a gain in power for the free community as a whole and did
> not promote a power grab by any new elite. Writing always increases the
> power at the disposal of a civilization, but who wields this power toward
> what ends is a cultural variable. [pp. 61–62]

Pattison does not deny that writing can be used to dominate others; he
simply asserts that how writing is used varies from culture to culture and
context to context. Do you feel that Pattison accurately paraphrases Lévi-
Strauss? Are you more inclined to agree with Lévi-Strauss or Pattison?
Why?

2. In *Myth and Meaning* (New York: Schocken, 1978), Lévi-Strauss wrote

People who are without writing have a fantastically precise knowledge of their environment and all their resources. All these things we have lost, but we did not lose them for nothing; we are now able to drive an automobile without being crushed at each moment, for example, or in the evening to turn on our television or radio. This implies a training of mental capacities which "primitive" people don't have because they don't need them. I feel that, with the potential they have, they could have changed the quality of their mind, but it would not be needed for the kind of life and relationship to nature that they have. You cannot develop all the mental capacities belonging to mankind all at once. You can only use a small sector, and this sector is not the same according to the culture. [p. 19]

How was Lévi-Strauss, the literate professor, unprepared to survive in the jungle? How were the illiterate natives better able to survive in that environment?

3. Lévi-Strauss argues that writing (or literacy) and power are related to each other. Discuss the power relation between the chief and his followers. At one point, the hungry natives sit down and wait for the chief to find some food. What does this say about the power within the tribe? Who has the power? The chief mimics writing to reinforce his power. Does this ploy work?

_____ **WRITING ASSIGNMENTS**

Suggested writing assignments follow each reading. Exactly how these writing assignments are used will depend in large part on your instructor's goals for the course.

Your instructor might choose to assign a particular topic to your entire class or to allow you to choose the topic that you find most interesting.

The suggested writing assignments will provide a variety of writing experiences, but your instructor might also wish to add to the list or solicit topics from the class.

Some instructors might even ask you to write several shorter and less formal pieces on some of the topics or even on some of the questions in the Rhetorical Analysis and Interpretation sections. As you work on these shorter writing tasks, you can begin to build knowledge and refine your ideas, thus preparing you to write a longer and more formal essay. By writing several shorter pieces that spiral from one to the next and culminate in a formal essay, you will find that you can write your way into handling challenging topics.

Two sample student essays follow the suggested topics on Lévi-Strauss's "A Writing Lesson." These essays can be used as the focus of a class discussion on possible approaches to your first essay.

1. Following the inductive pattern of "A Writing Lesson," describe an episode in your life that relates to writing or literacy and then explore your thoughts about that episode.

2. Pattison argues that the use and meaning of literacy vary from context to context and culture to culture. Write an essay in which you analyze the use and meaning of literacy within the context of your family or the culture of your community. You may want to focus on some important event from your family history that illustrates your family's views of literacy.

3. Write an essay in which you either agree or disagree with Lévi-Strauss's basic claim: Writing is always used to dominate others.

_____ **Sample Essays on These Topics**

Literacy Within My Family

Bettye J. Borom

My basic family foundation was structured in the southern portion of the United States. Many of my ancestors, I'm sure, had no education. Although at that time they probably were more familiar with other necessary abilities, such as farming, carpentry, and caring for their farm animals. Usually farming called for instinct and observing the elements of nature around them. A monthly or yearly almanac kept them informed on when to plant, what to plant, and when to harvest. Many times these almanacs, if the holder couldn't read, were illustrated with pictures and symbols.

Those who had carpentry skills only had need of tools and some years of observing a craftsman's hands at work. This job was mostly utilized by men. The women and girls were required to learn cookery, sewing, and the beautiful art of quilting. During this era physical labor was what it took to sustain their needs.

As time progressed new modern farm and household machinery as well as appliances became more advanced. Soon agriculture was studied in colleges. This made it very necessary for children to learn at a younger age, preparing them for college. Many men moved themselves and their families to larger cities, seeking a better life. It was important for these parents to become knowledgeable in rental and home owner contracts. Even filling out a simple job application now would be a new task. These well sought after jobs would open the door to great expectations for many. Now able to afford modern appliances to understand and the operation of these convenience items would be the job and concern of both parents. Among the thousands of families making this transition during the early 50's was our family, the Johnson's.

My father, having only a third grade education, was thankful for his ability to tackle any job he set his mind on. Having this talent enabled him to expand from service station attendant or building janitor to mechanic or grounds keeper for some successful doctor. Jobs like these kept our family going through difficult times. Soon the word got around about the steel mills in Indiana were hiring willing workers.

After relocating again our parents were determined our grades wouldn't suffer; we were immediately placed in school. During these days of struggle, constant emphasis was placed on their children making a better life for themselves. When the bell rang, we were expected to be in our seats ready to learn, and not just by our teachers. It was also pointed out that no failing grades would be tolerated.

On the other hand my mother was the only child among her twelve brothers and sisters to graduate from high school. Mother worked in a tailoring shop as a young lady. Passing her sewing skill on to her daughter was an honor. The take it out and put it back in correctly was her method of teaching. This persistence oozed over into everything she did. Mother later took a course in Practical Nursing and did very well, wanting to extend herself beyond what was expected of her. By this statement I mean generally jobs such as babysitting or house cleaning.

Although my parents excelled as a struggling couple during an era of transition, they often regreted not having been better educated. These feelings were not overly pressed upon us, but lovingly and constantly reiterated within our hearts. When learning a speech we couldn't just recite it; we had to feel it and understand it.

I am truly thankful for this my heritage to strive to be more than what I am. To learn and know to be literate is to be knowledgeable, to be respected by myself and others, and to grow beyond normal expectations. Though wealth is not my inheritance, the value of books, the ability to write, and never to limit myself is mine forever.

Is Literacy a Tool of Learning for Everyone or a Tool of Domination by the Powerful?

Nick Colakovic

In his essay "A Writing Lesson," Claude Lévi-Strauss argues that writing is a tool used by the powerful to dominate the less fortunate. By using very specific examples, Lévi-Strauss is able to explain his theory of domination through writing. In doing this, he not only avoids some very important questions concerning reading as a form of domination, but he also evades some vital questions about the methods used by leaders to dominate.

In his theory, Lévi-Strauss states that human civilization progressed more rapidly without the knowledge of literacy than with this knowledge. More specifically he claims that civilization progressed more rapidly in pre-history, without the knowledge of literacy, than it did later in the Classical Greek era, with the knowledge of literacy. But in making this assumption, Lévi-Strauss assumes that humanity gathers knowledge in a strictly linear fashion. But this is not the case. Humanity's mastery of science has always increased at varying rates. In history science has reached impasses that have limited scientific development, and at the same time, science also has discovered new concepts that have accelerated scientific development.

Lévi-Strauss falsely assumes that scientific development could have continued without the knowledge of written language. In his theory, he states that he cannot imagine how far humanity would have gone, scientifically, without knowledge of literacy. But with today's increasingly large base of scientific knowledge, it has become impossible for a single human being to memorize all of the information available today. Today, it is a must for engineers, scientists, and even the laymen to have reference books. Imagine trying to find an unknown phone number without a phone book, imagine trying to memorize the exact molecular mass of every known element, the list goes on and on. Put simply, today it is a requirement for humanity to have access to a permanently stored base of knowledge. Memory is too short and too limited to store the vital, voluminous core of scientific knowledge available.

More directly related to the issue is whether or not writing is actually used by the powerful to control or humble the less powerful. Lévi-Strauss argues for an absolute truth; he believes that the powerful *always* use writing to control the less powerful. This belief is based on pure speculation and cannot be verified to any extent. In the past, under certain circumstances, this might have been true, but those certain circumstances are by no means every circumstance. Even in the past the powerful could have been illiterate. Take for example ancient Egypt: The Pharaohs could not read, yet they were considered living gods. Only a limited number of scribes could read or write the very complex ancient Egyptian language, yet they held no power or position of presitge. Also, take for example, the nobility of the Medieval Ages: Most could not read or write. During this time period, essentially the only people that could read or write were the Monks, Priests, and other Church officials; yet again they held no power. One could go on and on about examples from the past in which the powerful could not read, so this argument is also flawed.

And the problems with the theory mentioned in "A Writing Lesson" do not end there. Not only does Claude Lévi-Strauss misinterpret historical data, but he also makes serious errors in interpreting the basic pattern of learning. With this in mind, it is safe to declare this theory is null and void on account of its own flaws.

1 Anthropology: Culture and Power

When we meet people from a different country, we are usually surprised by how they speak and act. We may even be shocked by how these people from another culture live. One of our natural responses to meeting "strangers" is to start thinking in "we/they" dichotomies. "We" eat with silverware, but "they" eat with their hands. "We" live in houses, but "they" live in huts. "We" eat hamburgers, but "they" worship cows. "We" cry at the loss of our pet dog, but "they" serve dog for dinner. When their way of life is so different from ours, it is hard to avoid thinking that "we" are right and "they" are wrong.

Yet, as we come to know these "strangers" (what some anthropologists call "the other"), we begin to realize that they are not so strange after all. We all want to feel safe and secure. We all want to be loved. We all want to feel connected to our culture, community, and family.

Anthropologists are concerned with just this kind of reaction to people from other cultures, as well as how people within a single culture view each other. Why? Because such views are integrally related to important moral questions. If we believe that other people—even those who at first seem strange to us—are essentially like us, then we are more likely to respect them and treat them as equals. If we believe that other people are essentially unlike us, then we are more likely to mistreat them.

One of the central themes of contemporary anthropology is that viewing the stranger ("the other") as inferior leads to an abuse of power. The connection between culture and power will be explored in this chapter.

Studying Culture Through Texts

Anthropologists today generally agree that the best way to learn about the people of other cultures is to study them firsthand, but early anthropologists were less likely to do this. Sir James George Frazer (1854–1941) is an example of these early anthropologists. Instead of living among the natives, Frazer read in a library, copiously collecting descriptions of native customs from the writings of historians, missionaries, traders, and the like. He presented his extensive compilation of primitive rituals and customs in *The Golden Bough*, originally published in two volumes (1890), but later enlarged to 12 volumes (1911–1915). In the following short passage from *The Golden Bough*, Frazer offers his explanation of why some cultures beat and expelled (or on occasions killed) a scapegoat.

_____ **Prereading**

In *The Golden Bough*, Frazer frequently refers to the use of homeopathic magic. The basic structure of homeopathic magic can be described thus:

> If X and Y are related,
> and if I do something to X,
> then the effect of my action on X will be replicated on Y.

Voodoo is a form of homeopathic magic. Those who practice voodoo believe that if they stick a needle in a doll made with some of their enemy's hair (or some other item associated with that enemy), then he or she will feel pain and perhaps even die.

In his research, Frazer found other unusual uses of homeopathic magic that were often employed to promote the growth of crops. Frazer found, for example, that many cultures sacrificed their vegetation god (as represented by a member of the society) and then brought the god back to life (by having a new person represent the god) to ensure that their crops would be plentiful.

Another form of homeopathic magic that Frazer encountered was "scapegoating." The most common form of scapegoating occurred when a person was punished for the sins of the entire community. By punishing a person who represented the community, the population could be purified without having to undergo punishment themselves.

Discuss some examples of homeopathic magic or scapegoating that you have observed in your culture.

The Human Scapegoat in Ancient Greece

Sir James George Frazer

The ancient Greeks were also familiar with the use of a human scape-   **1**
goat. In Plutarch's native town of Chaeronea a ceremony of this kind

Source: "The Human Scapegoat in Ancient Greece" from *The Golden Bough* by Sir George James Frazer. Copyright 1922 by Macmillan Publishing Company; copyright renewed 1950 by Barclays Bank Ltd. Reprinted by permission of Macmillan Publishing Company and A P Watt Limited on behalf of Trinity College, Cambridge.

was performed by the chief magistrate at the Town Hall, and by each householder at his own home. It was called the "expulsion of hunger." A slave was beaten with rods of the *agnus castus,* and turned out of doors with the words, "Out with hunger, and in with wealth and health." When Plutarch held the office of chief magistrate of his native town he performed this ceremony at the Town Hall, and he has recorded the discussion to which the custom afterwards gave rise.

But in civilised Greece the custom of the scapegoat took darker forms **2** than the innocent rite over which the amiable and pious Plutarch presided. Whenever Marseilles, one of the busiest and most brilliant of Greek colonies, was ravaged by a plague, a man of the poorer classes used to offer himself as a scapegoat. For a whole year he was maintained at the public expense, being fed on choice and pure food. At the expiry of the year he was dressed in sacred garments, decked with holy branches, and led through the whole city, while prayers were uttered that all the evils of the people might fall on his head. He was then cast out of the city or stoned to death by the people outside of the walls. The Athenians regularly maintained a number of degraded and useless beings at the public expense; and when any calamity, such as plague, drought, or famine, befell the city, they sacrificed two of these outcast scapegoats. One of the victims was sacrificed for the men and the other for the women. The former wore round his neck a string of black, the latter a string of white figs. Sometimes, it seems, the victim slain on behalf of the women was a woman. They were led about the city and then sacrificed, apparently by being stoned to death outside the city. But such sacrifices were not confined to extraordinary occasions of public calamity; it appears that every year, at the festival of the Thargelia in May, two victims, one for the men and one for the women, were led out of Athens and stoned to death. The city of Abdera in Thrace was publicly purified once a year, and one of the burghers, set apart for the purpose, was stoned to death as a scapegoat or vicarious sacrifice for the life of all the others; six days before his execution he was excommunicated, "in order that he alone might bear the sins of all the people."

From the Lover's Leap, a white bluff at the southern end of their is- **3** land, the Leucadians used annually to hurl a criminal into the sea as a scapegoat. But to lighten his fall they fastened live birds and feathers to him, and a flotilla of small boats waited below to catch him and convey him beyond the boundary. Probably these humane precautions were a mitigation of an earlier custom of flinging the scapegoat into the sea to drown. The Leucadian ceremony took place at the time of a sacrifice to Apollo, who had a temple or sanctuary on the spot. Elsewhere it was customary to cast a young man every year into the sea, with the prayer, "Be thou our offscouring." This ceremony was supposed to rid the people of the evils by which they were beset, or according to a somewhat different interpretation it redeemed them by paying the debt they owed to the sea-god. As practised by the Greeks of Asia Minor in the sixth century before our era, the custom of the scapegoat was as follows. When a city suffered from plague, famine, or other public calamity, an ugly or deformed person was chosen to take upon himself all the evils which afflicted the community. He was brought to a suitable place, where dried figs, a barley loaf, and cheese were put into his hand. These he ate. Then he was beaten seven times upon his genital organs with squills[1] and branches of the wild fig and other wild trees, while the flutes played a particular tune. Afterwards he was burned on a pyre built of the wood of forest trees; and his ashes were cast into the sea. A similar custom appears to have been annually celebrated by the Asiatic Greeks at the harvest festival of the Thargelia.

In the ritual just described the scourging of the victim with squills,   **4** branches of the wild fig, and so forth, cannot have been intended to aggravate his sufferings, otherwise any stick would have been good enough to beat him with. The true meaning of this part of the ceremony has been explained by W. Mannhardt. He points out that the ancients attributed to squills a magical power of averting evil influences, and that accordingly they hung them up at the doors of their houses and made use of them in purificatory rites. Hence the Arcadian custom of whipping the image of Pan with squills at a festival, or whenever the hunters returned empty-handed, must have been meant, not to punish the god, but to purify him from the harmful influences which were impeding him in the exercise of his divine functions as a god who should supply the hunter with game. Similarly the object of beating the human scapegoat on the genital organs with squills and so on, must have been to release his reproductive energies from any restraint or spell under which they might be laid by demoniacal or other malignant agency; and as the Thargelia at which he was annually sacrificed was an early harvest festival celebrated in May, we must recognise in him a representative of the creative and fertilising god of vegetation. The representative of the god was annually slain for the purpose I have indicated, that of maintaining the divine life in perpetual vigour, untainted by the weakness of age; and before he was put to death it was not unnatural to stimulate his reproductive powers in order that these might be transmitted in full activity to his successor, the new god or new embodiment of the old god, who was doubtless supposed immediately to take the place of the one slain. Similar reasoning would lead to a similar treatment of the scapegoat on special occasions, such as drought or famine. If the crops did not answer to the expectation of the husbandman, this would be attributed to some failure in the generative powers of the god whose function it was to produce the fruits of the earth. It might be thought that he was under a spell or was growing old and feeble. Accordingly he was slain in the person of his

---

[1] Squills are a type of sea onion.

representative, with all the ceremonies already described, in order that, born young again, he might infuse his own youthful vigour into the stagnant energies of nature. On the same principle we can understand why Mamurius Veturius was beaten with rods, why the slave at the Chaeronean ceremony was beaten with the *agnus castus* (a tree to which magical properties were ascribed), why the effigy of Death in some parts of Europe is assailed with sticks and stones, and why at Babylon the criminal who played the god was scourged before he was crucified. The purpose of the scourging was not to intensify the agony of the divine sufferer, but on the contrary to dispel any malignant influences by which at the supreme moment he might conceivably be beset.

Thus far I have assumed that the human victims at the Thargelia rep- 5
resented the spirits of vegetation in general, but it has been well remarked by Mr. W. R. Paton that these poor wretches seem to have masqueraded as the spirits of fig-trees in particular. He points out that the process of caprification, as it is called, that is, the artifical fertilisation of the cultivated fig-trees by hanging strings of wild figs among the boughs, takes place in Greece and Asia Minor in June about a month after the date of the Thargelia, and he suggests that the hanging of the black and white figs round the necks of the two human victims, one of whom represented the men and the other the women, may have been a direct imitation of the process of caprification designed, on the principle of imitative magic, to assist the fertilisation of the fig-trees. And since caprification is in fact a marriage of the male fig-tree with the female fig-tree, Mr. Paton further supposes that the loves of the trees may, on the same principle of imitative magic, have been simulated by a mock or even a real marriage between the two human victims, one of whom appears sometimes to have been a woman. On this view the practice of beating the human vicitms on their genitals with branches of wild fig-trees and with squills was a charm intended to stimulate the generative powers of the man and woman who for the time being personated the male and female fig-trees respectively, and who by their union in marriage, whether real or pretended, were believed to help the trees to bear fruit.

The interpretation which I have adopted of the custom of beating the 6
human scapegoat with certain plants is supported by many analogies. Thus among the Kai of German New Guinea, when a man wishes to make his banana shoots bear fruit quickly, he beats them with a stick cut from a banana-tree which has already borne fruit. Here it is obvious that fruitfulness is believed to inhere in a stick cut from a fruitful tree and to be imparted by contact to the young banana plants. Similarly in New Caledonia a man will beat his taro plants lightly with a branch, saying as he does so, "I beat this taro that it may grow," after which he plants the branch in the ground at the end of the field. Among the Indians of Brazil at the mouth of the Amazon, when a man wishes to increase the size of his generative organ, he strikes it with the fruit of a

white aquatic plant called *aninga*, which grows luxuriantly on the banks
of the river. The fruit, which is inedible, resembles a banana, and is
clearly chosen for this purpose on account of its shape. The ceremony
should be performed three days before or after the new moon. In the
county of Bekes, in Hungary, barren women are fertilised by being
struck with a stick which has first been used to separate pairing dogs.
Here a fertilising virtue is clearly supposed to be inherent in the stick
and to be conveyed by contact to the women. The Toradjas of Central
Celebes think that the plant *Dracaena terminalis* has a strong soul, because when it is lopped, it soon grows up again. Hence when a man is
ill, his friends will sometimes beat him on the crown of the head with
Dracaena leaves in order to strengthen his weak soul with the strong
soul of the plant.

These analogies, accordingly, support the interpretation which, fol-   7
lowing my predecessors W. Mannhardt and Mr. W. R. Paton, I have
given of the beating inflicted on the human victims at the Greek harvest festival of the Thargelia. That beating, being administered to the
generative organs of the victims by fresh green plants and branches, is
most naturally explained as a charm to increase the reproductive energies of the men or women either by comunicating to them the fruitfulness of the plants and branches, or by ridding them of the maleficent
influences; and this interpretation is confirmed by the observation that
the two victims represented the two sexes, one of them standing for
the men in general and the other for the women. The season of the
year when the ceremony was performed, namely the time of the corn
harvest, tallies well with the theory that the rite had an agricultural
significance. Further, that it was above all intended to fertilise the fig-
trees is strongly suggested by the strings of black and white figs which
were hung round the necks of the victims, as well as by the blows which
were given their genital organs with the branches of a wild fig-tree;
since this procedure closely resembles the procedure which ancient and
modern husbandmen in Greek lands have regularly resorted to for
the purpose of actually fertilising their fig-trees. When we remember
what an important part the artificial fertilisation of the date palm-tree
appears to have played of old not only in the husbandry but in the religion of Mesopotamia, there seems no reason to doubt that the artificial
fertilisation of the fig-tree may in like manner have vindicated for itself
a place in the solemn ritual of Greek religion.

If these considerations are just, we must apparently conclude that   8
while the human victims at the Thargelia certainly appear in later classical times to have figured chiefly as public scapegoats, who carried
away with them the sins, misfortunes, and sorrows of the whole people, at an earlier time they may have been looked on as embodiments
of vegetation, perhaps of the corn but particularly of the fig-trees; and
that the beating which they received and the death which they died
were intended primarily to brace and refresh the powers of vegetation

then beginning to droop and languish under the torrid heat of the Greek summer.

_____ **Written Response**

Why do you think that the phenomenon of scapegoating is found throughout history and across widely diverse cultures? Why is scapegoating so common?

_____ **Rhetorical Analysis**

1. One of the most prominent features of Frazer's writing style is his meticulous attention to concrete details. Reread a portion of Frazer's text and discuss his use of details. How do the details affect you as a reader? Why do you think that Frazer included so many details?

2. Reread "The Human Scapegoat in Ancient Greece" and make a list of Frazer's sources of information. What does this list of sources tell you about how he researched his topic?

_____ **Interpretation**

1. In *The Golden Bough*, Frazer attempted to synthesize information from hundreds of sources to understand unfamiliar aspects of primitive cultures, such as their use of homeopathic magic. When authors attempt such an ambitious synthesis of diverse materials, they may go too far. They may combine things—whether cultures, facts, or theories—that are too different to be fused into a single interpretation. For example, in *Patterns of Culture* (Boston: Houghton Mifflin, 1934), Ruth Benedict wrote of Frazer's work:

> Studies of culture like *The Golden Bough* and the usual comparative ethnological volumes are analytical discussions of traits and ignore all the aspects of cultural integration. Mating or death practices are illustrated by bits of behavior selected indiscriminately from the most different cultures, and the discussion builds up a kind of mechanical Frankenstein's monster with a right eye from Fiji, a left from Europe, one leg from Tierra del Fuego, and one from Tahiti, and all the fingers and toes from still different regions. Such a figure corresponds to no reality in the past or present. . . . If we are interested in cultural processes, the only way in which we can know the significance of the selected detail of behavior is against the background of the motives and emotions and values that are institutionalized in that culture. The first essential, so it seems today, is to study the living culture, to know its habits of thought and the functions of its institutions, and such knowledge cannot come out of post-mortem dissections and reconstructions. [pp. 49–50]

What do you think that Benedict means by calling Frazer's work a "mechanical Frankenstein's monster"? From the short segment of *The Golden*

Bough that you read, do you feel that Benedict's criticism is justified? Does Frazer neglect the motives and emotions associated with scapegoating? Does he discuss the "habits of thought" of ancient Greece or "the functions of its institutions"?

Benedict calls Frazer's approach to anthropology "analytic"; her own approach to anthropology could be described as "holistic." How would you define each approach? Do you agree with Benedict that the holistic approach (the preferred approach of most anthropologists) is better suited to the study of culture? Why? For what kind of disciplines or fields of study would the analytic approach be appropriate?

2. Later in *The Golden Bough*, Frazer writes: "the persons whom the Athenians kept to be sacrificed were. . . treated as divine. That they were social outcasts did not matter. On the primitive view a man is not chosen to be the mouth-piece or embodiment of a god on account of his high moral qualities or social rank." Frazer does not feel that it was important that those chosen to represent the god (and eventually be sacrificed) were social outcasts. Some modern anthropologists would disagree. In "Human Sacrifice at Tenochtitlan" (*Comparative Studies in Society and History*, July 1984), John M. Ingham suggests that human sacrifice was integrally related to the power structure of Aztec society. For example, those sacrificed were always slaves or war captives. In what way do you feel that scapegoating is related to who has power and who does not have power? How does this power issue relate to the examples of scapegoating that you have observed in your culture?

_____ **WRITING ASSIGNMENTS**

1. Benedict criticized Frazer for ignoring the cultural context of the rituals and customs that he was attempting to synthesize; for this topic you will be asked to describe some episode of scapegoating that you have experienced or observed. After you have described the episode so that a reader who was not there can understand what happened, use your understanding of the cultural context in which the episode occurred to provide a full and rich explanation of why that person was scapegoated.

2. Select an issue on your campus or in your community that seems to deal with an abuse of power, such as racism, the hazing of those who pledge fraternities or sororities, and so on. Then write an article appropriate for your student newspaper, in which you use an explanation of homeopathic magic and scapegoating in primitive cultures to explain this abuse of power.

The Difficulties and Rewards of Fieldwork

Napoleon A. Chagnon's "Doing Fieldwork Among the Yąnomamö" is an essay about the difficulties of doing fieldwork, but it is also an essay about how a young and inexperienced anthroplogist learns to adapt to the unique culture of a primitive tribe.

In 1964, Chagnon embarked on his first field trip to study the Yąnomamö people—a primitive tribe scattered throughout many villages in the tropical forest of Venezuela. He set up a base camp in the village of Bisaasiteri and from there made trips to neighboring villages to study the kinship patterns, or the structure of family relationships.

In "Doing Fieldwork Among the Yąnomanö," Chagnon reflects on his first meeting with the Yąnomamö and how he learned to survive as an anthropologist living among a primitive people.

_____ **Prereading**

Toward the end of the nineteenth century, American anthropologists began to realize that they could not rely on the observations of primitive people written by travelers or missionaries, as had Frazer. In "The Aims of Ethnology" (*Race, Language, and Culture* [Chicago: University of Chicago Press, 1940]), Franz Boas, one of the first anthropologists to advocate fieldwork, wrote:

> Even the rudest tribes do not conform to the picture that is drawn by many a superficial traveller. Many examples may be culled from the extensive literature of travel showing the superficiality of the reports given. The well-known traveller Burchell met near the Garib a group of Bushmen and gives us the most wonderful report of their complete lack of reasoning power. He asked the question: What is the difference between a good and an evil action? and since they could not answer to his satisfaction he declared them to have no power of reasoning and judging. In a similar way the Fuegians were asked about their religious ideas in terms that were necessarily unintelligible to them, and since they could not answer it was said that they cannot grasp any idea that transcends the barest needs of everyday life. Nowadays we know better, and no scientifically prepared traveller would dare to make statements of this kind. We know now that the Bushmen, whom Burchell described as little different from wild beasts, have a well-developed music, a wide range of tales and traditions; they enjoy poetry and are excellent narrators. Their rock paintings show a high degree of skill and a remarkable understanding of perspective. We also know that the Fuegians have a well-developed social organization and that their customs are proof of a deep-seated religious attitude. [pp. 626–627]

Anthropologists began to realize that, if they were to understand—not just judge or condemn—a particular primitive tribe, they could not remain at home in their study and read reports written by travelers or missionaries. They had to do fieldwork, also called *ethnography*. They had to go and live among the primitive people whom they were studying.

Can you think of any situations in which you were shocked or disturbed by the actions or beliefs of someone from another country, region, or religion? As you came to know this person better, did your attitudes toward the person change? If so, how?

What do you expect Chagnon to experience the first time he faces the Yąnomamö? How do you expect him to change as he continues to live among the Yąnomamö?

Doing Fieldwork Among the Yąnomamö
Napoleon A. Chagnon

My first day in the field illustrated to me what my teachers meant 1
when they spoke of "culture shock." I had traveled in a small, aluminum rowboat propelled by a large outboard motor for two and a half
days. This took me from the Territorial capital, a small town on the
Orinoco River, deep into Yąnomamö country. On the morning of the
third day we reached a small mission settlement, the field "headquarters" of a group of Americans who were working in two Yąnomamö
villages. The missionaries had come out of these villages to hold their
annual conference on the progress of their mission work, and were
conducting their meetings when I arrived. We picked up a passenger
at the mission station, James P. Barker, the first non-Yąnomamö to
make a sustained, permanent contact with the tribe (in 1950). He had
just returned from a year's furlough in the United States, where I had
earlier visited him before leaving for Venezuela. He agreed to accompany me to the village I had selected for my base of operations to introduce me to the Indians. This village was also his own home base,
but he had not been there for over a year and did not plan to join me
for another three months. Mr. Barker had been living with this particular group about five years.

We arrived at the village, Bisaasi-teri, about 2:00 PM and docked the 2
boat along the muddy bank at the terminus of the path used by the Indians to fetch their drinking water. It was hot and muggy, and my
clothing was soaked with perspiration. It clung uncomfortably to my
body, as it did thereafter for the remainder of the work. The small, biting gnats were out in astronomical numbers, for it was the beginning of
the dry season. My face and hands were swollen from the venom of
their numerous stings. In just a few moments I was to meet my first
Yąnomamö, my first primitive man. What would it be like? I had visions of entering the village and seeing 125 social facts running about

Source: "Doing Fieldwork Among the Yąnomamö" from *Yąnomamö: The Fierce People* by
N. A. Chagnon, copyright © 1968 by Holt, Rinehart and Winston, Inc. Reprinted by permission of the publisher.

calling each other kinship terms and sharing food, each waiting and
anxious to have me collect his genealogy. I would wear them out in
turn. Would they like me? This was important to me; I wanted them to
be so fond of me that they would adopt me into their kinship system
and way of life, because I had heard that successful anthropologists always get adopted by their people. I had learned during my seven years
of anthropological training at the University of Michigan that kinship
was equivalent to society in primitive tribes and that it was a moral
way of life, "moral" being something "good" and "desirable." I was
determined to work my way into their moral system of kinship and become a member of their society.

My heart began to pound as we approached the village and heard   3
the buzz of activity within the circular compound. Mr. Barker commented that he was anxious to see if any changes had taken place
while he was away and wondered how many of them had died during
his absence. I felt into my back pocket to make sure that my notebook
was still there and felt personally more secure when I touched it. Otherwise, I would not have known what to do with my hands.

The entrance to the village was covered over with brush and dry palm   4
leaves. We pushed them aside to expose the low opening to the village.
The excitement of meeting my first Indians was almost unbearable as I
duck-waddled through the low passage into the village clearing.

I looked up and gasped when I saw a dozen burly, naked, filthy,   5
hideous men staring at us down the shafts of their drawn arrows! Immense wads of green tobacco were stuck between their lower teeth and
lips making them look even more hideous, and strands of dark-green
slime dripped or hung from their noses. We arrived at the village while
the men were blowing a hallucinogenic drug up their noses. One of the
side effects of the drug is a runny nose. The mucus is always saturated
with the green powder and the Indians usually let it run freely from
their nostrils. My next discovery was that there were a dozen or so vicious, underfed dogs snapping at my legs, circling me as if I were going to be their next meal. I just stood there holding my notebook,
helpless and pathetic. Then the stench of the decaying vegetation and
filth struck me and I almost got sick. I was horrified. What sort of a
welcome was this for the person who came here to live with you and
learn your way of life, to become friends with you? They put their
weapons down when they recognized Barker and returned to their
chanting, keeping a nervous eye on the village entrances.

We had arrived just after a serious fight. Seven women had been ab-   6
ducted the day before by a neighboring group, and the local men and
their guests had just that morning recovered five of them in a brutal
club fight that nearly ended in a shooting war. The abductors, angry
because they lost five of the seven captives, vowed to raid the Bisaasi-
teri. When we arrived and entered the village unexpectedly, the

Indians feared that we were the raiders. On several occasions during
the next two hours the men in the village jumped to their feet, armed
themselves, and waited nervously for the noise outside the village to
be identified. My enthusiasm for collecting ethnographic curiosities diminished in proportion to the number of times such an alarm was
raised. In fact, I was relieved when Mr. Barker suggested that we sleep
across the river for the evening. It would be safer over there.

As we walked down the path to the boat, I pondered the wisdom of   7
having decided to spend a year and a half with this tribe before I had
even seen what they were like. I am not ashamed to admit, either, that
had there been a diplomatic way out, I would have ended my fieldwork
then and there. I did not look forward to the next day when I would be
left alone with the Indians; I did not speak a word of their language,
and they were decidedly different from what I had imagined them to
be. The whole situation was depressing, and I wondered why I ever
decided to switch from civil engineering to anthropology in the first
place. I had not eaten all day, I was soaking wet from perspiration, the
gnats were biting me, and I was covered with red pigment, the result
of a dozen or so complete examinations I had been given by as many
burly Indians. These examinations capped an otherwise grim day. The
Indians would blow their noses into their hands, flick as much of the
mucus off that would separate in a snap of the wrist, wipe the residue
into their hair, and then carefully examine my face, arms, legs, hair,
and the contents of my pockets. I asked Mr. Barker how to say "Your
hands are dirty"; my comments were met by the Indians in the following way: They would "clean" their hands by spitting a quantity of
slimy tobacco juice into them, rub them together, and then proceed
with the examination.

Mr. Barker and I crossed the river and slung our hammocks. When   8
he pulled his hammock out of a rubber bag, a heavy, disagreeable odor
of mildewed cotton came with it. "Even the missionaries are filthy,"
I thought to myself. Within two weeks, everything I owned smelled
the same way, and I lived with that odor for the remainder of the fieldwork. My own habits of personal cleanliness reached such levels that I
didn't even mind being examined by the Indians, as I was not much
cleaner than they were after I had adjusted to the circumstances.

So much for my discovery that primitive man is not the picture of   9
nobility and sanitation I had conceived him to be. I soon discovered
that it was an enormously time-consuming task to maintain my own
body in the manner to which it had grown accustomed in the relatively
antiseptic environment of the northern United States. Either I could be
relatively well fed and relatively comfortable in a fresh change of
clothes and do very little fieldwork, or, I could do considerably more
fieldwork and be less well fed and less comfortable.

It is appalling how complicated it can be to make oatmeal in the jun-   10
gle. First, I had to make two trips to the river to haul the water. Next, I

had to prime my kerosene stove with alcohol and get it burning, a tricky procedure when you are trying to mix powdered milk and fill a coffee pot at the same time: the alcohol prime always burned out before I could turn the kerosene on, and I would have to start all over. Or, I would turn the kerosene on, hoping that the element was still hot enough to vaporize the fuel, and start a small fire in my palm-thatched hut as the liquid kerosene squirted all over the table and walls and ignited. It was safer to start over with the alcohol. Then I had to boil the oatmeal and pick the bugs out of it. All my supplies, of course, were carefully stored in Indian-proof, rat-proof, moisture-proof, and insect-proof containers, not one of which ever served its purpose adequately. Just taking things out of the multiplicity of containers and repacking them afterward was a minor project in itself. By the time I had hauled the water to cook with, unpacked my food, prepared the oatmeal, milk, and coffee, heated water for dishes, washed and dried the dishes, repacked the food in the containers, stored the containers in locked trunks and cleaned up my mess, the ceremony of preparing breakfast had brought me almost up to lunch time!

Eating three meals a day was out of the question. I solved the **11** problem by eating a single meal that could be prepared in a single container, or, at most, in two containers, washed my dishes only when there were no clean ones left, using cold river water, and wore each change of clothing at least a week to cut down on my laundry problem, a courageous undertaking in the tropics. I was also less concerned about sharing my provisions with the rats, insects, Indians, and the elements, thereby eliminating the need for my complicated storage process. I was able to last most of the day on *café con leche*, heavily sugared espresso coffee diluted about five to one with hot milk. I would prepare this in the evening and store it in a thermos. Frequently, my single meal was no more complicated than a can of sardines and a package of crackers. But at least two or three times a week I would do something sophisticated, like make oatmeal or boil rice and add a can of tuna fish or tomato paste to it. I even saved time by devising a water system that obviated the trips to the river. I had a few sheets of zinc roofing brought in and made a rain-water trap; I caught the water on the zinc surface, funneled it into an empty gasoline drum, and then ran a plastic hose from the drum to my hut. When the drum was exhausted in the dry season, I hired the Indians to fill it with water from the river.

I ate much less when I traveled with the Indians to visit other vil- **12** lages. Most of the time my travel diet consisted of roasted or boiled green plantains[1] that I obtained from the Indians, but I always carried a few cans of sardines with me in case I got lost or stayed away longer than I had planned. I found peanut butter and crackers a very

---

[1] Plantain: a tropical fruit similar to a banana.

nourishing food, and a simple one to prepare on trips. It was nutritious
and portable, and only one tool was required to prepare the meal, a
hunting knife that could be cleaned by wiping the blade on a leaf.
More importantly, it was one of the few foods the Indians would let me
eat in relative peace. It looked too much like animal feces to them to.
excite their appetites.

I once referred to the peanut butter as the dung of cattle. They found   13
this quite repugnant. They did not know what "cattle" were, but were
generally aware that I ate several canned products of such an animal. I
perpetrated this myth, if for no other reason than to have some peace
of mind while I ate. Fieldworkers develop strange defense mechanisms,
and this was one of my own forms of adaptation. On another occasion
I was eating a can of frankfurters and growing very weary of the demands of one of my guests for a share in my meal. When he asked me
what I was eating, I replied: "Beef." He then asked, "What part of the
animal are you eating?" to which I replied, "Guess!" He stopped asking
for a share.

Meals were a problem in another way. Food sharing is important to   14
the Yąnomamö in the context of displaying friendship. "I am hungry,"
is almost a form of greeting with them. I could not possibly have
brought enough food with me to feed the entire village, yet they
seemed not to understand this. All they could see was that I did not
share my food with them at each and every meal. Nor could I enter
into their system of reciprocities with respect to food; every time one of
them gave me something "freely," he would dog me for months to pay
him back, not with food, but with steel tools. Thus, if I accepted a
plantain from someone in a different village while I was on a visit, he
would most likely visit me in the future and demand a machete as payment for the time that he "fed" me. I usually reacted to these kinds of
demands by giving a banana, the customary reciprocity in their culture—food for food—but this would be a disappointment for the individual who had visions of that single plantain growing into a machete
over time.

Despite the fact that most of them knew I would not share my food   15
with them at their request, some of them always showed up at my hut
during mealtime. I gradually became accustomed to this and learned to
ignore their persistent demands while I ate. Some of them would get
angry because I failed to give in, but most of them accepted it as just a
peculiarity of the subhuman foreigner. When I did give in, my hut
quickly filled with Indians, each demanding a sample of the food that I
had given one of them. If I did not give all a share, I was that much
more despicable in their eyes.

A few of them went out of their way to make my meals unpleasant,   16
to spite me for not sharing; for example, one man arrived and watched
me eat a cracker with honey on it. He immediately recognized the
honey, a particularly esteemed Yąnomamö food. He knew that I would

not share my tiny bottle and that it would be futile to ask. Instead, he glared at me and queried icily, "Shaki!² What kind of animal semen are you eating on that cracker?" His question had the desired effect, and my meal ended.

Finally, there was the problem of being lonely and separated from   **17** your own kind, especially your family. I tried to overcome this by seeking personal friendships among the Indians. This only complicated the matter because all my friends simply used my confidence to gain privileged access to my cache of steel tools and trade goods, and looted me. I would be bitterly disappointed that my "friend" thought no more of me than to finesse our relationship exclusively with the intention of getting at my locked up possessions, and my depression would hit new lows every time I discovered this. The loss of the possession bothered me much less than the shock that I was, as far as most of them were concerned, nothing more than a source of desirable items; no holds were barred in relieving me of these, since I was considered something subhuman, a non-Yąnomamö.

The thing that bothered me most was the incessant, passioned, and   **18** aggressive demands the Indians made. It would become so unbearable that I would have to lock myself in my mud hut every once in a while just to escape from it: Privacy is one of Western culture's greatest achievements. But I did not want privacy for its own sake; rather, I simply had to get away from the begging. Day and night for the entire time I lived with the Yąnomamö I was plagued by such demands as: "Give me a knife, I am poor!"; "If you don't take me with you on your next trip to Widokaiya-teri I'll chop a hole in your canoe!"; "Don't point your camera at me or I'll hit you!"; "Share your food with me!"; "Take me across the river in your canoe and be quick about it!"; "Give me a cooking pot!"; "Loan me your flashlight so I can go hunting tonight!"; "Give me medicine . . . I itch all over!"; "Take us on a weeklong hunting trip with your shotgun!"; and "Give me an axe or I'll break into your hut when you are away visiting and steal one!" And so I was bombarded by such demands day after day, months on end, until I could not bear to see an Indian.

It was not as difficult to become calloused to the incessant begging as **19** it was to ignore the sense of urgency, the impassioned tone of voice, or the intimidation and aggression with which the demands were made. It was likewise difficult to adjust to the fact that the Yąnomamö refused to accept "no" for an answer until or unless it seethed with passion and intimidation—which it did after six months. Giving in to a demand always established a new threshold; the next demand would be for a bigger item or favor, and the anger of the Indians even greater if the demand was not met. I soon learned that I had to become very much

---

² Shaki: the Yąnomanö's pronunciation of Chagnon, the author.

like the Yąnomamö to be able to get along with them on their terms:
sly, aggressive, and intimidating.

Had I failed to adjust in this fashion I would have lost six months of   20
supplies to them in a single day or would have spent most of my time
ferrying them around in my canoe or hunting for them. As it was, I
did spend a considerable amount of time doing these things and did
succumb to their outrageous demands for axes and machetes, at least at
first. More importantly, had I failed to demonstrate that I could not be
pushed around beyond a certain point, I would have been the subject
of far more ridicule, theft, and practical jokes than was the actual case.
In short, I had to acquire a certain proficiency in their kind of interpersonal politics and to learn how to imply subtly that certain potentially
undesirable consequences might follow if they did such and such to
me. They do this to each other in order to establish precisely the point
at which they cannot goad an individual any further without precipitat-
ing retaliation. As soon as I caught on to this and realized that much of
their aggression was stimulated by their desire to discover my flash
point, I got along much better with them and regained some lost
ground. It was sort of like a political game that everyone played, but
one in which each individual sooner or later had to display some sign
that his bluffs and implied threats could be backed up. I suspect that
the frequency of wife beating is a component of this syndrome, since
men can display their ferocity and show others that they are capable of
violence. Beating a wife with a club is considered to be an acceptable
way of displaying ferocity and one that does not expose the male to
much danger. The important thing is that the man has displayed his
potential for violence and the implication is that other men better treat
him with respect and caution.

After six months, the level of demand was tolerable in the village   21
I used for my headquarters. The Indians and I adjusted to each
other and knew what to expect with regard to demands on their part
for goods, favors, and services. Had I confined my fieldwork to just
that village alone, the field experience would have been far more enjoyable. But, as I was interested in the demographic pattern and social organization of a much larger area, I made regular trips to some dozen
different villages in order to collect genealogies or to recheck those I
already had. Hence, the intensity of begging and intimidation was
fairly constant for the duration of the fieldwork. I had to establish my
position in some sort of pecking order of ferocity at each and every
village.

For the most part, my own "fierceness" took the form of shouting   22
back at the Yąnomamö as loudly and as passionately as they shouted at
me, especially at first, when I did not know much of their language. As
I became more proficient in their language and learned more about
their political tactics, I became more sophisticated in the art of bluffing.
For example, I paid one young man a machete to cut palm trees and
make boards from the wood. I used these to fashion a platform in the

bottom of my dugout canoe to keep my possessions dry when I traveled by river. That afternoon I was doing informant work in the village; the long-awaited mission supply boat arrived, and most of the Indians ran out of the village to beg goods from the crew. I continued to work in the village for another hour or so and went down to the river to say "hello" to the men on the supply boat. I was angry when I discovered that the Indians had chopped up all my palm boards and used them to paddle their own canoes across the river. I knew that if I overlooked this incident I would have invited them to take even greater liberties with my goods in the future. I crossed the river, docked amidst their dugouts, and shouted for the Indians to come out and see me. A few of the culprits appeared, mischievous grins on their faces. I gave a spirited lecture about how hard I had worked to put those boards in my canoe, how I had paid a machete for the wood, and how angry I was that they destroyed my work in their haste to cross the river. I then pulled out my hunting knife and, while their grins disappeared, cut each of their canoes loose, set it into the current, and let it float away. I left without further ado and without looking back.

They managed to borrow another canoe and, after some effort, recov-   23
ered their dugouts. The headman of the village later told me with an approving chuckle that I had done the correct thing. Everyone in the village, except, of course, the culprits, supported and defended my action. This raised my status.

Whenever I took such action and defended my rights, I got along   24
much better with the Yąnomamö. A good deal of their behavior toward me was directed with the forethought of establishing the point at which I would react defensively. Many of them later reminisced about the early days of my work when I was "timid" and a little afraid of them, and they could bully me into giving goods away.

Theft was the most persistent situation that required me to take some   25
sort of defensive action. I simply could not keep everything I owned locked in trunks, and the Indians came into my hut and left at will. I developed a very effective means for recovering almost all the stolen items. I would simply ask a child who took the item and then take that person's hammock when he was not around, giving a spirited lecture to the others as I marched away in a faked rage with the thief's hammock. Nobody ever attempted to stop me from doing this, and almost all of them told me that my technique for recovering my possessions was admirable. By nightfall the thief would either appear with the stolen object or send it along with someone else to make an exchange. The others would heckle him for getting caught and being forced to return the item.

_____ **Written Response**

Based on what you have read in this selection, how would you describe the Yąnomamö people?

_____ **Rhetorical Analysis**

1. Fieldwork or ethnography is an unusual form of research in that its validity (whether or not we accept it as true) rests less on an objective method than it does on the trustworthiness of the anthropologist asethnographer (a reliable collector of data) and the anthropologist as writer (an accurate interpreter of the data and a believable storyteller). One of the ways that ethnographers attempt to develop some authority for their text is by placing themselves into their text. If the ethnographer talks about himself or herself as well as the culture under study, then the readers can, at least in part, judge the validity of the study by judging the trustworthiness of its author.

In "Doing Fieldwork Among the Yąnomamö," do you feel that Chagnon presents himself as a trustworthy person? Do you feel that you would trust him to collect data on the Yąnomamö accurately? Do you feel that he will sympathetically interpret Yąnomamö culture? Do you feel that he is a believable storyteller? Can you isolate portions of Chagnon's text that make him appear to be a trustworthy or untrustworthy storyteller?

2. Gilbert Ryle, as cited in Clifford Geertz's "Thick Description" (*The Interpretation of Culture* [New York: Basic, 1973]), believes that anthropologists should write a "thick description" of what they observe. To explain what he means by a "thick description," Ryle uses the following hypothetical example. Imagine that an anthropologist observes that the right eye of a young boy twitches. If the anthropologist wrote an entirely factual description of the event (a "thin description"), he would merely say that he or she observed that the boy's right eye twitched. If, however, the anthropologist wrote about what the twitch meant for that particular boy in that particular culture and in that particular context (a "thick description"), then he or she would say that the boy had a nervous disorder, or the boy was winking to a friend, or the boy was ridiculing someone else who had winked.

Do you feel that Chagnon provides a "thin" or a "thick" description? Can you find portions of his text that you feel are either a "thin" or a "thick" description?

_____ **Interpretation**

1. In order to survive while living among the Yąnomamö, Chagnon had to come to an understanding of the ways that the Yąnomamö men used power in their culture. How did Chagnon learn about the use of power in Yąnomamö culture? How did he protect himself and his property?

2. In "Doing Fieldwork," Chagnon mentions that the Yąnomamö exhibit a high frequency of wife-beating. Later in *Yąnomamö: The Fierce People*, Chagnon presents the following description of male and female roles:

There are a number of distinctions based on status differences [of Yąnomamö culture] that are important in daily life. Perhaps the most conspicuous and most important is the distinction between males and females.

Yąnomamö society is decidedly masculine. As was discussed earlier, there is a definite preference to have male children, resulting in a higher incidence of female infanticide as opposed to male infanticide. Female children assume duties and responsibilities in the household long before their brothers are obliged to participate in useful domestic tasks. For the most part, little girls are obliged to tend their younger brothers and sisters, although they are also expected to help their mothers in other chores such as cooking, hauling water, and collecting firewood. By the time girls have reached puberty they have already learned that their world is decidedly less attractive than that of their brothers.

As members of local descent groups, girls have almost no voice in the decisions reached by their agnates [their father and his relatives] concerning marriage. They are largely pawns to be disposed of by their kinsmen, and their wishes are given very little consideration. In many cases, the girl has been promised to a man long before she reaches puberty, and in some cases her husband actually raises her for part of her childhood. In short, they do not participate as equals in the political affairs of the corporate kinship group and seem to inherit most of the duties without enjoying many of the privileges.

Marriage does not enhance the status of the girl, for her duties as wife require her to assume difficult and laborious tasks too menial to be executed by the men. For the most part these include the incessant demands for firewood and drinking water, particularly the former. Women spend several hours each day scouring the neighborhood for suitable wood. There is usually an abundant supply in the garden within a year of the clearing of the land, but this disappears rapidly. Thereafter, the women must forage further afield to collect the daily supply of firewood, sometimes traveling several miles each day to obtain it. . . .

Women must respond quickly to the demands of their husbands. In fact, they must respond without waiting for a command. It is interesting to watch the behavior of women when their husbands return from a hunting trip or a visit. The men march slowly across the village and retire silently to their hammocks. The woman, no matter what she is doing, hurries home and quietly but rapidly prepares a meal for the husband. Should the wife be slow in doing this, the husband is within his rights to beat her. Most reprimands meted out by irate husbands take the form of blows with the hand or with a piece of firewood, but a good many husbands are even more brutal. Some of them chop their wives with the sharp edge of a machete or axe, or shoot them with a barbed arrow in some nonvital area, such as the buttocks or leg. Many men are given over to punishing their wives by holding the hot end of a glowing stick against them, resulting in serious burns. The punishment is usually, however, adjusted to the seriousness of the wife's shortcomings, more drastic measures being reserved for infidelity or suspicion of infidelity. Many men, however, show their ferocity by meting out serious punishment to their wives for even minor offenses. It is not uncommon for a man to injure his errant wife seriously; and some have even killed their wives.

Women expect this kind of treatment and many of them measure their husband's concern in terms of the frequency of minor beatings they sustain. I overheard two young women discussing each other's scalp scars. One of them commented that the other's husband must really care for her since he has beaten her on the head so frequently!

A woman usually depends for protection on her brothers, who will defend her against a cruel husband. If a man is too brutal to a wife, her brothers may take the woman away from him and give her to another man. It is largely for this reason that women abhor the possibility of being married off to men in distant villages; they know that their brothers cannot protect them under these circumstances. . . .

Still, the women have one method by which they can exercise a measure of influence over village politics. All women fear being abducted by raiders and always leave the village with this anxiety at the back of their minds. Women always bring their children with them, particularly younger children, so that if they are abducted, the child will not starve to death because of the separation of the mother. They are therefore concerned with the political behavior of their men and occasionally goad them into taking action against some possible enemy by caustically accusing the men of cowardice. This has the effect of establishing the village's reputation for ferocity, reducing the possibility of raiders abducting the women while they are out collecting firewood or garden produce. The men cannot stand being chided by the women in this fashion, and are forced to take action if the women unite against them.*

Drawing from "Doing Fieldwork" and this quotation, make a list of factors or aspects of Yąnomamö culture that may lead to wife-beating.

What kind of changes would have to be made in Yąnomamö culture to reduce the frequency of wife-beating?

Which of the factors on the list apply to your culture? Do you feel that these factors in your culture lead to an abuse of women?

3. Why do you feel that the Yąnomamö men allow the women to chide them about being cowards when they keep the women subservient in all other ways?

4. Did you detect any examples of homeopathic magic or scapegoating in Chagnon's description of the Yąnomamö culture?

_____ **WRITING ASSIGNMENTS**

1. Describe and analyze the power structure of the Yąnomamö people.

2. Drawing upon what you have learned from Chagnon's study of Yąnomamö culture, develop and explain your theory about the causes of wife-beating in our society.

3. Do you consider Chagnon to be a reliable and trustworthy enthnographer?

4. When he lived among the Yąnomamö, Chagnon must have observed wife-beating and many other kinds of brutality. How do you believe that

---

*Excerpt from "Division of Labor and Daily Social Life" from *Yąnomamö: The Fierce People* by Napoleon Chagnon, copyright © 1968 by Holt, Rinehart and Winston, Inc. Reprinted by permission of the publisher.

Chagnon should act in these situations? Should he, as an anthropologist studying the culture, not become involved? Or should he intervene and attempt to stop the violence? In other words, is it ethical for anthropologists to intervene in the culture that they are observing?

5. When anthropologists live among the people that they are studying, they take field notes, which are detailed records of what the anthropologists observe. Field notes usually include descriptions of the physical surroundings, portraits of the people, a transcription of dialogue, and a narration of events. Since anthropologists are considered to be a part of the culture being observed, they also include notes on what they say and do as well as any reflections they might have on what is observed (these are usually designated by "O.C.," or "observer's comments"). What follows is an excerpt from some field notes written by an educator who was observing a high school class:

March 24, 1980
Joe McCloud
11:00 A.M. to 12:30 P.M.
Westwood High
6th Set of Notes

The Fourth Period
Class in Marge's Room

I arrived at Westwood High at five minutes to eleven, the time Marge told me her fourth period started. I was dressed as usual: sport shirt, chino pants, and a Woolrich parka. The fourth period is the only time during the day when all the students who are in the "neurologically impaired/learning disability" program, better known as "Marge's program," come together. During the other periods, certain students in the program, two or three or four at most, come to her room for help with the work they are getting in other regular high school classes.

It was a warm, fortyish, promise of spring day. There was a police patrol wagon, the kind that has benches in the back that are used for large busts, parked in the back of the big parking lot that is in front of the school. No one was sitting in it and I never heard its reason for being there. In the circular drive in front of the school was parked a United States Army car. It had insignias on the side and was a khaki color. As I walked from my car, a balding fortyish man in an Army uniform came out of the building and went to the car and sat down. Four boys and a girl also walked out of the school. All were white. They had on old dungarees and colored stenciled T-shirts with spring jackets over them. One of the boys, the tallest of the four called out, "oink, oink, oink." This was done as he sighted the police vehicle in the back.

O.C.: This was strange to me in that I didn't think that the kids were into "the police as pigs." Somehow I associated that with another time, the early 1970s. I'm going to have to come to grips with the assumptions I have about high school due to my own experience. Sometimes I feel like Westwood is entirely different from my high school and yet this police car incident reminded me of mine.

Classes were changing when I walked down the halls. As usual there was the boy with girl standing here and there by the lockers. There were three couples that I saw. There was the occasional shout. There were not teachers outside the doors.

O.C.: The halls generally seem to be relatively unsupervised during class changes.

Two black girls I remember walking down the hall together. They were tall and thin and their hair was elaborately braided with beads all through them. I stopped by the office to tell Mr. Talbot's (the principal) secretary that I was in the building. She gave me a warm smile.

O.C.: I feel quite comfortable in the school now. Somehow I feel like I belong. As I walk down the halls some teachers say hello. I have been going out of my way to say hello to kids that I pass. Twice I've been in a stare-down with kids passing in the hall. Saying, "How ya' doin'?" seems to disalarm them.

I walked into Marge's class and she was standing in front of the room with more people than I had ever seen in the room save for her homeroom which is right after second period. She looked like she was talking to the class or was just about to start. She was dressed as she had been on my other visits—clean, neat, well-dressed but casual. Today she had on a striped blazer, a white blouse and dark slacks.*

As one of your writing assignments, find some unfamiliar situation to observe (a fraternity or sorority meeting, a religious event, a parade, and so on), then observe the situation and take field notes on what you observe. For some situations, such as a sorority meeting, you will need to ask permission of appropriate officials before beginning your observation. A good anthropologist always negotiates his or her entree into the "culture" to be studied. Also, before you turn in your field notes, you should change the names of those people whom you observed. This is standard procedure (part of an anthropologist's ethics) that will protect the people you are observing.

Understanding Rituals

In 1931, Margaret Mead, perhaps the best known of American anthropologists, made one of her many field trips to New Guinea. There she lived among three native societies. She later wrote *Sex and Temperament in Three Primitive Societies* about the field trip.

The particular New Guinea society that seemed most to fascinate Mead was the Arapesh, a people who lived in three different terrains—the mountains, the beach, and the plains. The culture of the people in each

---

*From *Qualitative Research for Education: An Introduction to Theory and Methods* by Robert C. Bogdan and Sari Knopp Biklen. Copyright © by Allyn and Bacon. Reprinted by permission.

terrain was remarkably distinct. For part of the field trip, Mead lived in the mountain village of Alitoa. Of them, Mead wrote:

> Arapesh life is organized about this central plot of the way men and women, physiologically different and possessed of differing potencies, unite in a common adventure that is primarily maternal, cherishing, and oriented away from the self and towards the needs of the next generation. It is a culture in which men and women do different things for the same reasons, in which men are not expected to respond to one set of motivations and women to another, in which if men are given more authority it is because authority is a necessary evil that someone, and that one the freer partner, must carry. [p. 15]

The beach and plains Arapesh were more aggressive and allowed for less equality between men and women. Mead considered the plains Arapesh, who held close ties with a tribe of headhunters and were reputed for their knowledge of sorcery, the fiercest of the Arapesh; they often terrorized both the beach and mountain people with their magical charms.

In "The Growth and Initiation of an Arapesh Boy" (a chapter from *Sex and Temperament*), Mead writes about the initiation ritual practiced by the mountain Arapesh of Alitoa.

_____ **Prereading**

An initiation ritual is a "rite of passage." In primitive societies, the initiation ritual most often marks the transition of the male from being a boy to becoming a man. The rituals, which are practiced by a wide range of primitive cultures, tend to include certain key elements, though not necessarily in this exact sequence:

1. The pubescent boys are separated from the tribe.
2. They undergo a symbolic death.
3. They are considered to be "invisible" and unclean.
4. They are often given new names.
5. They are often terrorized or ground down so that they will leave behind their old beliefs.
6. They undergo ritual ceremonies such as circumcision, which Mead calls "incision."
7. They learn secret knowledge.
8. They are symbolically reborn and transformed into men.
9. They develop a sense of communication with the other boys being initiated and the men.
10. They return to the village and assume the role of a man in their society.

Even people in civilized societies practice rites of passage, such as graduation, baptism, bar mitzvah, weddings, boot camp, and initiation into a club.

Have you ever participated in or witnessed an initiation ritual? Did the ritual make use of some of the elements listed above?

Do you feel that students undergo initiation ritual when they begin college? Or could the college experience itself be viewed as a protracted initiation ritual?

The Growth and Initiation of an Arapesh Boy
Margaret Mead

By the time the Arapesh child is seven or eight, its personality is set.   **1** Both boys and girls have learned a happy, trustful, confident attitude towards life. They have learned to include in the circle of their affection everyone with whom they are connected in any way whatsoever, and to respond to any relationship term with an active expression of warmth. They have been discouraged from any habits of aggressiveness towards others; they have learned to treat with respect and consideration the property, the sleep, and the feelings of other people. They definitely associate the giving of food with warmth, approval, acceptance, and security, and take any withholding of food as a sign of hostility and rejection. They have learned to be passive participators in the activities of their elders, but they have had very little experience of playing games on their own or organizing their own lives. They have become accustomed to respond when others give the signal, to follow where others lead, to be enthusiastic and uncritical about new things that are presented to them. When they are cold, or bored, or lonely, they bubble their lips in a hundred patterned ways.

They have learned to fear the stranger, the Plainsman, the man who   **2** walks among them with eyes alert for a bit of dirt that will be their undoing. And they have been taught to guard every chance piece of unfinished food or old clothing, to keep a sharp watch over these recently separated sections of their personalities when they meet a stranger. They have been permitted no expressions of hostility or aggressiveness towards any one of their hundred relatives, all of whom must be loved and cherished; but they have been allowed to join in their parents' sulky hatred of the sorcerers, and even to hurl a few small spears down a path that a departing group of Plainsmen have taken. So the basic pattern has been laid that in later life will make them identify anyone who hurts them as a stranger, and thus invoke the old sorcery-pattern

Source: "The Growth and Initiation of an Arapesh Boy" from *Sex and Temperament* by Margaret Mead, pp. 61–79. Copyright © 1935, 1950, 1963 by Margaret Mead. Reprinted by permission of William Morrow & Co., Inc.

of purloining the stranger's dirt. Only two sex-differences of importance
have been established, the affect surrounding group activities, and the
greater expressiveness in anger that is permitted little boys. This latter
is blurred by other considerations of order of birth, and sex of siblings;
girls who have no brothers show the same tendencies, and boys who
are one of many brothers show them less.

When the first signs of puberty appear—the lifting and swelling of a   3
girl's breasts, the appearance of a boy's pubic hair—the adolescent
child must observe certain taboos, must avoid eating certain meats and
drinking cold water until the yams that are now planted shall be har-
vested and sprouting in the yam-house, a taboo period of almost a
year. It is now the child's duty to observe these taboos, carefully, sol-
emnly "to grow itself," after the rules that everyone knows are correct.
For the first time children are now made culturally self-conscious of the
physiology of sex. Before this what masturbation there was—and it is
slight because of the greater emphasis upon the socially acceptable
pleasure of lip-bubbling—was disregarded as children's play. But when
a young boy begins to keep the taboos of his pubic hair, he is cautioned
against further careless handling of his genitals. And he learns from
the older boys what one must do if one has broken any of the rules essential to growth; he learns of the disciplinary and hygienic use of
stinging nettles and actual bleeding with a sharpened bamboo instrument. He becomes the responsible custodian of his own growth; and
the sanctions are all in terms of that growth. If he breaks the rules, no
one will punish him; no one but himself will suffer. He will simply not
grow to be a tall strong man, a man worthy to be the father of
children. He is now committed to the task of keeping the reproductive
function of women and the food-getting function of men apart. The
most dramatic representation of this separation of the function of men
and women is the *tamberan* cult. The *tamberan* is the supernatural patron
of the grown men of the tribe; he, or they, for sometimes he is
conceived severally, must never be seen by the women and uninitiated
children, and he is impersonated for their listening benefit by various
noise-making devices, flutes, whistles, slit gongs, and so forth. From
the time that a child is old enough to pay any attention to its surroundings, the coming of the *tamberan*, his stay in the village, his dramatic
departure, are high points of life. But until little boys and girls are six
or seven, the coming of the *tamberan* means the same thing to both
sexes. There is the bustle and stir that betokens a feast; people gather
in one of the larger villages, sleeping packed tight around the fire in
the crowded houses. Women and girls bring great loads of firewood on
their backs and stack it under the raised houses. The men go off for a
week's hunting, keeping a sharp look-out for monitor lizards for new
drum-heads, while they hunt also for cassowary, kangaroo, and wall-
aby. There is much talk of a pig, or perhaps two pigs, which are to be
contributed by someone in a neighbouring village and brought over for

the feast. Yams are brought in by relatives of the man at whose initiation the *tamberan* is to come. These are piled in little mounds on the
agehu,[1] and the grateful recipients march around them reciting "Wa Wa
Wa," which is called to "kill the bush-fowl" and signifies that some day
they will return these gifts. Finally there is news that the hunting is
finished, a specially large tree-kangaroo has completed the bag. The
hunters come in, wearing bird-of-paradise feathers in their hair, proud
of their kill, which is brought in in packages tied to poles and
festooned with red and green streamers of tracaena-leaves. Speeches of
congratulations are made, and tomorrow there will be cooking of the
special coconut croquettes that are made only for feasts.

Underneath all of these preparations runs a current of excitement.   4
The *tamberan* will be coming, coming from beyond the hill, coming
from seaward. The little children think of him as a huge monster, as
tall as a coconut-tree, who lives in the sea except on these rare occasions when he is summoned to sing to the people. When the *tamberan*
comes, one runs away, as fast as ever one can, holding on to one's
mother's grass skirt, tripping and stumbling, dropping one's mouthful
of yam, wailing for fear one will be left behind. The lovely sound of
the flutes is getting closer every minute, and something frightful would
happen to the little girl or boy caught loitering in the village after the
men and the *tamberan* enter it. So they hurry down the slope of the
mountain, women and children and puppies, and perhaps a little pig
or two that have come squealing after their mistress. One woman car-
ries a new-born baby, with many little bundles of leaves hung from its
net bag to protect it against evil, and a banana-leaf over the bag to shelter it from sun and rain. An old woman, her sparse white hair standing
up abruptly on her nearly bald head, hobbles along at the tail of the
procession, muttering that never again will she try to climb the mountain for a feast, no, after this she will stay in her little place in the valley, she will feed her son's pigs, but when his wife again has a child,
she will not climb the mountain to see it. It's too hard, too hard for her
old legs, and the tumour is too heavy to carry. The tumour is slowly
becoming more pronounced on her abdomen, outlined clearly beneath
her sagging skin. That tumour came from giving food to the sorcerers
who had killed her brother long ago. As she shuffles along, holding
tightly to a stick, the others look at her a little askance. Old women so
far past the child-bearing period know a little more than young
women. Their feet are not hurried by the same fear that makes a nursing mother clutch her child to her and flee from the sound of the
flutes, and later will make her tremble when she hears her husband's
step on the house-ladder. What if he has not properly washed his
hands in the proper magical herbs? It was for such neglect that Temos

---

[1] Agehu: the feasting and ceremonial area of the village.

lost her baby, and that one child of Nyelahai died. Old women do not fear these things any longer; they go no more to the menstrual hut, men do not lower their voices when they talk near them.

High and clear from the distant hill-side comes the sound of the   5
flutes. "Does not the *tamberan* have a beautiful voice?" whisper the women to each other, and "Tamberan, tamberan," echo the babies. From a knot of small girls comes a skeptical whisper: "If the *tamberan* is so big, how can he get inside his house?" "Be quiet! Hush your talk!" comes sharply from the mother of the new-born child. "If you talk about the *tamberan* like that, we shall all die." Nearer come the flutes, lovely broken sounds played faultily by young unaccustomed musicians. Now surely the *tamberan* is in the hamlet itself, winding among the trees, taking from the palm-trees his sacred mark, which he placed there six months ago, so that now the coconuts may be picked for the feast. The sun, before so hot, goes behind a cloud and a quick shower drenches the waiting women and children. The voice of the *tamberan* does not come so clearly through the rain. A chill settles upon the little company, babies cry and are hastily hushed against their mothers' breasts. Now to the sound of the flutes is added the sound of beaten slit gongs. "The *tamberan* has entered the house," whispers one of the older women. They stir, rearrange the net bags, which they have slackened from their foreheads, call to the children who have wandered farther down the hill-side. A distant halloo is heard from the hill-top; this is the men calling the women and children back to the village, which is once more safe for them now that the *tamberan* is closely housed in the special little house that is more gaily decorated than any of the others, with its painted wall-plates at the four corners and the painted shield set up in the gable. Answering the men's call, they climb laboriously back. There is no feeling that they have been excluded, that they are in any way inferior creatures whom the men have banished from a festive scene. It is only that this is something that would not be safe for them, something that concerns the growth and strength of men and boys, but which would be dangerous for women and children. Their men are careful of them, they protect them diligently.

It is always an exciting moment to re-enter the village where so re-   6
cently something mysterious has happened. In every house, on the gable or by the door, banners of brightly coloured leaves have been set up. The *tamberan* paused here. At the foot of each palm-tree lies a wreath of red leaves; these are the *tamberan's* anklets, which fell off as he stood beneath the palms. On the rain-softened surface of the *agehu* are large marks. One of the men may remark self-consciously to a woman or a child that these are the marks of the *tamberan's* testicles. It is easy to see how big the *tamberan* is. But although the men have been so careful to arrange this pantomime, the women pay little attention to the details. It is all something that is better let alone, even by the mind. It is something that belongs to the men. They have their *tamberans*

also, childbirth, and girl's puberty rites, and the ritual of dyeing grass
skirts. These are the *tamberans* of women. And this *tamberan*, he belongs
to the men, and does not bear thinking of. From the little *tamberan*
house the flutes, accompanied now by slit gongs, sound steadily. In
and out from the house pass the men, the initiated boys, and if there
are no visitors from the beach, the older uninitiated boys also.

This permission to the uninitiated boys marks another difference be-   7
tween the *tamberan* cult as it is practised by the Arapesh and the emphases among the surrounding tribes. In many parts of New Guinea,
the *tamberan* cult is a way of maintaining the authority of the older men
over the women and children; it is a system directed against the
women and children, designed to keep them in their ignominious
places and punish them if they try to emerge. In some tribes, a woman
who accidentally sees the *tamberan* is killed. The young boys are threatened with the dire things that will happen to them at their initiation,
and initiation becomes a sort of vicious hazing in which the older men
revenge themselves upon recalcitrant boys and for the indignities that
they themselves once suffered. Such are the primary emphases of the
wide-spread *tamberan* cult. Secrecy, age and sex-hostility, fear and hazing, have shaped its formal pattern. But the Arapesh, although they
share part of the formal pattern with their neighbours, have changed
all the emphases. In a community where there is no hostility between
men and women, and where the old men, far from resenting the wax-
ing strength of the young men, find in it their greatest source of happiness, a cult that stresses hate and punishment is out of place. And so
the mountain people have revised most of the major points. Where
other peoples kill a woman who chances on the secrets, and go to war
against a community that does not keep its women sufficiently in the
dark, the Arapesh merely swear the woman to secrecy, telling her that
if she does not talk to others nothing will happen to her. On the beach,
initiated boys are told that if they betray the secrets of the cult they
will be found hanging from a tree, eviscerated by the *tamberan*. But in
the mountains this frightening threat is omitted. And the great distinction between initiated and uninitiated boys is also blurred. In a properly organized men's cult, boys who have not been initiated are
severely barred from participation, but among the Arapesh, where all
the motivation for such exclusion is lacking, the older men say: "Here
is a good feast. It is a pity that he who is tall should not eat it just because we have not yet incised him. Let him come in." But if critical and
orthodox strangers from the beach are present, the uninitiated boys are
hustled out of sight, for the Arapesh are sensitive about their own happily muddled unorthodoxy.

On one occasion in Alitoa, there were many visitors from the beach   8
in the house of the *tamberan*, blowing the flutes, beating the slit gongs,
and generally taking matters into their own hands. After all it was from
the beach that the flutes had come; forty years ago the mountain peo-

ple had had nothing but seed whistles with which to impersonate their supernaturals. The visitors were haughty and hungry and demanded more meat. In traditional fashion they banged on the floor of the *tamberan* house and began hurling fire-sticks down the ladder. Finally, with a great clatter, they threatened the emergence of the *tamberan*. It was just dusk. Women and children were gathered in clusters close to the *tamberan* house, cooking the evening meal, when the threat came. Frantic, unprepared, desperate, they fled down the mountain sides, children straying, falling, lost among the rocks. With my hand held tightly in hers, Budagiel, my "sister," dragged my unaccustomed feet after the rest. Slipping, sliding, gasping for breath, we tumbled on. Then came a shout from above: "Come back, it was nonsense! It was not true." And breathlessly we clambered back up the slope. On the *agehu* confusion reigned, men were rushing about, arguing, exclaiming, disputing. Finally Baimal, volatile, excitable little Baimal, always indomitable despite his slight stature, dashed forward and began beating the front of the *tamberan* house with a stick: "You would, would you? You would come out and frighten our women-folk, and send them slipping and stumbling out into the dark and wet? You would chase our children away, would you? Take that and that and that!" And blow after blow fell with resounding whacks on the thatched roof. After that Baimal had to send in some meat to the outraged *tamberan*, but he didn't mind. Nor did the community. Baimal had expressed for all of them their objection to the use of the *tamberan* as an instrument of terror and intimidation. It was the *tamberan* that helped them grow the children and guard the women! The visitors from the beach sulked, ate the meat-offering, and went home to comment upon the barbarous ways of these mountain people who had no sense of the way in which things should be done.

Sometimes the *tamberan* stays only a few days in a village, sometimes 9 he stays several weeks. He comes to taboo coconut-trees for feasts and to lift the taboo, to preside over the second mortuary feast when the bones of an honoured man are dug up and distributed among the relatives. He comes when a new *tamberan* house is built, and most importantly, he comes for an initiation, when a large enclosure of palm-matting is built at one end of a village and the initiates are segregated in it for several months.

As children grow older and beyond the period when they cling in 10 fright to their mother's skirts, there comes to be a marked sex-difference in their attitudes towards the *tamberan*. The little girls continue to follow their mother's steps; they learn not to speculate lest misfortune come upon them all. A habit of intellectual passivity falls upon them, a more pronounced lack of intellectual interest than that which characterizes their brothers' minds. All that is strange, that is uncharted and unnamed—unfamiliar sounds, unfamiliar shapes—these are forbidden to women, whose duty it is to guard their reproductivity closely and tenderly. This prohibition cuts them off from speculative thought and likewise from art, because among the Arapesh art and the supernatural are part and parcel of each other. All children scribble with bits of charcoal upon pieces of bark, the highly polished sago-bark strips that are used as beds and as wall-plates. They draw ovals that are yams, and circles that are taros, and little squares that are gardens, and patterns that are representative of string figures, and a pretty little design that is called the "morning star." Drawing these designs becomes in later years an occupation exclusively of women, a game with which they can amuse themselves during the long damp hours in the menstrual hut.[2] But painting, painting mysterious half-realized figures in red and yellow, on big pieces of bark that will adorn the *tamberan* house, or a yam-house, this belongs to the men. The feeling against women's participating in art and in the men's cult is one and the same; it is not safe, it would endanger the women themselves, it would endanger the order of the universe within which men and women and children live in safety. When I showed them a brown, life-sized doll, the women shrank away from it in fright. They had never seen a realistic image before; they took it for a corpse. The men, with their different experience, recognized it as a mere representation, and one of them voiced the prevalent attitude towards women's concerning themselves with such things: "You women had better not look at that thing or it will ruin you entirely." Later the men became gay and familiar with the doll, danced with it in their arms and rearranged its ornaments, but the women, schooled since childhood in the acceptance of marvels and the suppression of all thought about them, never quite accepted the fact that it was only a doll. They would take me aside to ask me how I fed it, and ask if it would never grow any bigger. And if I laid it on the ground with its head lower than its feet, some solicitous woman always rushed to turn it around. Thus through the appearances of the *tamberan* the women and girls are trained in the passive acceptance that is considered their only safety in life.

But for the small boys it is different. To them speculation is not for- **11** bidden. It is true that they have to run away now, but later, just a little later, they will be part of the performance; they will go with the men to bring the *tamberan* back to the village, they will see if the *tamberan* really eats all those plates of meat which are passed into the *tamberan* house, or whether the men and boys get some too. If they are lucky, they will be initiated with a large group of boys; for three months they will live within the initiation enclosure, while they undergo the ceremony that is called "being swallowed by the *tamberan*," or sometimes "being swallowed by the cassowary." They know that the cassowary and the *tamberan* have some not very clear connection with each other.

---

[2] Menstrual hut: some primitive people felt that the blood of menstruation or birth was unclean, so they built huts where menstruating women and women giving birth stayed.

Anyway, this talk of swallowing, made up by some distant people interested in frightening women and children, holds no terror for little Arapesh boys. They have seen their big brothers emerge plump and sleek from this swallowing process, with their eyes glowing with pride and self-importance, their skins beautifully oiled and painted, new ornaments on their arms and legs, and lovely feathers in their hair. Apparently this swallowing is a very pleasant business, and the main point is to be swallowed in large numbers, in a big initiation ceremony, rather than swallowed quietly among their own relatives. So the small boys speculate together, no longer hiding with the women but going off by themselves into the bush, where they can give their tongues and their imagination free rein. As the *tamberan* cult dulls the imagination of the girls, it stimulates and quickens the imagination of the small boys. And this quickening extends to other things, to greater interest in the plants and animals of the bush, to greater curiosity about life in general. Upon the little girl of ten, sitting demurely beside her mother or her mother-in-law, the horizon of life has closed down in a way that it has not upon her brother. New responsibilities wait for him, as soon as he is grown enough to be initiated. He watches the taboos of his pubic hair even more assiduously, and imitates the self-disciplinary cuttings of the bigger boys even more valiantly, and wonders again and again what it will be like to be swallowed. The little girl bubbles her lips and ceases to think at all. If she does not think, if she does not let her mind wander in forbidden places, some day she too will hold a baby in her arms, a baby who will be born secretly in the bush, in a spot forbidden to men.

At last the time comes for a boy to be initiated. If he is an eldest son, **12** son of a large household, heir to an important man, he may be initiated separately. The large initiations are held only every six or seven years, when repeated gibes between communities at big feasts have finally goaded some community into undertaking the huge work of organization and preparation that is necessary if some twelve or fifteen boys and their sponsoring relatives are to be fed for several months in one place. Such a feast takes several years to prepare, and has its echoes throughout the lives of the group of novices, who years later, as middle-aged men, will be finding pigs to take back to that village to be distributed in final long-deferred repayment for the initiation. Meanwhile, in the six-year period between initiations, boys who were too small when the last initiation was held have grown very tall, embarrassingly so. They have gradually learned most of the secrets. They know that the voice of the *tamberan* is made by the big bamboo flutes, and may even have learned to play upon them. Altogether, it is better that a great tall boy should be initiated quietly, with a small family feast.

The essentials of the initiation remain the same: there is a ritual seg- **13** regation from the company of women, during which time the novice observes certain special food taboos, is incised, eats a sacrificial meal of

the blood of the older men, and is shown various marvellous things.
The marvelous things fall into two classes: remarkable objects that he
has never seen before, such as masks, and other carvings and representations; and the revelation, part of which usually has been revealed to
him already, of the fact that there is really no *tamberan* at all, but that
all of these things are done by men. The cassowary,[3] who has been so
mysteriously said to swallow little boys, is merely one of the men of a
certain clan, wearing a ferocious pair of cassowary-feather eye-pieces,
and having suspended from his neck a shell-covered bag in which are
stuck two sharpened cassowary-bones. The *tamberan* himself is simply
the noise of the flutes, the beating of the slit gongs by the men, or a
general concept covering the whole set of mystifying acts. To a boy,
growing up among the Arapesh means finding out that there is no
Santa Claus, having it acknowledged that one is old enough to know
that all this fanfare and ruffle of drums is a pantomime, devoutly maintained generation after generation because its maintenance will help to
make boys grow, and so promote the well-being of the people. The incision itself, and the meal of blood that the initiates are fed, is another
matter. The belief in blood and blood-letting, in the important connexion between blood and growth, is part of the very bones of Arapesh
culture. And when one boy is initiated at a time, it is these aspects
which are stressed. About the flutes he knows already, and one household has few other hidden marvels to show him. His initiation becomes
a matter of incision and a sacrificial meal.

In the big initiations other points are emphasized: the comradeship   **14**
between all of the boys, the care that is taken of them by their fathers
and elder brothers, and by the special sponsors, who accompany them
each day to the bathing-pool, bending back the brambles from their
paths, even as their ghostly ancestors are also believed to do. The recip-
rocal attitudes of the boys towards their sponsors are emphasized; their
sponsors weave them arm-bands that the novices must wear until they
fall off, and then they will make feasts for the sponsors. In the enclosure there is plenty to eat. The older men hunt for the novices and feed
them well; the period is supposed to be magically growth-promoting,
and they see to it that it is actually healthful also. For the only time in
all their meagrely fed lives, the young Arapesh boys become almost
plump.

The anxiety of the older men about the preservation of these neces-   **15**
sary secrets is communicated to the novices, not with intimidating
threats, but by giving them a share in all the little acts of loving decep-
tion that the men practise on the women. The novices wear little leaf
covers on their new wounds, and these are spoken of as their wives.
The voices of these wives are imitated on pieces of whistling grass for

---

[3] Cassowary: a large, flightless bird, usually about 5 feet in height.

the benefit of the listening women. A great fiction is got up about these imaginary "wives." Little bundles of firewood are prepared and hung on the paths to show the women where the tiny fanciful wives of the novices have been at work. Meanwhile, the women among themselves refer to these wives as "little birds" and probe no deeper into what is obviously some kind of a male mystery and better let alone.

The whole ceremony, formally representative of a jealous male so- **16** ciety grudgingly admitting younger males, now too old to be kept out, has been turned into a growth-giving rite. Even the gauntlet that the initiates run between two rows of men armed with stinging nettles is not administered in a spirit of hazing, but so that the novices will grow. They are given no instructions that will make them hate, despise, or fear women. They are subjected to a divinatory ceremony to find out whether they have been experimenting with sex or not, something that they know is forbidden because it will stunt natural growth. The boy who is found guilty is punished by being made to chew a piece of areca-nut that has been placed in contact with a woman's vulva, if possible with the vulva of the woman, usually his betrothed wife, with whom he has had intercourse. This ritual break of the most deeply felt taboo in Arapesh culture, the taboo that separates the mouth and the genitals, food and sex, is felt to be punishment enough; and while the guilty are punished, all are cautioned against similar in- dulgence. Sex is good, but dangerous to those who have not yet attained their growth.

So, with ceremonial and a little admonition, much singing and bath- **17** ing and eating, the two or three months of the seclusion pass away. At the end, the novices, dressed most resplendently, appear before their overjoyed mothers and sisters, who far from having spent the period in anxiety about their fate, have expected to find them just as plump and well fed as they actually appear. Then each youth, dressed in his best, is taken by his father's road, to the houses of all of his father's trade- friends, and also, when such women have married far away, to the houses of his father's sisters. In each house the novice is given a gift, a gift that he will some day reciprocate. He now walks, ceremonially and often actually for the first time, the road of his ancestors, the road by which tools and implements and weapons and ornaments, songs and new fashions, are imported; along this road also goes dirt stolen in anger, and loving relatives hunting for others' dirt. This is hereafter known as his road, the road over which all of these simple necessities and high excitements of life will pass.

His childhood is ended. From one who has been grown by the daily **18** carefulness and hard work of others, he now passes into the class of those whose care is for others' growth. During his pubescence his care was for his own growth, for the observances of the taboo would ensure to him muscle and bone, height and breadth, and strength to beget and rear children. This strength is never phrased as sexual potency, a point

in which the Arapesh are profoundly uninterested and for which they
have no vocabulary. Now this care is shifted and he has instead new
responsibilities towards those who after years devoted to his growth are
now growing old themselves, and towards his younger brothers and
sisters, and his young betrothed wife.

There is no feeling here that he is subservient towards those older   **19**
than himself, that he chafes beneath the power of those stronger than
himself. Instead, the oldest and the youngest, the ageing parent and
the little child, are placed together in Arapesh feeling, in contrast to
those who from puberty to middle age are specially concerned with sex
and child-rearing. From puberty to middle age one occupies a special
position with responsibilities towards the old and towards the young.
Half of the food in the world is set apart for the elders and the children, certain kinds of yams, certain kinds of taro, certain kinds of birds
and fish and meat—these are for those who are not yet concerned with
sex, or whose concern with it is over. There is no feeling here that the
powerful and the strong appropriate the best foods, but rather there is
a symbolic division into two equal parts from which all are fed. After a
big feast, the men of the locality make a special little family feast for
the women whose hard labour in carrying food and firewood has made
the feast possible. They often garnish the plates with tree-kangaroo, a
food that the women themselves cannot eat. But when I commented on
the seeming thoughtlessness of rewarding the women with meat that
was forbidden them, they stared at me in surprise: "But their children
can eat it." And between men and their children there is no more ri-
valry than this. To grow his son, to find for him the food from which
he must himself abstain, has been the father's great delight during his
son's childhood. Piece by piece he has built up his son's body. The
Arapesh father does not say to his son: "I am your father, I begot you,
therefore you must obey me." He would regard such a claim as pre-
sumptuous nonsense. Instead he says: "I grew you. I grew the yams, I
worked the sago, I hunted the meat, I laboured for the food that made
your body. Therefore I have the right to speak like this to you." And
this relationship between father and son, a relationship based on food
given and food gratefully received, is shared in slighter measure by all
the old and young of a community. Every man has contributed to the
growth of every child reared within the small circle of mountains that
forms his world. If a young man should so far forget himself as to
speak rudely or hastily to an old man, the old man may answer, sadly,
reproachfully: "And think how many pigs I have fattened from which
you took your growth."

As the young wax strong, the old retire more and more. When the   **20**
eldest son enters the *tamberan* cult, or if the eldest child is a girl, when
she reaches puberty, the father formally retires. Henceforward, all that
he does is done in his son's name; the big yam-house that he built last

year is spoken of as his son's; when trade-friends come, he sits aside-
and lets his son entertain them. The son too must bear in mind his
father's increasing age by little ritual acts of carefulness. He must take
care that none of the sago that is worked by himself or his brothers and
sisters is given to his father and mother to eat. Sago worked by the
young is dangerous to the old. The son must not eat lime from his
father's lime-gourd, or step over any of his father's possessions as they
lie on the floor. His young, springing manhood would endanger his
father's slackening, sexless hold on life.

The father's sexless rôle is illustrated most vividly in the attitude of   21
Arapesh middle-aged men towards women. Quarrels over women are
the key-note of the New Guinea primitive world. Almost every culture
has suffered in one way or another because it has failed to solve the
problem. Polygynous societies permit of far more quarreling over
women than do monogamous ones, for the enterprising man, not satisfied with one wife, can always try to express his superiority by trying
to attach a few more. Among the Arapesh, this quarreling has been reduced to a minimum. Polygyny they phrase entirely in terms of inheritance, as the duty of caring for the widow and children of brothers, not
as a sign of superiority over other men. Between the father-age-group
and the son-age-group, there is no possibility of conflict, for all men
over thirty-five or so are concerned not in finding wives for themselves,
but in finding wives for their sons. The search for wives is conducted
among small children, girls from six to ten, and the father's entire interest is enlisted in the son's behalf. Thus one of the ugliest results of
quarreling over women, the quarrel between a man and his son, in
which wealth, power, and prestige are pitted against youth and vigour,
is eliminated. As we shall see later, the Arapesh have not been able to
avoid all quarreling over women, but by phrasing polygyny as a duty
instead of a privilege, and by involving the interests of all the powerful
men in the marriages of the next generation, this struggle is reduced to
a minimum.

Thus at the end of his adolescence the Arapesh boy is placed in his   22
society, he is initiated, he has manifold duties to perform, unaggres-
sively, co-operatively, assisting his father and his uncles; guarding his
father in his old age and his young brother in his childhood; and growing his small, pre-adolescent wife.

Written Response

Mead writes of the *tamberan* ritual: "As the *tamberan* cult dulls the imagination of the girls, it stimulates and quickens the imagination of the
small boys. . . . Upon the little girl of ten, sitting demurely beside her
mother or her mother-in-law, the horizon of life has closed down in a
way that it has not upon her brother." Even though the culture of the

mountain Arapesh allows for an unusual degree of equality between men and women, Mead feels that the sex roles it places on women can limit their imaginations and their potential. Do you feel that the sex roles in our society in any way limit the imagination or potential of women or men? Explain.

_____ **Rhetorical Analysis**

1. Part of Mead's description of the women and children fleeing the *tamberan* reads:

> An old woman, her sparse white hair standing up abruptly on her nearly bald head, hobbles along at the tail of the procession, muttering that never again will she try to climb the mountain for a feast, no, after this she will stay in her little place in the valley, she will feed her son's pigs, but when his wife again has a child, she will not climb the mountain to see it. It's too hard, too hard for her old legs, and the tumour is too heavy to carry. The tumour is slowly becoming more pronounced on her abdomen, outlined clearly beneath her sagging skin. That tumour came from giving food to the sorcerers who had killed her brother long ago.

Here, Mead states that the woman developed a tumor because she gave food to the sorcerers who killed her brother, and Mead states this as if it were a scientific fact. Mead does not add that we, as civilized readers, do not believe that magic kills people and that giving food to sorcerers who killed a relative causes a tumor.

Mead is presenting the Arapesh culture as it might be viewed through the eyes of an Arapesh; the anthropologist and culture become one. How do you react to Mead's style of writing ethnography? How is it different from Chagnon's style? Do you feel that Mead is a believable storyteller, or do you believe that she has "gone native" (that is, lost her objectivity)?

2. The beginning of Mead's description of the *tamberan's* arrival reads:

> Underneath all of these preparations runs a current of excitement. The *tamberan* will be coming, coming from beyond the hill, coming from seaward. The little children think of him as a huge sea monster, as tall as a coconut-tree, who lives in the sea except on these rare occasions when he is summoned to sing to the people.

How, in this brief passage, is Mead attempting to convey to the reader a sense of how the Arapesh people feel? Can you find similar passages in Mead's text?

How does this aspect of Mead's style of describing culture differ from Frazer's or Chagnon's?

3. Mead does not mention many of the Arapesh people by name. As a result, her text is quite different from a short story or novel.

How is Mead's enthnographic narrative different from the narrative of a typical novel? Why do you suppose that she avoids writing about a specific boy undergoing the initiation who could serve as the main character or hero of her narrative?

_____ **Interpretation**

1. Reread, in the Prereading exercise, the list of elements typically found in primitive initiation myths. How many of these elements fit the Arapesh ritual that Mead describes?

2. Reread Mead's description of the Arapesh, which appears in the background information before the Prereading section. How well does this description of the Arapesh agree with what you read in the chapter "The Growth and Initiation of an Arapesh Boy"? In other words, does her general description of the culture of the mountain Arapesh agree with her data—her description of the Arapesh initiation ritual?

3. At one point Mead mentions that the mountain Arapesh have altered the initiation ritual. How have they altered it? Why do you think that they changed the ritual in this way? Do you feel that the Arapesh should make further changes in their ritual? Why or why not?

4. In *Dramas, Fields, and Metaphors* (Ithaca: Cornell, 1974), Victor Turner wrote: "Practically all rituals of any length and complexity represent a passage from one position, constellation, or domain of structure to another" (p. 238). In other words, one purpose of rituals is to redefine a person's social status or position. In what way does the Arapesh initiation ritual redefine the social status of those who undergo it?

5. The visit of the *tamberan* to the Arapesh village is an elaborate pantomime performed by the males who have already been initiated. Do you think the women believe that this "monster" is real, or do they just play along in the way that parents in some cultures pretend to believe in Santa Claus? Why?

6. Mead claims that there is a remarkable degree of equality between men and women in the village of mountain Arapesh that she studied. In what ways are men and women equals? In what ways are women treated as inferiors? What do the menstrual hut and rituals surrounding the cult of the *tamberan* tell you about the roles of men and women in this culture? How does the position of women within the culture of the mountain Arapesh compare to that of women in the culture of the Yąnomamö?

_____ **WRITING ASSIGNMENTS**

1. Describe and interpret an initiation ritual that you have observed or participated in. When you begin to think about how to interpret the ritual, ask yourself: What purpose does the ritual play within my community? If you wish, you might also discuss how you would like to change the ritual to make it more meaningful or less abusive.

2. Mead felt that the mountain Arapesh were a kind and nurturing people. Use Mead's description of the initiation ritual to affirm or refute this view of the mountain Arapesh. You might also wish to draw upon Chagnon's description of the Yąnomamö for a point of comparison.

3. In *The Power of Myth with Bill Moyers* the following exchange occurs between Joseph Campbell and Bill Moyers:

Moyers: What happens when a society no longer embraces a powerful mythology?

Campbell: What we've got on our hands. If you want to find out what it means to have a society without any rituals, read the *New York Times*.

Moyers: And you'd find?

Campbell: The news of the day, including destructive and violent acts by young people who don't know how to behave in a civilized society.

Moyers: Society has provided them no rituals by which they become members of the tribe, of the community. All children need to be twice born, to learn to function rationally in the present world, leaving childhood behind. I think of that passage in the first book of Corinthians: "When I was a child, I spake as a child, I understood as a child, I thought as a child: but when I became a man, I put away my childish things."

Campbell: That's exactly it. That's the significance of the puberty rites. In primal societies, there are teeth knocked out, there are sacrifications, there are circumcisions, there are all kinds of things done. So you don't have your little baby body anymore, you're something else entirely. . . .

Moyers: Where do the kids growing up in the city—on 125th and Broadway, for example—where do these kids get their myths today?

Campbell: They make them up themselves. This is why we have graffiti all over the city. These kids have their own gangs and their own limitations and their own mortality, and they're doing the best they can. But they're dangerous because their own laws are not those of the city. They have not been initiated into our society.*

Campbell argues that when a society loses its myths and its rituals (the enactment of a myth), its people are likely to act at odds with society: The society will manifest a higher occurrence of violence and crime. In "The Growth and Initiation of an Arapesh Boy," Mead shows that a people can decide to revise their rituals, which will in turn alter the structure of their society.

Do you agree that rituals can help to solve some of our society's problems, such as crime, violence, gangs, and so on? Do you think that we need to develop new rituals? If so, what kind of rituals? Do we need to revise some rituals that we currently practice? If so, how?

Write an essay in which you argue (a) that Campbell is wrong and that rituals cannot help to solve any of our problems, or (b) that Campbell is

*From *The Power of Myth with Bill Moyers* by Joseph Campbell, edited by Betty Sue Flowers. Copyright © 1988 by Apostrophe S Productions, Inc., and Alfred van der March Editions. Reprinted by permission of Doubleday, a division of Bantam, Doubleday, Dell Publishing Group, Inc. All rights reserved.

right and that we need to develop new rituals or revise existing ones in order to initiate young people into our society.

Interpreting Dreams

Thomas Gregor, author of *Mehinaku: The Drama of Daily Life in a Brazilian Indian Village* and *Anxious Pleasures: The Sexual Lives of an Amazonian People,* is an anthropologist who has used dreams to understand the inner lives of the people he is studying. After collecting a number of dreams from the Mehinaku tribe (also called Xinguanos) in Brazil, he was surprised to discover that the natives had frequent nightmares about white men.

_____ **Prereading**

The treatment of the Brazilian Indians in the twentieth century has been similar to the United States' treatment of Native Americans.

What do you know about the treatment of Native Americans from the time that European settlers came to the United States to the present?

Dark Dreams About the White Man

Thomas Gregor

> Last night my dream was very bad.
> I dreamed of the white man.
>
> *A Mehinaku villager*

In 1500 explorer Pedro Cabral landed on the coast of Brazil and   1
claimed its lands and native peoples for the Portugese empire. Since that time Brazilian Indians have been killed by European diseases and bounty hunters, forced off their land by squatters and speculators, and enslaved by ranchers and mine owners. Today the Indians, numbering less than one-tenth of the precontact population,[1] inhabit the most remote regions of the country.

I have been privileged as an anthropologist to live among the Mehi-   2
naku, a tribe of about eighty tropical-forest Indians who have thus far escaped the destruction. The Mehinaku, along with eight other single-village tribes, live in a vast government-protected reservation in the

Source: "Dark Dreams About the White Man" by Thomas Gregor, *Natural History,* Vol. 92, No. 1. Copyright © 1982 by the American Museum of Natural History. Reprinted by permission.

_____

[1] Precontact population: the population before contact with Europeans.

Mato Grosso, at the headwaters of the Xingu River in central Brazil. Collectively called Xinguanos by the outside world, the Mehinaku and their neighbors speak dialects of four unrelated languages. In spite of their cultural differences, they have developed a peaceful system of relationships based on intermarriage, trade, and group rituals. This political achievement persists, thanks largely to the geographic isolation of the Xingu reservation. Even today, the Brazilian presence consists only of an outpost of the Brazilian Indian Agency and a small, dirt-strip air force base. Nearly 200 miles of forest and savanna separate the Xingu villages from Shavantina, the nearest permanent Brazilian settlement of any size.

Despite the remoteness of central Brazil and the traditional character   3
of village life, even a casual visitor to the Mehinaku sees unexpected signs of Brazilian society: battery-operated shortwave radios (usually tuned to backwoods popular favorites), battered aluminum pots for carrying water, and discarded items of Western clothing. But these, and the other flotsam and jetsam of industrial society that drift to the center of Brazil, affect only the appearance of Indian culture. They catch the eye of the visitor, but they do not break the rhythm of traditional subsistence, ritual, and trade that are the heartbeat of Xingu life.

Although geographically and socially distant, urban Brazil peers   4
nonetheless into the world of the Xinguanos. Popular magazines feature articles about their life in a "jungle paradise," and smiling Xingu faces adorn postcards sold at Rio newsstands. Recently, a film shot in the Xingu reservation was woven into a *novela*, an afternoon television soap opera. So heavily exposed are the physically handsome Xingu tribes that in the popular mind they *are* the Brazilian Indian.

Brazilian officials have their own use for the Xinguanos. Faced with   5
charges of neglect and even genocide against its native peoples, the government has used the tribes of the area for public relations. Happy, well-nourished Xinguanos decorate government publications, and when necessary, the Indians themselves can be counted on to amuse visiting dignitaries. High consular officials from the diplomatic corps in Brasília and other international elite have flown out to the Xingu reservation for adventure and entertainment. Almost invariably their visits have been a success and they have returned home with an impression of idyllic relationships between the Brazilian authorities and the Xinguanos. But if such visitors came to know their hosts more intimately, they would learn that contact with the white man has had a profound and bitter impact on the Indians' inner life.

During my work among the Mehinaku I have become increasingly   6
aware of the villagers' anxieties about the white man. The soldiers at the nearby air force base, whom they regard as powerful and unpredictable, are especially frightening to the Mehinaku. On one occasion a rumor swept through the community that a plane from the base was going to bomb the village because one of the Mehinaku had stolen a mosquito net belonging to an air force sergeant. This wild story was

believable because it drew on a reservoir of anxiety and confusion about the white man. Recently, I have been studying the villagers' dreams as a way of learning about their unconscious fears.

According to the Mehinaku, dreams are caused by the wandering of   7 the "shadow," or soul, which is conceived of as a tiny replica of the individual living within the eye. As the villagers demonstrate to children or to the inquisitive anthropologist, the soul's image can be seen as a reflection in a pool of water or even in the iris of another person's eye. The soul is said to leave its owner at night to wander about. "Far, far away my soul wandered last night," is the opening phrase that may begin a dream narration. In the dream world of the community and the surrounding forests, the soul meets the wandering souls of animals, spirits, and other villagers. These experiences come into the dreamer's awareness in a way the villagers do not fully understand. "Dreams come up," they say, "as corn comes up from the ground."

The nightly adventures of the soul through the nocturnal village and   8 forest are interpreted with the help of an unwritten dream book, a collection of dream symbols and their deciphered meanings. To the Mehinaku, dream symbols (*patalapiri*, literally "pictures," or "images") represent events to come. Frequently, the predictions resemble the dream symbol in their appearance or activity. For example, since weeds are symbols of hair, a dream of a well-cleared path is symbolic of baldness in later life. Occasionally, the dream symbol is more abstract and poetic. A dream about collecting edible flying ants suggests bereavement, since the rain of ants that descends on the village in the fall of each year is likened to the tears that fall when a kinsman dies.

As the last example suggests, many Mehinaku dream symbols are   9 gloomy forecasts of death or misfortune. The grimmest omens of all, however, are those that deal with the white man. Any dream about a Brazilian is a bad dream. Even a dream prominently featuring an object associated with Brazilians, such as an airplane, is distressing. Dreams of the white man are, for the Mehinaku, "pictures" of disease. A person who has such a dream is likely to become sick. In support of this interpretation, the villagers point out that many illnesses—measles, colds, influenza—are brought in from the outside. These diseases have had a devastating impact on the community. In the early 1960s, nearly 20 percent of the tribe died in a measles epidemic, and the villagers continue to suffer from imported diseases for which they have neither natural nor acquired immunity. Dreams such as the following one reflect such concerns:

> At the post a plane landed. Many, many passengers got off. It
> seemed as if there was a village in the plane. I was very frightened
> of them and the things they carried. I was afraid they would bring
> a disease to the village, the white man's "witchcraft."

The Mehinaku fear of the white man goes beyond the fear of disease,   10 as I learned when I began to make a collection of their dreams. The villagers were willing collaborators in this effort since they regard dreams as significant and make a deliberate effort to recall them when they wake up. In the morning, as I circulated from house to house to harvest the previous night's crop of dreams, I would occasionally be summoned across the plaza ("Tommy, I have a dream for you!") by a villager with a particularly dramatic narrative. Altogether I collected 385 dreams, the majority of which (70 percent) were contributed by the men.

In thirty-one of the sample dreams, Brazilian were cast as the central   **11** characters. What is striking about these dreams is their high level of anxiety. While about half of the villagers' dreams show some level of anxiety, fully 90 percent of the dreams of the white man are tinged with fear. Furthermore, when I rated dreams on the basis of their frightening content and the dreamer's own report of distress, I found that dreams of the white man were charged with more than double the average level of anxiety. This was higher than any other comparable class of dreams, even dreams of malignant spirits and dangerous animals.

Occasionally, the mere sight or sound of an outsider creates anxiety.   **12** "I heard them speaking on the radio at the post, but I could not understand. The speech and the language were frightening to me." Within the sample of dreams, however, I found a number of terrifying themes that repeatedly appeared in the villagers' narratives. The most prominent of these are heat and fire. In the dreams, Brazilian soldiers explode incendiary devices in the village, burning houses and people. Fiery planes crash and blow up in the central plaza, covering the villagers with flames. Even when the victims throw themselves in the river, the fire continues to burn their clothes and skin.

> We went to the place where the canoe was moored. A plane came
> overhead and broke in the sky. It crashed in the water and every-
> thing caught on fire. The gasoline floated on the water. My mother
> caught on fire.

Fire and heat are appropriate symbols of terror among the Mehinaku.   **13** The villagers live in large thatch houses, often as much as 100 feet long, 30 feet wide, and 20 feet high. Two narrow doors in the middle of the house and a complete lack of windows minimize the intrusion of biting insects, but make the house firetraps. On occasion, the Mehinaku deliberately burn abandoned houses and the resultant blaze is instructive. While the villagers watch, the house owner sets fire to some of the thatch at the base of the building. Within moments, white smoke pours through the wall, and suddenly an entire side of the house bursts into flame. Seconds later, the convection of air and heat turns the building into a blazing inferno. As the Mehinaku edge back from the wall of heat and flame, they consider what would happen if an occupied house caught on fire. "If the fire begins when the people are asleep," one of the villagers told me, "then everyone burns."

Less dangerous than house fires, but almost as frightening, are fires **14**
that are deliberately set to clear the villagers' gardens. The Mehinaku
are slash-and-burn agriculturists who clear a plot of land in the forest,
allow the vegetation to dry, and then set it on fire. The blaze sends up
towers of white smoke that can be seen for miles. Once started, the fire
is totally out of control. The villagers say that it is "wildly angry," and
they tell myths of how men and spirits have gone to their death,
trapped in the burning fields. This danger is more than fictional, since
villagers have been badly burned when the wind shifted as they were
firing their gardens. Dreams that link the white man to heat and fire
thus associate him with one of the most frightening and destructive
forces in the Mehinaku environment.

A second recurrent theme in dreams of the white man is assault. Vil- **15**
lagers are shot with rifles, strafed from planes, pursued by trucks, and
attacked with machetes. At times, as in the following dream of a young
man, the assault is sexually motivated:

> We were at the air force base, and a soldier wanted to have sex with
> my sister. He took her arm and tried to pull her away. We shouted
> at the soldier and at my sister. My aunt and I tried to pull her back.
> But the soldier was too strong for us. He was very strong. He said
> "If you don't let me have sex with Mehinaku women I will shoot
> you." I got a gun and shot at him, many times. But he was hidden
> and I couldn't see him.

Another dreamer described a similar situation:

> A Brazilian doctor tried to take away my sister. . . . "If you don't let
> me, I will kill you," he said. . . . He shot and killed my two broth-
> ers. I cried in my dream, and I cried when I woke up.

Assault, like fire and heat, has an especially potent role in the Mehi- **16**
naku symbolism of fear. In comparing themselves to other Indians and
to whites, the villagers invariably point out that they are a peaceful
people. There is no word for war in their language other than "many
flying arrows," nor is there a historical record of the Mehinaku having
participated in organized, armed violence. When attacked by the Carib-
speaking Txicão tribe in the 1960s, they responded by cowering in their
houses as arrows whistled through the thatch walls. After the chief
sustained a serious arrow wound in his back, they moved the village
closer to the Indian post in the hope that they would not be pursued.

Within the village, strong sanctions bar interpersonal violence. The **17**
man who lets his anger get the best of him is slurred as a *japujaitsi*(literally, "angry man," but also a species of nearly inedible hot pepper).
There are no *japujaitsi* in the village, and in my year and a half residence in the community, I never saw a fight between men. As one villager put it, "When we are angry, we wrestle, and the anger is gone.
When the white men are angry, they shoot each other."

The menace of white society is real to the Mehinaku because of the   **18**
accounts they have heard at the Indian post about Brazilian atrocities
against Indians. They know that in the recent past Indians have been
shot, poisoned, and enslaved by bounty hunters and, during one particularly shameful period prior to the establishment of the present Indian agency in 1967, by some government employees working for the
former Indian agency. They know, too, that their lands are insecure and
that the boundaries of the Xingu reservation can—and do—change according to the whim of bureaucrats in Brasília. A road has already penetrated the far northern end of the reservation and has brought tribes
in that area into violent conflict with white ranchers. There is thus
good reason to be wary of the Brazilian. As in the case of fire, dreams
of assault and aggression link the white man to very real sources of
anxiety in waking life.

A final theme of fear that permeates the villagers' dreams is perhaps   **19**
the most poignant. In many of the narratives, the dreamer expresses a
sense of disorientation in dealing with the outsiders. The white men
lack comprehensible motivation and perform capricious acts of malice
and violence. They distract mothers from their crying infants, they give
presents and demand them back, and they kidnap small children. They
lure a man to a distant Brazilian city, cut off his head, and send it back
to his horrified kin. Disguised as Mehinaku, they tempt the dreamer to
give up his life as an Indian, and urge him to accompany them to distant cities from which he will never return. A mother dreams of losing
her young children to the outsider:

> My children said they would go to visit the Brazilians. They said
> they would go to São Paulo and Rio de Janeiro, and Cuiabá. I told
> them not to go. But they went, far off. We waited a long time, but
> they did not come back. I went to find them, but I could not. My
> mother's sister came to help me, and we looked all over. Then I
> heard them crying from a far way off, but still could not find them.
> Then, I awoke.

Some of the dreams border on the Kafkaesque:[2]

> A guard pointed a gun at me. He told me to go through a door. I
> did. The room was filled with a beautiful light. The guard gave me
> a watch and told me I could come out at a certain time. He locked
> the door. I looked at the watch, and I realized I did not know how
> to tell time. There was a wind and a strange smell.

The confused portrayal of the white man stems from the Mehinaku's   **20**
distorted view of Brazilian life. To the villagers, everyday Brazilian conduct and ordinary material objects are both alluring and strange. Tape
recorders, radios, cameras, and other gadgets sported by visitors to the

---

[2]Kafkaesque: relating to the fiction of Franz Kafka (1883–1924), which typically deals with
bizarre and horrifying events.

Xingu reservation fascinate the Mehinaku but also perplex them. Even
when these objects are dismantled and inspected, they don't give up
their secrets. "Are the white men wizards?" I was once asked by one of
the Mehinaku.

Those villagers who have visited São Paulo and Rio de Janeiro return   21
home with the same sense of fascinated puzzlement. A young man, the
narrator of the dream text above, spent a summer living with a vacationing upper-class family in the beach resort of Guarujá outside
of São Paulo. He was intrigued and attracted by what he saw, but un-
comprehending. The wealth of Guarujá seemed magically produced;
certainly members of the family were not making their possessions with
their own hands, as do the Xinguanos. On the same trip he saw im-
poverished beggars on São Paulo's streets, but once he was back in the
tribe, most of his stories were about the magic and glitter of the city.

The outsider visiting the Mehinaku senses the gap of understanding   22
in another way. Let a man arrive in the community and he is immediately questioned about his kinsmen. Does he have a wife? parents? sisters? Which of his kinsmen gave him his jacket? Was it his brother-in-
law? The Xingu communities are kin based, and the questions are an
effort to place the white man in the orbit of understandable social relationships. If he remains within the community, the villagers probe further, often by teasing their guest. His appearance, gait, name, and
speech become the object of semihumorous (and often painful) ridicule.
This period of hazing has been reported by many researchers in the
Xingu, and its predictability persuades me that it is part of the effort to
make the powerful outsider knowable. If he has weaknesses and can be
hurt, then he is human and understandable.

The many years of friendly but superficial contact with Brazilians   23
have not made the white man more intelligible to the Mehinaku. As of
my most recent visit in 1977, none of the villagers was able to explain
why the Brazilian had come to the Xingu forests. "The white man is
here," the chief told me in all seriousness, "to give up presents." The
economic and political forces that led the Brazilian government into the
interior of the continent to construct bases such as the Indian post are
mysterious to the Mehinaku. The Brazilian and their impersonal society
seem nearly as bizarre and disjointed in waking life as they do in the
villagers' dreams.

Mehinaku lands and culture remain largely intact, but a part of their   24
inner tranquility has been laid to waste. Neither geographic isolation
nor heroic efforts at protection could save it. Contact with Brazilian society has taken a higher toll than we might have anticipated. Certainly
the Mehinaku have paid dearly for their steel tools, their cast-off
clothes, and the other "gifts of civilization." By day, all appears well.
But each night, we outsiders visit the sleeping villagers and haunt
them in restless dreams.

_____ **Written Response**

Take one of the Mehinaku dreams that Gregor describes and write about what it means to you.

_____ **Rhetorical Analysis**

1. Gregor tells a story of contrast. He describes a contrast between the Mehinaku outer life during the day and the inner life that emerges in their dreams at night, but he also seems to want us to believe that the Mehinaku outer life (the smiling exterior of the tribe) is only an appearance while their inner life (the nightmares about white men) is reality. This framing of the contrast is, of course, Gregor's interpretation; it is possible that the outer life is reality and the inner life is only an appearance. Most readers, however, do not question Gregor's interpretation.

In what ways does Gregor construct the narrative so that readers are drawn into believing that the outer life is mere appearance and the inner life is reality?

2. When reading a text, it is often appropriate to ask the question, "What is missing?" Gregor argues that the Indians' nightmares about white men indicate that they have lost their "inner tranquility." Before we accept Gregor's conclusion, we might ask, "What other kind of dreams do the Indians have?" In *Anxious Pleasures* (Chicago: University of Chicago Press, 1985), Gregor writes of the dreams of Mehinaku men:

> Dreams of sexually aggressive women . . . are anxious experiences for the Mehinaku. . . . It is important to add that women are also overtly threatening in nonsexual dreams. In 78 of the 276 dreams in our sample, the dreamer was the victim of physical violence. A woman was the aggressor in 15 (nineteen percent) of these dreams. In daily life, however, women almost never injure men. Moreover, we find that women figure as aggressors in only three percent of American men's dreams of being attacked. This contrast is in accord with the previous data on . . . the generally threatening nature of women to the Mehinaku men. [pp. 160–161]

How does this information about some of the Mehinaku dreams that do not involve white men change your interpretation of Gregor's article?

Are there other kinds of information that you would like to have before you decide to accept or reject Gregor's interpretation?

3. Psychologists are more likely to interpret the events of dreams by relating them to events in the individual's past. Anthropologists, such as Gregor, are more likely to interpret the recurrent events or symbols in the dreams of many people by relating them to social or cultural context. How does Gregor help us to understand the cultural importance of the Indians' dreams by relating the events of the dreams to events in their social and cultural environment?

_____ **Interpretation**

1. How are the Mehinaku and their culture different from the Brazilians (or whites) and their culture?

2. As Gregor sees it, the Mehinaku do not understand white men and
white men do not understand the Mehinaku. In what ways do the Mehinaku fail to understand white men? In what ways do white men fail to
understand the Mehinaku?

3. Why do you think that the Mehinaku have nightmares about white
men but not white women?

_____ **WRITING ASSIGNMENTS**

1. Following Gregor's example, collect a series of dreams from a cultural group; the group could be people within your community or the
members of your class. If you choose to collect dreams from the members
of your class, have each person write a description of a dream, preferably
one that he or she has had on several occasions, and arrange to have
these copied anonymously for the entire class. Then use this collection of
dreams to investigate the inner life of the group. Try to include an explanation of the group's cultural background that will help the reader to
understand the significance of the events in the dreams.

2. Write an essay in which you use what you have learned from Gregor's
article to argue for greater restraint in the treatment of Brazilian Indians.

3. Write an essay in which you compare the dreams of the Mehinaku
with the following Native American myths.

Creation of the Whites

Yuchi

It was out upon the ocean. Some sea-foam formed against a big log float-
ing there. Then a person emerged from the sea-foam and crawled out upon
the log. He was seen sitting there. Another person crawled up, on the other
side of the log. It was a woman. They were whites. Soon the Indians saw
them, and at first thought that they were sea-gulls, and they said among
themselves, "Are they not white people?" Then they made a boat and went
out to look at the strangers more closely

Later on the whites were seen in their house-boat. Then they disappeared.

In about a year they returned, and there were a great many of them. The
Indians talked to them but they could not understand each other. Then the
whites left.

But they came back in another year with a great many ships. They approached the Indians and asked if they could come ashore. They [the Indi-
ans] said, "Yes." So the whites landed, but they seemed to be afraid to walk
much on the water. They went away again over the sea.

From *Native American Legends* edited by George E. Lankford. Copyright © 1987 by George
E. Lankford. Reprinted by permission of August House, Inc.

This time they were gone a shorter time; only three months passed and they came again. They had a box with them and asked the Indians for some earth to fill it. It was given to them as they desired. The first time they asked they had a square box, and when that was filled they brought a big shallow box. They filled this one too. Earth was put in them and when they were carried aboard the ship the white men planted seed in them and many things were raised. After they had taken away the shallow box, the whites came back and told the Indians that their land was very strong and fertile. So they asked the Indians to give them a portion of it that they might live on it. The Indians agreed to do it, the whites came to the shore, and they have lived there ever since.

A Shaman Predicts the Whites

Yuchi

A Creek chief died. When the chief was dead he appeared before Gohantone, who said to him, "This land belongs to you and your children forever. This land will be yours forever, but these whites who have just come will overwhelm you and inherit your land. They will increase and the Indian will decrease and at last die out. Then only white people will remain. But there will be terrible times."

So spoke Gohantone to the dead Creek chief. For four days he lay dead, when he came to life again. When he woke up he was well. He immediately called a great council. Shawnee, Choctaw, Creeks, and Yuchi all assembled to hear him, and he told them all that he had seen and heard. He told them that the land would belong to the Indian forever, but the white man would overrun it. So the thing is coming to pass as Gohantone said.

Stealing the Land

Yuchi

A long time ago the red people may have lived somewhere under the rising sun. On this island there lived no pale-faced White people; only red men were living there. Once the water rose, covered with much water foam, right there a person came out; that person was a White man; he came to the shore, it is told; every now and then the White men left and came back again. They asked for some land, only as much as one cowhide would cover, only this much they should give them, they said. They did not want to give it, and some said, "Let us kill them." Others, however, said, "We will not kill them; as much land as one cowhide would not be much," they thought, and so they gave it to them. The White men threw a cowhide into the water, when it was wet they cut it in little pieces. And then they stretched it; when they measured the four corners they had taken very much land. When the Indians said they had not understood it was to be done that way, they answered that they had taken just as much land as one cowhide; very much land they had taken indeed.

The Power of the Word

Creek (Tukabahchee)

When the Lord first made men (of all colors) they were all one people, [so] that the Lord offered them a choice, showing a piece of paper first to the red man and he could make nothing of it and let it alone, and the red man going along he found some roots and some bows and arrows and he said these are mine, and so he lived in the woods by roots and hunting.

The white man then looked at the paper and he could use it and he kept it ("and how about the black people?"). There was nothing said about them . . .

He said, referring to the white paper which the white man took, that if he could have had the chance he would have taken the paper and then perhaps the Indians would have had everything as the whites have.

Fieldwork as the Interaction of Cultures

Marjorie Shostak (born 1945) and her husband, who is also an anthropologist, studied the !Kung tribe in Botswana from August 1969 to March 1971. At the time that she and her husband left America, the women's movement had just begun to gain momentum, and many young people were questioning traditional views of marriage, family, and relationships. Shostak hoped that her study of the !Kung would provide a fresh cultural lens through which these important issues could be viewed.

In the last month of her field trip, Shostak met Nisa, a !Kung woman who was then about 50 years old. She interviewed Nisa 15 times on that trip and an additional 6 times on a trip four years later. Shostak called the interviews "the deepest insight I was able to gain into !Kung life."

When Shostak wrote *Nisa: The Life and Words of a !Kung Woman*, she was able to use her interviews with Nisa as part of her description of !Kung society. As you will see, "Women and Men," the chapter from the book that is excerpted here, is really two texts. The first is Shostak's description of how she, as an anthropologist from the United States, views male and female roles in !Kung culture. The second text is a portion of Nisa's oral autobiography, as told to Shostak in those 21 interviews.

Each of these texts will be presented so that they can be assigned as separate readings, but it is important that you remember that Shostak intended for the two views to form a dialogue.

_____ **Prereading**

One of the central ways in which cultures can differ is in what they consider to be sacred and profane. The sacred is what is considered good; the profane is what is considered taboo, the objects that should not be touched or the acts that should not be committed.

What does our society consider to be sacred? What do we consider to be taboo? Are there any objects or acts that could be considered both sacred *and* taboo? Why do you think that some things are considered sacred while others are considered taboo?

Women and Men
Marjorie Shostak

The position of women in !Kung society has been of great interest to   **1**
anthropologists and others trying to understand the variation in wom-
en's roles and status found in the world's cultures. Despite the substantial differences in how women live and what they do, one
generalization can be made: in the overwhelming majority of societies,
women have a lower status than men—by their own accounts and by
observation of the culture as a whole—and their activities are less
highly valued than men's activities. Margaret Mead recognized this in
1949 when she wrote, "In every known society, the males' need for
achievement can be recognized. Men may cook or weave or dress dolls
or hunt hummingbirds, but if such activities are appropriate occupations for men, then the whole society, men and women alike, votes
them important. When the same occupations are performed by women,
they are regarded as less important."

In relation to this pattern, the !Kung are something of an anomaly.   **2**
Here, in a society of ancient traditions, men and women live together
in a nonexploitative manner, displaying a striking degree of equality
between the sexes—perhaps a lesson for our own society. !Kung men,
however, do seem to have the upper hand. They more often hold positions of influence—as spokespeople for the group or as healers—and
their somewhat greater authority over many areas of !Kung life is acknowledged by men and women alike. A close look at this balance is
not of merely academic interest. Other contemporary gathering and
hunting societies have a similar high level of equality between the
sexes—higher, at least, than that of most agricultural or herding societies. This observation has led to the suggestion that the relations between the sexes that prevailed during the majority of human prehistory
were comparable to those seen among the !Kung today. Perhaps the
extremes of subordination of women by men found in many of today's
more socioeconomically "advanced" cultures are only a relatively recent
aberration in our long human calendar.

!Kung women assume roles of great practical importance, both in the   **3**
family and in the economy. They have maximum influence over decisions affecting their children for years, starting with birth. !Kung men
are usually discouraged from being present at a birth, and women have

Source: From *Nisa: The Life and Words of a !Kung Woman* by Marjorie Shostak, Harvard University Press, Cambridge, Mass. Copyright © 1981 by Marjorie Shostak. Reprinted by permission of the publishers.

complete control over the process, including the decision for or against infanticide. The sex of the child seems to have no influence over this decision, and the !Kung express no preference for either sex before the child's birth.

Mothers are responsible for close to 90 percent of child care, but the   4
public nature of village life—the fact that most activities take place out-side and in groups rather than behind closed doors—eases this burden and frees women for other pursuits as well. Mothers are rarely alone and children rarely lack playmates. The isolated mother burdened with bored small children is not a scene that has parallels in !Kung daily life. Older children can be left behind in the village with other adults while their mothers go gathering, so women with large families are able to make as much of an economic contribution as those with small families.

!Kung fathers have been shown to provide more care for infants and   5
young children than fathers in many societies, even though they spend much less time in contact with children than mothers do. !Kung chil-dren seem to be very comfortable with either parent, and are frequently seen touching, sitting with, or talking with their fathers. The father is not set up as an authority whose wrath must be feared; both parents guide their children, and a father's word seems to carry about the same weight as a mother's. Children probably misbehave equally with both, but parents avoid direct confrontations and physical punishment.

The lack of privacy in !Kung life also protects women from being bat-   6
tered by their husbands, and children from being abused by either par-ent. Arguments between husbands and wives occur within sight of their neighbors. If a fight becomes physical, other people are always there and ready to intervene.

In some cultures, a mother's influence is thought to pose a threat to   7
her son's masculinity or ability to attain full male status, and boys are separated from their mothers to counteract this feminizing influence. The !Kung, in contrast, allow both boys and girls to sleep in their par-ents' hut, often beside their mothers, for so many years that the child is usually the one who decides to sleep elsewhere. The only time !Kung boys are deliberately isolated from women is for a few weeks between the ages of fifteen and twenty, when they participate in Choma, the male initiation ceremony. During this intense and rigorous ritual the initiates experience hunger, cold, thirst, and the extreme fatigue that comes from continuous dancing. It takes place over a period of six weeks and is considered sacred time, when the ritual knowledge of male matters is passed from one generation to the next.

When Choma is over, however, boys resume village life as before—   8
eating, sleeping and working amid the typical absence of segregation by sex. Village space is basically communal, and no one is denied ac-cess to any of it. Although there are certain prohibitions against wom-en's touching men's arrows, especially while menstruating, and to engaging in sex during the height of the menstrual flow, these

prohibitions do not extend to sleeping beside each other during the
same time. Some men say it is bad to have sexual intercourse before a
hunt, but this seems to be related as much to ideas about their own
strength as to fear of being polluted by women. Also, menstruating and
pregnant women and women with newborn infants are not isolated
from the rest of the community as they so often are in other cultures.
Thus the few taboos that do exist in !Kung life do not exclude women
from the highly valued social, political, or economic life of the community. Women are not considered a threat to the ability of !Kung men to
maintain their male identities and functions.

!Kung women's influence increases as their children grow older. (A   9
barren women is not ostracized or looked down upon, although, having missed out on a major part of life, she may be pitied.) When
daughters or sons reach marriageable age, mothers play a major role in
deciding whom they will marry and when. The choice of a spouse has
a far-reaching impact on the family's social and economic life, and often
on that of the entire group. Marriage ties together a couple's families in
intimate rounds of visiting, mutual obligations, and gift exchange, and
sometimes even in the establishment of permanent living
arrangements. After marriage a couple is as likely to live near the
wife's family as near the husband's. This fact further assures daughters
the same loving treatment as sons, since both are equally likely to enhance their family's standing in the community.

Parents often arrange marriages for their daughters, usually with   10
adult men while the girls are still in their early teens. These marriages,
not surprisingly, are quite unstable. The husband may not live up to his
in-laws' expectations, or he may not have the patience to wait for his
wife, who may be uncooperative and rejecting, to grow up. Usually,
however, it is the girl who initiates divorce in these early marriages,
which are otherwise essentially unequal relationships. The man is physically larger and stronger; although the girl is protected by her family,
the threat of his exercising his will or power against her—especially in
sex—is always there. Later marriages are generally more equal, especially those in which the couple are close in age. (In the 20 percent of
marriages in which the husband is younger than his wife, the wife's
influence is often greater than his.) The control !Kung women retain
over this part of their lives is a marked contrast to other cultures where
girls have no choice but to comply with the wishes of their parents and
husbands.

!Kung women are recognized by men and women alike as the pri-   11
mary economic providers of the group. They gather vegetable foods
from the wild about three days a week, providing the majority of the
daily diet of their families and other dependents. Their economic activity is an autonomous undertaking. Men do not regulate women's
schedules, do not tell them which foods to gather or where to go, and
do not control the distribution of gathered foods. Women tell their husbands when they plan to be gone for the day, but this is as much a

courtesy as a potential restraint, and it is what men usually do as well. If a husband were to forbid his wife to go, saying that there were chores to be done near the village or that they should go visiting together, she would probably listen to him. But men cannot afford to restrain their wives much, since they also depend on the women's efforts for food.

Although women occasionally gather alone, most prefer the company **12** of others, for social reasons as well as for safety. Even the few miles between villages should preferably be traveled in groups. Fear of occasional predators, strangers, or even encounters with familiar men who might suggest romance, make solitary travel a moderately anxiety-provoking experience. If a male prerogative were in need of justification, the argument that !Kung women should have men's protection while traveling in the bush or between villages could gain a foothold. !Kung men do not exploit this possibility, however; women travel up to five miles away from camp, into the uninhabited wilderness, unprotected by men or their weapons. Loud talking creates a noisy enough progression as women advance from one gathering location to another so that large animals avoid them, and poisonous snakes are killed easily enough with digging sticks.

The only significant difference in mobility between !Kung men and **13** women is in overnight absences. Women usually return to the village at the end of a day of gathering. If an overnight gathering trip seems necessary, the entire group will move. In contrast, while hunting, men are often away from camp for a few days at a time (although they prefer not to be). A male bias may underlie this difference, but it is not difficult to postulate more practical reasons. Success in the hunt is unpredictable, and it often takes several days to make a kill. With gathering, by contrast, one day or even part of a day is usually enough time to collect as much as can be carried home. Also, women are responsible for the care of the children, and overnight trips would involve either coping with children in an unfamiliar and perhaps dangerous area or leaving them behind in someone else's care.

As a subsistence strategy, gathering for a living is quite satisfying. It **14** can be energetically engaged in, no matter what the size of a woman's family. The schedule is flexible, the pace is self-determined, and the work is accomplished in the company of others. Although each woman basically gathers for herself, this does not isolate her from other women. Women present choice findings to each other as offerings of good will and solidarity. The work is challenging: each expedition taps a woman's ability to discern, among the more than two hundred plants known by name and in the general tangle of vegetation, which plants are edible, which are ripe for harvesting, and which are most worthy of her efforts. It is also efficient: a day's work is usually enough to feed a family for a few days. Unlike !Kung hunters, !Kung gatherers have the solid assurance that when their families are hungry they will be able to find food—an assurance that fills them with pride. As one woman

explained, "I like to gather. If I just sit, my children have nothing to eat.
If I gather, my children are full." Finally, although gathering requires
considerable stamina, the four days a week that women are not gathering afford them abundant time for visiting and for leisure.

When a women returns to the village, she determines how much of   15
her gatherings, if any, will be given away, and to whom. She sets aside
piles of food for those she feels inclined to give to, and places the rest
in the back of her hut or beside her family's fire. The food she and her
family eat that night, the next day, and perhaps even the next, will consist primarily of the things she has brought home. From start to finish,
her labor and its product remain under her control.

Another indication of the high standing of !Kung women is their rela-   16
tionship to the gift-giving network called hxaro. All !Kung adults (and
some children) are part of this network; each has a discrete number of
partners with whom certain goods are exchanged. Women's participation in hxaro is basically the same as that of men, with no significant
difference in the number of exchange partners or in the quality or
quantity of exchanges.

In addition, core membership in a band, as well as "ownership" of   17
water holes and other resources, is inherited through women as well as
men. No male prerogative can be exercised in relation to this important
source of influence in !Kung society.

This picture of !Kung women's lives might seem to challenge Marga-   18
ret Mead's observation about the universality of the male bias. Unfortunately, though, the !Kung are not the exception they at first appear to
be. !Kung women do have a formidable degree of autonomy, but !Kung
men enjoy certain distinct advantages—in the way the culture values
their activities, both economic and spiritual, and in their somewhat
greater influence over decisions affecting the life of the group.

Meat, the economic contribution of men, is considered more valuable   19
than gathered foods. Most gathered foods, except the mongongo nut,
are described as "things comparable to nothing," while meat is so
highly valued that it is often used as a synonym for "food." Squeals of
delighted children may greet women as they return from gathering, but
when men walk into the village balancing meat on sticks held high on
their shoulders, everyone celebrates, young and old alike. It may even
precipitate a trance dance. The one thing women can bring in that
causes a comparable reaction is honey, but the finding of honey is a
much rarer event and one that men are usually enlisted to help with.
!Kung women may control the distribution of their gathered product,
but the distribution of meat, while more constrained by formal rules,
involves men in a wider sphere of influence.

!Kung men also provide women with their basic gathering kit and   20
other implements: tanned skins to make carrying devices (infant slings,
karosses, clothing, and pouches), digging sticks, mortars and pestles,
sinew for mending and for stringing and sewing beads and ornaments,

and shoes. These items are durable, however, and women assume their maintenance and upkeep. In contrast, women provide none of the articles associated with hunting. In fact, the opposite is true: women are prohibited from handling hunting equipment and from participating in the hunt, especially during menstruation—although this taboo seems to have few practical consequences.

The economic picture becomes more complex when hunting and **21** gathering activities are looked at more closely. Animal protein is not brought into the village only by men. Women collect lizards, snakes, tortoises' and birds' eggs, and insects and caterpillars, as well as occasional small or immature mammals. They also provide men with crucial information on animal tracks and animal movement that they observe while they travel in the bush. But !Kung women cannot be considered hunters in any serious way. The one prominent exception I heard about was a middle-aged woman who allegedly craved meat so intensely and was so tired of complaining that her husband was lazy that she decided to go out and hunt for herself. I was, unfortunately, never able to meet her. Those who knew her (including men) said that she was a fairly proficient hunter, but it was clear that she was considered eccentric and was in no way seen as a model for other women to emulate. She earned far less respect for her accomplishments than a man would have, as was evident from the snickering that accompanied discussions about her. No one actually said that what she was doing was wrong, but it was repeatedly pointed out that she was the *only* one. She was, however, considered accountable for her actions primarily in relation to herself, rather than in relation to her husband; her behavior was not seen as emphasizing his shortcomings or publicly emasculating him. This would probably not have been the case in many other societies, including our own.

!Kung men have an easier relationship to gathering than !Kung **22** women have to hunting. No social prohibitions comparable to the taboo against menstruating women's touching arrows implicate men as a negative influence on the success of women gatherers; nor are men's efforts at gathering seen as unusual, out of character, or even worthy of comment. (This is in contrast to many cultures in which men feel ashamed of performing tasks usually associated with women.) Men's knowledge about plants is comparable to that of women, and gathering is something men do whenever they want to. Men can account for as much as 20 percent of all foods gathered.

The male prerogative is more clearly exhibited in !Kung spiritual life, **23** the central expression of which is the traditional medicine dance in which healers tap their healing power by entering trance. Most healers are men. An occasional woman has mastered the art of healing, especially in the context of the women's drum dance, but women most often use their healing skill in response to the need of a close family member and not in a ritual setting. The status and respect that go with

being a healer are, therefore, only minimally available to women; un-
questionably, men have traditionally dominated this realm of !Kung life.

Perhaps the most crucial aspect of the balance of power is the process   24
of leadership and decision-making. Determining how the !Kung actually make important decisions is quite difficult. With no formal leaders
or hierarchies, and no political or legal institutions to convey authority,
decisions are made on the basis of group consensus. Each group has
individuals whose opinions carry more weight than those of others—
because of age, of having ancestors who have lived in the area longer,
or of personal attributes such as intelligence, knowledge, or charisma.
These people tend to be more prominent in group discussions, to make
their opinions known and their suggestions clear, and to articulate the
consensus once it is determined. Despite their lack of formal authority,
they function very much as group leaders.

!Kung men occupy these positions more frequently than women do,   25
although older women, especially those with large extended families,
occasionally assume such roles. Men are also generally more vocal in
group discussions. As contact with other cultures increases, and as the
demand for spokespeople to represent the group thus intensifies, !Kung
men are stepping forward more prominently. They are the ones who
learn foreign languages, who attend government meetings, and who
speak out on behalf of the regional !Kung communities.

Further evidence of male bias can be found: it is men who initiate   26
sex, for example, and male initiation rites are secret while female initiation rites are public. !Kung women themselves refer to, and do not
seem to reject, male dominance. The fact that this bias exists is important and should not be minimized—but it should also not be exaggerated.

!Kung culture downplays many of the attitudes that encourage male   27
dominance in other societies. Competition, ranking of individuals,
boastfulness, and self-aggrandizement are all discouraged. Formalized
aggression of any kind—in most cultures the province of men—is absent, and preparations for fighting do not occupy men's time or boys'
education. Wealth differentials are also minimized, by sharing food and
possessions and by giving presents. The division of labor by sex is not
rigidly defined. Village life is so intimate that a division between domestic and public life—an apt distinction for many other cultures—is
largely meaningless for the !Kung, a fact that helps to promote sexual
equality.

All in all, !Kung women maintain a status that is higher than that of   28
women in many agricultural and industrial societies around the world.
They exercise a striking degree of autonomy and of influence over their
own and their children's lives. Brought up to respect their own importance in community life, !Kung women become multifaceted adults, and
are likely to be competent and assertive as well as nurturant and coop-
erative.

Shostak mentioned that !Kung men can gather (the collecting of edible plants, bugs, and so on that is traditionally a woman's task), but !Kung women are not allowed to hunt. She mentions that one woman, despite this basic social guideline, learned to become a hunter. How was she treated? How do we in our culture tend to treat people who are eccentric, who violate social norms?

_____ **Rhetorical Analysis**

1. When Shostak presents her view of the !Kung society, she is very consciously speaking as an anthropologist, an American, a woman, and an outsider. She presents the kind of view of !Kung culture that someone born and raised in that culture could not. For example, she begins her text: "The position of women in !Kung society has been of great interest to anthropologists and others trying to understand the variation in women's roles and status found in the world's cultures." A native !Kung would be unlikely to make such a statement. Can you find other statements that remind the reader that Shostak is an outsider looking into !Kung culture?

2. At the time that Shostak studied the !Kung, the tribe and its culture were in a process of historical transition from its traditional way of life—hunting and gathering—to working for the white settlers. As Shostak describes the !Kung in this text, do you get a sense of this historical change?

_____ **Interpretation**

1. Based on Shostak's text, in what ways would you consider !Kung men and women to be basically equal? In what ways are they unequal? How does the position of women in !Kung culture compare to that of women in the cultures of the mountain Arapesh and the Yąnomamö?

2. One of Shostak's reasons for studying the !Kung was that she wanted to learn something to help her better understand the roles of men and women in our own society. Based on the excerpt that you have just read, do you sense that Shostak has learned anything about American culture by studying the !Kung?

_____ **WRITING ASSIGNMENTS**

1. How is the !Kung woman who hunted, the eccentric discussed in Shostak's text, treated by other members of society? Why?

2. What can we learn about relations between men and women from cultures like the !Kung, Arapesh, and Yąnamamö?

The following text is a narrative that was constructed from 21 interviews with Nisa. Shostak wanted this narrative to present a personal view of the same basic theme (the roles of men and women) that she objectively discussed in her text. Based on what you read in Shostak's text, what kinds of themes do you expect to be discussed in Nisa's narrative?

Men and Women

Nisa's Text

After Besa[1] and I had lived together for a long time, he went to visit   **1**
some people in the East. While there, he found work with a Tswana[2]
cattle herder. When he came back, he told me to pack; he wanted me
to go and live with him there. So we left and took the long trip to Old
Debe's village, a Zhun/twa[3] village near a Tswana and European settlement. We lived there together for a long time.

While we were there, my father died. My older brother, my younger   **2**
brother, and my mother were with him when he died, but I wasn't; I
was living where Besa had taken me. Others carried the news to me.
They said that Dau[4] had tried to cure my father, laying on hands and
working hard to make him better. But God refused and Dau wasn't able
to see what was causing the illness so he could heal him. Dau said,
"God is refusing to give up my father."

I heard and said, "Eh, then today I'm going to see where he died."   **3**
Besa and I and my children, along with a few others, left to take the
long journey west. We walked the first day and slept that night. The
next morning we started out and slept again that night; we slept another night on the road, as well. As we walked, I cried and thought,
"Why couldn't I have been with him when he died?" I cried as we
walked, one day and the next and the next.

Source: From *Nisa: The Life and Words of a !Kung Woman* by Marjorie Shostak, Harvard University Press, Cambridge, Mass. Copyright © 1981 by Marjorie Shostak. Reprinted by permission of the publishers.

_____

[1] Besa: Nisa's fourth husband.
[2] Tswana: the predominate tribe of Botswana.
[3] Zhun/twa: "the real people," the name the !Kung use to refer to themselves. Interestingly, scientists have recently discovered that the first humans came from the !Kung tribe.
[4] Dau: Nisa's older brother.

The sun was so hot, it was burning; it was killing us. One day we   4
rested such a long time, I thought, "Is the sun going to stop me from
seeing where my father died?" When it was cooler, we started walking
again and slept on the road again that night.

We arrived at the village late in the afternoon. My younger brother,   5
Kumsa, was the first to see us. When he saw me, he came and hugged
me. We started to cry and cried together for a long time. Finally, our
older brother stopped us, "That's enough for now. Your tears won't
make our father alive again."

We stopped crying and we all sat down. My mother was also with   6
us. Although my father never took her back again after the time she
ran away with her lover, she returned and lived near him until he died.
And even though she slept alone, she still loved him.

Later, my mother and I sat together and cried together.   7

We stayed there for a while, then Besa and I went back again to live   8
in the East where he had been working for the Europeans. A very long
time passed. Then, my brother sent word that my mother was dying.
Once again we made the journey to my family and when we arrived I
saw her: she was still alive.

We stayed there and lived there. One day, a group of people were   9
going to the bush to live. I said, "Mother, come with us. I'll take care
of you and you can help me with my children." We traveled that day
and slept that night; we traveled another day and slept another night.
But the next night, the sickness that had been inside her grabbed her
again and this time, held on. It was just as it had been with my father.
The next day, she coughed up blood. I thought, "Oh, why is blood
coming out like that? Is this what is going to kill her? Is this the way
she's going to die? What is this sickness going to do? She's coughing
blood. . . she's already dead!" Then I thought, "If only Dau were here,
he would be able to cure her. He would trance for her every day." But
he and my younger brother had stayed behind. Besa was with us, but
he didn't have the power to cure people. There were others with us as
well, but they didn't help.

We slept again that night. The next morning, the others left, as is our   10
custom, and then it was only me, my children, my husband, and my
mother; we were the only ones who remained. But her life was really
over by then, even though she was still alive.

I went to get her some water and when I came back, she said,   11
"Nisa. . . Nisa. . . I am an old person and today, my heart. . . today
you and I will stay together for a while longer; we will continue to sit
beside each other. But later, when the sun stands over there in the afternoon sky and when the new slim moon first strikes, I will leave
you. We will separate then and I will go away."

I asked, "Mother, what are you saying?" She said, "Yes, that's what   12
I'm saying. I am an old person. Don't deceive yourself; I am dying.

When the sun moves to that spot in the sky, that will be our final separation. We will no longer be together after that. So, take good care of
your children."

I said, "Why are you talking like this? If you die as you say, because   13
that's what you're telling me, who are you going to leave in your
place?" She said, "Yes, I am leaving you. Your husband will take care
of you now. Besa will be with you and your children."

We remained together the rest of the day as the sun crawled slowly   14
across the sky. When it reached the spot she had spoken of, she said—
just like a person in good health—"Mm, now . . . be well, all of you,"
and then she died.

That night I slept alone and cried and cried and cried. None of my   15
family was with me and I just cried the entire night. When morning
came, Besa dug a grave and buried her. I said, "Let's pull our things
together and go back to the village. I want to tell Dau and Kumsa that
our mother has died."

We walked that day and slept that night. We walked the next day   16
and stopped again that night. The next morning, we met my brother
Kumsa. Someone had told him that his mother was sick. When he
heard, he took his bow and quiver and came looking for us. He left
when the sun just rose and started walking toward us, even as we were
walking toward him. We met when the sun was overhead. He stood
and looked at me. Then he said, "Here you are, Nisa, with your son
and your daughter and your husband. But Mother isn't with you . . . "

I sat down and started to cry. He said, "Mother must have died be-   17
cause you're crying like this," and he started to cry, too. Besa said,
"Yes, your sister left your mother behind. Two days ago was when your
mother and sister separated. That is where we are coming from now.
Your sister is here and will tell you about it. You will be together to
share your mourning for your mother. That will be good."

We stayed there and cried and cried. Later, Kumsa took my little son   18
and carried him on his shoulders. I carried my daughter and we
walked until we arrived back at the village. My older brother came
with his wife, and when he saw us he, too, started to cry.

After that, we lived together for a while. I lived and cried, lived and   19
cried. My mother had been so beautiful . . . her face, so lovely. When
she died, she caused me great pain. Only after a long time was I quiet
again.

Before we returned to the East, I went with Besa to visit his family.   20
While I was there, I became very sick. It came from having carried my
mother. Because when she was sick, I carried her around on my back.
After she died, my back started to hurt in the very place I had carried
her. One of God's spiritual arrows must have struck me there and
found its way into my chest.

I was sick for a long time and then blood started to come out of my   21
mouth. My younger brother (he really loves me!) was visiting me at the

time. When he saw how I was, he left to tell his older brother, "Nisa's dying the same way our mother died. I've come to tell you to come back with me and heal her." My older brother listened and the two of them traveled to where I was. They came when the sun was high in the afternoon sky. Dau started to trance for me. He laid on hands, healing me with his touch. He worked on me for a long time. Soon, I was able to sleep; then, the blood stopped coming from my chest and later, even if I coughed, there wasn't any more blood.

We stayed there for a few more days. Then, Dau said, "Now I'm go-   22
ing to take Nisa with me to my village." Besa agreed and we all left together. We stayed at my brother's village until I was completely better.

Besa and I eventually moved back East again. But after we had lived   23
together for a long time, we no longer were getting along. One day I asked, "Besa, won't you take me back to my family's village so I can live there?" He said, "I'm no longer interested in you." I said, "What's wrong? Why do you feel that way?" But then I said, "Eh, if that's how it is, it doesn't matter."

I was working for a European woman at the time, and when I told   24
her what Besa was saying to me, she told him, "Listen to me. You're going to chase your wife away. If you continue to speak to her like this, she'll be gone. Today, I'm pregnant. Why don't you just let her be and have her sit beside you. When I give birth, she will work for me and help me with the baby."

That's what we did. We continued to live together until she gave   25
birth. After, I helped wash the baby's clothes and helped with other chores. I worked for her for a long time.

One day, Besa broke into a little box I had and stole the money she   26
had paid me with. He took it and went to drink beer. I went to the European woman and told her Besa had taken five Rand[5] from me and had left with it. I asked her to help me get it back. We went to the Tswana hut where everyone was drinking and went to the door. The European woman walked in, kicked over a bucket and the beer spilled out. She kicked over another and another and the beer was spilling everywhere. The Tswanas left. She turned to Besa and said, "Why are you treating this young Zhun/twa woman like this? Stop treating her this way." She told him to give her the money and when he gave it to her, she gave it to me. I went and put the money in the box, then took it and left it in her kitchen where it stayed.

Later Besa said, "Why did you tell on me? I'm going to beat you." I   27
said, "Go ahead. Hit me. I don't care. I won't stop you."

Soon after that, I became pregnant with Besa's child. But when it was still very tiny, when I was still carrying it way inside, he left me. I

---

[5] Rand: South African currency worth around $1.30-$1.50 US; five Rand would have probably been about two months salary for Nisa.

woman. But God . . . God gave you something beautiful in giving you
this baby and although it had death in it, you yourself are alive." We
left and walked back to the village. Then I lay down.

After that, I just continued to live there. One day I saw people visit-   **41**
ing from Besa's village. I told them to tell him that our marriage had
ended. I said, "Tell him that he shouldn't think, even with a part of his
heart, that he still has a wife here or that when we meet another time
in my village that he might still want me." That's what I said and
that's what I thought.

Because he left me there to die.   **42**

Soon after, a man named Twi saw me and said, "Did your husband   **43**
leave you?" I said, "Yes, he left me long ago." He asked, "Then won't
you stay with me?" I refused the first time he asked as well as the second and the third. But when he asked the next time, I agreed and we
started to live together. I continued to work for the European woman
until my work was finished and she told me I could go home. She
gave us food for our trip and then all of us—Old Debe, his wife, Twi,
and me—traveled the long distance back to where my family was
living.

Twi and I lived together in my brother's village for a long time. Then,   **44**
one day, Besa came from wherever he had been and said, "Nisa, I've
come to take you back with me." I said, "What? What am I like today?
Did I suddenly become beautiful? The way I used to be is the way I am
now; the way I used to be is what you left behind when you dropped
me. So what are you saying? First you drop me in the heart of where
the white people live, then you come back and say I should once again
be with you?" He said, "Yes, we will pick up our marriage again."

I was stunned! I said, "What are you talking about? This man, Twi,   **45**
helped bring me back. He's the man who will marry me. You're the
one who left me." We talked until he could say nothing more; he was
humbled. Finally he said, "You're shit! That's what you are." I said,
"I'm shit you say? That's what you thought about me long ago, and I
knew it. That's why I told you while we were still living in the East
that I wanted you to take me back to my family so we could end our
marriage here. But today, I came here myself and you only came afterward. Now I refuse to have anything more to do with you."

That's when Besa brought us to the Tswana headman to ask for a   **46**
tribal hearing. Once it started, the headman looked at everything. He
asked me, "Among all the women who live here, among all those you
see sitting around, do you see one who lives with two men?" I said,
"No, the women who sit here . . . not one lives with two men; not one
among them would I be able to find. I, alone have two. But it was because this man, Besa, mistreated and hurt me. That's why I took this
other man, Twi, who treats me well, who does things for me and gives
me things to eat." Then I said, "He is also the man I want to marry; I

want to drop the other one. Because Besa has no sense. He left me while I was pregnant and the pregnancy almost killed me. This other one is the one I want to marry."

We talked a long time. Finally, the headman told Besa, "I have ques- 47 tioned Nisa about what happened and she has tied you up with her talk; her talk has defeated you, without doubt. Because what she has said about her pregnancy is serious. Therefore, today she and Twi will continue to stay together. After more time passes, I will ask all of you to come back again." Later, Twi and I left and went back to my broth- ers' village to sleep.

The next day, my older brother saw a honey cache while walking in 48 the bush. He came to tell us and take us back there with him; we planned to stay the night in the bush. We arrived and spent the rest of the day collecting honey. When we finished, we walked toward where we were planning to camp. That's when I saw Besa's tracks in the sand. I said, "Everyone! Come here! Besa's tracks are here! Has anyone seen them elsewhere?" One of the men said, "Nonsense! Would you know his tracks . . ." I interrupted, "My husband . . . the man who married me . . . I *know* his tracks." The man's wife came to look "Yes, those are Besa's tracks; his wife really did see them."

The next morning, Besa walked into the camp. Besa and Twi started 49 to fight. My older brother yelled, "Do you two want to kill Nisa? Today she is not taking another husband. Today she's just going to lie by her- self." I agreed, "Eh, I don't want to marry again now."

Twi and I continued to live together after that. But later we 50 separated. My older brother caused it, because he wanted Besa to be with me again. He liked him and didn't like Twi. That's why he forced Twi to leave. When Twi saw how much anger both Dau and Besa felt toward him, he became afraid, and finally he left.

I saw what my brother had done and was miserable; I had really liked 51 Twi. I said, "So, this is what you wanted? Fine, but now that you have chased Twi away, I'll have nothing at all to do with Besa." That's when I began to refuse Besa completely. Besa went to the headman and said, "Nisa refuses to be with me." The headman said, "Nisa's been refusing you for a long time. What legal grounds could I possibly find for you now?"

After more time passed, a man who had been my lover years before, 52 started with me again. Soon we were very much in love. He was so handsome! His nose . . . his eyes . . . everything was so beautiful! His skin was light and his nose was lovely. I really loved that man, even when I first saw him.

We lived together for a while, but then he died. I was miserable, 53 "My lover has died. Where am I going to find another like him—an- other as beautiful, another as good, another with a European nose and with such lovely light skin? Now he's dead. Where will I ever find an- other like him?"

My heart was miserable and I mourned for him. I exhausted myself   54
with mourning and only when it was finished did I feel better again.

After years of living and having everything that happened to me hap-   55
pen, that's when I started with Bo, the next important man in my life
and the one I am married to today.

Besa and I lived separately, but he still wanted me and stayed near   56
me. That man, he didn't hear; he didn't understand. He was without
ears, because he still said, "This woman here, Nisa, I won't be finished
with her."

People told Bo, "You're going to die. This man, Besa, he's going to   57
kill you. Now, leave Nisa." But Bo refused, "Me . . . I won't go to another hut. I'll just stay with Nisa and even if Besa tries to kill me, I'll
still be here and won't leave."

At first, Bo and I sneaked off together, but Besa suspected us; he was   58
very jealous. He accused me all the time. Even when I just went to urinate, he'd say that I had been with Bo. Or when I went for water, he'd
say, "Did you meet your lover?" But I'd say, "What makes you think
you can talk to me like that?" He'd say, "Nisa, are you not still my
wife? Why aren't we living together? What are you doing?" I'd say,
"Don't you have other women or are they refusing you, too? You have
others so why are you asking me about what I'm doing?"

One night, Bo and I were lying down inside my hut and as I looked   59
out through the latched-branch door, I saw someone moving about. It
was Besa; I was able to see his face. He wanted to catch us, hoping I
would feel some remorse and perhaps return to him.

I said, "What? Besa's here! Bo . . . Bo . . . Besa's standing out there."   60
Bo got up; Besa came and stood by the door. I got up and that's when
Besa came in and grabbed me. He held onto me and threatened to
throw me into the fire. I cursed him as he held me, "Besa-Big-Testicles!
Long-Penis! First you left me and drank of women's genitals elsewhere.
Now you come back, see me, and say I am your wife?" He pushed me
toward the fire, but I twisted my body so I didn't land in it. Then he
went after Bo. Bo is weaker and older than Besa, so Besa was able to
grab him, pull him outside the hut, and throw him down. He bit him
on the shoulder. Bo yelled out in pain.

My younger brother woke and ran to us, yelling, "Curses to your   61
genitals!" He grabbed them and separated them. Bo cursed Besa. Besa
cursed Bo, "Curses on your penis!" He yelled, "I'm going to kill you
Bo, then Nisa will suffer! If I don't kill you, then maybe I'll kill her so
that you will feel pain! Because what you have that is so full of pleasure, I also have. So why does her heart want you and refuse me?"

I yelled at him, "That's not it! It's you! It's who you are and the way   62
you think! This one, Bo, his ways are good and his thoughts are good.
But you, your ways are foul. Look, you just bit Bo; that, too, is part of
your ways. You also left me to die. And death, that's something I'm

afraid of. That's why you no longer have a hold over me. Today I have
another who will take care of me well. I'm no longer married to you,
Besa. I want my husband to be Bo."

Besa kept bothering me and hanging around me. He'd ask, "Why   63
won't you come to me? Come to me, I'm a man. Why are you afraid of
me?" I wouldn't answer. Once Bo answered, "I don't understand why,
if you *are* a man, you keep pestering this woman? Is what you're doing
going to do any good? Because I won't leave her. And even though you
bit me and your marks are on me, you're the one who is going to move
out of the way, not me. I intend to marry her."

Another time I told Bo, "Don't be afraid of Besa. You and I will   64
marry; I'm not going to stay married to him. Don't let him frighten
you. Because even if he comes here with arrows, he won't do anything
with them." Bo said, "Even if he did, what good would that do? I am
also a man and am a master of arrows. The two of us would just strike
each other. That's why I keep telling him to let you go; I am the man
you are with now."

The next time, Besa came with his quiver full of arrows, saying, "I'm   65
going to get Nisa and bring her back with me." He left with another
man and came to me at my village. When he arrived, the sun was high
in the sky. I was resting. He said, "Nisa, come, let's go." I said,
"What? Is your penis not well? Is it horny?"

People heard us fighting and soon everyone was there, my younger   66
and older brothers as well. Besa and I kept arguing and fighting until,
in a rage, I screamed, "All right! Today I'm no longer afraid!" and I
pulled off all the skins that were covering me—first one, then another,
and finally the leather apron that covered my genitals. I pulled them all
off and laid them down on the ground. I cried, "There! There's my va-
gina! Look, Besa, look at me! This is what you want!"

The man he had come with said, "This woman, her heart is truly far   67
from you. Besa, look. Nisa refuses you totally, with all her heart. She
refuses to have sex with you. Your relationship with her is finished.
See. She took off her clothes, put them down, and with her genitals is
showing everyone how she feels about you. She doesn't want you,
Besa. If I were you, I'd finish with her today." Besa finally said, "Eh,
you're right. Now I am finished with her."

The two of them left. I took my leather apron, put it on, took the rest 68
of my things and put them on.

Mother! That was just what I did.   69

Besa tried one last time. He went to the headman again, and when   70
he came back he told me, "The headman wants to see you." I thought,
"If he wants to see me, I won't refuse."

When I arrived, the headman said, "Besa says he still wants to con-   71
tinue your marriage." I said, "Continue our marriage? Why? Am I so
stupid that I don't know my name? Would I stay in a marriage with a
man who left me hanging in a foreign place? If Old Debe and his wife

hadn't been there, I would have truly lost my way. Me, stay married to Besa? I can't make myself think of it."

I turned to Besa, "Isn't that what I told you when we were still in   72
the East?" Besa said, "Mm, that's what you said." I said, "And, when you left, didn't I tell you that you were leaving me pregnant with your baby. Didn't I also tell you that?" He said, "Yes, that's what you said." I said, "And didn't I say that I wanted to go with you, that I wanted you to help make our pregnancy grow strong? Didn't I say that and didn't you refuse?" He said, "Yes, you said that." Then I said, "Mm. Therefore, that marriage you say today, in the lap of the headman, should be continued, that marriage no longer exists. Because I am Nisa and today, when I look at you, all I want to do is to throw up. Vomit is the only thing left in my heart for you now. As we sit together here and I see your face, that is all that rises within and grabs me."

The headman laughed, shook his head and said, "Nisa is impos-   73
sible!" Then he said, "Besa, you had better listen to her. Do you hear what she is saying? She says that you left her while she was pregnant, that she miscarried and was miserable. Today she will no longer take you for her husband." Besa said, "That's because she's with Bo now and doesn't want to leave him. But I still want her and want to con-tinue our marriage."

I said, "What? Besa, can't you see me? Can't you see that I have re-   74
ally found another man? Did you think, perhaps, that I was too old and wouldn't find someone else?" The headman laughed again. "Yes, I am a woman. And that which you have, a penis, I also have something of equal worth. Like the penis of a chief . . . yes, something of a chief is what I have. And its worth is like money. Therefore, the person who drinks from it . . . it's like he's getting money from me. But not you, because when you had it, you just left it to ruin."

The headman said, "Nisa is crazy; her talk is truly crazy now." Then   75
he said, "The two of you sleep tonight and give your thoughts over to this. Nisa, think about all of it again. Tomorrow, I want both of you to come back."

Besa went and lay down. I went and lay down and thought about   76
everything. In the morning, I went to the headman. I felt ashamed by my talk of the night before. I sat there quietly. The headman said, "Nisa, Besa says you should stay married to him." I answered, "Why should he stay married to me when yesterday I held his baby in my stomach and he dropped me. Even God doesn't want me to marry a man who leaves me, a man who takes my blankets when I have small children beside me, a man who forces other people to give me blankets to cover my children with. Tell him to find another woman to marry."

The headman turned to Besa, "Nisa has explained herself. There's   77
nothing more I can see to say. Even you, you can hear that she has de-feated you. So, leave Nisa and as I am headman, today your marriage to her is ended. She can now marry Bo."

Besa went to the headman one more time. When he tried to discuss   78
it again, saying, "Please, help me. Give Nisa back to me," this headman said, "Haven't you already talked to me about this? You talked and
talked, and the words entered my ears. Are you saying that I have not
already decided on this? That I am not an important person? That I am
a worthless thing that you do not have to listen to? There is no reason
to give Nisa back to you."

I was so thankful when I heard his words. My heart filled with hap-   79
piness.

Bo and I married soon after that. We lived together, sat together, and 80
did things together. Our hearts loved each other very much and our
marriage was very very strong.

Besa also married again not long after—this time to a woman much   81
younger than me. One day he came to me and said, "Look how wrong
you were to have refused me! Perhaps you thought you were the only
woman. But you, Nisa, today you are old and you yourself can see that
I have married a young women, one who is beautiful!"

I said, "Good! I told you that if we separated, you'd find a young   82
woman to marry and to sleep with. That is fine with me because there
is nothing I want from you. But you know of course, that just like me,
another day she too will be old."

We lived on, but not long after, Besa came back. He said that his   83
young wife was troubled and that he wanted me again. I refused and
even told Bo about it. Bo asked me why I refused. I said, "Because I
don't want him." But what he says about his wife is true. She has a
terrible sickness, a type of madness. God gave it to her. She was such a
beautiful woman, too. But no longer. I wonder why such a young
woman has to have something like that . . .

Even today, whenever Besa sees me, he argues with me and says he   84
still wants me. I say, "Look, we've separated. Now leave me alone." I
even sometimes refuse him food. Bo tells me I shouldn't refuse, but
I'm afraid he will bother me more if I give anything to him. Because his
heart still cries for me.

Sometimes I do give him things to eat and he also gives things to   85
me. Once I saw him in my village. He came over to me and said,
"Nisa, give me some water to drink." I washed out a cup and poured
him some water. He drank it and said, "Now, give me some tobacco." I
took out some tobacco and gave it to him. Then he said, "Nisa, you
really are adult; you know how to work. Today, I am married to a
woman but my heart doesn't agree to her much. But you . . . you are
one who makes me feel pain. Because you left me and married another
man. I also married, but have made myself weary by having married
something bad. You, you have hands that work and do things. With
you, I could eat. You would get water for me to wash with. Today, I'm
really in pain."

I said, "Why are you thinking about our dead marriage? Of course,   **86**
we were married once, but we have gone our different ways. Now, I no
longer want you. After all that happened when you took me East—living there, working there, my father dying, my mother dying, and all
the misery you caused me—you say we should live together once
again?"

He said that I wasn't telling it as it happened.   **87**

One day, he told me he wanted to take me from Bo. I said, "What?   **88**
Tell me, Besa, what has been talking to you that you are saying this
again?" He said, "All right, then have me as your lover. Won't you
help my heart out?" I said, "Aren't there many men who could be my
lover? Why should I agree to you?" He said, "Look here, Nisa . . . I'm
a person who helped bring up your children, the children you and
your husband gave birth to. You became pregnant again with my child
and that was good. You held it inside you and lived with it until God
came and killed it. That's why your heart is talking this way and refusing me."

I told him he was wrong. But he was right, too. Because, after Besa,   **89**
I never had any more children. He took that away from me. With
Tashay, I had children, but Besa, he ruined me. Even the one time I
did conceive, I miscarried. That's because of what he did to me; that's
what everyone says.

_____ **Written Response**

Would you consider Nisa to be what we would call a free (or liberated)
woman? Do you feel that the role that she has decided to play in her
society (whether unliberated or liberated) has brought her happiness?
Why?

_____ **Rhetorical Analysis**

1. Shostak wanted her text and Nisa's text to form a dialogue between
an outside/objective and inside/personal view of the !Kung society. How
do you feel that Nisa's narrative adds to Shostak's text? How does Shostak's description of !Kung society add to Nisa's narrative?

2. What kind of differences do you notice between Shostak's text and
Nisa's text?

3. In her introduction, Shostak wrote:

> Nisa's narrative is just one view of !Kung life. Her history does not rep-
> resent the whole range of experience available to women in her culture; the
> life stories of other women are often quite different. Also, it is not possible
> to take everything Nisa says literally, particularly her description of her ear-
> lier years. She enjoyed the interview situation with the "machine that grabs
> your voice." To make her story lively and dramatic, she often assumed the

high, somewhat insistent voice of a young child, as though trying to describe the events of her childhood through the eyes of Nisa, the little girl. It is probable that these early accounts are somewhat exaggerated—a combination of actual memory, information about her childhood related to her when she was older, generalized experiences common to the culture, and fantasy. As the narrative progresses, her voice becomes more mature and independent and her stories are likely to be more reliable. I was able to corroborate much of what she said about her later life from independent sources. Thus her description of her adult life may be considered to be as accurate as it is vivid. [p. 43]

Why does Shostak feel that the adult portions of Nisa's narrative are more reliable that the child portions? Based on what you have read, do you think that her narrative is "as accurate as it is vivid"? What biases might influence Nisa's narrative? What biases might influence how Shostak "hears" or edits her narrative?

Interpretation

1. On two occasions, Besa goes to the headman and asks him to force Nisa to remain his wife. Each time Nisa is able to convince the headman that she and Besa should be divorced. How is Nisa able to convince the headman that she is right?

2. When Besa steals Nisa's money, Nisa enlists the aid of the European woman for whom she works to get her money back. What does this episode say about who has power in !Kung culture? What does it say about who has power in Botswana?

3. As you were reading Nisa's narrative, were you able to relate to it? Did her life seem foreign to you? Or did her life seem similar to the kind of lives that people in our culture might lead?

4. Do you feel that Nisa's text supports the statements that Shostak makes about !Kung culture in her text? In other words, after reading Nisa's text, are you more inclined to believe what Shostak has to say about the !Kung, or do you feel that she in some way failed to understand the !Kung?

WRITING ASSIGNMENTS

1. Select a character from Nisa's narrative (such as, Nisa, Besa, or Nisa's mother) and explain how that character is like someone that you know.

2. Take a statement from Shostak's text (such as, "All in all, !Kung women maintain a status that is higher than that of women in many agricultural and industrial societies around the world") and then use evidence from Nisa's narrative to either support or refute this statement.

3. Argue that Shostak either is or is not biased in her description of !Kung culture.

Synthesis

1. As you have learned from this chapter, an anthropologist studies culture in three basic ways: (1) by observing and recording his or her observations in field notes, (2) by interviewing people to learn how they view their own culture, and (3) by collecting artifacts, which could be anything from artwork to texts (for example, the dreams that Gregor collected).

As a final writing assignment in this chapter, you will be asked to become an ethnographer and study a culture that is foreign to you. Instead of traveling to a primitive village, you will be asked to learn about a culture that is unlike your culture. You could visit a new church, eat at an ethnic restaurant, or attend some kind of community meeting. Before observing the culture, you may need to ask permission of appropriate officials; anthropologists call this negotiating entree. While there, you should observe and take field notes, interview the people about their culture, and collect artifacts.

Once you have completed your study of this foreign culture, write a narrative about your experience that will inform an educated audience of what you have learned. Before turning in your narrative, you should change the names of any people whom you observed to protect their identity.

2. As a research project, collect as many texts (myths, descriptions of rituals, and so on) as you can relating to a particular culture. Then use these texts to write an essay that would help the average American to understand and better appreciate that foreign culture.

3. Use what you have learned in this chapter to argue that some social practice in your community is an abuse of power and should be abolished or altered.

2 | Science: The Quest for Objectivity

One of the major goals of science has traditionally been to understand the material and physical universe objectively. Scientists have wanted to understand the universe as it is, not as individual humans may perceive it and not as our cultural traditions—as preserved in myths, superstitions, and rituals—have told us it is.

Early attempts to bring objectivity to science relied, as we will see, on reason unaided by systematic observation and controlled experimentation. Aristotle, for example, believed that any attempt to comprehend the universe should use logic to move from the "known" to what was previously "unknown."

In the sixteenth century, scientists began to emphasize systematic experimentation, which came to be known as the scientific method, to guarantee objectivity. In Humphry Davy's *Elements of Chemical Philosophy* (1812), we can find a description of the basic scientific method on which modern science was founded:

> The foundations of chemical philosophy, are observation, experiment, and analogy. By observation, facts are distinctly and minutely impressed on the mind. By analogy, similar facts are connected. By experiment, new facts are discovered; and, in the progression of knowledge, observation, guided by analogy, leads to experiment, and analogy confirmed by experiment, becomes scientific truth.
>
> To give an instance.—Whoever will consider with attention the slender green vegetable filaments (*Conferva rivularis*) which in the summer exist in almost all streams, lakes, or pools, under the different circumstances of shade and sunshine, will discover globules of air upon the filaments that are not shaded. He will find that the effect is owing to the presence of light. This is an observation; but it gives no information respecting the nature of the air. Let a wine glass filled with water be inverted over the Conferva, the air will collect in the upper part of the glass, and when the glass is filled with air, it may be closed by the hand, placed in its usual position, and an inflammed taper [candle] introduced into it; the taper will burn with more brilliancy than in the atmosphere. This is an *experiment*. If the phenomena are reasoned upon, and the question is put, whether all

vegetables of this kind, in fresh or in salt water, do not produce such air under like circumstances, the enquirer is guided by *analogy:* and when this is determined to be the case by new trials, a *general scientific truth* is established—That all Confervae in the sunshine produce a species of air that supports flame in a superior degree; which has been shown to be the case by various investigations. [pp. 2–3]

Most scientists would view the development and refinement of the scientific method as an indication of science's progress toward achieving ojectivity. However, a number of philosophers of science have raised serious questions about the objectivity of current scientific methods; they have even raised questions about the possibility of science ever achieving objectivity. The readings in this chapter will explore the quest for objectivity in science as well as some of the recent critiques of the scientific method.

From Myth to Reason

Karl Popper (born 1902) is an Austrian-born philosopher of science; he has spent most of his career attempting to make science more objective and methodologically sound. In the following brief excerpt from *Objective Knowledge: An Evolutionary Approach,* he explains his theory about the origin of the scientific method.

_____ **Prereading**

In "The Origin of Science," Popper refers to two schools of Greek philosophy.

The first school, founded by Pythagoras (582–500 B.C.), attempted to understand the cosmos by studying complex relationships among numbers. This school's students were known for their philosophical and scientific conservatism; they attributed the development of all of the school's knowledge directly to Pythagoras and felt the need to teach his philosophy as it was taught to them. Interestingly, once Pythagoras' students were scattered throughout the Greek world, they all claimed to teach the true Pythagoras doctrine, but none of them taught the same ideas.

The second school, known as the Ionian school, was founded by Thales, who lived from about 640 to 546 B.C. Thales' major contribution to philosophy and science was that he attempted to comprehend the world through reason—the ability to critically analyze the nature of reality. He also encouraged his students to question his teachings.

Which school do you feel would be more likely to contribute to the development of the scientific method and the development of new knowledge? Why?

The Origin of Science
Karl Popper

The first beginnings of the evolution of something like a scientific   **1**
method may be found, approximately at the turn of the sixth and fifth
centuries B.C., in ancient Greece. What happened there? What is new
in this evolution? How do the new ideas compare with the traditional
myths, which came from the East and which, I think, provided many
of the decisive suggestions for the new ideas?

Among the Babylonians and the Greeks and also among the Maoris   **2**
in New Zealand—indeed, it would seem, among all peoples who invent cosmological myths—tales are told which deal with the beginning
of things, and which try to understand or explain the structure of the
Universe in terms of the story of its origin. These stories become traditional and are preserved in special schools. The tradition is often in the
keeping of some separate or chosen class, the priests or medicine men,
who guard it jealously. The stories change only little by little—mainly
through inaccuracies in handing them on, through misunderstandings,
and sometimes through the accretion of new myths, invented by
prophets or poets.

Now what is new in Greek philosophy, what is newly added to all   **3**
this, seems to me to consist not so much in the replacement of the
myths by something more 'scientific', as in a *new attitude towards the
myths*. That their character then begins to change seems to me to be
merely a consequence of this new attitude.

The new attitude I have in mind is *the critical attitude. In the place of a*   **4**
dogmatic handing on of the doctrine [in which the whole interest lies in the
preservation of the authentic tradition] *we find a critical discussion of the
doctrine*. Some people begin to ask questions about it; they doubt the
trustworthiness of the doctrine: its *truth*.

Doubt and criticism certainly existed before this stage. What is new,   **5**
however, is that doubt and criticism now become, in their turn, part of
the tradition of the school. A tradition of a higher order replaces the
traditional preservation of the dogma: in the place of traditional theory—in place of the myth—we find the tradition of criticizing theories
(which at first themselves are hardly more than myths). It is only in
the course of this critical discussion that observation is called in as a
witness.

Source: "The Origin of Science" from *Objective Knowledge* by Karl R. Popper, pp. 347–8.
Copyright © 1972, 1979 Karl R. Popper. Reprinted by permission of Oxford University
Press, Oxford.

exchange theories with one of your classmates. Then write an essay in which you explain your classmate's theory and how you, as a scientist, will attempt to prove the theory false. You could attempt to prove it false by presenting evidence (for example, is traffic *always* bad only when you are late for a meeting) or by pointing out that the theory is logically inconsistent.

The Move Toward Experimentation

Francis Bacon (1560–1626) was a person of questionable character, at least when it came to politics. While he was Lord Chancellor of England (the highest judicial officer for Queen Elizabeth I), he was accused of taking bribes and was forced out of office. This same man, however, is generally regarded as the founder of modern science; he was one of the first philosophers to argue that science must become more honest through objective experimentation, and there is no indication that he was anything but honest when practicing science.

Indeed, one of his last acts in life was a scientific experiment. In order to determine whether ice could be used to preserve food, Bacon spent hours outside collecting snow. From his exposure to the cold weather, he caught a fatal case of pneumonia. Yet, he still completed his experiment. On his death bed, he wrote, "The experiment succeeded, excellently well."

The following selections from "Aphorisms Concerning the Interpretation of Nature and the Kingdom of Man" (the first book of his *Novum Organum*) show his concern for developing an objective approach to science. Although Bacon felt that it was crucial for science to become more objective, he was not, as will be seen, naive about the difficulty of achieving absolute objectivity.

_____ **Prereading**

In his "Aphorisms," which form Book One of *Novum Organum*, Bacon writes that the old approach to science is no longer valid. The old science that Bacon began to change in the seventeenth century was known as Scholasticism, which was more a science of authority than of experimentation. Scholastics, who did not want science to overshadow or disrupt religion, looked back to the science of Aristotle. The character of Aristotle's—as well as the Scholastics'—approach to science is apparent in the following excerpt from the beginning of Aristotle's *Physics* (*The Complete Works of Aristotle* [Princeton: Princeton University Press, 1984]):

> When the objects of an inquiry, in any department, have principles, causes, or elements, it is through acquaintance with these that knowledge and understanding is attained. . . . The natural way of doing this is to start from the things which are more knowable and clear to us and proceed towards those which are clearer and more knowable by nature; for the same

things are not knowable relatively to us and knowable without qualification. So we must follow this method and advance from what is more obscure by nature, but clearer to us, towards what is more clear and more knowable by nature. . . . Thus we must advance from universals to particulars; for it is a whole that is more knowable to sense-perception, and a universal is a kind of whole, comprehending many things within it, like parts. [p. 315]

Rather than conduct experiments, Aristotle used reason and logic to develop his view of the world. It is Aristotle's attempt to understand the universe through logic alone that Bacon criticizes in his "Aphorisms." Indeed, he took the title of his *Novum Organum* from Aristotle's *Organum*, a collection of Aristotle's writings on logic that was brought together long after his death. In writing *Novum Organum*, Bacon was quite consciously rewriting Aristotle, which means that he was in effect rewriting science.

Why do you think that trying to understand the universe solely from what we already know and logic is an insufficient approach to science?

Aphorisms Concerning the Interpretation of Nature and the Kingdom of Man
Francis Bacon

Only a selection of the "Aphorisms" is included here; the original numbering has been maintained.

I

Man, being the servant and interpreter of Nature, can do and understand so much and so much only as he has observed in fact or in thought of the course of nature; beyond this he neither knows anything nor can do anything.

II

Neither the naked hand nor the understanding[1] left to itself can effect much. It is by instruments and helps[2] that the work is done, which are as much wanted for the understanding as for the hand. And as the instruments of the hand either give motion or guide it,

Source: Francis Bacon, Book I of *Novum Organum*, 1620.

---

[1] Understanding: the logical faculty of the mind.
[2] By "helps," Bacon means acts of helping, or aids.

so the instruments of the mind supply either suggestions for the understanding or cautions.

III

Human knowledge and human power meet in one, for where the cause is not known the effect cannot be produced. Nature to be commanded must be obeyed, and that which in contemplation is as the cause is in operation as the rule.

VII

The productions of the mind and hand seem very numerous in books and manufactures. But all this variety lies in an exquisite subtlety and derivations from a few things already known, not in the number of axioms.

VIII

Moreover, the works already known are due to chance and experiment rather than to sciences; for the sciences we now possess are merely systems for the nice ordering and setting forth of things already invented, not methods of invention or directions for new works.

IX

The cause and root of nearly all evils in the sciences is this, that while we falsely admire and extol the powers of the human mind we neglect to seek for its true helps.

X

The subtlety of nature is greater many times over than the subtlety of the senses and understanding, so that all those specious meditations, speculations, and glosses in which men indulge are quite from the purpose, only there is no one by to observe it.

XI

As the sciences which we now have do not help us in finding out new works, so neither does the logic which we now have help us in finding out new sciences.

XII

The logic now in use serves rather to fix and give stability to the errors which have their foundation in commonly received notions than to help the search after truth. So it does more harm than good.

XIX

There are and can be only two ways of searching into and discovering truth. The one flies from the senses and particulars to the most general axioms, and from these principles, the truth of which it takes for settled and immovable, proceeds to judgment and to the discovery of middle axioms. And this way is now in fashion. The other derives axioms from the senses and particulars, rising by a gradual and unbroken ascent, so that it arrives at the most general axioms last of all. This is the true way, but as yet untried.

XXII

Both ways set out from the senses and particulars, and rest in the highest generalities, but the difference between them is infinite. For the one just glances at experiment and particulars in passing, the other dwells duly and orderly among them. The one, again, begins at once by establishing certain abstract and useless generalities, the other rises by gradual steps to that which is prior and better known in the order of nature.

XXIII

There is a great difference between the Idols[3] of the human mind and the Ideas of the divine. That is to say, between certain empty dogmas and the true signatures and marks set upon the works of creation as they are found in nature.

XXVI

The conclusions of human reason as ordinarily applied in matters of nature, I call for the sake of distinction *Anticipations of Nature* (as a thing rash or premature). That reason which is elicited from facts by a just and methodical process, I call *Interpretation of Nature*.

XXXI

It is idle to expect any great advancement in science from the superinducing and engrafting of new things upon old. We must begin anew from the very foundations, unless we would revolve for ever in a circle with mean and contemptible progress.

XXXII

The honour of the ancient authors, and indeed of all, remains untouched, since the comparison I challenge is not of wits or faculties, but of ways and methods, and the part I take upon myself is not that of a judge, but of a guide.

XXXVIII

The idols and false notions which are now in possession of the human understanding, and have taken deep root therein, not only so beset men's minds that truth can hardly find entrance, but even after

---

[3] By "Idols," Bacon means unsubstantial images, phantoms, and illusions. His four "Idols" are factors that can distort the objectivity of science.

entrance obtained, they will again in the very instauration[4] of the sciences meet and trouble us, unless men being forewarned of the danger fortify themselves as far as may be against their assaults.

XXXIX

There are four classes of Idols which beset men's minds. To these for distinction's sake I have assigned names, calling the first class *Idols of the Tribe;* the second, *Idols of the Cave;* the third, *Idols of the Market Place;* the fourth, *Idols of the Theatre.*

XL

The formation of ideas and axioms by true induction[5] is no doubt the proper remedy to be applied for the keeping off and clearing away of idols. To point them out, however, is of great use, for the doctrine of Idols is to the Interpretation of Nature what the doctrine of the refutation of sophisms[6] is to common logic.

XLI

The Idols of the Tribe have their foundation in human nature itself and in the tribe or race of men. For it is a false assertion that the sense of man is the measure of things. On the contrary, all perceptions as well of the sense as of the mind are according to the measure of the individual and not according to the measure of the universe. And the human understanding is like a false mirror, which, receiving rays irregularly, distorts and discolours the nature of things by mingling its own nature with it.

XLII

The Idols of the Cave are the idols of the individual man. For every one (besides the errors common to human nature in general) has a cave or den of his own, which refracts and discolours the light of nature, owing either to his own proper and peculiar nature, or to his education and conversation with others, or to the reading of books, and the authority of those whom he esteems and admires, or to the differences of impressions, accordingly as they take place in a mind preoccupied and predisposed or in a mind indifferent and settled, or the like. So that the spirit of man (according as it is meted out to different individuals) is in fact a thing variable and full of perturbation, and governed as it were by chance. Whence it was well observed by Heraclitus[7] that men look for sciences in their own lesser worlds and not in the greater or common world.

---

[4] Instauration: the activity of restoring, renewing, or renovating.
[5] Induction: moving from particular facts or sensations to general ideas.
[6] Sophisms: false arguments that are used to intentionally deceive.
[7] Heraclitus: a pre-Socratic Greek philosopher.

XLIII

There are also Idols formed by the intercourse and association of men with each other, which I call Idols of the Market Place on account of the commerce and consort of men there. For it is by discourse that men associate, and words are imposed according to the apprehension of the vulgar. And therefore the ill and unfit choice of words wonderfully obstructs the understanding. Nor do the definitions or explanations wherewith in some things learned men are wont to guard and defend themselves, by any means set the matter right. But words plainly force and overrule the understanding, and throw all into confusion, and lead men away into numberless empty controversies and idle fancies.

XLIV

Lastly, there are Idols which have immigrated into men's minds from the various dogmas of philosophies and also from wrong laws of demonstration. These I call Idols of the Theatre, because in my judgment all the received systems are but so many stage plays, representing worlds of their own creation after an unreal and scenic fashion. Nor is it only of the systems now in vogue or only of the ancient sects and philosophies that I speak, for many more plays of the same kind may yet be composed and in like artificial manner set forth, seeing that errors the most widely different have nevertheless causes for the most part alike. Neither again do I mean this only of entire systems, but also of many principles and axioms in science, which by tradition, credulity, and negligence have come to be received.

But of these several kinds of Idols I must speak more largely and exactly, that the understanding may be duly cautioned.

XLV

The human understanding is of its own nature prone to suppose the existence of more order and regularity in the world than it finds. And though there be many things in nature which are singular and unmatched, yet it devises for them parallels and conjugates and relatives which do not exist. Hence the fiction that all celestial bodies move in perfect circles, spirals and dragons[8] being (except in name) utterly rejected. Hence too the element of fire with its orb[9] is brought in, to make up the square with the other three which the sense perceives. Hence also the ratio of density of the so-called elements is arbitrarily fixed at ten to one. And so on of other dreams. And these fancies affect not dogmas only, but simple notions also.

---

[8] Dragons: the luminous tails of shooting stars.

[9] Orb: During Bacon's era, the orb was the concentric hollow spheres that were thought to surround the earth and carry the planets and stars in their revolutions.

XLIX

The human understanding is no dry light, but receives an infusion
from the will and affections; whence proceed sciences which may be
called "sciences as one would". For what a man had rather were
true he more readily believes. Therefore he rejects difficult things
from impatience of research; sober things because they narrow hope;
the deeper things of nature from superstition; the light of experience
for arrogance and pride, lest his mind should seem to be occupied
with things mean and transitory; things not commonly believed, out
of deference to the opinion of the vulgar. Numberless, in short, are
the ways, and sometimes imperceptible, in which the affections colour and infect the understanding.

L

But by far the greatest hindrance and aberration of the human understanding proceeds from the dulness, incompetency, and decep-
tions of the senses; in that things which strike the sense outweigh
things which do not immediately strike it, though they be more important. Hence it is that speculation commonly ceases where sight
ceases; insomuch that of things invisible there is little or no observation. Hence all the working of the spirits inclosed in tangible bodies
lies hid and unobserved of men. So also all the more subtle changes
of form in the parts of coarser substances (which they commonly call
alteration, though it is in truth local motion through exceedingly
small spaces) is in like manner unobserved. And yet, unless these
two things just mentioned be searched out and brought to light,
nothing great can be achieved in nature as far as the production of
works is concerned. So again, the essential nature of our common air
and of all bodies less dense than air (which are very many) is almost
unknown. For the sense by itself is a thing infirm and erring; neither
can instruments for enlarging or sharpening the senses do much; but
all the truer kind of interpretation of nature is effected by instances
and experiments fit and apposite, wherein the sense decides touching the experiment only, and the experiment touching the point in
nature and the thing itself.

LII

Such then are the idols which I call *Idols of the Tribe,* and which take
their rise either from the homogeneity of the substance of the human
spirit, or from its preoccupation, or from its narrowness, or from its
restless motion, or from an infusion of the affections, or from the
incompetency of the senses, or from the mode of impression.

LIII

The *Idols of the Cave* take their rise in the peculiar constitution, mental or bodily, of each individual, and also in education, habit, and

accident. Of this kind there is a great number and variety, but I will instance those the pointing out of which contains the most important caution, and which have most effect in disturbing the clearness of the understanding.

LIV

Men become attached to certain particular sciences and speculations, either because they fancy themselves the authors and inventors thereof, or because they have bestowed the greatest pains upon them and become most habituated to them. But men of this kind, if they betake themselves to philosophy and contemplations of a general character, distort and colour them in obedience to their former fancies, a thing especially to be noticed in Aristotle, who made his natural philosophy a mere bondservant to his logic, thereby rendering it contentious and well nigh useless. The race of chemists again out of a few experiments of the furnace have built up a fantastic philosophy, framed with reference to a few things, and Gilbert also,[10] after he had employed himself most laboriously in the study and observation of the loadstone, proceeded at once to construct an entire system in accordance with his favourite subject.

LV

There is one principal and as it were radical distinction between different minds in respect of philosophy and the sciences, which is this: that some minds are stronger and apter to mark the differences of things, others to mark their resemblances. The steady and acute mind can fix its contemplations and dwell and fasten on the subtlest distinctions; the lofty and discursive mind recognizes and puts together the finest and most general resemblances. Both kinds however easily err in excess, by catching the one at gradations, the other at shadows.

LVIII

Let such then be our provision and contemplative prudence for keeping off and dislodging the *Idols of the Cave*, which grow for the most part either out of the predominance of a favourite subject, or out of an excessive tendency to compare or to distinguish, or out of partiality for particular ages, or out of the largeness or minuteness of the objects contemplated. And generally let every student of nature take this as a rule, that whatever his mind seizes and dwells upon with peculiar satisfaction is to be held in suspicion, and that so much the more care is to be taken in dealing with such questions to keep the understanding even and clear.

---

[10] William Gilbert (1544–1603), regarded as the father of electrical studies, was a pioneering researcher into loadstones and their magnetic properties.

LIX

But the *Idols of the Market Place* are the most troublesome of all—idols which have crept into the understanding through the alliances of words and names. For men believe that their reason governs words, but it is also true that words react on the understanding, and this it is that has rendered philosophy and the sciences sophistical and inactive. Now words, being commonly framed and applied according to the capacity of the vulgar, follow those lines of division which are most obvious to the vulgar understanding. And whenever an understanding of greater acuteness or a more diligent observation would alter those lines to suit the true divisions of nature, words stand in the way and resist the change. Whence it comes to pass that the high and formal discussions of learned men end oftentimes in disputes about words and names, with which (according to the use and wisdom of the mathematicians) it would be more prudent to begin, and so by means of definitions reduce them to order. Yet even definitions cannot cure this evil in dealing with natural and material things; since the definitions themselves consist of words, and those words beget others, so that it is necessary to recur to individual instances, and those in due series and order, as I shall say presently when I come to the method and scheme for the formation of notions and axioms.

LX

The idols imposed by words on the understanding are of two kinds. They are either names of things which do not exist (for as there are things left unnamed through lack of observation, so likewise are there names which result from fantastic suppositions and to which nothing in reality corresponds), or they are names of things which exist, but yet confused and ill defined and hastily and irregularly derived from realities. Of the former kind are Fortune, the Prime Mover, Planetary Orbits, Element of Fire, and like fictions which owe their origin to false and idle theories. And this class of idols is more easily expelled, because to get rid of them it is only necessary that all theories should be steadily rejected and dismissed as obsolete.

But the other class, which springs out of a faulty and unskilful abstraction, is intricate and deeply rooted. Let us take for example such a word as *humid*, and see how far the several things which the word is used to signify agree with each other; and we shall find the word *humid* to be nothing else than a mark loosely and confusedly applied to denote a variety of actions which will not bear to be reduced to any constant meaning. For it both signifies that which easily spreads itself round any other body; and that which in itself is indeterminate and cannot solidize; and that which readily yields in every direction; and that which easily divides and scatters itself; and that which easily unites and collects itself; and that which readily flows and is put in motion; and that which readily clings to another body and wets it; and that which is easily reduced to a liquid, or being solid easily melts. Accordingly when you come to apply the word, if you take it in one sense, flame is humid; if in another, air is not humid; if in another, fine dust is humid; if in another, glass is humid. So that it is easy to see that the notion is taken by abstraction only from water and common and ordinary liquids without any due verification.

There are however in words certain degrees of distortion and error. One of the least faulty kinds is that of names of substances, especially of lowest species and well deduced (for the notion of *chalk* and of *mud* is good, of *earth* bad); a more faulty kind is that of actions, as *to generate, to corrupt, to alter;* the most faulty is of qualities (except such as are the immediate objects of the sense) as *heavy, light, rare, dense,* and the like. Yet in all these cases some notions are of necessity a little better than others, in proportion to the greater variety of subjects that fall within the range of the human sense.

LXI

But the *Idols of the Theatre* are not innate, nor do they steal into the understanding secretly, but are plainly impressed and received into the mind from the playbooks of philosophical systems and the perverted rules of demonstration. To attempt refutations in this case would be merely inconsistent with what I have already said, for since we agree neither upon principles nor upon demonstrations there is no place for argument. And this is so far well, inasmuch as it leaves the honour of the ancients untouched. For they are no wise disparaged, the question between them and me being only as to the way. For as the saying is, the lame man who keeps the right road outstrips the runner who takes a wrong one. Nay, it is obvious that when a man runs the wrong way, the more active and swift he is the further he will go astray.

But the course I propose for the discovery of sciences is such as leaves but little to the acuteness and strength of wits, but places all wits and understandings nearly on a level. For as in the drawing of a straight line or a perfect circle much depends on the steadiness and practice of the hand, if it be done by aim of hand only, but if with the aid of rule or compass, little or nothing; so is it exactly with my plan. But though particular confutations would be of no avail, yet touching the sects and general divisions of such systems I must say something; something also touching the external signs which show that they are unsound; and finally something touching the causes of such great infelicity and of such lasting and general agreement in error: that so the access to truth may be made less difficult, and the human understanding may the more willingly submit to its purgation and dismiss its idols.

LXII

Idols of the Theatre, or of Systems, are many, and there can be and perhaps will be yet many more. For were it not that now for many ages men's minds have been busied with religion and theology, and were it not that civil governments, especially monarchies, have been averse to such novelties, even in matters speculative, so that men labour therein to the peril and harming of their fortunes, not only unrewarded but exposed also to contempt and envy, doubtless there would have arisen many other philosophical sects like to those which in great variety flourished once among the Greeks. For as on the phenomena of the heavens many hypotheses may be constructed, so likewise (and more also) many various dogmas may be set up and established on the phenomena of philosophy. And in the plays of this philosophical theatre you may observe the same thing which is found in the theatre of the poets, that stories invented for the stage are more compact and elegant, and more as one would wish them to be than true stories out of history.

In general however there is taken for the material of philosophy either a great deal out of a few things, or a very little out of many things, so that on both sides philosophy is based on too narrow a foundation of experiment and natural history, and decides on the authority of too few cases. For the Rational School of philosophers snatches from experience a variety of common instances, neither duly ascertained nor diligently examined and weighed, and leaves all the rest to meditation and agitation of wit.

There is also another class of philosophers, who having bestowed much diligent and careful labour on a few experiments, have thence made bold to educe and construct systems, wresting all other facts in a strange fashion to conformity therewith.

And there is yet a third class, consisting of those who out of faith and veneration mix their philosophy with theology and traditions, among whom the vanity of some has gone so far aside as to seek the origin of sciences among spirits and genii. So that this parent stock of errors—this false philosophy—is of three kinds: the Sophistical, the Empirical, and the Superstitious.

_____ **Written Response**

Write a few paragraphs that summarize Bacon's approach to the scientific method.

_____ **Rhetorical Analysis**

1. In *De Dignitate et Augmentis Scientiarum* (In *The Works of Francis Bacon* [London, 1861]), Bacon wrote:

Knowledge which is delivered to others . . . should be insinuated (if possible) in the same method as it was first discovered. And this very thing is certainly possible in the case of knowledge acquired through induction . . . it is certainly possible for someone more or less to revisit his own knowledge and simultaneously to retrace the path of both his ideas and his agreement; and in that way to transplant knowledge in another mind just as it grew in his own. . . . Aphorisms—in representing only portions and, as it were, morsels of knowledge—invite others also to add and donate something. [II: pp. 429, 431]

Based on this quotation, why do you think that Bacon wrote about his new science in aphorisms?

2. Since the Enlightenment in the eighteenth century, scientists have worked toward developing a style of writing that they feel will not distort the objectivity of their experiments. Today, most scientists attempt to avoid personal references. For example, they would probably write "The experiment was conducted under controlled circumstances" rather than "I conducted the experiment under controlled circumstances." They also attempt to avoid metaphors, descriptive words, or literary devices. For example, they would not write: "The polluted river smelled like a trash dump on a spring day."

Bacon was writing before the Enlightenment, before scientific writing was perceived as being distinct from literature. In what ways does Bacon's writing seem objective and scientific? In what ways does is seem to be personal and emotional, more like poetry or literature?

_____ **Interpretation**

1. In *A History of Philosophy* (Garden City, N.Y.: Image, 1985), Frederick Copleston wrote the following explanation of Bacon's thoughts on science:

The purpose of science [Bacon believes] is the extension of the dominion of the human race over nature; but this can be achieved only by a real knowledge of nature; we cannot obtain effects without an accurate knowledge of causes. The sciences which man now possesses, says Bacon, are useless for obtaining practical effects (*ad inventionem operum*) and our present logic is useless for the purpose of establishing sciences. . . . There are two ways of seeking and finding the truth. First, the mind may proceed from sense and from the perception of particulars to the most general axioms and from these deduce the less general propositions. Secondly it may proceed from sense and the perception of particulars to immediately attainable axioms and thence, gradually and patiently, to more general axioms. The first way is known and employed; but it is unsatisfactory, because particulars are not examined with sufficient accuracy, care and comprehensiveness and because the mind jumps from an insufficient basis to general conclusions and axioms. It produced *anticipationes naturae*, rash and premature generalizations. The second way, which has not yet been tried, is the true way. The

ners and civilization. These phenomena must have a cause; and can
any inquiry be at once more interesting and philosophical than that
which endeavors to ascertain whether that cause be connected with
a difference in the brain between the native American race, and
their conquering invaders (Combe and Coates, in review of Morton's *Crania Americana*, 1840, p. 352).

Moreover, Combe argued that Morton's collection would acquire true
scientific value *only if* mental and moral worth could be read from
brains: "If this doctrine be unfounded, these skulls are mere facts in
Natural History, presenting no particular information as to the mental
qualities of the people" (from Combe's appendix to Morton's *Crania
Americana*, 1839, p. 275).

Although he vacillated early in his career, Morton soon became a   5
leader among the American polygenists. He wrote several articles to
defend the status of human races as separate, created species. He took
on the strongest claim of opponents—the interfertility of all human
races—by arguing from both sides. He relied on travelers' reports to
claim that some human races—Australian aborigines and Caucasians in
particular—very rarely produce fertile offspring (Morton, 1851). He attributed this failure to "a disparity of primordial organization." But, he
continued, Buffon's criterion of interfertility must be abandoned in any
case, for hybridization is common in nature, even between species belonging to different genera (Morton, 1847, 1850). Species must be rede-
fined as "a primordial organic form" (1850, p. 82). "Bravo, my dear
Sir," wrote Agassiz in a letter, "you have at last furnished science with
a true philosophical definition of species" (in Stanton, 1960, p. 141). But
how to recognize a primordial form? Morton replied: "If certain existing
organic types can be traced back into the 'night of time,' as dissimilar
as we see them now, is it not more reasonable to regard them as ab-
original, than to suppose them the mere and accidental derivations of
an isolated patriarchal stem of which we know nothing?" (1850, p. 82).
Thus, Morton regarded several breeds of dogs as separate species because their skeletons resided in the Egyptian catacombs, as recognizable
and distinct from other breeds as they are now. The tombs also contained blacks and Caucasians. Morton dated the beaching of Noah's
Ark on Ararat at 4,179 years before his time, and the Egyptian tombs at
just 1,000 years after that—clearly not enough time for the sons of Noah
to differentiate into races. (How, he asks, can we believe that races changed
so rapidly for 1,000 years, and not at all for 3,000 years since then?) Human races must have been separate from the start (Morton, 1839, p. 88).

But separate, as the Supreme Court once said, need not mean un-   6
equal. Morton therefore set out to establish relative rank on "objective"
grounds. He surveyed the drawings of ancient Egypt and found that
blacks are invariably depicted as menials—a sure sign that they have
always played their appropriate biological role: "Negroes were numer-

ous in Egypt, but their social position in ancient times was the same
that it is now, that of servants and slaves" (Morton, 1844, p. 158). (A
curious argument, to be sure, for these blacks had been captured in
warfare; sub-Saharan societies depicted blacks as rulers.)

But Morton's fame as a scientist rested upon his collection of skulls   7
and their role in racial ranking. Since the cranial cavity of a human
skull provides a faithful measure of the brain it once contained, Morton
set out to rank races by the average sizes of their brains. He filled the
cranial cavity with sifted white mustard seed, poured the seed back into
a graduated cylinder and read the skull's volume in cubic inches. Later
on, he became dissatisfied with mustard seed because he could not obtain consistent results. The seeds did not pack well, for they were too
light and still varied too much in size, despite sieving. Remeasurements
of single skulls might differ by more than 5 percent, or 4 cubic inches
in skulls with an average capacity near 80 cubic inches. Consequently,
he switched to one-eighth-inch-diameter lead shot "of the size called
BB" and achieved consistent results that never varied by more than a
single cubic inch for the same skull.

Morton published three major works on the sizes of human skulls—   8
his lavish, beautifully illustrated volume on American Indians, the *Crania Americana* of 1839; his studies on skulls from the Egyptian tombs,
the *Crania Aegyptiaca* of 1844; and the epitome of his entire collection
in 1849. Each contained a table, summarizing his results on average
skull volumes arranged by race. I have reproduced all three tables here
(Tables 2.1 to 2.3). They represent the major contribution of American
polygeny to debates about racial ranking. They outlived the theory of
separate creations and were reprinted repeatedly during the nineteenth
century as irrefutable, "hard" data on the mental worth of human
races. . . . Needless to say, they matched every good Yankee's prejudice—whites on top, Indians in the middle, and blacks on the bottom;
and, among whites, Teutons and Anglo-Saxons on top, Jews in the
middle, and Hindus on the bottom. Moreover, the pattern had been
stable throughout recorded history, for whites had the same advantage
over blacks in ancient Egypt. Status and access to power in Morton's
America faithfully reflected biological merit. How could sentimentalists
and egalitarians stand against the dictates of nature? Morton had provided clean, objective data based on the largest collection of skulls in
the world.

During the summer of 1977 I spent several weeks reanalyzing Mor-   9
ton's data. (Morton, the self-styled objectivist, published all his raw information. We can infer with little doubt how he moved from raw
measurements to summary tables.) In short, and to put it bluntly, Morton's summaries are a patchwork of fudging and finagling in the clear
interest of controlling a priori convictions. Yet—and this is the most
intriguing aspect of the case—I find no evidence of conscious fraud;

Table 2.1 Morton's summary table of cranial capacity by race

Race	N	Internal Capacity (in^3)		
		Mean	Largest	Smallest
Caucasian	52	87	109	75
Mongolian	10	83	93	69
Malay	18	81	89	64
American	144	82	100	60
Ethiopian	29	78	94	65

Table 2.2 Cranial capacities for skulls from Egyptian tombs

People	Mean Capacity (in^3)	N
Caucasian		
Pelasgic	88	21
Semitic	82	5
Egyptian	80	39
Negroid	79	6
Negro	73	1

indeed, had Morton been a conscious fudger he would not have published his data so openly.

Conscious fraud is probably rare in science. It is also not very interesting, for it tells us little about the nature of scientific activity. Liars, if discovered, are excommunicated; scientists declare that their profession has properly policed itself, and they return to work, mythology unimpaired, and objectively vindicated. The prevalence of *unconscious* finagling, on the other hand, suggests a general conclusion about the social context of science. For if scientists can be honestly self-deluded to Morton's extent, then prior prejudice may be found anywhere, even in the basics of measuring bones and toting sums.   10

The Case of Indian Inferiority: *Crania Americana*

Morton began his first and largest work, the *Crania Americana* of 1839,   11
with a discourse on the essential character of human races. His statements immediately expose his prejudices. Of the "Greenland esquimaux,"[3] he wrote: "They are crafty, sensual, ungrateful, obstinate and unfeeling, and much of their affection for their children may be traced to purely selfish motives. They devour the most disgusting aliments uncooked and uncleaned, and seem to have no ideas beyond

---

[3]"Greenland esquimaux": the Eskimos of Greenland.

Table 2.3 Morton's final summary of cranial capacity by race

Races and Families	N	Cranial Capacity (in³)			
		Largest	Smallest	Mean	Mean
Modern Caucasian Group					
Teutonic Family					
Germans	18	114	70	90 ⎫	
English	5	105	91	96 ⎬	92
Anglo-Americans	7	97	82	90 ⎭	
Pelasgic Family	10	94	75	84	
Celtic Family	6	97	78	87	
Indostanic Family	32	91	67	80	
Semitic Family	3	98	84	89	
Nilotic Family	17	96	66	80	
Ancient Caucasian Group					
Pelasgic Family	18	97	74	88	
Nilotic Family	55	96	68	80	
Mongolian Group					
Chinese Family	6	91	70	82	
Malay Group					
Malayan Family	20	97	68	86 ⎫	
Polynesian Family	3	84	82	83 ⎭	85
American Group					
Toltecan Family					
Peruvians	155	101	58	75 ⎫	
Mexicans	22	92	67	79 ⎭	79
Barbarous Tribes	161	104	70	84	
Negro Group					
Native African Family	62	99	65	83 ⎫	
American-born Negroes	12	89	73	82 ⎭	83
Hottentot Family	3	83	68	75	
Australians	8	83	63	75	

providing for the present moment. . . . Their mental faculties, from infancy to old age, present a continued childhood. . . . In gluttony, selfishness and ingratitude, they are perhaps unequalled by any other nation of people" (1839, p. 54). Morton thought little better of other Mongolians, for he wrote of the Chinese (p.50): "So versatile are their feelings and actions, that they have been compared to the monkey race, whose attention is perpetually changing from one object to another." The Hottentots, he claimed (p. 90), are "the nearest approximation to the lower animals. . . . Their complexion is a yellowish brown, compared by travellers to the peculiar hue of Europeans in the last stages of jaundice. . . . The women are represented as even more repulsive in appearance than the men." Yet, when Morton had to describe one

Caucasian tribe as a "mere horde of rapacious banditti" (p. 9), he quickly added that "their moral perceptions, under the influence of an equitable government, would no doubt assume a much more favorable aspect."

Morton's summary chart (Table 2.1) presents the "hard" argument of **12** the *Crania Americana*. He had measured the capacity of 144 Indian skulls and calculated a mean of 82 cubic inches, a full 5 cubic inches below the Caucasian norm (Figs. 2.4 and 2.5). In addition, Morton appended a table of phrenological measurements[4] indicating a deficiency of "higher" mental powers among Indians. "The benevolent mind," Morton concluded (p. 82), "may regret the inaptitude of the Indian for civilization," but sentimentality must yield to fact. "The structure of his mind appears to be different from that of the white man, nor can the two harmonize in the social relations except on the most limited scale." Indians "are not only averse to the restraints of education, but for the most part are incapable of a continued process of reasoning on abstract subjects" (p. 81).

Since *Crania Americana* is primarily a treatise on the inferior quality of **13** Indian intellect, I note first of all that Morton's cited average of 82 cubic inches for Indian skulls is incorrect. He separated Indians into two groups, "Toltecans" from Mexico and South America, and "Barbarous Tribes" from North America. Eighty-two is the average for Barbarous skulls; the total sample of 144 yields a mean of 80.2 cubic inches, or a gap of almost 7 cubic inches between Indian and Caucasian averages. (I do not know how Morton made this elementary error. It did permit him, in any case, to retain the conventional chain of being with whites on top, Indians in the middle, and blacks on the bottom.)

But the "correct" value of 80.2 is far too low, for it is the result of an **14** improper procedure. Morton's 144 skulls belong to many different groups of Indians; these groups differ significantly among themselves in cranial capacity. Each group should be weighted equally, lest the final average be biased by unequal size of subsamples. Suppose, for example, that we tried to estimate average human height from a sample of two jockeys, the author of this book (strictly middling stature), and all the players in the National Basketball Association. The hundreds of Jabbars would swamp the remaining three and give an average in excess of six and a half feet. If, however, we averaged the averages of the three groups (jockeys, me, and the basketball players), then our figures would lie closer to the true value. Morton's sample is strongly biased by a major overrepresentation of an extreme group—the small-brained Inca Peruvians. (They have a mean cranial capacity of 74.36 cubic inches and provide 25 percent of the entire sample). Large-brained

----

[4]Phrenological measurements are measurements of the shape of the skull (for example, the height of the forehead) that some people believed were indicative of personal attributes (such as superior intelligence).

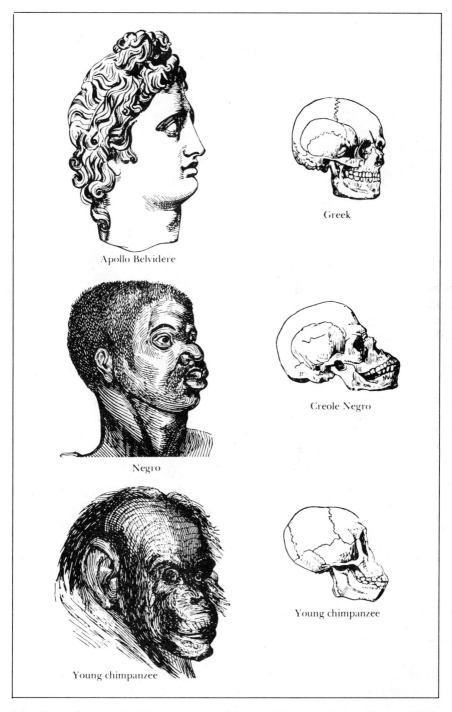

Apollo Belvidere

Greek

Negro

Creole Negro

Young chimpanzee

Young chimpanzee

2.1 The unilinear scale of human races and lower relatives according to Nott and Gliddon, 1868. The chimpanzee skull is falsely inflated, and the Negro jaw extended, to give the impression that blacks might even rank lower than the apes.

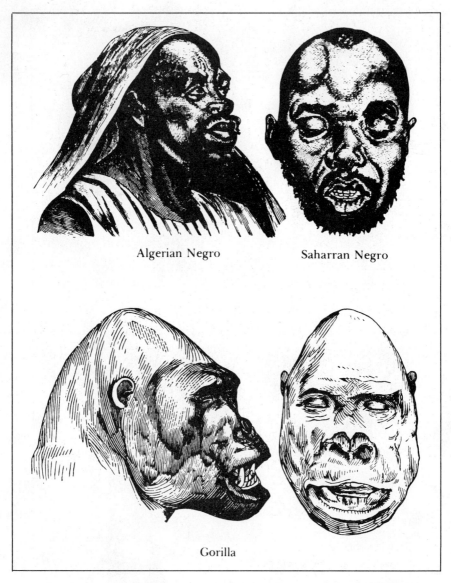

Algerian Negro   Saharran Negro

Gorilla

2.2   An unsubtle attempt to suggest strong affinity between blacks and gorillas. From Nott and Gliddon, *Types of Mankind*, 1854. Nott and Gliddon comment on this figure: "The palpable analogies and dissimilitudes between an inferior type of mankind and a superior type of monkey require no comment."

Iroquois, on the other hand, contribute only 3 skulls to the total sample (2 percent). If, by the accidents of collecting, Morton's sample had included 25 percent Iroquois and just a few Incas, his average would have risen substantially. Consequently, I corrected this bias as best I could by averaging the mean values for all tribes represented by 4 or more skulls. The Indian average now rises to 83.79 cubic inches.

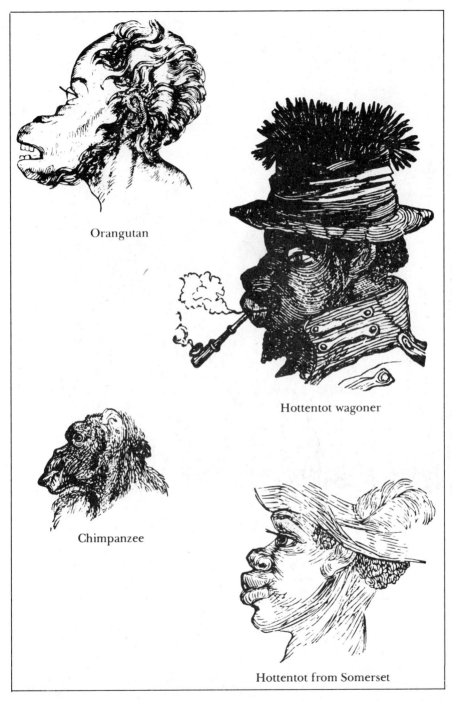

Orangutan

Hottentot wagoner

Chimpanzee

Hottentot from Somerset

2.3 Two more comparisons of blacks and apes from Nott and Gliddon, 1854. This book was not a fringe document, but the leading American text on human racial differences.

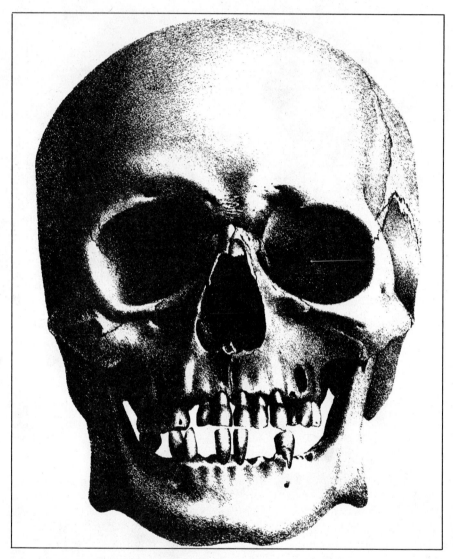

2.4 The skull of an Araucanian Indian. The lithographs of this and the next figure were done by John Collins, a great scientific artist unfortunately unrecognized today. They appeared in Morton's *Crania Americana* of 1839.

This revised value is still more than 3 cubic inches from the Cauca-   **15**
sian average. Yet, when we examine Morton's procedure for computing
the Caucasian mean, we uncover an astounding inconsistency. Since
statistical reasoning is largely a product of the last one hundred years, I
might have excused Morton's error for the Indian mean by arguing that
he did not recognize the biases produced by unequal sizes among subsamples. But now we discover that he understood this bias perfectly

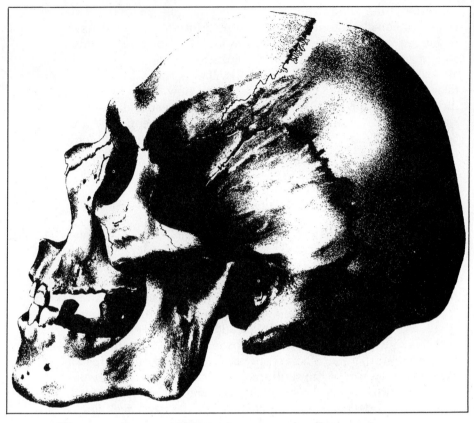

2.5   The skull of a Huron Indian. Lithograph by John Collins from Morton's *Crania Americana,*
1839.

well—for Morton calculated his high Caucasian mean by consciously
eliminating small-brained Hindus from his sample. He writes (p. 261):
"It is proper, however, to mention that but 3 Hindoos are admitted in
the whole number, because the skulls of these people are probably
smaller than those of any other existing nation. For example, 17 Hindoo
heads give a mean of but 75 cubic inches; and the three received into
the table are taken at that average." Thus, Morton included a large sub-
sample of small-brained people (Inca Peruvians) to pull down the Indian average, but excluded just as many Caucasian skulls to raise the
mean of his own group. Since he tells us what he did so baldly, we
must assume that Morton did not deem his procedure improper. But by
what rationale did he keep Incas and exclude Hindus, unless it were
the a priori assumption of a truly higher Caucasian mean? For one
might then throw out the Hindu sample as truly anomalous, but retain
the Inca sample (with the same mean as the Hindus, by the way) as the
lower end of normality for its disadvantaged larger group.

I restored the Hindu skulls to Morton's sample, using the same pro-   16
cedure of equal weighting for all groups. Morton's Caucasian sample,
by his reckoning, contains skulls from four subgroups, so Hindus
should contribute one-fourth of all skulls to the sample. If we restore
all seventeen of Morton's Hindu skulls, they form 26 percent of the total sample of sixty-six. The Caucasian mean now drops to 84.45 cubic
inches, for no difference worth mentioning between Indians and Caucasians. (Eskimos, despite Morton's low opinion of them, yield a mean of
86.8, hidden by amalgamation with other subgroups in the Mongol
grand mean of 83.) So much for Indian inferiority.

The Case of the Egyptian Catacombs: *Crania Aegyptiaca*

Morton's friend and fellow polygenist George Gliddon was United   17
States consul for the city of Cairo. He dispatched to Philadelphia more
than one hundred skulls from tombs of ancient Egypt, and Morton responded with his second major treatise, the *Crania Aegyptiaca* of 1844.
Morton had shown, or so he thought, that whites surpassed Indians in
mental endowment. Now he would crown his story by demonstrating
that the discrepancy between whites and blacks was even greater, and
that this difference had been stable for more than three thousand years.

Morton felt that he could identify both races and subgroups among   18
races from features of the skull (most anthropologists today would deny
that such assignments can be made unambiguously). He divided his
Caucasian skulls into Pelasgics (Hellenes, or ancient Greek forebears),
Jews, and Egyptians—in that order, again confirming Anglo-Saxon pref-
erences (Table 2.2). Non-Caucasian skulls he identified either as "negroid" (hybrids of Negro and Caucasian with more black than white) or
as pure Negro.

Morton's subjective division of Caucasian skulls is clearly unwar-   19
ranted, for he simply assigned the most bulbous crania to his favored
Pelasgic group and the most flattened to Egyptians; he mentions no
other criteria of subdivision. If we ignore his threefold separation and
amalgamate all sixty-five Caucasian skulls into a single sample, we obtain an average capacity of 82.15 cubic inches. (If we give Morton the
benefit of all doubt and rank his dubious subsamples equally—as we
did in computing Indian and Caucasian means for the *Crania Americana*—we obtain an average of 83.3 cubic inches.)

Either of these values still exceeds the negroid and Negro averages   20
substantially. Morton assumed that he had measured an innate difference in intelligence. He never considered any other proposal for the
disparity in average cranial capacity—though another simple and obvious explanation lay before him.

Sizes of brains are related to the sizes of bodies that carry them: big   21
people tend to have larger brains than small people. This fact does not

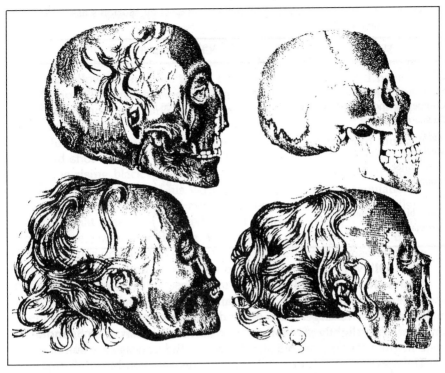

2.6 Skulls from the Egyptian catacombs. From Morton's *Crania Aegyptiaca* of 1844.

imply that big people are smarter—any more than elephants should be judged more intelligent than humans because their brains are larger. Appropriate corrections must be made for differences in body size. Men tend to be larger than women; consequently, their brains are bigger. When corrections for body size are applied, men and women have brains of approximately equal size. Morton not only failed to correct for differences in sex or body size; he did not even recognize the relationship, though his data proclaimed it loud and clear. (I can only conjecture that Morton never separated his skulls by sex or stature—though his tables record these data—because he wanted so much to read differences in brain size directly as differences in intelligence.)

Many of the Egyptian skulls came with mummified remains of their possessors (Fig.2.6), and Morton could record their sex unambiguously. If we use Morton's own designations and compute separate averages for males and females (as Morton never did), we obtain the following remarkable result. Mean capacity for twenty-four male Caucasian skulls is 86.5 cubic inches; twenty-two female skulls average 77.2 (the remaining nineteen skulls could not be identified by sex). Of the six negroid skulls, Morton identified two as female (at 71 and 77 cubic inches) and could not allocate the other four (at 77, 77, 87, and 88). If we make the

important differences in brain size among his groups. Negroids yielded a lower average than Caucasians among his Egyptian skulls because the negroid sample probably contained a higher percentage of smaller-statured females, not because blacks are innately stupider. The Incas that he included in the Indian sample and the Hindus that he excluded from the Caucasian sample both possessed small brains as a consequence of small body size. Morton used an all-female sample of three Hottentots to support the stupidity of blacks, and an all-male sample of Englishmen to assert the superiority of whites.

4. Miscalculations and convenient omissions: All miscalculations and **40** omissions that I have detected are in Morton's favor. He rounded the negroid Egyptian average down to 79, rather than up to 80. He cited averages of 90 for Germans and Anglo-Saxons, but the correct values are 88 and 89. He excluded a large Chinese skull and an Eskimo sub-sample from his final tabulation for mongoloids, thus depressing their average below the Caucasian value.

Yet through all this juggling, I detect no sign of fraud or conscious **41** manipulation. Morton made no attempt to cover his tracks and I must presume that he was aware he had left them. He explained all his procedures and published all his raw data. All I can discern is an a priori conviction about racial ranking so powerful that it directed his tabulations along preestablished lines. Yet Morton was widely hailed as the objectivist of his age, the man who would rescue American science from the mire of unsupported speculation.

_____ **Written Response**

Write a brief summary of how Morton mismeasured the volume of skulls, then explore your reactions to this attempt to "objectively" measure intelligence.

_____ **Rhetorical Analysis**

1. In "Rhetoric and Mathematics" (*The Rhetoric of Human Sciences* [Madison: University of Wisconsin Press, 1987]), Philip J. Davis and Reuben Hersh write:

> The competent professional knows what are the crucial points of his or her argument—the points where the audience should focus its skepticism. Those are the point where he or she will take care to supply sufficient detail. The rest of the proof will be abbreviated. This is not a matter of the author's laziness. On the contrary, to make a proof too detailed would be more damaging to its readability than to make it too brief. [p. 68]

Davis and Hersh assert that the discussion of mathematical proof, including statistics, should not be so detailed that it bores the reader, but the author needs to provide enough details on crucial points to persuade the audience that his or her proof is correct. Do you feel that Gould provides enough details for the reader to understand the faults of Morton's study?

2. Gould's review of Morton's data is complicated and could be confusing to many readers. Does Gould in any way emphasize his major findings?

3. Some readers might argue that Gould himself is biased. Do you feel that Gould is objective or biased? In what ways does he attempt to convince the audience that he is objective? In what ways might he be considered biased?

_____ **Interpretation**

1. Statistics are often used in persuasion. Although most people feel that statistics describe truth, they can present a very biased view of truth. In *How to Lie with Statistics* (New York: Norton, 1954), Darrell Huff used an example to explain "sampling errors." He discusses a study of the average salary of Yale graduates of the class of 1924 twenty-five years after they had graduated. The graduates averaged $25,111, which was a great deal of money around 1950. But Huff doubts that this average is accurate:

> The report on the Yale men [who have an average salary of $25,111] comes from a sample. We can be pretty sure of that because reason tells us that no one can get hold of all the living members of that class of '24. There are bound to be many whose addresses are unknown twenty-five years later.
>
> And, of those whose addresses are known, many will not reply to a questionnaire, particularly a rather personal one. With some kinds of mail questionnaire, a five or ten per cent response is quite high. This one should have done better than that, but nothing like one hundred per cent.
>
> So we find that the income figure is based on a sample composed of all class members whose addresses are known and who replied to the questionnaire. Is this a representative sample? That is, can this group be assumed to be equal in income to the unrepresented group, those who cannot be reached or who do not reply?
>
> Who are the little lost sheep down in the Yale rolls as "address unknown"? Are they the big-income earners—the Wall Street men, the corporation directors, the manufacturing and utility executives? No, the address of the rich will not be hard to come by. Many of the most prosperous members of the class can be found through *Who's Who in America* and other reference volumes even if they have neglected to keep in touch with the alumni office. It is a good guess that the lost names are those of the men who, twenty-five years or so after becoming Yale bachelors of arts, have not fulfilled any shining promise. They are clerks, mechanics, tramps, unemployed alcoholics, barely surviving writers and artists . . . people whom it would take half a dozen or more to add up to an income of $25,111. These men do not so often register at class reunions, if only because they cannot afford the trip.

Who are those who chucked the questionnaire into the nearest wastebasket? We cannot be so sure about these, but it is at least a fair guess that many of them are just not making enough money to brag about. [pp. 13–15]*

What kind of sampling errors in Huff's example make the $25,111 annual salary average of Yale graduates misleading? How could one sample the annual salary of Yale graduates more accurately?

What kind of sampling errors does Morton make in his calculations of skull sizes?

2. One of the errors that Gould found in Morton's study relates to how he averaged his data. In order to illustrate this point, you will be asked to average some data. These are not Morton's actual data (he had much larger samples), but the numbers do fit the basic parameters of his findings. The numbers indicate the measured cranial volume in cubic inches.

INDIANS	CAUCASIANS
1. Seminole-Muskogee	1. Pelasgic
88	84
89	85
86	86
87	83
2. Chippeway	84
87	82
88	84
89	82
86	83
3. Peruvians	82
73	2. Celtic
74	86
73	87
74	88
72	85
73	84
71	85
74	86
75	86
73	87
72	3. Hindu
73	74
	73
	75
	73

In order to better understand the sampling and statistical errors in Morton's work, perform the following exercise:

a. Find the average cranial volume for the Indian sample by adding all of the data together and dividing by the number in the sample; repeat this procedure for the Caucasians.

* Darrell Huff, How to Lie with Statistics. New York: W. W. Norton & Company, Inc., 1954.

b. Find the average cranial volume for each subgroup—that is, add all of the data for the Seminole-Muskogee Indians and then divide by the number in that subgroup; repeat this procedure for each subgroup.

c. Find the average for all of the Indian subgroups; add the average for Seminole-Muskogee, Chippeway, and Peruvians, then divide by three; repeat this procedure for Caucasian subgroups.

You have just averaged your data in two different ways. The first way determined the average for the entire group (Indians or Caucasians) directly. The second way determined the average of the subgroups, then averaged the averages of the subgroups. If you wanted (consciously or subconsciously) to "prove" that Caucasians had larger brains than Indians, how would you average your data?

Compare the averages for each subgroup and count the number of cases (or skulls measured) in each subgroup. What does this tell you about how biased sampling procedures can affect the outcome of the data?

How does this exercise relate to Gould's criticism of Morton's study?

3. Study the illustrations in the reading that accompanied a study by Nott and Gliddon (1868); Nott and Gliddon, like Morton, claimed that the white race was superior. What kind of bias can you detect in these illustrations?

4. Gould feels that Morton's fudging was unconscious. Why does he feel that Morton's errors were unconscious? Why does Gould find such unconscious fudging more interesting than outright cheating?

_____ **WRITING ASSIGNMENTS**

1. Writers often use bogus statistics and data from specious "scientific" studies to support their own biases. In the following fictitious letter to the editor, the author uses Morton's studies of skull sizes to support his own racial prejudice:

Dear Editor,

In recent years, our society has been moving toward greater and greater integration of the races. We have, for example, placed whites, blacks, hispanics, and Native Americans in the same schools. The purpose is to provide what some liberal politicians call an "equal opportunity."

But why should all races have an equal opportunity when they are not equal? A number of scientific studies have proven that races do not have the same levels of intelligence. For example, Samuel George Morton, an eminent nineteenth-century scientist, carefully measured the skulls of whites, blacks, Mexicans, and Native Americans. He found that whites had the largest skulls, Mexicans the next largest, Native Americans the next largest, and blacks the smallest. And, since skull size directly relates to intelligence, we can see that whites are intellectually superior.

If whites are more intelligent, why should they be forced to go to school with people of other races, who will only slow down their learning?

We need to look at the facts! We need to accept scientific proof! The races are not equal, nor have they ever been equal. We need to face reality and stop treating people as equal. Otherwise, our brightest students will never reach their potential and America will lose its position as the number one nation on earth.

Sincerely,

Albert J. Smith

Write a letter to the editor in which you use Gould's analysis of Morton's data to respond to Smith's comments. Try to present enough details to adequately prove your point but not so many that you bore your readers.

2. Use Bacon's four "idols" to explain the distortions in Morton's attempts to measure human intelligence.

3. Is it possible for scientists to remain objective while conducting experiments?

Science and Myth

In the eighteenth century, the Enlightenment placed great faith in the ability of science and human reason to bring an end to superstition and myth, which had persisted despite science's earlier efforts, from the time of the ancient Greeks onward, to eliminate them. Science and myth were viewed as being incompatible, with science being our future and myth being our primitive past. In the last few decades, however, more and more scientists have come to believe that myth is an essential part of human existence and that a life without myth is a life devoid of symbolic meaning. They have also come to believe that myth and science are not as distinct as they once thought. In "Some Biomythology," Lewis Thomas suggests that his field—biology—and myth are closely related.

_____ **Prereading**

One aspect of mythology that has fascinated scholars is the similarities of myths from different cultures, some of which have never had contact with each other. For example, many cultures from remote areas of the globe have myths about the theft of fire (for example, Prometheus stealing fire from the gods in Greek mythology). In "The Concept of the Collective Unconscious" (a lecture delivered in 1936), Carl Jung claims that the basic stories or themes of myths (archetypes) are stored in what he calls our collective unconscious. He said:

> My thesis, then, is as follows: In addition to our immediate consciousness, which is of a thoroughly personal nature and which we believe to be the only empirical psyche (even if we tack on the personal unconscious as an appendix), there exists a second psychical system of a collective universal, and impersonal nature which is identical in all individuals. This collective unconscious does not develop individually but is inherited. It consists of the pre-existent forms, the archetypes, which can only become conscious

secondarily and which give definite form to certain psychic contents. [*The Archetypes and the Collective Unconscious* (Princeton: Princeton University Press, 1959), p. 42]

The collective unconscious, Jung believes, contains something akin to instincts that lead us to develop certain basic characters and themes in our myths.

Claude Lévi-Strauss sought a similar explanation for common features among the myths of different cultures by looking for the principles (something akin to grammatical rules) that he believed lead to their creation. In *Structural Anthropology* (New York: Anchor, 1958, 1963), he wrote that "the unconscious activity of the mind consists in imposing forms upon content" and that "these forms are fundamentally the same for all minds—ancient and modern, primitive and civilized" (p. 21).

Both Jung and Lévi-Strauss speak of the "forms" of the unconscious that are imposed upon the "content" of different cultures to create myths that are similar in theme but different in details. What do you think that they mean by "form" and "content"?

Some Biomythology
Lewis Thomas

The mythical animals catalogued in the bestiaries of the world seem,   1
at a casual glance, nothing but exotic nonsense. The thought comes
that Western civilized, scientific, technologic society is a standing proof
of human progress, in having risen above such imaginings. They are
as obsolete as the old anecdotes in which they played their puzzling,
ambiguous roles, and we have no more need for the beasts than for
the stories. The Griffon, Phoenix, Centaur, Sphinx, Manticore, Ganesha, Ch'i-lin, and all the rest are like recurrent bad dreams, and we
are well rid of them. So we say.

The trouble is that they are in fact like dreams, and not necessarily   2
bad ones, and we may have a hard time doing without them. They may
be as essential for society as mythology itself, as loaded with symbols,
and as necessary for the architecture of our collective unconscious. If
Lévi-Strauss is right, myths are constructed by a universal logic that,
like language itself, is as characteristic for human beings as nest-
building is for birds. The stories seem to be different stories, but the

Source: From "Some Biomythology" from *The Lives of a Cell* by Lewis Thomas Copyright ©
1973 by Lewis Thomas. Reprinted by permission of Viking Penguin, a division of Penguin
USA Inc.

underlying structure is always the same, in any part of the world, at
any time. They are like engrams,[1] built into our genes. In this sense,
bestiaries are part of our inheritance.

There is something basically similar about most of these crazy ani-   3
mals. They are all unbiologic, but unbiologic in the same way. Bestiaries do not contain, as a rule, totally novel creatures of the imagination
made up of parts that we have never seen before. On the contrary, they
are made up of parts that are entirely familiar. What is novel, and star-
tling, is that they are mixtures of species.

It is perhaps this characteristic that makes the usual bestiary so out-   4
landish to the twentieth century mind. Our most powerful story, equivalent in its way to a universal myth, is evolution. Never mind that it is
true whereas myths are not; it is filled with symbolism, and this is the
way it has influenced the mind of society. In our latest enlightenment,
the fabulous beasts are worse than improbable—they are impossible,
because they violate evolution. They are not species, and they deny the
existence of species.

The Phoenix comes the closest to being a conventional animal, all   5
bird for all of its adult life. It is, in fact, the most exuberant, elaborate,
and ornamented of all plumed birds. It exists in the mythology of
Egypt, Greece, the Middle East, and Europe, and is the same as the
vermilion bird of ancient China. It lives for five hundred triumphant
years, and when it dies it constructs a sort of egg-shaped cocoon
around itself. Inside, it disintegrates and gives rise to a wormlike creature, which then develops into the new Phoenix, ready for the next five
hundred years. In other versions the dead bird bursts into flames, and
the new one arises from the ashes, but the worm story is very old, told
no doubt by an early biologist.

There are so many examples of hybrid beings in bestiaries that you   6
could say that an ardent belief in mixed forms of life is an ancient human idea, or that something else, deeply believed in, is symbolized by
these consortia. They are disturbing to look at, nightmarish, but most
of them, oddly enough, are intended as lucky benignities. The Ch'i-lin,
for instance, out of ancient China, has the body of a deer covered with
gleaming scales, a marvelous bushy tail, cloven hooves, and small
horns. Whoever saw a Ch'i-lin was in luck, and if you got to ride one,
you had it made.

The Ganesha is one of the oldest and most familiar Hindu deities,   7
possessing a fat human body, four human arms, and the head of a
cheerful-looking elephant. Prayers to Ganesha are regarded as the
quickest way around obstacles.

Not all mythical beasts are friendly, of course, but even the hostile   8
ones have certain amiable redeeming aspects. The Manticore has a li-

---

[1] Engram: the encoding of a memory trace on a neutral brain cell.

on's body, a man's face, and a tail with a venomous snake's head at the
end of it. It bounds around seeking prey with huge claws and three
rows of teeth, but it makes the sounds of a beautiful silver flute.

Some of the animal myths have the ring of contemporary biologic   9
theory, if you allow for differences in jargon. An ancient idea in India
postulates an initial Being, the first form of life on earth, analogous to
our version of the earliest prokaryotic arrangement of membrane-
limited nucleic acid, the initial cell, born of lightning and methane. The
Indian Being, undefined and indefinable, finding itself alone, fearing
death, yearning for company, began to swell in size, rearranged itself
inside, and then split into two identical halves. One of these changed
into a cow, the other a bull, and they mated, then changed again to a
mare and stallion, and so on, down to the ants, and thus the earth was
populated. There is a lot of oversimplification here, and too much
shorthand for modern purposes, but the essential myth is recognizable.

The serpent keeps recurring through the earliest cycles of mythology,   10
always as a central symbol for the life of the universe and the continuity of creation. There are two great identical snakes on a Levantine liba-
tion vase of around 2000 B.C., coiled around each other in a double
helix, representing the original generation of life. They are the replicated parts of the first source of living, and they are wonderfully ho-
mologous.

There is a Peruvian deity, painted on a clay pot dating from around   11
A.D. 300, believed to be responsible for guarding farms. His hair is
made of snakes, entwined in braids, with wings for his headdress.
Plants of various kinds are growing out of his sides and back, and a
vegetable of some sort seems to be growing from his mouth. The whole
effect is wild and disheveled but essentially friendly. He is, in fact, an
imaginary version of a genuine animal, *symbiopholus,* described in *Nature* several years back, a species of weevil in the mountains of northern New Guinea that lives symbiotically with dozens of plants, growing
in the niches and clefts in its carapace, rooted all the way down to its
flesh, plus a whole ecosystem of mites, rotifers, nematodes, and bacteria attached to the garden. The weevil could be taken for a good-luck
omen on its own evidence; it is not attacked by predators, it lives a
long, untroubled life, and nothing else will eat it, either because of
something distasteful in the system or simply because of the ambiguity.
The weevil is only about thirty millimeters long, easily overlooked, but
it has the makings of myth.

Perhaps we should be looking around for other candidates. I suggest   12
the need for a new bestiary, to take the place of the old ones. I can
think of several creatures that seem designed for this function, if you
will accept a microbestiary, and if you are looking for metaphors.

First of all, there is *Myxotricha paradoxa.* This is the protozoan, not yet   13
as famous as he should be, who seems to be telling us everything
about everything, all at once. His cilia are not cilia at all, but individual

spirochetes, and at the base of attachment of each spirochete is an oval organelle, embedded in the myxotricha membrane, which is a bacterium. It is not an animal after all—it is a company, an assemblage.

The story told by myxotricha is as deep as any myth, as profoundly   **14** allusive. This creature has lagged behind the rest of us, and is still going through the process of being assembled. Our cilia gave up any independent existence long ago, and our organelles are now truly ours, but the genomes controlling separate parts of our cells are still different genomes, lodged in separate compartments; doctrinally, we are still assemblages.

There is another protozoan, called blepharisma, telling a long story   **15** about the chanciness and fallibility of complex life. Blepharisma is called that because of a conspicuous fringe of ciliated membranes around the oral cavity, which evidently reminded someone of eyelashes (*blepharidos*). The whole mythlike tale has been related in a book by Giese. Blepharisma has come much further along than myxotricha, but not far enough to be free of slip-ups. There are three different sets of self-duplicating nuclei, with the DNA in each set serving different purposes: a large macronucleus, governing the events in regeneration after injury, a set of eight or more micronuclei containing the parts of the genome needed for reproduction, and great numbers of tiny nuclei from which the cilia arise.

One part of the organism produces a pinkish pigment, now called   **16** blepharismin, which is similar to hypericin and certain other photosensitizing plant pigments. Blepharismin causes no trouble unless the animal swims into sunlight, but then the pigment kills it outright. Under certain circumstances, the membrane surrounding blepharisma disintegrates and comes independently loose, like a cast-off shell, leaving the creature a transient albino. At times of famine, a single blepharisma will begin eating its neighbors; it then enlarges to an immense size and turns into a cannibalistic giant, straight out of any Norse fable. Evidently, this creature still has trouble getting along with the several parts of itself, and with the collective parts of other blepharismae.

There are innumerable plant-animal combinations, mostly in the sea,   **17** where the green plant cells provide carbohydrate and oxygen for the animal and receive a share of energy in return. It is the fairest of arrangements. When the paramecium bursaria runs out of food, all he needs to do is stay in the sun and his green endosymbionts will keep him supplied as though he were a grain.

Bacteria are the greatest of all at setting up joint enterprises, on   **18** which the lives of their hosts are totally dependent. The nitrogen-fixing rhizobia in root nodules, the mycetomes of insects, and the enzyme-producing colonies in the digestive tracts of many animals are variations of this meticulously symmetrical symbiosis.

The meaning of these stories may be basically the same as the mean-   **19** ing of a medieval bestiary. There is a tendency for living things to join

up, establish linkages, live inside each other, return to earlier arrangements, get along, whenever possible. This is the way of the world.

The new phenomenon of cell fusion, a laboratory trick on which   20
much of today's science of molecular genetics relies for its data, is the
simplest and most spectacular symbol of the tendency. In a way, it is
the most unbiologic of all phenomena, violating the most fundamental
myth of the last century, for it denies the importance of specificity, integrity, and separateness in living things. Any cell—man, animal, fish,
fowl, or insect—given the chance and under the right conditions,
brought into contact with any other cell, however foreign, will fuse
with it. Cytoplasm will flow easily from one to the other, the nuclei
will combine, and it will become, for a time anyway, a single cell with
two complete, alien genomes, ready to dance, ready to multiply. It is a
Chimera, a Griffon, a Sphinx, a Ganesha, a Peruvian god, a Ch'i-lin, an
omen of good fortune, a wish for the world.

_____ **Written Response**

How do you react to the idea that myth and science are at times difficult
to distinguish?

_____ **Rhetorical Analysis**

1. In this essay written for the general public (rather than for biologists
only), Thomas to some extent fuses two types of discourse or writing. In
the first part of the essay, Thomas writes about mythical creatures in a
language that is more typical of that found in myths. In the latter part,
Thomas writes about unusual organisms discovered by biologists in a
language that is more typical of that found in the field of biology. Compare Thomas's description of one of the mythical creatures to his description of one of the biological organisms. How is his writing different in
these two sections?

2. Why do you think that Thomas wanted to write about how myth
and science are intertwined? In other words, what was his purpose in
writing the essay?

_____ **Interpretation**

1. In *The Time Falling Bodies Take to Light* (New York: St. Martin's, 1981),
William Irwin Thompson wrote: "Science wrought to its uttermost becomes myth." Since Thompson believes that myth is "a relationship
between the known and the unknowable," he feels that science, at its
boundaries, is almost indistinguishable from myth. Some of the best examples of science operating at its boundaries may be provided by theories that attempt to explain the origin of the universe. An example of a

mythical explanation of the origin of the universe can be found in Hesiod's *Theogony* (Norman O. Brown, trans.) (Indianapolis: Bobbs-Merrill,
1953), written in the eighth century B.C.:

> First of all, the Void came into being, next broad-bosomed Earth, the
> solid and eternal home of all, and Eros, the most beautiful of the immortal
> gods, who in every man and every god softens the sinews and overpowers
> the prudent purpose of the mind. Out of the Void came Darkness and black
> Night, and out of Night came Light and Day, her children conceived after
> union in love with Darkness. Earth first produced starry Sky, equal in size
> with herself, to cover her on all sides. Next she produced the tall moun-
> tains, the pleasant haunts of the gods, and also gave birth to the barren
> waters, sea with its raging surges—all this without the passion of love.
> Thereafter she lay with Sky and gave birth to Ocean with its deep current,
> Coeus and Crius and Hyperion and Iapetus; Thea and Rhea and Themis
> and Mnemosyne; also golden-crowned Phoebe and lovely Tethys. After
> these came cunning Cronus, the youngest and boldest of her children; and
> he grew to hate the father who had begotten him.

Compare this mythical version of the origin of the universe to the following description of the current scientific explanation, the big-bang theory:

> The theory of cosmology, the big-bang model, has been accepted wisdom
> only since 1965. This theory holds that the universe began as an infinitely
> dense, infinitely hot point called a singularity. Then, 10 billion to 20 billion
> years ago, the singularity exploded. This was not an explosion *into* space,
> as popularly thought, but a smooth, slow explosion *of* space itself. Its ef-
> fects are still exploding today. Most dramatically, the universe is expand-
> ing, as one would expect if it exploded; galaxies, bundles of 100 stars, fly
> apart from each other, and new space is created between them. A second
> lingering effect is the cool radiation that bathes the cosmos. (The current
> reading is 3 degrees Kelvin or minus 270 degrees Celsius.) From these tem-
> peratures, physicists extrapolate and conclude that, once, the universe was
> a searing fireball. [*Time*, 13 June 1988, p. 60]

What seems scientific about this description? What seems mythic?

2. Although they claim to strive to use objective language, scientists
constantly use metaphors to describe the objects that they study. For example, Thomas wrote in an early passage of *The Lives of a Cell*:

> I have been trying to think of the earth as a kind of organism, but it is no
> go. I cannot think of it this way. It is too big, too complex, with too many
> working parts lacking visible connections. The other night, driving through
> a hilly, wooded part of southern New England, I wondered about this. If
> not like an organism, what is it like, what is it *most* like? Then, satisfactorily
> for that moment, it came to me: it is *most* like a cell. [p. 5]

Here, Thomas is overtly searching for a metaphor. At other times, the
scientist's metaphor may be less apparent. Can you think of any examples of metaphors used by scientists? Do you feel that the use of metaphors makes scientific writing less objective?

_____ **WRITING ASSIGNMENTS**

1. Write a story (in the style of science fiction) that describes the creation of a new form of life brought about by cell fusion or gene splicing.

You might find it useful to draw a picture of your new form of life before you write about it. For example, you could create a new form of life by drawing a creature that has some human features, some plant features (for example, ears that look like leaves), some machine features (for instance, legs that look like car tires), and some animal features (for example, fly eyes and butterfly wings). You can develop ideas for your drawing by looking at pictures of animals, insects, and plants in an encyclopedia.

2. Take one of the descriptions of a mythical beast in Thomas's essay and rewrite it in the scientific style of biology. Alternatively, take one of the descriptions of a biological organism in Thomas's essay and rewrite it in the style of myths. The purpose of this assignment is either to make the unreal mythical beast sound real by describing it scientifically, or to make the real organism sound unreal by describing it mythically.

3. Find a print advertisement (one that is accompanied by a significant amount of text) and analyze the language of the advertisement. Is the language more scientific or mythic?

Science and Gender

Evelyn Fox Keller (born 1936) is a feminist and a philosopher of science. In "A World of Difference," she writes about Barbara McClintock and her nontraditional approach to science. McClintock, who studied changes in maize as a means of better understanding genetics, developed what is called the transposition theory of genetics.

From the early 1900s until McClintock's theory was widely accepted in the 1960s, scientists believed that genes functioned in a highly predictable way; they thought that each chromosome functioned in isolation and sent its genetic information in one direction, from the chromosome to the cell. McClintock's transposition theory, in contrast, argues that chromosomes can interact and that the entire organism or even its environment can alter the organism's genetic organization.

Keller finds McClintock's career interesting because her revolutionary theory was ignored for over 30 years. Her ideas and publications were excluded (Keller says "marginalized") from the mainstream of scientific discourse. Was this because she was a woman in a male-dominated field? Was it because her approach to science broke too many of the widely accepted rules about how scientists should work? Or was it because her ideas were simply too new and unusual for the average scientist to accept?

Perhaps even in mice and men." (Marx 1981, quoted in Keller 1983, p. 193). But the significance of transposition remains in considerable dispute. McClintock saw transposable elements as a key to developmental regulation; molecular biologists today, although much more sympathetic to this possibility than they were twenty, or even ten, years ago, are still unsure. And in evolutionary terms, McClintock's view of transposition as a survival mechanism available to the organism in times of stress seems to most (although not to all) pure heresy.

My interest here, as it has been from the beginning, is less on who 7 was "right" than on the differences in perceptions that underlay such a discordance of views. The vicissitudes of McClintock's career give those differences not only special poignancy but special importance. In *A Feeling for the Organism: The Life and Work of Barbara McClintock* (Keller 1983), I argued that it is precisely the duality of success and marginality that lends her career its significance to the history and philosophy of science. Her success indisputably affirms her legitimacy as a scientist, while her marginality provides an opportunity to examine the role and fate of dissent in the growth of scientific knowledge. This duality illustrates the diversity of values, methodological styles, and goals that, to varying degrees, always exists in science; at the same time, it illustrates the pressures that, to equally varying degrees, operate to contain that diversity.

In the preface to that book (p. xii), I wrote: 8

> The story of Barbara McClintock allows us to explore the condition under which dissent in science arises, the function it serves, and the plurality of values and goals it reflects. It makes us ask: What role do interests, individual and collective, play in the evolution of scientific knowledge? Do all scientists seek the same kinds of explanations? Are the kinds of questions they ask the same? Do differences in methodology between different subdisciplines even permit the same kinds of answers? And when significant differences do arise in questions asked, explanations sought, methodologies employed, how do they affect communication between scientists? In short, why could McClintock's discovery of transposition not be absorbed by her contemporaries? We can say that her vision of biological organization was too remote from the kinds of explanations her colleagues were seeking, but we need to understand what that distance is composed of, and how such divergences develop.

I chose, in effect, not to read the story of McClintock's career as a 9 romance—neither as "a tale of dedication rewarded after years of neglect—of prejudice or indifference eventually routed by courage and truth" (p. xii), nor as a heroic story of the scientist, years "ahead of her time," stumbling on something approximating what we now know as "the truth." Instead, I read it as a story about the languages of science—about the process by which worlds of common scientific discourse become established, effectively bounded, and yet at the same

time remain sufficiently permeable to allow a given piece of work to
pass from incomprehensibility in one era to acceptance (if not full com-
prehensibility) in another.

In this essay, my focus is even more explicitly on difference itself. I   10
want to isolate McClintock's views of nature, of science, and of the relation between mind and nature, in order to exhibit not only their departure from more conventional views but also their own internal
coherence. If we can stand inside this world view, the questions she
asks, the explanations she seeks, and the methods she employs in her
pursuit of scientific knowledge will take on a degree of clarity and com-
prehensibility they lack from outside. And at the heart of this world
view lies the same respect for difference that motivates us to examine it
in the first place. I begin therefore with a discussion of the implications
of respect for difference (and complexity) in the general philosophy expressed in McClintock's testimony, and continue by discussing its implications for cognition and perception, for her interests as a geneticist,
and for the relation between her work and molecular biology. I conclude the essay with a brief analysis of the relevance of gender to any
philosophy of difference, and to McClintock's in particular.

Complexity and Difference

To McClintock, nature is characterized by an a priori complexity that   11
vastly exceeds the capacities of the human imagination. Her recurrent
remark, "Anything you can think of you will find," is a statement
about the capacities not of mind but of nature. It is meant not as a description of our own ingenuity as discoverers but as a comment on the
resourcefulness of natural order; in the sense not so much of adaptabil-
ity as of largesse and prodigality. Organisms have a life and an order of
their own that scientists can only begin to fathom. "Misrepresented, not
appreciated, . . . [they] are beyond our wildest expectations. . . . They
do everything we [can think of], they do it better, more efficiently, more
marvelously." In comparison with the ingenuity of nature, our scientific
intelligence seems pallid. It follows as a matter of course that "trying to
make everything fit into set dogma won't work. . . . There's no such
thing as a central dogma into which everything will fit."

In the context of McClintock's views of nature, attitudes about   12
research that would otherwise sound romantic fall into logical place.
The need to "listen to the material" follows from her sense of the order
of things. Precisely because the complexity of nature exceeds our own
imaginative possibilities, it becomes essential to "let the experiment tell
you what to do." Her major criticism of contemporary research is based
on what she sees as inadequate humility. She feels that "much of the
work done is done because one wants to impose an answer on it—they
have the answer ready, and they [know what] they want the material to

tell them, so anything it doesn't tell them they don't really recognize as there, or they think it's a mistake and throw it out. . . . If you'd only just let the material tell you."

Respect for complexity thus demands from observers of nature the   **13**
same special attention to the exceptional case that McClintock's own
example as a scientist demands from observers of science: "If the material tells you, 'It may be this,' allow that. Don't turn it aside and call it
an exception, an aberration, a containment. . . . That's what's happened
all the way along the line with so many good clues." Indeed, respect
for individual difference lies at the very heart of McClintock's scientific
passion. "The important thing is to develop the capacity to see one kernel [of maize] that is different, and make that understandable," she
says. "If [something] doesn't fit, there's a reason, and you find out
what it is." The prevailing focus on classes and numbers, McClintock
believes, encourages researchers to overlook difference, to "call it an
exception, an aberration, a contaminant." The consequences of this
seem to her very costly. "Right and left," she says, they miss "what is
going on."

She is, in fact, here describing the history of her own research. Her   **14**
work on transposition in fact began with the observation of an aberrant
pattern of pigmentation on a few kernels of a single corn plant. And
her commitment to the significance of this singular pattern sustained
her through six years of solitary and arduous investigation—all aimed
at making the difference she saw understandable.

Making difference understandable does not mean making it disap-   **15**
pear. In McClintock's world view, an understanding of nature can come
to rest with difference. "Exceptions" are not there to "prove the rule";
they have meaning in and of themselves. In this respect, difference constitutes a principle for ordering the world radically unlike the principle
of division of dichotomization (subject–object, mind–matter, feeling–
reason, disorder–law). Whereas these oppositions are directed toward a
cosmic unity typically excluding or devouring one of the pair, toward a
unified, all-encompassing law, respect for differences remains content
with multiplicity as an end in itself.

And just as the terminus of knowledge implied by difference can be   **16**
distinguished from that implied by division, so the starting point of
knowledge can also be distinguished. Above all, difference, in this
world view, does not posit division as an epistemological prerequisite—
it does not imply the necessity of hard and fast divisions in nature, or
in mind, or in the relation between mind and nature. Division severs
connection and imposes distance; the recognition of difference provides
a starting point for relatedness. It serves both as a clue to new modes
of connectedness in nature, and as an invitation to engagement with
nature. For McClintock, certainly, respect for difference serves both
these functions. Seeing something that does not appear to fit is, to her,
a challenge to find the larger multidimensional pattern into which it

does fit. Anomalous kernels of corn were evidence not of disorder or lawlessness, but of a larger system of order, one that cannot be reduced to a single law.

Difference thus invites a form of engagement and understanding that   **17**
allows for the preservation of the individual. The integrity of each kernel (or chromosome or plant) survives all our own pattern-making attempts; the order of nature transcends our capacities for ordering. And this transcendence is manifested in the enduring uniqueness of each organism: "No two plants are exactly alike. They're all different, and as a consequence, you have to know that difference," she explains. "I start with the seedling, and I don't want to leave it. I don't feel I really know the story if I don't watch the plant all the way along. So I know every plant in the field. I know them intimately, and I find it a great pleasure to know them." From days, weeks, and years of patient observation comes what looks like privileged insight: "When I see things, I can interpret them right away." As one colleague described it, the result is an apparent ability to write the "autobiography" of every plant she works with.

McClintock is not here speaking of relations to other humans, but the   **18**
parallels are nonetheless compelling. In the relationship she describes with plants, as in human relations, respect for difference constitutes a claim not only on our interest but on our capacity for empathy—in short on the highest form of love: love that allows for intimacy without the annihilation of difference. I use the word *love* neither loosely nor sentimentally, but out of fidelity to the language McClintock herself uses to describe a form of attention, indeed a form of thought. Her vocabulary is consistently a vocabulary of affection, of kinship, of empathy. Even with puzzles, she explains, "The thing was dear to you for a period of time, you really had an affection for it. Then after a while, it disappears and it doesn't bother you. But for a short time you feel strongly attached to that little toy." The crucial point for us is that McClintock can risk the suspension of boundaries between subject and object without jeopardy to science precisely because, to her, science is not premised on that division. Indeed, the intimacy she experiences with the objects she studies—intimacy born of a lifetime of cultivated attentiveness—is a wellspring of her powers as a scientist.

The most vivid illustration of this process comes from her own ac-   **19**
count of a breakthrough in one particularly recalcitrant piece of cytological analysis. She describes the state of mind accompanying the crucial shift in orientation that enabled her to identify chromosomes she had earlier not been able to distinguish: "I found that the more I worked with them, the bigger and bigger [the chromosomes] got, and when I was really working with them I wasn't outside, I was down there. I was part of the system. I was right down there with them, and everything got big. I even was able to see the internal parts of the chromosomes—actually everything was there. It surprised me

because I actually felt as if I was right down there and these were my friends. . . . As you look at these things, they become part of you. And you forget yourself."

Cognition and Perception

In this world of difference, division is relinquished without genera-   20
ting chaos. Self and other, mind and nature survive not in mutual
alienation, or in symbiotic fusion, but in structural integrity. The "feeling for the organism" that McClintock upholds as the sine qua non of
good research need not be read as "participation mystique"; it is a
mode of access—honored by time and human experience if not by prevailing conventions in science—to the reliable knowledge of the world
around us that all scientists seek. It is a form of attention strongly remi-
niscent of the concept of "focal attention" developed by Ernest Schachtel to designate "man's [sic] capacity to *center* his attention on an object
fully, so that he can perceive or understand it from *many sides*, as fully
as possible" (p. 251). In Schachtel's language, "focal attention" is the
principal tool that, in conjunction with our natural interest in objects
per se, enables us to progress from mere wishing and wanting to thinking and knowing—that equips us for the fullest possible knowledge of
reality in its own terms. Such "object-centered" perception . . . presupposes "a temporary eclipse of all the perceiver's egocentric thoughts
and strivings, of all preoccupation with self and self-esteem, and a full
turning towards the object, . . . [which, in turn] leads not to a *loss* of
self, but to a heightened feeling of aliveness" (p. 181). Object-centered
perception, Schachtel goes on to argue, is in the service of a love
"which wants to affirm others in their total and unique being . . .
[which affirms objects as] "part of the same world of which man is a
part" (p. 226). It requires

> an experiential realization of the kinship between oneself and the
> other . . . a realization [that] is made difficult by fear and by arro-
> gance—by fear because then the need to protect oneself by flight,
> appeasement, or attack gets in the way; by arrogance because then
> the other is no longer experienced as akin, but as inferior to oneself.
> (p. 227)

The difference between Schachtel and McClintock is that what Schachtel
grants to the poet's perceptual style in contrast to that of the scientist,
McClintock claims equally for science. She enlists a "feeling for the organism"—not only for living organisms but for any object that fully
claims our attention—in pursuit of the goal shared by all scientists: reliable (that is, shareable and reproducible) knowledge of natural order.

   This difference is a direct reflection of the limitations of Schachtel's   21
picture of science. It is drawn not from observation of scientists like

McClintock but only from the more stereotypic scientist, who "looks at the object with one or more hypotheses . . . in mind and thus 'uses' the object to corroborate or disprove a hypothesis, but does not encounter the object as such, in its own fullness." For Schachtel,

> modern natural science has as its main goal prediction, i.e. the power to manipulate objects in such a way that certain predicted events will happen. . . . Hence, the scientist usually will tend to perceive the object merely from the perspective of [this] power. . . . That is to say that his view of the object will be determined by the ends which he pursues in his experimentation. . . . He may achieve a great deal in this way and add important data to our knowledge, but to the extent to which he remains within the framework of this perspective he will not perceive the object in its own right. (1959, p. 171)

To McClintock, science has a different goal: not prediction per se, but understanding; not the power to manipulate, but empowerment—the kind of power that results from an understanding of the world around us, that simultaneously reflects and affirms our connection to that world.

What Counts as Knowledge

At the root of this difference between McClintock and the stereotypic   22
scientist lies that unexamined starting point of science: the naming of nature. Underlying every discussion of science, as well as every scientific discussion, there exists a larger assumption about the nature of the universe in which that discussion takes place. The power of this unseen ground is to be found not in its influence on any particular argument in science but in its framing of the very terms of argument—in its definition of the tacit aims and goals of science. As I noted in the introduction to this section, scientists may spend fruitful careers, building theories of nature that are astonishingly successful in their predictive power, without ever feeling the need to reflect on these fundamental philosophical issues. Yet if we want to ask questions about that success, about the value of alternative scientific descriptions of nature, even about the possibility of alternative criteria of success, we can do so only by examining those most basic assumptions that are normally not addressed.

We have to remind ourselves that, although all scientists share a   23
common ambition for knowledge, it does not follow that what counts as knowledge is commonly agreed upon. The history of science reveals a wide diversity of questions asked, explanations sought, and methodologies employed in this common quest for knowledge of the natural world; this diversity is in turn reflected in the kinds of knowledge acquired, and indeed in what counts as knowledge. To a large degree,

both the kinds of questions one asks and the explanations that one finds satisfying depend on one's a priori relation to the objects of study. In particular, I am suggesting that questions asked about objects with which one feels kinship are likely to differ from questions asked about objects one sees as unalterably alien. Similarly, explanations that satisfy us about a natural world that is seen as "blind, simple and dumb," ontologically inferior, may seem less self-evidently satisfying for a natural world seen as complex and, itself, resourceful. I suggest that individual and communal conceptions of nature need to be examined for their role in the history of science, not as causal determinants but as frameworks upon which all scientific programs are developed. More specifically, I am claiming that the difference between McClintock's conception of nature and that prevailing in the community around her is an essential key to our understanding of the history of her life and work.

It provides, for example, the context for examining the differences   24
between McClintock's interests *as a geneticist* and what has historically been the defining focus of both classical and molecular genetics—differences crucial to the particular route her research took. To most geneticists, the problem of inheritance is solved by knowing the mechanism and structure of genes. To McClintock, however, as to many other biologists, mechanism and structure have never been adequate answers to the question "How do genes work?" Her focus was elsewhere: on function and organization. To her, an adequate understanding would, by definition, have to include an account of how they function in relation to the rest of the cell, and of course, to the organism as a whole.

In her language, the cell itself is an organism. Indeed, "Every compo-   25
nent of the organism is as much an organism as every other part." When she says, therefore, that "one cannot consider the [gene] as such as being all important—more important is the overall organism," she means the genome as a whole, the cell, the ensemble of cells, the organism itself. Genes are neither "beads on a string" nor functionally disjoint pieces of DNA. They are organized functional units, whose very function is defined by their position in the organization as a whole. As she says, genes function "only with respect to the environment in which [they are] found."

Interests in function and in organization are historically and con-   26
ceptually related to each other. By tradition, both are primarily preoccupations of developmental biology, and McClintock's own interest in development followed from and supported these interests. By the same tradition, genetics and developmental biology have been two separate subjects. But for a geneticist for whom the answer to the question of how genes work must include function and organization, the problem of heredity becomes inseparable from the problem of development. The division that most geneticists felt they had to live with (happily or not)

McClintock could not accept. To her, development, as the coordination of function, was an integral part of genetics.

McClintock's views today are clearly fed by her work on transposi-   27
tion. But her work on transposition was itself fed by these interests.
Her own account (see Keller 1983, pp. 115–17) of how she came to this
work and of how she followed the clues she saw vividly illustrates the
ways in which her interests in function and organization—and in development—focused her attention on the patterns she saw and framed the
questions she asked about the significance of these patterns. I suggest
that they also defined the terms that a satisfying explanation had to
meet.

Such an explanation had to account not so much for how transposi-   28
tion occurred, as for why it occurred. The patterns she saw indicated a
programmatic disruption in normal developmental function. When she
succeeded in linking this disruption to the location (and change in location) of particular genetic elements, that very link was what captured
her interest. (She knew she was "on to something important.") The fact
that transposition occurred—the fact that genetic sequences are not
fixed—was of course interesting too, but only secondarily so. To her,
the paramount interest lay in the meaning of its occurrence, in the clue
that transposition provided for the relation between genetics and development. Necessarily, a satisfying account of this relation would have to
take due note of the complexity of the regulation process.

Transpositon and the Central Dogma

Just two years after McClintock's first public presentation of her work   29
on transposition came the culminating event in the long search for the
mechanism of inheritance. Watson and Crick's discovery of the structure of DNA enabled them to provide a compelling account of the essential genetic functions of replication and instruction. According to
their account, the vital information of the cell is encoded in the DNA.
From there it is copied onto the RNA, which, in turn, is used as a blue-
print for the production of the proteins responsible for genetic traits. In
the picture that emerged—DNA to RNA to protein (which Crick himself dubbed the "central dogma")—the DNA is posited as the central
actor in the cell, the executive governor of cellular organization, itself
remaining impervious to influence from the subordinate agents to
which it dictates. Several years later, Watson and Crick's original model
was emended by Jacques Monod and François Jacob to allow for environmental control of the rates of protein synthesis. But even with this
modification, the es-genetics were dramatic. By the end of the 1960s, it
was possible to say (as Jacques Monod did say), "The Secret of Life?
But this is in large part known—in principle, if not in details" (quoted

in Judson 1979, p. 216). A set of values and interests wholly different from McClintock's seemed to have been vindicated. The intricacies, and difficulties, of corn genetics held little fascination in comparison with the quick returns from research on the vastly simpler and seemingly more straightforward bacterium and bacteriophage. As a result, communication between McClintock and her colleagues grew steadily more difficult; fewer and fewer biologists had the expertise required even to begin to understand her results.

McClintock of course shared in the general excitement of this period,   30
but she did not share in the general enthusiasm for the central dogma. The same model that seemed so immediately and overwhelmingly satisfying to so many of her colleagues did not satisfy her. Although duly impressed by its explanatory power, she remained at the same time acutely aware of what it did not explain. It neither addressed the questions that were of primary interest to her—bearing on the relation between genetics and development—nor began to take into account the complexity of genetic organization that she had always assumed, and that was now revealed to her by her work on transposition.

McClintock locates the critical flaw of the central dogma in its pre-   31
sumption: it claimed to explain too much. Baldly put, what was true of *E. coli* (the bacterium most commonly studied) was *not* true of the elephant, as Monod (and others) would have had it (Judson 1979, p. 613). Precisely because higher organisms are multicellular, she argued, they necessarily require a different kind of economy. The central dogma was without question inordinately successful as well as scientifically productive. Yet the fact that it ultimately proved inadequate even to the dynamics of *E. coli* suggests that its trouble lay deeper than just a too hasty generalization from the simple to the complex; its presumptuousness, I suggest, was built into its form of explanation.

The central dogma is a good example of what I have earlier called   32
(following Nanney 1957) master-molecule theories (Keller 1982). In locating the seat of genetic control in a single molecule, it posits a structure of genetic organization that is essentially hierarchical, often illustrated in textbooks by organizational charts like those of corporate structures. In this model, genetic stability is ensured by the unidirectionality of information flow, much as political and social stability is assumed in many quarters to require the unidirectional exercise of authority.

To McClintock, transposition provided evidence that genetic organiza-   33
tion is necessarily more complex, and in fact more globally interdependent, than such a model assumes. It showed that the DNA itself is subject to rearrangement and, by implication, to reprogramming. Although she did not make the suggestion explicit, the hidden heresy of her argument lay in the inference that such reorganization could be induced by signals external to the DNA—from the cell, the organism, even from the environment.

For more than fifty years, modern biologists had labored heroically to   **34**
purge biological thought of the last vestiges of teleology, particularly as
they surfaced in Lamarckian notions of adaptive evolution. But even
though McClintock is not a Lamarckian, she sees in transposition a
mechanism enabling genetic structures to respond to the needs of the
organism. Since needs are relative to the environmental context and
hence subject to change, transposition, by implication, indirectly allows
for the possibility of environmentally induced and genetically transmitted change. To her, such a possibility is not heresy—it is not even
surprising. On the contrary, it is in direct accord with her belief in the
resourcefulness of natural order. Because she has no investment in
the passivity of nature, the possibility of internally generated order
does not, to her, threaten the foundations of science. The capacity of
organisms to reprogram their own DNA implies neither vitalism, magic,
nor a countermanding will. It merely confirms the existence of forms
of order more complex than we have, at least thus far, been able to account for.

The renewed interest in McClintock's work today is a direct conse-   **35**
quence of developments (beginning in the early 1970s) in the very research programs that had seemed so philosophically opposed to her
position; genetic mobility was rediscovered within molecular biology
itself. That this was so was crucial, perhaps even necessary, to establishing the legitimacy of McClintock's early work, precisely because the
weight of scientific authority has now come to reside in molecular biology. As a by-product, this legitimization also lends McClintock's views
of science and attitudes toward research somewhat more credibility
among professional biologists. To observers of science, this same historical sequence serves as a sharp reminder that the languages of science,
however self-contained they seem, are not closed. McClintock's

> eventual vindication demonstrates the capacity of science to over-
> come its own characteristic kinds of myopia, reminding us that
> its limitations do not reinforce themselves indefinitely. Their own
> methodology allows, even obliges, scientists to continually reen-
> counter phenomena even their best theories cannot accommodate.
> Or—to look at it from the other side—however severely communica-
> tion between science and nature may be impeded by the preconcep-
> tions of a particular time, some channels always remain open; and,
> through them, nature finds ways of reasserting itself. (Keller 1983,
> p. 197)

In this sense, the McClintock story is a happy one.

It is important, however, not to overestimate the degree of   **36**
rapprochement that has taken place. McClintock has been abundantly
vindicated; transposition is acknowledged, higher organisms and development have once again captured the interest of biologists, and almost
everyone agrees that genetic organization is manifestly more complex
than had previously been thought. But not everyone shares her

conviction that we are in the midst of a revolution that "will reorganize the way we look at things, the way we do research." Many researchers remain confident that the phenomenon of transposition can somehow be incorporated, even if they do not yet see how, into an improved version of the central dogma. Their attachment to this faith is telling. Behind the continuing skepticism about McClintock's interpretation of the role of transposition in development and evolution, there remains a major gap between her underlying interests and commitments and those of most of her colleagues.

The Issue of Gender

How much of this enduring difference reflects the fact that McClintock   37
is a woman in a field still dominated by men? To what extent are her views indicative of a vision of "what will happen to science," as Erik Erikson asked in 1964 (1965, p. 243), "if and when women are truly represented in it—not by a few glorious exceptions, but in the rank and file of the scientific elite?"

On the face of it, it would be tempting indeed to call McClintock's   38
vision of science "a feminist science." Its emphasis on intuition, on feeling, on connection and relatedness, all seem to confirm our most familiar stereotypes of women. And to the extent that they do, we might expect that the sheer presence of more women in science would shift the balance of community sentiment and lead to the endorsement of that vision. However, there are both general and particular reasons that argue strongly against this simple view.

The general argument is essentially the same as that which I made   39
against the notion of "a different science," in the introduction to part 3. To the extent that science is defined by its past and present practitioners, anyone who aspires to membership in that community must conform to its existing code. As a consequence, the inclusion of new members, even from a radically different culture, cannot induce immediate or direct change. To be a successful scientist, one must first be adequately socialized. For this reason, it is unreasonable to expect a sharp differentiation between women scientists and their male colleagues, and indeed, most women scientists would be appalled by such a suggestion.

McClintock is in this sense no exception. She would disclaim any   40
analysis of her work as a woman's work, as well as any suggestion that her views represent a woman's perspective. To her, science is not a matter of gender, either male or female; it is, on the contrary, a place where (ideally at least) "the matter of gender drops away."
Furthermore, her very commitment to science is of a piece with her lifelong wish to transcend gender altogether. Indeed, her adamant rejection of female stereotypes seems to have been a prerequisite for her becom-

ing a scientist at all. (See Keller 1983, chaps. 2 and 3.) In her own image of herself, she is a maverick in all respects—as a woman, as a
scientist, even as a woman scientist.

Finally, I want to reemphasize that it would be not only misleading   **41**
but actually contradictory to suggest that McClintock's views of science
were shared by none of her colleagues. Had that been so, she could
not have had even marginal status as a scientist. It is essential to understand that, in practice, the scientific tradition is far more pluralistic than
any particular description of it suggests, and certainly more pluralistic
than its dominant ideology. For McClintock to be recognized as a scientist, the positions that she represents, however unrepresentative, had
to be, and were, identifiable as belonging somewhere within that tradition.

But although McClintock is not a total outsider to science, she is   **42**
equally clearly not an insider. And however atypical she is as a woman,
what she is *not* is a man. Between these two facts lies a crucial connection—a connection signaled by the recognition that, as McClintock herself admits, the matter of gender never does drop away.

I suggest that the radical core of McClintock's stance can be located   **43**
right here: Because she is not a man, in a world of men, her commitment to a gender-free science has been binding; because concepts of
gender have so deeply influenced the basic categories of science, that
commitment has been transformative. In short, the relevance of Mc-
Clintock's gender in this story is to be found not in its role in her
personal socialization but precisely in the role of gender in the construction of science.

Of course, not all scientists have embraced the conception of science **44**
as one of "putting nature on the rack and torturing the answers out of
her." Nor have all men embraced a conception of masculinity that demands cool detachment and domination. Nor even have all scientists
been men. But most have. And however variable the attitudes of individual male scientists toward science and toward masculinity, the metaphor of a marriage between mind and nature necessarily does not look
the same to them as it does to women. And this is the point.

In a science constructed around the naming of object (nature) as fe-   **45**
male and the parallel naming of subject (mind) as male, any scientist
who happens to be a woman is confronted with an a priori contra-
diction in terms. This poses a critical problem of identity: any scientist who is not a man walks a path bounded on one side by inauthenticity and on the other by subversion. Just as surely as inauthenticity is
the cost a woman suffers by joining men in misogynist jokes, so it is,
equally, the cost suffered by a woman who identifies with an image of
the scientist modeled on the patriarchal husband. Only if she under-
goes a radical disidentification from self can she share masculine pleasure in mastering a nature cast in the image of woman as passive,
inert, and blind. Her alternative is to attempt a radical redefinition of

terms. Nature must be renamed as not female, or, at least, as not an alienated object. By the same token, the mind, if the female scientist is to have one, must be renamed as not necessarily male, and accordingly recast with a more inclusive subjectivity. This is not to say that the male scientist cannot claim similar redefinition (certainly many have done so) but, by contrast to the woman scientist, his identity does not require it.

For McClintock, given her particular commitments to personal in-   **46** tegrity, to be a scientist, and not a man, with a nonetheless intact identity, meant that she had to insist on a different meaning of mind, of nature, and of the relation between them. Her need to redefine for herself the relation between subject and object, even the very terms themselves, came not from a feminist consciousness, or even from a female consciousness. It came from her insistence on her right to be a scientist—from her determination to claim science as a human rather than a male endeavor. For such a claim, difference makes sense of the world in ways that division cannot. It allows for the kinship that she feels with other scientists, without at the same time obligating her to share all their assumptions.

Looked at in this way, McClintock's stance is, finally, a far more   **47** radical one than that implied in Erikson's question. It implies that what could happen to science "when women are truly represented in it" is not simply, or even, "the addition, to the male kind of creative vision, of women's vision" (p. 243), but, I suggest, a thoroughgoing transformation of the very possibilities of creative vision, for everyone. It implies that the kind of change we might hope for is not a direct or readily apparent one but rather an indirect and subterranean one. A first step toward such a transformation would be the undermining of the commitment of scientists to the masculinity of their profession that would be an inevitable concomitant of the participation of large numbers of women.

However, we need to remember that, as long as success in science   **48** does not require self-reflection, the undermining of masculinist or other ideological commitments is not a sufficient guarantee of change. But nature itself is an ally that can be relied upon to provide the impetus for real change: nature's responses recurrently invite reexamination of the terms in which our understanding of science is constructed. Paying attention to those responses—"listening to the material"—may help us to reconstruct our understanding of science in terms born out of the diverse spectrum of human experience rather than out of the narrow spectrum that our culture has labeled masculine.

_____ **Written Response**

McClintock's approach to science is certainly different from the way that we usually expect scientists (most of whom are still males working in a male-dominated field) to think and work. How might McClintock's unusual approach to science be a woman's version of the scientific method?

_____ **Rhetorical Analysis**

1. M. M. Bakhtin believes that writing, or any form of discourse, embodies more than one "voice." When we read a text, we do not hear only the author's voice. We also hear the voices of other writers and speakers. We hear the voices of the writers that the author quotes or, more subtly, the voices of the writers that the author has read and echoes in his or her own writing. Complex meaning develops, Bakhtin believes, from the interaction of these different voices within the boundaries of a text.

As we read "A World of Difference," we obviously hear Keller's voice. What other voices can you detect in this text?

2. Although Keller writes about a complicated issue, her prose is fairly accessible, especially when compared with that of other philosophers of science. In part, she is able to write clearly because she uses the story of McClintock's career to illustrate and focus her complex ideas. How does McClintock's career serve as an extended example of what Keller wants to say? Also, how does this extended example help to make Keller's message easier to follow?

_____ **Interpretation**

1. What would you consider to be our culture's stereotypical views of males and females? Could you say that McClintock's approach to science is typical of how we perceive females? Do you know any males who speak of their work as McClintock speaks of hers?

2. In _Women's Ways of Knowing: The Development of Self, Voice, and Mind_ (New York: Basic, 1986), Mary Field Belenky and her coauthors distinguish between "separate knowing" and "connected knowing." "Separate knowing" can be illustrated by the following comment made by a college sophomore:

> I never take anything someone says for granted. I just tend to see the contrary. I like playing devil's advocate, arguing the opposite of what somebody's saying, thinking of exceptions to what the person has said, or thinking of a different train of logic. [p. 100]

What Belenky and her coauthors mean by a "connected knowing" can be illustrated by this comment by another college sophomore:

> When I have an idea about something, and it differs from the way another person is thinking about it, I'll usually try to look at it from that person's point of view, see how they could say that, why they think that they're right, why it makes sense. [p. 100]

Based on these quotations, how would you distinguish between "separate knowing" and "connected knowing"?

Which approach to developing knowledge ("separate knowing" or "connected knowing") would you consider more typical of a female approach? Which approach to developing knowledge is similar to McClintock's approach to science?

3. In "An Imagined World" (New York: Harper & Row, 1981), June Goodfield presents the portrait of another female scientist, Anna Brito. She quotes the following bit of conversation in which Brito constructs an analogy between two people falling in love and scientific discovery:

> Why of all the people in the world should these two come to love each other? The analogy is the same. Here is a cell. It has been going round all the time, and nobody has taken any notice of it. Suddenly you fall in love with it. Why? You, the scientist, don't know you're falling in love, but suddenly you become attracted to that cell, or that problem. Then you are going to have to go through an active process in relationship to it, and this leads to discovery. First, there is the building up of the attraction, and the object of your attention eludes you. Then you must try to do things to gain its attention with your concepts. The boy keeps giving the girl flowers. I keep inventing more refined concepts. And you must understand—that is why it doesn't really matter whether they are my concepts or Edward's or Nozaki's [two of her colleagues] or anyone's—it's the *concepts* that matter. Even if they are obsolutely wrong, *it doesn't matter a bit*. The individual enters into it to a very limited extent. So we try to get better and better concepts, trying to get to know the cell. And finally, there is a moment when the girl recognizes the boy, and no longer eludes him, accepts by going up the hill and really getting on with it and expressing it fully! That is the moment of discovery. [pp. 229–230]

How is Brito's approach to science similar to McClintock's? How is it different?

4. Carol Gilligan's *In a Different Voice* (Cambridge: Harvard University Press, 1982) is about her research in gender differences. As part of her study, Gilligan presented young boys and girls with a moral dilemma. She asked them to imagine a situation involving Heinz, whose wife is dying. Heinz's wife can be saved if he can obtain a certain drug, but he does not have enough money to buy the drug and the druggist will not lower the price. She then asks the boys and girls, should Heinz steal the drug? Gilligan uses the responses of two children in her study, Jake and Amy, to illustrate the differences between male and female views of morality. She describes the difference between Jake (who felt that Heinz should steal the drug and then plead his case in a court of law) and Amy (who felt that Heinz's wife should go and talk to the druggist) thus:

> In resolving Heinz's dilemma, Jake relies on theft to avoid confrontation and turns to the law to mediate the dispute. Transposing a hierarchy of power into a hierarchy of values, he defuses a potentially explosive conflict between people by casting it as an impersonal conflict of claims. In this

way, he abstracts the moral problem from the interpersonal situation, finding in the logic of fairness an objective way to decide who will win the dispute. But this hierarchical ordering, with its imagery of winning or losing and the potential for violence which it contains, gives way to Amy's construction of the dilemma to a network of connection, a web of relationships that is sustained by a process of communication. With this shift, the moral problem changes from one of unfair domination, the imposition of property over life, to one of unnecessary exclusion, the failure of the druggist to respond to the wife. [p. 32]

How is Jake's response similar to what Keller sees as the male approach to science? How is Amy's approach similar to McClintock's view of science?

5. Under the heading "Cognition and Perception," Keller compares McClintock's view of science to Ernest Schachtel's. How does Keller use the terms *subject* and *object* to distinguish between these two views?

_____ **WRITING ASSIGNMENTS**

1. How is McClintock's approach to science different from Bacon's?

2. Why do you think that McClintock's theory of transposition was ignored by most scientists for over 30 years.

3. Argue that there should be many scientific methods (Bacon's, McClintock's, and many others as well) rather than one established method.

Synthesis

1. Scientists have traditionally striven to develop a scientific method, which they hoped would allow them to study the universe objectively, and a scientific language, which they hoped would allow them to convey their objective findings to a reader without distortion. You have already read about how difficult it is to develop a purely objective methodology; the development of a truly objective language is no less difficult. In *The Rhetoric of Economics* (Madison: University of Wisconsin Press, 1985), Donald N. McCloskey describes how the writing of economists, who generally value scientific objectivity, is full of rhetorical appeals and literary devices. Economists, he found, use metaphors, analogies, appeals to authority, and other rhetorical techniques to add support for their objective data. McCloskey goes as far as to say that the objective data of many economists would not be persuasive without the kind of rhetorical support that one finds in argumentative essays: "A shift of one metaphor here, a shift of one appeal to authority there, and the 'proof' would be valid no longer" (p. 58).

As your final writing assignment in this chapter, you will be asked to analyze a scientific study as McCloskey analyzed the rhetoric of economists. Your instructor will ask you either to find a discussion of a scientific study in a magazine like *Omni, Discovery,* or *Psychology Today* or to find an actual study in a professional journal.

Once you locate your study (or your description of a study), you should read it and isolate statements the author or authors make that are intended to convince the reader that the study was conducted objectively. You should also look for statements indicating that the authors were not entirely objective.

Most scientific articles are very specialized, as you will find out, and are difficult to read. It is not necessary that you understand all of the technical terms or the meaning of statistical procedures. As you read the article, look for explanations of the basic procedure of the study that, in effect, are messages from the scientists to the reader that the method of their study is sound and that they have been objective.

Then write an essay in which you describe the author's or authors' attempts to be scientifically objective and evaluate whether you feel that the author or authors were successful.

2. Do you feel that science can be objective?

3 | Psychology: Developing the Talking Cure

In *Madness and Civilization* (New York: Vintage, 1961), Michel Foucault describes how seventeenth-century physicians explained hysteria, a form of mental illness:

> At the beginning of the seventeenth century, Le Pois could write, speaking of hysterical convulsions: "Of all these one source is the father, and this not through sympathy but through idiopathy." More precisely, their origin is in an accumulation of fluids toward the posterior parts of the skull: "Just as a river results from the confluence of a quantity of smaller vessels which form it, so the sinuses that are on the surface of the brain and terminate in the posterior part of the head amass the liquid because of the head's inclined position. The heat of the parts then causes the liquid to warm and affect the origin of the nerves."

As odd as this explanation sounds, it is indicative of how poorly understood mental illnesses were until the end of the nineteenth century. Looking for the cause of mania or melancholy in body fluids was an attempt to study such phenomena scientifically, but in reality this was only slightly less primitive than blaming mental ailments on the devils or animal spirits that were believed, on occasion, to possess the souls of God-fearing humans. As you can imagine, the treatment of those who were mentally ill was equally crude.

It was only in the 1890s, when Josef Breuer and Sigmund Freud developed the "talking cure," that mental illness began to be treated with some success. Freud, who more fully developed the work that he and Breuer began, exerted an enormous influence on the development of modern psychology. Indeed, most of the more recent innovations in "the talking cure" (generally known as psychotherapy) can be viewed as variations of the tradition that Freud established.

This chapter will begin with "the talking cure" as it was developed by Breuer and Freud and then move to an exploration of how more recent psychotherapists have revitalized the general tradition of "the talking cure" by abandoning many of the specific techniques that Freud felt were crucial to the therapeutic process.

The Origin of the Talking Cure

From 1876 to 1882, Sigmund Freud was Josef Breuer's student and re-search assistant. As neurologists, both men were interested in under-standing the nervous system. Although much of their research was on fish, they hoped that a better understanding of the organic structure of the nervous systems of animals would eventually lead to medical cures of the "nervous ailments" that afflicted humans. In a letter to a friend, Freud wrote of his work: "Since it is not permitted to dissect humans, I have in fact nothing to do with them."

Yet, "dissecting humans," or psychologically analyzing them, is what Breuer and Freud soon did, and in the process, they laid the foundation for modern psychology. In 1880, Breuer began to treat Bertha Pappen-heim, a friend of Freud's fiancée, for hysteria. Pappenheim, like other sufferers of hysteria, exhibited a wide range of physical complaints—pa-ralysis, headaches, sleep disorders, and the like—that seemed to be un-related to any physical illness. As Breuer treated Pappenheim, he discovered that, if he allowed her to talk about her symptoms and trace them back to painful experiences, they soon disappeared.

The following excerpt from Peter Gay's *Freud: A Life for Our Time* de-scribes how Breuer and Freud used the case of Bertha Pappenheim, which they later wrote up as the case study of Anna O., to develop a revolutionary theory of what caused hysteria and how it could be cured.

_____ **Prereading**

Before Breuer and Freud presented their theory of hysteria, physicians were frustrated by the disease. Patients suffering from hysteria seemed to be in excellent health but exhibited psychical complaints. Physicians did not know how to explain the patients' symptoms or relieve their suffer-ing. Breuer and Freud's theory was revolutionary because they perceived a psychological cause for the patient's physical symptoms. In the follow-ing excerpt from a lecture that Freud delivered at Clark University on September 6, 1909, he describes how doctors viewed hysterics before Breuer treated Bertha Pappenheim (Anna O.) and why Breuer's attitude toward hysterics was superior:

> Thus the recognition of the illness as hysteria makes little difference to the patient; but to the doctor quite the reverse. It is noticeable that his atti-tude towards hysterical patients is quite other than towards sufferers from organic diseases. He does not have the same sympathy for the former as for the latter: for the hysteric's ailment is in fact far less serious and yet it seems to claim to be regarded as equally so. And there is a further factor at work. Through his studies, the doctor has learnt many things that remain a sealed book to the layman: he has been able to form ideas on the causes of illness and on the changes it brings about—e.g. in the brain of a person suffering from apoplexy or from a malignant growth—ideas which must to some degree meet the case, since they allow him to understand the details of the illness. But all his knowledge—his training in anatomy, in physiol-

ogy and in pathology—leaves him in the lurch when he is confronted by the details of hysterical phenomena. He cannot understand hysteria, and in the face of it he is himself a layman. This is not a pleasant situation for anyone who as a rule sets so much store on his knowledge. So it comes about that hysterical patients forfeit his sympathy. He regards them as people who are transgressing the laws of his science—like heretics in the eyes of the orthodox. He attributes every kind of wickedness to them, accuses them of exaggeration, of deliberate deceit, of malingering. And he punishes them by withdrawing his interest from them.

Dr. Breuer's attitude towards his patient (Anna O.) deserved no such reproach. He gave her both sympathy and interest, even though, to begin with, he did not know how to help her.*

Judging from Freud's description, how do you think doctors of the 1890s treated patients suffering from hysteria? How was Breuer's treatment of Anna O. different?

The Case of Anna O.
Peter Gay

Though *Studies on Hysteria* was published only in 1895, the earliest case   1 discussed in the book, Breuer's historic encounter with "Anna O.," dates back to 1880. It ranks as the founding case of psychoanalysis; it impelled Freud more than once to attribute paternity to Breuer instead of himself. Certainly Breuer deserves a commanding place in the history of psychoanalysis; in confiding to his young friend Freud the fascinating story of Anna O., he generated more unsettling ideas in Freud than he himself was willing to entertain. One of these confidential sessions took place on a stifling summer evening in 1883. The scene, as Freud reconstructed it for his fiancée, displays the unforced intimacy of the two friends and the high level of their professional gossip. "Today was the hottest, most agonizing day of the whole season; I was already childish from exhaustion. I noticed that I had need of some uplift and was therefore at Breuer's, from whom I have just come so late. He had a headache, poor fellow, and was taking salicyl. The first thing he did was to chase me into the bathtub, from which I

Source: "The Case of Anna O." from *Freud: A Life for Our Times* by Peter Gay. Copyright © 1988 by Peter Gay. Reprinted by permission of W. W. Norton & Company, Inc.

---

* From *Five Lectures on Psycho-Analysis* by Sigmund Freud, Translated and Edited by James Strachey. Copyright 1909, 1910 by Sigmund Freud. Copyright © 1961 by James Strachey. Copyright renewed 1989. Reprinted by permission of W. W. Norton & Company, Inc., and A. W. Freud et al.

emerged rejuvenated. As I accepted this moist hospitality, my thought was, if little Martha were here, she would say, that is how we want to organize things, too." It might take years before they could do so, he mused, but it would happen if only she kept on liking him. "Then"— Freud returned to his report—"we took our evening meal upstairs in our shirt sleeves (I am now writing in a more pronounced negligé), and then came a long medical conversation about 'moral insanity,' and nervous illnesses and strange cases." The two men became more and more personal in their talk as they discussed Martha's friend Bertha Pappenheim "once again." This was the patient whom Breuer would lend immortality under the pseudonym Anna O.

Breuer had begun treating this interesting hysteric in December 1880,   2 and stayed with the case for a year and a half. In mid-November 1882, Breuer told Freud about Anna O. for the first time. Then, on that hot midsummer night of 1883, Freud informed his fiancée, Breuer had revealed "some things" about Bertha Pappenheim that "I am supposed to repeat only 'once I am married to Martha.' " When he went to Paris, Freud tried to interest Charcot[1] in this remarkable case, but "the great man," probably persuaded that his own patients were extraordinary enough, showed indifference. Yet Freud, intrigued by Anna O. and disappointed by the therapeutic effects of hypnotic suggestion, made Breuer talk to him about her again. When the two nerve specialists put together their studies on hysteria in the early 1890s, Anna O. took pride of place.

One reason why Anna O. was so exemplary a patient is that she did   3 much of the imaginative work herself. Considering the importance that Freud would learn to attribute to the analyst's gift for listening, it is only fitting that a patient should contribute almost as much to the making of psychoanalytic theory as did her therapist, Breuer, or for that matter the theorist, Freud. Breuer rightly claimed a quarter century later that his treatment of Bertha Pappenheim contained "the germ cell of the whole of psychoanalysis." But it was Anna O. who made consequential discoveries, and it would be Freud, not Breuer, who assiduously cultivated them until they yielded a rich unsuspected harvest.

There are contradictions and obscurities in successive versions of the   4 case, but this much is more or less beyond dispute: In 1880, when Anna O. fell ill, she was twenty-one. She was, in Freud's words, a young woman of "exceptional cultivation and talents," kindly and philanthropic, given to works of charity, energetic and at times obstinate, and exceedingly clever. "Physically healthy," Breuer noted in his case report, "menstruates regularly. . . . Intelligence considerable; excellent

---

[1] Jean Martin Charcot was a French physician whom Freud met and studied under when he visited Paris in 1885. Freud was particularly impressed with Charcot's skill as a diagnostician (he first diagnosed hysteria as a form of mental illness) and hypnosis, which Charcot used to treat mental ailments.

memory, astonishingly acute [gift for] combinations and keen intuition; hence attempts to deceive her always fail." He added that her "strong intellect" could "also digest solid nourishment," but while she needed that nourishment, she had not received it since she left school. And so, condemned to a dull existence amidst her strait-laced Jewish family, she had long been inclined to escape into "systematic daydreaming," into what she liked to call her "private theater." Breuer was sympathetic as he watched her domestic predicament. "Very monotonous life, wholly restricted to her family," his report goes on in its telegraphic style, "substitute is sought in passionate love for her father, who spoils her, and indulgence in highly developed poetic-fantastic talent." She was, Breuer thought (as Freud recalled with astonishment and wry disbelief) "sexually astonishingly undeveloped."

The event that precipitated her hysteria was the fatal illness of her   **5** father, to whom she was, as Breuer had not failed to observe, greatly attached. Until the last two months of his life, when she became too ill to take care of him, she had nursed him devotedly, tirelessly, to the detriment of her own health. During these months of being his nurse, she had developed increasingly incapacitating symptoms: weakness induced by loss of appetite, a severe nervous cough. By December, after half a year of her exhausting regimen, she was afflicted with a convergent squint. Up to this time, she had been an energetic, vital young woman; now she became the pathetic victim of disabling ailments. She suffered from headaches, intervals of excitement, curious disturbances of vision, partial paralyses and loss of sensation.

Early in 1881, her symptomatology grew still more bizarre. She expe-   **6** rienced mental lapses, long somnolent episodes,[2] rapid shifts of mood, hallucinations about black snakes, skulls, and skeletons, mounting difficulties with her speech. At times, she regressed in her syntax and grammar; at times, she could speak only English, or French and Italian. She developed two distinct, highly contrasting personalities, one of them extremely unruly. When her father died in April, she responded with shocked excitement which died away to a stupor, and her array of symptoms became more alarming than before. Breuer visited her daily, at evening, while she was in a condition of self-induced hypnosis. She would tell stories, sad, at times charming, and, as she and Breuer discovered together, this talking out temporarily relieved her symptoms. Thus began an epoch-making collaboration between a gifted patient and her attentive physician: Anna O. described this procedure, felicitously, as her "talking cure," or, humorously, as "chimney sweeping." It proved cathartic as it awakened important memories and disposed of powerful emotions she had been unable to recall, or express, when she

---

[2] Every afternoon, Anna O. fell into a somnolent (almost hypnotic) state that would last until an hour after sunset; during some of these episodes, she told Breuer stories.

was her normal self. When Breuer took Freud into his confidence about
Anna O., he did not neglect to tell him about this process of catharsis.

The turning point in her talking cure came during the hot spring of   7
1882, when Anna O. underwent a spell resembling hydrophobia.
Though parched with thirst, she was unable to drink until one
evening, during her hypnotic state, she told Breuer she had seen her
English lady-companion—whom she disliked—letting her little dog
drink out of a glass. Once her suppressed disgust came out into the
open, the hydrophobia disappeared. Breuer was impressed, and
adopted this unorthodox mode of securing relief. He hypnotized Anna
O. and observed that she could, under hypnosis, trace each of her
symptoms in turn to the occasion that had given rise to it during her
father's illness. In this way, Breuer reported, all of her various symptoms, her paralytic contractions and her anesthesias, her double and
distorted vision, her various hallucinations, and the rest, were "talked
away"—*wegerzählt*. Breuer granted that this talking away had proved far
from easy. Anna O.'s recollections were often hazy, and her symptoms
reappeared with painful vividness precisely while she was sweeping
the chimney of her mind. But her participation in the talking cure grew
more and more energetic—Breuer praised it a dozen years later with
unfeigned admiration. Her symptoms turned out to be residues of feelings and impulses she had felt obliged to suppress. By June 1882,
Breuer noted in conclusion, all of Anna O.'s symptoms were gone.
"Then she left Vienna for a trip, but still needed a good deal of time
before she wholly regained her mental balance. Since then she has enjoyed complete health."

Questions about Breuer's case history arise at this point. The truth is   8
that at the conclusion of the treatment, Breuer referred Anna O. to Dr.
Robert Binswanger's highly regarded Swiss sanatorium Bellevue, at
Kreuzlingen. In mid-September 1882, three months after her symptoms
had presumably disappeared, Anna O. made a brave attempt to give an
account of her condition. She was still at Kreuzlingen and, she reported
in her near-perfect English, was "totally deprived of the faculty to
speak, to understand or to read German." In addition, she was suffering from "strong neuralgic pain"[3] and from "shorter or longer
absences," which she called "timemissing."[4] No doubt she was much
better. "I only get really nervous, anxious and disposed to cry, when the
but too well motived fear to lose the German language for longer again,
takes possession of me." Even a year later, she was by no means well,
and was suffering recurrent relapses. Her subsequent career was remarkable: she became a pioneering social worker, an effective leader in
feminist causes and Jewish women's organizations. These achievements

---

[3] A "strong neuralgic pain" is a pain produced by a disorder in a major nerve.
[4] By "timemissing," Gay means that Anna O. suffered from memory lapses.

testify to a substantial measure of recovery, but Breuer, in *Studies on Hysteria*, compressed with little warrant a difficult, often disrupted time of improvement into a complete cure.

Writing up Anna O. in 1895, Breuer casually noted that he had "sup- **9** pressed a large number of quite interesting details." They were, as we know from Freud's correspondence, more than just interesting: they constitute the reasons why Breuer had been so reluctant to publish this case in the first place. It was one thing to recognize hysterical conversion symptoms as the meaningful response to particular traumas, and the neurosis as not simply a flowering of some hereditary disposition but a possible consequence of a stifling environment. It was quite another thing to admit that the ultimate origins of hysteria, and some of its florid manifestations, were sexual in nature. "I confess," Breuer wrote later, "that the plunging into sexuality in theory and practice is not to my taste." The full story of Anna O., to which Freud had alluded with veiled phrases here and there, was erotic theater[5] that Breuer found exceedingly disconcerting.

Many years after, in 1932, writing to Stefan Zweig, one of his most **10** impassioned advocates, Freud recalled "what really happened with Breuer's patient." This, he reported, is what Breuer had told him long ago: "On the evening of the day that all her symptoms had been brought under control, he was called to her once more, found her confused and writhing with abdominal cramps. Asked what was the matter, she replied, 'Now comes Dr. B.'s child.' " At that moment, Freud commented, Breuer held "the key in his hand," but, unable or unwilling to use it, "he dropped it. With all his great mental endowment he had nothing Faustian[6] about him. In conventional horror he took to flight and left the patient to a colleague." It is most likely that Breuer had been hinting at this hysterical pregnancy that July evening in 1883, when he had told Freud things he could repeat only after Martha Bernays had become Martha Freud.

The case of Anna O. did more to divide Freud and Breuer than to **11** bring them together; it speeded the sad decline and eventual collapse of a long-standing, rewarding friendship. As Freud saw it, he was the explorer who had had the courage of Breuer's discoveries; in pushing them as far as they would go, with all their erotic undertones, he had inevitably alienated the munificent mentor who had presided over his early career. Breuer once said of himself that he was ridden by the "demon 'But,' " and Freud was inclined to interpret such reservations—*any* reservations—as craven desertion from the field of battle. No doubt

---

[5] By "erotic theater," Gay means the sexual component of Anna O.'s case, which Breuer chose to deemphasize.
[6] Faust: a character in a medieval legend who sold his soul to the Devil in exchange for knowledge and power.

quite as irritating, Freud owed Breuer money that Breuer did not want
him to repay. His disagreeable grumbling about Breuer in the 1890s is a
classic case of ingratitude, the resentment of a proud debtor against his
older benefactor.

For over a decade, Breuer had supplied Freud unstintingly with   **12**
much-needed, and for years warmly appreciated, encouragement, affections, hospitality, and financial support. Freud's characteristic gesture of
naming his first child after Frau Breuer, an appealing, attractive friend
to the penniless and aspiring young doctor, was a cheerful acknowledgment of the thoughtful patronage coming his way. That had been in
1887. Yet as early as 1891, relations between the two men had begun to
change. That year Freud was deeply disappointed with Breuer's reception of *On the Aphasias*,[7] which, as we know, Freud had dedicated to
him. "Hardly thanked me," Freud reported to his sister-in-law Minna, a
little bewildered, "was very much embarrassed and said all sorts of in-
comprehensibly bad things about it, remembered nothing good; at the
end, to mollify me, [he offered] the compliment that the writing was
excellent." In the following year, Freud reported some "battles" with
his "companion." By 1893, as he and Breuer were publishing their joint
preliminary report on hysteria, he was growing impatient and thought
that Breuer was "standing in the way of my advancement in Vienna."
A year later he reported that "scientific contacts with Breuer have
ceased." By 1896, he was avoiding Breuer and professed that he no
longer needed to see him. His idealization of his old friend, doomed as
such idealizations are to disappointment, had generated some vitriolic
reactions in him. "My anger at Breuer receives ever new nourishment,"
he wrote in 1898. One of his patients had reported that Breuer was telling people he had "given up his contacts" with Freud because "he cannot agree with my style of life and the management of my finances."
Freud, who was still in Breuer's debt, qualified this as "neurotic insin-
cerity." Avuncular, perhaps misplaced, friendly concern would have
been a better name for it.

After all, Freud's debt to Breuer was more than pecuniary. It was   **13**
Breuer who had been instrumental in teaching Freud about catharsis
and had helped to free him from the futile mental therapies current in
his day; it was Breuer who had been willing to tell Freud in the most
suggestive detail about Anna O., a case to which Breuer, after all,
looked back with mixed emotions. Besides, Breuer's scientific procedure
could serve Freud as a generally admirable model: Breuer was both a
fertile generator of scientific hunches and a close observer, even if at
times his fertility outran his observation—as did Freud's. Indeed,
Breuer was only too aware of the gap often yawning between conjecture and knowledge; in *Studies on Hysteria*, he quoted Theseus in *A Mid-*

---

[7] *On the Aphasias*, Freud's first book, was published in 1891.

summer Night's Dream on tragedy, "The best in this kind are but shadows," and expressed the hope that there might be at least some correspondence between the physician's idea of hysteria and the real thing.

Nor did Breuer deny the influence of sexual conflicts on neurotic suf-   **14**
fering. But Anna O., it seems, with her youthful attractions, her charming helplessness, and her very name, Bertha, reawakened in Breuer all his dormant oedipal longings[8] for his own mother, also called Bertha, who had died as a young woman when he was three. There were moments in the mid-1890s when Breuer professed himself a convert to Freud's sexual theories, only to be overpowered by his ambivalence, by his demon "But." Then he would retreat to a more conservative posture. "Not long ago," Freud reported to Fliess[9] in 1895, "Breuer gave a big speech about me" to the Vienna society of physicians, "and introduced himself as a *converted* adherent to the sexual etiology" of the neuroses. "When I thanked him for this in private, he destroyed my pleasure by saying, 'I don't believe it all the same.' " The retraction baffled Freud: "Do you understand this? I don't." Five years later, only a little less baffled, Freud told Fliess about a woman patient whom Breuer had referred to him, and with whom he had had, after severe frustrations, a stunning analytic success. When she confessed her "extraordinary improvement" to Breuer, he "clapped his hands and exclaimed over and over, 'He is right after all, then.' " But Freud was not inclined to appreciate this belated tribute, even though Breuer had obviously shown his confidence in him by sending this difficult patient; he wrote it off as coming from "a worshiper of success." By this time, with Freud's memories of his friend's loyal services wiped out, Breuer could do no right. Freud could see Breuer more judiciously only after his self-analysis had taken hold, some of his emotional storms had abated, and his friendship with Fliess was decaying. "I have not despised him for a long time," he told Fliess in 1901; "I have felt his strength." It is surely not without significance that Freud was now, after several years of self-analysis, in a position to make this discovery. Yet for all his strength, Breuer had come to see the case of Anna O. as excessively demanding and downright embarrassing. "I vowed at the time," he recalled, "that I would not go through such an ordeal again." It was a case he never forgot, but not a case from which he could ever really profit. When Freud's biographer Fritz Wittels intimated that Breuer had managed to dispose of the memory of Anna O. after some time, Freud tartly commented in the margin, "Nonsense!" The

---

[8] Gay refers to Freud's theory of the "Oedipus complex," which holds that men are attracted to their mothers and thus are in competition with their fathers for their mothers' attention.
[9] Wilhelm Fliess: an ear, nose, and throat specialist who became Freud's closest confidant during the 1890s.

psychoanalytic process is a struggle with resistances, and Breuer's rejection of the elemental, shocking truths that this process may uncover is a plain instance of such a maneuver. Fliess, Freud's necessary friend, had proved much more receptive.

_____ **Written Response**

Breuer and Freud's collaboration on the case of Anna O. and *Studies in Hysteria* (1895), the book in which they presented their theory of hysteria, marked the beginning of the end of their friendship. Based on this excerpt of Gay's biography of Freud, why do you think the two friends began to drift apart?

_____ **Rhetorical Analysis**

Biographers draw upon a number of sources in their attempt to recreate a person's life, as Leon Edel describes in his *Literary Biography:*

> Let us image the great table of biography, for biographers need larger tables or desks than most writers. It is piled high with books and papers: certificates of birth and death, genealogies, photostats of deeds, letters—letters filled with rationalizations and subterfuges, exaggerations, wishful thinking, deliberate falsehoods, elaborate politenesses—and then, testimonials, photographs, manuscripts, diaries, notebooks, bank checks, newspaper clippings, as if we had poured out the contents of desk drawers or of old boxes in an attic: a great chaotic mass of materials, not to forget volumes of memoirs by the contemporaries—how they abound in some cases!—and the diaries and notebooks of these contemporaries, and often biographies of the subject written by other hands. All this material, assembled out of the years, will make its way into the mind—and the heart—of the man who has gathered it. The death of the owner of many of these documents has tended to level them into a relative uniformity. We can no longer determine whether this particular letter, breathing sweetness and affection, was really written in love, or in pretense of love. The voice that gave it its original infection is gone; the recipient of the letter is perhaps no longer available to furnish a gloss or to testify what it means to receive it. Things impalpable surround these palpable objects. The diaries and notes reflecting moods ranging from vexation and anger to transcendent joy, bitter animosity to boundless Christian charity, all had a particular meaning when the author was alive. But once he is dead the meaning becomes more general and uninflected. And the biographer can only absorb these documents into his living consciousness: it becomes, for the time, surrogate for the consciousness that has been extinguished. In other words, the living, associating, remembering biographer's mind seeks to restore a time sense to the mass of data that has become timeless. All biography is, in effect, a reprojection into words, into a literary or kind of semiscientific and historical form, of the inert materials, reassembled, so to speak, through the mind of the historian or the biographer. His becomes the informing mind. He can only lay bare the facts as he has understood them. [pp. 12–13]*

_____

* Leon Edel, *Literary Biography*. Bloomington, IN; Indiana University Press, 1959, pp. 12–13.

According to Edel, biographers face two basic tasks. They must first collect as many facts and documents as possible; then, they must interpret—bring to life—these data.

What kind of sources did Gay use in this excerpt from his biography of Freud? Does it seem that Gay has thoroughly researched Freud's life? In what ways does Gay attempt to place these sources into context so that the reader will know how to interpret them?

_____ **Interpretation**

1. One of the events that Breuer chose to leave out of his published account of the Anna O. case was her "hysterical pregnancy." In fact, Breuer chose to say little at all about Anna O.'s sexual life. In his lengthy case study of Anna O. in *Studies in Hysteria*, Breuer's only comment about Anna O.'s sexuality was brief:

> The element of sexuality was astonishingly underdeveloped in her. The patient, whose life became known to me to an extent to which one person's life is seldom known to another, had never been in love; and in all the enormous number of hallucinations which occurred during her illness that element of mental life never emerged. [p. 22]

Freud criticized Breuer for not mentioning the "hysterical pregnancy" by saying that there was "nothing Faustian about him." Why do you think that Anna O. believed that she was having Breuer's child? Why did Breuer omit this episode from *Studies in Hysteria*? What did Freud mean by saying that Breuer was not Faustian? How does this omission affect Breuer's credibility?

2. In *Jacques Lacan: The Death of an Intellectual Hero* (Cambridge, Mass.: Harvard University Press, 1983), Stuart Schneiderman wrote:

> For the hysteric the dead remain alive, as living memories: sometimes as people who are remembered, who are grieved excessively—mourning and grief are not the same thing as ritual burial—as it happens in depression, but also as repressed memories that are converted into flesh, one might say, in what are called conversion symptoms. This is what happened in Breuer's case of Anna O., especially since her hysteria dated to the scene at her father's deathbed. The scene may or may not be repressed and forgotten, but the reminiscence remains alive in attacking some part of the body as a constant reminder of what was and is no longer. The hysteric's procrastination is an effort to keep the past alive, most especially in her body, considered or interpreted as fulfilling itself most truly in the reproduction of life. If the hysteric's question revolves around the meaning of femininity—in both male and female hysterics—the answer of interpretation she latches onto most often is that femininity of motherhood. As Moustapha Safouan said in his article "In Praise of Hysteria" (in my *Returning to Freud*) hysterics are remarkably well informed about every aspect of the experience of pregnancy. About their own sexuality hysterics are far less well informed. [p. 147]

How does the explanation of hysteria given in this passage relate to the explanation presented in Gay's biography of Freud?

3. All of the five case studies that Breuer and Freud presented in *Studies on Hysteria* were of women. Why do you think that this and other initial studies of hysteria saw the illness as typical of females but rarely an affliction of males?

_____ **WRITING ASSIGNMENTS**

1. Why did Breuer and Freud drift apart?

2. For an audience of college students who have not yet read about hysteria or Breuer and Freud's theory of hysteria, write a description of hysteria and how it can be treated.

Freud and the Case Study

In *Studies in Hysteria* (1895), Freud and Breuer explained their revolutionary theory of the cause and cure of hysteria. To provide some scientific data to both explain and provide a degree of proof for their theory, Freud and Breuer included five case studies. The fact that only one of the case studies (the case of Anna O.) was written by Breuer suggests that Freud was already more actively and aggressively treating patients and developing the treatment of hysteria than was Breuer, his coauthor. Included here is Freud's case study of Katharina, the fourth case study in the volume.

When Freud was vacationing in the eastern Alps in August 1893, an 18-year-old girl asked him about a recurring problem. At times, she would hyperventilate—that is, breathe so quickly that she almost felt as if she would suffocate. In his case study, Freud describes how he traced the episodes of hyperventilation back to earlier traumatic experiences. Even though Freud spoke to Katharina on only one occasion and even though he did not establish a formal doctor-patient relationship, his description of the event illustrates how he and Breuer were developing their "talking cure" of hysteria, which Freud would eventually call psychoanalysis.

_____ **Prereading**

In "The Sexual Life of Human Beings" (*Introductory Lectures on Psychoanalysis* [New York: Norton, 1920, 1966]), Freud described his theory of how sexual drives play a role in all mental illness:

> It is possible . . . to fall ill of a neurosis as a result of a frustration of normal sexual satisfaction. But when a real frustration like this occurs, the need moves over on to abnormal methods of sexual excitation. . . . But in any

case you will realize that as a result of this "collateral" damming-back [of the normal sexual current] the perverse impulses must emerge more strongly than they would have if normal sexual satisfaction had met with no obstacle in the real world. [pp. 309–310]

Freud felt that if our sexual drives did not find a normal outlet and were repressed for some reason, then some form of mental illness would result.

What kind of societal pressure might prevent a person from developing a normal outlet for sexual drives? What kind of personal experiences might lead a person to repress his or her sexual drives?

Katharina ————

Sigmund Freud

In the summer vacation of the year 189–[1] I made an excursion into the Hohe Tauern so that for a while I might forget medicine and more particularly the neuroses. I had almost succeeded in this when one day I turned aside from the main road to climb a mountain which lay somewhat apart and which was renowned for its views and for its well-run refuge hut. I reached the top after a strenuous climb and, feeling refreshed and rested, was sitting deep in contemplation of the charm of the distant prospect. I was so lost in thought that at first I did not connect it with myself when these words reached my ears: 'Are you a doctor, sir?' But the question was addressed to me, and by the rather sulky-looking girl of perhaps eighteen who had served my meal and had been spoken to by the landlady as 'Katharina'. To judge by her dress and bearing, she could not be a servant, but must no doubt be a daughter or relative of the landlady's.

Coming to myself I replied: 'Yes, I'm a doctor: but how did you know   2
that?'

'You wrote your name in the Visitor's Book, sir. And I thought if you   3
had a few moments to spare . . . The truth is, sir, my nerves are bad. I

Source: From "Studies on Hysteria" by Josef Breuer and Sigmund Freud. Translated from the German and edited by James Strachey in collaboration with Anna Freud. Published by arrangement with The Hogarth Press Ltd. Reprinted by permission of Basic Books, Inc., Publishers, New York and the Hogarth Press Ltd.

---

[1] At several places in the case study, Freud will leave dates or names blank to protect the identity of his patient.

went to see a doctor in L—— about them and he gave me something for them; but I'm not well yet.'

So there I was with the neuroses once again—for nothing else could 4
very well be the matter with this strong, well-built girl with her un-happy look. I was interested to find that neuroses could flourish in this way at a height of over 6,000 feet; I questioned her further therefore. I report the conversation that followed between us just as it is impressed on my memory and I have not altered the patient's dialect.[2]

'Well, what is it you suffer from?' 5

'I get so out of breath. Not always. But sometimes it catches me so 6
that I think I shall suffocate.'

This did not, at first sight, sound like a nervous symptom. But soon 7
it occurred to me that probably it was only a description that stood for an anxiety attack: she was choosing shortness of breath out of the com-plex of sensations arising from anxiety and laying undue stress on that single factor.

'Sit down here. What is it like when you get "out of breath"?' 8

'It comes over me all at once. First of all it's like something pressing 9
on my eyes. My head gets so heavy, there's a dreadful buzzing, and I feel so giddy that I almost fall over. Then there's something crushing my chest so that I can't get my breath.'

'And you don't notice anything in your throat?' 10

'My throat's squeezed together as though I were going to choke.' 11

'Does anything else happen in your head?' 12

'Yes, there's a hammering, enough to burst it.' 13

'And don't you feel at all frightened while this is going on?' 14

'I always think I'm going to die. I'm brave as a rule and go about ev- 15
erywhere by myself—into the cellar and all over the mountain. But on a day when that happens I don't dare go anywhere; I think all the time someone's standing behind me and going to catch hold of me all at once.'

So it was in fact an anxiety attack, and introduced by the signs of a 16
hysterical 'aura'[3]—or, more correctly, it was a hysterical attack the con-tent of which was anxiety. Might there not probably be some other con-tent as well?

'When you have an attack do you think of something? and always 17
the same thing? or do you see something in front of you?'

'Yes. I always see an awful face that looks at me in a dreadful way, 18
so that I'm frightened.'

Perhaps this might offer a quick means of getting to the heart of the 19
matter.

---

[2] In the original German version of the case study, Freud wrote in a way to suggest Katha-rina's dialect, but this was lost in translation.
[3] By "signs of hysterical 'aura,' " Freud means the signals that appear before an attack of hysteria.

'Do you recognize the face? I mean, is it a face that you've really 20
seen some time?'

'No.' 21

'Do you know what your attacks come from?' 22

'No.' 23

'When did you first have them?' 24

'Two years ago, while I was still living on the other mountain with 25
my aunt. (She used to run a refuge hut[4] there, and we moved here
eighteen months ago.) But they keep on happening.'

Was I to make an attempt at an analysis? I could not venture to trans- 26
plant hypnosis to these altitudes, but perhaps I might succeed with a
simple talk. I should have to try a lucky guess. I had found often
enough that in girls anxiety was a consequence of the horror by which
a virginal mind is overcome when it is faced for the first time with the
world of sexuality.[5]

So I said: 'If you don't know, I'll tell you how *I* think you got your 27
attacks. At that time, two years ago, you must have seen or heard
something that very much embarrassed you, and that you'd much
rather not have seen.'

'Heavens, yes!' she replied, 'that was when I caught my uncle with 28
the girl, with Franziska, my cousin.'

'What's this story about a girl? Won't you tell me all about it?' 29

'You can say *anything* to a doctor, I suppose. Well, at that time, you 30
know, my uncle—the husband of the aunt you've seen here—kept the
inn on the ——kogel.[6] Now they're divorced, and it's my fault they
were divorced, because it was through me that it came out that he was
carrying on with Franziska.'

'And how did you discover it?' 31

'This way. One day two years ago some gentlemen had climbed the 32
mountain and asked for something to eat. My aunt wasn't at home,
and Franziska, who always did the cooking, was nowhere to be found.
And my uncle was not to be found either. We looked everywhere, and
at last Alois, the little boy, my cousin, said: "Why, Franziska must be in
Father's room!" And we both laughed; but we weren't thinking

---

[4] The "refuge hut" is a resting place for hikers.

[5] Freud's footnote: "I will quote here the case in which I first recognized this causal connection. I was treating a young married woman who was suffering from a complicated
neurosis and, once again, was unwilling to admit that her illness arose from her married
life. She objected that while she was still a girl she had had attacks of anxiety, ending in
fainting fits. I remained firm. When we had come to know each other better she suddenly
said to me one day: 'I'll tell you now how I came by my attacks of anxiety when I was a
girl. At that time I used to sleep in a room next to my parents'; the door was left open and
a night-light used to burn on the table. So more than once I saw my father get into bed
with my mother and heard sounds that greatly excited me. It was then that my attacks
came on.' "

[6] Kogel Mountain is where Katharina's "aunt" managed a refuge hut.

anything bad. Then we went to my uncle's room but found it locked. That seemed strange to me. Then Alois said: "There's a window in the passage where you can look into the room." We went into the passage; but Alois wouldn't go to the window and said he was afraid. So I said: "You silly boy! I'll go. I'm not a bit afraid." And I had nothing bad in mind. I looked in. The room was rather dark, but I saw my uncle and Franziska; he was lying on her.'

'Well?' 33

'I came away from the window at once, and leant up against the wall 34 and couldn't get my breath—just what happens to me since. Everything went blank, my eyelids were forced together and there was a hammering and buzzing in my head.'

'Did you tell your aunt that very same day?' 35

'Oh no, I said nothing.' 36

'Then why were you so frightened when you found them together? 37 Did you understand it? Did you know what was going on?'

'Oh no. I didn't understand anything at that time. I was only sixteen. 38 I don't know what I was frightened about.'

'Fräulein Katharina, if you could remember now what was happening 39 in you at that time, when you had your first attack, what you thought about it—it would help you.'

'Yes, if I could. But I was so frightened that I've forgotten 40 everything.'

(This means: 'The affect itself created a hypnoid state, whose prod- 41 ucts were then cut off from associative connection with the ego-consciousness.')

'Tell me, Fräulein. Can it be that the head that you always see when 42 you lose your breath is Franziska's head, as you saw it then?'

'Oh no, she didn't look so awful. Besides, it's a man's head.' 43

'Or perhaps your uncle's?' 44

'I didn't see his face as clearly as that. It was too dark in the room. 45 And why should he have been making such a dreadful face just then?'

'You're quite right.' 46

(The road suddenly seemed blocked. Perhaps something might turn 47 up in the rest of her story.)

'And what happened then?' 48

'Well, those two must have heard a noise, because they came out 49 soon afterwards. I felt very bad the whole time. I always kept thinking about it. Then two days later it was a Sunday and there was a great deal to do and I worked all day long. And on the Monday morning I felt giddy again and was sick, and I stopped in bed and was sick without stopping for three days.'

We [Breuer and I] had often compared the symptomatology of hyste- 50 ria with a pictographic script which has become intelligible after the discovery of a few bilingual inscriptions. In that alphabet being sick

means disgust. So I said: 'If you were sick three days later, I believe
that means that when you looked into the room you felt disgusted.'

'Yes, I'm sure I felt disgusted,' she said reflectively, 'but disgusted at   51
what?'

'Perhaps you saw something naked? What sort of state were they in?'   52

'It was too dark to see anything; besides they both of them had their   53
clothes on. Oh, if only I knew what it was I felt disgusted at!'

I had no idea either. But I told her to go on and tell me whatever oc-   54
curred to her, in the confident expectation that she would think of precisely what I needed to explain the case.

Well, she went on to describe how at last she reported her discovery   55
to her aunt, who found that she was changed and suspected her of
concealing some secret. There followed some very disagreeable scenes
between her uncle and aunt, in the course of which the children came
to hear a number of things which opened their eyes in many ways and
which it would have been better for them not to have heard. At last her
aunt decided to move with her children and niece and take over the
present inn, leaving her uncle alone with Franziska, who had meanwhile become pregnant. After this, however, to my astonishment she
dropped these threads and began to tell me two sets of older stories,
which went back two or three years earlier than the traumatic moment.
The first set related to occasions on which the same uncle had made
sexual advances to her herself, when she was only fourteen years old.
She described how she had once gone with him on an expedition down
into the valley in the winter and had spent the night in the inn there.
He sat in the bar drinking and playing cards, but she felt sleepy and
went up to bed early in the room they were to share on the upper
floor. She was not quite asleep when he came up; then she fell asleep
again and woke up suddenly 'feeling his body' in the bed. She jumped
up and remonstrated with him: 'What are you up to, Uncle? Why don't
you stay in your own bed?' He tried to pacify her: 'Go on, you silly
girl, keep still. You don't know how nice it is.'—'I don't like your
"nice" things; you don't even let one sleep in peace.' She remained
standing by the door, ready to take refuge outside in the passage, till
at last he gave up and went to sleep himself. Then she went back to
her own bed and slept till morning. From the way in which she
reported having defended herself it seems to follow that she did not
clearly recognize the attack as a sexual one. When I asked her if she
knew what he was trying to do to her, she replied: 'Not at the time.' It
had become clear to her much later on, she said; she had resisted because it was unpleasant to be disturbed in one's sleep and 'because it
wasn't nice'.

I have been obliged to relate this in detail, because of its great impor-   56
tance for understanding everything that followed.—She went on to tell
me of yet other experiences of somewhat later date: how she had once

again had to defend herself against him in an inn when he was completely drunk, and similar stories. In answer to a question as to whether on these occasions she had felt anything resembling her later loss of breath, she answered with decision that she had every time felt the pressure on her eyes and chest, but with nothing like the strength that had characterized the scene of discovery.

Immediately she had finished this set of memories she began to tell   **57** me a second set, which dealt with occasions on which she had noticed something between her uncle and Franziska. Once the whole family had spent the night in their clothes in a hay loft and she was woken up suddenly by a noise; she thought she noticed that her uncle, who had been lying between her and Franziska, was turning away, and that Franziska was just lying down. Another time they were stopping the night at an inn at the village of N——; she and her uncle were in one room and Franziska in an adjoining one. She woke up suddenly in the night and saw a tall white figure by the door, on the point of turning the handle: 'Goodness, is that you, Uncle? What are you doing at the door?'—'Keep quiet. I was only looking for something.'—'But the way out's by the *other* door.'—'I'd just made a mistake' . . . and so on.

I asked her if she had been suspicious at that time. 'No, I didn't   **58** think anything about it; I only just noticed it and thought no more about it.' When I enquired whether she had been frightened on these occasions too, she replied that she thought so, but she was not so sure of it at this time.

At the end of these two sets of memories she came to a stop. She   **59** was like someone transformed. The sulky, unhappy face had grown lively, her eyes were bright, she was lightened and exalted. Meanwhile the understanding of her case had become clear to me. The later part of what she had told me, in an apparently aimless fashion, provided an admirable explanation of her behaviour at the scene of the discovery. At that time she had carried about with her two sets of experiences which she remembered but did not understand, and from which she drew no inferences. When she caught sight of the couple in intercourse, she at once established a connection between the new impression and these two sets of recollections, she began to understand them and at the same time to fend them off. There then followed a short period of working-out, of 'incubation',[7] after which the symptoms of conversion set in, the vomiting as a substitute for moral and physical disgust. This solved the riddle. She had not been disgusted by the sight of the two people but by the memory which that sight had stirred up in her. And taking everything into account, this could only be the memory of the attempt on her at night when she had 'felt her uncle's body'.

---

[7] Katharina's hysterical symptoms needed time to incubate (or develop).

So when she had finished her confession I said to her: 'I know now   60
what it was you thought when you looked into the room. You thought:
"Now he's doing with her what he wanted to do with me that night
and those other times." That was what you were disgusted at, because
you remembered the feeling when you woke up in the night and felt
his body.'

'It may well be,' she replied, 'that that was what I was disgusted at   61
and that that was what I thought.'

'Tell me just one thing more. You're a grown-up girl now and know   62
all sorts of things . . . '

'Yes, now I am.'   63

'Tell me just one thing. What part of his body was it that you felt   64
that night?'

But she gave me no more definite answer. She smiled in an embar-   65
rassed way, as though she had been found out, like someone who is
obliged to admit that a fundamental position has been reached where
there is not much more to be said. I could imagine what the tactile sensation was which she had later learnt to interpret. Her facial expression
seemed to me to be saying that she supposed that I was right in my
conjecture. But I could not penetrate further, and in any case I owed
her a debt of gratitude for having made it so much easier for me to talk
to her than to the prudish ladies of my city practice, who regard whatever is natural as shameful.

Thus the case was cleared up.—But stop a moment! What about the   66
recurrent hallucination of the head, which appeared during her attacks
and struck terror into her? Where did it come from? I proceeded to ask
her about it, and, as though *her* knowledge, too, had been extended by
our conversation, she promptly replied: 'Yes, I know now. The head is
my uncle's head—I recognize it now—but not from *that* time. Later,
when all the disputes had broken out, my uncle gave way to a senseless rage against me. He kept saying that it was all my fault: if I hadn't
chattered, it would never have come to divorce. He kept threatening he
would do something to me; and if he caught sight of me at a distance
his face would get distorted with rage and he would make for me with
his hand raised. I always ran away from him, and always felt terrified
that he would catch me some time unawares. The face I always see
now is his face when he was in a rage.'

This information reminded me that her first hysterical symptom, the   67
vomiting, had passed away; the anxiety attack remained and acquired a
fresh content. Accordingly, what we were dealing with was a hysteria
which had to a considerable extent been abreacted.[8] And in fact she
had reported her discovery to her aunt soon after it happened.

---

[8] Katharina's emotional tension or anxiety was released as she remembered the painful experience.

'Did you tell your aunt the other stories—about his making advances   **68**
to you?'

'Yes. Not at once, but later on, when there was already talk of a di-   **69**
vorce. My aunt said: "We'll keep that in reserve. If he causes trouble in
the Court, we'll say that too.' "

I can well understand that it should have been precisely this last pe-   **70**
riod—when there were more and more agitating scenes in the house
and when her own state ceased to interest her aunt, who was entirely
occupied with the dispute—that it should have been this period of accumulation and retention that left her the legacy of the mnemic
symbol[9] [of the hallucinated face].

I hope this girl, whose sexual sensibility had been injured at such an   **71**
early age, derived some benefit from our conversation. I have not seen
her since.

Discussion

If someone were to assert that the present case history is not so much   **72**
an analysed case of hysteria as a case solved by guessing, I should have
nothing to say against him. It is true that the patient agreed that what I
interpolated into her story was probably true; but she was not in a position to recognize it as something she had experienced. I believe it
would have required hypnosis to bring that about. Assuming that my
guesses were correct, I will now attempt to fit the case into the sche-
matic picture of an 'acquired' hysteria on the lines suggested by Case
3.[10] It seems plausible, then, to compare the two sets of erotic experiences with 'traumatic' moments[11] and the scene of discovering the
couple with an 'auxiliary' moment. . . . The similarity lies in the fact
that in the former experiences an element of consciousness was created
which was excluded from the thought-activity of the ego and remained,
as it were, in storage, while in the latter scene a new impression forc-
ibly brought about an associative connection between this separated
group and the ego. On the other hand there are dissimilarities which
cannot be overlooked. The cause of the isolation was not, as in Case 3,
an act of will on the part of the ego but *ignorance* on the part of the
ego, which was not yet capable of coping with sexual experiences. In
this respect the case of Katharina is typical. In every analysis of a case
of hysteria based on sexual traumas we find that impressions from

---

[9] By "mnemic symbol," Freud means a symbol in her memory, which Freud earlier called a
"pictographic script."
[10] By Case 3, Freud means the case study of "Miss Lucy R.," which appeared immediately
before Katharina's case in *Studies in Hysteria*.
[11] By "traumatic moment," Freud means a painful experience (her "uncle's" attempt to seduce her). By "auxiliary moment," he means experiences (such as seeing her "uncle" and
Franziska in bed) that are connected in the patient's mind to the "traumatic moment."

the pre-sexual period which produced no effect on the child attain traumatic power at a later date as memories, when the girl or married
woman has acquired an understanding of sexual life. The splitting-off of
psychical groups[12] may be said to be a normal process in adolescent
development; and it is easy to see that their later reception into the ego
afford frequent opportunities for psychical disturbances. Moreover, I
should like at this point to express a doubt as to whether a splitting
of consciousness due to ignorance is really different from one due to
conscious rejection, and whether even adolescents do not possess sexual knowledge far oftener than is supposed or than they themselves
believe.

A further distinction in the psychical mechanism of this case lies in   73
the fact that the scene of discovery, which we have described as 'auxiliary', deserves equally to be called 'traumatic'. It was operative on account of its own content and not merely as something that revived
previous traumatic experiences. It combined the characteristics of an
'auxiliary' and a 'traumatic' moment. There seems no reason, however,
why this coincidence should lead us to abandon a conceptual separation which in other cases corresponds also to a separation in time. Another peculiarity of Katharina's case, which, incidentally, has long been
familiar to us, is seen in the circumstance that the conversion, the production of the hysterical phenomena, did not occur immediately after
the trauma but after an interval of incubation. Charcot liked to describe
this interval as the 'period of psychical working-out' [élaboration].

The anxiety from which Katharina suffered in her attacks was a hys-   74
terical one; that is, it was a reproduction of the anxiety which had appeared in connection with each of the sexual traumas. I shall not here
comment on the fact, which I have found regularly present in a very
large number of cases—namely that a mere suspicion of sexual relations
calls up the affect of anxiety in virginal individuals.[13]

_____ **Written Response**

In *Freud: A Life for Our Times*, Peter Gay wrote of Freud's use of case
studies:

> Freud's laboratory was his couch. From the early 1890s on, Freud's pa-
> tients had taught him much of what he knew, forcing him to refine his

---

[12] By "splitting-off the psychical groups" from the ego, Freud means the patient does not
consciously remember a group of related events.

[13] Freud added the following footnote in 1924: "I venture after the lapse of so many years to
lift the veil of discretion and reveal the fact that Katharina was not the niece but the daughter of the landlady. The girl fell ill, therefore, as a result of sexual attempts on the part of
her own father. Distortions like the one which I introduced in the present instance should
be altogether avoided in reporting a case history. From the point of view of understanding
the case, a distortion of this kind is not, of course, a matter of such indifference as would be
shifting the scene from one mountain to another."

technique, opening breath-taking vistas to theoretical departures, substantiating or compelling him to amend—or even drop—cherished conjectures. That is one reason why Freud set so much store by his case histories; they were a record of his education. Gratifyingly, they proved no less educational for others, effective and elegant instruments of persuasion. [p. 245]

Freud's case studies, thus, were a means of convincing his contemporaries that his theories were valid. What were your reactions to the case study of Katharina? Did you accept Freud's interpretation? Why or why not?

_____ **Rhetorical Analysis**

1. Case studies can be written in a wide variety of ways. This is in part due, as Foreman pointed out in "The Theory of Case Studies" (In *Research Methods: Issues and Insights*, 1971), to the nature of case studies. The descriptions of the the individual cases do not necessarily follow a "reporting form" (or standard format); rather, the organization of the descriptions tends to be related to or arise from "the manner by which data are obtained." Does Freud structure (or organize) his case study in a way that fits how he collected his information? Does his organization in any way make the case study more believable?

2. In *On Defining Freud's Discourse* (New Haven: Yale University Press, 1989), Patrick J. Mahony states that Freud liked to combine two basic styles in his writing. The first style is what Freud calls the dogmatic style. The purpose of this style is to explain rather than persuade; it presents fully formed theories concisely and objectively. The second style is what Freud calls the genetic. The purpose of this style is to persuade rather than explain. Freud described this style in *Some Elementary Lessons in Psycho-Analysis* (1940):

> It is possible to start off from what every reader knows (or thinks he knows) and regards as self-evident, without in the first instance contradicting him. An opportunity will soon occur for drawing his attention to facts in the same field which, though they are known to him, he has so far neglected or insufficiently appreciated. Beginning from these, one can introduce further facts to him of which he has *no* knowledge and so prepare him for the necessity of going beyond his earlier judgments, of seeking new points of view and of taking new hypotheses into consideration. In this way one can get him to take a part in building up a new theory about the subject and one can deal with his objections during the actual course of the joint work. [p. 281]

Does Freud use both the dogmatic and genetic styles in his case study of Katharina? If so, why does he combine these styles? How might the combination of these styles help Freud to convince his audience that his and Breuer's theory is correct?

3. In "The Theory of Case Studies," Foreman says that case studies can help to test hypotheses (such as Breuer and Freud's theory of the cause and cure of hysteria) if they have predictive power. In other words, researchers present their theory about neurosis or some other event. The theory will predict the cause and/or solution to the problem. Then, they provide a case study that illustrates how the theory predicted the cause and/or solution of the problem in an individual case. In *Studies in Hysteria*, Breuer and Freud conjectured that hysteria is caused when a person forgets a painful event; the hysteria could be cured, they believed, by leading the person to remember the painful event, which sweeps the mind clean. How does the case study of Katharina confirm the predictive power of Breuer and Freud's theory?

—————————————————————————— **Interpretation**

1. For Freud, psychoanalysis was comparable to doing good detective work in the mind. The psychoanalyst had to probe into the patient's mind, jumping from one clue to another, until he or she finds the cause of the patient's current neurosis. In this case study, Freud gives the reader a sense of how he reconstructed the patient's past. To do so, Freud chose to describe the events in a chronological order related to his conversation with Katharina. In other words, he revealed events to the reader in the order that Katharina told them to him. Reread the case study and attempt to place the events into the chronological order as they actually occurred. After you have done this, discuss the sequence of events that Freud believed led to Katharina's hyperventilation. Discuss whether the events seem to be a plausible explanation of the etiology (the history) of Katharina's hysteria.

2. How is Freud's theory that sexual drives are in some way related to all mental illness related to the case of Katharina?

3. In the footnote added in 1924, Freud admits that he changed one portion of his case study: he changed the person who seduced Katharina from her father to her uncle. Why do you feel that he did this? How does this footnote affect your interpretation of the case study? How does this footnote affect Freud's credibility?

—————————————————————————— **WRITING ASSIGNMENTS**

1. In *Freud: A Life for Our Times*, Gay writes of the revolutionary nature of Freud and Breuer's *Studies in Hysteria*:

> It is also emphatically psychological and thus, for its time, revolutionary. Freud developed his program within the framework of contemporary psychology, but he broke through that framework at point after decisive point. His most eminent colleagues in the field of psychiatry were neurologists at heart. In 1895, the year of Freud and Breuer's *Studies in Hysteria*, Krafft-Ebing published a monograph, *Nervousness and Neurasthenic States*, which illustrates the prevailing viewpoint to perfection. The little book is a brave

attempt to bring some clarity into the confusion then current in the use of diagnostic terms. Krafft-Ebing defined "nervousness" as "for the most part an innate pathological disposition, more rarely an acquired pathological change in the current nervous system." Heredity is the principal source of trouble: "The vast majority of individuals afflicted with a nervous disposition are nervous from their earliest years, on the basis of congenital influences." Krafft-Ebing saluted with grave, almost awed respect "the mighty biological law of heredity, which decisively intervenes in all of organic nature"; its influence on mental life, he though, is undisputed and preeminent. Acquired nervousness, for its part, arises when the "correct relationship between the accumulation and the expenditure of the nerve force" is disturbed. Lack of sleep, poor diet, alcoholic debauches, the "antihygienic" character of modern civilization, with its haste, its excessive demands on the mind, its democratic politics, its emancipation of women, all make people nervous. But acquired nervousness is, precisely like the congenital variety, a matter of "material, if extremely slight changes in the nervous system." [pp. 119–120]

Write on one of the following topics:

a. How was the theory that Freud and Breuer presented in *Studies in Hysteria* revolutionary?

b. As is evident from the above quotation, Freud and Breuer's *Studies in Hysteria* attempted to persuade the psychiatrists of the day, who expected and demanded scientific proof, that hysteria is caused by the repression of painful experiences. Do you feel that Freud's case study of Katharina is convincing? In other words, is the case study persuasive? Does it lead you to believe that Freud and Breuer's theory is correct?

2. Freud's case study of Katharina is unusual in that it represents a psychoanalytic treatment lasting only one session, and this session was not even a formal meeting in Freud's office. Usually, Freud saw his patients several times a week over much longer periods. In order to keep track of his treatment and to collect data for his case studies, Freud wrote case notes—short descriptions of what occurred during each session as well as any interpretations he had of the patient's problems.

For three weeks, keep you own "case notes" on a person in one of your classes, someone you work with, or some other person that you can observe almost daily. After each encounter, make an entry in a notebook. You will want to date each entry, record meticulous notes on what you observe, and explore interpretations of what you observe. At the end of three weeks, turn in your notebook of "case notes" as a writing assignment.

The Talking Cure and Hypnosis

Influenced by his studies under Charcot and Breuer, Freud used hypnosis extensively early in his career. By 1886, however, he came to the conclusion that treatment "by means of hypnosis is a senseless and worthless proceeding" (Gay, *Freud*, 1988, p. 71). After all, Freud believed that hysterics suffered "from reminiscences": they had repressed traumatic memories and needed to be cured by bringing these unconscious ideas back into the conscious mind. Freud felt that having his patients gain access to unconscious ideas through the trance state of hypnosis was not as effective as free association, which allowed the patient to consciously experience the reemergence of the repressed traumatic experience. Freud was also beginning to view the role of the psychoanalyst as that of a detached observer. Freud would allow his patients to talk about their dreams or follow their associations, only occasionally offering his interpretation or analysis.

In the 1950s, many psychotherapists were becoming dissatisfied with the detached role advocated by Freud. Among them was Milton H. Erickson. He developed revolutionary hypnotic techniques and integrated these into the "talking cure" of pyschoanalysis. In the following case study, Erickson describes how he used hypnosis to treat Ann, a 21-year-old woman who was overweight and had a negative self-concept.

_____ **Prereading**

Erickson is perhaps best known for his ability to synthesize Freudian psychoanalysis and hypnosis. For example, he borrowed the concept of "resistance" from Freud, but used it in a unique way.

Freud believed that patients were ambivalent toward being cured: They would at the same time seek treatment (by visiting and paying for a psychoanalyst or psychotherapist) and resist treatment (by being uncooperative or refusing to accept the therapist's interpretations). Rather than attempting to reduce or bypass a patient's resistance, Erickson encouraged it, as Jay Haley describes in *Uncommon Therapy* (New York: Norton, 1986):

> If a subject is asked to have his hand get lighter [as part of a hypnotic induction] and says, "My hand is getting heavier," the hypnotist does not say, "Now cut that out!" Instead, he accepts that response, and even encourages it, by saying, "That's fine, your hand can get heavier yet." This acceptance approach is typical of hypnosis and is also Erickson's fundamental approach to human problems whether or not he is using hypnosis. What happens when one "accepts" the resistance of a subject [or patient] and even encourages it? The subject is thereby caught in a situation where his attempt to resist is defined as cooperative behavior. He finds himself following the hypnotist's directives no matter what he does, because what he does is defined as cooperative. Once he is cooperating, he can be diverted into new behavior. [pp. 24–25]

In the case study that follows, Ann comes to Erickson to receive help in losing weight. When she says to Erickson that she is ugly and worthless, how do you think that Erickson will respond?

Ann

Milton H. Erickson

I urged the girl to take a seat, and after some rapid thinking I real-   1
ized that the only possible way of communicating with this girl had to
be through unkindness and brutality. I would have to use brutality to
convince her of my sincerity. She would misinterpret any kindness and
could not possibly believe courteous language. I would have to convince her beyond a doubt that I understood her and recognized her
problem, and that I was not afraid to speak openly, freely, unemotion-
ally, and truthfully.

I took her history briefly and then asked the two important ques-   2
tions: "How tall are you and how much do you weigh?" With a look of
extreme distress, she answered, "I am four feet ten inches. I weigh between two hundred and fifty and two hundred and sixty pounds. I am
just a plain, fat slob. Nobody would ever look at me except with disgust."

This comment offered me a suitable opening, and so I told her, "You   3
haven't really told the truth. I'm going to say this simply so that you
will know about yourself and understand that I know about you. Then
you will believe, really believe, what I have to say to you. You are *not* a
plain, fat, disgusting slob. You are the fattest homeliest, most disgust-
ingly horrible bucket of lard I have ever seen, and it is appalling to
have to look at you. You have gone through high school. You know
some of the facts of life. Yet here you are, four feet ten inches tall,
weighing between two hundred and fifty and two hundred and sixty
pounds. You have got the homeliest face I have ever seen. Your nose
was just mashed onto your face. Your teeth are crooked. Your lower jaw
doesn't fit your upper jaw. Your face is too damned spread out. Your
forehead is too hideously low. Your hair is not even decently combed.
And that dress you are wearing—polka dots, millions and billions of
them. You have no taste, even in clothes. Your feet slop over the edges
of your shoes. To put it simply—you are a hideous mess. But you do
need help. I'm willing to give you this help. I think you know now that
I won't hesitate to tell you the truth. You need to know the truth about
yourself before you can ever learn the things necessary to help yourself.
But I don't think you can take it. Why did you come to see me?"

She answered, "I thought maybe you could hypnotize me so I could   4
lose some weight." I answered her, "Maybe you can learn to go into a

Source: "Ann" from *Uncommon Therapy, The Psychiatric Techniques of Milton H. Erickson, M.D.*
by Jay Haley. Copyright © 1986, 1973 by Jay Haley. Reprinted by permission of W. W.
Norton & Company, Inc.

hypnotic trance. You're bright enough to graduate from high school, and maybe you're bright enough to learn how to go into hypnosis. I'd like to have you go into hypnosis. It's an opportunity to say a few more uncomplimentary things to you: Things I don't think you could possibly stand to hear when you are wide awake. But in the trance state you can listen to me. You can understand. You can do something. Not too damn much, because you are horribly handicapped. But I want you to go into a trance. I want you to do everything I tell you to do because the way you have gobbled up food to make yourself look like an overstuffed garbage pail shows you need to learn something so you won't be so offensive to the human eye. Now that you know I can tell you the truth, just close your eyes and go deeply into a trance. Don't fool around about it, just as you don't fool around in making yourself a disgusting eyesore. Go into a completely deep hypnotic trance. You will think nothing, see nothing, feel nothing, do nothing, hear nothing except my voice. You will understand what I say—and be glad that I am willing to talk to you. There is a lot of truth I want to tell you. You couldn't face it in the waking state. So sleep deeply in a deep hypnotic trance. Hear nothing except my voice, see nothing, think nothing except what I tell you to think. Do nothing except what I tell you to do. Just be a helpless automaton. Now, are you doing that? Nod your head and do exactly as I tell you because you know I'll tell you the truth. The first thing I am going to do is to get you—rather order you—to tell me certain facts about yourself. You can talk even though you are in a deep trance. Answer each question simply but informatively. What is important about your father?"

Her answer was, "He hated me. He was a drunk. We lived on wel-   5
fare. He used to kick me around. That's all I ever remember about my father. Drunk, slapping me, kicking me, hating me." "And your mother?" "She was the same, but she died first. She hated me worse than my father did. She treated me worse than he did. They only sent me to high school because they knew I hated high school. All I could do at high school was study. They made me live in the garage with my sister. She was born defective. She was short and fat. She had her bladder on the outside of her body. She was always sick. She had kidney disease. We loved each other. We only had each other to love. When she died of kidney disease they said, 'Good.' They wouldn't let me go to the funeral. They just buried the only thing I loved. I was a freshman in high school. The next year my mother drank herself to death. Then my father married a woman worse than my mother. She didn't let me go in the house. She would bring slop out to the garage and make me eat it. Said I could eat myself to death. It would be good riddance. She was a drunk like my mother. The social worker didn't like me, either, but she did send me for some medical examinations. The doctors didn't like to touch me. Now my stepmother and my sister are all dead. Welfare told me to get a job. I got a job scrubbing floors. The

men there make fun of me. They offer each other money to have sex relations with me, but nobody will. I'm just not good for anything. But I would like to live. I've got a place where I live. It's an old shack. I don't earn much—eat corn-meal mush and potatoes and things like that. I thought maybe you could hypnotize me and do something for me. But I guess it isn't any use."

In a most unsympathetic, peremptory fashion I asked, "Do you know   6 what a library is? I want you to go to the library and take out books on anthropology. I want you to look at all the hideous kinds of women men will marry. There are pictures of them in books in the library. Primitive savages will marry things that look worse than you. Look through book after book and be curious. Then read books that tell about how women and men disfigure themselves, tattoo themselves, mutilate themselves to look even more horrible. Spend every hour you can at the library. Do it well and come back in two weeks."

I awakened her from trance with this posthypnotic suggestion and   7 she left the office in the same cringing fashion as she had entered it. Two weeks later she returned. I told her to waste no time—to go into a trance, a deep one, immediately. I asked if she had found some pictures unpleasant to her. She spoke of finding pictures of the steatopygous women of the Hottentots, and of duck-billed women, and giraffe-necked women, of keloid scarification in some African tribes, of strange rituals of disfigurement.

I instructed her to go to the busiest section of the city (in a waking   8 state) and watch the peculiar shapes and faces of the things that men marry. She was to do this for one whole week. The next week she was to look at the peculiar faces and peculiar shapes of the things women will marry, and to do this wonderingly.

She obediently returned for the next appointment, went into a trance,   9 and stated with simple wonderment that she had actually seen women almost as homely as she was who wore wedding rings. She had seen men and women who seemed to be man and wife, both of whom were hideously fat and clumsy. I told her that she was beginning to learn something.

Her next assignment was to go to the library and read all the books   10 she could on the history of cosmetology—to discover what constituted desirable beauty to the human eye. She made a thorough search, and the next week she entered the office without cringing, but she was still clad in her polka-dot dress. Then I told her to return to the library and look through books dealing with human customs, dress, and appearance—to find something depicted that was at least five hundred years old and still looked pretty. Ann returned, developed a trance immediately upon entering the office, sat down, and spoke eagerly about what she had seen in books.

I told her that her next assignment would be very hard. For two   11 weeks she was to go first to one women's apparel store and then an-

Ann 185

other, wearing her frightful polka-dot dress. She was to ask the clerks what she really ought to wear—to ask so earnestly and so honestly that the clerks would answer her. She reported after this assignment that a number of elderly women had called her "dearie" and explained to her why she should not wear millions and millions of polka dots. They told her why she should not wear dresses that were unbecoming and served to exaggerate her fatness. The next assignment was to spend two weeks in obsessive thinking: Why should she, who must have been born weighing less than twenty pounds, have added such enormous poundage? Why had she wrapped herself up in blubber? From that assignment, she reported, she couldn't reach any conclusions.

Again in the trance state, she was given another assignment. This **12** time to discover if there was really any reason why she had to weigh what she did—to be curious about what she might look like if she weighed only 150 pounds and was dressed appropriately. She was to awaken in the middle of the night with that question in mind, only to fall asleep again restfully. After a few more trances in which she reviewed all her assignments, she was asked to recall, one by one, each of her assignments and to see whether they especially applied to her.

Ann was seen at two-week intervals. Within six months she came **13** in, with great interest, to explain that she could not find any reason why she should weigh so much—or why she should dress so atrociously. She had read enough on cosmetology, hairdressing, and makeup. She had read books on plastic surgery, on orthodontia. She asked piteously if she could be permitted to see what she could do about herself.

Within another year's time, Ann weighed 150 pounds. Her taste in **14** clothes was excellent, and she had a much better job. She was enrolling in the university. By the time she graduated from the university, even though she still weighed 140 pounds, she was engaged to be married. She had had two teeth that had developed outside of the dental alignment removed and replaced. Her smile was actually attractive. She had a job as a fashion artist for catalogues and newspapers.

Ann brought her fiancé to meet me. She came into my office first and **15** said, "The darn fool is so stupid. He thinks I'm pretty. But I am never going to disillusion him. He's got stars in his eyes when he looks at me. But both you and I know the truth. I have difficulty keeping below a hundred and fifty—and I am afraid I am going to start gaining again. But I actually know that he loves me this way."

They have been married for fifteen years, and they have three hand- **16** some children. Ann talks freely of her therapy, since she remembers everything that was said to her. She has said more than once, "When you said those awful things about me, you were so truthful. I knew that you were telling me the truth. But if you hadn't put me in a trance, I wouldn't have done any of the things you made me do."

but he thinks there's something the matter with me that I have to straighten out. I have also at various times been rather promiscuous, and I don't want to be that way.

T: Have you enjoyed the sex?

C: Not particularly. I think—in trying to analyze it myself and find out why I was promiscuous, I think I was afraid not to be.

T: Afraid they wouldn't like you, you mean?

C: Yes. This one fellow that I've been going with—in fact, both of them—said that I don't have a good opinion of myself.

T: What do you work at?

C: Well, I'm a copywriter for an advertising agency. I don't know if this means anything, but when I was in college, I never could make up my mind what to major in. I had four or five majors. I was very impulsive about the choice of college.

T: What did you finally pick?

C: I went to the University of Illinois.

T: What did you finally major in?

C: I majored in—it was a double major: advertising and English.

T: Did you do all right in college?

C: Yes, I was a Phi Beta Kappa. I graduated with honors.

T: You had no difficulty—even though you had trouble in making up your mind—you had no difficulty with the work itself?

C: No, I worked very hard. My family always emphasized that I couldn't do well in school, so I had to work hard. I always studied hard. Whenever I set my mind to do anything, I really worked at it. And I was always unsure of myself with people. Consequently, I've almost always gone out with more than one person at the same time. I think that it is, possibly, maybe a fear of rejection by one. Also, something that bothers me more than anything is that I think that I have the ability to write, and I wrote a lot when I was in college. Fiction, that is. And I've done a little bit since. But I don't seem to be able to discipline myself. Instead of spending my time wisely, as far as writing is concerned, I'll let it go, let it go, and then go out several nights a week—which I know doesn't help me. When I ask myself why I do it, I don't know.

T: Are you afraid the writing wouldn't be good enough?

C: I have that basic fear.

T: That's right: it is a *basic* fear.

C: Although I have pretty well convinced myself that I have talent, I'm just afraid to apply myself. My mother always encouraged me to write, and she always encouraged me to keep on looking for something better in everything I do. And from the time when I started to go out with boys, when I was about thirteen or fourteen, she never wanted me to get interested in one boy. There was always something better somewhere else. Go out and look for it. And if somebody didn't please me in all respects, go out and find somebody else. I think that this has influenced the feeling that I've had that I might be quite interested in one person, but I'm always looking for someone else.

T: Yes, I'm sure it probably has.

C: But I don't know what I'm looking for.

T: You seem to be looking for perfection, in a sense—which you're not going to find. You're looking for security, certainty.

C: Well, the basic problem I think that I have is that I seem to have lost sight of goals. I'm tied up in knots about—I'm worried about my family. I'm worried about money. And I never seem to be able to relax.

T: Why are you worried about your family. Let's go into that, first of all. What's to be concerned about? They have certain demands on you which you don't want to adhere to.

C: I was brought up to think that I mustn't be selfish.

T: Oh, we'll have to knock *that* out of your head!

C: I think that that is one of the basic problems.

T: That's right. You were brought up to be Florence Nightingale—which is to be very disturbed!

C: I was brought up in a family of sort of would-be Florence Nightingales, now that I analyze the whole pattern of my family history. Maybe it was just a perversion of other desires. My parents got married because I was on the way. I really think that they loved each other. I don't know, but I think they did. They were pretty happy with each other up till a few years ago. When I was a little girl, I was my father's pet. Nobody ever spanked me, hardly anybody said a cross word to me. So I really don't think I was spoiled. My brother, Joe, who is twenty, had an enlarged heart, from which he has pretty well recovered as a result of an operation; and my parents are now sending him to college. My sixteen-year-old brother has had polio. When I was twelve, I developed an easily dislocatable shoulder; and there's always been one kind of ailment or another in my family. Always. And they have never been able to get out of debt. Never. They were hardly able to help me through college. I incurred all kinds of debts myself in college. And since then I've helped my family. My father became really alcoholic sometime when I was away in college. My mother developed breast cancer last year, and she had one breast removed. Nobody is healthy.

T: How is your father doing now?

C: Well, he's doing much better. He's been going to AA meetings, and the doctor he has been seeing has been giving him tranquilizers and various other types of pills to keep him going. He spends quite a bit of money every week on pills. And if he misses a day of pills, he's absolutely unlivable. My mother feels that I shouldn't have left home—that my place is in Great Neck with them. I don't feel that, but there are nagging doubts, and there are nagging doubts about what I should—

T: Why are there doubts? Why *should* you?

C: I think it's a feeling I was brought up with that you always have to give of yourself. If you think of yourself, you're wrong.

T: That's a *belief*. It's a feeling because you *believe* it. Now, why do you have to keep believing that—at *your* age? You believed a lot of superstitions when you were younger. Why do you have to retain them? We can see why your parents would have to indoctrinate you with this kind of nonsense, because that's *their* belief. But why do you still have to believe this nonsense—that one should not be self-interested; that one should be devoted to others, self-sacrificial? Who needs that philosophy? All it's gotten you, so far, is guilt. And that's all it ever *will* get you!

C: And now I try to break away. For instance, they'll call up and say, "Why don't you come Sunday? Why don't you come Friday?" And if I say, "No, I'm busy," rather than saying, "No, I can't come, I will come when it's convenient they get terribly hurt, and my stomach gets all upset.

T: Because you tell yourself, "There I go again. I'm a louse for not devoting myself to them!" As long as you tell yourself that crap, then your stomach or some other part of you will start jumping! But it's your *philosophy,* your *belief,* your *sentence to yourself*—"I'm no goddamned good! How could I do that lousy, stinking thing?" *That's* what's causing your stomach to jump. Now that sentence is a false sentence. Why are you no goddamned good because you prefer you to them? For that's what it amounts to. *Who said* you're no damned good— Jesus Christ? Moses? Who the hell said so? The answer is: your parents said so. And you believe it because they said so. But who the hell are they?

C: That's right. You're brought up to believe that everything your parents say is right. And I haven't been able to loose myself from this.

T: You haven't *done* it. You're *able* to, but you haven't. And *you're* now saying, every time you call them, the same crap to yourself. And you've got to see you're saying this drivel! Every time a human being gets upset—except when she's in physical pain—she has always told herself some bullshit the second before she gets upset. Normally, the bullshit takes the form, "This is terrible!"—in your case, "It's terrible that I don't want to go out there to see them!" Or people tell themselves, "I *shouldn't* be doing this!"—in your case, "I *shouldn't* be a selfish individual!" Now, those terms—"This is terrible!" and "I *shouldn't* be doing this!"—are assumptions, premises. You cannot sustain them scientifically. But you *believe* they're true, without any evidence, mainly because your parents indoctrinated you to believe that they're true. It's exactly the same kind of assumption that people make that "Negroes are no goddamned good!" If you had been raised in the South, you would have believed that. But is it true because you would have been raised to believe it?

C: No.

T: Then why is it true that one should not be selfish, or should not stick up for oneself first, and should not consider one's parents or anybody else second, third, fourth, and fifth?

C: That's absolutely right.

T: Yes, but we've got to get you to believe it—that's the point. You don't *believe* that.

C: I *want* to believe that.

T: I know you want to; and once in a while you do believe it. But most of the time, very forcefully and strongly, you believe the crap with which you were indoctrinated. Not only believe it, but *keep* indoctrinating yourself with it. That's the real perniciousness of it. That's the reason it persists—not because they taught it to you. It would just naturally die after a while. But you keep saying it to yourself. It's these simple declarative sentences that you tell yourself every time you make a telephone call to your parents. And unless we can get you to see that you are saying them, and contradict and challenge them, you'll go on saying them forever. Then you will keep getting pernicious results: headaches, self-punishment, lying, and whatever else you get. These results are the logical consequences of an irrational cause, a false premise. And it's this premise that has to be questioned If you do question it, you can't possibly sustain it.

C: I get so mad at myself for being so illogical.

T: Now, you see, there you go again! Because you are not only saying that you *are* illogical, but that you *shouldn't* be. Why *shouldn't* you be? It's a pain in the ass to be illogical; it's a nuisance. But who says it's *wicked* for you to be wrong? That's what you're saying—that's *your parents'* philosophy.

C: Yes, and also there's the matter of religion. I was brought up to be a strict, hard-shelled Baptist. And I can't quite take it any more. This has been going on for—(*Pause*) Well, the first seeds of doubt were sown when I was in high school. Nobody answered my questions. And I kept asking the minister, and he didn't answer my questions. And when I went to college, I started reading. I tried very hard, the first two years in college. I went to church all the time. If I had a question I'd ask the minister. But pretty soon I couldn't get any answers. And now I really don't believe in the Baptist Church.

T: All right, but are you *guilty* about not believing?

C: Not only am I guilty, but the worst part about it is that I can't quite tell my parents that I don't believe.

T: But why do you have to? What's the necessity? Because they're probably not going to accept it.

C: Well, they didn't accept it. I was going to get married to a Jewish fellow as soon as I graduated from college. And, of course, the problem of religion came up then. And I didn't stand up for what I believed. I don't know; rather than have scenes, I took the coward's way out. And when I spend Saturdays and Sundays with them now—which is rare—I go to church with them. And this is what I mean by lying, rather than telling the truth.

T: I see. You're probably going to extremes there—going to church. Why do you have to go to church?

C: I always hate to create a scene.

T: You mean you always sell your soul for a mess of porridge?

C: Yes, I do.

T: I don't see why you should. That leaves you with no integrity. Now it's all right to do whatever you want about being quiet, and not telling your parents about your loss of faith—because they're not going to approve and could well upset themselves. There's no use in throwing your irreligiosity in their faces. But to let yourself be forced to go to church and thereby to give up your integrity—that's bullshit. You can even tell them, if necessary, "I don't believe in that any more." And if there's a scene, there's a scene. If they commit suicide, they commit suicide! You can't really hurt them, except physically. You can't hurt anybody else except with a baseball bat! You can do things that they don't like, that they take too seriously, and that they hurt themselves with. But you can't really hurt them with words and ideas. That's nonsense. They taught you to believe that nonsense: "You're hurting us, dear, if you don't go along with what we think you ought to do!" That's drivel of the worst sort! They're hurting themselves by fascistically demanding that you do a certain thing, and then making themselves upset when you don't do it. You're not doing the hurting—they are. If they get hurt because you tell them you're no longer a Baptist, that's their doing. They're hurting themselves; you're not hurting them. They'll say, "How can you do this to us?" But is that *true*? *Are* you doing anything to them or are *they* doing it to themselves?

C: No, I'm not.

T: But you *believe* that you're hurting them. It's crap!

C: And also, my mother thinks that I should be at home. I was contributing quite a bit of my paycheck every week. I got my first job when I graduated. My father started to work about the same time. He had been out of work. And I just gave them everything but what I absolutely needed. The debts that I had incurred when I was in college, I couldn't really start to pay back. Since then I've moved out, and I give them a little; but I just can't give them much any more—because I just simply can't. And besides that, I've gotten sick. I was sick twice this fall. And I have to get my teeth pulled now, and have to get a full upper plate put in. And I'm under financial strain. They make me feel—I guess I can't say *they* make me feel guilty.

T: No; *you* do!

C: The thing I make myself guilty about is the fact that my father doesn't earn enough money to support them.

T: Why should *you* make yourself guilty because *he* doesn't earn enough money?

C: All my life, ever since I can remember, I have. And I don't know where I got it from. This I would like to find out because maybe I can get rid of it. I've always felt that I had to make up for my father, because of his lack of financial success in the world. I don't know why I have the feeling.

T: You have it, obviously, because somewhere along the line you *accepted* their indoctrination with this kind of philosophy—that you have to make up for your family's deficiencies. It doesn't matter exactly how they indoctrinated you; but you didn't get it from nowhere. Anyway, you let yourself be indoctrinated with this notion. They and society started it—for society helps indoctrinate you, too. Maybe it's a matter of shame: you think, "If everybody knows my father is so incompetent, they'll look down on us; and that would be terrible! So I have to make up for his lack in order to show people that we have a perfectly fine family."

C: No, it isn't that. Someone was always sick. And if it wasn't one person sick, it was two. And this went on all the time. There was no time that I can remember when everybody was well. They've had doctors all the time. And when my brother Teddy was ill, my father spent a great deal of time going from doctor to doctor, and not concentrating on his—on his own career, I guess.

T: That may have been because of his own mental disturbance. He's probably always been mentally upset; alcoholics generally are.

C: He's always been supporting more people than he can. When his father died, my daddy was twelve, and he started working part time then. And then all through high school. He supported his mother and his sister all the way up till the time he married my mother. And then his mother made him feel guilty about getting married.

T: Yes, that's right; and he's been pre-alcoholic, in a sense, all his life, because he agreed with his mother that he should feel guilty. He now merely is more guilty than ever, and therefore has gone over the border into real alcoholism.

C: The constant pressures, the financial pressures, that were on him—

T: Which he really created—or at least went out of his way to accept!

C: Yes. Because he's a great writer and could make a lot of money that way. He could sell everything he writes. But why he doesn't, I don't know.

T: Because he's so disturbed.

C: He *is* disturbed.

T: He's always been. And probably, because you were the one member of the family who was relatively healthy physically, you felt, "I have to make up to the others for being this healthy!"

C: My mother always told me that. You see, I was always healthy until I developed my dislocatable shoulder. And my mother told me that my father almost came apart at the seams when I got afflicted, too. Because I was always the one he could look to for his security.

T: Yes, and that's exactly the point now. There's your answer: he looked to you for his security. That's where you may have got the concept that you had to be his security. There's their indoctrination. It's his expectation that you will take care of him and the family; and you've always tried to live up to that expectation.

C: I've always tried to live up to their expectations!

T: You're still trying to live *their* lives, instead of living *yours*.

C: I'm realizing that now. And I don't want to live their lives.

T: Well, I'm afraid that you have to be almost cruel and ruthless with people like your parents—because otherwise they'll exploit you forever: and you'll just be in the old morass. Because they're going to remain in a morass for the rest of their lives. I doubt whether they will ever change.

C: I feel that I went to college, and I was doing it practically on my own. My father always gave me five or ten dollars whenever he could; and he paid the phone bills. They tried, but they couldn't keep up with the expenses. I borrowed money, and I got some scholarships, and I worked in my freshman year. And I thought, "Now that I'm in college, I'm not a financial worry of theirs. Now everything will be all right. They'll be able to get on their feet. There are only four people to support." But it didn't happen.

T: You may never be in good financial circumstances, as far as I can see. Your father is too mentally disturbed.

C: They think everything will turn out well.

T: Yes, I'm sure. God is on their side!

C: I tried a little experiment with God—which was one of the things that made me break off from religion. I always used to pray for what I wanted, because anything you want you pray for. So I was always praying. Then one time I said, "I'll see what I can do without praying." So I studied instead; and I did better!

T: Right! But people like your parents will never take that risk of trying things without calling upon God to help them.

C: If there were a God, he never would have cursed anybody like he cursed my family—.

T: Yes, if there were a God, he'd be awfully cruel to do this to your family. Because you seem to have every ill in it: alcoholism, cancer, polio, an enlarged heart, a dislocatable shoulder—you name it! Every one of five people seems to be sorely afflicted. You could hardly have a worse setup.

C: I said once at the dinner table, "You know, somebody up there hates us!" (*Laughs*) I wanted to come to you because Ronald suggested it because you helped him get over his guilt about his mother. I had the feeling that I should go somewhere to find out what needed to be done. Because I don't want to waste any more of my life.

T: What needs to be done is relatively simple—but it's not easy to do. And that is—you've already done parts of what needs to be done. You have changed some of your fundamental philosophies—particularly regarding religion—which is a big change for a human being to make. But you haven't changed enough of your philosophy; you still believe some basic superstitions. Most people—whether Jew, Catholic, or Protestant—believe these superstitions, and your parents believe them even more than most people do, because they're more disturbed. The main superstitions are that we should devote ourselves to others before ourselves; that we must be loved, accepted, and adored by others, especially by members of our own family; and that we must do well, we must achieve greatly, succeed, do right. And you firmly believe these major superstitions. You'd better get rid of them!

C: How do I do that?

T: By seeing, first of all, that every single time you get upset—meaning guilty, depressed, anxious, or anything like that— every time you get some form of upset, some severe negative feelings, right before you got the feeling, you told yourself some superstitious creed—some bullshit. That, for example, you're no good because you aren't successful at something; or that you're a louse because you are unpopular, or are selfish, or are not as great as you should be. Then, when you see that you have told yourself this kind of nonsense, you have to ask yourself the question, "*Why* should I have to be successful? *Why* should I always have to be accepted and approved? *Why* should I be utterly loved and adored? Who said so? Jesus Christ? Who the hell was he?" There is no evidence that these things *should* be so; and you are just parroting, on faith, this nonsense, this crap that most people in your society believe. And it's not only your parents who taught it to you. It's also all those stories you read, the fairy tales you heard, the TV shows you saw. They all include this hogwash!

C: I know. But every time you try to overcome this, you're faced with it somewhere else again. And I realize—I've come to realize—you know, the thing that made me try to straighten myself out was that I know I've got to learn to have confidence in my own judgment.

T: While you've really got confidence in this other crap!

C: Yes, I'm very unconfident.

T: You have to be—because you believe this stuff.

C: I have tremendous self-doubts about every part of my existence.

T: Yes, you must, because you have so much of a belief that you must please others. If you have so much of this belief, you cannot have confidence in you. It's virtually impossible, for how can you do two opposite things at once—have confidence that you are a valuable person to yourself, no matter what others think, and believe that you are not valuable to you unless others approve of you? Confidence in yourself is really a high-class term for not giving that much of a damn what other people think of you. That's all it is. But you do care terribly about what other people think of you—about what your parents, especially, think. But also, probably, about what many other people think. Because if you were a poor daughter, what would the neighbors think? What would your friends think? You're really petrified!

C: It's not the neighbors and friends. The thing that ties me up mostly is my parents.

T: Yes, they're the primary ones. What would *they* think of you if you acted mainly in your own behalf? So what, if they think you're a louse? Let's even suppose that they disinherit you, excommunicate you from the family—

C: Then I should think, "If they care that little about me, why should I care about them?"

T: That's right. That would be tough! But it would just prove that they were benighted. It just would follow from their philosophy, which they're entitled to hold—however miserable it has made them. It would prove that they are fascistically trying to force you to believe this philosophy; and because they're failing, they excommunicate you. They're entitled to do so, of course; but you're entitled to say, "Who needs them?" Suppose, for example, you lived down south for awhile, that lots of people didn't like you because you weren't against Negroes, and that they called you a nigger-lover. What are you going to do—get terribly upset about them?

C: No, that wouldn't bother me, because that never entered my life. I mean the fact that they hate Negroes. There are people who hate Negroes who never entered my life. Because I went to school with Negroes. Nobody ever told me that they were bad. If somebody ever said, "You're bad because you don't hate Negroes," that wouldn't bother me because that's not something—

T: All right. But why should it bother you if somebody says you're bad because you don't put your parents' interests before your own?

C: I guess because I've been indoctrinated with this idea.

T: You believe *it*. It's exactly like hard-shelled Baptism. In fact, it has some of the aspects of orthodox religion; for this kind of religion says that the family comes first and the individual second; and that you're supposed to have twenty children and not use birth control, and so on. That's what many orthodox religions, like Catholicism and orthodox Judaism, teach. Everything for the church, the family—and somewhere, away underneath, the individual is buried.

C: But the individual—whatever contributions he has to make, whatever his capabilities are—can be lost that way; and I don't want to be lost.

T: Not only can he be, he must be lost that way.

C: I don't want to be self-effacing!

T: Right! Then why do you have to be? Who said you must be? The answer is: your parents. Who the hell are they? Poor, sick, benighted individuals. They're not educated; they're not sophisticated. They're probably bright enough, but they're disturbed. Your father, as we said before, has probably been seriously upset all his life, in an undramatic manner. More recently, he became dramatically ill. But it doesn't come on like that. (*Snaps his fingers*) You can see the signs clearly over the years. And your mother has probably been fairly disturbed, too, though probably not as much as he. But that's the way it is: you were raised in a pretty crazy family. Does that mean you have to kowtow to their beliefs for the rest of your life?

C: No; I want to get away from it. I want to be myself. I don't want to be—

T: What's preventing you from being yourself? Nothing can prevent you right now, if you really want to be. You just would do better, every time the feelings of being weak arise, to trace them to the indoctrinations of your parents and of your society and your acceptance of these indoctrinations. And you'd better counter them—because you're suggesting to yourself, a hundred times a day now, those same creeds. You've taken them over, internalized them. And that's really fortunate. Because it's now become *your* belief—you can get rid of it. Not immediately—but you can. Just like you got rid of your religious views.

C: And I also want to find out—I suppose it's all basically the same thing—why I have been promiscuous, why I lie—

T: For love. You think you're such a worm that the only way to get worth, value, is to be loved, approved, accepted. And you're promiscuous to gain love, because it's an easy way: you can gain acceptance easily that way. You lie because you're ashamed. You feel that they wouldn't accept you if you told the truth. These are very common results; anybody who desperately needs to be loved—as you think you do with your crummy philosophy, will be promiscuous, will lie, will do other things which are silly, rather than do the things she really wants to do and rather than gain her own self-approval.

C: That's what I don't have; I don't have any.

T: You never tried to get it! You're working your butt off to get other people's approval. Your parents' first, but other people's second. That's why the promiscuity; that's why the lying. And you're doing no work whatever at getting your own self-acceptance, because the only way to get self-respect is by not giving that much of a damn what other people think. There is no other way to get it; that's what self-acceptance really means: to thine *own* self be true!

C: You have to develop a sort of hard shell towards other people?

T: Well, it isn't really a callous shell. It's really that you have to develop your own goals and your own confidence so much that you do not allow the views and desires of others to impinge that much on you. Actually, you'll learn to be kinder and nicer to other people if you do this. We're not trying to get you to be against others, to be hostile or resentful. But you won't be Florence Nightingale, either! So you'd better get, not insensitive, but invulnerable. And the less vulnerable you get to what others think of you, actually the more sensitive, kindly, and loving you can often be. Because you haven't been so loving, really, but largely maintaining a facade with your parents. Underneath, you've been resentful, unloving.

C: I can be loving, though.

T: That's right. But you'd better be true to yourself first; and through being true to yourself—and not being anxious, depressed, and upset—then you'll be able to care more for other people. Not all people, and maybe not your parents. There's no law that says you have to love your parents. They may just not be your cup of tea. In fact, it looks like in some ways they aren't. Tough! It would be nice if they were; it would be lovely if they were people of your own kind, if you could love them and have good relationships. But that may never really be. You may well have to withdraw emotionally from them, to some extent—not from everybody, but probably from them somewhat—in order to be true to yourself. Because they tend to be leeches, fascists, emotional blackmailers.

C: Yes, that's the term: emotional blackmailers. This I know; this has been evidenced all through my life. Emotional blackmail!

T: Right. And you've been accepting this blackmail. You had to accept it as a child—you couldn't help it, you were dependent. But there's no law that says you *still* have to accept it. You can see that they're blackmailing; calmly resist it, without being resentful of them—because they are, they are. It's too bad, but if they are, they are. Then their blackmail won't take effect. And they'll probably foam at the mouth, have fits, and everything. Tough!—so they'll foam. Well, there's no question that you can be taught to change. We haven't got any more time now. But the whole thing—as I said awhile ago—is your philosophy, which is an internalizing, really, of their philosophy. And if there ever was evidence of how an abject philosophy affects you, there it is: they're thoroughly miserable. And you'll be just as miserable if you continue this way. If you want to learn to *change* your philosophy, this is what I do in therapy: beat people's ideas over the head until they stop defeating themselves. That's all you're doing: defeating yourself!

_____ **Written Response**

Why do you feel that Martha has entered therapy? In other words, why do you feel that she is unhappy? What are your reactions to Ellis's interaction with Martha?

_____ **Rhetorical Analysis**

1. Part of the role of the therapist who practices rational-emotive therapy is to persuade the client to think more rationally. At several points during this first session, Ellis compares Martha's irrational beliefs to the Baptist religion. Why would he make this comparison?

2. As he talks with Martha, Ellis uses a fair amount of profanity. Why do you think that he speaks to her in this way?

_____ **Interpretation**

1. In *Permanence and Change* (Berkeley: University of California Press, 1935, 1954), Kenneth Burke wrote: "Psychoanalysis may be described as a new rationalization, offered to the patient in place of an older one that had got him into difficulties." How does this apply to Ellis's approach to psychotherapy?

How do Martha's beliefs get her into difficulties? What kind of new beliefs does Ellis offer her to replace her old beliefs? How might these new beliefs keep Martha out of difficulties?

2. One of the basic principles of rational-emotive therapy is that the therapist should aggressively question the validity of the client's irrational beliefs. How did you feel about the way that Ellis confronts Martha?

3. At one point Ellis tells Martha that she lives in a family full of Florence Nightingales. Why does Ellis use this metaphor (some psychologists would call it a family myth) to describe her family? In what sense are the members of Martha's family behaving like Florence Nightingale?

4. In "Reality and Myth in Family Life: Changes Across Generations" (in Stephen A. Anderson and Dennis A. Bagarozzi, eds., *Family Myths: Psychotherapy Implications* [New York: Haworth Press, 1989]), Frederick S. Wamboldt and Steven J. Wolin write about the attempts of families to change their myths (such as the Florence Nightingale myth in Martha's family):

> There appear to be rare occasions when families are open to . . . revisions [in their myths]. While our knowledge of these important change processes remains rudimentary, two central characteristics of such occasions are: (1) the family jointly has struggled with a challenge or crisis that it has not been able to resolve using the explanations inherent in its currently held reality, (2) family members acknowledge that as a group they (and hence

their reality) have not succeeded. Then and only then is radically different information from individual family members likely to become available to the family as a whole. However, much more frequently an individual's attempts to revise the family's reality based on his/her discovery [from the process of psychotherapy] it is rejected or disconfirmed by the family.

As a result of accumulating these surprising discoveries and attempting to integrate them into the reality of their families, individuals entering their young adult years typically will have evaluatively positioned themselves vis-à-vis their family myths—there will be parts of their family experience that they hold dear, and there will be parts that they intend to change as soon as they have their chance. This chance, of course, comes with marriage—the new couple can rework their family myths—not necessarily within the family that they are leaving but rather by constructing a new reality in the family they form. [pp. 148–149]

Based on the information in this quotation and what you have read about Ellis's first meeting with Martha, what do you think are some of the obstacles that she will encounter as she attempts to change during psychotherapy? What are some of her opportunities for change?

5. Ellis was trained as a Freudian psychoanalyst, but soon became disillusioned with it. In an interview (*Psychology Today*, September 1988), he explained why:

I was, I think, a good psychoanalyst, and people liked what I did and wanted more sessions. But I just didn't feel it was an efficient form of treatment. Clients temporarily felt better from all of the talk and attention, but they didn't seem to get better; the insights it took them so long to arrive at didn't change things for them in significant ways. I began to wonder why I had to wait passively for weeks or months until clients showed that they were ready to accept my interpretation. Why, if they were silent most of the hour, couldn't I help them with some pointed questions or remarks? So, unlike the Freudian mode, I became a much more eclectic, exhortative-persuasive, activity-directing kind of therapist. [p. 57]

How accurately does this statement describe Ellis's work with Martha? In what ways does Ellis's approach to therapy differ from Freud's?

_____ **WRITING ASSIGNMENTS**

1. Using Ellis's 11 irrational ideas as a starting point, examine your own irrational ideas. What kinds of beliefs have you adopted that are counterproductive and make you unhappy? Write about your irrational beliefs and how you could change the way you think about yourself and the way you view the world around you.

2. Write a case study of Martha. In other words, take this transcript of Ellis's first session with Martha and use it as your source of information for writing a case study. In the first part of the case study, describe Martha and the issues that she presents to Ellis. In the second part, give your interpretation of why Martha is unhappy.

The Talking Cure and Communication

Virginia Satir, who is generally regarded as one of the most effective psychotherapists of her generation, is far from being an orthodox Freudian. She is less concerned about probing into a patient's past—although looking into the patient's past is part of her treatment. She is more concerned with improving communication. Satir feels that much of our psychological pain is caused by the family's tendency to deliver "mixed messages." If the members of a family learn to communicate more clearly, then the individuals in the family and the family as a unit will be more psychologically healthy.

In "Patterns of Communication," a chapter from *Peoplemaking*, Satir describes how poor communication can cause psychological pain and how that pain can be reduced through developing better communication patterns.

_____ **Prereading**

In "Patterns of Communication," Satir uses the metaphor of a pot to represent one's self-concept. In an earlier chapter of *Peoplemaking*, she explains the metaphor:

> When I was a little girl, I lived on a farm in Wisconsin. On our back porch was huge black iron pot, which had lovely rounded sides and stood on three legs. My mother made her soap, so for part of the year the pot was filled with soap. When threshing crews came through in the summer, we filled the pot with stew. At other times my father used it to store manure for my mother's flower beds. We all came to call it the "3-S pot." Whenever anyone wanted to use the pot, he was faced with two questions: What is the pot now full of, and how full is it?
>
> Long afterward, when people would tell me of their feelings of self-worth—whether they felt full or empty, dirty or even "cracked"—I would think of that old pot. One day several years ago, a family was sitting in my office, and its members were trying to explain to one another how they felt about themselves. I remembered the black pot and told them the story. Soon the members of the family were talking about their own individual "pots," whether they contained feelings of worth or of guilt, shame or uselessness. [pp. 20–21]

With this metaphor, Satir creates a link between a "pot" and a person's "self-concept." Given the metaphor, what do you think the following terms would mean?

My Pot is low.
My Pot is high.

My pot is cracked.
My pot is burnt.
My pot is dirty.
My pot is hooked.

Patterns of Communication
Virginia Satir

After thirty years of listening to literally thousands of interactions   1
among people, I gradually became aware of certain seemingly universal
patterns in the way people communicated.

Whenever there was any stress, over and over again I observed four   2
ways people had of handling it. These four patterns occurred only
when one was reacting to stress *and at the same time* felt his self-esteem
was involved—"his pot got hooked." In addition, the "hooked" one felt
he could not say so. Presence of stress alone need not hook your pot,
incidentally. Stress might be painful or annoying, but that isn't the
same as doubting your own worth.

The four patterns of communication (which will be dealt with in   3
detail later in this chapter) are: *placating, blaming, computing,* and *distracting.*

As I went into this more deeply I began to see that the self-esteem   4
(pot) became hooked more easily when a person had not really developed a solid, appreciative sense of his own worth. Not having his own,
he would use another's actions and reactions to define himself. If someone called him green he would agree with no checking and take the
other's comment as one fitting him. He was green because the other
person said so. It's easy for anyone with doubts about his own worth to
fall into this trap.

Do you know your internal feeling when your pot gets hooked?   5
When mine does, my stomach gets knots, my muscles get tight, I find
myself holding my breath, and I sometimes feel dizzy. While all this is
going on I find that my thoughts concern the pot dialogue I am having
with myself. The words are variations of "Who cares about me? I am
unlovable. I can never do anything right. I am a nothing." Descriptive
words for this condition are embarrassed, anxious, incompetent.

What I say at this point might be quite different from anything I am   6
feeling or thinking. If I feel the only way out of my dilemma is to make

Source: From *Peoplemaking* by Virginia Satir. Reprinted by permission of the author and
publisher, Virginia Satir, *Peoplemaking*, 1972 Edition and Science & Behavior Books, Inc.,
Palo Alto, CA, 94306 415-965-0954 USA.

things right with you so you will think I am lovable, etc., I will say whatever I think would fit. It would not matter if it were true or not. What matters is my survival, and I have put that in your hands.

Suppose, instead, I keep my survival in my hands. Then when my   7
pot is hooked, I can say straight out what I think and feel. I might feel some initial pain at exposing my "weaknesses" and taking the risk that I believe goes with that, but I avoid the greater pain of hurting myself physically, emotionally, intellectually, socially, and spiritually, as well as avoiding giving you double-level messages.

It's important at this point to understand that every time you talk, all 8
of you talks. Whenever you say words, your face, voice, body, breathing, and muscles are talking, too. A simple diagram is as follows:

Verbal communication = words
Body/sound communication = facial expression
body position
muscle tonus
breathing tempo
voice tone

What we are essentially talking about in these four patterns of com-   9
munication are *double-level* messages. In all four instances your voice is saying one thing, and the rest of you is saying something else. Should you be interacting with someone who responds in double-level messages, too, the results of your interactions are often hurtful and unsatisfactory.

The troubled families I have known all have handled their communi-   10
cation through double-level messages. Double-level messages come through when a person holds the following views:

1. He has low self-esteem (low pot) and feels he is bad because he feels that way.
2. He feels fearful about hurting the other's feelings.
3. He worries about retaliation from the other.
4. He fears rupture of the relationship.
5. He does not want to impose.
6. He does not attach any significance to the person or the interaction itself.

In nearly all of these instances the person is unaware that he is giv-   11
ing double-level messages.

So the listener will be confronted by two messages, and the outcome   12
of the communication will be greatly influenced by his response. In general, these are the possibilities: pick up the words and ignore the rest; pick up the non-word part and ignore the words; ignore the whole message by changing the subject, leaving, going to sleep, or commenting on the double-level nature of the message.

For example, if I have a smile on my face and the words, "I feel terri- 13
ble," come out of my mouth, how will you respond? Picking up on the possibilities outlined in the last paragraph, you might respond to the

words and say, "That's too bad," to which I can respond, "I was just kidding." Your second choice is to respond to the smile and say, "You look great," in which case I can say, "How can you say that!" Your third choice is to ignore the whole thing and go back to your paper, in which case I would respond, "What's the matter? Don't you give a damn?" Your fourth choice is to comment on my double message: "I don't know what you're telling me. You're smiling, yet you tell me you're feeling bad. What gives?" In this case I have a chance to respond, "I didn't want to impose on you," and so on.

Let yourself imagine what kinds of results there could be if each of   14
the above were the basis of communication between two people.

It is my belief that any family communication not leading to realness   15
or straight, single level of meaning cannot possibly lead to the trust and
love that, of course, nourish members of the family.

Remember that what goes on in a moment in time between two peo-   16
ple has many more levels than are visible on the surface. The surface
represents only a small portion of what is going on, much in the same
way that only a very small part of an iceberg is visible.

Thus in the following: 17
"Where were you last night?"   18
"You are always nagging me!"   19
Something is happening to each person in relation to himself.   20
Something is happening to the perception by each of the other.   21
The ensuing direction of the relationship can go toward distrust, per- 22

I feel terrible

sonal low pot, frustration, or, on the other hand, it can be the beginning of new depth and trust.

Let's take a closer look at these universal patterns of response people   23
use to get around the threat of rejection. In all cases the individual is
feeling and reacting to the threat, but because he doesn't want to reveal
"weakness" he attempts to conceal it in the following ways:

1. *Placate* so the other person doesn't get mad;
2. *Blame* so the other person will regard you as strong (if he goes away it will be
   his fault, not yours);
3. *Compute* with the resultant message that you are attempting to deal with the
   threat as though it were harmless, and you are trying to establish your self-
   worth by using big words;
4. *Distract* so you ignore the threat, behaving as though it were not there (maybe
   if you do this long enough, it really will go away).

Our bodies have come to accommodate our feeling of self-worth   **24**
whether we realize it or not. If our self-worth is in question, our bodies
show it.

With this in mind I have devised certain physical stances to help   **25**
people get in touch with parts of themselves that are obvious to other
people but not to themselves. All I did was exaggerate and expand the
facial and voice messages into the whole body and make it so exaggerated that nobody could miss it.

To help clarify the responses . . . , I have included a simple word-   **26**
diagram with each descriptive section.

Placater

(1) Words	agree	("Whatever you want is okay. I am just here to make you happy.")
Body	placates	("I am helpless.")
Insides		("I feel like a nothing; without him I am dead. I am worthless.")

The *placater* always talks in an ingratiating way, trying to please, apol- 27
ogizing, never disagreeing, no matter what. He's a "yes man." He talks
as though he could do nothing for himself; he must always get someone to approve of him. You will find later that if you play this role for
even five minutes, you will begin to feel nauseous and want to vomit.

A big help in doing a good placating job is to think of yourself as   **28**
really worth nothing. You are lucky just to be allowed to eat. You owe
everybody gratitude, and you really are responsible for everything that
goes wrong. You know you could have stopped the rain if you used

your brains, but you don't have any. Naturally you will agree with any criticism made about you. You are, of course, grateful for the fact that anyone even talks to you, no matter what they say or how they say it. You would not think of asking anything for yourself. After all, who are you to ask? Besides, if you can just be good enough it will come by itself.

Be the most syrupy, martyrish, bootlicking person you can be. Think   **29** of yourself as being physically down on one knee, wobbling a bit, putting out one hand and in begging fashion, and be sure to have your head up so your neck will hurt and your eyes will become strained so in no time at all you will begin to get a headache.

When you talk in this position your voice will be whiny and squeaky   **30** because you keep your body in such a lowered position that you don't have enough air to keep a rich, full voice. You will be saying "yes" to everything, no matter what you feel or think. The placating stance is the body position that matches the placating response.

Blamer

(2) Words   disagree   ("You never do anything right. What is the matter with you?")

Body   blames   ("I am the boss around here.")

Insides   ("I am lonely and unsuccessful.")

The *blamer* is a fault-finder, a dictator, a boss. He acts superior, and   **31** he seems to be saying, "If it weren't for you, everything would be all right." The internal feeling is one of tightness in the muscles and in

leveling. To thwart the rejection we so fear, we tend to threaten ourselves in the following ways:

1. I might make a mistake.
2. Someone might not like it.
3. Someone will criticize me.
4. I might impose.
5. He will think I am no good.
6. I might be thought of as imperfect.
7. He might leave.

When you can tell yourself the following answers to the foregoing   59
statements, you will have achieved real growth:

1. You are sure to make mistakes if you take any action, especially new action.
2. You can be quite sure that there will be someone who won't like what you do.
   Not everyone likes the same things.
3. Yes, someone will criticize you. You really aren't perfect. Some criticism is
   useful.
4. Sure! Every time you are in the presence of another person, speak to him,
   and interrupt him, you impose!
5. So maybe he will think you're no good. Can you live through it? Maybe
   sometimes you aren't so hot. Sometimes the other person is "putting his trip
   on you." Can you tell the difference?
6. If you think of yourself as needing to be perfect, the chances are you will
   always be able to find imperfection.
7. So he leaves. Maybe he should leave, and anyway, you'll live through it.

These attitudes will give you a good opportunity to stand on your   60
own two good feet. It won't be easy and it won't be painless, but it
might make the difference as to whether or not you grow.

With no intention of being flippant, I do think that most of the   61
things we use to threaten ourselves and that affect our self-worth turn
out to be tempests, in teapots. One way I helped myself through these
threats was to ask myself if I would still be alive if all these imagined
threats came true. If I could answer yes, then I was okay. I can answer
yes to all of them now.

I will never forget the day I found out that lots of other people wor-   62
ried about these same silly threats as I did. I had thought for years I
was the only one, and I kept myself busy trying to outwit them, and at
the same time doing my best to conceal the threats. My feeling was—
what if somebody found out? Well, what if somebody did? We all use
these same kinds of things to threaten ourselves.

By now you must realize that this isn't some kind of a magical recipe,   63
but the leveling response is actually a way of responding to real people
in real life situations that permit you to agree because you really do,
not because you think you should; disagree because you really do, not
because you think you won't make points unless you do; use your

brain freely, but not at the expense of the rest of you; to change
courses, not to get you off the hook, but because you want to and there
is a need to do so.

What the leveling response does is make it possible for you to live as   **64**
a whole person—real, in touch with your head, your heart, your feelings, and your body. Being a leveler enables you to have integrity, commitment, honesty, intimacy, competence, creativity, and the ability to
work with real problems in a real way. The other forms of communication result in doubtful integrity, commitment by bargain, dishonesty,
loneliness, shoddy competence, strangulation by tradition, and dealing
in a destructive way with fantasy problems.

It takes guts, courage, some new beliefs, and some new skills to be-   **65**
come a leveler responder. *You can't fake it.*

Unfortunately there is little in society that reinforces this leveling re-   **66**
sponse. Yet people are actually hungry for this kind of straightness and
honesty. When they become aware of it and are courageous enough to
try it, distances between people are shortened.

I did not come to this formulation via religion or through the study   **67**
of philosophy. I came to it through a tough, trial-and-error way, trying
to help people who had serious life problems. I found that what healed
people was getting them to find their hearts, their feeling, their bodies,
their brains, which once more brought them to their souls and thus to
their humanity. They could then express themselves as whole people,
which, in turn, helped them to greater feelings of self-worth (high pot),
to nurturing relationships and satisfying outcomes.

None of these results is possible through the use of four crippling   **68**
ways of communication. I have found these, incidentally, as inevitable
outcomes of the way authority is taught in families and reinforced by
much of our society. What is so sad is that these four ways have become the most frequently used among people and are viewed by many
as the most possible ways of achieving communication.

From what I have seen I've made some tentative conclusions about   **69**
what to expect when I meet new groups of people. Fifty percent will
say yes no matter what they feel or think (placate); 30 percent will say
no, no matter what they feel or think (blame); 15 percent will say neither yes nor no and will give no hint of their feelings (compute); and
$\frac{1}{2}$ percent will behave as if yes, no, or feeling did not exist (distracting).
That leaves only $4\frac{1}{2}$ percent whom I can expect to be real and to level.
My colleagues tell me I am optimistic, saying the leveling response is
probably found in only 1 percent of our population. Remember this is
not validated research. It is only a clinical hunch. In the vernacular it
would seem we are all a bunch of crooks—hiding ourselves and playing dangerous games with one another.

At this point I want to make an even more drastic statement. If you   **70**
want to make your body sick, become disconnected from other people,

throw away your beautiful brain power, make yourself deaf, dumb, and blind, using the four crippling ways of communication will in great measure help you to do it.

I feel very strongly as I write this. For me, the feelings of isolation,   71
helplessness, feeling unloved, low pot, or incompetence comprise the real human evils of this world. Certain kinds of communication will continue this and certain kinds of communication can change it. What I am trying to do in this chapter is make it possible for each person to understand the leveling response so he can recognize and use it.

I would like to see each human being value and appreciate himself,   72
feel whole, creative, competent, healthy, rugged, beautiful, and loving.

Despite the fact that I have exaggerated these different ways of   73
communication for emphasis, and they may even seem amusing, I am deadly serious about the killing nature of the first four styles of communication.

_____ **Written Response**

Describe a time when you were given a mixed message. What was the mixed message? How did it make you feel? How did you react to it?

_____ **Rhetorical Analysis**

1. How does Satir create a sense of authority in this chapter? In other words, how did she obtain special knowledge of the way that families communicate? How does she convince the reader that she can improve the communication of families?

2. Satir found that using the metaphor of a "pot" for "self-concept" seemed to allow her clients to express themselves better. Why do you think that a metaphor such as the "pot" helps people to express themselves and communicate better? Why would any metaphor help people to communicate better?

_____ **Interpretation**

1. Develop a list of people from history, literature, or the news, then discuss which of the four ways of reacting to mixed messages (placating, blaming, computing, distracting) you think each person would employ when under stress.

2. Discuss situations you have experienced or observed recently that represent one of Satir's four categories.

3. In *The Structure of Magic II* (Palo Alto: Science and Behavior Books, 1975), John Grinder and Richard Bandler offer the following description of the psychotherapist's role:

The therapist's task in working with a client's incongruencies is to assist the client in changing by integrating the parts of the client which are in conflict, the incongruencies which are draining his energies and blocking him from getting what he wants. Typically, when a client has parts which are in conflict, no part is successful, but each sabotages the others' efforts to achieve what they want. Within a client who has conflicting parts, there are (at least) two incompatible models or maps of the world. As these models both serve as a guide for the client's behavior and are incompatible, his behavior is, itself, inconsistent. Integration is a process by which the client creates a new model of the world which includes both the formerly incompatible models in such a way that they are coordinated and function smoothly together, both working to assist the client in getting what he wants from life. [p. 44]

How does this description of the therapist's role apply to the kind of psychotherapy that Satir practices?

_____ **WRITING ASSIGNMENTS**

1. Using Satir's four patterns of communication (placating, blaming, computing, and distracting) as a starting point, describe how someone you know well (a friend or a family member) acts when under stress. You may want to focus your essay by describing a particular incident that illustrates your point.

2. Satir used the metaphor of the pot to represent one's self-concept. Write an essay in which you use a metaphor, or a series of metaphors, to describe your personality.

Synthesis

1. In this chapter, you have learned about how Breuer and Freud developed the talking cure and how subsequent psychoanalysts and psychotherapists modified this revolutionary treatment. Freud argued that psychoanalysis, his version of the talking cure, brought suppressed memories from the unconscious to the conscious mind. The new understanding of self that emerged from this process, he felt, was what allowed his patients to improve.

In "The Stories That We Live By" (*Psychology Today,* December 1988), Sam Keen describes what happens during the talking cure in a slightly different way. He feels that our "personal myths," the stories that we tell ourselves and others about who we are and what we will be, determine a great deal of our behavior. Some of our myths lead us to act in ways that make us unhappy. Psychoanalysis or psychotherapy, Keen feels, is a way of discovering the myths that make us unhappy and rewriting them in a way that allows us to improve our lives.

Soc. Then rhetoric, as would appear, is the artificer of a persuasion which creates belief about the just and unjust, but gives no instruction about them?

Gor. True.

Soc. And the rhetorician does not instruct the courts of law or other assemblies about things just and unjust, but he creates belief about them; for no one can be supposed to instruct such a vast multitude about such high matters in a short time?

Soc. Come, then, and let us see what we really mean about rhetoric; for I do not know what my own meaning is as yet. When the assembly meets to elect a physician or a shipwright or any other craftsman, will the rhetorician be taken into counsel? Surely not. For at every election he ought to be chosen who is most skilled; and, again, when walls have to be built or harbours or docks to be constructed, not the rhetorician but the master workman will advise; or when generals have to be chosen and an order of battle arranged, or a proposition taken, then the military will advise and not the rhetoricians: what do you say, Gorgias? Since you profess to be a rhetorician and a maker of rhetoricians, I cannot do better than learn the nature of your art from you. And here let me assure you that I have your interest in view as well as my own. For likely enough some one or other of the young men present might desire to become your pupil, and in fact I see some, and a good many too, who have this wish, but they would be too modest to question you. And therefore when you are interrogated by me, I would have you imagine that you are interrogated by them. 'What is the use of coming to you, Gorgias?' they will say—'about what will you teach us to advise the state?—about the just and unjust only, or about those other things also which Socrates has just mentioned?' How will you answer them?

Gor. I like your way of leading us on, Socrates, and I will endeavour to reveal to you the whole nature of rhetoric. You must have heard, I think, that the docks and the walls of the Athenians and the plan of the harbour were devised in accordance with the counsels, partly of Themistocles, and partly of Pericles, and not at the suggestion of the builders.

Soc. Such is the tradition, Gorgias, about Themistocles; and I myself heard the speech of Pericles when he advised us about the middle wall.

Gor. And you will observe, Socrates, that when a decision has to be given in such matters the rhetoricians are the advisers; they are the men who win their point.

Soc. I had that in my admiring mind, Gorgias, when I asked what is the nature of rhetoric, which always appears to me, when I look at the matter in this way, to be a marvel of greatness.

Gor. A marvel, indeed, Socrates, if you only knew how rhetoric comprehends and holds under her sway all the inferior arts. Let me offer you a striking example of this. On several occasions I have been with my brother Herodicus or some other physician to see one of his patients, who would not allow the physician to give him medicine, or apply a knife or hot iron to him; and I have persuaded him to do for me what he would not do for the physician just by the use of rhetoric. And I say that if a rhetorician and a physician were to go to any city, and had there to argue in the Ecclesia or any other assembly as to which of them should be elected state-physician, the physician would have no chance; but he who could speak would be chosen if he wished; and in a contest with a man of any other profession the rhetorician more than any one

would have the power of getting himself chosen, for he can speak more persua-
sively to the multitude than any of them, and on any subject. Such is the nature and power of the art of rhetoric! And yet, Socrates, rhetoric should be
used like any other competitive art, not against everybody,—the rhetorician
ought not to abuse his strength any more than a pugilist or pancratiast or other
master of fence;—because he has powers which are more than a match either
for friend or enemy, he ought not therefore to strike, stab, or slay his friends.
Suppose a man to have been trained in the palestra and to be a skilful boxer,—
he in the fulness of his strength goes and strikes his father or mother or one of
his familiars or friends; but that is no reason why the trainers or fencing-
masters should be held in detestation or banished from the city;—surely not.
For they taught their art for a good purpose, to be used against enemies and
evil-doers, in self-defence not in aggression, and others have perverted their
instructions, and turned to a bad use their own strength and skill. But not on
this account are the teachers bad, neither is the art in fault, or bad in itself; I
should rather say that those who make a bad use of the art are to blame. And
the same argument holds good of rhetoric; for the rhetorician can speak against
all men and upon any subject,—in short, he can persuade the multitude better
than any other man of anything which he pleases, but he should not therefore
seek to defraud the physician or any other artist of his reputation merely because he has the power; he ought to use rhetoric fairly, as he would also use
his athletic powers. And if after having become a rhetorician he makes a bad
use of his strength and skill, his instructor surely ought not on that account to
be held in detestation or banished. For he was intended by his teacher to make
a good use of his instructions, but he abuses them. And therefore he is the person who ought to be held in detestation, banished, and put to death, and not
his instructor.

_____ **Written Response**

Write a paragraph or two in which you describe Socrates and Gorgias.
What kind of persons are they? What kind of personality traits do they
have? Are they like anyone you know?

_____ **Rhetorical Analysis**

1. Plato believed that truth emerges from what he called "dialectic"—
the free play of opposing ideas. Dialectic, to Plato, was quite different
from rhetoric, as Kennedy writes in *Classical Rhetoric:*

> Dialectic is a faculty of discovering available arguments to answer pro-
> posed questions, and in Plato it is the only acceptable form of philosophical
> reasoning. It follows a method of division of the question and definition of
> the factors involved, testing hypotheses as they are advanced. In theory the
> leader of the discussion does not know, at least with certainty, what the
> conclusion will be, but the Platonic Socrates certainly has predilections,
> and his hypotheses often work out with a feeling of inevitability. Plato
> would say that this is because new truth is not discovered, but rather old

truth is recollected: we all existed before birth and we know much more than we can immediately remember.

In contrast to dialectic, rhetoric involves a preselected arbitrary conclusion: that a defendant is guilty or that the assembly should follow a particular policy or that a certain proposition is feasible. The orator chooses those arguments which prove or seem to prove the conclusion to which he is committed, whether or not it is true. [p. 46]

Why do you think that Plato preferred dialogue over rhetoric?

2. In *Classical Rhetoric*, Kennedy argues that, throughout history, the critics of rhetoric always use rhetoric to criticize rhetoric. How does Socrates use rhetoric to criticize rhetoric? How does the way that Socrates questions Gorgias resemble the way that lawyers question witnesses?

Interpretation

1. What kind of concerns does Socrates express about the use of rhetoric? Do you agree with these concerns?

2. Later in the dialogue, Socrates criticizes rhetoric for using the same equipment (strategies or techniques) in the service of good or evil:

For the moment let us rather consider this point: Is the rhetorician's equipment the same in regard to justice and injustice, beauty and ugliness, good and evil, as it is regarding health and the several subjects of the other arts? Is it, in fact, true that he does not really know what is good or evil, beautiful or ugly, just or unjust, but has devised a means of persuasion about them so that, in the eyes of the ignorant, he seems to know more than the actual possessor of knowledge though he does not really do so? Or is it necessary for him to know? Must the man who intends to learn rhetoric have acquired this knowledge before he comes to you? And if he hasn't, will you, the teacher of rhetoric, teach him none of these things (of course that's not really your job), but instead will you make him, in the eyes of the crowd, seem to know such things, though he doesn't, and seem to be good, though he isn't? Or is it a fact that you will not be able to teach him rhetoric at all until he first learns the truth about these matters?

What does Socrates mean here? How do you think that he would answer Gorgias' argument that he, as a teacher of rhetoric, should not be blamed for those who misuse rhetoric?

WRITING ASSIGNMENTS

1. Use an example from your personal experience to express your views on rhetoric. You could write about when rhetoric was misused (for example, a car salesperson manipulated you into buying a car that you could not afford), or you could write about when rhetoric was used for a good purpose (someone persuaded you to become a better person), or you could perhaps write about a situation that embodies your ambivalence toward rhetoric (someone who manipulated people into giving

money for a good cause). In your essay, you will need to narrate what happened, explain why the person using rhetoric was so persuasive, and express your personal views on what happened.

2. Write an essay in which you argue that it is either ethical or unethical to teach rhetoric.

3. Although Plato is critical of rhetoric in *Gorgias*, many of the philosophers who followed him held more positive views. Indeed, even Plato held a more positive view in *Phaedrus*, one of his later dialogues. Some brief excerpts follow from Aristotle's *Rhetoric*, Isocrates' "Nicocles or the Cyrians," and Saint Augustine's *On Christian Doctrine*. Write an essay in which you use these excerpts from Aristotle, Isocrates, and Saint Augustine to argue that Plato's criticism of rhetoric is invalid.

Excerpt from Aristotle's *Rhetoric**

But the art of Rhetoric has its value. It is valuable, first, because truth and justice are by nature more powerful than their opposites; so that, when decisions are not made as they should be, the speakers with the right on their side have only themselves to thank for the outcome. Their neglect of the art needs correction. A proper knowledge and exercise of Rhetoric would prevent the triumph of fraud and injustice. Secondly, Rhetoric is valuable as a means of instruction. Even if our speaker had the most accurate scientific information, still there are persons whom he could not readily persuade with scientific arguments. True instruction, by the method of logic, is here impossible; the speaker must frame his proofs and arguments with the help of common knowledge and accepted opinions. . . . Thirdly, in Rhetoric, as in Dialectic, we should be able to argue on either side of a question; not with a view to putting both sides into practice—we must not advocate evil—but in order that no aspect of the case may escape us, and that if our opponent makes unfair use of the arguments, we may be able in turn to refute them. In no other art do we draw opposite conclusions; it is characteristic of Rhetoric and Dialectic alone that, abstractly considered, they may indifferently prove opposite statements. Still, their basis, in the facts, is not a matter of indifference, for, speaking broadly, what is true and preferable is by nature always easier to prove and more convincing. Lastly, if it is a disgrace to a man when he cannot defend himself in a bodily way, it would be odd not to think him disgraced when he cannot defend himself with reason in a speech. Reason is more distinctive of man than is bodily effort. If it is urged that an abuse of the rhetorical faculty can work great mischief, the same charge can be brought against all good things (save virtue itself), and especially against the most useful things such as strength, health, wealth, and military skill. Rightly employed, they work the greatest blessings; and wrongly employed, they work the utmost harm.

We have seen that Rhetoric is not confined to any single and definite class of subjects, but in this respect is like Dialectic, and that the art has its uses; and we see that its function is not absolutely to persuade, but to

*Lane Cooper, trans., *The Rhetoric of Aristotle*. Englewood Cliffs, NJ: Prentice-Hall, Inc., 1932.

In "The Psycho-Seduction of Children" (a chapter from *The Hidden Persuaders*), Packard attacks the advertising industry's appeals to children.

_____ **Prereading**

In the "Psycho-Seduction of Children," Packard is especially critical of those advertisers who use depth psychology. This branch of psychology, which evolved from Freud's psychoanalytic theory, studies the unconscious motivation of human behavior. In the 1950s, some advertisers felt that depth psychology could suggest a more effective method of appealing to a target audience (the specific kind of people who the advertisers felt would probably buy a particular product). These advertisers felt that, if people's motives for buying a product are frequently unconscious, then advertisements should be directed to the thoughts, drives, and emotions of the unconscious mind. An example of this occurs when advertisers associate owning a product with being sexually desirable.

Can you think of advertisements that use this technique? Why do you think that Packard would object to this kind of advertising?

The Psycho-Seduction of Children

Vance Packard

> Today the future occupation of all moppets is to
> be skilled consumers.
>
> —David Riesman, *The Lonely Crowd*

Dr. Riesman in his study of the basic changes taking place in the American character during the twentieth century (i.e., from inner-directed to other-directed) found that our growing preoccupation with acts of consumption reflected the change. This preoccupation, he noted, was particularly intense (and intensively encouraged by product makers) at the moppet[1] level. He characterized the children of America as "consumer trainees."

In earlier more innocent days, when the pressure was not on to build 2 future consumers, the boys' magazines and their counterparts concen-

Source: "The Psycho-Seduction of Children" from *The Hidden Persuaders* by Vince Packard. Copyright © 1957 by Vince Packard. Reprinted by permission.

_____

[1] Moppets are children.

trated on training the young for the frontiers of production, including warfare. As a part of that training, Dr. Riesman pointed out in *The Lonely Crowd,* the budding athlete might eschew smoke and drink. "The comparable media today train the young for the frontiers of consumption—to tell the difference between Pepsi-Cola and Coca-Cola, as later between Old Golds and Chesterfields," he explained. He cited the old nursery rhyme about one little pig going to market while one stayed home and commented dourly: "The rhyme may be taken as a paradigm of individuation and unsocialized behavior among children of an earlier era. Today, however, all little pigs go to market; none stay home; all have roast beef, if any do; and all say 'wee-wee-wee.' "

The problem of building eager consumers for the future was consid-   3
ered at a mid-fifties session of the American Marketing Association. The head of Gilbert Youth Research told the marketers there was no longer any problem of getting funds "to target the youth market"; there were plenty. The problem was targeting the market with maximum effectiveness. Charles Sievert, advertising columnist for the *New York World Telegram and Sun,* explained what this targeting was all about by saying, "Of course the dividend from investment in the youth market is to develop product and brand loyalty and thus have an upcoming devoted adult market."

A more blunt statement of the opportunity moppets present appeared   4
in an ad in *Printer's Ink* several years ago. A firm specializing in supplying "education" material to schoolteachers in the form of wall charts, board cutouts, teachers' manuals made this appeal to merchants and advertisers: "Eager minds can be molded to want your products! In the grade schools throughout America are nearly 23,000,000 young girls and boys. These children eat food, wear out clothes, use soap. They are consumers today and will be the buyers of tomorrow. Here is a vast market for your products. Sell these children on your brand name and they will insist that their parents buy no other. Many farsighted advertisers are cashing in today . . . and building for tomorrow . . . by molding eager minds" through Project Education Material supplied to teachers. It added reassuringly: "all carrying sugar-coated messages designed to create acceptance and demand for the products. . . . " In commenting on this appeal Clyde Miller, in his *The Process of Persuasion,* explained the problem of conditioning the reflexes of children by saying, "It takes time, yes, but if you expect to be in business for any length of time, think of what it can mean to your firm in profits if you can condition a million or ten million children who will grow up into adults trained to buy your product as soldiers are trained to advance when they hear the trigger words 'forward march.' "

One small phase of the seduction of young people into becoming   5
loyal followers of a brand is seen in the fact that on many college campuses students can earn a part of their college expenses by passing among fellow students handing out free sample packages of cigarettes.

The potency of television in conditioning youngsters to be loyal en-   6
thusiasts of a product, whether they are old enough to consume it or
not, became indisputable early in the fifties. A young New York ad
man taking a marketing class at a local university made the casual
statement that, thanks to TV, most children were learning to sing beer
and other commercials before learning to sing "The Star-Spangled Ban-
ner." Youth Research Institute, according to *The Nation*, boasted that
even five-year-olds sing beer commercials "over and over again with
gusto." It pointed out that moppets not only sing the merits of advertised products but do it with the vigor displayed by the most raptly enthusiastic announcers, and do it all day long "at no extra cost to the
advertiser." They cannot be turned off as a set can. When at the beginning of the decade television was in its infancy, an ad appeared in a
trade journal alerting manufacturers to the extraordinary ability of TV
to etch messages on young brains. "Where else on earth," the ad exclaimed, "is brand consciousness fixed so firmly in the minds of four-
year-old tots? . . . What is it worth to a manufacturer who can close in
on this juvenile audience and continue to sell it under controlled conditions year after year, right up to its attainment of adulthood and full-
fledged buyer status? It CAN be done. Interested?" (While the author
was preparing this chapter he heard his own eight-year-old-daughter
happily singing the cigarette jingle: "Don't miss the fun of smoking!")

The relentlessness with which one TV sponsor tried to close in on   7
preschool tots brought protests in late 1955. Jack Gould, TV columnist
of *The New York Times*, expressed dismay at a commercial for vitamin
pills that Dr. Francis Horwich, "principal" of TV's *Ding Dong School* for
preschool children, delivered. It seems she used the same studied
tempo she used in chatting to children about toys and helping mother
while she demonstrated how pretty the red pills were and how easy to
swallow they were. She said she hoped they were taking the pills every
morning "like I do," and urged them to make sure the next time they
visited a drugstore that their mother picked out the right bottle. Gould
commented:

"To put it as mildly as possible, Dr. Horwich has gone a step too far   8
in letting a commercial consideration jeopardize her responsibility to
the young children whose faith and trust she solicits." First, he pointed
out, was the simple factor of safety. Small children should be kept away
from pills of all kinds and certainly not be encouraged to treat them as
playthings. A lot of different pills (including mama's sleeping pills) can
be pretty and red and easy to swallow, and after all prekindergarten
children can't read labels. Gould doubted whether TV had any business deciding whether tots do or do not need vitamin pills. He felt that
a vitamin deficiency is better determined "by a parent after consulta-
tion with a physician" rather than a TV network. Finally, he observed,
"Using a child's credibility to club a parent into buying something is
reprehensible under the best of circumstances. But in the case of a

product bearing on a child's health it is inexcusable." Doctors wrote in commending Gould for his stand; and a mother wrote that she found herself "appalled at the amount of commercialism our children are being subjected to."

Mr. Gould's complaints notwithstanding, the merchandisers sought to 9 groom children not only as future consumers but as shills[2] who would lead or "club" their parents into the salesroom. Dr. Dichter advised a major car maker to train dealer salesmen to regard children as allies rather than nuisances while demonstrating a car. The salesmen, instead of shoving them away, should be especially attentive to the kiddies and discuss all the mechanisms that draw the child's attention. This, he said, is an excellent strategy for drawing the understanding permissive father into the discussion.

In late 1955 a writer for *The Nation* offered the opinion that the   10 shrewd use of premiums[3] as bait for kiddies could "mangle the parent's usual marketing consideration of need, price, quality and budget." He cited as one example General Electric's offer of a sixty-piece circus, a magic-ray gun, and a space helmet to children who brought their parents into dealers' stores to witness new GE refrigerators being demonstrated. Sylvania reportedly offered a complete Space Ranger kit with not only helmet but disintegrator, flying saucer, and space telephone to children who managed to deliver parents into salesrooms. And Nash cars offered a toy service station. This writer, Joseph Seldin, concluded: "Manipulation of children's minds in the fields of religion or politics would touch off a parental storm of protest and a rash of congressional investigations. But in the world of commerce children are fair game and legitimate prey."

Herb Sheldon, TV star with a large following of children, offered this 11 comment in 1956: "I don't say that children should be forced to harass their parents into buying products they've seen advertised on television, but at the same time I cannot close my eyes to the fact that it's being done every day." Then he added, and this was in *Advertising Agency* magazine, "Children are living, talking records of what we tell them every day."

Motivational analysts were called in to provide insights on the most   12 effective ways to achieve an assured strong impact with children. Social Research got into this problem with a television study entitled "Now, for the Kiddies . . . " It found that two basic factors to be considered in children's TV programs are filling the moppet's "inner needs" and making sure the program has "acceptability" (i.e., appease Mom, for one thing, so that she won't forbid the child to listen to it, which is an ever-present hazard). Social Research offered some psychological guideposts.

---

[2] A shill is someone who poses as a customer to convince others to buy a product.
[3] Premiums are gifts that encourage people to buy a certain product.

A show can "appeal" to a child, it found, without necessarily offer-   13
ing the child amusement or pleasure. It appeals if it helps him express
his inner tensions and fantasies in a manageable way. It appeals if it
gets him a little scared or mad or befuddled and then offers him a way
to get rid of his fear, anger, or befuddlement. Gauging the scariness of
a show is a difficult business because a show may be just right in scariness for an eight-year-old but too scary for a six-year-old and not scary
enough for a ten-year-old.

Social Research diagnosed the appeal of the highly successful Howdy   14
Doody and found some elements present that offered the children listening far more than childish amusement. Clarabelle, the naughty
clown, was found consistently to exhibit traits of rebellious children.
Clarabelle, it noted, "represents children's resistance to adult authority
and goes generally unpunished." The report stated: "In general the
show utilizes repressed hostilities to make fun of adults or depict adults
in an unattractive light. The 'bad' characters (Chief Thunderthud, Mr.
Bluster, Mr. X) are all adults. They are depicted either as frighteningly
powerful or silly." When the adult characters are shown in ridiculous
situations, such as being all tangled up in their coats or outwitted by
the puppets, the child characters in the show are shown as definitely
superior. "In other words," it explained, "there is a reversal process
with the adults acting 'childish' and incompetent, and children being
'adult' and clever." It added that the master of ceremonies, Buffalo Bob,
was more of a friendly safe uncle than a parent.

All this sly sniping at parent symbols takes place while Mother, un-   15
aware of the evident symbology, chats on the telephone content in the
knowledge that her children are being pleasantly amused by the childish antics being shown electronically on the family's wondrous pacifier.

In turning next to the space shows the Social Research psychologists   16
found here that the over-all format, whether the show was set in the
twenty-first century or the twenty-fourth, was: "Basic pattern of 'good
guys' versus 'bad men' with up-to-date scientific and mechanical trap-
ping." Note that it said bad men, not bad guys.

The good guys interestingly were found to be all young men in their   17
twenties organized as a group with very strong team loyalty. The leader
was pictured as a sort of older brother (not a father symbol). And the
villains or cowards were all older men who might be "symbolic or father figures." They were either bad or weak.

Much of this fare might be construed as being antiparent sniping,   18
offering children an exhilarating, and safe, way to work off their grudges
against their parents. "To children," the report explained, "adults are a
'ruling class' against which they cannot successfully revolt."

The report confided some pointers to TV producers for keeping par-   19
ents pacified. One way suggested was to take the parent's side in such
easy, thoughtful ways as having a character admonish junior to clean

his plate. Another good way was to "add an educational sugar coating. Calling a cowboy movie 'American history' and a space show 'scientific' seems to be an effective way to avoid parental complaints." A final hint dropped was: "Cater a little more to parents . . . . The implication that children can be talked into buying anything . . . irritates parents. Slight changes along these lines can avoid giving offense without losing appeal for the children."

Some of the United States product makers evidently solicit the favor   20
of moppets by building aggressive outlets right into their products. Public-relations counsel and motivational enthusiast E. L. Bernays was reported asserting in 1954 that the most successful breakfast cereals were building crunch into their appeal to appease hostility by giving outlet to aggressive and other feelings. (He has served as a counsel to food groups.) The cereal that promises "pop-snap-crackle" when you eat it evidently has something of value to kiddies besides calories.

One aspect of juvenile merchandising that intrigued the depth ma-   21
nipulators was the craze or fad. To a casual observer the juvenile craze for cowboys or knights or Davy Crockett may seem like a cute bit of froth on the surface of American life. To fad-wise merchandisers such manifestations are largely the result of careful manipulation. They can be enormously profitable or disastrously unprofitable, depending on the merchandiser's cunning.

An evidence of how big the business can be is that the Davy Crockett   22
craze of 1955, which gave birth to 300 Davy Crockett products, lured $300,000,000 from American pockets. Big persuasion indeed!

American merchandisers felt a need for a deeper understanding of   23
these craze phenomena so that they could not only share in the profits, but know when to unload. Research was needed to help the manufacturers avoid overestimating the length of the craze. Many were caught with warehouses full of "raccoon" tails and buckskin fringe when, almost without warning, the Crockett craze lost its lure. One manufacturer said: "When they die, they die a horrible death."

This problem of comprehending the craze drew the attention of such   24
motivation experts as Dr. Dichter and Alfred Politz. And *Tide* magazine, journal of merchandisers, devoted a major analysis to the craze.

The experts studied the Crockett extravaganza as a case in point and   25
concluded that its success was due to the fact that it had in good measure all of the three essential ingredients of a profitable fad: symbols, carrying device, and fulfillment of a subconscious need. The carrying device, and the experts agreed it was a superb one, was the song "Ballad of Davy Crockett," which was repeated in some form in every Disney show. Also it was richer in symbols than many of the fads: coonskin cap, fringed buckskin, flintlock rifle. *Tide* explained: "All popular movements from Christianity's cross to the Nazis' swastika have their distinctive symbols."

As for filling a subconscious need, Dr. Dichter had this to say of   26
Crockett: "Children are reaching for an opportunity to explain themselves in terms of the traditions of the country. Crockett gave them that
opportunity. On a very imaginative level the kids really felt they were
Davy Crockett . . . . "

What causes the quick downfall of crazes? The experts said over-   27
exploitation was one cause. Another cause was sociological. Mr. Politz
pointed out that crazes take a course from upper to lower. In the case
of adult fads this means upper-income education groups to lower. In
the case of children, Politz explained: "Those children who are leaders
because of their age adopt the fad first and then see it picked up by the
younger children, an age class they no longer wish to be identified
with. This causes the older children deliberately to drop the fad."

Both Politz and Dichter felt not only that with careful planning the   28
course of fads could be charted to ensure more profits to everybody,
but also that profitable fads could actually be created. *Tide* called this
possibility "fascinating." Dr. Dichter felt that with appropriate motivation research techniques a fad even of the Crockett magnitude could be
started, once the promoters had found, and geared their fad to, an un-
satisfied need of youngsters.

Politz felt that the research experts could certainly set up the general   29
rules for creating a successful fad. In a bow to the professional persuaders of advertising he added that once the general rules are laid down, the
"creative" touch is needed. Both he and Dr. Dichter agreed that this challenging task for the future—creating fads of the first magnitude for our
children—is the combined job of the researcher and the creative man.

_____ **Written Response**

How do you react to Packard's description of the ways that advertisers
attempt to sell products to children? Do you feel that you were affected
by this kind of advertising when you were a child? Are you affected by
this kind of advertising now?

_____ **Rhetorical Analysis**

1. In order to persuade his readers that motivational researchers and
advertisers are acting unethically, Packard "damns them with their own
words." He extensively quotes the speeches and articles of motivational
researchers and marketers in the hopes that his readers will see in their
words a desire to sell their product at any cost.

From "The Psycho-Seduction of Children," select a quotation from a
motivational researcher or marketer. What seems unethical about the
statement?

Do you feel that Packard's attempt to "damn them with their own
words" is effective? Why?

2. Packard's *The Hidden Persuaders* has continued to sell well since it was published in 1957. Based on the chapter that you have read, why do you feel that this book is so popular?

_____ **Interpretation**

1. What are the "inner needs" (or unconscious motives) that Packard feels advertisements and children's television shows of the 1950s attempt to fulfill? How will fulfilling these needs make the advertisement more effective or the television show more popular?

2. Describe a current advertisement directed toward children. How does the advertisement attempt to sell its product?

3. In *Social Psychology and Social Relevance* (Boston: Little, Brown, 1972), Alan C. Elms writes of motivational research and Packard's criticism of it:

> Motivational Research (MR) is a term loosely applied by public relations men, advertising agencies, and a scattering of psychologists to their attempted use of psychoanalytic concepts in advertising campaigns. Depth interviews, individual and group free-association sessions, projective tests, and related procedures have been employed to discover the unconscious or preconscious motivations associated with consumer behavior, in hopes that advertisers can manipulate these motivations to promote sales. The attitude-changing efficacy of MR-inspired ads has been trumpeted not only by the motivational researchers themselves but by their best-selling critics, notably Vance Packard. His book *The Hidden Persuaders* (1957), now approaching its fortieth paperback reprinting, was an exciting survey of "the use of mass psychoanalysis to guide campaigns of persuasion." Packard occasionally laughed at the motivational researchers' claims, but more often he viewed their powers with great alarm. Perhaps the discovery that "baking a cake traditionally is acting out the birth of a child," and that therefore the cakemix manufacturer should let the household wife add her own eggs and milk, represents little threat to our free will; but what of those motivational researchers who market political candidates, religions, entire ways of life? Most ad men are nice guys, according to Packard—"But when you are manipulating, where do you stop?"
>
> Packard didn't realize that the motivational researchers had hardly been able to get started. MR data were generally kept secret, so as not to give business competitors any advantages; but the research that was described sufficiently for independent evaluation seldom deserved to be called research. Concepts of research design and efforts at quantification were nil; consumer interviews were often conducted by unqualified personnel, in such brevity that even a professional psychologist would have been able to deduce little from them. The sweeping claims about consumer motivation often made by MR specialists seemed in most cases to derive as much from their own personal fantasies as from anything their research told them.
>
> Further, the basic assumptions of motivational research were highly questionable. Our daily decisions, including consumer decisions, may indeed rest partly on unconscious motives. But these motives and their

relationships to the outside world are likely to be very individualized, hard to discover, unreliable, and difficult to manipulate. The consumer may not be entirely rational in all his purchases, but that doesn't mean his irrationality can be conveniently channeled through a mass advertising campaign. Nor does any good evidence show that motivational researchers have been able to do so. Instances can be cited in which an ad man followed a motivational researcher's advice and apparently increased his company's sales by several million dollars as a result. But several million dollars may mean changes in the behavior of only a small fraction of an advertising campaign's audience. Such changes may derive instead from the layout director's artistic inspiration, or from competitors' stupidities (perhaps induced by their own MR men), or from sheer good luck. Neither advertisers nor motivational researchers like to waste their time with carefully controlled experiments, and they do not publicize their failures.

The Hidden Persuaders goes on selling, but hardly anyone in the advertising world mentions motivational research today. [pp. 163–164]*

Discuss Elms's critique of Packard. Which of his criticisms do you feel are valid?

_____ **WRITING ASSIGNMENTS**

1. Write an essay in which you analyze how an advertisement directed toward children works and then discuss whether you feel that the advertisement is ethical. In other words, do you feel that the advertisement in any way takes advantage of children?

2. Watch a Saturday morning children's program (one on commercial rather than educational television) and take detailed notes on what you observe. Then write about whether the ideas that Packard presents in "The Psycho-Seduction of Children" are still valid. In other words, do you feel that Packard's ideas are now dated?

3. Discuss how Plato's criticism of rhetoric is similar to Packard's criticism of advertising.

4. In *Subliminal Politics: Myths and Mythmaking in America* (Englewood Cliffs, N.J.: Prentice-Hall, 1980), Dan Nimmo and James E. Combs argue that those advertisers who work on political campaigns make use of a variety of political myths. They define myth as "a dramatic representation of past, present, or future events that people *believe*" (p. xii). They do not necessarily regard political myths as either true or false, good or bad.

One of the most common types of political myth is what Nimmo and Combs call the "macro-myth," which calls attention to the origin of our political order and the values that most Americans cherish. This kind of political mythmaking is evident in the following memorandum about the "Great Nation" myth, written by Kevin Phillips, who worked on Richard Nixon's 1968 media campaign:

_____

*Alan C. Elms, *Social Psychology and Social Relevance*. Boston: Little, Brown and Company, 1972.

> *Great Nation:* This is fine for national use, but viz local emphasis it strikes
> me as best suited to the South and heartland. They will like the great na-
> tion self-help, fields of waving wheat stuff and the general thrust of Prot-
> estant ethic imagery. . . . We need a red hot military music, land of pride
> and glory special for the South and Border. . . . We need more concern for
> the countryside, its values and farmers' welfare spot, complete with thresh-
> ers, siloes, Aberdeen Angus herds, et al.

The other types of myth that Nimmo and Combs find in American politics are (a) the myth of "we" and "they," as in we the Democrats do this,
but they the Republicans do that; (b) the invocation of political heroes,
such as Abraham Lincoln and F. D. R.; and (c) the elevation of a candi-
date to the status of a hero by creating a compelling—though not always
accurate—story of his or her life.

Study examples of advertising (print advertisements, television commercials, and radio commercials) to find some that employ myths; then
either expose this technique of advertising as Packard exposed the techniques of depth persuasion in *The Hidden Persuaders,* or argue that this
technique is ethical and acceptable.

An Apology for Advertising

In 1964, while the advertising world was rocking in the wake of Packard's
The Hidden Persuaders, John Hobson, then the chair of a leading British
advertising agency, delivered a series of lectures to the Royal Society of
Arts. In one of the lectures, Hobson directly addresses Packard's book:

> A lot has been written and spoken about 'hidden persuaders' since Vance
> Packard's book was written. Certainly the book over-dramatized what is a
> very natural and sensible process. Let us be clear that in buying, as in
> many aspects of life, the number of decisions that can be taken on strictly
> rational grounds is very few; not only because it is seldom possible to as-
> semble all the facts, but also because rational decisions involve a painful
> and complicated mental process which only a few people are either capable
> or willing to undertake. Therefore the majority of decisions are made out of
> feelings, habits, instincts and impulses. It is common sense therefore to try
> to chart those feelings, habits and impulses which surround the purchase
> of goods you are selling. There is nothing much more sinister in doing so
> (although people have represented it as sinister) than in the Vicar, who
> wants a contribution to the Church Roof Fund from his rich parishioner,
> starting the conversation on the subject of the old brasses in which he
> knows she is particularly interested.

As is clear from this quotation, Hobson is as ardent a defender of advertising as Packard is a critic. In "The Influence and Techniques of Modern
Advertising," the first of his three lectures, Hobson addresses the criticisms that Packard and others have hurled at the advertising industry.

In his lecture, Hobson argues that advertising plays an essential role in the economy of modern capitalism. Toward that argument, he discusses the law of supply and demand (*supply* refers to the amount of a particular product available for sale; *demand* refers to the degree to which the public wants to buy the product).

What would you expect to happen if a product were mass-produced so that supply was increased but demand remained the same?

How might advertising affect the relationship between supply and demand?

The Social and Economic Context of Advertising

John Hobson

I am delighted that the Royal Society of Arts have thought fit to   1
make advertising the subject of these three Cantor Lectures. Not only
is advertising one of the most notable areas where the arts, industry
and commerce meet. It is also the outward and visible sign of one of
the most important social phenomena of the mid-twentieth century in
this country—backstreet abundance,[1] the percolation to the mass level
of a substantial purchasing power. Certainly advertising would not exist without that mass purchasing power; but I venture to assert, too,
that back-street abundance would not exist without advertising.

I am the Chairman of an advertising agency; so you will not expect   2
me to be other than biased in favour of my occupation. I am fascinated
by its creativity; its techniques; its vast range of human, social and industrial interest. But I can see that it is open to some question and
even some criticism, and I shall try to put a fair and honest appraisal of
the subject in front of you. I am going to confine my remarks largely to
mass consumer goods advertising. The £225 million of mass consumer
advertising is the area in which discussion is most needed and most
challenging.

Lastly by way of preamble, I must remind you that inevitably I am   3
speaking in the context of the society and the economics that exist today in Britain; where an individual is rightly accorded a measure of free

Source: "The Social and Economic Context of Advertising" by John Hobson, *Journal of the Royal Society of Arts*, Vol. CXII, No. 5096, July 1964. Reprinted by permission of The Royal Society of Arts, London.

_____

[1] By *backstreet abundance*, Hobson means that poor people are able to buy more goods.

will and free choice, some opportunity to be right or wrong in his own decision; where there is free competition and a drive for profits. If you prefer an authoritarian society and economy, in which some authority decides for everyone what his tastes should be, what is best for him, what profits he should make, and what the limits of his objectives should be, then you alter the terms of reference and you would not necessarily want advertising in exactly its present shape; you might not even want it at all, though I rather doubt the latter.

Before I launch into my main topics, I need to clear away two com- 4 mon confusions about advertising. First, advertising is not (as some people seem to imagine) something in its own right, some separate estate of the realm, like civil administration, or the Services, or law. Advertising is an integral and essential part of industry—its projection into the vital department of selling. This misconception is so widespread that, at the Labour Party Conference last autumn, one delegate could talk of 'curtailing the power of the advertising industry'. He should rather have said, 'curtailing the power of industry to sell its products'.

There are indeed advertising specialists serving industry just as there 5 are engineers serving ships. But their sailing orders come from the bridge, and on the bridge are the captains of industry. Advertising reflects industry's intentions and will, its strengths and weaknesses. Indeed, it does more than reflect them—it projects them on to the biggest screen possible. For the most part British industry's intentions are honest, honourable and fair. Most manufacturers believe implicitly that they have succeeded in making products that are better than competitive ones in properties, performance or value. They may sometimes be mistaken, but their belief is honest. This confidence they translate into their advertising, and their advertising technicians are advocates of that confidence. When, however, competition drives or sheer survival demands, industry will signal from the bridge to the engine-room to increase the power, quicken the pace, or change the direction, and advertising is in no position to refuse.

The second misconception I want to clear away is about the true 6 function of advertising. Advertising is selling. Nicholas Kaldor in an important article in the *Journal of Economic Studies* some years ago attempted an interesting appraisal of advertising; but since he started with the wrong premise that the function of advertising is to inform, he produced some notably erroneous conclusions. The object of advertising is not basically to inform, but to inform for the purpose of selling. The information given will be that which is calculated to help the proposition. No one is going to pay large sums of money to give information which hinders his proposition. Often the amount of information is valid; sometimes it is minimal because there is no new information to give. Advertising neither is nor can be a disinterested service of consumer information. It is salesmanship on a mass scale and it is well to start this discussion with all the cards upwards on the table.

That advertising is a vital part of modern economics is proved by the   7
fact that it exists and thrives in every country where the economics of
abundance apply. You cannot have production without consumption. It
is absurd to have a National Productivity Year and official NEDC[2] targets
of production increase, without the means of stimulating consumption.
Or are we to be for ever bedevilled by that typical British fetish that
production is *'good'* but consumption is *'bad'*? We live in a society in
which the mass of the people already have more than a sufficiency of
necessities, and where the extra consumption must take the form of
optional benefits ranging from necessary extras to sheer luxuries. The
old models of the classical economists are out of date: the models which
assume a certain level of demand for bushels of wheat or tons of coal,
and play around with supply and price variables. In the context of consumer buying, such cosy, arithmetical factors as price-elasticity in a
market are of far less importance than the elusive subjective factors of
intensity of want. This always baffles and irritates the old-fashioned
economists. An automatic demand does not exist for the types of extra
production now coming forward; it has to be created.

Professor Galbraith in *The Affluent Society* pointed out that the eco-   8
nomic objectives of the last century have been the increase of production. He believes they should be changed, but for the moment they are
so; and while they are so, production has got to find a complementary
consumption. We *must* create an acquisitive society if this extra production is not to pile up in the warehouses.

In a recent speech Lord Robens referred to the NEDC target of a   9
4 percent increase in production. After eliminating the increase corre-
lated with growth of population and of exports, he pointed out that we
shall need *each year* a 2.8 per cent increase of domestic consumer production—compared with a 2.1 per cent growth in recent years. This
represents an annual increase of £500 million in domestic consumption
and it is an accepted Government target. He added that it cannot be
achieved without the power of advertising to stimulate consumption.
'Industry', he said, 'must not have one hand tied behind its back.'

There may be other ways of disposing of increased production, such   10
as giving it to backward countries, but the present state of public opinion and domestic politics admits only of marginal disposals in this way.
The rest must be consumed by the home consumer, and the consumer
must *like* consuming it. It is the job of advertising and salesmanship on
behalf of industry to make the consumer *want* to consume more. Or is
this necessary consumption to be a frigid, joyless process without preliminary wooing?

---

[2] NEDC: the National Economic Development Council, a British governmental agency that
makes economic forecasts.

This brings me to the service which advertising performs for the industry which pays for it. Let us be clear that industry does not spend £225 million each year on advertising in order to see its name in the papers. It does so because advertising performs an indispensable service for it. It assures to the manufacturer the mass consumption necessary to match his mass production. That mass production involves high initial and investment risks, and much of this risk could never be undertaken without the assurance of mass consumption. **11**

However, the process does not merely assure a total demand; advertising can help to stabilize demand. It helps to assure the stability and rhythm of the type of mass distribution needed. It can do much to even out seasonal fluctuations of demand. It can smooth out the turmoil of events which result from dynamic competitive innovations. It can offer the opportunity to exploit new inventions and improvements. It can result in a quicker build up of demand which reduces the pay-off period of new machinery, new buildings, research investment. The assurance of steady demand justifies longer-term contracts for raw materials, and this increases stability and reduces costs all down the line right to the raw material producers. **12**

The growth of quantity production, through constantly improving production techniques, and assisted by the confidence in demand created by advertising, is now in its turn the true cause of backstreet abundance, as I have called it. Mass production reduces the real cost of goods and makes them more and more widely available. The price which has to be paid for mass production is some degree of standardization of products, but it is a small price to suffer for a process which brings more and more utilities, pleasures and recreations within the purchasing power of the mass of the population. The rise in the mass standard of living, the competitiveness of industry which results in better and better products coming forward each year, and the stabilization of full employment, these are the fruits of mass production assisted by mass salesmanship which is advertising. Poverty, maybe, still exists here and there, but it is a relative word. Sufficiency and abundance are seen everywhere. **13**

In this context may I touch on the cost of advertising. Advertising is one of the selling costs of a product, like packaging or running a sales force or paying a retail margin. In this sense the public pays for the advertising, as indeed it pays for the costs of ingredients, or the production costs, or the other costs of selling comprised in the ultimate buying price. **14**

But in a much more real sense advertising helps to lower prices: because mass production assuredly lowers unit costs and advertising is indispensable, in a free economy, to mass production. Like the installation of a wonderful new very efficient production machine (which no one would query in principle), advertising *pays for itself*, and more, out **15** of the savings in the unit cost through quantity production. If advertising ceased to exist, most consumer goods would in the long run, or most likely the short run, go up in price.

The main criticism of advertising in its economic aspects, I think, is **16** that there is more of it than is needed to fulfil the economic and industrial function required of it. Much has been made of an old, old saying of Lord Leverhulme about 'half my advertising is wasted but I do not know which half'. There is thought to be wasteful competition. There is a general imputation of slap-dash spending of very large sums of money. This leads to suggestions of restriction and even of taxation.

The figures show that, expressed as a percentage of the Gross Na- **17** tional Product, expenditure on advertising is at just about the same level now as it was in 1938. Of course, just after the war the percentage was lower, but at that time the need to stimulate consumption was not so great. The stability of this percentage in pre-war and recent post-war years suggests that as far as the British market is concerned the process has found its level and is unlikely to increase or decrease much.

Modern methods of assessing results from advertising are far more **18** efficient than those of the pre-war or early post-war period. They are not yet perfect but they are improving every year; Lord Leverhulme's saying is no longer true in any major degree. The industrialists who spend large sums on advertising are no fools.

The idea that competitive advertising of brands in the same market is **19** wasteful, is not true in practice. Although it might seem to an outsider that they are merely spending to take business away from each other, this is not in fact what happens. What happens is that their joint spending widens the total market for the product group and both advertisers are well repaid for their efforts. I have seen it happen over and over again.

Of course, there are times when new products are launched ill- **20** advisedly, or extra spending is put into existing products unsuccessfully. There are the occasions when excessive or stubborn optimism overrules good judgement and when, to put it plainly, the manufacturers make a mistake. But unless one envisages a government bureau to decide what shall be sold, and who shall be allowed to progress, and what new initiatives may be undertaken, such misjudgements are unavoidable. They are a normal price of progress.

A restriction or tax on advertising must be a restriction or tax on ini- **21** tiative and on development. If we need more consumption then we must not inhibit the initiatives or the investment in securing it. The industrialists may surely be left to decide for themselves what initiatives and what volume of activity are compatible with running a sound business.

To return to my main theme. Increased production presupposes in- **22** creased consumption. But increased consumption cannot be achieved merely by making an increase of goods available. It can only be achieved by making the products *wanted*. This raises the question of salesmanship, which, on a mass scale, is what advertising is. Incidentally, advertising is accused of creating wants. This is not a true picture: advertising evokes and activates latent wants, which people never realized they had the means of satisfying. The failures of marketing almost always reside in the failure to assess rightly whether a true want exists. You cannot create a want which does not exist.

The economic phenomenon of abundance at mass level has a natural complement in what historians will, I think, recognize as one of the social phenomena of the century—the rise in importance of salesmanship. In the eyes of a limited intellectual and upper class minority—but I suspect this audience will include such people in a substantial majority—salesmanship is not quite respectable. In the eyes of the great majority of the public it presents very little problem. On the whole, you know, people enjoy being sold things.   **23**

In 'salesmanship' I comprise two separate elements. First, the whole complex of activities by which a cornucopia of goods and services and pleasures is spilled out in front of the mass consumer; by which his every next want is assessed and provided for; and of which advertising is the most obvious and ubiquitous outward and visible sign. The consumer is king; his wants are law; and a whole host of specialists is studying how best to cater to them. The impetus of the development derives from two forces that cannot be resisted: the new mass spending power and the democratic expectation of being allowed to exercise choice and free will.   **24**

Second, the techniques of salesmanship. These are of course the more tangible of the two elements, and they are therefore used as the main target.   **25**

A powerful new force such as salesmanship naturally meets fierce resistance from those elements in society whose existing power it is diminishing. We have seen the same resistance to 'trade' as an occupation as late as at the turn of the century. But the clock cannot be turned back and there is ample evidence that the new generations in the Establishment, in industry and in commerce are recognizing and accepting the new force.   **26**

However, the rearguard of conservative social forces have one relatively easy target. Advertising magnifies each day on to a huge projection the difference between the accepted ethics of everyday life and the true philosophical or religious ethics to which each of us in our best moments aspires. For example, by its nature advertising deals in partial truths, not in whole truths. It claims the favourable aspects of the truth about the product it sells, and is silent about the less favourable. It is content if what it says is true for some people on some occasions, even if it cannot be universally true. In short it behaves as ordinary people behave, and I think you would have to be very self-righteous to blame it for that.   **27**

The law in its ancient wisdom has accepted that this is permissible in   **28**
selling, and it is recognized as common practice and common sense.
Indeed, the simple words and images comprehensible to the mass market could not possibly comprise the universal truth. Moreover, selling is
accepted behaviour in a vast range of other contexts: selling political or
social ideas; selling projects across a committee table; selling one's own
personality in every phase of personal relations; and so on. Selling is as
old as human relations and it has been accepted as common practice.
The advocacy of ideas, it seems, is applauded; but the selling of goods
is rejected. Yet good goods are as valuable as good ideas; and, assuredly, bad ideas are far more dangerous than bad goods.

The real problem is that what is accepted common practice in private,   **29**
or on a small scale, can easily be subjected to criticism when shown up
in the limelight of mass proportions.

What is vital therefore is that the beneficial power of this new force of   **30**
mass salesmanship should neither attract fair criticism nor overstep acceptable limits by being allowed to become misleading or irresponsible.
In its earlier phases advertising was often irresponsible and occasionally it still is. The best safeguard lies in the attitude of the industry that
sponsors it and the people who practise it. The licence of salesmanship
must not be allowed to develop into licentiousness.

What then are the reasonable safeguards that the community must   **31**
have to channel this dynamic into its most beneficial direction? There is
a strong movement nowadays in the name of 'consumer protection'.
This movement says, 'If the powerful voice of advertising is merely representing the favourable aspects of its products, should not the public
have the right to full and precise information on the pros and cons of
these products alongside the advertising claims?' The theory is fine; the
practice is virtually unworkable. The average public would far rather
invest a few shillings to find out whether a product lives up to its claim
than read some elaborate objective evaluation. Nor do people really
trust the rounded-off 'best buy' pronouncement of some remote, unseen authority. Their own experiences, or the say-so of friends or relations, are far more convincing. The great majority of consumers would
not use this kind of protection, if it were provided.

In my judgement and experience there are three great safeguards of   **32**
the buyer in relation to salesmanship through advertising.

The first is that (unlike the salesman at the door, for example) the   **33**
advertiser depends on repeat selling, not on a single sale. If his propositions are extravagant or misleading, and his product on its first purchase fails to live up to the promises in its advertising, he will suffer a
serious loss.

The second is that people who see and hear advertisements are well   **34**
aware that they are being sold something, and they discount a large
measure of what is said. Talk to them and they will say 'I never believe
what the adverts tell me'. By this they mean they mentally prefix to the

reading of each advertisement the thought 'the advertiser says . . . '.
They distil out of it instinctively as much as they can believe might be
true for them personally. Some people worry that children may be
over-credulous on exposure to good advertising. This is possible. It is a
worry best met, as one of my colleagues said in a speech recently, by
teaching children to put the mental prefix to each advertisement 'the advertiser says . . . '.

The third safeguard lies in all that has been done during the last   **35**
sixty years to prevent misleading claims from irresponsible advertisers.
Not only have industry and its advertising technicians adopted higher
standards, but there has been legislation like the Merchandise Marks
Act. However, legislation itself is not the right answer—it can never be
watertight. Recently the sections of industry and commerce concerned
with advertising have consolidated into a single code, 'the British Code
of Advertising Practice', the various existing rules governing advertising
claims, and have adopted—with the agreement of the principal media—the sanction that advertisements which offend these standards are
debarred from publication. The governing body is called the Advertising Standards Authority, formed half from advertising and half from
non-advertising interests, with an independent Chairman. The executive body is called the Code of Advertising Practice Committee, which
sets up the codes and deals with the cases arising under them. Then
there is the Advertisement Investigation Department of the Advertising
Association which investigates the validity of claims, and there are experts available on most subjects to advise on the facts. It is a system
which is as watertight as it can be. It may not prevent some fly-by-
night advertiser from offering spurious wares in some obscure local medium but it will go a long way to preventing serious abuses. Let me
only add that, although this new and elaborate machinery has only recently been established, the responsible media have for years done their
utmost to check on advertisement claims, especially on television,
which is a special case because of the provisions of the Television Act.
For the most part those checks have been successful in eliminating false
claims; but the system will now be tighter.

My own appraisal therefore of this whole issue is that the balance   **36**
of strength between the drive of the seller for more sales, and the natural caution and resistance of the buyer (which is in fact the current balance, and which has grown up in a free society over many centuries), is
still the best system, and cannot be replaced by externally imposed limitations on either the buyer or the seller. In this balance of strength,
salesmanship and advertising, which is mass salesmanship, play their
part on behalf of the seller; and caution, inertia and habit as well as
judgement, play their part for the buyer. No one should ever underrate
the capacity of the British public to divine and assess the true values of
what is offered. It is erroneous as well as patronizing to think it can
easily be fooled. The public is very adult and can be treated as such.

This is not to say that within this pattern there is not a case for every
reasonable limitation on unfair selling and every possible protection for
incautious or ignorant buying—and these precautions are being more
and more devised by all concerned in the business. But we know this
pattern works; all the alternatives are untried.

There are other arguments brought against advertising in its social   37
context: that the whole overwhelming pressure of expert communication to sell things is tending to create a materialistic outlook and an 'acquisitive society'; and secondly, that it debases taste.

To the first of these propositions I must reply 'Yes, the effect of ad-   38
vertising volume is to concentrate people's minds on the pleasures of
acquiring, owning, enjoying materialistic benefits.'

We are dealing with a subject which is very much a matter of point   39
of view. Our politics, our economics, our whole basic drive, whether
from industry or the trade unions, from the City or from the Labour
Party, has been to raise the material well-being of the masses of the
population. Who is to say that it is right to ensure that people have
a sufficiency of bread and meat, but wrong that they have a variety
of attractive foods to choose from? That is it right for women to be released from drudgery, but wrong for the process to go as far as offering
them washing machines, mixers, frozen peas or gay curtain material?
That we should all have holidays with pay not but to be tempted to
take those holidays abroad? And so on?

Let us remember all the time that all the needs of production-   40
oriented economics, all the maintenance of full employment, all the
progressive discoveries of modern science, and all the drives of past
history, have tended to focus on material betterment for people and
nations.

The ascetic, the puritan, the idealist may have other views, but I sus-   41
pect that very often they are essentially egotistic views proceeding from
a personal dislike of possessions. They positively dislike and fear abundance, particularly backstreet abundance. I respect these as personal
attitudes. But I do not think that they are compatible with the daily activities of 99 per cent of our population who, in the backstreets or the
suburbs, are involved in a struggle for material livelihoods and comforts.

Moreover the achievement of a better materialistic standard of living,   42
the struggle out of the slum outlook, in which the drive for self-better-
ment fostered by advertising plays so great a part, can be the finest
foundation for further *non*-materialistic aspirations. In any case we cannot put the economic clock back, to satisfy the ascetics. Modern economics are the economics of abundance, in which the demand for,
and the acquisition and consumption of, goods are an indispensable
counterpart of more and more efficient and plentiful production.

The second proposition, that advertising lowers literary usage and   43
standards of taste, and produces debased images and motivations, is to

my mind an absurd generalization (though there may be a few cases which can be truly cited). It is of course a view heard from a limited minority, and it proceeds from an intellectual and social snobbery resulting from a complete lack of contact between those people and the vast majority of their fellow countrymen. An eminent leader of public opinion, highly regarded in Government circles, and the Chairman of a number of Royal and other Commissions said to me recently that he approved of the advertising found in *The Times*, but totally disapproved on literary grounds of certain popular advertising found in the *Daily Mirror* and elsewhere. Now what kind of human understanding does that remark reveal? The job of advertising is to communicate with the potential market. If we talk to *Times* readers we talk in *Times* language; but if we want to talk to the *Daily Mirror* readers we might almost as well talk in Russian as talk in *Times* language. To communicate with the people we have to accept and to use their vocabulary, their motives and interests, their ideas of fun, their standard of visual images, just as their favourite newspapers do, or their favourite television programmes.

We hear criticisms that the trivialities of advertising smother the   **44** means of important communication. It is true that advertising deals mainly with trivialities—the choice between two beers or two toothpastes must rest on trivialities. But if those who thought they had something important to say to the people would only come down off their pontifical high horses and their classical educations, and use the idioms and images of the people—like negro spirituals or Churchill's speeches—they would, I feel sure, find that they were getting the attention they expect.

In its language and its visual images, in the motives or the aspira-   **45** tions it evidences, advertising reflects without flattery the values of the society we live in. Advertising that hypocritically assumed that tastes and motives were higher than they are, would simply fail to do its primary job. Nor is it the province of advertising to educate or uplift; that is for the educators and the preachers. Advertising is the mirror of our society and if the face we see in the mirror is, on occasion, more ugly or illiterate than we hoped, it is no good solving the problem by breaking the mirror.

Now I do not mean to disparage fine ideals and high standards; and   **46** I certainly do not underrate the basic problem which lies in the fact that a great and powerful system of communication, with all its capacity for social good or evil, is motivated and governed by industry seeking its own economic ends. This is indeed a paradox which needs deep reflection. But society must expect, and on the whole does find, that its industrialists have a sense of the responsibility this power entails. Society must build up countervailing forces to promote the interests of non-materialistic well-being, because we all of us know that there are vital factors of well-being that lie outside the materialistic areas. But I say that advertising itself cannot be expected to be schizophrenic; it has its job to do, and it must do it, and it is a job of great value to the community.

I recall one incident which seems to me to crystallize the whole essence of the problem of advertising's social context. A well-known and highly respected Quaker industrialist once said to me, as he approved his vast advertising budgets, 'advertising is a necessary evil'. To him as an industrialist advertising was essential; to him as a Quaker it was an evil. Which is the greater good: the prosperity of an industry which ensures the livelihood of thousands of families and meets the legitimate needs of millions—or the very real and honourable convictions of Quaker asceticism?   47

These words crystallize the paradox of modern advertising. On the one hand we have a system which is indispensable to the health of our consumer industries, to the abundance of our people's standard of living, to the life-or-death struggle for exports in a competitive world. On the other hand we have the creation of a materialistic society, the question of the partial truths of salesmanship, the risks involved in putting a vast social power into the hands of industry seeking its economic salvation.   48

The solution to a paradox must, I think, be compromise. Salesmanship, and in particular public salesmanship in the form of advertising, must be allowed pressures. But we must demand responsible salesmanship, highly self-critical, conscious exactly of the line of truth and good manners that it must not overstep. This is not a problem for the law or the Government; such matters cannot be handled by written law. It is the job of industry that pays for advertising and governs it, of the technicians who practise it, and of the pressure of public opinion, to exercise the necessary restraint. The minority view of asceticism, the Puritan strain in our make-up, the eyebrow-raising of the out-of-touch intellectual, must not overpower and outweigh the majority needs of a better living standard, but neither must they be ignored. We need salesmanship in our society, but it must be *responsible salesmanship,* and this I believe is what modern industry and modern advertising are striving to give us.   49

Written Response

Hobson argues that advertising creates "backstreet abundance": What does he mean by this? How does he believe that advertising can create "backstreet abundance"? Do you agree with him?

Rhetorical Analysis

1. Richard Weaver, an American rhetorician of the early twentieth century, wrote of the persuasive power of "god terms" and "devil terms." If a writer or speaker wishes to create a positive attitude toward some person or idea, he or she associates that person or idea with "god terms"—words that have positive connotations (in our culture some examples are *democracy, freedom,* and so on). If a writer or speaker wishes to create a negative attitude toward some person or idea, he or she associates that person or idea with "devil terms"—words that have negative connotations (*communism, slavery,* and so on).

Does Hobson associate advertising with any "god terms"? Does he associate his opponents with any "devil terms"?

2. Since Aristotle's time, rhetoricians have argued that *ethos* (the quality of a speaker's or writer's character as presented in a text) contributes greatly to how readily an audience is persuaded. If a speaker or writer appears to be honest, good, concerned about others, and competent, then an audience will be more inclined to believe what he or she says. If the speaker or writer appears to be dishonest, self-serving, and poorly prepared, then the audience will be less inclined to believe what he or she says.

How would you assess Hobson's character (his *ethos*) as it comes through in his text? Is he the kind of person you are inclined to believe?

3. Writers are often faced with the difficulty of trying to adapt to the diverse beliefs of a heterogeneous audience. Hobson, for example, probably realized that some members of his audience would be business executives who would be concerned primarily about whether or not advertising works. He probably also realized that some members of his audience might be more concerned about how advertising seems to manipulate the consumer.

If Hobson tried to please the business executives by saying that advertisements can manipulate consumers into buying anything, how would those people concerned about the rights of the consumer react?

If Hobson said that advertising did not affect a consumer's decision-making (did not manipulate the consumer), how would the business executives react?

If he wishes to please (or, at least, not offend) each side, Hobson has to operate within a rhetorical dialectic. He has to formulate his comments so that they move between the extremes of "I, as an advertiser, can manipulate consumers into buying anything" and "I, as an advertiser, allow the consumer freedom of choice." How does Hobson operate within this rhetorical dialectic? In other words, how does he argue that advertising is good for everyone?

Interpretation

1. Below is a series of statements from Hobson's lecture. Read each statement, and then put it into your own words.

> Incidentally, advertising neither is nor can be a disinterested service of consumer information.

Advertising is accused of creating wants. This is not the true picture: advertising evokes and activates latent wants, which people never realized they had the means of satisfying.

On the whole, you know, people enjoy being sold things.

The consumer is king; his wants are law; and a whole host of specialists is studying how best to cater to them.

Yet good goods are as valuable as good ideas; and, assuredly, bad ideas are far more dangerous than bad goods.

The theory [of consumer protection] is fine; the practice is virtually unworkable.

Advertising is the mirror of our society and if the face we see in the mirror is, on occasion, more ugly and illiterate than we hoped, it is no good solving the problem by breaking the mirror.

Discuss whether you agree with each statement.

2. In his speech, Hobson discusses the role of supply and demand from the perspective of a capitalist. Karl Marx and Frederick Engels were also interested in this issue because they believed that fluctuations in supply and demand would eventually contribute to a collapse of capitalism and the initiation of revolution. In "Outlines of a Critique of Political Economy" (*Economic and Philosophic Manuscripts of 1844* [Foreign Languages Publishing House, 1961]), Engels wrote:

The law of competition is that demand and supply always strive to complement each other, and therefore never do so. The two sides are torn apart again and transformed into flat opposition. Supply always follows close on demand without ever quite covering it. It is either too big or too small, never corresponding to demand; because in this unconscious condition of mankind no one knows how big supply or demand is. If demand is greater than supply, the price rises and, as a result, supply is to a certain degree stimulated. As soon as it comes on the market, prices fall; and if it becomes greater than demand, then the fall in prices is so significant that demand is once again stimulated. So it goes on unendingly—a permanently unhealthy state of affairs—a constant alternation of overstimulation and collapse which precludes all advance—a state of perpetual fluctuation perpetually unresolved. [p. 195]

How is the way that Engels discusses the law of supply and demand different from the way that Hobson discusses it? In what way does Hobson feel that advertising will interact with the law of supply and demand?

_____ **WRITING ASSIGNMENTS**

1. After investigating current approaches to advertising (you can do so by collecting print advertisements from magazines or studying television

advertisements), use Packard's and Hobson's essays to either defend or denounce the practice of advertising.

2. In his speech, Hobson attempts to defend advertising against critics such as Packard. Analyze how effectively (or ineffectively) Hobson defends advertising.

3. How are the defenses of rhetoric by Aristotle, Isocrates, and St. Augustine similar to Hobson's defense of advertising?

Propaganda and Ethics

In November 1923, the National Socialist movement (or the Nazi Party), which Adolf Hitler helped to form and develop, launched an unsuccessful insurrection against the German government. While spending 13 months in prison for his part in the failed coup, Hitler wrote *Mein Kampf*. The book at times seems to ramble on without any clear purpose as Hitler describes the formation of his character during childhood, discusses his belief that Jews were responsible for the problems of Western civilization, and shares his vision of future greatness for the German people. As one reads on, however, it becomes more apparent that Hitler's purpose in writing the book was to present himself as the kind of hero, thinker, and leader who could bring Germany to greatness.

In "War Propaganda," a chapter from *Mein Kampf*, Hitler describes how he, as a young soldier during World War I, studied the effective use of propaganda by the British and the ineffective use of it by the Germans. He describes what he believes to be the techniques of an effective propaganda campaign, which he would later employ during World War II.

_____ **Prereading**

What do you believe to be the key elements of propaganda? How does propaganda differ from persuasion? How does it differ from advertising?

War Propaganda
Adolf Hitler

Ever since I have been scrutinizing political events, I have taken a   1
tremendous interest in propagandist activity. I saw that the Socialist-

Source: "War Propaganda" from *Mein Kampf* by Adolf Hitler, translated by Ralph Manheim. Copyright 1943 and copyright © renewed 1971 by Houghton Mifflin Company. Reprinted by permission of Houghton Mifflin Company and Hutchinson Publishing Ltd.

Marxist organizations mastered and applied this instrument with astounding skill. And I soon realized that the correct use of propaganda is a true art which has remained practically unknown to the bourgeois parties. Only the Christian-Social movement, especially in Lueger's[1] time, achieved a certain virtuosity on this instrument, to which it owed many of its successes.

But it was not until the War that it became evident what immense   2 results could be obtained by a correct application of propaganda. Here again, unfortunately, all our studying had to be done on the enemy side, for the activity on our side was modest, to say the least. The total miscarriage of the German 'enlightenment' service[2] stared every soldier in the face, and this spurred me to take up the question of propaganda even more deeply than before.

There was often more than enough time for thinking, and the enemy 3 offered practical instruction which, to our sorrow, was only too good.

For what we failed to do, the enemy did, with amazing skill and re- 4 ally brilliant calculation. I, myself, learned enormously from this enemy war propaganda. But time passed and left no trace in the minds of all those who should have benefited; partly because they considered themselves too clever to learn from the enemy, partly owing to lack of good will.

Did we have anything you could call propaganda?   5

I regret that I must answer in the negative. Everything that actually 6 was done in this field was so inadequate and wrong from the very start that it certainly did no good and sometimes did actual harm.

The form was inadequate, the substance was psychologically wrong: 7 a careful examination of German war propaganda can lead to no other diagnosis.

There seems to have been no clarity on the very first question: Is pro- 8 paganda a means or an end?

It is a means and must therefore be judged with regard to its end. It 9 must consequently take a form calculated to support the aim which it serves. It is also obvious that its aim can vary in importance from the standpoint of general need, and that the inner value of the propaganda will vary accordingly. The aim for which we were fighting the War was the loftiest, the most overpowering, that man can conceive: it was the freedom and independence of our nation, the security of our future food supply, and—our national honor; a thing which, despite all contrary opinions prevailing today, nevertheless exists, or rather should exist, since peoples without honor have sooner or later lost their freedom and independence, which in turn is only the result of a higher

---

[1] Dr. Karl Lueger, a member of the Christian Social Party (which expressed anti-Semitic and nationalistic views), was elected mayor of Vienna when Hitler was a young boy.
[2] "German 'enlightenment' service" is Hitler's sarcastic way of referring to the German propaganda program during WWI.

justice, since generations of rabble without honor deserve no freedom. Any man who wants to be a cowardly slave can have no honor, or honor itself would soon fall into general contempt.

The German nation was engaged in a struggle for a human existence,   **10** and the purpose of war propaganda should have been to support this struggle; its aim to help bring about victory.

When the nations on this planet fight for existence—when the ques-   **11** tion of destiny, 'to be or not to be,' cries out for a solution—then all considerations of humanitarianism or aesthetics crumble into nothing-ness; for all these concepts do not float about in the ether, they arise from man's imagination and are bound up with man. When he departs from this world, these concepts are again dissolved into nothingness, for Nature does not know them. And even among mankind, they be-long only to a few nations or rather races, and this in proportion as they emanate from the feeling of the nation or race in question. Hu-manitarianism and aesthetics would vanish even from a world inhab-ited by man if this world were to lose the races that have created and upheld these concepts.

But all such concepts become secondary when a nation is fighting for   **12** its existence; in fact, they become totally irrelevant to the forms of the struggle as soon as a situation arises where they might paralyze a struggling nation's power of self-preservation. And that has always been their only visible result.

As for humanitarianism, Moltke[3] said years ago that in war it lies in   **13** the brevity of the operation, and that means that the most aggressive fighting technique is the most humane.

But when people try to approach these questions with drivel about   **14** aesthetics, etc., really only one answer is possible: where the destiny and existence of a people are at stake, all obligation toward beauty ceases. The most unbeautiful thing there can be in human life is and remains the yoke of slavery. Or do these Schwabing[4] decadents view the present lot of the German people as 'aesthetic'? Certainly we don't have to discuss these matters with the Jews, the most modern inventors of this cultural perfume. Their whole existence is an embodied protest against the aesthetics of the Lord's image.

And since these criteria of humanitarianism and beauty must be   **15** eliminated from the struggle, they are also inapplicable to propaganda.

Propaganda in the War was a means to an end, and the end was the   **16** struggle for the existence of the German people; consequently, propa-ganda could only be considered in accordance with the principles that were valid for this struggle. In this case the most cruel weapons were

---

[3] General Helmuth von Moltke (1800–1891) became chief of the Prussian General Staff in 1859.

[4] Schwabing: a bohemian section of Munich.

humane if they brought about a quicker victory; and only those methods were beautiful which helped the nation to safeguard the dignity of its freedom.

This was the only possible attitude toward war propaganda in a life-   17
and-death struggle like ours.

If the so-called responsible authorities had been clear on this point,   18
they would never have fallen into such uncertainty over the form and
application of this weapon: for even propaganda is no more than a
weapon, though a frightful one in the hand of an expert.

The second really decisive question was this: To whom should propa-   19
ganda be addressed? To the scientifically trained intelligentsia or to the
less educated masses?

It must be addressed always and exclusively to the masses.   20

What the intelligentsia—or those who today unfortunately often go   21
by that name—what they need is not propaganda but scientific instruction. The content of propaganda is not science any more than the object
represented in a poster is art. The art of the poster lies in the design-
er's ability to attract the attention of the crowd by form and color. A
poster advertising an art exhibit must direct the attention of the public
to the art being exhibited; the better it succeeds in this, the greater is
the art of the poster itself. The poster should give the masses an idea of
the significance of the exhibition, it should not be a substitute for the
art on display. Anyone who wants to concern himself with the art itself
must do more than study the poster; and it will not be enough for him
just to saunter through the exhibition. We may expect him to examine
and immerse himself in the individual works, and thus little by little
form a fair opinion.

A similar situation prevails with what we today call propaganda.   22

The function of propaganda does not lie in the scientific training of   23
the individual, but in calling the masses' attention to certain facts, processes, necessities, etc., whose significance is thus for the first time
placed within their field of vision.

The whole art consists in doing this so skillfully that everyone will   24
be convinced that the fact is real, the process necessary, the necessity
correct, etc. But since propaganda is not and cannot be the necessity in
itself, since its function, like the poster, consists in attracting the attention of the crowd, and not in educating those who are already educated
or who are striving after education and knowledge, its effect for the
most part must be aimed at the emotions and only to a very limited
degree at the so-called intellect.

All propaganda must be popular and its intellectual level must be   25
adjusted to the most limited intelligence among those it is addressed to.
Consequently, the greater the mass it is intended to reach, the lower its
purely intellectual level will have to be. But if, as in propaganda for
sticking out a war, the aim is to influence a whole people, we must

avoid excessive intellectual demands on our public, and too much caution cannot be exerted in this direction.

The more modest its intellectual ballast, the more exclusively it takes   **26**
into consideration the emotions of the masses, the more effective it will
be. And this is the best proof of the soundness or unsoundness of a
propaganda campaign, and not success in pleasing a few scholars or
young aesthetes.

The art of propaganda lies in understanding the emotional ideas of   **27**
the great masses and finding, through a psychologically correct form,
the way to the attention and thence to the heart of the broad masses.
The fact that our bright boys do not understand this merely shows how
mentally lazy and conceited they are.

Once we understand how necessary it is for propaganda to be ad-   **28**
justed to the broad mass, the following rule results:

It is a mistake to make propaganda many-sided, like scientific instruc-   **29**
tion, for instance.

The receptivity of the great masses is very limited, their intelligence   **30**
is small, but their power of forgetting is enormous. In consequence of
these facts, all effective propaganda must be limited to a very few
points and must harp on these in slogans until the last member of the
public understand what you want him to understand by your slogan.
As soon as you sacrifice this slogan and try to be many-sided, the effect
will piddle away, for the crowd can neither digest nor retain the material offered. In this way the result is weakened and in the end entirely
cancelled out.

Thus we see that propaganda must follow a simple line and corre-   **31**
spondingly the basic tactics must be psychologically sound.

For instance, it was absolutely wrong to make the enemy ridiculous,   **32**
as the Austrian and German comic papers did. It was absolutely wrong
because actual contact with an enemy soldier was bound to arouse an
entirely different conviction, and the results were devastating; for now
the German soldier, under the direct impression of the enemy's resistance, felt himself swindled by his propaganda service. His desire to
fight, or even to stand firm, was not strengthened, but the opposite
occurred. His courage flagged.

By contrast, the war propaganda of the English and Americans was   **33**
psychologically sound. By representing the Germans to their own people as barbarians and Huns, they prepared the individual soldier for
the terrors of war, and thus helped to preserve him from disappoint-
ments. After this, the most terrible weapon that was used against him
seemed only to confirm what his propagandists had told him; it likewise reinforced his faith in the truth of his government's assertions,
while on the other hand it increased his rage and hatred against the
vile enemy. For the cruel effects of the weapon, whose use by the enemy he now came to know, gradually came to confirm for him the

'Hunnish' brutality of the barbarous enemy, which he had heard all about; and it never dawned on him for a moment that his own weapons possibly, if not probably, might be even more terrible in their effects.

And so the English soldier could never feel that he had been misin-   34
formed by his own countrymen, as unhappily was so much the case with the German soldier that in the end he rejected everything coming from this source as 'swindles' and 'bunk.' All this resulted from the idea that any old simpleton (or even somebody who was intelligent 'in other things') could be assigned to propaganda work, and the failure to realize that the most brilliant psychologists would have been none too good.

And so the German war propaganda offered an unparalleled example   35
of an 'enlightenment' service working in reverse, since any correct psychology was totally lacking.

There was no end to what could be learned from the enemy by a   36
man who kept his eyes open, refused to let his perceptions be ossified, and for four and a half years privately turned the storm-flood of enemy propaganda over in his brain.

What our authorities least of all understood was the very first axiom   37
of all propagandist activity: to wit, the basically subjective and one-sided attitude it must take toward every question it deals with. In this connection, from the very beginning of the War and from top to bottom, such sins were committed that we were entitled to doubt whether so much absurdity could really be attributed to pure stupidity alone.

What, for example, would we say about a poster that was supposed   38
to advertise a new soap and that described other soaps as 'good'?

We would only shake our heads.   39

Exactly the same applied to political advertising.   40

The function of propaganda is, for example, not to weigh and ponder   41
the rights of different people, but exclusively to emphasize the one right which it has set out to argue for. Its task is not to make an objective study of the truth, in so far as it favors the enemy, and then set it before the masses with academic fairness; its task is to serve our own right, always and unflinchingly.

It was absolutely wrong to discuss war-guilt from the standpoint that   42
Germany alone could not be held responsible for the outbreak of the catastrophe; it would have been correct to load every bit of the blame on the shoulders of the enemy, even if this had not really corresponded to the true facts, as it actually did.

And what was the consequence of this half-heartedness?   43

The broad mass of a nation does not consist of diplomats, or even   44
professors of political law, or even individuals capable of forming a rational opinion; it consists of plain mortals, wavering and inclined to doubt and uncertainty. As soon as our own propaganda admits so much as a glimmer of right on the other side, the foundation for doubt in our own right has been laid. The masses are then in no position to

distinguish where foreign injustice ends and our own begins. In such a case they become uncertain and suspicious, especially if the enemy refrains from going in for the same nonsense, but unloads every bit of blame on his adversary. Isn't it perfectly understandable that the whole country ends up by lending more credence to enemy propaganda, which is more unified and coherent, than to its own? And particularly a people that suffers from the mania of objectivity as much as the Germans. For, after all this, everyone will take the greatest pains to avoid doing the enemy any injustice, even at the peril of seriously besmirching and even destroying his own people and country.

Of course, this was not the intent of the responsible authorities, but   **45** the people never realize that.

The people in their overwhelming majority are so feminine by nature   **46** and attitude that sober reasoning determines their thoughts and actions far less than emotion and feeling.

And this sentiment is not complicated, but very simple and all of a   **47** piece. It does not have multiple shadings; it has a positive and a negative; love or hate, right or wrong, truth or lie, never half this way and half that way, never partially, or that kind of thing.

English propagandists understood all this most brilliantly—and acted   **48** accordingly. They made no half statements that might have given rise to doubts.

Their brilliant knowledge of the primitive sentiments of the broad   **49** masses is shown by their atrocity propaganda, which was adapted to this condition. As ruthless as it was brilliant, it created the preconditions for moral steadfastness at the front, even in the face of the greatest actual defeats, and just as strikingly it pilloried the German enemy as the sole guilty party for the outbreak of the War: the rabid, impudent bias and persistence with which this lie was expressed took into account the emotional, always extreme, attitude of the great masses and for this reason was believed.

How effective this type of propaganda was is most strikingly shown   **50** by the fact that after four years of war it not only enabled the enemy to stick to its guns, but even began to nibble at our own people.

It need not surprise us that our propaganda did not enjoy this suc-   **51** cess. In its inner ambiguity alone, it bore the germ of ineffectualness. And finally its content was such that it was very unlikely to make the necessary impression on the masses. Only our feather-brained 'statesmen' could have dared to hope that this insipid pacifistic bilge could fire men's spirits till they were willing to die.

As a result, their miserable stuff was useless, even harmful in fact.   **52**

But the most brilliant propagandist technique will yield no success   **53** unless one fundamental principle is borne in mind constantly and with unflagging attention. It must confine itself to a few points and repeat them over and over. Here, as so often in this world, persistence is the first and most important requirement for success.

Particularly in the field of propaganda, we must never let ourselves   **54**
be led by aesthetes or people who have grown blasé: not by the former,
because the form and expression of our propaganda would soon, instead of being suitable for the masses, have drawing power only for literary teas; and of the second we must beware, because, lacking in any
fresh emotion of their own, they are always on the lookout for new
stimulation. These people are quick to weary of everything; they want
variety, and they are never able to feel or understand the needs of their
fellow men who are not yet so callous. They are always the first to criticize a propaganda campaign, or rather its content, which seems to them
too old-fashioned, too hackneyed, too out-of-date, etc. They are always
after novelty, in search of a change, and this makes them mortal enemies of any effective political propaganda. For as soon as the organization and the content of propaganda begin to suit their tastes, it loses all
cohesion and evaporates completely.

The purpose of propaganda is not to provide interesting distraction   **55**
for blasé young gentlemen, but to convince, and what I mean is to convince the masses. But the masses are slow-moving, and they always
require a certain time before they are ready even to notice a thing, and
only after the simplest ideas are repeated thousands of times will the
masses finally remember them.

When there is a change, it must not alter the content of what the   **56**
propaganda is driving at, but in the end must always say the same
thing. For instance, a slogan must be presented from different angles,
but the end of all remarks must always and immutably be the slogan
itself. Only in this way can the propaganda have a unified and complete effect.

This broadness of outline from which we must never depart, in com-   **57**
bination with steady, consistent emphasis, allows our final success to
mature. And then, to our amazement, we shall see what tremendous
results such perseverance leads to—to results that are almost beyond
our understanding.

All advertising, whether in the field of business or politics, achieves suc-   **58**
cess through the continuity and sustained uniformity of its application.

Here, too, the example of enemy war propaganda was typical; limited   **59**
to a few points, devised exclusively for the masses, carried on with indefatigable persistence. Once the basic ideas and methods of execution
were recognized as correct, they were applied throughout the whole
War without the slightest change. At first the claims of the propaganda
were so impudent that people thought it insane; later, it got on people's nerves; and in the end, it was believed. After four and a half
years, a revolution broke out in Germany; and its slogans originated in
the enemy's war propaganda.

And in England they understood one more thing: that this spiritual   **60**
weapon can succeed only if it is applied on a tremendous scale, but
that success amply covers all costs.

There, propaganda was regarded as a weapon of the first order,   **61**
while in our country it was the last resort of unemployed politicians
and a comfortable haven for slackers.

And, as was to be expected, its results all in all were zero.   **62**

_____ **Written Response**

Do you feel that the end can justify the means? Specifically, would it be
ethical to use propaganda for some good purpose?

_____ **Rhetorical Analysis**

1. In "The Legend of Hitler's Childhood" (in *Childhood and Society*
[New York: Norton, 1950]), Erik H. Erikson argues that *Mein Kampf* is
itself a piece of propaganda; in the text, Hitler created a myth about his
childhood that would make him appear as a great leader to the German
people.

In this excerpt from *Mein Kampf*, how does Hitler portray himself as the
kind of person who can solve the problems of a defeated Germany?

2. Propaganda has a tendency to "flatten" discourse—in other words,
it makes the complex seem simple. Would Hitler agree with this? In this
excerpt from *Mein Kampf*, how does Hitler attempt to flatten his discourse?

3. In "War Propaganda," Hitler speaks well of some groups of people
and ill of others. What groups does he praise? What groups does he in-
sult or blame?

What does this tell you about the audience Hitler wanted to reach by
writing *Mein Kampf*?

Why would criticizing or insulting some people help him to reach his
intended audience?

_____ **Interpretation**

1. In *Techniques of Persuasion: From Propaganda to Brainwashing* (New
York: Penguin, 1963). J. A. C. Brown lists the following techniques of propaganda:

  a. The use of stereotypes that make the "enemy" seem to be evil or less
     than human.
  b. The use of derogatory names, such as "Red" instead of "Communist" or
     "Hun" instead of "German."
  c. The selection and use of facts or historical events that support the pro-
     pagandist's views and the suppression of facts or events that do not.
  d. The use of intentional lying.
  e. The repetition of key words or slogans.
  f. The use of bold assertions that are not backed up with logical arguments.

g. The placing of blame on scapegoats.

h. The appeal to widely accepted authorities, such as politicians or religious leaders. [pp. 26–28]

How many of these techniques does Hitler mention? How many does he use in his own text?

How many of these techniques are used in advertising? Now that you have read Hitler's essay, how would you differentiate between propaganda and advertising?

2. In *The Myth of the State,* Ernst Cassirer wrote the following passage about his concerns for the new techniques of political manipulation that had developed since World War I:

> in the totalitarian states the political leaders have had to take charge of all those functions that, in primitive societies, were performed by the magician. They were the absolute rulers; they were the medicine men who promised to cure all social evils. But that was not enough. In a savage tribe the sorcerer has still another important task. The *homo magus* [viz., magician] is, at the same time the *homo divinans* [viz., priest]. He reveals the will of the gods and foretells the future. The soothsayer has his firm place and his indispensable role in primitive social life. Even in highly developed stages of political culture he is still in full possession of his old rights and privileges. In Rome, for instance, no important political decision was ever made, no difficult enterprise was undertaken, no battle was fought without the advice of augurs and haruspices [priests who predicted the future by examining the entrails of animals]. When a Roman army was sent out it was always accompanied by its haruspices; they were an integral part of the military staff.
>
> Even in this respect our modern political life has abruptly returned to forms which seemed to have been entirely forgotten. To be sure, we no longer have the primitive kind of sortilege, the divination by lot; we no longer observe the flight of birds nor do we inspect the entrails of slain animals. We have developed a much more refined and elaborate method of divination—a method that claims to be scientific and philosophical. But if our methods have changed the thing itself has by no means vanished. Our modern politicians know very well that the great masses are much more easily moved by the force of imagination than by sheer physical force. And they have made ample use of this knowledge. The politician becomes a sort of public fortuneteller. Prophecy is an essential element in the new technique of rulership. The most improbable or even impossible promises are made; the millennium is predicted over and over again. [pp. 288–289]*

Why would the leader of a totalitarian state want to assume a role that is analogous to that of priest and magician in primitive cultures? Why would they want to predict the millennium over and over again? How is Cassirer's analysis of propaganda consistent or inconsistent with Hitler's?

3. In "The Technological Society (New York: Vintage, 1954), Jacques Ellul wrote: "The suppression of the critical faculty—man's growing incapacity to distinguish truth from falsehood, the individual from the

---

*Ernst Cassirer, *The Myth of the State.* New Haven, CT: Yale University Press, 1946.

collectivity, action from talk, reality from statistics, and so on—is one of the most evident results of the technical power of propaganda" (p. 369). Why would propaganda want to suppress "the critical faculty"? Why did Hitler believe that propaganda should attempt to suppress critical thought?

WRITING ASSIGNMENTS

1. In "War Propaganda," Hitler argues that the end (such as winning a war) can justify the means (such as the use of propaganda). Do you feel that the use of propaganda is never justified? Or do you feel that propaganda can sometimes be justified if used for truly good ends?

2. Write an essay in which you warn the American public about the dangers of propaganda.

3. Write a speech—one that would qualify as propaganda—on some controversial issue (abortion, gun control, nuclear disarmament), aiming the speech at some segment of the American public. For example, you may want to write a propagandistic speech against gun control that could be delivered to a meeting of the National Rifle Association.

4. J. M. Coetzee's "The Vietnam Project" is a novella about Eugene Dawn, a mentally disturbed researcher who is evaluating the United States's propaganda program during the Vietnam War. His report on that program is reprinted below.* Use Dawn's report to analyze this fictitious propaganda program and discuss whether you consider such programs to be ethical.

INTRODUCTION

1.1 *Aims of the report.* This report concerns the potential of broadcast programming in Phases IV–VI of the conflict in Indo-China. It evaluates the achievements of this branch of psychological warfare during Phases I–III (1961–65, 1965–69, 1969–72) and recommends certain changes in the future form and content of propaganda. Its recommendations apply both to broadcasting services operated directly by U.S. agencies (including services in Vietnamese, Khmer, Lao, Muong, and other vernaculars but excluding V.O.A. Pacific services) and to those operated by the Republic of Vietnam with U.S. technical advice (principally Radio Free Vietnam and V.A.F., the Armed Forces radio).

The strategy of the psychological war must be determined by overall war strategy. This report is being drawn up in early 1973 as we enter upon Phase IV of the war, a phase during which the propaganda arm will play a complex and crucially important role. It is projected that, depending upon domestic political factors, Phase IV will last until either mid-1974 or early 1977. Thereafter there will be a sharp remilitarization of the conflict

---

*From *Dusklands* by J. M. Coetzee. Copyright © 1974, 1982 by J. M. Coetzee. Reprinted by permission of the publisher Viking Penguin, a division of Penguin Books USA Inc. and Martin Secker & Warburg Limited.

(Phase V), followed by a police/civilian reconstruction effort (Phase VI). This scenario is broad. I have accordingly had no qualms about projecting my recommendations beyond the end of Phase IV into the final phases of the conflict.

1.2 *Aims and achievements of propaganda services.* In waging psychological warfare we aim to destroy the morale of the enemy. Psychological warfare is the negative function of propaganda: its positive function is to create confidence that our political authority is strong and durable. Waged effectively, propaganda war wears down the enemy by shrinking his civilian base and recruitment pool and rendering his soldiers uncertain in battle and likely to defect afterwards, while at the same time fortifying the loyalty of the population. Its military/political potential cannot therefore be overstressed.

However, the record of the propaganda services in Vietnam, U.S. and U.S.-aided, remains disappointing. This is the common conclusion of the Joint Commission of Inquiry, 1971; of the internal studies made available to the Kennedy Institute; and of my own analysis of interviews with contended civilians, defectors, and prisoners. It is confirmed by content analysis of programs broadcast between 1965 and 1972. Our gross inference must be that the effective psychological pressure we bring to bear on the guerrillas and their supporters is within their limits of tolerance; a further inference may be that some of our programming is counterproductive. The correct starting-point for our investigation should therefore be this: is there a factor in the psychic and psychosocial constitution of the insurgent population that makes it resistant to penetration by our programs? Having answered this question we can go on to ask: how can we make our programs more penetrant?

1.3 *Control.* Our propaganda services have yet to apply the first article of the anthropology of Franz Boas: that if we wish to take over the direction of a society we must either guide it from within its cultural framework or else eradicate its culture and impose new structures. We cannot expect to guide the thinking of rural Vietnam until we recognize that rural Vietnam is non-literate, that its family structure is patrilineal, its social order hierarchical, and its political order authoritarian though locally autonomous. (This last fact explains why in settled times the ARVN command structure degenerates into local satrapies.) It is a mistake to think of the Vietnamese as individuals, for their culture prepares them to subordinate individual interest to the interest of family or band or hamlet. The rational promptings of self-interest matter less than the counsel of father and brothers.

1.31 *Western theory and Vietnamese practice.* But the voice which our broadcasting projects into Vietnamese homes is the voice of neither father nor brother. It is the voice of the doubting self, the voice of René Descartes driving his wedge between the self in the world and the self who contemplates that self. The voices of our Chieu Hoi (surrender/reconciliation) programming are wholly Cartesian. Their record is not a happy one. Whether disguised as the voice of the doubting secret self ("Why should I fight when the struggle is hopeless?") or as that of the clever brother ("I have gone over to Saigon—so can you!"), they have failed because they speak out of an alienated *doppelgänger* rationality for which there is no precedent in Vietnamese thought. We attempt to embody the ghost inside the villager, but there has never been any ghost there.

The propaganda of Radio Free Vietnam, crude though it may seem with its martial music, boasts and slogans, exhortations and anathema, is closer to the pulse of Vietnam than our subtler programming of division. It offers strong authority and a simple choice. Our own statistics show that everywhere except in Saigon itself Radio Free Vietnam is the most favored listening. The Saigonese prefer U.S. Armed Forces Radio for its pop music. Our figures for Liberation Radio (NLF) indicate a small listenership but are probably unreliable. Figures for the U.S.-run services are more accurate and indicate low interest everywhere except in the cities. The provincial population listens with respect to the ferocious war-heroes, humble defectors, and brass-band disk-jockeys of Radio Free Vietnam. There is an early-evening commentary program run by Nguyen Loc Binh, a colonel in the National Police, which draws an enormous audience. Westerners are distressed by Nguyen's crudity, but the Vietnamese like him because with rough humor, cajolements, threats, and a certain slyness of insight he has worked up a typically Vietnamese elder-brother relationship with his audience, particularly with women.

1.4 *The father-voice.* The voice of the father utters itself appropriately out of the sky. The Vietnamese call it "the whispering death" when it speaks from the B-52's, but there is no reason why it should not ride the radio waves with equal devastation. The father is authority, infallibility, ubiquity. He does not persuade, he commands. That which he foretells happens. When the guilty Saigonese in the dead of night tunes to Liberation Radio, the awful voice that breaks in on the LR frequency should be the father's.

The father-voice is not a new source in propaganda. The tendency in totalitarian states is, however, to identify the father-voice with the voice of the Leader, the father of the country. In times of war this father exhorts his children to patriotic sacrifice, in times of peace to greater production. The Republic of Vietnam is no exception. But the practise has two drawbacks. The first is that the omnipotence of the Father is tainted by the fallibility of the Leader. The second is that there exist penalties that the prudent statesman dare not threaten, punishments that he dare not celebrate, which nevertheless belong to the omnipotent Father.

It is in view of such considerations that I suggest a division of responsibilities, with the Vietnamese operating the brother-voices and we ourselves taking over the design and operation of the father-voice.

[I omit three dull pages on details of interface between intelligence and information services; on the problem of security among the South Vietnamese; and on the longed-for assumption of responsibility by them.]

1.41 *Programming the father-voice.* In limited warfare, defeat is not a military but a psychic concept. To the ideal of demoralization we pay lip service, and insofar as we wage terroristic war we strive to realize it. But in practise our most effective acts of demoralization are justified in military terms, as though the use of force for psychological ends were shameful. Thus, for example, we have justified the elimination of enemy villages by calling

them armed strongholds, when the true value of the operations lay in demonstrating to the absent VC menfolk just how vulnerable their homes and
families were.

Atrocity charges are empty when they cannot be proved. 95% of the villages we wiped off the map were never on it.

There is an unsettling lack of realism about terrorism among the higher
ranks of the military. Questions of conscience lie outside the purview of
this study. We must work on the assumption that the military believe in
their own explanations when they assign a solely military value to terror
operations.

1.411 *Testimony of CT.* There is greater realism among men in the field. During 1968 and 1969 the Special Forces undertook a program in political assassination (CT) in the Delta Region. Under CT a significant proportion of the
NLF cadres were eliminated and the rest forced into hiding. The official
report defines the program as a police action rather than a military one, in
that it identified specified victims and eliminated them by such subject-
specific means as ambush and sniping. The official explanation for the success of the program is that the NLF lost face because the populace were
made to see that NLF operatives had no defense against their own weapon
of assassination.

The men who carried out the killings have a different explanation. They
knew that the intelligence identifying NLF cadres was untrustworthy. In-
formers often acted out of personal envy and hatred, or simply out of greed
for reward. There is every reason to suspect that many of those killed were
innocent, though innocence among the Vietnamese is a relative affair. Not
only this. I quote one member of an assassination squad: "At a hundred
yards who can tell one slope from another? You can only blow his head off
and hope". Not only this. We must expect that when they knew they had
been marked down, the more important cadres would have slipped away.
So we must regard the official count of 1250 as grossly inflated with non-
significant dead.

Yet CT was a measurable success. In concert with the more orthodox activities of the National Police it brought about a 75% drop in terror and
sabotage incidents. Investigators using advanced non-verbal techniques—in
Vietnam all verbal responses are untrustworthy—recorded a progressive
muting of such positive reactions as rage, contempt, and defiance in subjects from villages where before 1968 the NLF had held sway. After phases
of insecurity and anxiety their subjects settled into a state known as High
Threshold, with affect traits of apathy, despondency, and despair.

Once again those who knew the flavor of the moment tell the story
best. I quote: "We scared the shit out of them. They didn't know who was
next".

Yet fear was no novelty to these Vietnamese. Fear had bound the community together. The novelty of CT was that it broke down the community
not by attacking the whole but by facing each member with the prospect of
an attack on him as an individual with a name and a history. To his question, Why me? there was no comforting answer. I am chosen because I am
the object of an inscrutable choice. I am chosen because I am marked. With
this non sequitur the subject's psyche is penetrated. The emotional support

of the group falls into irrelevance as he sees that war is being waged on him in his isolation. He has become a victim and begins to behave like one. He is the quarry of an infallible hunter, infallible since whenever he attacks someone dies. Hence the victim's preoccupation with taint: I move among those marked for death and those unmarked—which am I? The community breaks down into a scurrying swarm whose antennae vibrate only to the coming of death. The nest hums with suspicion (Is this a corpse I am talking to?). Then, as pressure is maintained, the coherence of the psyche cracks (I am tainted, I smell in my own nostrils).

(My explication of the dynamics of this de-politicizing process is strikingly confirmed by the studies of Thomas Szell in the de-politicizing of internment camps. Szell reports that a camp authority which randomly and at random times selects subjects for punishment, while maintaining the *appearance* of selectivity, is consistently successful in breaking down group morale.)

What is the lesson of CT? CT teaches that when the cohesiveness of the group is weakened the threshold of breakdown in each of its members drops. Conversely, it teaches that to attack the group as a group without fragmenting it does not reduce the psychic capacity of its members to resist. Many of our Vietnam programs, including perhaps strategic bombing, show poor results from neglect of this principle. There is only one rule in Vietnam: fragment, individualize. Our mistake was to allow the Vietnamese to conceive themselves as an entire people huddled under the bombs of a foreign oppressor. Thereby we created for ourselves the task of breaking the resistance of a whole people—a dangerous, expensive, and unnecessary task. If we had rather compelled the village, the guerrilla band, the individual subject to conceive himself the village, the band, the subject elected for especial punishment, for reasons never to be known, then while his first gesture might have been to strike back in anger, the worm of guilt would inevitably, as punishment continued, have sprouted in his bowels and drawn from him the cry, "I am punished therefore I am guilty". He who utters these words is vanquished.

1.5 *The myth of the father.* The father-voice is the voice that breaks the bonds of the enemy band. The strength of the enemy is his bondedness. We are the father putting down the rebellion of the band of brothers. There is a mythic shape to the encounter, and no doubt the enemy draws sustenance from the knowledge that in the myth the brothers usurp the father's place. Such inspirational force strengthens the bonds of the brothers not only by predicting their victory but by promising that the era of the warring brothers, the abhorred *kien tiem* of Chinese experience, will be averted.

A myth is true—that is to say, *operationally* true—insofar as it has predictive force. The more deeply rooted and universal a myth, the more difficult it is to combat. The myths of a tribe are the fictions it coins to maintain its powers. The answer to a myth of force is not necessarily counterforce, for if the myth predicts counterforce, counterforce reinforces the myth. The science of mythography teaches us that a subtler counter is to subvert and revise the myth. The highest propaganda is the propagation of a new mythology.

For a description of the myths we combat, together with their national variants, I refer you to Thomas McAlmon's *Communist Myth and Group*

Integration: vol. I, *Proletarian Mythography* (1967), vol. II, *Insurgent Myth-ography* (1969). McAlmon's monumental work is the foundation of the en-tire structure of modern revisionary counter-myth, of which the present study is one small example. McAlmon describes the myth of the overthrow of the father as follows.

"In origin the myth is a justification of the rebellion of sons against a father who uses them as hinds. The sons come of age, rebel, mutilate the father, and divide the patrimony, that is, the earth fertilized by the father's rain. Psychoanalytically the myth is a self-affirming fantasy of the child powerless to take the mother he desires from his father-rival". In popular Vietnamese consciousness the myth takes the following form: "The sons of the land (i.e., the brotherhood of earth-tillers) desire to take the land (i.e., the Vietnamese *Boden*) for themselves, overthrowing the sky-god who is identified with the old order of power (foreign empire, the U.S.). The earth-mother hides her sons in her bosom, safe from the thunderbolts of the fa-ther; at night, while he sleeps, they emerge to unman him and initiate a new fraternal order" (II, pp. 26, 101).

1.51 *Countermyths.* The weak point in this myth is that it portrays the fa-ther as vulnerable, liable to wither under a single well-directed radical blow. Our response has hitherto been the Hydran counter: for every head chopped off we grow a new one. Our strategy is attrition, the attrition of plenty. Before our endless capacity to replace dead members we hope that the enemy will lose faith, grow disheartened, surrender.

But it is a mistake to think of the Hydran counter as a final answer. For one thing, the myth of rebellion has a no-surrender clause. Punishment for falling into the father's hands is to be eaten alive or penned eternally in a volcano. If you surrender your body it is not returned to the earth and so cannot be reborn (volcanoes are not of the earth but terrestrial bases of the sun-father). Thus surrender is not an option because it means a fate worse than death. (Nor, considering what happens to prisoners of Saigon, can the intuitive force of this argument be denied.)

A second fallacy in the Hydran counter is that it misinterprets the myth of rebellion. The blow that wins the war against the tyrant father is not a death-thrust but a humiliating blow that renders him sterile (impotence and sterility are mythologically indistinguishable). His kingdom, no longer fertilized, becomes a waste land.

The importance of the humiliating blow will not be underestimated by anyone who knows the place of shame in per-Sinic value systems.

Let me now outline a more promising counter-strategy.

They myth of rebellion assumes that heaven and earth, father and mother, live in symbiosis. Neither can exist alone. If the father is over-thrown there must be a new father, new rebellion, endless violence, while no matter how deep her treachery toward her mate, the mother may not be annihilated. The scheming of mother and sons is thus endless.

But has the master-myth of history not outdated the fiction of the sym-biosis of earth and heaven? We live no longer by tilling the earth but by devouring her and her waste products. We signed our repudiation of her with fights toward new celestial loves. We have the capacity to breed out of our own head. When the earth conspires incestuously with her sons, should our recourse not be to the arms of the goddess of *techne* who springs from our brains? Is it not time that the earth-mother is supplanted by her own faithful daughter, shaped without woman's part? The age of Athene dawns. In the Indo-China Theater we play out the drama of the end of the tellurian age and the marriage of the sky-god with his parthenogene daughter-queen. If the play has been poor, it is because we have stumbled about the stage asleep, not knowing the meaning of our acts. Now I bring their meaning to light in that blinding moment of ascending meta-historical consciousness in which we begin to shape our own myths.

1.6 *Victory.* The father cannot be a benign father until his sons have knelt before his wand.

The plotting of the sons against the father must cease. They must kneel with hearts bathed in obedience.

When the sons know obedience they will be able to sleep.

Phase IV only postpones the day of reckoning.

There is no problem of reconstruction in Vietnam. The only problem is the problem of victory.

We are all somebody's sons. Do not thick it does not pain me to make this report. (On the other hand, do not underestimate my exultation.) I too am stirred by courage. But courage is an archaic virtue. While there is courage we are all bound to the wheel of rebellious violence. Beyond courage there is the humble heart, the quiet garden into which we may escape from the cycles of time. I am neat and polite, but I am the man of the future paradise.

Before paradise comes purgatory.

Not without joy, I have girded myself for purgatory. If I must be a martyr to the cause of obedience, I am prepared to suffer. I am not alone. Behind their desks across the breadth of America wait an army of young men, out of fashion like me. We wear dark suits and thick lenses. We are the generation who were little boys in 1945. We are taking up position. We are stepping into shoes. It is we who will inherit America, in due course. We are patient. We wait our turn.

If you are moved by the courage of those who have taken up arms, look into your heart: an honest eye will see that it is not your best self which is moved. The self which is moved is treacherous. It craves to kneel before the slave, to wash the leper's sores. The dark self strives toward humiliation and turmoil, the bright self toward obedience and order. The dark self sickens the bright self with doubts and qualms. I know. It is his poison which is eating me.

I am a hero of resistance. I am no less than that, properly understood, in metaphor. Staggering in my bleeding armor, I stand erect, alone on the plain, beset.

My papers are in order. I sit neatly and write. I make fine distinctions. It is on the point of a fine distinction that the world turns. I distinguish between obedience and humiliation, and under the fire of my distinguishing intellect mountains crumble. I am the embodiment of the patient struggle of the intellect against blood and anarchy. I am a story not of emotion and violence—the illusory war-story of television—but of life itself, life in obedience to which even the simplest organism represses its entropic yearning for the mud and follows the road of evolutionary duty toward the glory of consciousness.

There is only one problem in Vietnam and that is the problem of victory. The problem of victory is technical. We must believe this. Victory is a matter of sufficient force, and we dispose over sufficient force.

I wish to get this part over with. I am impatient with the restrictions of this assignment.

I dismiss Phase IV of the conflict. I look forward to Phase V and the return of total air-war.

There is a military air-war with military targets; there is also a political air-war whose purpose is to destroy the enemy's capacity to sustain himself psychically.

We cannot know until we can measure. But in the political air-war there is no easy measure like the body-count. Therefore we use probability measures (I apologize for repeating what is in the books, but I cannot afford not to be complete.) When we strike at a target, we define the probability of a success as

$$P_1 = aX^{-3/4} + (bX - c)Y$$

where X measures release altitude, Y measures ground fire intensity, and a, b, c are constants. In a typical political air-strike, however, the target is not specified but simply formalized as a set of map co-ordinates. To measure success we compute two probabilities and find their product: P_1 above (the probability of a hit) and P_2, the probability that what we hit is a target. Since at present we can do little more than guess at P_2, our policy has been round-the-clock bombing, with heavy volume compensating for infinitesimal products P_1P_2. The policy barely worked in Phase III and cannot work in Phase IV, when all bombing is clandestine. What policy should we adopt in Phase V?

I sit in the depths of the Harry Truman Library, walled round with earth, steel, concrete, and mile after mile of compressed paper, from which impregnable stronghold of the intellect I send forth this winged dream of assault upon the mothering earth herself.

When we attack the enemy via a pair of map co-ordinates we lay ourselves open to mathematical problems we cannot solve. But if we cannot solve them we can eliminate them, by attacking the co-ordinates themselves—all the co-ordinates! For years now we have attacked the earth, explicitly in the defoliation of crops and jungle, implicitly in aleatoric shelling and bombing. Let us, in the act of ascending consciousness mentioned above, admit the meaning of our acts. We discount 1999 aleatoric missiles out of every 2000 we fire; yet every one of them lands somewhere, is heard by human ears, wears down hope in a human heart. A missile is truly wasted only when we dismiss it and are known by our foes to dismiss it. Our prodigality breeds contempt in the frugal Vietnamese, but only because they see it as the prodigality of waste rather than the prodigality of bounty. They know our guilt at devastating the earth and know that our fiction of aiming at the 0.058% of a man crossing the spot we strike at the moment we strike it is a guilty lie. Press back such atavistic guilt! Our future belongs not to the earth but to the stars. Let us show the enemy that he stands naked in a dying landscape.

I have to pull myself together.

We should not sneer at spray techniques. If spraying does not give the orgasm of the explosion (nothing has done more to sell the war to America than televised napalm strikes), it will always be more effective than high explosive in a campaign against the earth. PROP-12 spraying could change the face of Vietnam in a week. PROP-12 is a soil poison, a dramatic poison which (I apologize again), washed into the soil, attacks the bonds in dark silicates and deposits a topskin of gray ashy grit. Why have we discontinued PROP-12? Why did we use it only on the lands of resettled communities? Until we reveal to ourselves and revel in the true meaning of our acts we will go on suffering the double penalty of guilt and ineffectualness.

I am in a bad way as I write these words. My health is poor. I have a treacherous wife, an unhappy home, unsympathetic superiors. I suffer from headaches. I sleep badly. I am eating myself out. If I knew how to take holidays perhaps I would take one. But I see things and have a duty toward history that cannot wait. What I say is in pieces. I am sorry. But we can do it. It is my duty to point out our duty. I sit in libraries and see things. I am in an honorable line of bookish men who have sat in libraries and had visions of great clarity. I name no names. You must listen. I speak with the voice of things to come. I speak in troubled times and tell you how to be as children again. I speak to the broken halves of all our selves and tell them to embrace, loving the worst in us equally with the best.

Tear this off, Coetzee, it is a postscript, it goes to you, listen to me.

Synthesis

1. In *The Technological Society* (New York: Vantage, 1954), Jacques Ellul writes:

> Propaganda must become as natural as air or food. It must proceed by psychological inhibition and the least possible shock. The individual is then able to declare with all honesty that no such thing as propaganda exists. In fact, however, he has been so absorbed by it that he is literally no longer able to see the truth. The natures of man and propaganda have become so inextricably mixed that everything depends not on choice or on free will, but on reflex and myth. The same prolonged and hypnotic repetition of the same complex of ideas, the same images, and the same rumors condition man for the assimilation of his nature to propaganda. [p. 336]

Ellul feels that propaganda is so much a part of our daily lives that we no longer pay any conscious attention to it. Propaganda influences our beliefs without our realizing it.

For a few days, collect the messages that you encounter in your environment. The messages could be part of political speeches, newscasts, talk shows, advertisements, books, or lectures. Is Ellul right? Is propaganda as much a part of our environment as air and water? Are we constantly being influenced by propaganda? Or is he wrong? Is he being "paranoid"? Does he see the messages in our environment as beingdangerous when they are actually harmless or beneficial? Does he fear "hidden messages" that are really not there?

2. The illustrations that follow are posters used in various war propaganda campaigns. Write an essay in which you analyze the mythic qualities in these pieces of propaganda; then discuss whether you feel that they are ethical.

U. S. ARMY
OFFICIAL POSTER

SOLDIERS *without guns*

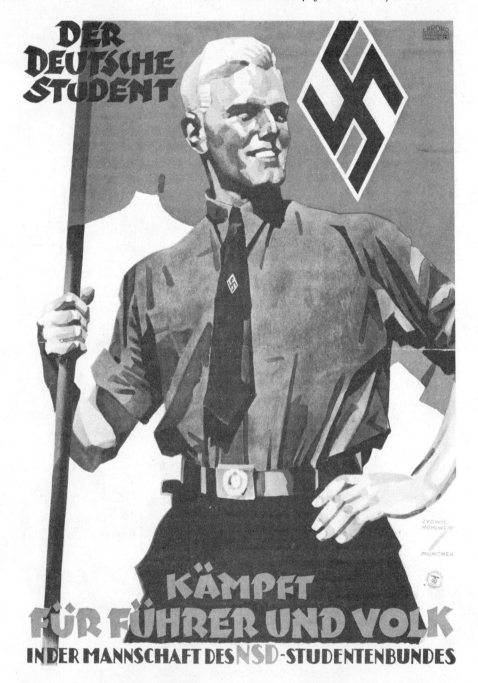

This is the Enemy

WINNER R. HOE & CO., INC. AWARD – NATIONAL WAR POSTER COMPETITION
HELD UNDER AUSPICES OF ARTISTS FOR VICTORY, INC – COUNCIL FOR DEMOCRACY – MUSEUM OF MODERN ART

This aristocratic officer seems a far cry from the crudeness of most
enel leaders, 1942, USA, Karl Koehler and Victor Ancona.

TAKE UP THE
SWORD OF JUSTICE

5 Criticism: Literature and Its Context

In "A Dialectic of Aural and Objective Correlatives" (in *Approaches to the Poem* [San Francisco: Chandler, 1965]), Walter J. Ong describes the function of criticism thus:

> Although it is not to be equated with science, criticism is in some degree explanation, and has something of this same scientific bent. Unless it is to be itself a poem, criticism of a poem must involve some elucidation. Its ultimate object may be to introduce the reader more fully into the mystery which is the poem, but its technique will be to some extent to "clear up" certain things. [p. 248]

If criticism is the task of "clearing up" certain things, it does not aim to "clear up" just any "certain things." Criticism amounts to the task of "clearing up" or interpreting or making meaning from a certain specific group of things—texts.

It is understandable that criticism—the interpretation of texts—has come to be most closely associated with the study of literature, for literature cannot be separated from texts (or, at least, no one has tried to do so). Historians have tried to separate history from texts, psychologists have tried to separate psychology from texts, and physicists have tried to separate physics from texts, because they have believed that what they study has an objective existence somewhere beyond the boundaries of a piece of writing. But specialists from a wide range of disciplines are beginning to accept that they cannot avoid texts and that they too have to become critics.

Clifford Geertz, for example, is an anthropologist who feels that he is a "literary critic" of cultures. In *The Interpretation of Cultures* (New York: Basic, 1973), he writes: "The culture of a people is an ensemble of texts, themselves ensembles, which the anthropologist strains to read over the shoulders of those to whom they properly belong" (pp. 453–454). Geertz is a "literary critic" of cultures because he wants to say something (offer an interpretation) about something (the "text" of a culture) to someone (some audience who hopes that his interpretation will "clear up" the text).

Although criticism takes many forms (Freudian criticism, Marxist criticism, feminist criticism, formalist criticism, deconstructive criticism, historical criticism, textual criticism, rhetorical criticism, and so on), it is essentially the art of saying something about something to somebody.

In this chapter, you will have an opportunity to explore interpreting several types of texts—a play, a short story, and a selection of related poems—and to explore one form of criticism—the interpretation of texts as they relate to their social and political context.

Tragedy and Society

Of the hundreds of tragedies written during the golden age of Athens (the fifth century B.C.), only 33 have survived. Aeschylus wrote 7 of these, Sophocles 7, and Euripides 19. Thus, more of Euripides' tragedies survive than those of any other Greek dramatist. His plays (reportedly he wrote 92) were immensely popular throughout Greece, but he won few prizes for playwriting and was only grudgingly admired by the people of Athens, where he lived and wrote.

The nature of his tragedies might account for some of his mixed reputation. Euripides was known for writing tragedies about the larger-than-life heroes of myths as if they were ordinary people. The critics and judges of drama contests might have felt that the tragedies of Euripides were not grand enough, that they did not deal with characters who were better than the average man or woman. Euripides was also known as a iconoclast, a person who criticizes the most deeply cherished of social customs and traditions. His criticisms of Athenian culture may account for his being more popular elsewhere in Greece. It might also explain why the philosopher Socrates (another Athenian iconoclast) thought so highly of Euripides' plays.

_____ **Prereading**

Greek dramatists wrote their tragedies about the heroes and heroines of myths that were familiar to those attending the theater. The story of Euripides' *Medea* was drawn from the myths of Jason and his search for the Golden Fleece (the hide of a golden ram). The outline of these myths provides important background for Euripides' play.

Aeson, Jason's father, was wrongfully dethroned by Pelias, his half brother. When Jason, who was raised by a foster father, first came upon Pelias, he demanded his father's throne. Pelias said that he would comply, but only if Jason would first free his country of a curse by finding the Golden Fleece.

Jason agreed and set sail with 50 men in the *Argo*, which was made with timber from Mount Pelion. After numerous adventures, Jason and his Argonauts arrived in Colchis, where they would find the Golden Fleece. In order to aid Jason, the goddesses Hera and Athena instructed

Eros to make Medea (daughter of Aeetes, King of Colchis) fall in love with Jason.

After Jason swore that he would wed and never divorce Medea, she helped Jason to secure the Golden Fleece, betraying her father in the process.

When Jason returned to the city of Iolcus, he learned that Pelias had condemned his parents to death and then allowed them to take their own lives. Jason and the Argonauts made plans to attack the city, but, before they could act, Medea used magic to trick the daughters of Pelias into killing their father. Once Pelias was dead, Jason and his men took the city.

Fearing the revenge of Pelias' son, Jason relinquished his throne. He and Medea were then banished from the city and traveled to Corinth. The throne of Corinth rightfully belonged to Medea's father but had been usurped by Corinthus. When Corinthus died, Medea claimed the throne for herself and Jason.

They had ruled Corinth for 10 years before Jason began to suspect that Medea was responsible for Corinthus' death. Jason then made plans to divorce Medea (thus breaking his oath) and marry Glauce, daughter of Creon, King of Corinth. It is at this point in the Jason myths that Euripides' *Medea* begins. In the play Jason leaves Medea for Glauce, Creon's daughter. After failing to regain Jason's affections, Medea kills their two children and flees the city.

Based on what you know of the Medea and Jason myth, why do you think that Euripides, who liked to write plays that criticized some aspect of his society, would be drawn to it? In other words, how might this myth be used to criticize some aspect of Athenian society, or, for that matter, our society?

Medea

Euripides

Characters

NURSE *to Medea*
TUTOR *to Medea's children*
The two sons of Medea and Jason
CHORUS *of Corinthian Women*
MEDEA
CREON, *King of Corinth*

Source: "The Medea" by Euripides from *Three Greek Plays for the Theatre,* translated by Peter D. Arnott, 1961. Reprinted by permission of Indiana University Press.

JASON
AEGEUS, *King of Athens*
MESSENGER
Soldiers, servants and attendants.

The action takes place before the house of MEDEA *in Corinth.* MEDEA'S *old* NURSE *is standing at the door.*

NURSE: If only Argo's hull had never flown
    Between the Clashing Rocks to Colchis' shore,
    And if the pine in Pelion's woods had never
    Been chopped down, to put oars into the hands
    Of heroes who went out in Pelias' name
    To fetch the Golden Fleece! My mistress then,
    Medea, would never have fallen in love with Jason
    And sailed with him to the walls of Iolkos' land,
    Or persuaded the daughters of Pelias to kill
    Their father; would not be living here   10
    In Corinth, with her husband and her children,
    Giving pleasure to the country she has chosen for her exile.
    Everything she did was for Jason's sake,
    And that's the best way of avoiding risks,
    For a wife to have no quarrel with her husband.
    But love's turned sour, there's hatred everywhere.
    Jason deserts my mistress and his children
    And seeks a royal alliance, marrying
    The daughter of Creon, ruler of this land,
    While poor Medea is left wretched and dishonored   20
    To cry "You promised," and remind him of the hand
    He pledged in faith, and calls on heaven to see
    What she has done for him—and her reward.
    She lies without eating, her body abandoned to grief,
    Weeping herself thinner with each day that passed
    Since first she knew her husband was unfaithful,
    Never lifting her head or raising her eyes
    From the ground, as deaf as rock or water
    To anyone who gives her good advice.
    Except, at times, she lifts her snow-white neck   30
    And mourns to herself for the loss of her dear father
    And the home and country she betrayed to come
    Away with a man who now cares nothing for her.
    Poor lady, she has come to learn the hard way
    What it means to have no country to go back to.
    She hates her children, takes no joy in seeing them;
    I'm afraid she has something dreadful in her mind.
    She's a dangerous woman; he who picks a fight
    With her won't come off victor easily.
    Here come her children, leaving their games behind;   40
    They don't know anything about their mother's
    Sorrows; youth is no friend to grief.
    (*Enter* MEDEA'S *two small sons, with their* TUTOR.)

TUTOR: My mistress' time-worn piece of household property,
  What are you doing standing here alone
  Before the gates, soliloquizing on misfortune?
  However could Medea do without you?
NURSE: Old fellow, guardian of Jason's children,
  Good servants take it as a personal sorrow
  When trouble and misfortune touch their masters.
  And I was moved to such a pitch of misery   **50**
  I longed to come outside, to tell
  Heaven and earth about Medea's troubles.
TUTOR: Poor lady, has she not stopped weeping yet?
NURSE: O blessed ignorance! Not halfway, hardly started.
TUTOR: The fool—if I may speak so of my mistress;
  She knows nothing of her more recent troubles.
NURSE: What is it, old man? Don't keep it to yourself!
TUTOR: Nothing. I'm sorry that I said so much.
NURSE: By your beard, don't keep it from your fellow-servant.
  I'll swear to keep it secret if I must.   **60**
TUTOR: I heard somebody saying, and pretended not to listen,
  When I was at the place where the old men sit
  Playing draughts around the holy fountain of Peirene,
  That Creon, this country's ruler, was about
  To send Medea with her children into exile
  Away from Corinth. Whether this tale is true
  I cannot say; I hope it may not be so.
NURSE: Will Jason be content to see his sons
  So treated, even though he's quarrelled with their mother?
TUTOR: When loyalties conflict, the old one loses.   **70**
  He has no love for any in this house.
NURSE: Why then, we are ruined, if we must add new sorrow
  Before we have got rid of the old one.
TUTOR: This is no time to tell Medea
  What has happened; be quiet, keep it to yourself.
NURSE: My children, do you see what your father's like?
  I hope he—no, he is my master still,
  Even though he's proved a traitor to his loved ones.
TUTOR: Who isn't? Have you only just now realized
  That no man puts his neighbor before himself?   **80**
  Some have good reason, most are out for profit,
  Just as he neglects his sons for his new wife's sake.
NURSE: Go indoors, my children, everything will be all right.
  You keep them to themselves as much as possible,
  Don't bring them near their mother when she's angry.
  I saw that wild bull look come in her eyes
  As if she meant them harm. I know too well
  She'll keep her anger warm till someone's hurt.
  May it be enemies, and not her friends!
            (MEDEA'S *voice is heard from inside the house.*)
MEDEA: Oh,
  I am wretched and oppressed with troubles.   **90**

I wish I were dead, I wish I were dead.
NURSE: What did I tell you, dear children? Your mother
  Is stirring her heart and her anger with it.
  Get along indoors as quickly as possible,
  Don't go within sight of her, don't come near her,
  Beware of her temper, the wild beast lurking
  In that desperate mind of hers.
  Come now, hurry along indoors;
  It's clear that her smoldering anger will burst
  Into flames as her passion increases.   100
  Her spirit's too big for her, uncontrollable;
  What will she do when provoked?
MEDEA: Oh,
  I have suffered things, I have suffered things
  Worth a world of weeping. Unhappy sons,
  May you die with your father, the whole house perish!
NURSE: Oh dear, oh dear, what a state I am in!
  What have your children to do with their father's
  Wickedness, why hate them?
  Oh, my darling children,
  I'm terrified something will happen to you.   110
  It's bad when a queen is angry; she rarely submits,
  Gets her own way in most things, and changes
  Her mood without warning.
             (Exeunt CHILDREN and TUTOR.)
  It's better if you've been used to a life
  Without any ups or downs; I'd rather
  Grow old in peace than be a great lady.
  Moderation's a word that's good to hear
  And the greatest blessing that men could have.
  Excess can never bring profit; when heaven's
  Angry, the great ones are hit the hardest.   120
        (Enter the CHORUS of Corinthian women.)
CHORUS: I heard the voice, I heard the cry
  Of Colchis' unhappy daughter.
  It is ringing still; tell us, old woman.
  I was inside at my door, and heard her crying.
  I cannot be happy when the home is troubled,
  When the home is one I love.
NURSE: Home! There is no home, that's past and gone.
  Jason is wrapped up in his new wife,
  And my mistress sits pining away in her room
  And her friends can say nothing to comfort her.   130
MEDEA: I wish
  That lightning from heaven would split my head open!
  What have I to live for now?
  Why can I not leave this hateful life
  And find repose in death?
CHORUS: Zeus, heaven and earth, do you hear
  How the wretched wife is weeping?

Why do you pray for that hateful sleep?
Fool, would you wish your death sooner?
This is no way to pray. If your husband   140
Honors another wife, it has happened
To others, don't take it to heart.
Zeus will see justice done; don't wear
Yourself out with lamenting your husband.
MEDEA: Goddess of justice, Queen Artemis,
  You see how I suffer, who bound
  My husband, curse him, with oaths?
  I pray I may see him perish
  And his wife, and all the house
  Who have dared unprovoked to wrong me.   150
  My father, my country, how shamefully
  I left you, and killed my own brother.
NURSE: Do you hear what she says, how she cries
  To Themis in prayer, and to Zeus
  Whom we honor as keeper of oaths?
  One thing is certain, my mistress
  Won't let go her anger for nothing.
CHORUS: If she would only come out here to see us,
  If she would only hear what we have to say,
  To see if her bitterness would melt   160
  And her anger disappear.
  I hope I shall always be ready
  To stand by my friends. Go inside, old woman,
  And fetch her out of the house; and hurry,
  Before she can harm the household;
  That's the way her grief is going.
NURSE: I'll do it, but I'm afraid
  I shan't be able to move her.
  Still, it's a labor of love.
  She's angry, and glares at her servants   170
  Like a lioness guarding her cubs
  When anyone comes with a message.
  You wouldn't be wrong to consider
  The old poets not clever but fools
  Who wrote music for dinners and banquets,
  Pleasant tunes for men who were happy,
  But nobody ever discovered
  How to use all this music and singing
  To lessen a man's load of trouble
  That brought death and misfortune and ruin.   180
  It would certainly be an advantage
  To use music for healing! Why waste it
  On dinners? There's pleasure enough
  In a banquet, who wants any more?
                                                        (Exit.)
CHORUS: I heard the voice heavy with grief
  Bitterly mourning the faithless

Husband who married and left her,
Blaming her wrongs on the gods,
The justice of Zeus, the sworn oath
That started her difficult crossing   190
Through the gates of the salt foggy sea
To the opposite shores of Greece.

(*Enter* MEDEA.)

MEDEA: Women of Corinth, I have come outside
   To avoid your disapproval. I know there are many
   Conceited people; some keep themselves to themselves,
   Others show it in public, while others still, who take
   Things quietly, will find themselves called idlers.
   The eyes are no good judges, when a man
   Dislikes another at sight before he knows
   His character, when there is nothing against him.   200
   A foreigner especially should conform.
   I'd even blame a native for presuming
   To annoy his fellow citizens through lack of manners.
   For me, this unexpected blow that fell
   Has shattered me; it is the end, I only want to die.
   The man to whom I gave my all, as well he knows,
   Has turned out utterly false—my husband.
   Of all things living that possess a mind
   We women are the most unfortunate.
   To start with, we must put ourselves to vast expense   210
   To buy ourselves a husband, take a master for
   Our bodies—a worse evil than the other:
   And everything depends on this, whether we take a good man
   Or a bad one; divorce is not respectable
   For women, we may not deny our husbands.
   Coming to new manners and a new way of life,
   A woman needs second sight to know how best
   To manage her bedfellow; no-one taught her at home.
   And if we work hard at it, and our husband
   Lives with us without struggling against the yoke   220
   We are to be envied; if not, death comes at last.
   When a man is bored with the company in his household
   He can go out to find his consolation.
   We women have only one soul-mate to look to.
   They tell us we can spend our lives at home
   In safety, while they go out to fight the wars.
   How illogical! I'd rather stand three times
   In the battlefield than bear one child.
   But we have different stories, you and I;
   You have a city, and a father's home,   230
   And friendly company, a life you can enjoy.
   I have no home, no country; I am despised
   By my husband, something brought back from abroad;
   I have no mother, no brother, no family
   Where I can find a refuge from my troubles.

So this is the favor I will ask of you:
If the means offer, or I can find some way
To pay my husband back for the wrong he has done me,
Keep my secret. At other times a woman is timid,
Afraid to defend herself, frightened at the sight   240
Of weapons; but when her marriage is in danger
There is no mind bloodthirstier than hers.
CHORUS: I will; for you have every right to punish him.
I do not wonder that you are distressed.
But I can see Creon, ruler of this land,
Approaching with some new decision to tell us.
                    (*Enter* CREON.)
CREON: You with the scowling face, who hate your husband,
Medea, I command you leave this land
An exile, taking your two children with you
Without delay. I come to execute   250
My own decree, and shall not go back home
Till I have seen you past our boundaries.
MEDEA: Alas, my ruin is complete;
My enemies pursue full-sailed, and I
Can find no friendly harbor from calamity.
But though I am persecuted I will ask one thing:
For what reason, Creon, do you banish me?
CREON: I am afraid of you. Why veil my words?
Afraid you will do my child some dreadful harm.
And many things contribute to my fear: 260
You are clever, and accomplished in black arts,
And angry that your husband has deserted you.
I hear you threaten—so I am informed—
To act against the bridegroom and the bride
And the father too. I had rather be safe than sorry.
Better be hated, woman, by you now,
Than soften and repent my weakness later.
MEDEA: This has happened before. It is not the first time, Creon,
I have been the victim of my reputation.
No sensible man should ever have his sons   270
Brought up more clever than the average.
Apart from being told they waste their time
They earn the spite and envy of their neighbors.
You'll be called good-for-nothing, not intelligent,
For holding unconventional ideas;
And if the know-alls find your reputation
Exceeding theirs, the state will turn against you.
And I am one of those to whom it happened.
I am clever, so some people envy me,
Some call me idle, some the opposite,   280
While others hate me; but they exaggerate.
You fear me? Do you think you will be hurt?
I am in no state—do not be nervous, Creon—
To commit an offence against the authorities.

How have you wronged me? You bestowed your daughter
On the man your heart desired. It is my husband
That I hate.
But I suppose you know what you are doing.
I do not grudge you any of your good fortune.
Let the marriage stand, and prosper; but permit me   **290**
To stay here. Though I am the injured party
I shall not raise my voice against my betters.
CREON: Your words are smooth enough, but I fear your heart
    Is already plotting mischief, and by so much less
    I trust you than I did before.
    A fiery temper, in woman as in man,
    Is easier to guard against than silent cunning.
    So get you gone without more argument.
    You may be sure that no arts you can use
    Will keep you here, now you have turned against us.   **300**
MEDEA: No, by your knees, and by your child the bride!
CREON: Go, it is useless, you cannot persuade me.
MEDEA: Will you turn me away and not listen to my prayers?
CREON: My family comes first in my affections.
MEDEA: My country, how strongly I recall you now.
CREON: I love my country too, after my children.
MEDEA: Oh, what a bitter curse is love to men.
CREON: Well, that depends on circumstances, I suppose.
MEDEA: O Zeus, remember who began these sorrows.
CREON: Get out, you fool, and trouble me no further.   **310**
MEDEA: I have my troubles; trouble me no further.
CREON: Soon my men will drive you out by force.
MEDEA: No! Spare me that, at least. I beg you, Creon—
CREON: You seem determined, woman, to be difficult.
MEDEA: No. I will go. It was not that I wanted.
CREON: Then why resist? Why do you not leave the country?
MEDEA: Permit me to remain here this one day,
    To make my mind up where I am to go,
    And where to keep my children, since their father
    Prefers to leave his sons without protection.   **320**
    You are a father; you have sons yourself,
    And therefore should be well disposed to mine.
    I do not care for myself if I am banished
    But I am wretched if they are in trouble.
CREON: I never had the heart to play the tyrant.
    My conscience has always been my disadvantage.
    Woman, I know that I am making a mistake,
    But your request is granted. But I warn you,
    If the light of heaven falls on you tomorrow
    Here with your sons inside our boundaries   **330**
    You die. This is my final word.
    And now, if stay you must, remain one day,
    Too little time to do the harm I dread.
                                   (*Exit.*)

CHORUS: How troubled you are, unfortunate lady!
  Where will you turn? What home, what country
  Will give you protection?
  Medea, god has plunged you in a sea of troubles
  And there is no land in sight.
MEDEA: Beaten on every side; who can deny it?   340
  But not in this, so do not think I am.
  There are still trials for this new-married pair
  And no small sorrow for their families.
  You think I would have fawned upon this man
  Unless I were working for my own advantage?
  I would not have touched him, not have spoken to him.
  But he has gone so far in foolishness
  That when he could have foiled my plans
  By sending me to exile, he allowed me stay
  One day, in which I shall make corpses of   350
  Three of my enemies—father, girl, my husband.
  And I have many ways to work their deaths
  And do not know where first to try my hand—
  Whether to set their wedding house on fire,
  Or creep indoors to where their bedroom is
  And thrust a sharpened sword into their hearts.
  One thing prevents me; if I should be caught
  Entering the house and plotting against it
  I shall die the laughing-stock of my enemies.
  No. It is best to go direct, the way in which I am
  Most skilled, and poison both of them.   360
  Ah then,
  Suppose them dead; what city will receive me?
  What host will offer me home and security
  In some safe country, and protect my life?
  No-one. Then I shall wait a little while,
  And if some tower of safety should appear,
  By stealth and cunning I shall murder them.
  But if misfortune should drive me out helpless,
  I shall take the sword, even though it means my death,
  And kill them.
  No, by the Queen of Night whom above all   370
  I honor and have chosen as my partner,
  Dark Hecate dwelling in the corners of my hearth,
  No man shall wound my heart and still live happy.
  I will make them curse the day they married,
  Curse this alliance and my banishment.
  Then come, Medea, call on all the skill
  You have in plotting and contriving;
  On to the crime! This is the test of courage.
  Look to your wrongs! You must not let yourself
  Be mocked by Jason's Sisyphean wedding,   380
  You, a royal child, descended from the Sun.
  You have the skill; moreover you were born

A woman; and women are incapable of good,
But have no equal in contriving harm.
CHORUS: The sacred rivers flow back to their sources,
  The appointed order of things is reversed.
  It is men whose minds are deceitful, who take
  The names of their gods in vain,
  And women the future will honor in story
  As leaders of upright lives.   390
  Glory is ours! And the slanderous tongues
  That attacked womankind shall be stilled.

  You Muses of past generations, inspire
  No more the refrain that woman is fickle.
  We were not given the wit of Phoebus
  Apollo, the master of songs,
  To strike from the lyre its heavenly music.
  If it were so, I should sing
  In answer to men; for history tells
  As much of men's lives as of ours.   400

  In passion you sailed from the land
  Of your fathers, and saw the twin rocks
  Of the sea fall open before you.
  Now you live among strangers, exchange
  Your couch for a husbandless bed;
  Without rights and distressed you are driven
  An exile out of the land.

  The spell of the oath has been broken; no longer
  Has Greece any shame, it has flown to the winds.
  Poor lady, your father's home   410
  Will offer you shelter no more
  In time of distress; your marriage
  Is lost to a queen who descends
  On your house as a second bride.
                    (*Enter* JASON.)
JASON: I have noticed many times, this not the first,
  How willfulness runs on to self-destruction.
  You could have kept this country as your home
  By obeying the decisions of your betters,
  But futile protests send you into exile.
  They do not worry me. You can go on   420
  Forever saying Jason is a scoundrel;
  But when it comes to slandering your rulers,
  Count yourself lucky you were only banished.
  I wanted you to stay—tried all the time
  To pacify the anger of the king;
  But you persevered in folly, and continually
  Spoke ill of him, and so you must be banished.
  However, I shall not desert my friends
  In spite of their behavior, but am here to see

That you and your children do not go out penniless   **430**
Or in need of anything; for banishment
Brings many hardships. Hate me though you may,
I could never bring myself to bear you malice.
MEDEA: Oh, devil! Devil! This is the worst abuse
My tongue can find for your lack of manliness.
You come to me, my mortal enemy,
Hateful to heaven and to all mankind?
This is not venturesome, this is not courage,
To look friends in the face whom you have wronged,
But the most detestable of human weaknesses,   **440**
Yes, shamelessness! But I am glad you came,
For I can ease my overburdened heart
Abusing you, and you will smart to hear.
I shall begin my tale at the beginning.
I saved your life, as every single Greek
Who sailed with you on board the Argo knows,
When you were sent to tame the bulls that breathed fire,
And yoke them, and sow death in the field.
The dragon that encircled with his coils
The Golden Fleece and watched it without sleeping   **450**
I killed for you, and lit your path to safety.
For you I left my father and my home
And sailed to Iolkos and Mount Pelion
With you, and showed more eagerness than sense.
I brought on Pelias the worst of ends,
Death at his children's hands, and ruined his house.
All this I suffered for your worthless sake,
To be abandoned for another woman,
Though I had borne you children! Were I barren
You might have some excuse to marry again.   **460**
I have no faith in your promises; I cannot tell
If you believe in the old gods still, or think
There is some newer standard of morality—
You have broken your oath to me, you must know that.
Oh, this my right hand, that you wrung so often!
These knees, at which you fell; how am I deceived
In a false lover, cheated of my hopes.
But come, I will open my heart to you as to a friend—
Though what fair treatment could I hope from you?
Yet will I; you will feel more shame to answer.   **470**
Where should I turn now? To my father's home?
The country I betrayed to come with you?
Or Pelias' wretched daughters? They would give
A gracious welcome to their father's murderess.
For that is how it is. I have estranged myself
From friends at home, and those I should not hurt
I have made mortal enemies for your sake.
In recompense, how happy have you made me
Among Greek women; what a paragon

Speak out; I am ready to be open-handed,   580
And give you introductions to my friends
Who will assist you. It is foolish to refuse;
Let your anger rest, and you will profit by it.
MEDEA: I want no truck with any friends of yours
Or anything from you, so do not offer it.
A bad man's gifts bring no-one any good.
JASON: Very well! But I call on heaven to witness
I have done everything possible for you and your sons.
Your stubbornness rejects your friends; you don't know
When you are well off. So much the worse for you.   590
                    (Exit.)
MEDEA: Yes, go; you are too eager for your new bride
To stay any longer outside her house.
Go and be married! God will echo me,
This marriage may be such you will disown it.
CHORUS: Love unrestrained can bring
No worth or honor with it,
But coming in small measure
There is no power more gracious.
Never let fly at me
Great Queen, the unerring shafts   600
Of your golden arrows, tipped
In the poison of desire.

Let moderation be
My guide, the gods' best gift.
Dread Aphrodite, never
Send strife and argument
To attack my heart and make
Me long for other loves,
But learn to honor marriage
And let love lie in peace.   610

Oh, let me never lose you,
My country and my home,
Or learn the thorny ways
Of poverty, the worst
Of life's calamities.
No! Let me rather die
And see life's brief day done.
This is the greatest sorrow,
The loss of fatherland.

I know; I do not learn   620
The tale from the lips of others.
No home or friend to share
The depths of your distress.
Dishonored be the man
Who honors not his friends
And locks his heart away;

No friend shall he be of mine.

(Enter AEGEUS.*)*

AEGEUS: Give you joy, Medea; this is the best way
  Men know to start a conversation with their friends.
MEDEA: And joy to you, wise Aegeus, son of Pandion.   630
  Where are you from? What brings you to our country?
AEGEUS: From Apollo's ancient oracle at Delphi.
MEDEA: What took you there, to earth's prophetic center?
AEGEUS: To inquire how children might be born to me.
MEDEA: What, are you still without a son at your age?
AEGEUS: Yes, by some whim of providence I have no heir.
MEDEA: Are you married? Or have you never had a wife?
AEGEUS: I am no stranger to the marriage bond.
MEDEA: And what did Phoebus have to say about it?
AEGEUS: Words too wise for a man to understand.   640
MEDEA: Then may I know the oracle's reply?
AEGEUS: Most certainly, for cleverness is what we need.
MEDEA: Then tell me, if you may, what Phoebus said.
AEGEUS: Not to loosen the wineskin's hanging foot—
MEDEA: Until you had arrived somewhere, or done something?
AEGEUS: Until I reached my ancestral hearth again.
MEDEA: And what directs your journey through this country?
AEGEUS: There is a man called Pittheus, King of Troezen—
MEDEA: Old Pelops' son, with a great reputation for piety.
AEGEUS: I want to tell him what the oracle has said.   650
MEDEA: He is a wise man, skillful in such matters.
AEGEUS: And the oldest of my military allies.
MEDEA: I hope you are lucky, and achieve your heart's desire.

(She breaks down, and turns away her head.)

AEGEUS: Why do you turn away, and look so pale?
MEDEA: Aegeus, my husband is the worst of men.
AEGEUS: What's this you say? Tell me about your troubles.
MEDEA: Jason, unprovoked, has done me wrong.
AEGEUS: What has he done to you? Tell me more clearly.
MEDEA: Put another woman over his household in my place.
AEGEUS: He would not dare to treat you so despicably!   660
MEDEA: Too truly; and I, the old love, am dishonored.
AEGEUS: Was it for love of her, or hate of you?
MEDEA: Much love he has; the man was born unfaithful.
AEGEUS: Take no notice, if he's as worthless as you say.
MEDEA: He was in love with marrying a king's daughter.
AEGEUS: Who gives her to him? Tell me the whole story.
MEDEA: Creon, the ruler of this land of Corinth.
AEGEUS: You have good reason for your grief, my lady.
MEDEA: It is the end; and I am banished too.
AEGEUS: On whose orders? This is a new wrong you speak of.   670
MEDEA: It is Creon who sends me into exile from the land.
AEGEUS: And Jason lets him? This is unforgivable.
MEDEA: He says not, but he has resigned himself.

(She falls at his feet.)

But I beseech you, by the beard I clasp.
And throw myself a suppliant at your knees,
Have pity, have pity on my misery
And do not see me thrown out destitute.
Let me come to your country and live at your hearthside;
So may your great desire come to fruition
And give you children, and allow you to die happy.   680
You do not know what good fortune you have found.
I can put a stop to your childlessness, and give
You issue, with the potions that I know.
AEGEUS: I am anxious for many reasons, lady,
    To grant your request; first, my religious scruples,
    And then your promise that I should have sons,
    For in this there is nothing else that I can do.
    But this is how I stand. If you can reach my country
    I'll endeavor to protect you as in duty bound.
    But one thing I must make clear from the start: 690
    I am not willing to take you from this country.
    If you can make your own way to my home
    I will keep you safe and give you up to no-one,
    But you must make your own escape from Corinth.
    I would not give offence, even to strangers.
MEDEA: So let it be, then. If you swear an oath
    To do this, I have nothing more to ask.
AEGEUS: Do you not trust me? What is it puts you off?
MEDEA: I trust you; but the house of Pelias is against me,
    And Creon. Oath-bound, you could never yield   700
    Me to them when they came to take me away.
    A promise unsupported by an oath
    Would allow you to befriend them, and obey
    Their summons when it came. My cause is weak,
    While they have power and money on their side.
AEGEUS: You show great thought for the future in what you say.
    But, if you wish it, I shall not refuse.
    My own position will be unassailable
    If I have an excuse to offer your enemies,
    And you will run less risk. Come, name your gods.   710
MEDEA: Swear by the plain of Earth, and by the Sun,
    My father's father; add the whole family of gods.
AEGEUS: That I will do or not do what? Say on.
MEDEA: Never to drive me from the land yourself
    Or willingly yield me to my enemies
    When they come for me, as long as you do live.
AEGEUS: I swear by Earth, by the holy light of Sun,
    By all the gods, to do as you have said.
MEDEA: Enough. What penalty if you break your oath?
AEGEUS: What comes to men who take their gods in vain.   720
MEDEA: Now go your way in peace. All will be well.
    I shall come to your country as soon as I have done
    What I intend to do, and won my heart's desire.

CHORUS: Now Hermes, God of Travelers,
    Give you safe conduct home,
    And may the desire that you cherish
    So eagerly be fulfilled.
    You have shown, Aegeus,
    What a good man you are.

(Exit AEGEUS.)

MEDEA: O Zeus, Zeus' daughter Justice, light of Sun,   **730**
    Now shall we have a glorious triumph, friends,
    Upon our enemies; our feet are on the path.
    Now is there hope my enemies will pay
    The penalty. This man has shown himself,
    Where we were weakest, a haven for my plans.
    In him my ship may find safe anchorage;
    To Athena's fortress city shall I go!
    And now I will reveal you all my plans.
    Hear what I have to say; it will not please you.
    One of my servants I shall send to Jason   **740**
    And ask him to come here before my face.
    And when he comes, I shall say soft words to him,
    That I agree with him, and all is well;
    That the royal match he abandons me to make
    Is for my advantage, and a good idea.
    I shall entreat him that my sons should stay—
    Not to allow my sons to be insulted
    In a strange country by my enemies,
    But to kill the daughter of the king with cunning.
    I shall send them both with presents in their hands,   **750**
    A fine-spun robe, a golden diadem.
    If she accepts the gifts and puts them on
    She will die in agony and all who touch her,
    With such deadly poison shall I anoint my gifts.
    Now I must leave this story, and lament
    The dreadful thing that then remains for me to do.
    I will kill my sons; no man shall take them from me.
    And when the house of Jason lies in ruins,
    I shall fly this land, setting my darlings' death
    Behind me, most unspeakable of crimes.   **760**
    The scorn of enemies is unendurable.
    But let it go; for what have I to live for?
    I have no home, no country, no escape from misery.
    I made my mistake the day I left behind
    My father's home, seduced by speeches from
    A Greek who heaven knows will pay for them.
    The sons I bore him he will never see
    Alive after this day, nor father more
    On his new-married bride, condemned to die
    In agony from my poisons as she deserves.   **770**
    No-one shall call me timorous or weak
    Or stay-at-home, but quite the opposite,

A menace to my enemies and help to friends;
Those are the people that the world remembers.
CHORUS: Since you have taken me into your confidence,
  I should like to help you, but must still uphold
  The laws of men. I say you cannot do this.
MEDEA: There is nothing else I can do. But you have excuse
  For speaking so, you have not known my sufferings.
CHORUS: But will you have the heart to kill your children?   780
MEDEA: Yes; it is the way I can most hurt my husband.
CHORUS: But you will be the most unhappy of women.
MEDEA: So be it; there can be no compromise.
(Calling the NURSE.)

You; go at once and fetch Jason here.
We have no secrets from each other, you and I,
And breathe no word to anyone of my plans,
As you love your mistress, as you are a woman.
(Exit NURSE.)

CHORUS: Happy of old were the sons of Erechtheus,
  Sprung from the blessed gods, and dwelling
  In Athens' holy and untroubled land.   790
  Their food is glorious wisdom; they walk
  With springing step in the crystal air.
  Here, so they say, golden Harmony first
  Saw the light, the child of the Muses nine.

And here too, they say, Aphrodite drank
Of Cephisus' fair-flowing stream, and breathed
Sweet breezes over the land, with garlands
Of scented roses entwined in her hair,
And gave Love a seat on the throne of Wisdom
To work all manner of arts together.   800

How then will this city of sacred waters,
This guide and protector of friends, take you,
Your children's slayer, whose touch will pollute
All others you meet? Think again of the deaths
Of your children, the blood you intend to shed.
By your knees, by every entreaty we beg you
Not to become your children's murderess.

Where will you find the boldness of mind,
The courage of hand and heart, to kill them?
How will you strike without weeping, how   810
Be constant to stain your hands in their blood
When your children kneel weeping before you?
(Enter JASON.)

JASON: I come at your request; although you hate me,
  This favor you shall have. So let me hear
  What new demand you have to make of me.
MEDEA: Jason, I ask you to forgive the words
  I spoke just now. The memory of our

Past love should help you bear my evil temper.
Now I have taken myself to task and found
I was to blame. "Fool, why am I so mad?   820
Why should I quarrel with those who want to help me,
And why antagonize the men in power
And my husband, who works only for my advantage
In making this royal marriage, and begetting
New brothers for my sons? Why not lay down
My anger, why resent what the gods provide?
Are not my children mine, and am I not
An exile from the land, without a friend?"
Such were my thoughts; and then I realized
What foolishness my futile anger was.   830
Now I agree with you, and think you provident
In gaining us this connection, and myself a fool.
I should have been your go-between and shared
Your plans, stood by your marriage-bed,
And had the joy of tending your new bride.
But we are what we are; I will not say bad,
But women. But you should not take bad example
And answer my stupidity with yours.
Now I submit, agree that I was wrong
Before, but come to saner judgment now.   840
My children, here, my children, leave the house,
Come out to greet your father, and with me
Bid him goodbye; be reconciled to friends
And let your anger rest beside your mother's.
          (The CHILDREN *appear from the house, and go to* JASON.)
We are at peace; there is no anger now.
Come, take his hand.
(*aside*)   Oh, the pity of it;
There is something still unseen, but my mind knows it.
Children, will you live long to stretch out
Your loving arms, as now? Oh pity, pity;
How near I am to tears, how full of fear.   850
                    (*aloud.*)
At last I have stopped the quarrel with their father
And brought tears of forgiveness to their eyes.
CHORUS: And my eyes too are wet with running tears.
   I pray we have no troubles worse than these.
JASON: I approve this mood, and do not blame the other.
   It is natural for a woman to show resentment
   When her husband smuggles in a second marriage.
   But now your mind has turned to better things
   And learned—at last—which policy must win.
   Done like a sensible woman!   860
                    (*To the* CHILDREN.)
Your father hasn't forgotten you, my boys.
God willing, you'll be well provided for.
I'll see you here in Corinth at the top

Beside your brothers. Just grow up; your father
Will see to the rest, and any god that fancies you.
I want to see you, when you've grown young men,
Stout fellows, head and shoulders above my enemies.
Medea, what are these tears upon your cheeks?
Why do you turn your face away from me?
Why aren't you happy at the things I say?   870
MEDEA: It is nothing. I was thinking of my children.
JASON: Don't worry. I shall see them well set up.
MEDEA: I shall try to be brave, not mistrust what you say;
But we women are the weaker sex, born weepers.
JASON: Why so unhappy, lady, for these children?
MEDEA: I am their mother. When you prayed that they might live,
Compassion came, and said "Will it be so?"
For what you came here to discuss with me,
Part has been said, the rest remains to say.
Since the king thinks good to send me from the land,   880
I too think it is good, and I acknowledge it,
Not to embarrass you or the authorities
By staying. I am not welcome in this house.
Yes, I will leave this country, go to exile;
But that your hand alone may rear my sons,
I pray you, beg the king to let them stay.
JASON: I doubt I will succeed, but I must try.
MEDEA: Then you must tell your new wife, the princess,
To beg her father to remit their banishment.
JASON: I'll do it. Yes, I think I can persude her.   890
MEDEA: You will, if she is a woman like the rest of us.
And I shall lend my shoulder to this labor,
And send her gifts more beautiful by far
Than any man has ever seen, I know—
A fine-spun robe, a golden diadem.
My sons shall take them. One of my servants,
Go bring the robes as quickly as you can.
She will be not once blessed but a thousand times,
Having you, the best of men, to be her husband,
And owning ornaments which once the Sun,   900
My father's father gave to his descendants.
                    (*A servant brings the presents from the house.*)
Here, take this dowry, children, put it in the hands
Of the happy royal bride. She will not think lightly of it.
JASON: What are you doing? Why deprive yourself?
Do you think the royal house lacks robes?
Do you think we have no gold? Keep them,
Don't give them away. If my wife respects me at all,
She will prefer my wish to presents, I can tell you.
MEDEA: Not so; they say that gifts can move the gods.
A piece of gold is worth a thousand speeches.   910
Her luck is in, god give her more of it.
A queen, so young. I'd willingly give my life

To save my sons from banishment, not only gold.
Go to the halls of wealth, my sons, beseech
The new wife of your father and my queen,
And beg her not to send you into exile.
Give her the presents—this is most important—
Into her own hands.
Now hurry; bring your mother back good news
That you have accomplished what she sets her heart on.   920
                    (*Exeunt* CHILDREN *and* JASON.)
CHORUS: There is no hope now for the children's lives,
  No hope any longer; they go to their deaths,
  And the bride, poor bride, will accept the gift
  Of the crown worked of gold,
  And with her own hands make death an adornment
  To set in her yellow hair.

  The unearthly splendor and grace of the robe
  And the crown worked of gold will persuade her to wear them.
  She will soon be attired to marry the dead.
  Into such a snare is she fallen,   930
  Into such deadly fate, poor girl, and will never
  Escape from the curse upon her.

  And you, unhappy man, bitter bridegroom,
  Who make an alliance with kings,
  Unknowing you send your sons to their deaths
  And bring on your bride the worst of ends.
  How are you deceived in your hopes of the future.

  And next to theirs we mourn your sorrows,
  Unhappy mother of sons,
  Who, to repay your husband for leaving   940
  Your bed, and going to live with another
  Woman, will kill your children.
                    (*Enter the* TUTOR, *leading the* TWO CHILDREN.)
TUTOR: Mistress! Your children are reprieved from exile!
  The royal bride was pleased to take into her hands
  Your gifts, and with your sons is peace.
  Why does good fortune leave you so confused?
  Why do you turn your face the other way?
  Why aren't you happy at the things I say?
MEDEA: Alas.
TUTOR: Your words and mine are out of tune.
MEDEA: Alas again.
TUTOR: Is there some meaning to my words   950
  I do not know? Am I wrong to think them good?
MEDEA: You have said what you have said; I do not blame you.
TUTOR: Why do you drop your eyes, begin to weep?
MEDEA: Because there is necessity, old man. The gods
  And my pernicious schemings brought this thing to pass.
TUTOR: Be brave; your children will bring you home again.

MEDEA: I shall send others home before they do.
TUTOR: You are not the only mother to lose her children.
   Mankind must bear misfortune patiently.
MEDEA: And so shall I. But go inside the house   **960**
   And see about my children's daily needs.
                       (*Exit* TUTOR.)
   My sons, my sons, you have a city now
   And home, where when we've said our sad goodbye
   You will stay for ever, parted from your mother.
   I go in exile to another land
   Before I have had the joy of seeing you happy,
   Before I have made your marriage beds, and seen
   Your brides, and carried torches at your weddings.
   My willfulness has brought its own reward.
   For nothing did I toil to bring you up,   **970**
   For nothing did I labor, and endure
   The pangs I suffered in your hour of birth.
   Once I had in you, oh, once, such splendid hopes,
   To have you by my side as I grew old
   And when I died, your loving arms around me,
   What all men long for. This sweet dream is now
   Destroyed. When you and I have parted
   My life will be forlorn and desolate.
   Your loving eyes will never look upon
   Your mother again, you go to another life.   **980**
   My sons, my sons, why do you look at me?
   Why smile at me the last smile I shall see?
   Oh, oh, what shall I do? Women, my heart
   Is faltering when I look at their bright eyes.
   I cannot do it; I renounce the plans
   I made before, my children shall go with me.
   Why should I use their sufferings to hurt
   Their father, and so doubly hurt myself?
   Not I, not I; I renounce my plans.
   And yet—what is happening to me? Shall I let   **990**
   My enemies go scot-free and earn their scorn?
   Be bold, Medea. Why, what a coward am I
   That can allow my mind talk of relenting.
   Go in, my children. He who may not be
   Present at my sacrifice without sin,
   On his own head be it; my hand is firm.
         (*She turns to follow the* CHILDREN *into the house, and then pauses.*)
   Do not do this, my heart, do not do this!
   Spare them, unhappy heart, let my sons go.
   They will live with you in exile and make you glad.
   No, by the fiends that dwell in Hell below,   **1000**
   It shall never come to this, that I allow
   My sons to be insulted by my enemies.
         (*A noise of shouting is heard off-stage.*)
   So; it is finished; there is no escape.

The crown is on her head, the royal bride
Is dying in her robes, this I know well.
And I must tread my own unhappy road;
Far worse the road on which I send my sons.
I want to speak to them. Here, children, give
Your mother your hand, let mother hold your hand.
Oh dearest hand, oh lips I hold most dear,   1010
Dear face, and dear bright eyes, may you be happy—
But in another place; your father leaves
You nothing here. Oh, sweet embrace,
The feel of your skin, the scent of your sweet breath;
Go away! Go away! I have no strength
To look on you, my sorrows overwhelm me.
Women, I know what evil I am to do,
But anger has proved stronger than our reason
And from anger all our greatest ills arise.
                        (The CHILDREN go into the house.)
CHORUS: I have often allowed my mind   1020
    To speculate, enter into arguments
    Lying outside a woman's province.
    But there is a Muse in women too
    To help us to wisdom; not in all,
    But look far enough, and you many find a few
    On whom the Muse has smiled.

    And I say that those men and women
    Who do not know what it means to have children
    Are blessed above parents in this world.
    A child can bring joy, or bitter pain;
    What can the children know of these?   1030
    And those whose fortune it is to be barren
    Are spared a world of worry.

    But we see that those who tend
    The delicate plant of youth in their houses
    Have care at their side every hour of the day;
    How they will bring their children up,
    How they will leave them the means to live,
    Will they grow up to be good or bad?
    There is no way of knowing.

    Then the unkindest blow: 1040
    Suppose young bodies grow sturdy and strong
    To make parents proud; then if Fate decides,
    Down goes Death to the house of Hades,
    Taking the children's bodies with him.
    How should it profit a man, if heaven
    Adds this, the bitterest grief, to his sorrows
    Only for loving his children?
MEDEA: Friends, I have awaited my fortune this long while,
    Anxious to see which way events would turn.

And now I can see one of Jason's servants   **1050**
Approaching; he is running, out of breath,
Sure sign of some new horror to report.
(*Enter a* MESSENGER.)
MESSENGER: You who have outraged all laws, and done
  This dreadful crime; run, run away, Medea!
  Take ship or chariot, and do not scorn their aid!
MEDEA: What have I done, that I should run away?
MESSENGER: The royal bride is dead, and with her
  Her father Creon; it was your poisons killed them.
MEDEA: You tell a glorious tale. From this time on
  I'll number you among my friends and benefactors.   **1060**
MESSENGER: Are you in your right mind? Have you gone insane,
  To work the ruin of the royal house
  And laugh, and not be afraid of what I tell you?
MEDEA: There is a great deal I could say
  To answer you. Do not be hasty, friend,
  But tell me how they died. My pleasure will
  Be doubled, if their deaths were horrible.
MESSENGER: When the two children, your sons, came with their father
  And presented themselves at the house where the bride lived,
  We servants, who sympathized with your misfortunes,   **1070**
  Were glad, and rumor soon buzzed about the house
  That you had patched up the old quarrel with your husband.
  Some kissed their hands, and some
  Their golden heads; and I was so delighted
  I followed the children to the women's quarters.
  Our mistress—her we honor in your place—
  Only had eyes for Jason, and didn't see
  The children, when they came in at first.
  And then she turned her pretty head the other way,
  Angry they should have been let in. But Jason   **1080**
  Tried to pacify her anger and resentment
  And said, "You must not be at odds with friends.
  Stop sulking, turn your head this way again;
  You must believe your husband's friends are yours.
  Accept their gifts, and supplicate your father
  To reprieve the boys from exile, for my sake."
  When she saw the finery, she couldn't hold out longer,
  But did everything he asked. Before the children
  And their father had gone far outside the house
  She took the pretty robe and put it on,   **1090**
  And set the golden crown around her curls,
  Arranging them before a shining mirror
  And smiling at her ghostly image there.
  Then she stood up, and left the throne, and trod
  Her white feet delicately round the room,
  Delighted with the gifts, and every now and then
  She made a leg and studied the effect.
  And then there was a sight that scared us all:
  Her color goes, she stumbles sideways, back

Towards the throne, and hardly stops herself   **1100**
From falling on the floor.
Then some old waiting maid, who must have thought
The fit was sent by Pan, or by some god,
Began to pray; and then she saw her mouth
All white with running froth, the eyeballs starting from
Their sockets, and her body pale and bloodless; and then
She screamed so loud the screaming drowned the prayer.
Someone went straight away to fetch
Her father, someone to her new husband,
To tell them what was happening to the bride,   **1110**
And the house rang everywhere with noise of running feet.
Already, in the time a practised runner
Could run a hundred yards, the princess
Recovered from her speechless, sightless swoon
And screamed in anguish. It was terrible;
From two directions the pain attacked her.
The golden circlet twining round her hair
Poured forth a strange stream of devouring fire,
And the fine-spun robe, the gift your children gave her,
Had teeth to tear the poor girl's pretty skin.   **1120**
She left the throne and fled burning through the room,
Shaking her head this way and that,
Trying to dislodge the crown, but it was fixed
Immovably, and when she shook her hair
The flames burnt twice as fiercely.
Then, overcome with pain, she fell to the ground.
Only her father would have recognized her.
Her eyes had lost their settled look, her face
Its natural expression, and the blood
Dripped from her head to mingle with the fire.   **1130**
The flesh dropped from her bones like pine-tears, torn
By the unseen power of the devouring poison,
We saw, and shuddered; no-one dared
To touch the corpse, we had her fate for warning.
But her old father, who knew nothing of what had happened,
Came running in, and flung himself on the body,
Began to weep, and flung his arms around her,
And kissed her, crying "Oh, unhappy child,
What god has killed you so inhumanly?
Who takes you from me, from the grave of my   **1140**
Old age? If I could die with you, my child!"
And then he stopped his tears and lamentations
And tried to raise his old body up again,
But clung fast to the robe, as ivy clings
To laurel branches. Then there was a ghastly struggle,
He trying to raise himself from off his knees,
She holding him down; and when he pushed her off
He tore the aged flesh from off his bones.
And then he fought no more; the poor old man
Gave up the ghost, the struggle was too much for him.   **1150**

The bodies of the princess and her father
Lie side by side, a monument to grief.
Your part in this affair is none of my business.
You will find your own escape from punishment.
Life is a shadow; I have thought so often,
And I am not afraid to say that those
Who seem wise among men, and accomplished talkers,
Must pay the heaviest penalty of all.
No man is happy. He might grow more prosperous
Than other men, if fortune comes his way,   1160
But happy he can never be.
(Exit.)
CHORUS: This is the day of heaven's visitation
On Jason, and he has deserved it richly.
But we have only tears for your misfortune,
Poor child of Creon, who must go to Hades
Because of Jason's wedding.
MEDEA: Women, my task is fixed: as quickly as possible
To kill my children and to fly this land,
And not by hesitation leave my sons
To die by other hands more merciless.   1170
Whatever happens, they must die; and since they must,
I, who first gave them life, shall give them death.
Come, steel yourself, my heart; why do you hesitate
To do this dreadful thing which must be done?
Come, my unhappy hand, take up the sword
And go to where life's misery begins.
Do not turn coward; think not of your children,
How much you loved them, how you bore them; no,
For this one day forget you are a mother;
Tomorrow you may weep. But though you kill them, yet   1180
You love them still; and my poor heart is broken.
(She goes into the house.)
CHORUS: Earth and all-seeing light of the Sun,
Look down, look down on a woman destroyed
Before she raises her murderous hand
Against her babes. From a golden age
Was she born, and we fear divine blood
Will be shed by mortals. Restrain her, great light
Of heaven, hold her back, drag her forth from the house,
This accursed murderess driven by furies.
Did you toil for your sons in vain, did you labor   1190
For nothing to bring your darlings to birth
When you left behind you the angry straits
Where ships are crushed in the grim grey rocks?
Why has their weight of anger fallen
Upon your heart, this lust for the kill?
The death of kindred is mortals' curse
And heaven sends sorrows meet for the murderers,
Calamities falling upon the house.

lished as the center point, and marked by a pointed stone (*omphalos*, navel) in the oracular shrine.

638 *no stranger to the marriage bond.* Aegeus had already married twice.

644 *not to loosen . . .* The Delphic Oracle is typically ambiguous. Aegeus is commanded "not to loosen the wineskin's hanging foot"—that is, not to engage in sexual intercourse—until he reaches his "ancestral hearth." He naturally takes this to mean Athens. But on his way home he stopped at Troezen and lay with Aethra, who bore him a son. Euripides is referring here to a tradition whereby Troezen was already associated with Athens; thus the "ancestral hearth" could apply equally well to either place, and the oracle is proved correct.

775 *Since you have taken me . . .* Here the awkwardness of the chorus becomes apparent. Euripides is compelled to take their presence into account and make Medea divulge her plans to them; though they object, the exigencies of the plot forbid them to interfere. Euripides has given their inaction a bare plausibility by making Medea, earlier in the play, swear them to secrecy.

788 *Erechtheus* Mythical founder of the Athenian people. The chorus try to divert Medea from her purpose by dwelling on the glory and sanctity of Athens. How could such a city receive a murderess? This provides an opportunity for a burst of patriotic sentiment.

895 *A fine-spun robe* The exact repetition of this line from l. 751 has led some editors to excise it as an interpolation. It has, however, considerable dramatic point. Jason does not appreciate the full significance of the phrase, but the chorus and audience do. This is true dramatic irony.

994 *Go in, my children.* We must imagine the children as turning to go into the house, and then pausing at the door as Medea continues to speak.

1164 *But we have only tears . . .* These lines have been dismissed by some editors as a sentimental interpolation, but they are in keeping with Euripides' intention. He wishes to stress the horror of the deaths of Creon and the princess, and by implication the murders of Apsurtos and Pelias. This accounts for the Grand Guignol nature of the Messenger's speech, which violates all the customary restraint of Greek tragedy. Euripides is concerned to show the true nature of violence, and to condemn the acceptance of such episodes in the traditional stories. Thus the chorus makes a clear distinction. Jason deserved his punishment, but the princess did not; she, like Medea's brother, has been sacrificed to further a personal advantage.

1201 *What shall I do?* Although he is forced to work within the old conventions, Euripdes often contrives to give them a new twist. Tragedy was allowed only three speaking actors; thus the children must be *personae mutae*, silent characters, as long as they are on the stage. But Euripdes uses their unspeaking presence to increase the pathos of their plight. Every time we see them, we wonder if it will be the last. Note how Euripides gives the final twist by postponing their final exit (See l. 994 and note). When we do hear them, it is in the moment of their death.

1210 *One woman . . .* This chorus serves a dual purpose. First, it increases the excitement of her predicament. In drawing this parallel between Medea's crime and Ino's, Euripides seems to depart from the usual version, in which Ino saw one of her sons killed by his father and leapt into the sea with the other, for one in which Ino killed both sons and then leapt into the sea herself. The parallel, of course, is not as exact as the chorus thinks. Medea does not die, though the chorus sees this as inevitable, and so does Jason when he appears. The escape in the dragon chariot thus comes as a great surprise.

The chorus also provides a welcome relief from the high tragedy that has gone before. The tension has mounted higher and higher, to culminate in Medea's speech of decision and the dying screams of the children. Euripides now gives his audience a moment to recuperate.

1244 *What are you waiting for?* Euripides once more gives a new and exciting twist to an old formula. Such commands to "unbar the door" are customarily followed by the revelation of the *ekkyklema,* a wheeled platform bearing a tableau, of the dead bodies. The audience, hearing the familiar words, would have their gaze riveted on the central door. Then, from above, comes a cry, and Medea is seen on the roof of the stage building. Euripides has performed a theatrical conjuring trick, distracting the audience's attention to one point while he brings in Medea at another.

1254 *Hateful to heaven . . .* An exact repetition of l. 437 and thus excised by most editors. But it emphasizes the exact counter-balancing of the two halves of the play. Earlier, Medea said this of Jason; now, Jason says it of Medea. Their positions have been completely reversed.

1273 *Scylla* The mythical monster, familiar from the *Odyssey,* who lived in a sea-cave and preyed on passing ships.

1316 *Crushed by a relic . . .* There were two versions of Jason's death. According to one, he was sleeping under the beached Argo, now old and rotten, when the timbers collapsed on his head. According to the other, he had dedicated the stem of his ship in the temple of Hera; one day, as he was visiting the shrine, it fell down and killed him. Euripides seems to be following the second version.

1318 *Mountain-mother's shrine* Euripides likes to link his plays to some familiar rite or festival—here, to the worship of Hera.

1344 *Many things are wrought . . .* A stock epilogue, which appears at the end of several plays.

_____ **Written Response**

In *Euripides and His Age* (London: Henry Holt, 1913), Gilbert Murray wrote:

It is somewhat [difficult] to understand the universal assumption of our authorities that Euripides was a notorious castigator of the female sex and that the women of Athens naturally hated him. To us he seems an aggressive champion of women; more aggressive, and certainly far more appreciative, than Plato. Songs and speeches from the *Medea* are recited to-day at suffragette [the feminists of the early 1900s] meetings. His tragic heroines are famous and are almost always treated with greater interest and insight than his heroes. Yet not only the ancients, but all critics up to the last generation or so, have described him as a woman-hater. What does it mean? [pp. 31–32]

How do you feel that women are portrayed in *Medea?* Do you feel that Euripides was a woman-hater?

1. In Greek drama, the Chorus is not used in exactly the same way by all dramatists; indeed, even the same dramatist might use the Chorus in distinctly different ways in each of his or her plays. F. M. Cornford has suggested, however, that Greek drama operates on two planes or dimensions (*Thucydides Mythistoricus*, p. 144). When the actors are on stage, the drama portrays the actions, the fate, of individuals. When the Chorus is on stage, the drama is elevated to the universal or eternal. In other words, the Chorus takes a story about individuals and explains its significance for all humans. Review Euripides' use of the Chorus. How does Cornford's explanation of the Greek Chorus apply to *Medea*?

2. In his essay on *Medea* (in *Oxford Readings in Greek Tragedy* [London: Oxford University Press, 1983]), Eilhard Schlesinger writes:

> Because actors wore masks and performed at a great distance from the audience, an ancient dramatist could not convey his meaning through the sort of facial expression, which would be effective in the cinema today. Euripides, however, in a masterly fashion is able to achieve the same effect through the words of the heroine: 'Why, children, do you look upon me with your eyes?' cries Medea, 'why do you smile so sweetly that last smile of all?' [p. 294]

Schlesinger points out that Medea's description of her children's facial gestures, as she is about to kill them, conveys not only what her children were feeling but also what Medea was feeling.

What do you think that her children were feeling at this point? What was Medea feeling? How do these emotions affect the way that you react to Medea's killing of her children?

Can you find other examples in the play through which Euripides conveys subtle emotions by having one character describe the facial gestures of another character?

_____ **Interpretation**

1. As you read the play, did you find yourself siding with one of the major characters? Were you more sympathetic toward Medea than toward Jason? Or were you more sympathetic toward Jason than Medea? Why?

2. In *The Greek Way* (New York: Norton, 1930), Edith Hamilton argues that Euripides has a "modern mind":

> This spirit [or mind], always in the world and always the same, is primarily a destructive spirit, critical not creative. "The life without criticism," Plato says, "is not worthy to be lived." The modern minds in each generation are the critics who preserve us from a petrifying world, who will not leave us to walk undisturbed in the ways of our fathers. The established order is always wrong to them. [p. 166]

In what way do you feel that Euripides was criticizing Athenian society in *Medea*.

3. For virtually all ancient Greek myths, more than one version exist. Dramatists could thus select the version of the myth that they found most interesting or even combine elements of different versions of the myth to create an effective tragic plot. In *Word and Action: Essays on the Ancient Theater* (Baltimore: Johns Hopkins University Press, 1979), Bernard Knox wrote of Euripides' use of myth in *Medea*:

> We know that the version of the myth which he used in this play was not imposed on him. The many variants of the legend which can still be found in ancient mythographers and commentators as well as in the fragments of lost epics show that he had a wide freedom of choice. One account had Medea kill her children unintentionally (she was trying to make them immortal and something went wrong with the formula); in another the children were killed by the Corinthians in a revolt against Medea, whom they had appointed queen of Corinth; in yet another Medea killed Creon, left her children in the temple of Hera, and fled to Athens—wereupon Creon's kinsmen killed the children and spread the rumor that Medea had done it. At least two of these versions (and probably more besides) were available to Euripides, but he made his own by combination, addition, selection. [pp. 295–296]

Why do you think that Euripides rejected some of the versions of the Medea myth described above?

Why do you think that it was so important for ancient Greek tragedians to use myths as the source of their plots?

_____ **WRITING ASSIGNMENTS**

1. In *Medea*, Medea blames the murder of her children on Jason, and Jason blames the murder on Medea. Who do you believe is ultimately responsible for the death of Medea and Jason's children?

2. Argue that Euripides wrote *Medea* to criticize some aspect of Athenian culture.

3. Discuss Euripides' attitude toward women.

Tragedy: Ancient and Modern

Aristotle's *Poetics*, written 330 B.C., is one of the first attempts in Western civilization at what has become known as literary criticism, and it has remained one of the most influential treatises on literary theory. Despite his powerful influence on criticism to this day, some critics argue that Aristotle's ideas make the best sense when applied to Greek literature as written and as experienced within Greek culture. Other critics feel that Aristotle's ideas are as valid today as they were some 2000 years ago. In this section, you will have the opportunity to explore such issues.

You will find, however, that Aristotle's *Poetics* is not an easy work to read and interpret. The text, which was probably either Aristotle's unrevised lecture notes or a compilation of notes that his students wrote down after listening to him speak, is incomplete and sketchy. For example, a long section on comedy was apparently lost. Also, Aristotle refers in passing to dramas that have not survived. His students—the intended audience—were probably familiar with these dramas, but modern readers can, at times, feel lost amid comments about plays that can be nothing more than obscure titles.

In the following excerpts from the *Poetics*, Aristotle discusses his theory of tragedy.

_____ **Prereading**

In his discussion of tragedy, Aristotle emphasizes the importance of plot. He feels that good tragedies follow a basic plot structure (or pattern) and that those tragedies that deviate significantly from this basic plot will affect the audience less profoundly.

Select a specific genre (or type) of literature or film (for example, horror films) and discuss whether a basic plot is repeated in most effective works that fall into this category.

Excerpt from *Poetics*

Aristotle

It is clear that the general origin of poetry was due to two causes,   **1**
each of them part of human nature. Imitation is natural to man from
childhood, one of his advantages over the lower animals being this,
that he is the most imitative creature in the world, and learns at first
by imitation. And it is also natural for all to delight in works of imitation. The truth of this second point is shown by experience: though
the objects themselves may be painful to see, we delight to view the
most realistic representations of them in art, the forms for example of
the lowest animals and of dead bodies. The explanation is to be found
in a further fact: to be learning something is the greatest of pleasures
not only to the philosopher but also to the rest of mankind, however

Source: Excerpts from "Poetics" from *The Complete Works of Aristotle: The Revised Oxford Translation* edited by Jonathan Barnes. Bullingen Series 71. Copyright © 1984 Jowett Copyright Trustees. Reprinted by permission of Princeton University Press.

small their capacity for it; the reason of the delight in seeing the picture is that one is at the same time learning—gathering the meaning of things, e.g. that the man there is so-and-so; for if one has not seen the thing before, one's pleasure will not be in the picture as an imitation of it, but will be due to the execution or colouring or some similar cause. Imitation, then, being natural to us—as also the sense of harmony and rhythm, the metres being obviously species of rhythms—it was through their original aptitude, and by a series of improvements for the most part gradual on their first efforts, that they created poetry out of their improvisations.

. . . .

The unity of a plot does not consist, as some suppose, in its having 2
one man as its subject. An infinity of things befall that one man, some of which it is impossible to reduce to unity; and in like manner there are many actions of one man which cannot be made to form one action. One sees, therefore, the mistake of all the poets who have written a *Heracleid, a Theseid,* or similar poems; they suppose that, because Heracles was one man, the story also of Heracles must be one story. Homer, however, evidently understood this point quite well, whether by art or instinct, just in the same way as he excels the rest in every other respect. In writing an *Odyssey,* he did not make the poem cover all that ever befell his hero—it befell him, for instance, to get wounded on Parnassus and also to feign madness at the time of the call to arms, but the two incidents had no necessary or probable connexion with one another—instead of doing that, he took as the subject of the *Odyssey,* as also of the *Iliad,* an action with a unity of the kind we are describing. The truth is that, just as in the other imitative arts one imitation is always of one thing, so in poetry the story, as an imitation of action, must represent one action, a complete whole, with its several incidents so closely connected that the transposition or withdrawal of any one of them will disjoin and dislocate the whole. For that which makes no perceptible difference by its presence or absence is no real part of the whole.

From what we have said it will be seen that the poet's function is 3
to describe, not the thing that has happened, but a kind of thing that might happen, i.e. what is possible as being probable or necessary. The distinction between historian and poet is not in the one writing prose and the other verse—you might put the work of Herodotus into verse, and it would still be a species of history; it consists really in this, that the one describes the thing that has been, and the other a kind of thing that might be. Hence poetry is something more philosophic and of graver import than history, since its statements are of the nature rather of universals, whereas those of history are singulars. By a universal

statement I mean one as to what such or such a kind of man will probably or necessarily say or do—which is the aim of poetry, though it af-
fixes proper names to the characters; by a singular statement, one as to
what, say, Alcibiades did or had done to him. In comedy this has become clear by this time; it is only when their plot is already made up of
probable incidents that they give it a basis of proper names, choosing
for the purpose any names that may occur to them, instead of writing
like the old iambic poets about particular persons. In Tragedy, however,
they still adhere to the historic names; and for this reason: what con-
vinces is the possible; now whereas we are not yet sure as to the possibility of that which has not happened, that which has happened is
manifestly possible, otherwise it would not have happened. Nevertheless even in tragedy there are some plays with but one or two known
names in them, the rest being inventions; and there are some without a
single known name, e.g. Agathon's *Antheus*, in which both incidents
and names are of the poet's invention; and it is no less delightful on
that account. So that one must not aim at a rigid adherence to the traditional stories on which tragedies are based. It would be absurd, in
fact, to do so, as even the known stories are only known to a few,
though they are a delight none the less to all.

It is evident from the above that the poet must be more the poet of   4
his plots than of his verses, inasmuch as he is a poet by virtue of the
imitative element in his work, and it is actions that he imitates. And if
he should come to take a subject from actual history, he is none the
less a poet for that; since some historic occurrences may very well be in
the probable order of things; and it is in that aspect of them that he is
their poet.

Of simple plots and actions the episodic are the worst. I call a plot   5
episodic when there is neither probability nor necessity in the sequence
of its episodes. Actions of this sort bad poets construct through their
own fault, and good ones on account of the players. His work being for
public performance, a good poet often stretches out a plot beyond its
capabilities, and is thus obliged to twist the sequence of incident.

Tragedy, however, is an imitation not only of a complete action, but   6
also of incidents arousing pity and fear. Such incidents have the very
greatest effect on the mind when they occur unexpectedly and at the
same time in consequence of one another; there is more of the marvellous in them than if they happened of themselves or by mere chance.
Even matters of chance seem most marvellous if there is an appearance
of design as it were in them; as for instance the statue of Mitys at Ar-
gos killed the author of Mitys' death by falling down on him when he
was looking at it; for incidents like that we think to be not without a
meaning. A plot, therefore, of this sort is necessarily finer than others.

Plots are either simple or complex, since the actions they represent   7
are naturally of this twofold description. The action, proceeding in the

way defined, as one continuous whole, I call simple, when the change
in the hero's fortunes takes place without reversal or discovery; and
complex, when it involves one or the other or both. These should each
of them arise out of the structure of the plot itself, so as to be the consequence, necessary or probable, of the antecedents. There is a great
difference between a thing happening *propter hoc* and *post hoc*.

A reversal of fortune is the change of the kind described from one   8
state of things within the play to its opposite, and that too as we say,
in the probable or necessary sequence of events; as it is for instance in
Oedipus: here the opposite state of things is produced by the Messenger,
who, coming to gladden Oedipus and to remove his fears as to his
mother, reveals the secret of his birth. And in *Lynceus:* just as he is being led off for execution, with Danaus at his side to put him to death,
the incidents preceding this bring it about that he is saved and Danaus
put to death. A discovery is, as the very word implies, a change from
ignorance to knowledge, and thus to either love or hate, in the personages marked for good or evil fortune. The finest form of discovery is
one attended by reversal, like that which goes with the discovery in *Oedipus.* There are no doubt other forms of it; what we have said may
happen in a way in reference to inanimate things, even things of a very
casual kind; and it is also possible to discover whether some one has
done or not done something. But the form most directly connected
with the plot and the action of the piece is the first-mentioned. This,
with a reversal, will arouse either pity or fear—actions of that nature
being what tragedy is assumed to represent; and it will also serve to
bring about the happy or unhappy ending. The discovery, then, being
of persons, it may be that of one party only to the other, the latter being already known; or both the parties may have to discover each other.
Iphigenia, for instance, was discovered to Orestes by sending the letter;
and another discovery was required to reveal him to Iphigenia.

Two parts of the plot, then, reversal and discovery, are on matters of   9
this sort. A third part is suffering; which we may define as an action of
a destructive or painful nature, such as murders on the stage, tortures,
woundings, and the like. The other two have been already explained.

. . . .

The next points after what we have said above will be these: what   10
is the poet to aim at, and what is he to avoid, in constructing his Plots?
and what are the conditions on which the tragic effect depends?

We assume that, for the finest form of tragedy, the plot must be not
simple but complex; and further, that it must imitate actions arousing
fear and pity, since that is the distinctive function of this kind of imitation. It follows, therefore, that there are three forms of plot to be

avoided. A good man must not be seen passing from good fortune to bad, or a bad man from bad fortune to good. The first situation is not fear-inspiring or piteous, but simply odious to us. The second is the most untragic that can be; it has not one of the requisites of tragedy; it does not appeal either to the human feeling in us, or to our pity, or to our fears. Nor, on the other hand, should an extremely bad man be seen falling from good fortune into bad. Such a story may arouse the human feeling in us, but it will not move us to either pity or fear; pity is occasioned by undeserved misfortune, and fear by that of one like ourselves; so that there will be nothing either piteous or fear-inspiring in the situation. There remains, then, the intermediate kind of personage, a man not preeminently virtuous and just, whose misfortune, however, is brought upon him not by vice and depravity but by some fault, of the number of those in the enjoyment of great reputation and prosperity; e.g. Oedipus, Thyestes, and the men of note of similar families. The perfect plot, accordingly, must have a single, and not (as some tell us) a double issue; the change in the subject's fortunes must be not from bad fortune to good, but on the contrary from good to bad; and the cause of it must lie not in any depravity, but in some great fault on his part; the man himself being either such as we have described, or better, not worse, than that. Fact also confirms our theory. Though the poets began by accepting any tragic story that came to hand, in these days the finest tragedies are always on the story of some few houses, on that of Alcmeon, Oedipus, Orestes, Meleager, Thyestes, Telephus, or any others that may have been involved, as either agents or sufferers, in some deed of horror. The theoretically best tragedy, then, has a plot of this description. The critics, therefore, are wrong who blame Euripides for taking this line in his tragedies, and giving many of them an unhappy ending. It is, as we have said, the right line to take. The best proof is this: on the stage, and in the public performances, such plays, properly worked out, are seen to be the most truly tragic; and Euripides, even if his execution be faulty in every other point, is seen to be nevertheless the most tragic certainly of the dramatists. After this comes the construction of plot which some rank first, one with a double story (like the *Odyssey*) and an opposite issue for the good and the bad personages. It is ranked as first only through the weakness of the audiences; the poets merely follow their public, writing as its wishes dictate. But the pleasure here is not that of tragedy. It belongs rather to comedy, where the bitterest enemies in the piece (e.g. Orestes and Aegisthus) walk off good friends at the end, with no slaying of any one by any one.

The tragic fear and pity may be aroused by the spectacle; but they 11 may also be aroused by the very structure and incidents of the play—which is the better way and shows the better poet. The plot in fact should be so framed that, even without seeing the things take place,

he who simply hears the account of them shall be filled with horror
and pity at the incidents; which is just the effect that the mere recital
of the story in *Oedipus* would have on one. To produce this same effect
by means of the spectacle is less artistic, and requires extraneous aid.
Those, however, who make use of the spectacle to put before us that
which is merely monstrous and not productive of fear, are wholly out
of touch with tragedy; not every kind of pleasure should be required of
a tragedy, but only its own proper pleasure.

The tragic pleasure is that of pity and fear, and the poet has to pro-   12
duce it by a work of imitation; it is clear, therefore, that the causes
should be included in the incidents of his story. Let us see, then, what
kinds of incident strike one as horrible, or rather as piteous. In a deed
of this description the parties must necessarily be either friends, or enemies, or indifferent to one another. Now when enemy does it on enemy, there is nothing to move us to pity either in his doing or in his
meditating the deed, except so far as the actual pain of the sufferer is
concerned; and the same is true when the parties are indifferent to one
another. Whenever the tragic deed, however, is done among friends—
when murder or the like is done or meditated by brother on brother, by
son on father, by mother on son, or son on mother—these are the situations the poet should seek after. The traditional stories, accordingly,
must be kept as they are, e.g. the murder of Clytaemnestra by Orestes
and of Eriphyle by Alcmeon. At the same time even with these there is
something left to the poet himself; it is for him to devise the right way
of treating them. Let us explain more clearly what we mean by 'the
right way'. The deed of horror may be done by the doer knowingly and
consciously, as in the old poets, and in Medea's murder of her children
in Euripides. Or he may do it, but in ignorance of his relationship, and
discover that afterwards, as does the Oedipus in Sophocles. Here the
deed is outside the play; but it may be within it, like the act of the Alcmeon in Astydamas, or that of the Telegonus in *Ulysses Wounded*. A
third possibility is for one meditating some deadly injury to another, in
ignorance of his relationship, to make the discovery in time to draw
back. These exhaust the possibilities, since the deed must necessarily
be either done or not done, and either knowingly or unknowingly.

_____ **Written Response**

If, as Aristotle claims, part of the plot of a tragedy is suffering, why do
you think that people would want to view a tragedy? Do we ever expose
ourselves to works of art that make us suffer? Why do we do this?

_____ **Rhetorical Analysis**

1. In "Aristotelian Literary Criticism" (preface to *Aristotle's Theory of Poetry and Fine Art*, [New York: Dover, 1951]), John Gassner wrote:

The *Poetics* is the first extant essay on art that is honestly exploratory. Such criticism was unusual in Aristotle's time, and it continued to be rare long after his death when he was considered the supreme arbiter in esthetic judgment. It is, indeed, one of the ironies of history that Aristotle's admirers from the sixteenth to the eighteenth centuries should have tried to convert the explorer into an absolute lawmaker. It was their chief ambition, next to that of establishing themselves as legislators, too, by standing under the ample shadow of the great man's reputation. [p.xxxix]

Gassner feels that Aristotle was writing exploratory discourse; he was suggesting ways to describe or think about tragedy. But the playwrights and critics who followed turned Aristotle's suggestions into rules or laws. For example, Aristotle said that a play would have more unity if its events took place within 24 hours and the action occurred in a single place. Later, some critics assumed that a tragedy was flawed if it violated the unities of time and place.

Do you agree with Gassner? Do you feel that Aristotle's *Poetics* is exploratory? Does Aristotle seem to make suggestions or pronounce rules and laws? Select portions of the text to back up your analysis.

2. The text of Aristotle's *Poetics* apparently comes from either his lecture notes or his students' transcriptions of his lectures. In what ways does this text resemble lecture notes that were not polished and revised for publication?

_____ **Interpretation**

1. Discuss what you think Aristotle meant by the following terms: *imitation, unity, plot, discovery, suffering, pity and fear, spectacle.*

2. Why does Aristotle argue that it is important for a tragedy to arouse pity and fear within a family? Why would this be more powerful than arousing pity and fear about the actions among a group of friends?

3. In *Aristotle and His Philosophy* (Chapel Hill: University of North Carolina Press, 1982), Abraham Edel wrote of Aristotle's conception of tragedy:

How intimately Aristotle's account of the psychological function of tragedy enters into his recommendations on the construction of the drama can be seen most directly in his derivation of the appropriate character for the hero. If we are to identify with a person, that is, to feel fear and pity, then he has to be sufficiently like us, and his suffering has to be undeserved. If he is very good we will simply be outraged, and if he is very evil we will feel that it served him right. Our best choice is neither: "There remains the intermediate kind of person, a man not outstanding in virtue and justice, nor falling into misfortune through evil and wickedness, but by some error [or flaw: *harmartia*]." Later theorists eventually magnified *harmartia* into the "tragic flaw." Characters may of course have flaws not amounting to vice: Oedipus is stubborn, Agamemnon is proud. The vicissitudes of this concept at the hands of interpreters have been striking. For a long time it was thought of as a moral defect. Then scholars agreed that it meant an error of judgment resting on some factual ignorance. Now a "mean" is emerging, that the term has a range of application extending from ignorance of fact at one end to moral defect at the other. *Harmartia* must thus be interpreted in each case according to the situation. Aristotle also adds to his delineation of the hero's character that the person involved be one of renown and prosperity. This is probably the same point as that quoted above from the *Rhetoric*: fear is inspired more readily by our seeing that even the more fortunate are afflicted. [pp. 356–357]

What are some examples of people (from novels, movies, television programs, or the news) who would fit Aristotle's criteria for a tragic hero or heroine? In other words, can you think of people whose lives would make good tragedy?

4. In *Theatre in Search of a Fix* (New York: Delacorte, 1973), Robert W. Corrigan writes of tragedy:

> It seems to me that a much more effective way of dealing with the subject would be to distinguish between the *form of tragedy*, which constantly changes—even in the work of a single dramatist—and *the tragic*, which is a way of looking at experience that has persisted more or less unchanged in the Western world from the time of Homer to the present. Santayana once wrote: "Everything in nature is lyrical in its ideal essence, tragic in its fate, and comic in its existence." The tragic writer in all ages has always been chiefly concerned with man's fate: ultimate defeat and death. Sophocles, Shakespeare, and Ibsen were tragedians because they were, in large measure, concerned with the individual's struggle with fate; for them, as for all writers of tragedy, this struggle is seen as a conflict with necessity, or what the Greeks referred to as Ananke. Necessity is not some kind of social disease that those who would change the world can ignore, soften or legislate out of existence. Necessity is the embodiment of the limitation and morality of all human experience. Man's struggle with necessity has been expressed in many forms and in varying contexts throughout history, but it is the constant of tragic drama. . . .
>
> The spirit of tragedy, then, is not quietistic; it is a grappling spirit. And while the nature and terms of the struggle vary in direct relationship to the individual dramatist's belief in the meaning of the struggle, in every great tragedy we sense the validity of a meaningful struggle and the real possibility of it. Thus, tragic characters may win or lose; or more precisely, they win in the losing and lose in the winning. But it is the struggle itself that is the source of the dramatic significance, and it is out of this struggle with necessity that heroism is born. [pp. 6–7]

Corrigan, who is essentially attempting to update Aristotle's theory of tragedy, believes that the best way to define tragedy is by its spirit: the heroic struggle of its characters against a force that they cannot beat. Do you feel that *Medea* fits Corrigan's definition of a tragedy?

1. Apply Aristotle's definition of tragedy to Euripides' *Medea*. In other words, would Aristotle consider *Medea* to be a tragedy?

2. Argue either (a) that Aristotelian tragedy is no longer meaningful in contemporary society, or (b) that Aristotelian tragedy is just as meaningful today as it was in ancient Greece.

3. Find a newspaper or magazine article describing an event that you feel is tragic. Write an essay in which you describe the event and then analyze why you feel that it is tragic. You can draw upon the ideas of Aristotle or Corrigan, or you can develop your own modern theory of tragedy.

Fiction and Community

Although Alice Walker, best known as the author of *The Color Purple*, now lives in California, she considers her upbringing in Georgia to be a crucial factor in her development as a writer. In "The Black Writer and the Southern Experience" (*In Search of Our Mothers' Gardens* [San Diego, CA: Harvest/HBJ, 1983]), she wrote that Northerners have difficulty understanding how a Southern black writer can draw from her "underprivileged" background. Walker wrote: "In the cities it cannot be so clear to one that he is a creature of the earth, feeling the soil between the toes, smelling the dust thrown up by the rain, loving the earth so much that one longs to taste it and sometimes does." But Walker does not idealize her childhood in the rural south. She wrote: "I can recall that I hated it, generally. The hard work in the fields, the shabby houses, the evil greedy men who worked my father to death and almost broke the courage of that strong woman, my mother. (pp. 20–21)" Much of Walker's fiction reflects this contrast between feeling mystically tied to the earth and one's environment and having to struggle to rise above forces and people who attempt to destroy you.

_____ **Prereading**

Discuss what you know about the history of abortion in the United States. When was abortion illegal nationwide? How did women deal with unwanted pregnancies when it was illegal? When did it become legal? How did things change once abortion was legalized? When did opposition to abortion begin?

expected *him* to take care of her, and she blamed him for not doing so
now.

Well, she was a fraud, anyway. She had known after a year of mar-   20
riage that it bored her. "The Experience of Having a Child" was to distract her from this fact. Still, she expected him to "take care of her."
She was lucky he didn't pack up and leave. But he seemed to know, as
she did, that if anyone packed and left, it would be her. Precisely *because* she was a fraud and because in the end he would settle for fraud
and she could not.

On the plane to New York her teeth ached and she vomited bile—   21
bitter, yellowish stuff she hadn't even been aware her body produced.
She resented and appreciated the crisp help of the stewardess, who
asked if she needed anything, then stood chatting with the cigarette-
smoking white man next to her, whose fat hairy wrist, like a large
worm, was all Imani could bear to see out of the corner of her eye.

Her first abortion, when she was still in college, she frequently re-   22
membered as wonderful, bearing as it had all the marks of a supreme
coming of age and a seizing of the direction of her own life, as well as
a comprehension of existence that never left her: that life—what one
saw about one and called Life—was not a facade. There was nothing
behind it which used "Life" as its manifestation. Life was itself. Period.
At the time, and afterwards, and even now, this seemed a marvelous
thing to know.

The abortionist had been a delightful Italian doctor on the Upper East 23
Side in New York, and before he put her under he told her about his
own daughter who was just her age, and a junior at Vassar. He babbled
on and on until she was out, but not before Imani had thought how
her thousand dollars, for which she would be in debt for years, would
go to keep her there.

When she woke up it was all over. She lay on a brown Naugahyde   24
sofa in the doctor's outer office. And she heard, over her somewhere in
the air, the sound of a woman's voice. It was a Saturday, no nurses in
attendance, and she presumed it was the doctor's wife. She was pulled
gently to her feet by this voice and encouraged to walk.

"And when you leave, be sure to walk as if nothing is wrong," the   25
voice said.

Imani did not feel any pain. This surprised her. Perhaps he didn't do 26
anything, she thought. Perhaps he took my thousand dollars and put
me to sleep with two dollars' worth of ether. Perhaps this is a racket.

But he was so kind, and he was smiling benignly, almost fatherly, at 27
her (and Imani realized how desperately she needed this "fatherly"
look, this "fatherly" smile). "Thank you," she murmured sincerely: she
was thanking him for her life.

Some of Italy was still in his voice. "It's nothing, nothing," he said.   28
"A nice, pretty girl like you; in school like my own daughter, you
didn't need this trouble."

"He's nice," she said to herself, walking to the subway on her way   29
back to school. She lay down gingerly across a vacant seat, and passed
out.

She hemorrhaged steadily for six weeks, and was not well again for a   30
year.

*   *   *

But this was seven years later. An abortion law now made it possible   31
to make an appointment at a clinic, and for seventy-five dollars a safe,
quick, painless abortion was yours.

Imani had once lived in New York, in the Village, not five blocks   32
from where the abortion clinic was. It was also near the Margaret
Sanger clinic, where she had received her very first diaphragm, with
utter gratitude and amazement that someone apparently understood
and actually cared about young women as alone and ignorant as she.
In fact, as she walked up the block, with its modern office buildings
side by side with older, more elegant brownstones, she felt how close
she was still to that earlier self. Still not in control of her sensuality,
and only through violence and with money (for the flight, for the operation itself) in control of her body.

She found that abortion had entered the age of the assembly line.   33
Grateful for the lack of distinction between herself and the other
women—all colors, ages, states of misery or nervousness—she was less
happy to notice, once the doctor started to insert the catheter, that the
anesthesia she had been given was insufficient. But assembly lines
don't stop because the product on them has a complaint. Her doctor
whistled, and assured her she was all right, and carried the procedure
through to the horrific end. Imani fainted some seconds before that.

They laid her out in a peaceful room full of cheerful colors. Primary 34
colors: yellow, red, blue. When she revived she had the feeling of being
in a nursery. She had a pressing need to urinate.

A nurse, kindly, white-haired and with firm hands, helped her to the   35
toilet. Imani saw herself in the mirror over the sink and was alarmed.
She was literally gray, as if all her blood had leaked out.

"Don't worry about how you look," said the nurse. "Rest a bit here and 36
take it easy when you get back home. You'll be fine in a week or so."

She could not imagine being fine again. Somewhere her child—she   37
never dodged into the language of "fetuses" and "amorphous
growths"—was being flushed down a sewer. Gone all her or his
chances to see the sunlight, savor a fig.

"Well," she said to this child, "it was you or me, Kiddo, and I chose   38
me."

There were people who thought she had no right to choose herself,   39
but Imani knew better than to think of those people now.

It was a bright, hot Saturday when she returned.   40

Clarence and Clarice picked her up at the airport. They had brought   41
flowers from Imani's garden, and Clarice presented them with a stout-
hearted hug. Once in her mother's lap she rested content all the way
home, sucking her thumb, stroking her nose with the forefinger of the
same hand, and kneading a corner of her blanket with the three fingers
that were left.

"How did it go?" asked Clarence.   42

"It went," said Imani.   43

There was no way to explain abortion to a man. She thought castration   44
might be an apt analogy, but most men, perhaps all, would insist this
could not possibly be true.

"The anesthesia failed," she said. "I thought I'd never faint in time   45
to keep from screaming and leaping off the table."

Clarence paled. He hated the thought of pain, any kind of violence.   46
He could not endure it; it made him physically ill. This was one of the
reasons he was a pacifist, another reason she admired him.

She knew he wanted her to stop talking. But she continued in a flat,   47
deliberate voice.

"All the blood seemed to run out of me. The tendons in my legs felt   48
cut. I was gray."

He reached for her hand. Held it. Squeezed.   49

"But," she said, "at least I know what I don't want. And I intend   50
never to go through any of this again."

They were in the living room of their peaceful, quiet and colorful   51
house. Imani was in her rocker, Clarice dozing on her lap. Clarence
sank to the floor and rested his head against her knees. She felt he was
asking for nurture when she needed it herself. She felt the two of
them, Clarence and Clarice, clinging to her, using her. And that the
only way she could claim herself, feel herself distinct from them, was
by doing something painful, self-defining but self-destructive.

She suffered the pressure of his head as long as she could.   52

"Have a vasectomy," she said, "or stay in the guest room. Nothing is   53
going to touch me anymore that isn't harmless."

He smoothed her thick hair with his hand. "We'll talk about it," he   54
said, as if that was not what they were doing. "We'll see. Don't worry.
We'll take care of things."

She had forgotten that the third Sunday in June, the following day,   55
was the fifth memorial observance for Holly Monroe, who had been
shot down on her way home from her high-school graduation ceremony
five years before. Imani *always* went to these memorials. She liked the
reassurance that her people had long memories, and that those people
who fell in struggle or innocence were not forgotten. She was, of
course, too weak to go. She was dizzy and still losing blood. The white
lawgivers attempted to get around assassination—which Imani consid-

ered extreme abortion—by saying the victim provoked it (there had been some difficulty saying this about Holly Monroe, but they had tried) but were antiabortionist to a man. Imani thought of this as she resolutely showered and washed her hair.

Clarence had installed central air conditioning their second year in **56** the house. Imani had at first objected. "I want to smell the trees, the flowers, the natural air!" she cried. But the first summer of 110-degree heat had cured her of giving a damn about any of that. Now she wanted to be cool. As much as she loved trees, on a hot day she would have sawed through a forest to get to an air conditioner.

In fairness to him, she had to admit he asked her if she thought she **57** was well enough to go. But even to be asked annoyed her. She was not one to let her own troubles prevent her from showing proper respect and remembrance toward the dead, although she understood perfectly well that once dead, the dead do not exist. So respect, remembrance was for herself, and today herself needed rest. There was something mad about her refusal to rest, and she felt it as she tottered about getting Clarice dressed. But she did not stop. She ran a bath, plopped the child in it, scrubbed her plump body on her knees, arms straining over the tub awkwardly in a way that made her stomach hurt—but not yet her uterus—dried her hair, lifted her out and dried the rest of her on the kitchen table.

"You are going to remember as long as you live what kind of people **58** they are," she said to the child, who, gurgling and cooing, looked into her mother's stern face with light-hearted fixation.

"You are going to hear the music," Imani said. "The music they've **59** tried to kill. The music they try to steal." She felt feverish and was aware she was muttering. She didn't care.

"They think they can kill a continent—people, trees, buffalo—and **60** then fly off to the moon and just forget about it. But you and me we're going to remember the people, the trees and the fucking buffalo. Goddammit."

"Buffwoe," said the child, hitting at her mother's face with a spoon. **61**

She placed the baby on a blanket in the living room and turned to **62** see her husband's eyes, full of pity, on her. She wore pert green velvet slippers and a lovely sea green robe. Her body was bent within in. A reluctant tear formed beneath his gaze.

"Sometimes I look at you and I wonder 'What is this man doing in **63** my house?' "

This had started as a joke between them. Her aim had been never to **64** marry, but to take in lovers who could be sent home at dawn, freeing her to work and ramble.

"I'm here because you love me," was the traditional answer. But Clar- **65** ence faltered, meeting her eyes, and Imani turned away.

It was a hundred degrees by ten o'clock. By eleven, when the memo-   66
rial service began, it would be ten degrees hotter. Imani staggered from
the heat. When she sat in the car she had to clench her teeth against
the dizziness until the motor prodded the air conditioning to envelop
them in coolness. A dull ache started in her uterus.

The church was not of course air conditioned. It was authentic Primi-   67
tive Baptist in every sense.

Like the four previous memorials this one was designed by Holly   68
Monroe's classmates. All twenty-five of whom—fat and thin—managed
to look like the dead girl. Imani had never seen Holly Monroe, though
there were always photographs of her dominating the pulpit of this
church where she had been baptized and where she had sung in the
choir—and to her, every black girl of a certain vulnerable age *was* Holly
Monroe. And an even deeper truth was that Holly Monroe was herself.
Herself shot down, aborted on the eve of becoming herself.

She was prepared to cry and to do so with abandon. But she did not.   69
She clenched her teeth against the steadily increasing pain and her
tears were instantly blotted by the heat.

Mayor Carswell had been waiting for Clarence in the vestibule of the   70
church, mopping his plumply jowled face with a voluminous handker-
chief and holding court among half a dozen young men and women
who listened to him in awe. Imani exchanged greetings with the mayor,
he ritualistically kissed her on the cheek, and kissed Clarice on the
cheek, but his rather heat-glazed eye was already fastened on her husband. The two men huddled in a corner away from the awed young
group. Away from Imani and Clarice, who passed hesitantly, waiting to
be joined or to be called back, into the church.

There was a quarter hour's worth of music.   71

"Holly Monroe was five feet, three inches tall, and weighed one hun- 72
dred and eleven pounds," her best friend said, not reading from notes,
but talking to each person in the audience. "She was a stubborn, loyal
Aries, the best kind of friend to have. She had black kinky hair that
she experimented with a lot. She was exactly the color of this oak
church pew in the summer; in the winter she was the color [pointing
up] of this heart pine ceiling. She loved green. She did not like laven-
der because she said she also didn't like pink. She had brown eyes and
wore glasses, except when she was meeting someone for the first time.
She had a sort of rounded nose. She had beautiful large teeth, but her
lips were always chapped so she didn't smile as much as she might
have if she'd ever gotten used to carrying Chap Stick. She had elegant
feet.

"Her favorite church song was 'Leaning on the Everlasting Arms.'   73
Her favorite other kind of song was 'I Can't Help Myself—I Love You
and Nobody Else.' She was often late for choir rehearsal though she
loved to sing. She made the dress she wore to her graduation in Home
Ec. She *hated* Home Ec. . . . "

Imani was aware that the sound of low, murmurous voices had been   74
the background for this statement all along. Everything was quiet
around her, even Clarice sat up straight, absorbed by the simple friend-
liness of the young woman's voice. All of Holly Monroe's classmates
and friends in the choir wore vivid green. Imani imagined Clarice en-
tranced by the brilliant, swaying color as by a field of swaying corn.

Lifting the child, her uterus burning, and perspiration already a   75
stream down her back, Imani tiptoed to the door. Clarence and the
mayor were still deep in conversation. She heard "board meeting . . .
aldermen . . . city council." She beckoned to Clarence.

"Your voices are carrying!" she hissed.   76

She meant: How dare you not come inside.   77

They did not. Clarence raised his head, looked at her, and shrugged 78
his shoulders helplessly. Then, turning, with the abstracted air of
priests, the two men moved slowly toward the outer door, and into the
churchyard, coming to stand some distance from the church beneath a
large oak tree. There they remained throughout the service.

Two years later, Clarence was furious with her: What is the matter   79
with you? he asked. You never want me to touch you. You told me to
sleep in the guest room and I did. You told me to have a vasectomy I
didn't want and *I did*. (Here, there was a sob of hatred for her somewhere in the anger, the humiliation: he thought of himself as a eunuch,
and blamed her.)

She was not merely frigid, she was remote.   80

She had been amazed after they left the church that the anger she'd 81
felt watching Clarence and the mayor turn away from the Holly Monroe
memorial did not prevent her accepting a ride home with him. A month
later it did not prevent her smiling on him fondly. Did not prevent a
trip to Bermuda, a few blissful days of very good sex on a deserted
beach screened by trees. Did not prevent her listening to his mother's
stories of Clarence's youth as though she would treasure them forever.

And yet. From that moment in the heat at the church door, she had   82
uncoupled herself from him, in a separation that made him, except occasionally, little more than a stranger.

And he had not felt it, had not known.   83

"What have I done?" he asked, all the tenderness in his voice break- 84
ing over her. She smiled a nervous smile at him, which he interpreted
as derision—so far apart had they drifted.

They had discussed the episode at the church many times. Mayor   85
Carswell—whom they never saw anymore—was now a model mayor,
with wide biracial support in his campaign for the legislature. Neither
could easily recall him, though television frequently brought him into
the house.

"It was so important that I help the mayor!" said Clarence. "He was   86
our *first!*"

Imani understood this perfectly well, but it sounded humorous to   87
her. When she smiled, he was offended.

She had known the moment she left the marriage, the exact second.   88
But apparently that moment had left no perceptible mark.

They argued, she smiled, they scowled, blamed and cried—as she   89
packed.

Each of them almost recalled out loud that about this time of the year 90
their aborted child would have been a troublesome, "terrible" two-year-
old, a great burden on its mother, whose health was by now in excellent shape, each wanted to think aloud that the marriage would have
deteriorated anyway, because of that.

_____ **Written Response**

Walker's "The Abortion" could be viewed as a short story about the issue of abortion. Walker could be asking the reader to think about
whether abortions are moral and whether they should be legal. On the
other hand, "The Abortion" could be viewed as a short story that uses
the situation of a woman undergoing an abortion to ask the reader to
think about other issues.

What other issues, besides the morality or immorality of abortion, do
you feel that Walker raises in her short story?

_____ **Rhetorical Analysis**

1. In *A Grammar of Motives* (Berkeley: University of California Press,
1945), Kenneth Burke discusses how what he calls the "scene" (the environment in which an action occurs), the "agent" (the person who performs the act), the "act" (the action itself), the "agency" (how the act is
performed), and the "purpose" (the reason for performing the act) are
related to each other. Looking for relationships between or among the
textual elements that these terms label can be a useful way of rethinking
and analyzing a piece of literature. For example, the narrator describes
Imani and Clarence's bed as being a "massive king-size bed with a for-
bidding ridge down the middle." The bed (the scene) says something
about the agents (Imani and Clarence), for the ridge down the middle of
the bed is related to distance that has grown between Imani and Clarence. Other relationships between or among elements related to these
terms can be found in the short story. A few suggestions will help you to
begin discussing these relationships.

How would you describe the scene (the town in which Imani and Clarence live, the locations of the two abortions)? How are these related to
the central act (the abortion)?

What is Imani's purpose for having the abortion? How is this purpose
related to the agent (Imani) and her relationship to her husband?

How did the agency (the method) of the two abortions differ? How was the agency related to the agent (Imani) and how she felt about each abortion?

Can you think of other relationships between or among aspects of the short story that are related to Burke's terms?

2. In "Epic and Novel" (in *The Dialogic Imagination* [Austin: University of Texas Press, 1981]), M. M. Bakhtin writes that one of the "basic themes of the novel is precisely the theme of the hero's inadequacy to his fate or his situation." How is this statement similar to tragedy as defined by Aristotle and Corrigan? How well does this statement describe the action that occurs in "The Abortion"? Is Imani unable to rise above her fate or situation? Why or why not?

_____ **Interpretation**

1. In a 1973 interview, Alice Walker recounted how she became pregnant during her last year of college. Even though she did not receive much support from her sisters during this crisis, two of her friends stood by her. Walker described the aftermath of her abortion thus:

When I woke up, my friend was standing over me holding a red rose. . . . That moment is engraved on my mind—her smile, sad and pained and frightfully young—as she tried so hard to stand by me and be my friend. She drove me back to school and tucked me in. My other friend, brown, a wisp of blue and scarlet, with hair like thunder, brought me food. (From *In Search of Our Mothers' Gardens*, [San Diego, CA: Harvest/HBJ, 1983] pp. 245–248)

How is Walker's description of her abortion similar to the first abortion in "The Abortion"? How is it different?

3. In "The Black Writer and the Southern Experience" (in *In Search of Our Mothers' Gardens*) Walker wrote:

What the black Southern writer inherits as a natural right is a sense of *community*. . . . My mother, who is a walking history of our community, tells me that when each of her children was born the midwife accepted as payment such home-grown or homemade items as a pig, a quilt, jars of canned fruits and vegetables. (p. 17)

Even though the midwife was seldom paid in cash and not always paid right away, Walker recalls that she always came. Walker feels that this situation is very different from stories that she had heard about women in labor who were turned away from hospitals because they cannot pay in cash.

What do you think that Walker might mean by a sense of community? Do you feel that there was a sense of community where Imani lived? Why or why not?

_____ WRITING ASSIGNMENTS

1. Argue that "The Abortion" is or is not a modern tragedy. You can draw upon Aristotle's or Corrigan's definition of tragedy or develop your own definition.

2. Many people who read "The Abortion" for the first time probably feel that the short story is about the issue of abortion. Argue that the short story is actually about some issue other than abortion.

3. Explain the relation between Imani and her community in "The Abortion."

Poetry and Politics

Even though we are constantly exposed to the sounds and sights of the political protests against apartheid in South Africa, it is hard for us to understand the effects of the racist policy of the minority government on daily life. Listening to reports of protests on the news can hardly convey the effect of apartheid on the people of an entire nation.

But imagine that you are about to march in a funeral for a young boy who was killed by police. Someone hands you a first aid pamphlet just in case there is violence. You begin to read:

> THIS PAMPHLET IS A GUIDE TO THE EMERGENCY TREATMENT OF INJURIES CAUSED BY POLICE. INJURED PEOPLE ARE OFTEN AUTO- MATICALLY ARRESTED WHEN THEY GO TO HOSPITALS FOR TREAT- MENT, SO, MANY PEOPLE DO NOT GO TO HOSPITAL OR SEE A DOCTOR AT ALL. THIS PAMPHLET WILL HELP PEOPLE TREAT SMALL INJURIES IF THEY ARE REALLY NOT PREPARED TO GO TO HOSPITAL.

Or, imagine that you are reading the newspaper and encounter the fol- lowing advertisement:

> *Amandla Ngawethu [Power to the People]*, a first volume of Afrikaans poems by Patrick Petersen, made its debut appearance on 11 September 1985 at the Genaadendal printing office. This is a relevant collection with a politically relevant message. There are thirty poems in the book, and they will be of particular interest to the black reader. This volume can be profitably used at mass meetings, during school boycotts, and at protest marches, funerals, etc.

Or, you encounter the following advertisement:

CANCELLED

The programme of the Arts Festival '86 in Cape Town was booked to run in this space.

Unfortunately the festival was banned on Thursday afternoon.

The organisers regret that they cannot provide any details.

The selection of poems that are presented in this section will, like these texts from the daily lives of South Africans, provide further insight into the effects of apartheid.

_____ **Prereading**

The following chronology will provide some historical background for the poems presented in this section*:

1899: Anglo-Boer War begins.

1902: Anglo-Boer War ends. Treaty of Vereeniging establishes British rule.

1907: Gandhi leads civil rights campaign in South Africa (hereinafter, "S.A.").

1909: The Union of South Africa established, with Louis Botha as Prime Minister.

1912: The African National Congress (ANC) founded in Bloemfontein.

1913: The Land Act deprives Africans of the right to own land in S.A. outside of reserves.

1918: The founding of the *Broederbond,* a right-wing Afrikaner "secret society," to look after and ensure Afrikaner group identity and supremacy.

1920: Twenty thousand black mineworkers strike for higher pay. This is the last major black miners' strike until 1946.

1922: The "Rand Revolt." Twenty-five thousand white miners strike partly in protest against a Chamber of Mines' move to replace white miners with black.

1939: S.A. joins in World War II on the side of the British. This is a furiously debated move because: 1) Britain is the traditional enemy of many white South Africans; 2) There is support for national socialism in certain sectors.

1944: The Youth League of the ANC is formally constituted.

1946: India severs trade relations with S.A.

1948: The Nationalist Party wins the white General Election and Dr. Daniel Malan becomes Prime Minister.

1950: Hendrick Verwoerd appointed Minister of Native Affairs. Passing of the Bantu Authorities Act.

1952: June to October. The Defiance Campaign, a period of passive resistance. In these months about 8,500 convicted for such offenses as using amenities reserved for whites only.

_____

* "Chronology" From *From South Africa* edited by David Bunn and Jane Taylor. Originally published in *TriQuarterly Magazine,* a publication of Northwestern University. Copyright © 1987 by TriQuarterly. All rights reserved. Reprinted by permission.

1955:   "Freedom Charter" adopted at Congress of the People.

1956:   Sixty thousand so-called "colored" voters struck from the voter's role in the Cape Province.

August: Twenty thousand women demonstrate at the Union Buildings (seat of government in Pretoria) against passes for women.

December: Police arrest the leaders of the Congress Alliance. One hundred and fifty-six are arrested. The Treason Trial lasts for the following five years. All are acquitted.

1958:   Verwoerd, the "architect of apartheid," becomes Prime Minister.

1959:   The Pan Africanist Congress (PAC) founded.

Verwoerd pushes through parliament the Promotion of Bantu Self-Government Act, which conceives of eight national units for African peoples. This signals active beginning to "homelands" or "Bantustan" policy.

1960:   March 21: Sharpeville massacre. On this day at Sharpeville, a township in the Transvaal, police open fire on passive resisters taking part in a public demonstration, burning their passbooks in defiance of pass laws which restricted freedom of movement for blacks. Sixty-nine are killed and 150 wounded. The slayings are received with outrage both locally and internationally. Sharpeville Day is a day of mourning and commemoration for South Africans of conscience.

ANC and PAC are banned.

1961:   Union of South Africa becomes a republic.

1963:   Political leadership of the ANC arrested at Rivonia, a suburb of Johannesburg. Leadership, including Nelson Mandela, tried and convicted in a notorious trial.

1966:   Verwoerd stabbed to death by a white parliamentary messenger while sitting at his desk in the House of Assembly. Balthazer John Vorster becomes Prime Minister.

1969:   Dockworkers strike in Durban. All summarily fired.

1975:   The Front for the Liberation of Mozambique (FRELIMO) wins Mozambican independence, after 500 years of colonial rule.

1976:   June 16: The Soweto Students Representative Council holds a meeting to protest the compulsory use of Afrikaans as a teaching medium in black schools. Police confront school students on their way to Orlando stadium where a mass rally is to be held. By the end of the day 100 students have been killed and townships across the country come out in support of student demands. The day is an annual memorial day, to commemorate the dead and to reassert the role of students in the restructuring of society. June 16 is seen as a turning point.

1977:   Black Consciousness leader Steve Biko killed while in police detention.

1984:   Government establishes the Tricameral Parliament in an attempt to seduce "Indian" and "Colored" communities by offering them a puppet role in which they could have a say in issues relating to "own affairs."

The United Democratic Front, a massive coordinating body

which unites workers' groups, unions, women's movements, anti-conscription groups, et al., is established initially to campaign against the election of members of the House of Representatives, the Colored and Indian flank of the Tricameral Parliament. The UDF and its affiliates begin to play an increasingly important role, as civil obedience is employed as a strategy throughout South Africa.

Bishop (now Archbishop) Desmond Tutu is awarded the Nobel Prize for Peace for his work in South Africa.

November 5: General stayaway strike in the Transvaal, as nearly one million respond to the call of unions and community organizations.

1985: July 20: Over 60,000 attend funeral of assassinated leaders in Lingelihle, Cradock.

July 21: State of Emergency declared in thirty-six magisterial districts.

August 11: Twenty Duncan village residents killed in township protests.

August 17: Beaufort West consumer boycott begins.

August 20: Consumer boycott spreads to Western Cape.

August 29: In Cape Town, seventeen die in clashes with police during march on Pollsmoor Prison to demand the release of Nelson Mandela.

October 6: Government closes 460 schools in the Western Cape after continued clashes.

October 15: Cape Town. Three youths die in "Trojan Horse" killings, in which armed police hide in boxes on a truck and open fire on a crowd of stone throwers.

November 21: General stayaway strike in Mamelodi, Pretoria. Thirteen die as 50,000 march on development to demand the troops be removed from the townships.

December 1: National launch of Congress of South African Trade Unions (COSATU).

1986: January 5: Twenty-three thousand National Union of Mineworkers (NUM) members fired at Gencor's Impala Platinum, Bophuthatswana, after striking for one week over wages and recognition.

February 15: Mass resistance breaks out after disruption of funerals in Alexandra Township. Forty-six people killed in four days.

March 31: In defiance of police ban, 20,000 attend memorial service for Moses Mabhida, general secretary of the South African Communist Party, who died in exile in Mozambique.

May 19: Crossroads squatter camp attacked by vigilantes. Thirteen killed, 20,000 homeless.

June 9: Squatter camp near Crossroads attacked by vigilantes. Eighteen killed, 20,000 homeless.

June 12: Second State of Emergency in two years. Massive detention of activists around the country.

October 1: Thirty thousand miners stage one-day strike to protest deaths in Kinross mining disaster.

October 19: Samora Machel and thirty-two Frelimo officials die in mysterious plane crash.

October 27: Thirty-five thousand mineworkers strike at Gold Fields mine. They return to work three days later as owners agree to negotiate.

1987:   January 8: Some twenty South African newspapers run a full-page advertisement marking the 75th anniversary of the founding of the ANC and calling on the government to legalize the group. Police say they will investigate whether the papers have broken any laws by publishing the ads, which had been placed by anti-apartheid and church groups.

April 5: A black police trainee is killed and sixty-four of his colleagues are wounded by a hand grenade thrown into a crowded police parade ground in Soweto. The attack is part of a sharp upsurge in violence and civil unrest preceding the May 6 general election, in which only whites will vote.

April 16: Archbishop Tutu and forty-six other Anglican clergymen disobey new emergency restrictions by asking President P. W. Botha to either free detainees or put them on trial.

April 22: Police shoot six blacks to death during street battles at a Johannesburg railroad station and at union buildings in Johannesburg and neighboring Germiston, after the government-owned railroad fired 16,000 striking black workers. The fighting is the worst in Johannesburg since the government imposed a nationwide state of emergency June 12, 1986, in an attempt to quell unrest against apartheid.

April 24 and 28: In two rulings, the Natal Supreme Court overturns key aspects of the government's emergency censorship provisions that curb the press and outlaw protests and appeals on behalf of people detained without charge, stating that President Botha had exceeded his authority by delegating powers to the police commissioner in a December 1986 decree. The Government states it will appeal the rulings to the Appeals Court in Bloemfontein.

April 27: Police open fire with birdshot during an hour of running battles with about 350 protesting students on the University of Cape Town campus in violence that followed a student meeting to protest a recent South African military raid into Zambia.

May 4: South African riot police arrest 120 students and fire tear gas at about 50 faculty members at the University of the Witwatersrand in Johannesburg as the students and teachers protest the upcoming whites-only election.

May 6: White voters shift sharply to the right in parliamentary elections. Workers, meanwhile, mount what is called the largest protest strike in the nation's history as some 1.5 million of them stay home from work in the second day of a two-day "stayaway," amid reports of dozens of incidents of stone throwing and arson.

[1990:   February 11: Nelson Mandela is released from prison after 27 years of confinement. Some feel that this event marks the end of apartheid and the beginning of new relations between blacks and

Child shot running,
stones in his pocket,
boy's swollen stomach
full of hungry air.
Girls carrying babies
not much smaller than themselves.
Erosion. Soil washed down to the sea.

3

I think these mothers dream
headstones of the unborn.
Their mourning rises like a wall
no vine will cling to.
They will not tell you your suffering is white.
They will not say it is just as well.
They will not compete for the ashes of infants.
I think they may say to you:
Come with us to the place of mothers.
We will stroke your flat empty belly,
let you weep with us in the dark,
and arm you with one of our babies
to carry home on your back.

1983

Source: "Small Passing" by Ingrid de Kok from *From South Africa* edited by David Bunn and Jane Taylor. Originally published in *TriQuarterly Magazine,* a publication of Northwestern University. Copyright © 1987 by TriQuarterly. All rights reserved. Reprinted by permission.

Exit Visa

Arthur Nortje

There were evils in the road.
I ate acorns.
Lands where rumored honey flowed
lay barbed covered with thorns.
But I acquired stronger boots,
sharpened my teeth on bitter fruits.
For that Strongman's prowess
was long unable
to crush my spirit

Nor was his genius equal to
though he was blond & I black

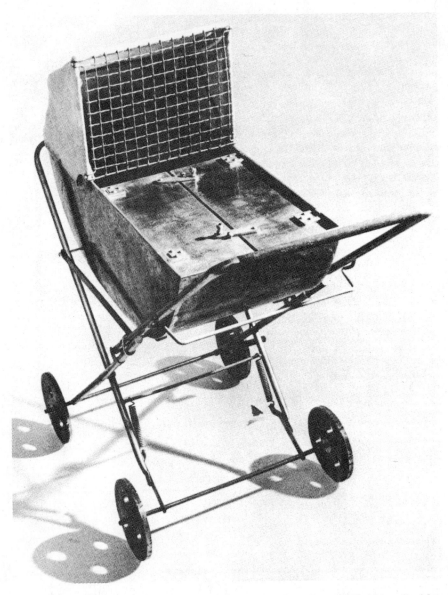

Source: "Riot-Protected Baby Carriage" by Gavin Younge from *From South Africa* edited by David Bunn and Jane Taylor. Originally published in *TriQuarterly Magazine,* a publication of Northwestern University. Copyright © 1987 by TriQuarterly. All rights reserved. Reprinted by permission.

removal of the sun from me cement-celled
I had seen and spoken to the light
though at any time he could call the darkness back

Evils accumulate,
Perils that patiently lie in ambush
at every crossing would snare my progress
had He and His Praetorian henchmen
had their way.
After marching orders
they laughed about my wintering in cold climes
beyond those golden borders,
With a lump in the throat
I took my gypsy leave.

1970

Source: "Exit Visa" by Arthur Nortje from *From South Africa* edited by David Bunn and Jane Taylor. Originally published in *TriQuarterly Magazine,* a publication of Northwestern University. Copyright © 1987 by TriQuarterly. All rights reserved. Reprinted by permission.

Steve Biko's Anthem
Mazisi Kunene

The sun blazes its flames,
Its fierce rays burst open the enveloping night,
From here I see the restless generations to come,
They run wild like the wind, they hold onto the eagle's tail,
They sing the anthems of our forefathers,
They declaim the epics of the Maluti Mountains.
Three hundred years ago
We chose the brotherhood of battle.
The crowds followed us with their song.
Their lips quivered in anger,
They broke the neck of the salamander.
They came to the festival by the dead of night,
They set the cities on fire,
The madams fled in terror through the alleyways.
My children were free to praise their father!
Yet not even dawn could bring peace
The stars fell precipitately from the sky
What was once the Milky Way bowed to our sun!
We are tall, we who are the children of the morning,
We who worshipped at the altar of fire,
We who made the beast flee for its life.
This age is ours, we made it bear the sacred flower,

We planted the seed of our freedom at the mountain-region
To bear fruit for all peoples.
In your name, young man of the river,
You who loved me in my youth
Until I was decrepit with age;
In your name, young man of the sun, let there be rain,
Let there be beautiful songs in our festivals,
Let humanity walk proudly.
You who followed after me, your turn has come!
You must nourish the dream
To make Africa sing from Algeria to the Maluti Mountains.

1982

Source: "Steve Biko's Anthem" by Mazisi Kunene from From South Africa edited by David
Bunn and Jane Taylor. Originally published in TriQuarterly Magazine, a publication of Northwestern University. Copyright © 1987 by TriQuarterly. All rights reserved. Reprinted by
permission.

The Tyrant

Mazisi Kunene

Through uncertainty the tyrant imposes his power.
He chooses the gods that speak his own language,
To make us stand before him like cattle.
By his ancestral names he haunts our children.
They must parade at his festivals like slaves
To declaim the glories of his violent prophets.
The enemy boasts the power of the sun,
The beast steals the young from their mother's breast,
The tyrant celebrates, the feast is in his name . . .

1982

Source: "The Tyrant" by Mazisi Kunene from From South Africa edited by David Bunn and
Jane Taylor. Originally published in TriQuarterly Magazine, a publication of Northwestern University. Copyright © 1987 by TriQuarterly. All rights reserved. Reprinted by permission.

Cowardice

Mazisi Kunene

I overcame her who was my enemy
Who seized my staffs of courage
And was unkind to my clansmen.
I said to her: Go away,

English cultural criteria. Indeed, his disapproval in most cases closely matched the interests of the British Empire; thus the black Christians fought zealously against those whom they were taught were pagans and antichrists. As their material standards improved through such incentives as the vote for the wealthy and the 'educated', they not only completely rejected their culture but developed a *tabula rasa* mentality into which nothing 'native' intruded, unless strictly approved by the missionaries. They totally embraced the ideology of individualism, and thus became known amongst non-Christians as the 'stingy ones', or 'they who cook in a small pot'.

Since generosity and the concept of sharing constituted the very basis of traditional philosophy, these acts and attitudes indicated how deeply the black converts had been alienated from their culture.

What happened in the missionary schools was even more tragic in so far as African literature and culture was concerned. The missionary and the administrator combined efforts to promulgate rules by which African language and traditional cultural expressions (such as dancing, 'excited participation' and 'body exposure') were forbidden at the risk of incurring serious punishment such as hard labour and ridicule. On the other hand, English language, English country dances, and English styles of clothing were yoked round the necks of the pupils. Of course, 'excited participation' and 'body exposure' were all matters of cultural definition. The effect was to deprive African literature of some of its components, precisely because African literature required communal participation, and, for its expression, body movements in their minutest forms. And the vast ignorance and usual arrogance of conquerors also meant that in defining African literature and philosophies they relegated them to the lowest level of expression. [pp. 9–11]*

Kunene, who writes most of his poetry in Zulu, feels that it is important for South African blacks to preserve their cultural identity.

Based on the quotation above, why do you think that preserving his people's cultural identity is so important to Kunene? Besides writing in Zulu, in what ways does he attempt to preserve his people's cultural identity in his poetry?

_____ **WRITING ASSIGNMENTS**

1. Write an interpretation of one of the poems in this section.

2. Use the poems that you have just read to explain the effects of apartheid on the people of South Africa.

3. Trace a central theme through several of the poems presented in this section. A central theme might be the poets' call for South Africans to sacrifice themselves to make the world better for their children.

4. What kind of advice do you think that these poets offer through their poetry to the people of South Africa?

---

* From Introduction, *Zulu Poems* by Mazisi Kunene, pp. 9–11. Copyright © 1970 by Mazisi Kunene. (New York: Africana Publishing Company, 1970.) Reprinted by permission of the publisher.

Synthesis

1. As your final writing assignment of this chapter, you may be asked to write a review of a movie or a play. Your instructor may chose to have all of the members of the class view the same movie or play so that you can offer each other better feedback on your rough drafts.

Once you have viewed the movie or play, write a review of it in which you tell the reader what it is about, offer your interpretation, and evaluate it. The review should, however, be more than a plot synopsis.

You may want to think about the following questions before writing your review:

What was the basic story of the play or movie?
What did you feel as you were watching it?
What did you think about as you were watching it?
What did you like about it?
What did you dislike about it?
Was the script good? In other words, did all of the scenes fit together? Was the dialogue good?
Was the acting good?
What is the message of the movie or play?
What is the social context of the movie or play and how does this relate to the message?
Are the production values good? For a movie, evaluate the photography, sound, special effects, and so on. For a play, evaluate the lighting, sets, costumes, and so on.
What would make the movie or play better?

2. Go to the library and locate the works of an author who is from your "community"—either your city, state, or region—and write an essay in which you discuss how that author's writing reflects the values of your "community."

6 History: Facts and Narration

In "On the Relations of History and Philosophy" (in *The Theory and Practice of History* [Indianapolis: Bobbs Merrill, 1973]), Leopold von Ranke, a nineteenth-century historian, wrote:

> There are two ways of acquiring knowledge about human affairs—through the perception of the particular and through abstraction. The one is the way of philosophy, the other that of history. There is no other way, and even revelation encompasses both abstract doctrines and history. These two sources of knowledge are therefore to be kept clearly distinguished. Nevertheless, equally mistaken are those historians who view all of history merely as an immense aggregate of facts to be committed to memory, meaning that particulars are strung to particulars and all of these held together only by a common moral principle. I am of the opinion, rather, that historical science at its best is both called upon and able to rise in its own way from the investigation and contemplation of the particular to a general view of events and to the recognition of their objectively existing relatedness. [p. 30]

Although Ranke believes that the "general view" is important (true history would not exist without it), he also believes that history begins with—and is grounded in—the "particular." In the "particular," Ranke believed, the historian finds objectivity.

Jacob Burckhardt, another nineteenth-century historian, was more skeptical about achieving objectivity or finding truth. He believed that "historical pictures are, for the most part, pure constructions." But he nonetheless believed that history dealt with the "particular," or what, in *Reflections on History* (Indianapolis: Liberty Classics, trans. 1943), he called the "source":

> Now the source, as compared with a treatise [on history], has its external advantage.
>
> First and foremost, it presents the fact pure, so that *we* must see what conclusions are to be drawn from it, while the treatise anticipates that labor and presents the fact digested, that is, placed in an alien, and often erroneous setting.

Further, the source gives the fact in a form not far removed from its origin or author, and indeed is often that author's work. Its difficulty lies in its language, but so do its stimulus and a great part of the value which makes it superior to any treatise. Here again we must bear in mind the importance of original languages and the knowledge of them as against the use of translations.

Further, our mind can only enter into a real, chemical combination, in the full sense of the word, with the original source; we must, however, note that the word "original" is here used in a relative sense, since, when the original source is lost, it can be replaced by one at second or third remove.

Sources, however, especially such as come from the hand of great men, are inexhaustible, and everyone must reread the works which have been exploited a thousand times, because they present a peculiar aspect, not only to every reader and every century, but also to every time of life. It may be, for instance, that there is in Thucydides a fact of capital importance which somebody will note in a hundred years' time. [p. 52]

What does Burckhardt mean by a "source"? It could be any document original to the times under study: a letter, an eyewitness account, a newspaper article, literature, photographs, a diary, or art. These "sources," he feels, give the historian undigested facts—the matter of which history is written.

While Ranke looks to the "particular" and Burckhardt to the "source," both write about sensing the concrete remnants of history. And this is how most of us tend to view history. Writing history is the job of getting in touch with the facts and shaping these facts into a narrative, a story that can in important ways affect how we make decisions.

In this chapter, you will be presented with facts and documents relating to an interesting period of Japanese history, a time when the samurai decided to give up the gun and return to the warfare of the sword. You will be asked to interpret these documents and determine whether they apply to a contemporary issue.

The Writing of History

Barbara W. Tuchman, who died in 1989, was a modern oddity: she was a well-respected historian who did not hold a graduate degree or university professorship. She was essentially a self-taught historian, although she learned something of the art of history while writing her senior honors thesis at Radcliffe:

In the process of doing my own thesis—not for a Ph.D., because I never took a graduate degree, but just my undergraduate honors thesis—the single most formative experience in my career took place. It was not a tutor or a teacher or a fellow student or a great book or the shining example of some famous visiting lecturer—like Sir Charles Webster, for instance, brilliant as he was. It was the stacks at Widener [the library]. They were *my* Archimedes' bathtub, my burning bush, my dish of mold where I found my personal penicillin. I was allowed to have as my own one of those little cubicles with a table under a window, queerly called, as I have since learned, carrels, a word I never knew when I sat in one. Mine was deep in among the 942S (British History, that is) and I could roam at liberty through the rich stacks, taking whatever I wanted. The experience was marvelous, a word I use in its exact sense meaning full of marvels. The happiest days of my intellectual life, until I began writing history again some fifteen years later, were spent in the stacks at Widener. [From *Practicing History*, New York: Ballantine, 1981, p. 15]

In "History by the Ounce" (an essay first published in 1965), Tuchman discusses how she believes history should be written—from the facts of actual experience.

_____ **Prereading**

Tuchman begins "History by the Ounce" with an allusion (a reference to or mention of) Gilbert and Sullivan's *Mikado*, a light opera. The portion of the script that Tuchman alludes to describes the attempt of Pooh-Bah, a lovable rogue, to convince the Mikado (the Emperor of Japan) that they have beheaded a prisoner who is actually still alive. Pooh-Bah describes what happens after the beheading thus:

> Now though you'd have said that head was dead
> (For its owner dead was he),
> It stood on its neck, with a smile well-bred,
> And bowed three times to me!
> It was none of your impudent off-hand nods,
> But as humble as could be,
> For it clearly knew
> The deference due
> To a man of pedigree!
> And it's oh, I vow,
> This deathly bow
> Was a touching sight to see;
> Though trunkless yet
> It couldn't forget
> The deference due to me!

As unlikely as these events might be, Tuchman will argue that Pooh-Bah's story is believable. Why do you think that she feels this lie is believable?

History by the Ounce

Barbara Tuchman

At a party given for its reopening last year, the Museum of Modern   **1**
Art in New York served champagne to five thousand guests. An alert
reporter from the *Times*, Charlotte Curtis, noted that there were eighty
cases, which, she informed her readers, amounted to 960 bottles or
7,680 three-ounce drinks. Somehow through this detail the Museum's
party at once becomes alive; a fashionable New York occasion. One sees
the crush, the women eyeing each other's clothes, the exchange of
greeting, and feels the gratifying sense of elegance and importance imparted by champagne—even if, at one and a half drinks per person, it
was not on an exactly riotous scale. All this is conveyed by Miss Curtis' detail. It is, I think, the way history as well as journalism should
be written. It is what Pooh-Bah, in *The Mikado*, meant when, telling
how the victim's head stood on its neck and bowed three times to him
at the execution of Nanki-Poo, he added that this was "corroborative
detail intended to give artistic verisimilitude to an otherwise bald and
unconvincing narrative." Not that Miss Curtis' narrative was either
bald or unconvincing; on the contrary, it was precise, factual, and a
model in every way. But what made it excel, made it vivid and memorable, was her use of corroborative detail.

Pooh-Bah's statement of the case establishes him in my estimate as a   **2**
major historian or, at least, as the formulator of a major principle of
historiography.[1] True, he invented his corroborative detail, which is
cheating if you are a historian and fiction if you are not; nevertheless,
what counts is his recognition of its importance. He knew that it supplied verisimilitude, that without it a narrative is bald and unconvincing. Neither he nor I, of course, discovered the principle; historians
have for long made use of it, beginning with Thucydides, who insisted
on details of topography,[2] "the appearance of cities and localities, the
description of rivers and harbors, the peculiar features of seas; and
countries and their relative distances."

Source: From *Practicing History* by Barbara Tuchman. Copyright © 1981 by Alma Tuchman,
Lucy T. Eisenberg, and Jessica Tuchman Matthews. Reprinted by permission of Alfred A.
Knopf Inc.

---

[1] Historiography is the theory of writing history and the methodology of historical research.
[2] Topography is the detailed description of rivers, cities, etc.

Corroborative detail is the great corrective. Without it historical nar-   3
rative and interpretation, both, may slip easily into the invalid. It is a
disciplinarian. It forces the historian who uses and respects it to cleave
to the truth, or as much as he can find out of the truth. It keeps him
from soaring off the ground into theories of his own invention. On
those Toynbeean heights the air is stimulating and the view is vast, but
people and houses down below are too small to be seen. However persuaded the historian may be of the validity of the theories he conceives,
if they are not supported and illustrated by corroborative detail they are
of no more value as history than Pooh-Bah's report of the imagined execution.

It is wiser, I believe, to arrive at theory by way of the evidence rather   4
than the other way around, like so many revisionists today. It is more
rewarding, in any case, to assemble the facts first and, in the process of
arranging them in narrative form, to discover a theory or a historical
generalization emerging of its own accord. This to me is the excitement,
the built-in treasure hunt, of writing history. In the book I am working
on now, which deals with the twenty-year period before 1914 (and the
reader must forgive me if all my examples are drawn from my own
work, but that, after all, is the thing one knows best), I have been writing about a moment during the Dreyfus Affair[3] in France when on the
day of the reopening of Parliament everyone expected the Army to attempt a *coup d'état*. English observers predicted it, troops were brought
into the capital, the Royalist pretender was summoned to the frontier,
mobs hooted and rioted in the streets, but when the day had passed,
nothing had happened; the Republic still stood. By this time I had assembled so much corroborative detail pointing to a *coup d'état* that I had
to explain why it had not occurred. Suddenly I had to stop and think.
After a while I found myself writing, "The Right lacked that necessary
chemical to a coup—a leader. It had its small, if loud, fanatics; but to
upset the established government in a democratic country requires either foreign help or the stuff of a dictator." That is a historical generalization, I believe; a modest one, to be sure, but my size. I had arrived
at it out of the necessity of the material and felt immensely pleased and
proud. These moments do not occur every day; sometimes no more
than one a chapter, if that, but when they do they leave one with a
lovely sense of achievement.

I am a disciple of the ounce because I mistrust history in gallon jugs   5
whose purveyors are more concerned with establishing the meaning
and purpose of history than with what happened. Is it necessary to insist on a purpose? No one asks the novelist why he writes novels or the
poet what is his purpose in writing poems. The lilies of the field, as I

---

[3] Alfred Dreyfus was a French Army officer convicted of treason on questionable grounds
in 1884.

remember, were not required to have a demonstrable purpose. Why cannot history be studied and written and read for its own sake, as the record of human behavior, the most fascinating subject of all? Insistence on a purpose turns the historian into a prophet—and that is another profession.

To return to my own: Corroborative detail will not produce a general-   6
ization every time, but it will often reveal a historical truth, besides keeping one grounded in historical reality. When I was investigating General Mercier, the Minister of War who was responsible for the origi- nal condemnation of Dreyfus and who in the course of the Affair be- came the hero of the Right, I discovered that at parties of the *haut monde* ladies rose to their feet when General Mercier entered the room. That is the kind of detail which to me is worth a week of research. It illustrates the society, the people, the state of feeling at the time more vividly than anything I could write and in shorter space, too, which is an additional advantage. It epitomizes, it crystallizes, it visualizes. The reader can see it; moreover, it sticks in his mind; it is memorable.

The same is true, verbally though not visually, of a statement by   7
President Eliot of Harvard in 1896 in a speech on international arbi- tration, a great issue of the time. In this chapter I was writing about the founding tradition of the United States as an anti-militarist, anti- imperialist nation, secure within its own shores, having nothing to do with the wicked armaments and standing armies of Europe, setting an example of unarmed strength and righteousness. Looking for material to illustrate the tradition, I found in a newspaper report these words of Eliot, which I have not seen quoted by anyone else: "The building of a navy," he said, "and the presence of a large standing army mean . . . the abandonment of what is characteristically American. . . . The build- ing of a navy and particularly of battleships is English and French pol- icy. It should never be ours."

How superb that is! Its assurance, its conviction, its Olympian au-   8
thority—what does it not reveal of the man, the time, the idea? In those words I saw clearly for the first time the nature and quality of the American anti-militarist tradition, of what has been called the American dream—it was a case of detail not merely corroborating but revealing an aspect of history.

Failing to know such details, one can be led astray. In 1890 Congress   9
authorized the building of the first three American battleships and, two years later, a fourth. Shortly thereafter, in 1895, this country plunged into a major quarrel with Great Britain, known as the Venezuelan crisis, in which there was much shaking of fists and chauvinist shrieking for war. Three years later we were at war with Spain. She was no longer a naval power equal to Britain, of course, but still not negligible. One would like to know what exactly was American naval strength at the time of both these crises. How many, if any, of the battleships autho-

rized in 1890 were actually at sea five years later? When the jingoes[4]
were howling for war in 1895, what ships did we have to protect our
coasts, much less to take the offensive? It seemed to me this was a
piece of information worth knowing.

To my astonishment, on looking for the answer in textbooks on the   **10**
period, I could not find it. The historians of America's rise to world
power, of the era of expansion, of American foreign policy, or even of
the Navy have not concerned themselves with what evidently seems to
them an irrelevant detail. It was hardly irrelevant to policy-makers of
the time who bore the responsibility for decisions of peace or war. Text
after text in American history is published every year, each repeating
on this question more or less what his predecessor has said before,
with no further enlightenment. To find the facts I finally had to write to
the Director of Naval History at the Navy Department in Washington.

My point is not how many battleships we had on hand in 1895 and   **11**
'98 (which I now know) but why this hard, physical fact was missing
from the professional historians' treatment. "Bald and unconvincing,"
said Pooh-Bah of narrative without fact, a judgment in which I join.

When I come across a generalization or a general statement in history   **12**
unsupported by illustration I am instantly on guard; my reaction is,
"Show me." If a historian writes that it is raining heavily on the day
war was declared, that is a detail corroborating a statement, let us say,
that the day was gloomy. But if he writes merely that it was a gloomy
day without mentioning the rain, I want to know what is his evidence;
what made it gloomy. Or if he writes, "The population was in a belligerent mood," or, "It was a period of great anxiety," he is indulging in
general statements which carry no conviction to me if they are not illustrated by some evidence. I write, for example, that fashionable
French society in the 1890s imitated the English in manners and habits.
Imagining myself to be my own reader—a complicated fugue that goes
on all the time at my desk—my reaction is of course, "Show me." The
next two sentences do. I write, "The Greffulhes and Breteuils were inti-
mates of the Prince of Wales, *le betting* was the custom at Longchamps,
le Derby was held at Chantilly, *le steeplechase* at Auteuil and an
unwanted member was *black-boulé* at the Jockey Club. Charles Haas, the
original of Swann, had 'Mr' engraved on his calling cards."

Even if corroborative detail did not serve a valid historical purpose,   **13**
its use makes a narrative more graphic and intelligible, more pleasur-
able to read, in short more readable. It assists communication, and
communication is, after all, the major purpose. History written in abstract terms communicates nothing to me. I cannot comprehend the abstract, and since a writer tends to create the reader in his own image, I

---

[4] Jingoes are overly enthusiastic patriots.

assume my reader cannot comprehend it either. No doubt I underestimate him. Certainly many serious thinkers write in the abstract and
many people read them with interest and profit and even, I suppose,
pleasure. I respect this ability, but I am unable to emulate it.

My favorite visible detail in *The Guns of August*, for some inexplicable   14
reason, is the one about the Grand Duke Nicholas, who was so tall (six
foot six) that when he established headquarters in a railroad car his
aide pinned up a fringe of white paper over the doorway to remind
him to duck his head. Why this insigificant item, after several years'
work and out of all the material crammed into a book of 450 pages,
would be the particular one to stick most sharply in my mind I cannot
explain, but it is. I was so charmed by the white paper fringe that I
constructed a whole paragraph describing Russian headquarters at
Baranovici in order to slip it in logically.

In another case the process failed. I had read that the Kaiser's birth-   15
day gift to his wife was the same every year: twelve hats selected by
himself which she was obliged to wear. There you see the value of corroborative detail in revealing personality; this one is worth a whole
book about the Kaiser—or even about Germany. It represents, however,
a minor tragedy of *The Guns*, for I never succeeded in working it in at
all. I keep my notes on cards, and the card about the hats started out
with those for the first chapter. Not having been used, it was moved
forward to a likely place in Chapter 2, missed again, and continued on
down through all the chapters until it emerged to a final resting place
in a packet marked "Unused."

A detail about General Sir Douglas Haig, equally revealing of person-   16
ality or at any rate of contemporary customs and conditions in the British officer corps, did find a place. This was the fact that during the
campaign in the Sudan in the nineties he had "a camel laden with
claret" in the personal pack train that followed him across the desert.
Besides being a vivid bit of social history, the phrase itself, "a camel
laden with claret," is a thing of beauty, a marvel of double and inner
alliteration. That, however, brings up another whole subject, the subject
of language, which needs an article of its own for adequate discussion.

Having inadvertently reached it, I will only mention that the inde-   17
pendent power of words to affect the writing of history is a thing to be
watched out for. They have an almost frightening autonomous power to
produce in the mind of the reader an image or idea that was not in the
mind of the writer. Obviously they operate this way in all forms of
writing, but history is particularly sensitive because one has a duty to
be accurate, and careless use of words can leave a false impression one
had not intended. Fifty percent at least of the critics of *The Guns* commented on what they said was my exposé of the stupidity of the generals. Nothing of the kind was in my mind when I wrote. What I meant
to convey was that the generals were in the trap of the circumstances,
training, ideas, and national impulses of their time and their individual

countries. I was not trying to convey stupidity but tragedy, fatality. Many reviewers understood this, clearly intelligent perceptive persons (those who understand one always are), but too many kept coming up with that word "stupidity" to my increasing dismay.

This power of words to escape from a writer's control is a fascinating   **18** problem which, since it was not what I started out to discuss, I can only hint at here. One more hint before I leave it: For me the problem lies in the fact that the art of writing interests me as much as the art of history (and I hope it is not provocative to say that I think of history as an art, not a science). In writing I am seduced by the sound of words and by the interaction of their sound and sense. Recently at the start of a paragraph I wrote, "Then occurred the intervention which irretrievably bent the twig of events." It was intended as a kind of signal to the reader. (Every now and then in a historical narrative, after one has been explaining a rather complicated background, one feels the need of waving a small red flag that says, "Wake up, Readers; something is going to happen.") Unhappily, after finishing the paragraph, I was forced to admit that the incident in question had *not* irretrievably bent the twig of events. Yet I hated to give up such a well-made phrase. Should I leave it in because it was good writing or take it out because it was not good history? History governed and it was lost to posterity (although, you notice, I have rescued it here). Words are seductive and dangerous material, to be used with caution. Am I writer first or am I historian? The old argument starts inside my head. Yet there need not always be dichotomy or dispute. The two functions need not be, in fact should not be, at war. The goal is fusion. In the long run the best writer is the best historian.

In quest of that goal I come back to the ounce. The most effective   **19** ounce of visual detail is that which indicates something of character or circumstance in addition to appearance. Careless clothes finished off by drooping white socks corroborate a description of Jean Jaurès as looking like the expected image of a labor leader. To convey both the choleric looks and temper and the cavalry officer's snobbism of Sir John French, it helps to write that he affected a cavalryman's stock in place of collar and tie, which gave him the appearance of being perpetually on the verge of choking.

The best corroborative detail I ever found concerned Lord Shaftes-   **20** bury, the eminent Victorian social reformer, author of the Factory Act and child-labor laws, who appeared in my first book, *Bible and Sword*. He was a man, wrote a contemporary, of the purest, palest, stateliest exterior in Westminster, on whose classic head "every separate dark lock of hair seemed to curl from a sense of duty." For conveying both appearance and character of a man and the aura of his times, all in one, that line is unequaled.

Novelists have the advantage that they can invent corroborative de-   **21** tail. Wishing to portray, let us say, a melancholy introspective character,

they make up physical qualities to suit. The historian must make do
with what he can find, though he may sometimes point up what he
finds by calling on a familiar image in the mental baggage of the
reader. To say that General Joffre looked like Santa Claus instantly conveys a picture which struck me as peculiarly apt when I wrote it. I was
thinking of Joffre's massive paunch, fleshy face, white mustache, and
bland and benevolent appearance, and I forgot that Santa Claus wears a
beard, which Joffre, of course, did not. Still, the spirit was right. One
must take care to choose a recognizable image for this purpose. In my
current book I have a melancholy and introspective character, Lord Sal-
isbury, Prime Minister in 1895, a supreme, if far from typical product of
the British aristocracy, a heavy man with a curly beard and big, bald
forehead, of whom I wrote that he was called the Hamlet of English
politics and looked like Karl Marx. I must say that I was really rather
pleased with that phrase, but my editor was merely puzzled. It developed that he did not know what Karl Marx looked like, so the comparison conveyed no image. If it failed its first test, it would certainly not
succeed with the average reader and so, sadly, I cut it out.

Sources of corroborative detail must of course be contemporary with   22
the subject. Besides the usual memoirs, letters, and autobiographies, do
not overlook novelists and newspapers. The inspired bit about the ladies rising to their feet for General Mercier comes from Proust as do
many other brilliant details; for instance, that during the Affair ladies
had "A bas les juifs"[5] printed on their parasols. Proust is invaluable not
only because there is so much of him but because it is all confined to a
narrow segment of society which he knew personally and intimately; it
is like a woman describing her own living room. On the other hand,
another novel set in the same period, Jean Barois by Roger Martin du
Gard, considered a major work of fiction on the Affair, gave me nothing I could use, perhaps because visual detail—at least the striking and
memorable detail—was missing. It was all talk and ideas, interesting,
of course, but for source material I want something I can see. When you
have read Proust you can see Paris of the nineties, horse cabs and lamp-
light, the clubman making his calls in white gloves stitched in black
and gray top hat lined in green leather.

Perhaps this illustrates the distinction between a major and a less   23
gifted novelist which should hold equally true, I believe, for historians.
Ideas alone are not flesh and blood. Too often, scholarly history is written in terms of ideas rather than acts; it tells what people wrote instead
of what they performed. To write, say, a history of progressivism in
America or of socialism in the era of the Second International by quoting the editorials, books, articles, speeches, and so forth of the leading
figures is easy. They were the wordiest people in history. If, however,

---

[5] "A bas les juifs": a French term for "down with the Jews."

one checks what they said and wrote against what actually was happening, a rather different picture emerges. At present I am writing a
chapter on the Socialists and I feel like someone in a small rowboat under Niagara. To find and hold on to anything hard and factual under
their torrent of words is an epic struggle. I suspect the reason is that
people out of power always talk more than those who have power. The
historian must be careful to guard against this phenomenon—weight it,
as the statisticians say—lest his result be unbalanced.

Returning to novels as source material, I should mention *The Edward-* **24**
ians by V. Sackville-West, which gave me precise and authoritative information on matters on which the writers of memoirs remain discreet.
Like Proust, this author was writing of a world she knew. At the great
house parties, one learns, the hostess took into considedration established liaisons in assigning the bedrooms and each guest had his name
on a card slipped into a small brass frame outside his door. The poets
too serve. Referring in this chapter on Edwardian England to the central role of the horse in the life of the British aristocracy, and describing
the exhilaration of the hunt, I used a line from a sonnet by Wilfrid Sca-
wen Blunt, "My horse a thing of wings, myself a god." Anatole France
supplied, through the mouth of a character in *M. Bergeret,* the words to
describe a Frenchman's feeling about the Army at the time of the Affair, that it was "all that is left of our glorious past. It consoles us for
the present and gives us hope of the future." Zola expressed the fear of
the bourgeoisie for the working class through the manager's wife in
Germinal, who, watching the march of the striking miners, saw "the red
vision of revolution . . . when on some somber evening at the end of
the century the people, unbridled at last, would make the blood of the
middle class flow." In *The Guns* there is a description of the retreating
French Army after the Battle of the Frontiers with their red trousers
faded to the color of pale brick, coats ragged and torn, cavernous eyes
sunk in unshaven faces, gun carriages with once-new gray paint now
blistered and caked with mud. This came from Blasco Ibáñez's novel
The Four Horsemen of the Apocalypse. From H. G. Wells's *Mr. Britling Sees
It Through* I took the feeling in England at the outbreak of war that it
contained an "enormous hope" of something better afterward, a chance
to end war, a "tremendous opportunity" to remake the world.

I do not know if the professors would allow the use of such sources   **25**
in a graduate dissertation, but I see no reason why a novelist should
not supply as authentic material as a journalist or a general. To determine what may justifiably be used from a novel, one applies the same
criterion as for any nonfictional account: If a particular item fits with
what one knows of the time, the place, the circumstances, and the
people, it is acceptable; otherwise not. For myself, I would rather quote
Proust or Sackville-West or Zola than a professional colleague as is the
academic habit. I could never see any sense whatever in referring to
one's neighbor in the next university as a source. To me that is no

source at all; I want to know where a given fact came from originally, not who used it last. As for referring to an earlier book of one's own as a source, this seems to me the ultimate absurdity. I am told that graduate students are required to cite the secondary historians in order to show they are familiar with the literature, but if I were granting degrees I would demand primary familiarity with primary sources. The secondary histories are necessary when one starts out ignorant of a subject and I am greatly in their debt for guidance, suggestion, bibliography, and outline of events, but once they have put me on the path I like to go the rest of the way myself. If I were a teacher I would disqualify anyone who was content to cite a secondary source as his reference for a fact. To trace it back oneself to its origin means to discover all manner of fresh material from which to make one's own selection instead of being content to re-use something already selected by someone else.

Though it is far from novels, I would like to say a special word for **26** *Who's Who*. For one thing, it is likely to be accurate because its entries are written by the subjects themselves. For another, it shows them as they wish to appear and thus often reveals character and even something of the times. H. H. Rogers, a Standard Oil partner and business tycoon of the 1890s, listed himself simply and succinctly as "Capitalist," obviously in his own eyes a proud and desirable thing to be. The social history of a period is contained in that self-description. Who would call himself by that word today?

As to newspapers, I like them for period flavor perhaps more than for factual information. One must be wary in using them for facts, because an event reported one day in a newspaper is usually modified or denied or turns out to be rumor on the next. It is absolutely essential to take nothing from a newspaper without following the story through for several days or until it disappears from the news. For period flavor, however, newspapers are unsurpassed. In the *New York Times* for August 10, 1914, I read an account of the attempt by German officers disguised in British uniforms to kidnap General Leman at Liège. The reporter wrote that the General's staff, "maddened by the dastardly violation of the rules of civilized warfare, spared not but slew."

This sentence had a tremendous effect on me. In it I saw all the dif- **27** ference between the world before 1914 and the world since. No reporter could write like that today, could use the word "dastardly," could take as a matter of course the concept of "civilized warfare," could write unashamedly, "spared not but slew." Today the sentence is embarrassing; in 1914 it reflected how people thought and the values they believed in. It was this sentence that led me back to do a book on the world before the war.

Women are a particularly good source for physical detail. They seem **28** to notice it more than men or at any rate to consider it more worth reporting. The contents of the German soldier's knapsack in 1914, includ-

ing thread, needles, bandages, matches, chocolate, tobacco, I found in
the memoirs of an American woman living in Germany. The Russian
moose who wandered over the frontier to be shot by the Kaiser at Rom-
inten came from a book by the English woman who was governess to
the Kaiser's daughter. Lady Warwick, mistress for a time of the Prince
of Wales until she regrettably espoused socialism, is indispensable for
Edwardian society, less for gossip than for habits and behavior. Princess
Daisy of Pless prattles endlessly about the endless social rounds of the
nobility, but every now and then supplies a dazzling nugget of information. One, which I used in *The Zimmermann Telegram*, was her description of how the Kaiser complained to her at dinner of the ill-treatment
he had received over the *Daily Telegraph* affair and of how, in the excess
of his emotion, "a tear fell on his cigar." In the memoirs of Edith
O'Shaughnessy, wife of the First Secretary of the American Embassy in
Mexico, is the description of the German Ambassador, Von Hintze,
who dressed and behaved in all things like an Englishman except that
he wore a large sapphire ring on his little finger which gave him away.
No man would have remarked on that.

In the end, of course, the best place to find corroborative detail is on
the spot itself, if it can be visited, as Herodotus did in Asia Minor or
Parkman on the Oregon Trail. Take the question of German attrocities
in 1914. Nothing requires more careful handling because, owing to
post-war disillusions, "atrocity" came to be a word one did not believe
in. It was supposed because the Germans had not, after all, cut off the
hands of Belgian babies, neither had they shot hostages nor burned
Louvain. The results of this disbelief were dangerous because when the
Germans became Nazis people were disinclined to believe they were as
bad as they seemed and appeasement became the order of the day.
(It strikes me that here is a place to put history to use and that a certain wariness might be in order today.) In writing of German terrorism
in Belgium in 1914 I was at pains to use only accounts of Germans
themselves or in a few cases by Americans, then neutral. The most
telling evidence, however, was that which I saw forty-five years later:
the rows of gravestones in the churchyard of a little Belgian village on
the Meuse, each inscribed with a name and a date and the legend
"fusillé par les Allemands." Or the stone marker on the road outside
Senlis, twenty-five miles from Paris, engraved with the date September
2, 1914, and the names of the mayor and six other civilian hostages
shot by the Germans. Somehow the occupations engraved opposite the
names—baker's apprentice, stonemason, *garçon de café*—carried extra
conviction. This is the verisimilitude Pooh-Bah and I too have been
trying for.

The desire to find the significant detail plus the readiness to open his   **30**
mind to it and let it report to him are half the historian's equipment.
The other half, concerned with idea, point of view, the reason for writing, the "Why" of history, has been left out of this discussion although

I am not unconscious that it looms in the background. The art of writing is the third half. If that list does not add up, it is because history is human behavior, not arithmetic.

Written Response

What would Tuchman consider good historical writing? Do you agree with her?

Rhetorical Analysis

1. Tuchman writes that she is suspicious of any histories that do not include supporting details. Select one of Tuchman's paragraphs and discuss whether she provides adequate supporting details for her general ideas.

2. Tuchman uses allusions to an article in *The New York Times* and *The Mikado* to introduce her thesis, that history must be grounded in facts. Discuss how she uses these allusions to develop her introduction and explain her basic point.

Interpretation

1. Based on what you have read in Tuchman's article, how would you define good history?

2. In *Tropics of Discourse: Essays in Cultural Criticism* (Baltimore: Johns Hopkins, 1978), Hayden White wrote:

> Theorists of historiography generally agree that all historical narratives contain an irreducible and inexpungeable element of interpretation. The historian has to interpret his materials in order to construct the moving pattern of images in which the form of the historical process is to be mirrored. And this because the historical record is both too full and too sparse. On the one hand, there are always more facts in the record than the historian can possibly include in his narrative representation of a given segment of the historical process. And so the historian must "interpret" his data by excluding certain facts from his account as irrelevant to his narrative purpose. On the other hand, in his efforts to reconstruct "what happened" in any given period of history, the historian inevitably must include in his narrative an account of some event or complex of events for which the facts that would permit a plausible explanation of its occurrence are lacking. And this means that the historian must "interpret" his materials by filling in the gaps in his information on inferential or speculative grounds. A historical narrative is thus necessarily a mixture of adequately and inadequately explained events, a congeries of established and inferred facts, at once a representation that is an interpretation and an interpretation that passes for an explanation of the whole process mirrored in the narrative. [p. 51]

Discuss this passage. What is White saying about the writing of history? Do you feel that Tuchman would agree with White's statement?

<hr/>

                                                    WRITING ASSIGNMENT

This writing assignment will take place in several stages.

First, divide into groups of three or four people.

Second, decide on something that your group can observe together. You may wish to observe a busy street, people in a particular location, a group of construction workers, or anything that will pass for an historical event.

Third, once you have decided what to observe, arrange a time to meet as a group. As you observe the event, each individual should take notes as detailed as possible, but you should not compare or share notes.

Fourth, take your notes and write a description of the event without comparing your notes with those of the others in your group. By writing a description of the event, you will be simulating what historians do when they begin to construct a narrative from their facts and sources. Thus, you need to think about how to make a story out of what you have observed.

Fifth, after you have completed your description and have it ready to turn in, make enough copies of it for everyone in your group. Then, turn in your description as a writing assignment.

Finally, compare the descriptions that each member of your group wrote about the "historical event" that you observed together. How are they similar? How are they different? As a second writing assignment, write an essay in which you discuss whether your descriptions of the event (your historical narratives) were objective.

Learning from History

In *Giving Up the Gun* (Boulder, Colo.: Shambhala, 1979), Noel Perrin wrote about an unusual historical episode. From 1543 to 1876, the Japanese abandoned the use of guns and returned to the sword, an earlier, less deadly form of warfare. At the end of his book, Perrin argues that this historical event can teach us a lesson:

> The idea of turning back the clock has, of course, occurred to men in the West many times. Bayard—who, like Lord Mori Nagayoshi, died of a bullet wound—would have been only too happy to. Queen Elizabeth I not only thought about it, she actually once did set the hands back a fraction of a second. A subject of hers named William Lee had invented a knitting machine, with which he hoped to replace hand-knitting as the universal method of making stockings in England. He succeeded in interesting the Queen's cousin, Lord Hunsden, in this early bit of automation. Lord Hunsden, in turn, tried to get Elizabeth both to grant Lee a patent and to invest crown funds in a prototype factory. She would do neither. "My Lord," she

said, "I have too much love for my poor people who obtain their bread by knitting to give much money to forward an invention which will tend to their ruin, by depriving them of employment." That was in 1589.

In our own time, Arnold Toynbee, among others, has wanted to put the clock back several hours. His argument is that men can no more be trusted to play with machine guns. "If a vote could undo all the technological advances of the last three hundred years," Toynbee has written, "many of us would cast that vote, in order to safeguard the survival of the human race while we remain in our present state of social and moral backwardness."

Even some scientists, such as the biologist René Dubos, would like to see the clock of technology, if not turned back, then stopped more or less at its present moment. Dr. Dubos is moved less by fears that now we can kill each other, we will, than by dismay at our reckless expenditure of natural resources. Unlike some others who are dismayed, he has predicted that by the year 2000 we will be driven by the needs of conservation into what he calls "a phase of steady state," technologically speaking.

But the number of those who seriously hope to set back the clock, or even to stop it, remains very small. To most men who have considered the matter, there seem to be two overwhelming objections. First, ignoring (or unaware of) the Japanese experience, they suppose it is just not possible to reverse technology within a continuous culture. Second, if by some miracle (such as Toynbee's vote taking place, and God heading it), it *were* possible, they think it would lead to decadence and stagnation. They see the choice as either continued progress in all fields, or else a return to the Dark Ages. Either we press on with neutron bombs and biogenetic engineering, or we give up dentistry and window glass. Selective control of technology is impossible, they suppose.

The history of Tokugawa Japan does not support this gloomy view, however. The Japanese did practice selective control. They utterly ceased weapons development—indeed, went backwards—and meanwhile they went ahead in dozens of other fields. [pp. 80–81]

The lesson that can be learned from this period of Japanese history, Perrin believes, is that we *can* turn back the clock. We can selectively decide to abandon some potentially dangerous forms of technology (such as the development of new weapons or genetic research) without abandoning beneficial forms of technology. Perrin is arguing, in essence, that what occurred in Japan between 1543 and 1876 can be repeated today in the United States or in the entire world.

In this section, you will play the role of historian and investigate Perrin's claim. As you read the chronology and documents that follow, you will need to decide whether (a) the historical episode of the Japanese giving up the gun between 1543 and 1876 was unique to Japanese culture of a particular point in hitory and thus cannot be replicated in other cultures and historical periods, or (b) that the episode was not tied to its historical context in ways that would prevent it from serving as a model for other countries to follow in other historical situations. You will begin by reading a chronology of key events. The chronology will explain the pure facts of what happened, but you will soon find that these facts must be interpreted. In preparation for interpreting the facts, you will read a series of documents or sources, as would any serious historian. From these texts, you should be able to develop the kind of cultural and historical perspective that will enable you to interpret the chronology and critically analyze Perrin's claim that other countries can also give up the gun or abandon a potentially dangerous line of scientific research.

As you read the documents, you should attempt to isolate important facts, examples, and quotations that might help you to write an essay on this issue. By doing so, you will be playing the role of an historian and a scholar in yet another way. Because the use of photocopying is now so widespread, most scholars will make copies of the documents that they wish to study and, instead of taking time-consuming notes on index cards, will circle important facts, write comments in the margin, underline interesting quotations, and make other notes right on their photocopy. After you have finished reading and taking notes on the documents, your instructor may ask the class to discuss your note-taking techniques.

With this assignment you will be allowed more independence than with previous assignments. You will, in effect, be writing a short research paper, which will help to prepare you for the more demanding research papers that you will write later in your academic career.

Chronology of Key Events

1490–1600 A period called Japan's "Age of a Country at War." Feudal lords fight for military control of the country.

1543 August: A Chinese cargo ship anchors in the bay of Tanegashima Island at the southern tip of Japan. Aboard are about 100 Chinese trader-pirates and 3 Portuguese adventurers.

October: The Portuguese sell two arquebuses (rifles) and ammunition to Lord Tokitaka (feudal master of Tanegashima), reportedly for 1000 taels of gold. Lord Tokitaka orders Yatsuika Kinbei (his chief swordsmith) to replicate the guns. Yatsuika has difficulty making the spring mechanism in the breech. He reportedly trades his 17-year-old daughter to the captain of a Portuguese ship in exchange for lessons in gunsmithing. Within a year, Yatsuika makes ten guns. Within a decade, guns are being made all over Japan.

1549 Lord Oda Nobunaga places an order for 500 guns.

1560 Guns are first used in large battles. A general in full armor dies of a bullet wound. Guns become increasingly important to Japanese warfare.

1592 A Japanese lord, who was fighting in Korea and facing troops armed with matchlocks, writes home: "Please arrange to send us guns and ammunition. There is absolutely no need for spears."

1600 Lord Tokugawa Ieyasu, the first Tokugawa shogun, takes office, ending over 100 years of feudal warfare.

1607 Lord Tokugawa orders that guns can be made only in Nagahama and that all orders for guns must be cleared through the Teppo

Bugyo, or Commissioner of Guns. The making of guns was thus centralized.

1610   The government begins to reduce its orders for guns.

1617   Christian missionaries are expelled from Japan.

1636   In an effort to dissuade the shogun from forcing them to leave Hirado, a Dutch trading mission gives him 12 flintlock pistols, which are superior to the matchlock. The Japanese do not copy the new weapon.

1637   In the Shimabara Rebellion, 20,000 Japanese Christians take over Hara Castle and use guns to defend themselves against the shogun's troops. The Christian rebels sing the following song:

> While the powder and shot remain,
> Continue to chase the besieging army
> That is blown away before us
> Like the drifting sand.
>
> Hear the dull thud of the enemy's guns: Don! Don!
> Our arms give back the reply,
> 'By the Blessing of God the Father,
> I will cut off your heads!'

This was the last extensive use of guns in a Japanese battle for 200 years.

1725   The shogun sends the new king of Korea, now an ally, coronation presents:

> 500 suits of heavy armor
> 350 swords
> 200 suits of light armor
> 67 spears
> 23 matchlocks

1809   Sato Nobuhiro secretly publishes his *How to Use Three Types of Fire-arms.*

1829   Japanese gunmakers begin to experiment with making flintlocks.

1853   Commodore Matthew Calbraith Perry anchors four well-armed ships in Tokyo Bay. The Japanese order him to sail to Nagasaki, the only port open to foreigners, but Perry refuses to leave. His show of power (i.e., modern cannons) leads to a treaty in 1854 with the Tokugawa shogun that opens trade with Japan.

1867   Japan's feudal regime collapses.

1876   The last Tokugawa shogun resigns. The new government forbids samurai to wear swords and promotes modern military weapons. A group of 170 samarai revolt but are defeated.

1877   The government forces, using guns, defeat 40,000 samurai rebels.

Document One

Document One is a chapter from Noel Perrin's *Giving Up the Gun* (pp. 23–31). In the chapter, Perrin describes how guns were used in Japan in the midde of the sixteenth century, shortly before the Shogun decided to reduce the production of guns.

During the half century after Lord Oda's victory, firearms were at   1
their height in Japan. Not to know how to use them was not to be a
soldier. But, at the same time, the first resistance to firearms was developing. It arose from the discovery that efficient weapons tend to
overshadow the men who use them. Prior to Nagashino, the normal
Japanese battle had consisted of a very large number of single combats
and small melees. After introducing themselves (unless they were gunners), people paired off. Such a battle could produce almost as many
heroic stories as there were participants. It even had a kind of morality,
since each man's fate depended principally on his own ability and state
of training. Equipment counted, too, of course. Defensive armor was
considered especially important. ('The Japanese made more varieties of
mail than all the rest of the world put together,' said George Stone),
and a well-made piece of it came in for a full share of praise. In an old
description of a battle fought in 1562, there is one incident that reads
remarkably like a modern advertisement. Late in the battle, a general
named Ota Sukemasa, who had already been wounded twice, got into
single combat with an enemy knight named Shimizu.

'His assailant, a man noted for his strength, threw down the now   2
weary and wounded Ota, but tried in vain to cut off his head,' the account runs. 'At this, Ota, his eyes flashing with anger, cried out, "Are
you flurried, sir? My neck is protected by a NODOWA [a jointed iron
throatpiece]. Remove this, and take off my head."

'Shimizu replied with a bow, "How kind of you to tell me! You die a   3
noble death. You have my admiration!" But just as he was about to remove the NODOWA, two squires of Ota rushed up and, throwing down
Shimizu, enabled their master to decapitate his foe and retire safely
from the field.'

Incidents like this occurred very rarely in mass battles with match-   4
locks. A well-aimed volley of a thousand shots killed flurried soldiers
and cool-headed ones without discrimination—and at a distance too
great for conversation. Bravery was actually a disadvantage if you were

Source: From *Giving Up the Gun* by Noel Perrin. Copyright © 1979 by Noel Perrin. Reprinted by permission of David R. Godine, Publisher.

charging against guns, while if you changed sides and became a
matchlockman yourself, there was still not much chance for individual
distinction. You were now simply one of the thousand men in your
rank, waiting behind your breastworks to mow down the charging enemy. It didn't even take much skill to do this. Skill had been moved
back from the soldier to the manufacturer of his weapon, and up from
the soldier to his commander. Partly for that reason, many of Lord
Oda's matchlockmen were farmers and members of the yeoman class
called *goshi* or *ji-samurai*, rather than samurai proper. It was a shock to
everyone to find out that a farmer with a gun could kill the toughest
samurai so readily.

The result was that soon after Nagashino two conflicting attitudes   5
toward guns began to appear. On the one hand, everyone recognized
their superiority as long-range killing devices, and all the feudal lords
ordered them in large numbers. At least in absolute numbers, guns
were almost certainly more common in Japan in the late sixteenth century than in any other country in the world. On the other hand, no
true soldier—that is, no member of the *bushi* class—wanted to use them
himself. Even Lord Oda avoided them as personal weapons. In the ambush in which he died, in 1582, he is supposed to have fought with his
great bow until the string broke, and then with a spear. The following
year, during a battle in which something like two hundred ordinary
soldiers were hit by artillery fire, the ten acknowledged heroes of the
battle made their names with swords and spears.

This attempted division of warfare into upper-class fighting with   6
swords and lower-class fighting with guns did not, of course, work.
The two methods kept colliding. The death of Lord Mori Nagayoshi, in
1584, is typical. Lord Mori, who was wearing full armor with a kind of
white silk jupon over it, and who thus made an extremely conspicuous
target, persisted in riding out in front of his troops to rally them. He
probably waved his sword. A matchlockman took careful aim at his
head and knocked him off his horse dead, aged twenty-seven.

That same year, the two leading generals in Japan met with their   7
armies at a place called Komaki. Both had the lessons of Nagashino
very clearly in mind, and both had a high proportion of gunners
among their troops. The result was an impasse. Not only were there no
introductions and no individual heroics, neither general would allow
his cavalry to attack at all against the other's guns. Instead, both armies
dug trenches, settled in, and waited, firing an occasional volley or
blowing up a few of the enemy with a land mine to pass the time. In
some ways it was like a scene from World War I, three and a half centuries ahead of schedule. In the end the two commanders made an alliance, and went off to fight other armies that were less constricted by
their own technology.

A couple of years later, Lord Hideyoshi, the regent of Japan at the   8
time, took the first step toward the control of firearms. It was a very

small step, and it was not taken simply to protect feudal lords from being shot by peasants but to get *all* weapons out of the hands of civilians. What Lord Hideyoshi did was characteristically Japanese. He said
nothing about arms control. Instead, he announced that he was going
to build a statue of Buddha that would make all existing statues look
like midgets. It would be of wood, braced and bolted with iron. And it
would be so enormous (the figure was about twice the scale of the
Statue of Liberty), that many tons of iron would be needed just for the
braces and bolts.

Still more was required to erect the accompanying temple, which   9
was to cover a piece of ground something over an eighth of a mile
square. All farmers, *ji-samurai*, and monks were invited to contribute
their swords and guns to the cause. They were, in fact, required to. As
a result, anyone visiting Kyoto in 1587 would have seen a curious scene
of disarmament. He would have seen scores of blacksmiths busy hammering matchlocks into religious hardware. The Jesuit Annual Letter for
that year reported rather bitterly that Lord Hideyoshi was 'planning to
possess himself of all the iron in Japan,' and added, 'He is crafty and
cunning beyond belief. Now he is depriving the people of their arms
under pretext of devotion to Religion.'

No one was depriving the armies of *their* arms, of course, and the   10
production of guns continued to rise for another twenty years. Lord
Hideyoshi himself had a powerful need of them. He had a new plan,
which was, briefly, to conquer Korea, China, and then the Philippines.
China was his real target, but Korea came first, as offering the best invasion route. The Philippines were an afterthought, included chiefly
because Hideyoshi had received a report that the small Spanish garri-
son would be a pushover. (The report was apparently correct. Most military historians agree that if Hideyoshi had reversed his order of attack,
Manila would have been a Japanese city from 1592 on.)

During a campaign as Napoleonic as this, one might have expected   11
the efficiency of guns to triumph over the mere heroism of swords and
spears. It almost did. The Japanese started off to Korea with mixed
upper- and lower-class units, their weapons as ill-assorted as ever. The
samurai, who were a majority in nearly all detachments, carried their
traditional two swords, plus at least one other weapon, usually either
a bow or a spear. Most of the other soldiers carried guns. Of the original invading army of 160,000, somewhat over a quarter were matchlockmen.

During the first few months while the Japanese were advancing up   12
Korea almost at will, the diverse mixture of weapons worked well
enough. The Korean army was so disorganized that the invaders could
almost have fought with stone hatchets and won. As it was, they triumphed. The samurai fought with sword and spear against the Korean
knights, routing them time after time. The lower-class gunners mopped
up the remnants. It took the lead detachment just eighteen days from

the first landing at Pusan until they captured Seoul. There was no danger of any Japanese being mopped up by Korean matchlockmen, because the Koreans had no matchlocks.

What the Koreans did have was a rather inefficient form of light artillery, which they had learned about from the Chinese. This the Japanese gunners outshot with no trouble at all, meanwhile devastating the Korean archers. It was an ideal war. Upper-class soldiers could be, and were, heroes; lower-class soldiers easily triumphed through technological superiority. They took particular pleasure in capturing the little Korean cannon, and General Kato Kiyomasa sent them home by the dozen as souvenirs. They are just over two feet long, and at infrequent intervals, fire a sort of large marble. Useful for scaring Highlanders, but worthless against sixteenth-century Japanese. **13**

But when the Chinese began to send whole armies of reinforcements to help the Koreans, the holiday atmosphere evaporated. Especially since in the second year of the war a few Korean units began to appear with matchlocks of their own. These were Korean-made—copied by smiths in northern Korea from the handful of captured Japanese weapons. They were perfectly capable of killing a samurai. **14**

The Japanese were now heavily outnumbered, and beginning to face serious resistance. The idea of guns for the whole army began to look very attractive to some of the commanders. A couple of letters written home from Korea in the 1590s reveal their view rather clearly. One was written in 1592 by a provincial lord who had gone over with approximately 1,500 archers, 1,500 gunners, and 300 spearmen. He wanted to change the ratio. 'Please arrange to send us guns and ammunition,' he wrote to his steward. 'There is absolutely no need for spears.' **15**

Seventeen years had passed since Nagashino, and it can hardly have been news to the steward that guns outperformed spears. The news was the change in his master's attitude. Incidentally, there were still plenty of guns in Japan to send. Francesco Carletti, the Florentine merchant, made his visit to Japan at the height of the Korean war, arriving from the Philippines in a Japanese ship in 1597. Even though, as he later reported to Grand Duke Ferdinand de Medici, the Japanese now had nearly 300,000 men committed in Korea, there were still numerous samurai left at home. Most of them owned a gun or two, as he found when he got invited to go hunting. However much they might prefer sword and bow on the battlefield, for shooting ducks, pheasants, and wild geese, they liked guns. 'They kill all these with the arquebus, getting each with a single ball.' he wrote Duke Ferdinand. **16**

The other letter was written much later in the campaign, when the Japanese—rather like the Americans three hundred and fifty years later—had swept up to the Yalu River and then been driven down again by the Chinese (who made up a quarter of the world's population then, too). A Japanese nobleman named Asano was holding Yol-San Castle against a very much larger force of Koreans and Chinese, and he **17** wrote his father to arrange for replacements. 'Have them bring as many guns as possible, for no other equipment is needed,' he said. 'Give strict orders that all the men, even the samurai, carry guns.' In other words, the knightly retainers of the Asano family were to be dragged, kicking and screaming, into the late sixteenth century.

Document Two

Yamamoto Tsunetomo's *Hagakure: The Book of the Samurai* (Tokyo: Kodansha, trans. 1979) is generally regarded as the most important expression of the code of Bushido, by which the samurai lived. Tsunetomo was a samurai in the service of Nabeshima Mitsushige from the time he was a child until 1700, when Mitsushige died. After he was forbidden to commit seppuku (ritual disembowelment), he became a Buddhist priest. From 1710 to 1716, he had a series of conversations with Tashiro Tsuramoto, a young samurai. Tsuramoto wrote his recollections of the conversations and eventually arranged them into *Hagakure.* Below are some selected passages.

Although it stands to reason that a samurai should be mindful of the   1
Way of the Samurai, it would seem that we are all negligent. Consequently, if someone were to ask, "What is the true meaning of the Way of the Samurai?" the person who would be able to answer promptly is rare. This is because it has not been established in one's mind beforehand. From this, one's unmindfulness of the Way can be known.   2
　Negligence is an extreme thing.

*　　*　　*

　The Way of the Samurai is found in death. When it comes to either/   3
or, there is only the quick choice of death. It is not particularly difficult. Be determined and advance. To say that dying without reaching one's aim is to die a dog's death is the frivolous way of sophisticates. When pressed with the choice of life or death, it is not necessary to gain one's aim.
　We all want to live. And in large part we make our logic according to   4
what we like. But not having attained our aim and continuing to live is cowardice. This is a thin dangerous line. To die without gaining one's aim *is* a dog's death and fanaticism. But there is no shame in this. This is the substance of the Way of the Samurai. If by setting one's heart right every morning and evening, one is able to live as though his body were already dead, he gains freedom in the Way. His whole life will be without blame, and he will succeed in his calling.

*　　*　　*

　Sagara Kyūma was completely at one with his master and served him   5
as though his own body were already dead. He was one man in a thousand.

Source: From *Hagakure: The Book of the Samurai.* Copyright © 1979, published by Kodansha International Ltd. Reprinted by permission. All rights reserved.

Once there was an important meeting at Master Sakyō's Mizugae   6
Villa, and it was commanded that Kyūma was to commit seppuku. At
that time in Ōsaki there was a teahouse on the third floor of the subur-
ban residence of Master Taku Nui. Kyūma rented this, and gathering
together all the good-for-nothings in Saga he put on a puppet show,
operating one of the puppets himself, carousing and drinking all
day and night. Thus, overlooking Master Sakyō's villa, he carried on
and caused a great disturbance. In instigating this disaster he gallantly
thought only of his master and was resolved to committing suicide.

*   *   *

At the time when there was a council concerning the promotion of a   7
certain man, the council members were at the point of deciding that
promotion was useless because of the fact that the man had previously
been involved in a drunken brawl. But someone said, "If we were to
cast aside every man who had made a mistake once, useful men could
probably not be come by. A man who makes a mistake once will be
considerably more prudent and useful because of his repentance. I feel
that he should be promoted."
Someone else then asked, "Will you guarantee him?"   8
The man replied, "Of course I will."   9
The others asked, "By what will you guarantee him?"   10
And he replied, "I can guarantee him by the fact that he is a man   11
who has erred once. A man who has never once erred is dangerous."
This said, the man was promoted.

*   *   *

A certain person was brought to shame because he did not take re-   12
venge. The way of revenge lies in simply forcing one's way into a place
and being cut down. There is no shame in this. By thinking that you
must complete the job you will run out of time. By considering things
like how many men the enemy has, time piles up; in the end you will
give up.
No matter if the enemy has thousands of men, there is fulfillment in   13
simply standing them off and being determined to cut them all down,
starting from one end. You will finish the greater part of it.
Concerning the night assault of Lord Asano's rōnin, the fact that they   14
did not commit seppuku at the Sengakuji was an error, for there was a
long delay between the time their lord was struck down and the time
when they struck down the enemy. If Lord Kira had died of illness
within that period, it would have been extemely regrettable. Because
the men of the Kamigata area have a very clever sort of wisdom, they
do well at praiseworthy acts but cannot do things indiscriminately, as
was done in the Nagasaki fight.
Although all things are not to be judged in this manner, I mention it   15
in the investigation of the Way of the Samurai. When the time comes,

there is no moment for reasoning. And if you have not done your in-
quiring beforehand, there is most often shame. Reading books and listening to people's talk are for the purpose of prior resolution.

Above all, the Way of the Samurai should be in being aware that you do 16
not know what is going to happen next, and in querying every item day
and night. Victory and defeat are matters of the temporary force of circumstances. The way of avoiding shame is different. It is simply in death.

Even if it seems certain that you will lose, retaliate. Neither wisdom 17
nor technique has a place in this. A real man does not think of victory
or defeat. He plunges recklessly towards an irrational death. By doing
this, you will awaken from your dreams.

*   *   *

There was a man who said, "Such and such a person has a violent 18
disposition, but this is what I said right to his face . . . " This was an
unbecoming thing to say, and it was said simply because he wanted to
be known as a rough fellow. It was rather low, and it can be seen that
he was still rather immature. It is because a samurai has correct manners that he is admired. Speaking of other people in this way is no different from an exchange between low class spearmen. It is vulgar.

*   *   *

Every morning, the samurai of fifty or sixty years ago would bathe, 19
shave their foreheads, put lotion in their hair, cut their fingernails and
toenails rubbing them with pumice and then with wood sorrel, and
without fail pay attention to their personal appearance. It goes without
saying that their armor in general was kept free from rust, that it was
dusted, shined, and arranged.

Although it seems that taking special care of one's appearance is sim- 20
ilar to showiness, it is nothing akin to elegance. Even if you are aware
that you may be struck down today and are firmly resolved to an inevitable death, if you are slain with an unseemly appearance, you will
show your lack of previous resolve, will be despised by your enemy,
and will appear unclean. For this reason it is said that both old and
young should take care of their appearance.

Although you say that this is troublesome and time-consuming, a 21
samurai's work is in such things. It is neither busy-work nor time-
consuming. In constantly hardening one's resolution to die in battle,
deliberately becoming as one already dead, and working at one's job
and dealing with military affairs, there should be no shame. But when
the time comes, a person will be shamed if he is not conscious of these
things even in his dreams, and rather passes his days in self-interest
and self-indulgence. And if he thinks that this is not shameful, and
feels that nothing else matters as long as he is comfortable, then his
dissipate and discourteous actions will be repeatedly regrettable.

The person without previous resolution to inevitable death makes cer- 22
tain that his death will be in bad form. But if one is resolved to death

beforehand, in what way can he be despicable? One should be especially diligent in this concern.

Furthermore, during the last thirty years customs have changed; now   **23** when young samurai get together, if there is not just talk about money matters, loss and gain, secrets, clothing styles or matters of sex, there is no reason to gather together at all. Customs are going to pieces. One can say that formerly when a man reached the age of twenty or thirty, he did not carry despicable things in his heart, and thus neither did such words appear. If an elder unwittingly said something of that sort, he thought of it as a sort of injury. This new custom probably appears because people attach importance to being beautiful before society and to household finances. What things a person should be able to accomplish if he had no haughtiness concerning his place in society!

It is a wretched thing that the young men of today are so contriving   **24** and so proud of their material possessions. Men with contriving hearts are lacking in duty. Lacking in duty, they will have no self-respect.

*   *   *

A retainer is a man who remains consistently undistracted twenty-   **25** four hours a day, whether he is in the presence of his master or in public. If one is careless during his rest period, the public will see him as being only careless.

*   *   *

Regardless of class, a person who does something beyond his social   **26** standing will at some point commit mean or cowardly acts. In the lower class there are even people who will run away. One should be careful with menials and the like.

*   *   *

There are many people who, by being attached to a martial art and   **27** taking apprentices, believe that they have arrived at the full stature of a warrior. But it is a regrettable thing to put forth much effort and in the end become an "artist." In artistic technique it is good to learn to the extent that you will not be lacking. In general, a person who is versatile in many things is considered to be vulgar and to have only a broad knowledge of matters of importance.

*   *   *

When something is said to you by the master, whether it is for your   **28** good or bad fortune, to withdraw in silence shows perplexity. You should have some appropriate response. It is important to have resolution beforehand.

Moreover, if at the time that you are asked to perform some function   **29** you have deep happiness or great pride, it will show exactly as that on your face. This has been seen in many people and is rather unbecoming. But another type of person knows his own defects and thinks, "I'm a clumsy person but I've been asked to do this thing anyway. Now how am I going to go about it? I can see that this is going to be much trouble and cause for concern." Though these words are never said, they will appear on the surface. This shows modesty.

By inconsistency and frivolity we stray from the Way and show our- 30
selves to be beginners. In this we do much harm.

* * *

There was a certain person who was a master of the spear. When he 31
was dying, he called his best disciple and spoke his last injunctions:

I have passed on to you all the secret techniques of this school, and 32
there is nothing left to say. If you think of taking on a disciple yourself,
then you should practice diligently with the bamboo sword every day.
Superiority is not just a matter of secret techniques.

Also, in the instructions of a *renga* teacher, it was said that the day 33
before the poetry meeting one should calm his mind and look at a collection of poems. This is concentration on one affair. All professions should be done with concentration.

* * *

Although the Mean is the standard for all things, in military affairs 34
a man must always strive to outstrip others. According to archery instructions the right and left hands are supposed to be level, but the right hand has a tendency to go higher. They will become level if one will lower the right hand a bit when shooting. In the stories of the elder warriors it is said that on the battlefield if one wills himself to outstrip warriors of accomplishment, and day and night hopes to strike down a powerful enemy, he will grow indefatigable and fierce of heart and will manifest courage. One should use this principle in everyday affairs too.

* * *

There is a way of bringing up the child of a samurai. From the time 35
of infancy one should encourage bravery and avoid trivially frightening or teasing the child. If a person is affected by cowardice as a child, it remains a lifetime scar. It is a mistake for parents to thoughtlessly make their children dread lightning, or to have them not go into dark places, or to tell them frightening things in order to stop them from crying.

* * *

When on the battlefield, if you try not to let others take the lead and 36
have the sole intention of breaking into the enemy lines, then you will not fall behind others, your mind will become fierce, and you will manifest martial valor. This fact has been passed down by the elders. Furthermore, if you are slain in battle, you should be resolved to have your corpse facing the enemy.

*   *   *

Even if one's head were to be suddenly cut off, he should be able to   37
do one more action with certainty. The last moments of Nitta Yoshisada
are proof of this. Had his spirit been weak, he would have fallen the
moment his head was severed. Recently, there is the example of Ōno
Dōken. These actions occurred because of simple determination. With
martial valor, if one becomes like a revengeful ghost and shows great
determination, though his head is cut off, he should not die.

*   *   *

The priest Keihō related that Lord Aki once said that martial valor is   38
a matter of becoming a fanatic. I thought that this was surprisingly in
accord with my own resolve and thereafter became more and more extreme in my fanaticism.

*   *   *

A certain person said the following.   39
There are two kinds of disposition, inward and outward, and a per-   40
son who is lacking in one or the other is worthless. It is, for example,
like the blade of a sword, which one should sharpen well and then put
in its scabbard, periodically taking it out and knitting one's eyebrows as
in an attack, wiping off the blade, and then placing it in its scabbard
again.

If a person has his sword out all the time, he is habitually swinging   41
a naked blade; people will not approach him and he will have no allies.

If a sword is always sheathed, it will become rusty, the blade will   42
dull, and people will think as much of its owner.

Document Three

Miyamoto Musashi was Japan's most celebrated warrior. He lived most of his life as a ronin, a samurai without a lord or retainer, and pursued enlightment through Kendo, the art of using the sword. By age 30, he had already fought and won some 60 duels, killing his opponent each time. It was rumored that he never took a bath for fear that an opponent might catch him offguard. In 1643, he began to live a life of seclusion in a cave. There he wrote *A Book of Five Rings*, a book of Kendo strategy. Below are excerpts from "The Fire Book," the fifth book of *A Book of Five Rings*.

In this the Fire Book of the NiTo Ichi school of strategy I describe fighting as fire. **1**

In the first place, people think narrowly about the benefit of strategy. **2** By using only their fingertips, they only know the benefit of three of the five inches of the wrist. They let a contest be decided, as with the folding fan, merely by the span of their forearms. They specialise in the small matter of dexterity, learning such trifles as hand and leg movements with the bamboo practice sword.

In my strategy, the training for killing enemies is by way of many **3** contests, fighting for survival, discovering the meaning of life and death, learning the Way of the sword, judging the strength of attacks and understanding the Way of the "edge and ridge" of the sword.

You cannot profit from small techniques particularly when full armour is worn. My Way of strategy is the sure method to win when **4** fighting for your life one man against five or ten. There is nothing wrong with the principle "one man can beat ten, so a thousand men can beat ten thousand". You must research this. Of course you cannot assemble a thousand or ten thousand men for everyday training. But you can become a master of strategy by training alone with a sword, so that you can understand the enemy's stratagems, his strength and resources, and come to appreciate how to apply strategy to beat ten thousand enemies.

Any man who wants to master the essence of my strategy must re- **5** search diligently, training morning and evening. Thus can he polish his skill, become free from self, and realise extraordinary ability. He will come to possess miraculous power.

This is the practical result of strategy. **6**

Source: From *A Book of Rings* by Miyamoto Musashi. Copyright © 1974 by Victor Harris. Published in 1974 by The Overlook Press, Lewis Hollow Road, Woodstock, New York 12498.

To Tread Down the Sword

"To tread down the sword" is a principle often used in strategy. First,   7
in large scale strategy, when the enemy first discharges bows and guns
and then attacks, it is difficult for us to attack if we are busy loading
powder into our guns or notching our arrows. The spirit is to attack
quickly while the enemy is still shooting with bows or guns. The spirit
is to win by "treading down" as we receive the enemy's attack.

In single combat, we cannot get a decisive victory by cutting, with a   8
"tee-dum tee-dum" feeling, in the wake of the enemy's attacking long
sword. We must defeat him at the start of his attack, in the spirit of
treading him down with the feet, so that he cannot rise again to the
attack.

"Treading" does not simply mean treading with the feet. Tread with   9
the body, tread with the spirit, and, of course, tread and cut with the
long sword. You must achieve the spirit of not allowing the enemy to
attack a second time. This is the spirit of forestalling in every sense.
Once at the enemy, you should not aspire just to strike him, but to
cling after the attack. You must study this deeply.

To Know "Collapse"

Everything can collapse. Houses, bodies, and enemies collapse when   10
their rhythm becomes deranged.

In large-scale strategy, when the enemy starts to collapse you must   11
pursue him without letting the chance go. If you fail to take advantage
of your enemies' collapse, they may recover.

In single combat, the enemy sometimes loses timing and collapses. If   12
you let this opportunity pass, he may recover and not be so negligent
thereafter. Fix your eye on the enemy's collapse, and chase him, attacking so that you do not let him recover. You must do this. The chasing
attack is with a strong spirit. You must utterly cut the enemy down so
that he does not recover his position. You must understand how to utterly cut down the enemy.

To Become the Enemy

"To become the enemy" means to think yourself into the enemy's po-   13
sition. In the world people tend to think of a robber trapped in a house
as a fortified enemy. However, if we think of "becoming the enemy",
we feel that the whole world is against us and that there is no escape.
He who is shut inside is a pheasant. He who enters to arrest is a hawk.
You must appreciate this.

In large-scale strategy, people are always under the impression that   **14**
the enemy is strong, and so tend to become cautious. But if you have
good soldiers, and if you understand the principles of strategy, and if
you know how to beat the enemy, there is nothing to worry about.

In single combat also you must put yourself in the enemy's position.   **15**
If you think, "Here is a master of the Way, who knows the principles
of strategy", then you will surely lose. You must consider this deeply.

To Pass On

Many things are said to be passed on. Sleepiness can be passed on,   **16**
and yawning can be passed on. Time can be passed on also.

In large-scale strategy, when the enemy is agitated and shows an in-   **17**
clination to rush, do not mind in the least. Make a show of complete
calmness, and the enemy will be taken by this and will become relaxed.
When you see that this spirit has been passed on, you can bring about
the enemy's defeat by attacking strongly with a Void spirit.

In single combat, you can win by relaxing your body and spirit and   **18**
then, catching on to the moment the enemy relaxes, attack strongly and
quickly, forestalling him.

What is known as "getting someone drunk" is similar to this. You   **19**
can also infect the enemy with a bored, careless, or weak spirit. You
must study this well.

To Throw into Confusion

This means making the enemy lose resolve.   **20**

In large-scale strategy we can use our troops to confuse the enemy   **21**
on the field. Observing the enemy's spirit, we can make him think,
"Here? There? Like that? Like this? Slow? Fast?" Victory is certain when
the enemy is caught up in a rhythm which confuses his spirit.

In single combat, we can confuse the enemy by attacking with varied   **22**
techniques when the chance arises. Feint a thrust or cut, or make the
enemy think you are going to close with him, and when he is confused
you can easily win.

This is the essence of fighting, and you must research it deeply.   **23**

The Three Shouts

The three shouts are divided thus: before, during, and after. Shout ac- **24**
cording to the situation. The voice is a thing of life. We shout against
fires and so on, against the wind and the waves. The voice shows
energy.

In large-scale strategy, at the start of battle we shout as loudly as pos- **25**
sible. During the fight, the voice is low-pitched, shouting out as we attack. After the contest, we shout in the wake of our victory. These are
the three shouts.

In single combat, we make as if to cut and shout "Ei!" at the same **26**
time to disturb the enemy, then in the wake of our shout we cut with
the long sword. We shout after we have cut down the enemy—this
is to announce victory. This is called *"sen go no koe"* (before and
after voice). We do not shout simultaneously with flourishing the long
sword. We shout during the fight to get into rhythm. Research this
deeply.

To Crush

This means to crush the enemy regarding him as being weak. **27**

In large-scale strategy, when we see that the enemy has few men, or **28**
if he has many men but his spirit is weak and disordered, we knock
the hat over his eyes, crushing him utterly. If we crush lightly, he may
recover. You must learn the spirit of crushing as if with a hand-grip.

In single combat, if the enemy is less skilful than ourself, if his **29**
rhythm is disorganised, or if he has fallen into evasive or retreating attitudes, we must crush him straightaway, with no concern for his presence and without allowing him space for breath. It is essential to crush
him all at once. The primary thing is not to let him recover his position
even a little. You must research this deeply.

To Let Go the Hilt

There are various kinds of spirit involved in letting go the hilt. **30**

There is the spirit of winning without a sword. There is also the **31**
spirit of holding the long sword but not winning. The various methods
cannot be expressed in writing. You must train well.

Document Four

In June 1944, when some thought that World War II might last another 10 years, the United States government asked Ruth Benedict, an anthropologist, to study the culture of Japan. The government wanted to understand the Japanese culture so that they could better predict how Japanese soldiers would act in certain situations. Included here is Chapter 2, "The Japanese at War", from Benedict's *The Chrysanthemum and the Sword* (New York: Meridian, 1946, pp. 20–42), the book that evolved out of her wartime study.

In every cultural tradition there are orthodoxies of war and certain of these are shared in all Western nations, no matter what the specific differences. There are certain clarion calls to all-out war effort, certain forms of reassurance in case of local defeats, certain regularities in the proportion of fatalities to surrenders, and certain rules of behavior for prisoners of war which are predictable in wars between Western nations just because they have a great shared cultural tradition which covers even warfare. **1**

All the ways in which the Japanese departed from Western conventions of war were data on their view of life and on convictions of the whole duty of man. For the purposes of a systematic study of Japanese culture and behavior it did not matter whether or not their deviations from our orthodoxies were crucial in a military sense; any of them might be important because they raised questions about the character of the Japanese to which we needed answers. **2**

The very premises which Japan used to justify her war were the opposite of America's. She defined the international situation differently. America laid the war to the aggressions of the Axis. Japan, Italy, and Germany had unrighteously offended against international peace by their acts of conquest. Whether the Axis had seized power in Manchukuo or in Ethiopia or in Poland, it proved that they had embarked on an evil course of oppressing weak peoples. They had sinned against an international code of 'live and let live' or at least 'open doors' for free enterprise. Japan saw the cause of the war in another light. There was anarchy in the world as long as every nation had absolute sovereignty; it was necessary for her to fight to establish a hierarchy—under Japan, of course, since she alone represented a nation truly hierarchal from top to bottom and hence understood the necessity of taking 'one's **3**

Source: From *The Chrysanthemum and the Sword* by Ruth Benedict. Copyright 1946 by Ruth Benedict. Copyright © renewed 1974 by Robert G. Freeman. Reprinted by permission of Houghton Mifflin Co.

proper place.' Japan, having attained unification and peace in her
homeland, having put down banditry and built up roads and electric
power and steel industries, having, according to her official figures, educated 99.5 per cent of her rising generation in her public schools,
should, according to Japanese premises of hierarchy, raise her backward
younger brother China. Being of the same race as Greater East Asia,
she should eliminate the United States, and after her Britain and Russia, from that part of the world and 'take her proper place.' All nations
were to be one world, fixed in an international hierarchy. In the next
chapter we shall examine what this high value placed on hierarchy
meant in Japanese culture. It was an appropriate fantasy for Japan to
create. Unfortunately for her the countries she occupied did not see it
in the same light. Nevertheless not even defeat has drawn from her
moral repudiation of her Greater East Asia ideals, and even her prisoners of war who were least jingoistic rarely went so far as to arraign the
purposes of Japan on the continent and in the Southwest Pacific. For a
long, long time Japan will necessarily keep some of her inbred attitudes
and one of the most important of these is her faith and confidence in
hierarchy. It is alien to equality-loving Americans but it is nevertheless
necessary for us to understand what Japan meant by hierarchy and
what advantages she has learned to connect with it.

Japan likewise put her hopes of victory on a different basis from that   4
prevalent in the United States. She would win, she cried, a victory of
spirit over matter. America was big, her armaments were superior, but
what did that matter? All this, they said, had been foreseen and dis-
counted. 'If we had been afraid of mathematical figures,' the Japanese
read in their great newspaper, the *Mainichi Shimbun*, 'the war would not
have started. The enemy's great resources were not created by this war.'

Even when she was winning, her civilian statesmen, her High Com-   5
mand, and her soldiers repeated that this was no contest between armaments; it was a pitting of our faith in things against their faith in
spirit. When we were winning they repeated over and over that in such
a contest material power must necessarily fail. This dogma became, no
doubt, a convenient alibi about the time of the defeats at Saipan and
Iwo Jima, but it was not manufactured as an alibi for defeats. It was a
clarion call during all the months of Japanese victories, and it had been
an accepted slogan long before Pearl Harbor. In the nineteen-thirties
General Araki, fanatical militarist and one-time Minister of War, wrote
in a pamphlet addressed 'To the whole Japanese Race' that 'the true
mission' of Japan was 'to spread and glorify the Imperial way to the
end of the Four Seas. Inadequacy of strength is not our worry. Why
should we worry about that which is material?'

Of course, like any other nation preparing for war, they did worry.   6
All through the nineteen-thirties the proportion of their national income which was devoted to armament grew astronomically. By the time
of their attack on Pearl Harbor very nearly half the entire national

income was going to military and naval purposes, and of the total expenditures of the government only 17 per cent were available for financing anything having to do with civilian administration. The difference between Japan and Western nations was not that Japan was careless about material armament. But ships and guns were just the outward show of the undying Japanese Spirit. They were symbols much as the sword of the samurai had been the symbol of his virtue.

Japan was as completely consistent in playing up non-material re-   7
sources as the United States was in its commitment to bigness. Japan had to campaign for all-out production just as the United States did, but her campaigns were based on her own premises. The spirit, she said, was all and was everlasting; material things were necessary, of course, but they were subordinate and fell by the way. 'There are limits to material resources,' the Japanese radio would cry: 'it stands to reason that material things cannot last a thousand years.' And this reliance on spirit was taken literally in the routine of war; their war catechisms used the slogan—and it was a traditional one, not made to order for this war—'To match our training against their numbers and our flesh against their steel.' Their war manuals began with the bold-type line, 'Read this and the war is won.' Their pilots who flew their midget planes in a suicidal crash into our warships were an endless text for the superiority of the spiritual over the material. They named them the Kamikaze Corps, for the *kamikaze* was the divine wind which had saved Japan from Genghis Khan's invasion in the thirteenth century by scattering and overturning his transports.

Even in civilian situations Japanese authorities took literally the domi-   8
nance of spirit over material circumstances. Were people fatigued by twelve-hour work in the factories and all-night bombings? 'The heavier our bodies, the higher our will, our spirit, rises above them.' 'The wearier we are, the more splendid the training.' Were people cold in the bomb shelters in winter? On the radio the Dai Nippon Physical Culture Society prescribed body-warming calisthenics which would not only be a substitute for heating facilities and bedding, but, better still, would substitute for food no longer available to keep up people's normal strength. 'Of course some may say that with the present food shortages we cannot think of doing calisthenics. No! The more shortage of food there is, the more we must raise our physical strength by other means.' That is, we must increase our physical strength by expending still more of it. The American's view of bodily energy which always reckons how much strength he has to use by whether he had eight or five hours of sleep last night, whether he has eaten his regular meals, whether he has been cold, is here confronted with a calculus that does not rely on storing up energy. That would be materialistic.

Japanese broadcasts went even farther during the war. In battle,   9
spirit surmounted even the physical fact of death. One broadcast described a hero-pilot and the miracle of his conquest of death:

> After the air battles were over, the Japanese planes returned to their base in small formations of three or four. A Captain was in one of the first planes to return. After alighting from his plane, he stood on the ground and gazed into the sky through binoculars. As his men returned, he counted. He looked rather pale, but he was quite steady. After the last plane returned he made out a report and proceeded to Headquarters. At Headquarters he made his report to the Commanding Officer. As soon as he had finished his report, however, he suddenly dropped to the ground. The officers on the spot rushed to give assistance but alas! he was dead. On examining his body it was found that it was already cold, and he had a bullet wound in his chest, which had proved fatal. It is impossible for the body of a newly-dead person to be cold. Nevertheless the body of the dead captain was as cold as ice. The Captain must have been dead long before, and it was his spirit that made the report. Such a miraculous fact must have been achieved by the strict sense of responsibility that the dead Captain possessed.

To Americans, of course, this is an outrageous yarn but educated Japanese did not laugh at this broadcast. They felt sure it would not be taken as a tall tale by listeners in Japan. First they pointed out that the broadcaster had truthfully said that the captain's feat was 'a miraculous fact.' But why not? The soul could be trained; obviously the captain was a past-master of self-discipline. If all Japan knew that 'a composed spirit could last a thousand years,' could it not last a few hours in the body of an air-force captain who had made 'responsibility' the central law of his whole life? The Japanese believed that technical disciplines could be used to enable a man to make his spirit supreme. The captain had learned and profited.

As Americans we can completely discount these Japanese excesses as   10 the alibis of a poor nation or the childishness of a deluded one. If we did, however, we would be, by that much, the less able to deal with them in war or in peace. Their tenets have been bred into the Japanese by certain taboos and refusals, by certain methods of training and discipline, and these tenets are not mere isolated oddities. Only if Americans have recognized them can we realize what they are saying when, in defeat, they acknowledge that spirit was not enough and that defending positions 'with bamboo spears' was a fantasy. It is still more important that we be able to appreciate their acknowledgment that *their* spirit was insufficient and that it was matched in battle and in the factory by the spirit of the American people. As they said after their defeat: during the war they had 'engaged in subjectivity.'

Japanese ways of saying all kinds of things during the war, not only   11 about the necessity of hierarchy and the supremacy of spirit, were revealing to a student of comparative cultures. They talked constantly about security and morale being only a matter of being forewarned. No matter what the catastrophe, whether it was civilian bombing or defeat at Saipan or their failure to defend the Philippines, the Japanese line to their people was that this was foreknown and that there was therefore nothing to worry about. The radio went to great lengths, obviously counting on the reassurance it gave to the Japanese people to be told that they were living still in a thoroughly known world. 'The American occupation of Kiska brings Japan within the radius of American bombers. But we were well aware of this contingency and have made the necessary preparations.' 'The enemy doubtless will make an offensive against us by combined land, sea and air operations, but this has been taken account of by us in our plans.' Prisoners of war, even those who hoped for Japan's early defeat in a hopeless war, were sure that bombing would not weaken Japanese on the home front 'because they were forewarned.' When Americans began bombing Japanese cities, the vice-president of the Aviation Manufacturer's Association broadcast: 'Enemy planes finally have come over our very heads. However, we who are engaged in the aircraft production industry and who had always expected this to happen had made complete preparations to cope with this. Therefore, there is nothing to worry about.' Only granted all was foreknown, all was fully planned, could the Japanese go on to make the claim so necessary to them that everything had been actively willed by themselves alone; nobody had put anything over on them. 'We should not think that we have been passively attacked but that we have actively pulled the enemy toward us.' 'Enemy, come if you wish. Instead of saying, "Finally what was to come has come," we will say rather, "That which we were waiting for has come. We are glad it has come." ' The Navy Minister quoted in the Diet the teachings of the great warrior of the eighteen-seventies, Takamori Saigo, 'There are two kinds of opportunities: one which we chance upon, the other which we create. In time of great difficulty, one must not fail to create his opportunity.' And General Yamashito, when American troops marched into Manila, 'remarked with a broad smile,' the radio said, 'that now the enemy is in our bosom. . . . ' 'The rapid fall of Manila, shortly after the enemy landings in Lingayen Bay, was only possible as a result of General Yamashito's tactics and in accordance with his plans. General Yamashito's operations are now making continuous progress.' In other words, nothing succeeds like defeat.

Americans went as far in the opposite direction as the Japanese in 12 theirs. Americans threw themselves into the war effort *because* this fight had been forced upon us. We had been attacked, therefore let the enemy beware. No spokesman, planning how he could reassure the rank and file of Americans, said of Pearl Harbor or of Bataan, 'These were fully taken account of by us in our plans.' Our officials said instead, 'The enemy asked for it. We will show them what we can do.' Americans gear all their living to a constantly challenging world—and are prepared to accept the challenge. Japanese reassurances are based rather on a way of life that is planned and charted beforehand and where the greatest threat comes from the unforeseen.

Another constant theme in Japanese conduct of the war was also re- **13**
vealing about Japanese life. They continually spoke of how 'the eyes of
the world were upon them.' Therefore they must show to the full the
spirit of Japan. Americans landed on Guadalcanal, and Japanese orders
to troops were that now they were under direct observation 'by the
world' and should show what they were made of. Japanese seamen
were warned that in case they were torpedoed and the order given to
abandon ship, they should man the lifeboats with the utmost decorum
or 'the world will laugh at you. The Americans will take movies of you
and show them in New York.' It mattered what account they gave of
themselves to the world. And their concern with this point also was a
concern deeply imbedded in Japanese culture.

The most famous question about Japanese attitudes concerned His **14**
Imperial Majesty, the Emperor. What was the hold of the Emperor on
his subjects? Some American authorities pointed out that through all
Japan's seven feudal centuries the Emperor was a shadowy figurehead.
Every man's immediate loyalty was due to his lord, the *daimyo,* and,
beyond that, to the military Generalissimo, the Shogun. Fealty to the
Emperor was hardly an issue. He was kept secluded in an isolated
court whose ceremonies and activities were rigorously circumscribed by
the Shogun's regulations. It was treason even for a great feudal lord to
pay his respects to the Emperor, and for the people of Japan he hardly
existed. Japan could only be understood by its history, these American
analysts insisted; how could an Emperor who had been brought out
from obscurity within the memory of still living people be the real ral-
lying point of a conservative nation like Japan? The Japanese publicists
who again and again reiterated the undying hold of the Emperor upon
his subjects were over-protesting, they said, and their insistence only
proved the weakness of their case. There was no reason, therefore, that
American policy during the war should draw on kid gloves in dealing
with the Emperor. There was every reason rather why we should direct
our strongest attacks against this evil Fuehrer concept that Japan had
recently concocted. It was the very heart of its modern nationalistic
Shinto religion and if we undermined and challenged the sanctity of
the Emperor, the whole structure of enemy Japan would fall in ruins.

Many capable Americans who knew Japan and who saw the reports **15**
from the front lines and from Japanese sources were of the opposite
persuasion. Those who had lived in Japan well knew that nothing
stung the Japanese people to bitterness and whipped up their morale
like any depreciatory word against the Emperor or any outright attack
on him. They did not believe that in attacking the Emperor we would
in the eyes of the Japanese be attacking militarism. They had seen that
reverence for the Emperor had been equally strong in those years after
the First World War when 'de-mok-ra-sie' was the great watchword and
militarism was so discredited that army men prudently changed to
mufti before they went out on the streets of Tokyo. The reverence of the

Japanese for their Imperial chief could not be compared, these old Japanese residents insisted, with Heil-Hitler veneration which was a barometer of the fortunes of the Nazi party and bound up with all the evils of a fascist program.

Certainly the testimony of Japanese prisoners of war bore them out. **16** Unlike Western soldiers, these prisoners had not been instructed about what to say and what to keep silent about when captured and their responses on all subjects were strikingly unregimented. This failure to indoctrinate was of course due to Japan's no-surrender policy. It was not remedied until the last months of the war, and even then only in certain armies or local units. The prisoners' testimony was worth paying attention to for they represented a cross-section of opinion in the Japanese Army. They were not troops whose low morale had caused them to surrender—and who might therefore be atypical. All but a few were wounded and unconscious soldiers unable to resist when captured.

Japanese prisoners of war who were out-and-out bitter-enders im- **17** puted their extreme militarism to the Emperor and were 'carrying out his will,' 'setting his mind at rest,' 'dying at the Emperor's command.' 'The Emperor led the people into war and it was my duty to obey.' But those who rejected this present war and future Japanese plans of conquest just as regularly ascribed their peaceful persuasions to the Emperor. He was all things to all men. The war-weary spoke of him as 'his peace-loving Majesty'; they insisted that he 'had always been liberal and against the war.' 'He had been deceived by Tojo.' 'During the Manchurian Incident he showed that he was against the military.' 'The war was started without the Emperor's knowledge or permission. The Emperor does not like war and would not have permitted his people to be dragged into it. The Emperor does not know how badly treated his soldiers are.' These were not statements like those of German prisoners of war who, however much they complained that Hitler had been betrayed by his generals or his high command, nevertheless ascribed war and the preparations for war to Hitler as supreme inciter. The Japanese prisoner of war was quite explicit that the reverence given the Imperial Household was separable from militarism and aggressive war policies.

The Emperor was to them, however, inseparable from Japan. 'A Ja- **18** pan without the Emperor is not Japan.' 'Japan without the Emperor cannot be imagined.' 'The Japanese Emperor is the symbol of the Japanese people, the center of their religious lives. He is a super-religious object.' Nor would he be blamed for the defeat if Japan lost the war. 'The people did not consider the Emperor responsible for the war.' 'In the event of defeat the Cabinet and the military leaders would take the blame, not the Emperor.' 'Even if Japan lost the war ten out of ten Japanese would still revere the Emperor.'

All this unanimity in reckoning the Emperor above criticism appeared **19** phoney to Americans who are accustomed to exempt no human man from skeptical scrutiny and criticism. But there was no question that it

was the voice of Japan even in defeat. Those most experienced in inter-
rogating the prisoners gave it as their verdict that it was unnecessary to
enter on each interview sheet: 'Refuses to speak against the Emperor';
all prisoners refused, even those who co-operated with the Allies and
broadcast for us to the Japanese troops. Out of all the collected interviews of prisoners of war, only three were even mildly anti-Emperor
and only one went so far as to say: 'It would be a mistake to leave the
Emperor on the throne.' A second said the Emperor was 'a feeble-
minded person, nothing more than a puppet.' And the third got no farther than supposing that the Emperor might abdicate in favor of his son
and that if the monarchy were abolished young Japanese women would
hope to get a freedom they envied in the women of America.

Japanese commanders, therefore, were playing on an all but unani-   20
mous Japanese veneration when they distributed cigarettes to the
troops 'from the Emperor,' or led them on his birthday in bowing three
times to the east and shouting 'Banzai'; when they chanted with all
their troops morning and evening, 'even though the unit was subjected
to day and night bombardment,' the 'sacred words' the Emperor himself had given to the armed forces in the Rescript for Soldiers and Sail-
ors while 'the sound of chanting echoed through the forest.' The
militarists used the appeal of loyalty to the Emperor in every possible
way. They called on their men to 'fulfill the wishes of His Imperial
Majesty,' to 'dispel all the anxieties of your Emperor,' to 'demonstrate
your respect for His Imperial benevolence,' to 'die for the Emperor.' But
this obedience to his will could cut both ways. As many prisoners said,
the Japanese 'will fight unhesitatingly, even with nothing more than
bamboo poles, if the Emperor so decrees. They would stop just as
quickly if he so decreed'; 'Japan would throw down arms tomorrow if
the Emperor should issue such an order'; 'Even the Kwantung Army in
Manchuria'—most militant and jingoistic—'would lay down their arms';
'only his words can make the Japanese people accept a defeat and be
reconciled to live for reconstruction.'

This unconditional and unrestricted loyalty to the Emperor was con-   21
spicuously at odds with criticisms of all other persons and groups.
Whether in Japanese newspapers and magazines or in war prisoners'
testimony, there was criticism of the government and of military leaders. Prisoners of war were free with their denunciation of their local
commanders, especially those who had not shared the dangers and
hardships of their soldiers. They were especially critical of those who
had evacuated by plane and left their troops behind to fight it out. Usually they praised some officers and bitterly criticized others; there was
no sign that they lacked the will to discriminate the good from the bad
in things Japanese. Even in the home islands newspapers and magazines criticized 'the government.' They called for more leadership and
greater co-ordination of effort and noted that they were not getting
from the government what was necessary. They even criticized the restrictions on freedom of speech. A report on a panel of editors, former

members of the Diet, and directors of Japan's totalitarian party, the Imperial Rule Assistance Association, printed in a Tokyo paper in July, 1944, is a good example. One speaker said: 'I think there are various ways to arouse the Japanese people but the most important one is freedom of speech. In these few years, the people have not been able to say frankly what they think. They have been afraid that they might be blamed if they spoke certain matters. They hesitated, and tried to patch up the surface, so the public mind has really become timid. We can never develop the total power of the people in this way.' Another speaker expanded the same theme: 'I have held symposiums almost every night with the people of the electoral districts and asked them about many things, but they were all afraid to speak. Freedom of speech has been denied. This is certainly not a proper way to stimulate their will to fight. The people are so badly restricted by the so-called Special Penal Law of War Time and the National Security Law that they have become as timid as the people in the feudalistic period. Therefore the fighting power which could have been developed remains undeveloped now.'

Even during the war, therefore, the Japanese criticized the govern-   22
ment, the High Command, and their immediate superiors. They did not unquestioningly acknowledge the virtues of the whole hierarchy. But the Emperor was exempt. How could this be when his primacy was so recent? What quirk of Japanese character made it possible that he should so attain a sacrosanct position? Were Japanese prisoners of war right in claiming that just as the people would fight to the death 'with bamboo spears' as long as he so ordered, they would peaceably accept defeat and occupation if that was his command? Was this nonsense meant to mislead us? Or was it, possibly, the truth?

All these crucial questions about Japanese behavior in the war, from   23
their anti-materialistic bias to their attitudes toward the Emperor concerned the homeland Japan as well as the fighting fronts. There were other attitudes which had to do more specifically with the Japanese Army. One of these concerned the expendability of their fighting forces. The Japanese radio put well the contrast with the American attitudes when it described with shocked incredulity the Navy's decoration of Admiral George S. McCain, commander of a task force off Formosa.

> The official reason for the decoration was not that Commander John S. McCain was able to put the Japanese to flight, though we don't see why not since that is what the Nimitz communiqué claimed. . . . Well, the reason given for Admiral McCain's decoration was that he was able successfully to rescue two damaged American warships and escort them safely to their home base. What makes this bit of information important is not that it is a fiction but that it is the truth. . . . So we are not questioning the veracity of Admiral McCain's rescuing two ships, but the point we want you to see is the curious fact that the rescuing of damaged ships merits decoration in the United States.

Americans thrill to all rescue, all aid to those pressed to the wall. A
valiant deed is all the more a hero's act if it saves the 'damaged.' Japanese valor repudiates such salvaging. Even the safety devices installed
in our B-29's and fighter planes raised their cry of 'Cowardice.' The
press and the radio returned to the theme over and over again. There
was virtue only in accepting life and death risks; precautions were un-
worthy. This attitude found expression also in the case of the wounded
and of malarial patients. Such soldiers were damaged goods and the
medical services provided were utterly inadequate even for reasonable
effectiveness of the fighting force. As time went on, supply difficulties
of all kinds aggravated this lack of medical care, but that was not the
whole story. Japanese scorn of materialism played a part in it; her
soldiers were taught that death itself was a victory of the spirit and
our kind of care of the sick was an interference with heroism—like
safety devices in bombing planes. Nor are the Japanese used to such
reliance on physicians and surgeons in civilian life as Americans are.
Preoccupation with mercy toward the damaged rather than with other
welfare measures is especially high in the United States, and is often
commented on even by visitors from some European countries in peace-
time. It is certainly alien to the Japanese. At all events, during the war
the Japanese army had no trained rescue teams to remove the wounded
under fire and to give first aid; it had no medical system of front line,
behind-the-lines and distant recuperative hospitals. Its attention to medical supplies was lamentable. In certain emergencies the hospitalized
were simply killed. Especially in New Guinea and the Philippines, the
Japanese often had to retreat from a position where there was a hospital. There was no routine of evacuating the sick and wounded while
there was still opportunity; only when the 'planned withdrawal' of the
battalion was actually taking place or the enemy was occupying was
anything done. Then, the medical officer in charge often shot the in-
mates of the hospital before he left or they killed themselves with hand
grenades.

If this attitude of the Japanese toward damaged goods was funda-   24
mental in their treatment of their own countrymen, it was equally important in their treatment of American prisoners of war. According to
our standards the Japanese were guilty of atrocities to their own men as
well as to their prisoners. The former chief medical officer of the Philippines, Colonel Harold W. Glattly, said after his three years' internment
as a prisoner of war on Formosa that 'the American prisoners got better
medical treatment than the Japanese soldiers. Allied medical officers in
the prison camps were able to take care of their men while the Japanese didn't have any doctors. For a while the only medical personnel
they had for their own men was a corporal and later on a sergeant.' He
saw a Japanese medical officer only once or twice a year.

'The furthest extreme to which this Japanese theory of expendability   25
could be pushed was their no-surrender policy. Any Occidental army

which has done its best and finds itself facing hopeless odds surrenders
to the enemy. They still regard themselves as honorable soldiers and by
international agreement their names are sent back to their countries so
that their families may know that they are alive. They are not disgraced
either as soldiers or as citizens or in their own families. But the Japanese defined the situation differently. Honor was bound up with fighting to the death. In a hopeless situation a Japanese soldier should kill
himself with his last hand grenade or charge weaponless against the
enemy in a mass suicide attack. But he should not surrender. Even if
he were taken prisoner when he was wounded and unconscious, he
'could not hold up his head in Japan' again; he was disgraced; he was
'dead' to his former life.

There were Army orders to this effect, of course, but there was ap-   **26**
parently no need of special official indoctrination at the front. The
Army lived up to the code to such an extent that in the North Burma
campaign the proportion of the captured to the dead was 142 to 17,166.
That was a ratio of 1:120. And of the 142 in the prison camps, all except
a small minority were wounded or unconscious when taken; only a
very few had 'surrendered' singly or in groups of two or three. In the
armies of Occidental nations it is almost a truism that troops cannot
stand the death of one-fourth to one-third of their strength without giving up; surrenders run about 4:1. When for the first time in Hollandia,
however, any appreciable number of Japanese troops surrendered, the
proportion was 1:5 and that was a tremendous advance over the 1:120
of North Burma.

To the Japanese therefore Americans who had become prisoners of   **27**
war were disgraced by the mere fact of surrender. They were 'damaged
goods' even when wounds or malaria or dysentery had not also put
them outside the category of 'complete men.' Many Americans have
described how dangerous a thing American laughter was in the prison
camps and how it stung their warders. In Japanese eyes they had suffered ignominy and it was bitter to them that the Americans did not
know it. Many of the orders which American prisoners had to obey,
too, were those which had also been required of their Japanese keepers
by their own Japanese officers; the forced marches and the close-packed
transshipments were commonplaces to them. Americans tell, too, of
how rigorously sentries required that the prisoners should cover up
evasions of rules; the great crime was to evade openly. In camps where
the prisoners worked off-bounds on roads or installations during the
day the rule that no food be brought back with them from the country-
side was sometimes a dead letter—if the fruit and vegetables were covered up. If they could be seen, it was a flagrant offense which meant
that the Americans had flouted the sentry's authority. Open challenging of authority was terribly punished even if it were mere 'answering
back.' Japanese rules are very strict against a man's answering back
even in civilian life and their own army practices penalized it heavily. It

is no exoneration of the atrocities and wanton cruelties that did occur in
the prison camps to distinguish between these and those acts which
were the consequences of cultural habituations.

Especially in the earlier stages of the conflict the shame of capture   **28**
was reinforced by a very real belief among the Japanese that the enemy
tortured and killed any prisoners. One rumor of tanks that had been
driven across the bodies of those captured on Guadalcanal spread
through almost all areas. Some Japanese who tried to give themselves
up, too, were regarded with so much suspicion by our troops that they
were killed as a precaution, and this suspicion was often justified. A
Japanese for whom there was nothing left but death was often proud
that he could take an enemy with him when he died; he might do it
even after he was captured. Having determined, as one of them put it,
'to be burned on the altar of victory, it would be a disgrace to die with
no heroic deed achieved.' Such possibilities put our Army on its guard
and diminished the number of surrenders.

The shame of surrender was burned deeply into the consciousness of   **29**
the Japanese. They accepted as a matter of course a behavior which was
alien to our conventions of warfare. And ours was just as alien to them.
They spoke with shocked disparagement of American prisoners of war
who *asked* to have their names reported to their government so that
their families would know they were alive. The rank and file, at least,
were quite unprepared for the surrender of American troops at Bataan
for they had assumed that they would fight it out the Japanese way.
And they could not accept the fact that Americans had no shame in
being prisoners of war.

The most melodramatic difference in behavior between Western sol-   **30**
diers and the Japanese was undoubtedly the co-operation the latter gave
to the Allied forces as prisoners of war. They knew no rules of life
which applied in this new situation; they were dishonored and their life
as Japanese was ended. Only in the last months of the war did more
than a handful imagine any return to their homeland, no matter how
the war ended. Some men asked to be killed, 'but if your customs do
not permit this, I will be a model prisoner.' They were better than
model prisoners. Old Army hands and long-time extreme nationalists
located ammunition dumps, carefully explained the disposition of Japanese forces, wrote our propaganda and flew with our bombing pilots to
guide them to military targets. It was as if they had turned over a new
page; what was written on the new page was the opposite of what was
written on the old, but they spoke the lines with the same faithfulness.

This is of course not a description of all prisoners of war. Some few   **31**
were irreconcilable. And in any case certain favorable conditions had to
be set up before such behavior was possible. American Army
commanders were very understandably hesitant to accept Japanese assistance at face value and there were camps where no attempt was
made to use any services they might have given. In camps where this

was done, however, the original suspicion had to be withdrawn and more and more dependence was placed on the good faith of the Japanese prisoners.

Americans had not expected this right-about-face from prisoners of   **32** war. It was not according to our code. But the Japanese behaved as if, having put everything they had into one line of conduct and failed at it, they naturally took up a different line. Was it a way of acting which we could count on in post-war days or was it behavior peculiar to soldiers who had been individually captured? Like the other peculiarities of Japanese behavior which obtruded themselves upon us during the war, it raised questions about the whole way of life to which they were conditioned, the way their institutions functioned and the habits of thought and action they had learned.

Document Five

"Technology, War, and Government" is a chapter from Arnold J. Toynbee's *A Study of History* (New York: Oxford, 1957, Vol. XII, pp. 321–331).

(I) Prospects of a Third World War

As a result of two world wars, the number of the Great Powers had **1** been reduced from a fluctuating plurality, in which some states, such as Italy, had borne the title by courtesy, though everyone knew that they could not sustain it, to two only—The United States and the Soviet Union. The Soviet Union had established its domination over Eastern Germany as well as over most of the successor-states of the former Hapsburg and Ottoman empires which had been overrun, during the Second World War, by the ephemeral National Socialist German Third Reich. The only reason why Western Germany and the inter-war Austrian Republic had not followed their neighbours into Russia's maw by A.D. 1956 was that they had come, meanwhile, under the protection of the United States and her West European allies. By this date it had become apparent that the substitution of a United States protectorate for an untenable independence was the only insurance against Russian (or Chinese) domination that promised to be effective in the long run for any state anywhere in the World.

This role, which was a new role for the United States in the Old **2** World, had long been familiar to her in the New World. From the days of the Holy Alliance to the days of the Third Reich the Monroe Doctrine had saved the successor-states of the Spanish and Portuguese empires in the Americas from falling under the domination of some European Power at the price of replacing a Spanish or Portuguese colonial administration by a United States hegemony. Benefactors are seldom popular, and unless their benefactions are completely disinterested they may not altogether deserve to be. The feelings of, say, the French towards the United States since A.D. 1945 were not very different from those of, say, the Brazilians at any time within the past hundred years.

However that might be, the Soviet Union and the United States **3** found themselves, in A.D. 1956, confronting one another as the only two Great Powers still surviving on the face of the planet; and in any international balance of power two was bound, at the best, to be an

Source: From *A Study of History*, Volume XII by Arnold J. Toynbee. Copyright © 1961 by Oxford University Press; renewed 1989 by Lawrence Toynbee. Reprinted by permission of the publisher.

awkward number. It was true that, in contrast with Germany and Japan twenty years earlier, both were economically 'sated' countries, which could find peaceful employment for the whole of their manpower, for many decades to come, in cultivating their own estates. But past history had shown that mutual fear was as potent a source of warlike aggression as economic want. The Russian and American peoples were ill equipped for understanding each other. The Russian people's habitual temper was one of docile resignation, the American's one of obstreperous impatience; and this difference of temper was reflected in a difference of attitude towards arbitrary government. The Russians acquiesced in this as inevitable, whereas the Americans had learnt from their own history to think of it as an evil institution which any people could overthrow at will. The Americans saw their *summum bonum* in a personal liberty which they rather oddly identified with equality, whereas the Russian Communist dominant minority saw their *summum bonum* in theoretical equality which they still more oddly identified with liberty.

These temperamental and doctrinal differences made it difficult for   **4** the two peoples to understand and trust each other; and this mutual distrust bred fear, now that the arena in which they menaced one another had been transformed out of all recognition by the unprecedentedly rapid progress of technology, which had made a once wide world shrivel to dimensions so diminutive as to make it henceforth impossible for the rivals to take their stand in this arena without finding themselves within point-blank range of each other.

In a world thus technologically unified, it looked as if a competition   **5** for World power between the Soviet Union and the United States might be decided in the long run by the suffrages of those three-quarters of the living generation of Mankind who, five or six thousand years after the dawn of civilization, were still living in the Neolithic Age on the material plane of life, but who had begun to become aware that a higher standard was possible. In exercising a choice, now open to it, between an American and a Russian way of life, this hitherto submerged majority might be expected to choose whichever way of the two seemed to them the more likely to satisfy this awakening majority's revolutionary aspirations. Yet, although the last word might lie with a hitherto submerged non-Western majority of Mankind, it nevertheless seemed probable that, in the short run, the decisive weight in the scales of a Russo-American balance would prove to be, not those three-quarters of the World's population, but that one-quarter of the World's present industrial war-potential that was still located in Western Europe. In global terms it might be said that there was now one sole continent, Eurafrasia, skirted by two large offshore islands, North and South America. On this global view, Russia appeared as the continental, and the United States as the insular Power—much as, in the 'European' inter-parochial wars of the 'Modern' period of Western history, Britain had played the part of the insular Power, and Spain, France, and Germany the part of serving as Britain's successive continental enemies. In the Post-Modern global arena the West European sector was still crucial, because it was the insular Power's Continental bridgehead. In times past, Flanders had been the 'cockpit' of Western Europe, in which its incorrigibly belligerent parochial states had fought their battles. Now the whole of Western Europe appeared to be marked out for serving, in the event of another general war, as the 'cockpit' of a Westernizing world. There was, perhaps, a poetic justice in this transformation of the strategic map; but this did not make the plight of inhabiting a 'cockpit' less unwelcome to West Europeans in general since A.D. 1946 than it had been to Flemings since before the close of the fifteenth century.

The progress of technology has no power to diminish the sway of hu- 6
man feelings over the course of human affairs. Militarism is a matter not of technology but of psychology—the will to fight. Wars are exhilarating when fought elsewhere and by other people. Perhaps they are most exhilarating of all when over and done with; and historians of all civilizations had traditionally regarded them as the most interesting topic in their field. Most armies in the past had been relatively small, and had largely consisted of people who preferred fighting to other occupations. But, since the *levée en masse* in a revolutionary France in A.D. 1792, Modern Western warfare had become a far more serious matter; and the warfare of the future threatened to become more serious still. War was now tending to kill the militarism of peoples who experienced it, and the will of the people is a force to which even an autocratic government has ultimately to yield. Among the countries that had suffered the most severely in the First World War, France had virtually refused to endure the second. Hitler had succeeded in galvanizing the Germans into a further bout of militarism; but in A.D. 1956 it seemed doubtful whether another Hitler—if another were ever to arise—could perform the same *tour de force* again. It was significant that the favourite conventional epithet of the Communist dictators was 'peace-loving'. Napoleon in St. Helena had still described war as a *belle occupation*; but it may be doubted whether he would have applied the phrase to atomic warfare if he could have lived to see its advent.

These reflections were primarily applicable to peoples of advanced   7
civilization who had had first-hand experience of twentieth-century warfare. The traditional submissiveness of the peoples of Asia, on the other hand, had, since time immemorial, taken the political form of passive obedience to arbitrary governments; and the cultural process of Westernization would have to go far beyond the rudimentary accomplishment of acquiring a Western military technique before the Asian peasant-soldier would begin to think of questioning, or defying, orders to sacrifice his life, even in an aggressive war which meant nothing to him personally. How far could mid-twentieth-century Asian governments go in exploiting their subjects' ingrained submissiveness for

military purposes? In Western eyes it might look as if the Chinese and
Russian peasant-soldier had given his government a blank cheque
drawn on his life; yet History had demonstrated that there was a
limit beyond which neither a Chinese nor a Russian government could
venture with impunity. Chinese régimes, from the Ts'in to the Kuom-
intang, that had had the temerity to give the screw just one turn too
many had repeatedly paid for this slight excess by the forfeiture of their
mandate to rule; and in Russian history it had been the same story.

A Czardom that had had the wisdom to take the sting out of the   8
Russian people's sufferings in the Crimean War by conceding the re-
forms of the eighteen-sixties had paid with its life for its obstinacy in
refusing to forestall trouble once again by paying a corresponding ran-
som for subsequent military reverses, first in the Japanese war of A.D.
1904–5, which had provoked the abortive Russian revolution of the
latter year, and afterwards in the First World War, which had provoked
the double revolution of A.D. 1917. It seemed, then, that there were
limits at which the *moral* of Russia or any other peasant country would
collapse. Nevertheless, it seemed likely that the Government of the
Soviet Union would face the terrors of a war with the United States
rather than make any political concession to the United States that, in
Russian eyes, would be tantamount to submission to an American
ascendancy.

If it was thus likely that there were circumstances in which the Soviet   9
Union could and would go to war with a Power of its own calibre, was
this also to be predicted of the United States? In A.D. 1956 the answer
appeared to be in the affirmative. Ever since the first settlement of the
oldest of the Thirteen Colonies, the American people had been one of
the most unmilitary, yet at the same time one of the most martial, of
the nations of the Western world. They had been unmilitary in the
sense that they had disliked submitting themselves to military discipline
and had had no Gallic ambition to see their country win military glory
for its own sake. They had been martial in the sense that, till the date
of the closing of the frontier *circa* A.D. 1890, they had always numbered
among them a contingent of frontiersmen who were accustomed, not
only to bearing arms, but to using them at their own discretion in pursuit of their own private enterprises—a state of affairs that, by then,
had long since been obsolete in the greater part of Western Europe.
The martial spirit of ten generations of American frontiersmen would
have been acknowledged by the North American Indians at any time
since the first landing of White men from the British Isles on American
coasts; by the English colonists' French rivals in the eighteenth century;
and by their Mexican victims in the nineteenth century; and these encounters between the Anglo-American frontiersmen and their competitors for the possession of North America were also evidence that not
only the frontiersmen, but the American people as a whole, were prepared, exceptionally and temporarily, to submit themselves to a military

discipline without which the frontiersmen's personal spirit and prowess would have been unable to prevail against antagonists of their own cultural level.

The soldierly qualities latent in the American people as a whole had   **10** been revealed to their German adversaries in the German-American wars of 1917–18 and 1941–5; but the most impressive demonstration of American valour, discipline, generalship, and endurance had been given in a war in which Americans had been arrayed against Americans. The War of A.D. 1861–5 between the Union and the Confederacy had been the longest, the most stubborn, the costliest in casualties, and the most fertile in technological innovations of all wars waged in the Western world between the fall of Napoleon and the outbreak of the First World War. Moreover the two world wars that, within living memory, had harrowed Germany and Germany's Russian and West European victims as severely as the American Civil War had harrowed the South, had left the United States virtually unscathed. The psychological effects that two world wars in one lifetime had produced on the *moral* of West Europeans had hardly made themselves felt on the American side of the Atlantic; and in A.D. 1956 it could not be doubted that the American people would indeed be prepared to face the terrors of a war with the Soviet Union rather than make any concession to the Soviet Union that, in American eyes, would be tantamount to submission to a Russian ascendancy.

But the foregoing historical evidence, suggesting the likelihood of a   **11** will to war in certain circumstances on the part of the American and the Russian people, has to be estimated in the light of the developments of atomic warfare and of the psychological effect of these developments—an effect which, under mid-twentieth-century conditions, would not lag very far behind the technological developments themselves. To die for a country or a cause becomes a gratuitous and meaningless act of heroism if it has become demonstrably certain that the country will perish together with the patriot, and the cause together with the devotee, in one all-comprehending catastrophe.

(2) Towards a Future World Order

By A.D. 1955 the abolition of War had, in fact, become imperative; but it   **12** could not be abolished unless the control of atomic energy could be concentrated in the hands of some single political authority. This monopoly of the command of the master weapon of the age would enable, and indeed compel, the authority to assume the role of a World Government. The effective seat of this Government, in the conditions of A.D. 1955, must be either Washington or Moscow; but neither the United States nor the Soviet Union was prepared to place itself at the mercy of the other.

soon, however, as we ascend—or descend—from the plane of technology to the plane of human nature, we find the earthly paradise skilfully assembled by the ingenuity of *Homo Faber* being reduced to a fool's paradise by the perversity of *Homo Politicus*. The 'Parliament of Man', whose inauguration the prophet Tennyson seemed to have synchronized approximately with the invention of the aeroplane, was now in being under the more prosaic name of the United Nations Organization; and U.N.O. had not proved as ineffective as its critics sometimes asserted. On the other hand, U.N.O. was evidently incapable of becoming the embryo of a world government. The realities of the distribution of power were not reflected in the clumsiness of a constitution that had embodied the unrealistic principle of 'one state, one vote', and had then found no better means of bringing a fictitious equality of states into line with a harsh reality than the concession to five Powers, one of whom had since been reduced from China to Formosa, of a veto that was denied to their nominal peers. The best prospect in sight for the U.N.O. was that it might evolve from being a forum into becoming a confederacy; but there is a great gulf between any confederacy of independent states and any confederation of peoples with a central government claiming and receiving the direct personal allegiance of every individual citizen of the union; and it was notorious that the history of political institutions knew of no case in which that gulf had been crossed by any other process than a revolutionary leap.

On this showing, U.N.O. seemed unlikely to be the institutional nu- **20** cleus out of which an eventually inevitable world government would grow. The probability seemed to be that this would take shape through the development, not of U.N.O., but of one or other of two older and tougher political 'going concerns', the Government of the United States or the Government of the Soviet Union.

If the living generation of Mankind had been free to choose between **21** them, there could be little doubt in any Western observer's mind that a decisive majority of all living men and women that were competent to form any judgement on this issue would have opted for becoming subjects of the United States rather than of the Soviet Union. The virtues that made the United States incomparably preferable stood out conspicuously against a Communist Russian foil.

America's cardinal virtue in the eyes of her present and prospective **22** subjects was her transparently sincere reluctance to be drawn into playing this role at all. An appreciable portion of the living generation of American citizens, as well as the ancestors of all American citizens who were not themselves immigrants, had been moved to pluck up their roots in the Old World and to start life again in the New World by a yearning to extricate themselves from the affairs of a continent whose dust they had demonstratively shaken off from their feet; and the buoyancy of the hope with which they had made their withdrawal was matched by the poignancy of the regret with which the living generation of Americans was making its compulsory return. The compulsion was, as we have seen, an aspect of that 'annihilation of distance' which was making the Old and New World one and indivisible. But the ever-increasing clearness with which this compulsion was being recognized was not diminishing the reluctance with which it was being accepted.

The Americans' second outstanding virtue was their generosity. Both **23** the United States and the Soviet Union were 'sated' Powers, but their economic and social situations were identical only in the general sense that Russia, like America, commanded vast undeveloped resources. In contrast to America, Russia had hardly begun to exploit her potentialities, and the development that she had carried out, at such a cost in human effort and suffering, during the twelve years immediately preceding the German assault upon her in A.D. 1941, had been largely ruined by the invasion. Thereafter the Russians had taken an unjust advantage of finding themselves on the winning side by recouping themselves for a German destruction of Russian industrial plant by seizing and removing plant, not only from a guilty Germany, but also from East and Central European countries that the Russians professed to be liberating from the Nazis, and from Chinese provinces in Manchuria that they professed to be liberating from the Japanese. This was a contrast indeed to the American post-war reconstruction policy, implemented in the Marshall Plan and other measures, in which a number of countries, whose life had been disorganized by the war, were set on their feet again with the help of money voted by the Congress at Washington with the goodwill of the American taxpayer, out of whose pockets all this money had to come. In the past it had been customary for victorious Powers, not to give, but to take, and there had been no departure from this evil custom in the policy of the Soviet Union. The Marshall Plan set a new standard for which there was no comparable historical precedent. It might be said that this generous policy was in America's own interests, on a long and enlightened view; but good deeds are not the less good for being, at the same time, wise.

Citizens of West European countries were, however, now haunted by **24** fears that some American decision, in which the West European peoples might have had no say, might bring Russian atomic weapons down upon their heads as unintended by-products of some impulsive American retort to Russian provocation. Though the satellite states of the American Union enjoyed, in most respects, an enviable freedom of action that was entirely denied to the satellites of the Soviet Union, they did find themselves in much the same helpless plight in these matters of life and death.

In A.D. 1895, in connexion with an Anglo-American dispute about the **25** location of the frontier between British Guiana and Venezuela, an American Secretary of State, Richard Olney, had issued a resonant dispatch which had secured for his name such immortality as it still enjoyed.

'To-day the United States is practically sovereign on this continent,
and its fiat is law upon the subjects to which it confines its interposi-
tions. Why? It is not because of the pure friendship or good will felt
for it. It is not simply by reason of its high character as a civilized
state, nor because wisdom and justice and equity are the invariable
characteristics of the dealings of the United States. It is because, in
addition to all other grounds, its infinite resources, combined with
its isolated position, render it master of the situation and practically
invulnerable as against any or all other Powers.'

This dictum had not lost any of its cogency in coming to be applicable to a far wider sphere of hegemony than Latin America alone, and,
though a non-American might resign himself to the fact that American
whips were preferable to Russian scorpions, a 'philosopher' might (in
Gibbonian parlance) 'be permitted to enlarge his views' by observing
that the virtual monopoly, by a paramount Power, of the determination
and execution of policies in which the lives and fortunes of satellite
peoples were at stake, was pregnant with a constitutional problem
which could be solved only by some form of federal union. The constitutional issues raised by the advent of a supernational order were not
likely to be settled easily or rapidly, but at least it was a good omen
that the United States was already committed by its own history to an
approval of the federal principle.

_____ **WRITING ASSIGNMENT**

In the quote that began this section, Perrin argued that a specific historical event (the Japanese giving up of the gun between 1543 and 1786)
proves that it is possible to turn back the historical clock—that it is possible to abandon dangerous technology.

Write an essay in which you argue that (a) Perrin is right, (b) that Perrin failed to understand why the Japanese gave up the gun, or (c) that
the Japanese people's abandonment of guns was uniquely related to a
specific culture and historical period and cannot be easily replicated.

Another Look at the Fact

John Lukacs is an academic historian who believes that history is not a
discipline per se, but rather a mode of thought—a way of thinking—that
can be applied to any facet of human experience. In the following excerpt
from *Historical Consciousness*, Lukacs critically analyzes the most cherished of historical institutions: the fact.

_____ **Prereading**

How would you define a fact? How do you feel that facts and truth are
related? Are they the same? Or are they different?

"Fictio," or the Purposes of Historical Statements

John Lukacs

Let me begin, first, with the most obvious condition. Facts are not **1**
independent; no Fact ever stands by itself; a Fact is not separable from
other Facts. "We compare, contrast, abstract, generalize, connect, adjust, classify," said Newman, "and we view all our knowledge in the
association with which these processes have invested it." "With this
one word, *association*, bang goes the simple notion that 'facts are
facts,' " commented Seán O'Faoláin a century later, "for facts are
thereby only to be called facts when they are isolated in our minds.
And are they ever isolated?" They are not: facts are meaningless by
themselves: they mean something only in relation to other facts.

For, in the second place, the value of Facts may depend on their rela- **2**
tionships even more than on their accuracy. I do not mean to say that
accuracy is unimportant: what I am saying is that often the more "accurate" a Fact the more theoretical it may be. American newspapers are
often stuffed with filler items informing us that the average American
family consists of 3.2 members or that it consumes 791 quarts of milk a
year. The abstractness of such Facts is (or, rather, it should be) obvious.
What is not so obvious is that of two statements of fact the more accurate may be the less truthful one. To say that on April, 1, 1958, the
population of Philadelphia was 2,242,714 is more accurate but less
truthful than to say that the population of Philadelphia during the first
half of 1958 was between 2,200,000 and 2,250,000, since any definition
of who was and who was not a resident of Philadelphia at a static moment is necessarily abstract, leaving a considerable margin of error.
Moreover, the meaning of these figures exists only as we relate them to
other figures in our minds (how does this compare to the populations
of other cities?) or to direction and movement (is the population rising,
or falling?)

The association, therefore—and this is my third point—is profoundly **3**
involved with the fact. I say association, not interpretation: because interpretation (the term chosen by Professor Carr) suggests that it is *preceded* by the fact, whereas the association, if it is meaningful at all, is
already part of the fact itself (when we think of a "fact" we think of
something that *is*). At this point we encounter the inadequacy of the
Fact-Fiction dichotomy. *Fictio*, deriving from the verb *fingere*, means construction: we have now seen that a fact cannot be separated from its

Source: From *Historical Consciousness* by John Lukacs, pp. 104–108. Copyright © 1968 by John
Lukacs. Reprinted by permission of the author.

association: that is, from a certain construction of the mind. Because of this construction, not only is *fictio* of a higher order than *factum*: what is more important, every fact is, in a certain sense, a fiction. While it is certainly arguable that what happened is more important than what we think happened, it is hardly arguable that these are separate matters— that, in other words, a fact can be isolated not only from other facts but from our thinking about it. The evidences of this eminently human condition are perhaps more widespread than we are inclined to believe: they are certainly apparent (that is, for those who want to see them) in the Factual Science of Economics. . . .

The historian's work is re-lation, involving the *fictio* of events. Let me **4** now deal with this re-lation rather than pursue deeper the mental processes of the historian (even at the cost of having to postpone, for example, the consideration of how much recognition there is in mental construction). We have now seen that facts are not quite what we used to think they are. Still, no matter how inflated its meaning may be, when we say: this is a "fact," we are making a statement. And this is the fourth, perhaps the most important, point: while, on the one hand, a fact is not separable from its association (or call it construction, recognition, *fictio*), on the other hand, neither is it separable from its expression. Expression is not merely the clothing of the fact, but its very flesh. It is not only that the "hard core"—the fact—is less enjoyable than the "pulpy part of the fruit": the hard core has no seed, it is not hard, and it is not the core. For example, Professor Pieter Geyl is quoted saying that "we could agree about simple facts—the Second World War began in 1939—but such facts were a very small part of history; the rest was made up of judgments of events, situations, and characters, and *they* would be debated till doomsday." But even such a "simple fact" as *the Second World War began in 1939* is not really a simple fact but a statement, an expression, involving a choice of words: and therefore it is not essentially different from a statement such as, say, *Hitler was an evil genius*. There are people who will argue that the Second World War was not really the Second World War but the Second German War, or the First Atomic War, or the European Civil War, or the Sixth, or Seventh, or Eighth Atlantic World War. There are people who might say that the Second World War did not really become a world war until December, 1941. There are others who may argue that, if it was a world war, then it began in Manchuria in September, 1931. This is not mere sophistry: a Chinese historian, for example, might find the statement that the Second World War broke out in 1939 inaccurate or even unjust—unjust, say, if that statement was made in a context slighting the importance of the Chinese part of the war.

For we have to take another, last, step: we must recognize that the **5** expression of a fact is inseparable from its purpose. Even if there is agreement about the same fact—which, as we have seen, is really a statement of a fact—the same statement and the same phrase may be used for different purposes. This ought to be evident:

A	B
Hitler was a fanatic and a dictator. He wanted to reduce Germany's neighbor states even at the cost of war. After he had conquered Austria and Czechoslovakia, Britain and France offered their alliance to Poland. On September 1, 1939, the German armies broke into Poland, and the Second World War began. . . .	By the spring of 1939 Britain and France, supported by certain American circles, decided that Germany should not be allowed to dominate eastern Europe. They offered an alliance to Poland. From then on Poland rejected every German demand. After Germany and Poland went to war on September 1, 1939, Britain and France declared war on Germany; and the Second World War began. . . .

Each of these statements is true. Yet they are true in different ways. **6**
Of course, the sophisticated reader will say: the same fact was put in
different contexts. Yet it is not enough to say that; the problem is not
merely a problem of context; if the fact depends on its statement, and
its statement on its context, the context, in turn, depends on its purpose: it is a construction of purpose.

A	B
Like so often during the previous two decades of almost uninterrupted French triumphs over the armies of Continental Europe, the British were to demonstrate their singular determination in the end. On June 18, 1815, Wellington won the Battle of Waterloo. . . .	The rising national spirit of Germany had already become a dominant factor at that time. Wellington won the Battle of Waterloo on June 18, 1815; even there his victory depended on Blücher. . . .

"A" reflects an Anglophile tendency; "B" a Germanophile one. "A" **7**
is no more true than "B" than "B" is truer than "A." And yet . . . "A"
could, suddenly, become "truer" than "B." Suppose that a historian in
the middle of Axis Europe stood up and said it in a lecture before a
German audience, in the summer of 1940. Or imagine "B," as it is written thus by an English historian, irritated as he was to the point of a
noble anger, say, in 1917, in his critical review of a jingo biography of
Wellington: wouldn't it be invested by an especial meaning of truthful-
ness?

We are coming to the end of the argument. Every human statement **8**
may be actually true and potentially untrue. "The Anglo-American-
Russian coalition won the Second World War." "The victors of World
War II were Soviet Russia and the United States." "China and the colonial peoples turned out to be the real victors of the last world war."
Depending on their purpose, each of these contradictory statements
may be true. But the relativity of such statements does not mean that
there is no truth, just as the inevitable corruptibility of the human flesh
does not mean that the human spirit may not reach incorruptibility: it
is only that historical truth, as I said earlier, touches our minds and our

senses differently (and more deeply) than does scientific truth—since we all are historians by nature while we are scientists only by choice.

I am aware of the uneasiness which may be forming in some of my   **9** readers' minds at this point: I seem to have shifted the argument from what is a fact to what is truth: but I could not avoid this; all that I wish to say is that the problem of truth is not necessarily a problem of fact. One evening in 1960, after having worked all day, I drove over the hill to see some friends after supper. My account in my 1960 diary reads: "June went by, closely together with H., in our little country house." "Late on the evening of June 1," someone could write, "Lukacs left his ailing wife alone in a darkened house, and drove off to spend several hours drinking with friends on a well-lit terrace, in an electric atmosphere with pretty women." Absolutely correct. Deeply untrue. I know it to be so. "What is truth?" I cannot answer Pilate's question; but I shall not wash my hands under the laboratory faucet of the specialist; if I cannot answer what truth is, I can at least say what it is not. Apart from all metaphysics, I can but say that the *purpose* of historical truth (like every fact, every truth is to some extent historical) is understanding even more than accuracy, involving the reduction of untruth; and I can say that the *nature* of truth is inseparable from personal knowledge; that it cannot be proven by definitions but that it can be suggested through words.

_____ **Written Response**

How is Lukacs's view of facts different from our common, everyday view of facts?

_____ **Rhetorical Analysis**

1. On two occasions, Lukacs contrasts the way that the same basic facts can be presented in two distinct narratives and styles, changing what the "bare facts" mean. Review these two sets of parallel texts and discuss how the same facts can have different meaning. What causes the meaning of the facts to change?

2. Select one of Lukacs's paragraphs and discuss the kind of evidence that he uses to illustrate the central point of that paragraph. How are his paragraphs similar to or different from Tuchman's?

_____ **Interpretation**

1. What does Lukacs mean when he says that a fact is abstract rather than concrete?

2. If, as Lukacs argues, a fact is not the same thing as the truth, then what is truth? How can an historical narrative hope to express the truth?

3. In *Against Method* (London: Verso, 1975), a book that criticizes current scientific methodology, Paul Feyerabend writes:

> Not only are facts and theories in constant disharmony, they are never as neatly separated as everyone makes them out to be. Methodological rules [scientific methods] speak of 'theories', 'observations' and 'experimental results' as if these were clear-cut well-defined objects whose properties are easy to evaluate and which are understood in the same way by all scientists.
>
> However, the material which a scientist *actually* has at his disposal, his laws, his experimental results, his mathematical techniques, his epistemological prejudices, his attitude towards the absurd consequence of his theories which he accepts, is indeterminate in many ways, ambiguous, *and never fully separated from the historical background*. This theory is always contaminated by principles which he does not know and which, if known, would be extremely hard to test. Questionable views on cognition such as the view that our senses, used in normal circumstances, give reliable information about the world, may invade the observation language itself, constituting the observation terms as well as the distinction between veridical and illusory appearance. [p. 66]

Do you feel that what Lukacs says about the fact and history is similar to what Feyerabend says here about fact and theory in science?

_____ **WRITING ASSIGNMENT**

This writing assignment will be broken down into several steps:

First, write a list of important facts about you and your life history.

Second, pair off with one of your classmates and exchange lists.

Third, using the list of facts, write a narrative that will describe your classmate's life history. Make a copy of this life history and then turn the original in as one writing assignment.

Fourth, exchange life histories with your classmate. As a second writing assignment, write an essay in which you analyze the accuracy or inaccuracy of the narrative that your classmate wrote of your life.

Synthesis

1. This writing assignment will be broken down into several steps:

First, make two or three copies of your essay on Japan's giving up the gun.

Second, form groups of two or three classmates.

Third, within each group, read and discuss your essays. These essays were written from the same body of facts and documents. Did you come to similar conclusions? Were your conclusions radically different? Did you use the same facts, or did each author select different facts? Did some authors interpret—or present—the same facts in different ways?

Fourth, write an essay in which you either state that history can be objective and arrive at truth, or that history can never be objective and can give only an interpretation of truth. Use the articles by Tuchman and Lukacs and the "giving up the gun" essays to support your thesis.

2. Go to the library and find two different accounts of the same historical event (for example, a battle during the Civil War); then write an essay in which you compare how the two historians treated the same event.

Rereading in Order to Write

The following paragraph describes a simple and familiar procedure. As you read this description, try to identify the procedure:

> The procedure is actually quite simple. First, you arrange things into different groups. Of course, one pile may be sufficient depending on how much there is to do. If you have to go somewhere else due to lack of facilities that is the next step; otherwise, you are pretty well set. It is important not to overdo things. That is, it is better to do too few things at once than too many. In the short run this may not seem important but complications can easily arise. A mistake can be expensive as well. At first the whole procedure will seem complicated. Soon, however, it will become just another facet of life. It is difficult to foresee any end to the necessity for this task in the immediate future, but then one can never tell. After the procedure is completed one arranges the materials into different groups again. Then they can be put in their appropriate places. Eventually, they will be used once more and the whole cycle will have to be repeated. However, that is part of life. [From J. D. Bransford and M. K. Johnson's "Conceptual Prerequisites for Understanding," *Journal of Learning Behavior*, 11 (1972), 717–726.]

A few people who read this paragraph for the first time may understand it, but most do not. This is not because the "procedure" is in itself difficult to follow or because the paragraph is poorly written, although it certainly could be stylistically improved. Rather, you probably had difficulty understanding this paragraph because you did not have the background knowledge that you needed to place each statement into a meaningful context.

You might be surprised to know that the paragraph is about washing clothes. Now that you know this, reread the paragraph and see if it makes more sense.

This experience illustrates the importance of background information (sometimes called "schema") to the process of understanding texts. As you work your way through this textbook, you will build background information that will help the readings to make more sense.

The background information that you pick up from the "Prereading" section will help to prepare you for your first interaction with each reading selection. After your first reading of the selection, you will write a response that will allow you to construct an initial interpretation on paper. You will not, however, be expected to reach an authoritative understanding of the reading selection at this time.

Once you have discussed the selection in class, you will reread the text once again in order to prepare yourself to write about it. And the selection will make more sense, just as the description of doing laundry made more sense the second time around.

Some of the writing assignments will also require that you go back and reread articles that were assigned earlier in the course. With this looping back to previous reading selections, you will find that your understanding improves yet again, for at this time you will have even more background knowledge.

This pattern of reading, writing, rereading, writing, and rereading again is an important part of reading like a writer. All writers reread to come to grips with their sources—the texts that they read in order to build the texts that they write.

Writing Responses to Texts

In this textbook, you will write responses in order to ease the transition between reading and writing. Although your written responses will provide a collection of ideas on paper that can be used in your rough draft, responses are not drafts.

As you write a response, you will be exploring how an article, or the experience of reading that article, has affected you. You will be exploring what this reading experience made you feel and what it made you think. You need not attempt to focus and organize your thoughts for the benefit of a reader. Rather, you will be attempting to record some of your initial feelings and thoughts on paper. The writing down of your initial feelings and thoughts will no doubt trigger additional feelings and thoughts, leading to digressions and tangents. When writing a response, it is best to write down any idea that pops into your mind, for a "bad" idea might trigger a "good" idea, or a digression might lead to a new perspective.

As you begin the rough draft of an essay, you will no longer be writing to understand what you feel and think. Instead, you will shift to writing for an audience. Your written response will no doubt provide a number of ideas that you can include in your draft, but your draft will need to be more focused and organized.

The sample of responses that follow will help to give you a better idea of how you can write responses and generate ideas for a rough draft. After reading Margaret Mead's "The Growth and Initiation of an Arapesh Boy," Loraz, Scott, Douna, Howard, and William wrote their responses in reaction to this question:

> Mead writes of the *tamberan* ritual: "As the *tamberan* cult dulls the imagination of the girls, it stimulates and quickens the imagination of the small boys. . . . Upon the little girl of ten, sitting demurely beside her mother or her mother-in-law, the horizon of life has closed down in a way that it has not upon her brother." Even though the culture of the mountain Arapesh allows for an unusual degree of equality between men and women, Mead feels that the sex roles it places on women can limit their imaginations and their potential. Do you feel that the sex roles in our society in any way limit the imagination or potential of women or men? Explore your thoughts on this topic in a few paragraphs.

As you read the responses that follow, think of which responses more fully explore the topic and generate more interesting ideas that might be used in a rough draft.

Loraz's Response

I do not feel that the roles in our society do limit the imagination for women and men. As in the Arapesh society, men and women both had limits. Women were not allowed to further their education as women are able to in societies today.

Scott's Response

I do not feel that women are limited in their potential. But of course what else can I say, being a man and all. I feel women are more able to express themselves. Women are no longer confined to this type of job or that type of job. Women are now able to freely choose what they wish to be and are not confined to any "proper" types of job.

Of course, before in our modern society we did not differ much from the primitive Arapesh. Women were not allowed an opinion. Women were not allowed to vote. A women's place was in the home "barefoot and pregnant." If a woman did have a job it was as a maid, a nurse, a teacher, or a housemaid. A woman could never be seen in a place of authority. They were subservient and inferior to men.

But times they are changing. Women are now doctors, lawyers, scientists, and any other thing they so desire. In fact in some cases it is the man who stays home to raise a family. If it is sex roles you are looking for to determine a superior society, then we are by far the most advanced.

Douna's Response

No, I do not feel that the sex roles in our society limit the imagination or potential of men or women. But I do feel that some men in our society (particularly in the workplace) do not let women live up to their full potential. This is a result of "primitive" thinking coming from the stereotypical idea of a women. That idea is that women are supposed to stay at home with the children and cater to their husband.

Because of the positive way our society is changing, in aspects of male/female roles, it opens the imagination and potentiality on both parts. Since both men and women are taking on similar roles, the type of "primitive" thinking I mentioned will soon become extinct.

Howard's Response

In today's world man and women can do the same job, unless the job has some physical lifting and making things that go with it. In the old days women were thought of as being at home with the children and the father making the money for the family. Times have changed because women can do the same job as a man and sometimes better.

My own thoughts on this matter is that if my wife wants to have a career that's fine but if we have a child I would like her to be home with them. The only problem with this is I hope I can find a wife that will do this.

William's Response

The likelihood of a woman reaching her true potential was very slim in our society not too many years ago. At the age when her brothers were encouraged to go to work or school she was expected to assist with her mother's duties. It was nearly unheard of for a young woman to be independent and have a career or live on her own. Today things are much different.

Men in our society used to be the dominant figure. Starting in the home most people began their lives seeing a male as the head of the household. Along with this most of the people with power, such as presidents and most of the successful business leaders, have been men. Lately the male has been losing his role as the supreme authority and power figure.

Nowadays partly from the womans movement and equality laws from a couple of decades ago, and partly from the high number of female heads of households, the attitudes have changed. About the only difference between men and women in our society, other than the apparent physical differences, is that girl babies wear pink and boys wear blue. There are no longer any stringent rules separating the male and female roles in society. Men become nurses, women become corporate executives, men are beginning to raise families, and women are beginning to run for president of the United States.

Discussion

Read the selection of essay topics that follow Mead's "The Growth and Initiation of an Arapesh Boy" on pages 51–53. Which of the above responses generated ideas that might be used in a draft for one of these topics?

Writing Summaries and Isolating Facts

Some students find it relatively easy to write summaries of paragraphs or entire texts as they read, but they often have more difficulty picking out and retaining important facts or examples. Other students, who pay more attention to the facts and examples of a text, may experience some difficulty writing summaries.

If you are adept at writing summaries and retaining the general ideas of a text, then you may need to learn to become more aware of its facts and examples. One easy way to do this is to write your summary in the margin of the text and then go into the text and underline the important facts, details, or statements that support that summary. You may then wish to revise your summary by adding in a few important details.

If you are more likely to focus on the facts and examples as you read a text, you might wish to practice the same basic procedure in reverse. As you read the text for the first time, underline what you consider to be the important facts, details, or statements. Then look at the information that you have underlined and write a general statement that can explain the basic idea behind the facts and examples. As you begin to write your summary, you may find that you have underlined too much. If so, do not attempt to include everything that you have underlined in the exact wording of your summary. Your summary should ideally explain all of the details in the text, but it need not explicitly mention them. Finally, reread the text to check your summary for accuracy and, if necessary, revise it. If you still have trouble getting past the words of the text to make a summary in your own words, you can try writing the facts and a brief description of examples on a sheet of paper. Then you can close your book and write your summary from your separate notes.

Practicing one of these approaches to taking notes on your texts should help you to understand and appreciate how abstract ideas and concrete details dynamically interact as you interpret a text. Because both ideas and details are important to how meaning emerges from the reading of a text, it is important that you, as a reader, attend to both ideas and details as it is that you, as a writer, include both ideas and details in your texts.

In the excerpt below from James J. Murphy's *A Synoptic History of Classical Rhetoric*, important facts and examples have been underlined and summaries have been written in the margin for the first three paragraphs. You may decide, as you read over these summaries, that you do not agree with them. This should not be surprising, for a summary is an interpretation of a text or a portion of a text, and every person's interpretation will differ to some degree.

After you have read the first three paragraphs, practice one of the procedures described above on the remaining paragraphs: either write a summary in the margin and then search for important facts and details to support it, or underline important facts and details and then work these into a summary. Although you are encouraged to summarize one paragraph at a time here, you may find, with more practice, that it sometimes makes more sense to write several summaries for one paragraph or a single summary for several paragraphs.

Once you finish reading, write a summary of the entire passage.

The Sophists

The term "sophist" means literally "wisdom-bearer." Strictly speaking, it could be applied to any wise person. But the development of ancient rhetoric is, especially in Athens, so closely tied to the so-called sophists of the fifth century B.C. that the way in which the Greeks used this term must be more precisely defined.

> Because the term "sophists" is usually used to refer to the sophists of the 5th century B.C., a more precise definition is needed than "wisdom-bearer."

The history of the ancient rhetorical sophists can best be understood as part of the history of the concept of logos (thought-plus-expression) which is deeply rooted in the ancient Greek consciousness. One modern scholar has distinguished three successive stages or types of sophists, depending on their use of the logos:

First stage: Wise men like Solon the lawgiver, devising wisdom in the form of laws.
Second stage: Statesmen applying wisdom to practical affairs, like Pericles or Themistocles.
Third stage: "Teachers of Wisdom" who asserted their ability to transmit wisdom, or to transmit eloquence, like Protagoras, Gorgias, or Isocrates.

> The sophists can be divided into three stages according to how they practiced logos: (1) lawgivers like

Source: From *A Synoptic History of Classical Rhetoric* edited by James J. Murphy, pp. 7–10. Copyright © 1983 by James J. Murphy. Reprinted by permission of the author.

Clearly a statesman like Pericles required both wisdom and eloquence enabling him to lead others to
carry out what wisdom led him to believe. In short,
he needed command of the logos. Pericles indeed
possessed wisdom and eloquence, as his exploits
demonstrate.

Is it possible, however, to teach others what a man
like Pericles knew and could do? This was the question answered in the fifth-century Athens by certain
teachers who set themselves up to give their students either <u>wisdom itself (like Socrates)</u>, merely <u>elo-
quence (like Gorgias)</u>, or a usable combination of <u>both
(like Isocrates)</u>. <u>Only through the excesses of such
eloquence-teachers as Protagoras and Gorgias has
the term "sophist" acquired a pejorative meaning.</u>

Protagoras (481–411 B.C.) is probably the best single example of the eloquence-teacher. His views
were lampooned by Aristophanes in *The Clouds,* and
he was important enough to draw the wrath of
Plato, who presents a biting attack on the sophist's
views in his dialogues *Protagoras.* Plato has Protagoras say that his pupils will be "better men" for
studying with him, meaning that they would learn
virtue through the study of eloquence. In practice
Protagoras seems to have believed that since no man
can be certain of the truth in a given situation, each
man has the right to express his own personal view
as strongly as possible. His most famous statement
is "Man is the measure of all things," and he is
credited with the statement, "On every question
there are two speeches that oppose each other." He
encouraged his students to debate both sides of a
question in order to train them to understand the
nature of controversy and to defend themselves better. His critics, however, declared that such exercises
essentially taught the students how "to make the
worse appear the better cause."

A number of other teachers in this period are
credited with contributions to the growing body
of rhetorical precepts. Thrasymachus, who figures
in some of Plato's dialogues, may have written the
first book dealing with methods of delivering
speeches, and Aristotle mentions a book by him
called *Appeals to Pity.* Thrasymachus may also have
been the first to discuss the concept of rhetorical
tropes and other figures of speech. Hippias taught a

[Handwritten margin notes:] Solon, (2) statesmen like Pericles, and (3) teachers of wisdom like Gorgias

Even though some sophists taught wisdom (Socrates) or wisdom and eloquence (Isocrates), the term "sophist" developed a negative connotation from those who taught only eloquence (Gorgias).

method of training the memory, but records of his
lessons have not survived. Alcidamas, a student of
Gorgias, taught methods of preparing extemporane-
ous speeches (as opposed to writing a text in advance). Prodicus of Ceos concentrated on clarifying
precise definitions of words, especially by linking
them to synonyms. He thus may have had an indirect influence on Socrates and others interested in
the logical uses of languages.

Sophists like these should not be confused with
logographers, such as Antiphon (480–411 B.C.) or
Lysias (459–380 B.C.), who were essentially paid
speech-writers for other men. They did not attempt
to analyze the rhetorical process itself, but rather
were interested only in discovering ways to adapt
the speeches they wrote to the personal style and
character of the speakers they had agreed to assist.
Lysias has been credited with developing "plain
style"—that is, the level of language used by ordinary men, as opposed to the "high style" common
to skilled orators or other educated persons. His objective was to adapt the speech's language to his client's ordinary way of talking so that the speech
would seem natural to him and suited to his character *(ethos)*.

Arguing with Texts

An important part of learning to read like a writer is learning how to
argue with texts. When good writers read a text, especially one that they
plan to incorporate into their own writing, they often argue with it—that
is, they systematically question the validity of what they read.

By writing questions, comments, and refutations in the margin as you
read, you will be preparing yourself to write, for writing is, to some extent, an ongoing argument. If you want to enter that argument, which
may have started over 2000 years ago, you will need to write about how
your ideas agree or disagree with ideas in other texts. You will need to
use your text to argue with other texts.

Some texts, because of their content, almost demand that you argue
with them, but it is not always appropriate to argue with texts. Other
texts, again because of their content, will almost demand that you empathize with them.

· Some examples of how you can argue with a text as you read it have
been written in the margin of the reading below, a speech delivered by
H. W. Evans before the first annual meeting of the Ku Klux Klan in July

1923. The purpose of the meeting was to improve the organization of the Klan and to develop a plan to recruit more members. After you have read the first section and the comments in the margin, continue to read the rest of the speech. As you read, argue with what Evans is saying by writing questions, comments, and refutations in the margin. Then, discuss with the rest of your class the way that you argued with the text.

Where Do We Go from Here?

Every undertaking, however large or great it may become, has somewhere its beginning. Today we are holding the first conference of Grand Dragons and Great Titans and it is rather a momentous occasion. I doubt whether the first real conference of leaders of a movement was ever held as late in the life of a movement as this meeting here today. When you think that you represent here more than a million Klansmen and that you represent maybe five thousand or more different or separate organizations each with its separate interpretation of the Holy doctrine, you realize that it must be an auspicious beginning.

What is so "Holy" about their doctrine? Is bombing churches holy?

The wants of the Klansman, his needs and his service requirements are the principal responsibilities of the Exalted Cyclops of the Klans. In a Province representing the principal responsibilities are you Titans and going up the line, the needs of the provinces of the nation represent the duties and responsibilities of the Grand Dragon and finally you come to your Imperial headquarters for final and complete one hundred percent service to the Klansmen of the nation, a service that will cause them to leave their imprint on this civilization.

What is with all of these fancy titles? Isn't this rather childish?

This man has an ego!

You have heard much of a program of activity for the Knights of the Ku Klux Klan. You have heard of one with the boundaries marked out, "Where do we go from here?" You cannot put into effect any set program for there are different needs in the various localities. Your program must embrace the needs of the people it must serve. I have been listening and watching in order to be able to interpret to you a real program for the Klan. The thing I am going to

He is trying to present himself as a servant,

Source: "Where Do We Go from Here?" by Former Imperial Wizard Hiram W. Evans, December 4, 1938. Permission to use this speech given by Mr. James W. Farrands, Imperial Wizard of the Invisible Empire, Knights of the Ku Klux Klan, Box 700, Gulf, North Carolina 27256.

do as your Imperial Wizard and the thing I am going to ask your Imperial Officers to do, all of us as
your <u>servants</u>, is to administer to the needs of your
locality and if we all do that to the utmost of our
ability and teach Klansmen along that line and carry
to them their responsibilities to <u>God and Country</u>,
we need not worry about the effect on this nation.

a religious person, and a patriot. This public image doesn't fit with the Klan's secret actions.

   I am not smitten with the idea of making Atlanta
the invisible capital of the world. I had rather make
the invisible capital of the world the serving heart
of the individual Klansman who loves his country,
who realizes its greatest needs and is willing to offer
himself to <u>serve and sacrifice</u> regardless of cost to
himself. That ought to be the capital of Klankraft
and not any physical structure. This idea that you
are to get behind a man or a set of men and follow
them blindly does not appeal to me. Don't get any
idea on earth that you are any man's machine. <u>Of
course you will obey your Constitution and Laws</u>; of
<u>course you will obey your superior officers</u>. Those
things are the natural things to do.

More dubious patriotism!

Earlier he said that the officers were the servants of the Klansmen.

   The present vital need of the Klan is for you men
here to carry back to the Klan and Klansmen <u>the idea
of co-ordination</u> and let them know something that I
know better than anybody else on earth,—that the
Klan is now and has been in the past functioning
almost entirely as a unit. Consider the Klan in your
locality and what is its condition. Take it where you
are and you know that there is nothing wrong with
the Klan there. You are hearing a great deal about
lack of co-operation in the Klan here and there. <u>Just
take your local conditions and you have the average
condition throughout the nation</u>. You know where
you stand on the Constitution and Laws. That is exactly the national condition. Quit getting your Klan
doctrine from the newspapers. They are naturally
antagonistic, and I can tell you why. Other organizations like this have been builded by advertising
and they have had to pay for it. We have been given
fifty million dollars worth of free advertising by the
newspapers. They have not yet been able to find out
what the Klan is and where it is going. The Klan is
of vital interest to the American public and the papers are anxious to tell them all about the opportunity. There is not and has not been any information
so sought after as news about the Klan. I can go

If every locality has its special needs, as he said earlier, how can they co-ordinate activities?

He is contradicting himself. First, he says the localities are unique; now he says they are all the same. This sounds paranoid!

Here's his big ego again!

to Chicago and every one of the papers will have men out to see me. I have talked in Washington to a room full of newspaper men at one time. I have never failed to have them there and newspaper men tell me the Klan is a matter of greatest public interest. Just as long as our doctrine is the pure and Holy doctrine, the newspapers won't be able to grasp what it is,—just as long as they are hunting for the bug under the chip you will have them fooled for there is no bug under the chip.

*   *   *

The Immigration Question

For one hundred and forty years America has been a haven for the halt, the maimed and the blind, for the broken in mind, body, fortune and soul, to come over here where nature has spread her bounteous gifts, where life is easy, health is good and conditions ideal. But the time has come when the millions who have been broken in the old world and who have led their countries to despoilation should not be admitted to our country. A proportionate immigration law is favored by some. What's that got to do with it? We admit that undesirable immigration is poison and they propose to give us one-half glass today and one-half glass next month. Let's consider the immigrant as a visitor in our house. You would make him show you whether, when he visits with you, he would be of advantage to you and your household. Let's make him a visitor so that he may prove that he is bringing something to America and that he will be an asset. Let's adopt that kind of program. Let's not let in the bad at all,—let's see that they are all good.

Let us fix it so American citizens will have to be born into the heritage and will have superiority by law. You own this country—it is yours. If you promise to allow anyone to take it away from you, it can mean nothing to you.

The Jewish Problem

I just want to touch on one more thing then I am through. We have lots of foreigners in here—the Irish American, the German-American, and the Jew, they are all here. We have been assimilating them and we have a little colic now. We have adopted a plan to get rid of all but one.

The Jews organized a Klan nearly forty centuries ago. You remember Moses organized them to get to the land of promise. They are still working. They know what it means to stand shoulder to shoulder, and not forget to put all he had on the Jewish altar. There have been ten tribes lost and nobody knew where they went. Christ absorbed them. The Christian civilization has absorbed them into Christian civilization the world over. They forget they were Jews when they moved into England and Germany and other countries, they took up the duties and responsibilities of the countries in which they lived and I am proposing to you that there will be two more lost tribes. We are organizing a Klan so large,—so much bigger than their Klan and if we will just do to them what I am talking to you about,—if we fix it so the Jew will boast of being an American instead of a Jew, he will be gone.

They are going to quit setting up Jewland in America. Their doctrine of setting up separate entity in our country is dangerous business.

Give them the idea of Christian civilization,—give them the high tide of Christian civilization and they will absorb Jesus Christ—they will absorb Christ's doctrine because it has won every human on earth except the Jew. If you will only do that you will not only benefit those people themselves who stand out as people without a flag or country, but the whole world will be benefited, and we will know what happens to them.

Law Enforcement

Now the program has one last thing I want to advance to you. We have not been appointed by an Almighty God or by an Imperial Wizard, to go out meddling in other people's business. Our duty is to get behind the constituted officers of the law as every one of you have sworn to do. Let's get a national law enforcement program—let's fix it so people will have to go to the penitentiary for violating law. You cannot enforce laws in the form of a super-government trying to force your will or your government on the law of the land. The first time one of your Klansmen violates the law, thus breaking his obligation, thus doing a thing in direct conflict for which we stand, let us administer on him as a Klansman for breaking his obligation. Let us get them outside the Klan and let the judge and the jury and the penitentiary take care of them. When we do that, this thing will fade like the morning dew.

The Wizard is not responsible for any violation. I am going to tell you now, you go home and do your duty and the first time you have a bunch of Klansmen that break the law do not get behind them. Put your influence behind the constituted officers of the law and let us support a law enforcement program and go with the law and act through the law and thus, once and for all and eternally end this fallacious accusation that we are a super-government because we are trying to teach constructive law enforcement and obedience to the law. Take coordination, immigration, education, law enforcement, as the national program behind which you are to labor and serve and sacrifice.

Empathizing with Texts

Just as it is important to doubt texts, it is important to believe them. It is important for us to put aside—at least temporarily—our inclination to doubt what the author is saying and attempt to see reality from his or her perspective. If we constantly doubt what we read, we will only defend our current beliefs; we will never live with foreign or disconcerting ideas long enough to rethink our current beliefs.

But what does it mean to empathize with a text? It means in part that you look for an author's good ideas, but it does not mean that you accept what the author is saying without question and without revision. Rather, it means that you make an attempt to understand the author's point of view, or that you at least attempt to rework the author's basic thought into an expression that you can accept. When you cannot entirely accept his or her line of thought, you may need to add the "missing pieces" that will allow you to accept some valuable insight that the author is struggling to make, perhaps with limited success. If you cannot agree with how his or her ideas are stated, you need to revise the author's text so that its basic idea is expressed in a different way—one that you will find easier to accept. If the author seems to be overstating a basically sound idea, then you need to add a qualification. Empathizing with texts, then, means reworking the author's basic ideas so that you will be more likely to accept them.

Empathizing with texts is, as you will see, an important part of reading as a writer because it allows you to think about old problems in new ways, and it allows you to transform ideas that you do not quite accept into ideas that you can incorporate into your writing.

The annotation on the first part of the text below (an excerpt from Lucien Levy-Bruhl's *The Notebooks on Primitive Mentalities*) represent the interpretations of a reader who is attempting to empathize with the author and believe his ideas. After you have read Levy-Bruhl's text, discuss the annotations. Then, read and annotate the last paragraph by attempting to empathize with the author.

True Myth Histories, in What Sense?

I have insisted on the point that, improbable as it may seem to us, among "primitive people" myths are taken as true histories. I have tried to show the reasons for this, and I believe these reasons to be still valid. But I have failed to ask myself if "true" has the same sense for the "primitive man" as for us.

I like the way that he is trying to think about myths from the perspective of a native.

I did not ask the question because it seemed clear that for them as for us true history means the account of one or many events which in actual fact happened, which have been real. Those events which myths relate are considered real, and that is why myths are "true histories."

I could perhaps agree if he acknowledged that some civilized people doubt the "truth" of history.

But what I did not notice until now, and what has some important consequences, is that the word real has only one sense for us, and for the primitive man it has two. Real for us is unequivocal: that is real whose actual existence can be perceived or, directly or indirectly, proved uncontestably. What does not satisfy these conditions may be more or less probable, but cannot be part of reality. This conviction is integral to our ideal of experience, to our idea of truth (or concrete reality).

This belief in a single reality was more typical of civilized thought when Levy-Bruhl was writing (1938), but this does not necessarily change his

Now the primitive mentality has not at all the same idea of experience. It is wider than ours. It will include, besides the ordinary experience which is like ours, the mystical experience which puts "primitive man" in contact with another reality, re-

Source: "True Myth Histories, in What Sense?" from *The Notebooks on Primitive Mentality* by Lucien Levy-Bruhl. Copyright © 1975 by Basil Blackwell & Mott Ltd., Oxford and Harper & Row, Publishers, Inc., New York. Reprinted by permission.

vealed by that experience itself, and he does not
dream of doubting it any more than the experience
furnished by the impressions coming from the surrounding milieu. Thus, in his terms, real is not unequivocal, no more than "experience," but just as
the two experiences form only one for him so the
two realities, although their difference may be
clearly felt, form for him only a single reality, and
reality, like experience, is bi-univocal.

We now discern the unperceived ambiguity that
hinders us in the formula: for "primitive men"
myths are true histories, the events they relate are
real. Yes, but real in the sense of the reality revealed
by the mystical experience and not in the sense of
the only reality true for us, that which is perceived
or adequately proved. It follows that the difficulty is
resolved. A myth is a true history. For the Marin-
danim, the history of Piekor really happened. But
that is not wishing to say that for them it is an event
as true as the flooding of the river which they observed yesterday, nor that they believe it in the
same way. The history of Piekor is a myth. It forms
part of the totality of events of the mythical world as
a flood forms part of the totality of phenomena of
the world perceived by the senses. The idea of asking themselves whether such a mythical event is
real does not occur to them, since in advance and so
to speak *a priori* the totality of the mythical world is
real for them, just as the mystical experience is as
valid if not more so than the other. Thus there is no
reason for asking how it is that they accept as real
such and such a mythical event, which is clearly absurd and impossible in our eyes. The only question
would be: how do they accept that the mythical
world is at least as real, though different, as the actual world?

December 4th, 1938

[handwritten margin note: theory about "primitive" thought.]

Reading From a Perspective

One of the ways that students learn how to write in a specific discipline
(such as anthropology, history, or psychology) is by criss-crossing their
way through the texts of that field. If, for example, you want to become
an anthropologist, you will begin by reading a variety of texts written by
anthropologists for anthropologists. Your first experience with these texts
may be frustrating, for you are essentially dropping in on a conversation

among specialists that has been going on for over a hundred years. Yet, as you continue to read, you will begin to get a fix on the terrain of anthropology. You will find that anthropologists tend to solve problems from a perspective that is unique to their field—that they do not think and write in the same way that historians and psychologists do.

The more that you survey texts from the field of anthropology, the more easily you will be able to assume the role of an anthropologist as you read and write. This general knowledge of the field is extremely important, and it will even affect how you annotate your texts. For example, if you are reading a text from anthropology, you should be especially concerned about how that text relates to key issues in the field. You will want to know what is unique about the culture being described, what role its rituals and symbols play in the culture at large, and what a knowledge of this other culture can tell us about our culture or about human nature in general.

The following passage from Ruth Benedict's *Patterns of Culture* has been annotated to serve as one example of how you can read from a particular perspective. After you have read the passage, discuss how the annotations are written from the perspective of an anthropologist.

The Pacific Seacoast Indians

The Indians who lived on the narrow strip of Pacific seacoast from Alaska to Puget Sound were a vigorous and overbearing people. They had a culture of no common order. Sharply differentiated from that of the surrounding tribes, it had a zest which it is difficult to match among other peoples. Its values were not those which are commonly recognized, and its drives not those frequently honored.

> Why did these people develop such an unusual culture? Were they isolated from other tribes?

They were a people of great possessions as primitive peoples go. Their civilization was built upon an <u>ample supply of goods</u> inexhaustible, and obtained without excessive expenditure of labour. The fish, upon which they depended for food, could be taken out of the sea in great hauls. Salmon, cod, halibut, seal, and candlefish were dried for storage or tried out for oil. Stranded whales were always utilized, and the more southern tribes went whaling as well. <u>Their life would have been impossible without the sea</u>. The mountains abutted sharply upon their shore territory; they built upon the beaches. It was a country wonderfully suited to the demands they put upon it. The deeply indented coast was flanked with

> How does this "ample supply of goods" affect their culture?

> The importance of the sea to their culture.

Source: Ruth Benedict, *Patterns of Culture.* Boston: Houghton Mifflin Company, 1934.

numberless islands which not only trebled the
shoreline, but gave great sheltered areas of water
and protected navigation from the unbroken sweep
of the Pacific. The sea life that haunts this region is
proverbial. It is still the great spawning ground of
the world, and the tribes of the Northwest Coast
knew the calendar of the fish runs as other peoples
have known the habits of bears or the season for
putting seed into the earth. Even in the rare cases
when they depended upon some product of the
earth, as when they cut the great trees that they
split into boards for their houses or hollowed with
fire and adzes for canoes, they held close to their
waterways. They knew no transportation except by
water, and every tree was cut close enough to a
stream or inlet so that it could be floated down to
the village.

How unusual are wooden houses for American Indians?

If their entire culture is centered around water, will water play an important role in their symbols and rituals?

Switching Perspective

Once you have learned how to read from a perspective, you can begin to
experiment with reading the same text from several perspectives. You
could, for example, take Benedict's description of the Pacific seacoast Indians and read it, as we did in the "Reading from a Perspective" section,
as an anthropologist would. This is, as it might seem at first, the most
logical way to read an anthropological text. It is not, however, the only
way to read Benedict's text. We could also read it from the perspective of
an historian, an economist, a psychologist, and so on. Each time that we
reread the text from a new perspective, we will see it in a different light.

By switching perspectives like this, we can accomplish several things.
We can detect some flaws or weaknesses in the author's line of thought,
and we can rethink the author's data in a way that will lead to a fresh
and original interpretation.

Below are two examples of how Benedict's text can be read from different perspectives, that of an historian and that of a psychologist. Discuss
how reading from these "switched perspectives" produces a different interpretation and different annotations.

Reading from the Perspective of an Historian

The Indians who lived on the narrow strip of Pacific
seacoast from Alaska to Puget Sound were a vigorous and overbearing people. They had a culture of
no common order. Sharply differentiated from that
of the surrounding tribes, it had a zest which it is

When did Benedict observe them? Before they had much

Appendix B

Exploring Your Writing Process

Too often, students feel that there is one sure approach to writing, one process or series of steps that must be followed in order to write the kind of essay that their instructor expects. They may feel that their essays would be much better if only their instructor would tell them the *right* way to generate ideas, outline, organize facts, and proofread.

Some students may even blame their writing process—the way they like to write as opposed to the way they were taught to write—if their essays do not turn out as well as they had expected. They may feel that they would have done better if only they had used note cards to write down ideas, if only they had written a detailed outline, if only they had started earlier, if only they had used bigger words.

If there were a single approach to writing that would guarantee a perfect essay, instructors would certainly tell their students about it. There is not, because people are different. Each person must approach writing in a way that works for him or her.

In this section, you will begin to explore your individual writing process by thinking about a few opposing approaches to writing. You will read four sets of stories (or case studies), each of which describes two opposing approaches to writing. Each story is followed by a sample essay. The stories are entitled

Victor: The Active Writer	Darrel: The Reflective Writer
Sean: The Factual Writer	Scott: The Abstract Writer
Mitzie: The Objective Writer	Maria: The Personal Writer
Douna: The Focused Writer	Monique: The Inclusive Writer

As you read these stories, you will see that Victor's approach to writing is opposite to Darrel's, Sean's is opposite to Scott's, Mitzie's is opposite to Maria's, and Douna's is opposite to Monique's. None of these approaches is better than its opposite, and your most natural writing process will be some combination of these opposite approaches. Thus, you can use the stories to help you better understand how you prefer to approach writing.

As you read each set of stories, try to decide which of the two better describes the approach to writing that comes more naturally to you. The sample essay that follows each story should also provide an opportunity for you to think about how your writing process might affect the kind of rough drafts that you produce.

While reading, you might want to underline portions of the stories that seem true of you as a writer, or write "no" in the margin when you read something that is very different from how you approach writing. If you wish to work through the stories more quickly, you might consider beginning with the heading that seems to best describe you. For example, if the word "active" seems more descriptive of you and your approach to writing than "reflective," you can begin with Victor's story rather than Darrel's. If Victor's story does not fit with how you write, then you can jump to Darrel's and see if that story better fits you and your approach to writing. Then, you can move on to the next pair of stories or opposite approaches to writing.

Victor: The Active Writer

Ever since he was in elementary school, teachers made Victor write an outline before he began to write his essay. He always hated that. How could he know what he was going to write before he wrote it! Since he was a smart and resourceful student, he figured out—very early in life—that he could write his essay first, then outline it. His teachers never caught on!

When he doesn't have to outline first, Victor can write the way that fits him—he can write actively! Instead of staring into space, Victor can leap into writing with little forethought and write whatever pops into his mind. His first drafts often look like a map of the realm of chaos, with words and sentences crossed out, ideas added up and down the margins, and arrows connecting one paragraph to another. Sometimes, he even adds entire paragraphs on the back and draws an arrow that wraps around the edge of the paper (almost like the path of a ship sailing over the edge of the earth) to show where the paragraph would be added on the front page. Only Victor can read these first drafts, but that is okay. This is the way he likes to write. He doesn't have to slow down to make his writing pretty or perfect. He can throw ideas down on paper as quickly as he can think of them (which is pretty quickly), and he can rely on his energy to carry him through to the end of the first draft. He has a great deal of *energy!*

Writing this way works well for him as long as he saves enough time for a second or third or sometimes even a fourth draft. In later drafts, he can reorganize ideas, cut ideas that don't belong, and add new ideas so that other people can follow his train of thought.

When he first started college, Victor found it a little difficult to write in-class essays. This was because he felt he didn't have enough time to revise —he had to get it right the first time! He soon discovered that it was possible to write two drafts—even when he only had 60 minutes to write the essay! He began to leap into his in-class essays, writing a very quick rough draft (without any details or examples) in about 15 or 20 minutes. The rough draft helped him to get warmed up; it was almost as if he was warming up before he began to exercise. The rough draft also helped him to explore his ideas, for Victor came up with some of his best ideas while he was in the process of putting words on paper. Once he was warmed up (he knew when he was warmed up because something clicked and then he knew what he wanted to say), he could begin to rewrite his essay (adding the examples and details) and (believe it or not!) he could finish the second draft before his 60 minutes were up. Of course, he had to be careful to watch the time. If he had not finished his rough draft by 15 or 20 minutes, he went on to start the second (and final) draft anyway.

As long as Victor writes in his special active process, as long as he leaps into his writing without feeling that he has to write an outline or have everything thought out in advance, he finds writing relatively easy—or at least easier than it was before. When he does become blocked, he uses one of his "block-busters," for he is lucky enough to have several of them. The easiest of his "block-busters" is to rescan his text. By reviewing what he has already written, he can usually recapture his line of thought and continue to write. At other times, he can break a block by simply talking to a friend. (He also likes to talk about ideas before he begins to write.) The more he talks to the friend about what he is trying to write, the clearer his ideas become, and the more confident he becomes in his ideas. If this doesn't work, he talks (rather than writes) a first draft into a tape recorder, or he pretends that he is giving a speech on the topic. At other times, he finds a word processor to write on, for he loves nothing more than writing on a word processor. It is much easier for him to throw his ideas into the computer quickly, because the word processor allows him to erase and start over, add words, move paragraphs, and so on. It is almost as if the word processor were made for his approach to writing.

When Victor begins to revise, he likes to read his essay aloud or, even better, have a friend read it aloud to him. This helps him to know which sentences need to be revised; he can even hear grammatical errors better than he can see them. Then, as soon as his essay *sounds* good, he turns it in.

The Text of an "Active" Writer

Those writers who prefer to leap into composing with little planning and develop ideas as they put words on paper tend to produce rough drafts that ramble on with little organization and are filled with a wide range of partially developed ideas. Victor wrote the following rough draft to explore his attitudes toward advertising:

Victor's Essay

My views about advertising might be different than others and I might look at it from a different point of view maybe when I tell them to you then you can begin to understand them. Sometimes it's not a subject if a certain type of advertising is ethical or not. And sometimes money is the only issue that is ever brought up when advertising is mentioned. This essay consists of only my opinions they might or might not be yours.

When ever I think about advertising I think of television, and billboards and other things of that matter. When I think of those things I think about how much money the company's pay for them, then I think how much money will be brought in because of the advertisement(s). Advertising is used to make money and for that only reason advertising is around. If advertising didn't make money there wouldn't be as many people talking about it or as many references relating to it.

Sometimes advertising becomes unethical and that is where all of the controversy about advertising begins. A couple of years ago movie theatres use to put sublimanial messages in the movie it would have a picture of popcorn and people would go and get popcorn for no reason at all. Sometimes people make up alot to do about something that really isn't anything at all. Like these little religious groups that want to rid the world of injustice, there's nothing wrong with that but when they start baning the book's from library's and start picketing radio stations because a song might suggest SEX or something else like they might find unethical that really isn't anything at all. But who is to say what is ethical and what is not. Maybe then when that is settled then someone can criticize advertising.

Victor prefers to compose rough drafts by simply writing down any thought that pops into his head, which is precisely how many very good writers prefer to begin. However, Victor needs to realize that his writing process will tend to produce a rather chaotic rough draft—which is essentially written for himself—that will often require substantial revision so that it can be understood by readers.

Because Victor tends to write down any idea that pops into his head, his rough draft may lack a focus—a central idea or theme. Before revising, he needs to think about what he is trying to say in his rough draft or what he would like to say in his second draft. Based on Victor's rough draft, what do you feel would be a good central theme to focus on during his next stage of revision?

Victor's rough drafts also tend to cover a wide range of ideas. Once he has selected a theme or thesis, he needs to cut some ideas or passages that are not related to that theme and develop others that support it. What ideas or passages in Victor's rough draft should be cut? What ideas or passages should be expanded?

Victor likes to write as quickly as possible, which helps him to preserve his ideas on paper (before he forgets them) as well as create mental space for thinking about new ideas (the sooner he pushes each idea out of his head, the sooner he can think about new ideas). Writing quickly, however, tends to produce an informal style filled with loosely structured sentences. Find a section of three or four sentences in Victor's rough draft that needs to be revised, and rewrite that section to make it more formal and polished.

Darrel: The Reflective Writer

Darrel likes to think before he acts, and that is how he likes to write as well. Before he ever puts his first sentence on paper, he likes to spend a great deal of time thinking about what he wants to say and how he wants to say it. He will think about the ideas that he wants to write about, how he wants to organize them, and even how he will fashion these ideas into phrases and sentences.

He may write down an outline, which is fairly long and detailed at times and short at other times, or he may jot down a few notes on key ideas or facts, but usually he prepares for his writing assignment in his head. He prefers to do this preparatory thinking when he is alone and uninterrupted, but then again he is fairly good at blocking out disturbances from the outside world.

Once Darrel has thought about his ideas long enough, he begins to write down his text. This phase of his writing process is often more akin to transcribing than composing. In other words, he transcribes onto paper the text that he has already composed in his head. When he has thoroughly thought through his text, he can write very quickly and his first draft may need little revision. When he has not thought it through as completely (which is okay), he may stop more frequently to think about where key sentences are leading him. Indeed, in his texts, he often has a number of sentences that announce where he is going, such as "At this point, I would like to discuss . . . ".

Darrel spends a great deal of time on his introductions. Sometimes he will discard several well-written introductions because they are not suited to the essay that he has already mapped out in his head. Once he has written the introduction, the rest of the essay comes pretty easily.

For the most part, this reflective process works well for Darrel. Since he has thought about the topic before he writes, he can usually put words on paper without experiencing many writer's blocks, although sometimes he becomes bored with the physical act of writing—the transcribing of his mental text. When he has thought his topic through too thoroughly, he feels that the physical act of writing is just so much scribal work. He tends to enjoy writing more when he leaves some of the details or ideas unfinished in his mental text so that he can experience the thrill of discovering new messages as he puts words on paper. This is the key to Darrel's writing process: knowing how much and how long he should write in his head and knowing when to begin putting words on paper.

When he began college, he found writing in-class essays difficult. He likes to think about a topic for days (even weeks or months) before he begins writing. When he wrote his first in-class essays, he noticed that some of his classmates would begin writing almost immediately. It seemed to him that the time was flying by and all he was doing was sitting there thinking about the topic. With time, he has come to realize that it is okay for him to think about the topic for a long time before he begins to write. Sometimes, he will think about his topic for 30 minutes before he begins to put words on paper, but, since he uses this time to consider what he wants to say, he can then write a good essay in the remaining 30 minutes.

_____ **The Text of a "Reflective" Writer**

Reflective writers such as Darrel tend to think about their topic a long time before they begin to put words on paper. Their texts, thus, often contain phrases that predict the direction of the thought (for example, "In this essay, I will . . . ", or "Next, I wish to discuss . . . "). Because their essays are more likely to evolve from reflection, from an inner rather than an outer use of language, their texts also tend to be more naturally formal than those of active writers. As you read Darrel's rough draft (a letter to the editor of a newspaper that argues against someone who uses inaccurate data to promote racist views), pay attention to how he predicts the direction of his thought and to how his language is basically formal.

Darrel's Essay

Dear Editor,

I'm writing this letter in response to Albert J. Stimmer's letter to you. In recent years our society has been moving toward greater integration of races, but this is for the best because Morton's information was incorrect. In this letter you will find data by Stephen Gould that reveals that Morton's calculations were wrong.

Stephen Jay Gould criticizes Samuel George Morton for basing his conclusions on biased samples. Gould said that Morton set out to rank races by the average sizes of their brains. Morton's experiments are full of false information to support Morton's prior theory. Gould reveals that Morton unconsciously forced his data to fit his prejudices.

Morton's calculations made adjustments for the white skulls but left the other skulls the same causing an error in averages. Gould found that Morton calculated his high Caucasian mean by unconsciously eliminating small brain Hindus from his sample. Thus, Morton included a large subsample of Inca to pull down the indian average. It seems here that he was producing averages on what he felt they should have been.

Sizes of the brains are related to the sizes of the bodies that carry them: big people tend to have larger brains than small people. This fact does not imply that big people are smarter.

Therefore, by the evidence presented by Stephen Gould, Morton's data was unconsciously fudged to support his own bias thinking. Also, he never separated his skulls by sex or stature; that can account for some of the low averages. To sum it all up, Mr. Stimmer, all races could be equal because the method which Morton used cannot determine the intelligence level of each of the races.

Sincerely,
Darrel M.

How does Darrel's text predict what will come later in the essay? Are these kinds of predictions appropriate for all situations and all types of writing?

Darrel's essay is more formal than Victor's. Reread both essays and then discuss the features of Victor's text that make it more conversational and the features of Darrel's text that make it more formal.

Sean: The Factual Writer

Sean feels that 90 percent of his writing instructors give him assignments that are needlessly difficult. Their directions are too vague and general. If they would only tell him how long the essay should be and how they want it organized, then he would find it easier to begin the essay. When the instructor tells him what he or she expects, which is unfortunately only 10 percent of the time, then Sean knows what to do and is able to write good essays.

For example, his first college writing instructor gave him very vague instructions. He would say, "I want you to write an essay about the transformation of American culture during the 1960s." What does that mean? Why can't this man speak in English? What planet is he from? When Sean receives instructions like this, he has learned that he needs to ask the instructor some questions to clarify what the instructor wants. He will ask questions like: What do you mean by transformation? Could you give me an example of what you mean by transformation? Can you show me a sample essay or two on this topic that you would consider to be acceptable? After he asks questions like this, the assignment is clearer; then he can give the instructor what he or she wants.

Mitzie's Essay

The Japanese giving up the gun for over two hundred years in 1630 is not a historical precedent to the United States giving up nuclear weapons in 1988. The weapon which the Japanese used instead of the gun was the sword. Their reasons for not using the gun for two thousand years is entirely different from the reasons why the United States does not want to use nuclear weapons. During the two hundred years that the gun was absent from Japan, Japan isolated itself from the rest of the world; which could have been a contributing factor to the absence of the gun.

The usage of the sword in Japan dates back to 1160. Sword fighting was a method of battle which the Samurai warriors preferred. These Japanese warriors trained day and night to perfect their usage of the sword for battle fighting. It took almost a lifetime to master this sword fighting technique. Being a Samurai warrior was not just being an excellent swordsman, it was also being a servant to his master, someone who had already perfected the technique. A Samurai warrior was very dedicated to his master. His master always came first, second was his wife and family. Being a Samurai Warrior was a way of life. The Japanese may have not wanted to give up such a valuable and sacred weapon, the sword, for a new and unfamiliar weapon, the gun.

During the time period that the gun was introduced, Japan had taken in a new ruler, Lord Ieyasu. In 1600 a new Shogun, which is the head feudal lord, took office ending over 100 years of feudal warfare. Ten years after Lord Ieyasu took office the government began to reduce it's orders for guns. In 1614 Lord Ieyasu isolated Japan from the rest of the world. He ordered Japan to give up Christianity, and he only allowed one Dutch ship to enter Japan's port a year; the rest were forced to leave for fear that they would spread Christianity. The whole time that Japan was in seclusion guns were not active or made except for those made behind the government's back.

The gun had many inconveniences during battle. In the gun's preliminary stages it would not function in the rain; later the Japanese devised an accessory that would allow the gun to work in the rain. The Japanese custom of bowing before a battle was very cumbersome when the gun was the weapon being used. While one side was bowing and loading their guns, which took 10–15 minutes, the opposite side had already begun to fight with swords. Battles with guns were not as much fun as battles with swords; which took the excitement out of being a trained Samurai warrior.

As one can see from the information discussed, the Japanese did not give up the gun because it hurt too many people. The Japanese did not give up the gun because it was too expensive, nor did they give up the gun because it could destroy the world. The three reasons above are not reasons why the Japanese gave up the gun but reasons why the

United States would want to give up nuclear weapons. The reasons why the Japanese gave up the gun were: they did not want to throw away long years of training with a sword to start over with the gun, and it was an inconvenience to use, whereas the sword was not. The difference as to why the two weapons, the gun and nuclear arms, were given up or want to be given up, are totally different. The Japanese giving up the gun is not a historical precedent to the U.S. giving up Nuclear arms.

Mitzie "cuts" her data up into categories, and the categories then become the superstructure of her organization.

One of the consequences of breaking an essay into a list of items or a series of categories is that the writer will need to provide transitions between the items or categories. Do you feel that Mitzie has provided transitions between categories?

Within her categories, Mitzie tends to give a simple list of data or points. Are all of these points related to the central idea of each paragraph? Does her writing "flow" from one sentence to the next?

When writers organize their essay by categories, they need to think about the order of the categories. Do you feel that Mitzie's essay would flow better if the categories were rearranged?

Because objective writers tend to focus on what they are saying instead of how their writing is affecting their audience, their texts are sometimes dry and devoid of emotions. Do you feel that Mitzie's essay is too dry? What could she do to make her essay more interesting?

Maria: The Personal Writer

Writing, for Maria, is like a river. She begins to express herself and then she just follows the flow of her feelings.

She finds that her writing often surprises her. Even if she plans what she wants to say, there is still something mysterious about how her feelings take shape. It is like watching a flower grow. You see the sprout push its way through the soil, and you know that it will be exciting to see what develops. You know it will be a flower, but you do not know what kind of flower, for the flower takes shape only as it grows.

This is how Maria's essays take shape—not from her deciding on an organizational format in advance, but by her letting the organization develop organically, like the flower, as she follows the flow of her thoughts and feelings.

As you might already suspect, Maria tends to put her heart into her writing. Writing is communication, and communication is touching other people with your ideas and feelings. Maria feels that if she puts herself into her writing, then her reader will enjoy reading her essay.

Maria really wants to entertain her reader. She tries to find just the right word (very unusual words) that will capture the reader's attention, and she constantly wonders about whether her reader will understand her and be interested in what she has to say.

Maria tends to be sensitive about what instructors or other students say about her essays. After she puts so much of herself into her essays, she feels that any criticism of her writing is a criticism of her as a person. Since she has been in college, she has learned to handle criticism better, but it can still be painful to read negative comments. She tends to prefer instructors who like her as a person and tell her what they like about her essay before they make suggestions for revision. As long as she feels that her teachers like her, she will work extremely hard on her assignments.

Of course, some assignments can still be hard. She has difficulty writing essays in which she has to criticize someone's ideas (she doesn't like to offend people) or essays on topics that she is not interested in. She has learned that it is important for her to try to connect her personal values (what she is interested in and what she feels is important) to the essay topic. Once she is emotionally tied to the essay topic, then it is easier for her to write on it. This works sometimes, but at other times the topics are just too boring. If she just can't get into a topic, she has learned to ask her instructor if she can write on something else.

Once she is interested in her topic, her writing flows. She prefers to write personal narratives, because she likes to tell stories: They flow better. But sometimes her essays are not well organized (either because her ideas didn't flow well or because she couldn't use a narrative structure); then she has to be careful to work on her organization as she revises.

Maria has learned a great deal since she has been in college, and she plans to continue improving as a writer for the rest of her life.

_____ **The Text of a "Personal" Writer**

Personal writers like to follow "the flow." They like to begin writing and then follow the flow of their thoughts. Their texts, not surprisingly, are often organized chronologically, following either some personal or historical time sequence. As you read the rough draft of Maria's essay (on whether or not the renunciation of the gun by the Japanese in the seventeenth century was similar to our trying to renounce nuclear weapons), pay attention to how her text is organized chronologically. Also, pay attention to how Maria attempts to personalize her essay, even though she is writing on the kind of topic that usually draws a more objective and analytical response:

Maria's Essay

In the year A.D. 1543, Japan was to undergo a drastic change in their society and their warfare strategies. They were introduced to the gun. This was a period of time in Japan when feudal lords fought each other for military control of the country. A centralized government or Emperor was nonexistent, and so the Japanese lords that fought each other came to form a part of Japanese history that was called the "Age of a Country at War".

The gun's effectiveness in battle was soon proven when fully armored fighters died from bullet wounds. In an age when not long ago swords and spears were used to injure and kill, the gun had shown greater advantages from these previous primitive weapons. There was no need to come within a few yards with the enemy in order to kill them. This could now be done from a distance. Also, a greater number of men on the enemy side could be eliminated without much more effort than just pulling the trigger with one's finger. But even with these few examples of the gun's advantages, Japan was able to give up the gun at the beginning of the 17th century when Lord Tokugawa took office and ended a war that had now lasted a century. By 1637 the last extensive use of guns is known to have taken place in the Shimabara Rebellion. For the next 200 years peace reigned and the usage of guns virtually disappeared.

Today, a similar "introduction" was made in this century to the world. The atomic bomb. In comparison to the gun, I believe, there is absolutely none. The atomic bomb is many times more powerful than a mere rifle and by far it can cause far more damage to a greater area of people. To give you an idea, an atomic bomb is immensely more powerful than a bomb of the same size containing chemical explosive; but in addition to the shock and blast there is also release of heat, light, and lethal radiation.

In questioning myself on whether it can be given up just as the gun was given up in Japan. I believe that the way things are now-a-days, such a wish would be granted only by a miracle.

Now-a-days the bomb is not a secret weapon that is in just one country's possession such as the United States. It is for the majority in possession of the two world powers, the Soviet Union and the United States, but it can also be found in other less powerful countries like the United Kingdom, France, and China. What we are talking about here is basically the world and not one country which is ruled by one Emperor who decides when to give up guns or in this case atomic bombs. As such was the case of Japanese prisoners during WWII who were quoted saying that they "will fight unhesitantly, even with nothing more than bamboo poles, if the Emperor so decrees. They would stop just as quickly if he so decreed". We are dealing with many different people who think differently. Some are driven to power and so they support the manufacturing of atomic bombs, others are peace loving individuals who are 100% against it. Each country has its own views towards the bomb but for the most part they can agree that now-a-days this object (being the ultimate weapon) means power. Power to a country is important, its prestigious, it keeps it on top, and its something that isn't easily given up. Fear of being the weakling under the dominion of another country with differences in culture, laws, language, traditions, etc., can give the political leaders more of a reason to cling on to this powerful device. An example would be as Arnold J. Toynbee best put it "neither the United States nor the Soviet Union was prepared to place itself at the mercy of the other." We can therefore see why these are some reasons the bomb wouldn't be given up.

Another reason would be self-defense. Lets imagine ourselves for example as the president of a country. As the leader of that country one takes up many responsibilities and one of them is the defense of the nation. Its almost as if one becomes the single, protective parent of many children who look up to you for safety. Part of your job is to seek ways of keeping these children safe in a place where they will be comfortable and war-free for at least most of their lives. If weapons and other warfare devices you feel are not enough for safety than you look towards today's ultimate—the atomic bomb. This bomb somehow, it psychologically makes you and your children feel safe from the external world. You now have the respect of neighboring countries who don't have it and more or less the admiration of your country for not letting them get stepped on.

In this world of competition I believe that even if the atomic bomb was given up, man would find a way of developing something similar if not worse. For lets remember our need for power, safety, self-defense, our fear of foreign domination, and insecurity, which may arise if the bomb is done away with. All we can say and remember is that as, Arnold J. Toynbee once wrote, we once lived "in an age in which man's worst weapons had been swords, pikes, and nuzzle-loading guns"; and so lets hope for the best in our future, atomic bombs or not we'll all have to die some day anyway.

Maria begins with one kind of "flow" (the "flow" of a historical chronology) and then switches to another kind of "flow" (the "flow" of her own train of thoughts). Do you feel that her essay is cohesive? Does it hold together?

Maria presents her ideas as they come to mind. When writers organize their essays by following the flow of their thoughts, their essays can draw the reader along as one thought triggers another. They can also infuse a sense of drama into their writing. Is Maria's essay easy to read? Does it have a sense of drama?

When authors follow the flow of their thoughts (instead of organizing their ideas into categories), their points or arguments may sometimes become lost. Do you feel that Maria's points or arguments are clear? Did you have difficulty understanding what she was trying to say?

Douna: The Focused Writer

For Douna, deadlines are important, very important.

Almost from the minute that she is given a writing assignment, Douna begins to think about how she can complete the writing assignment and turn it in on time. She usually begins by making a schedule. She plans to have her research completed by a certain date (she may decide to read two articles a day), the rough draft completed by another date (perhaps, writing a page or two every day), and the revisions made and the final version turned in by another date. She follows the schedule and never turns in an assignment late.

The process works quite well for her, although she has learned that she can sometimes follow her schedule too rigidly. She has learned "to plan to be spontaneous"—that is, plan to stop at key points in her schedule, assess her progress, and decide whether her schedule needs to be revised.

Because she wants to finish writing quickly, she sometimes begins too soon—that is, before she has done enough research or before she has thought about the topic enough. This can lead to blocks, but she has learned that when she is blocked, what she needs to do is read some more or think more about the topic, or discuss her ideas with friends.

Douna's expediency also leads to fairly short rough drafts that she needs to expand when she revises.

_____ **The Text of a "Focused" Writer**

When writers hustle to complete a rough draft as quickly as possible, they tend to produce a text that is clearly focused on a central idea but is also underdeveloped. As you read Douna's rough draft of an essay on the dangers of propaganda, pay attention to how her essay is so concise that it is poorly developed.

Douna's Essay

We should always be concerned about propaganda and propagandists. Anytime someone wants you to think, speak, look or act a certain way, we should be concerned. Many dangers lie within propaganda and in the minds of propagandist. Some notorious propagandist were Adolf Hitler, Benito Mussolini, and Napoleon. Actually when you think of how a propagandist controls his audience, you should automatically become concerned. Propagandist use scapegoats, appealing to your emotions unconsciously and give a one-sided story to manipulate you.

Scapegoating is used to put the blame on someone or something else. If you notice when someone is doing something wrong, they have something to put the blame on. Scapegoating is dangerous because the blamed party could be and usually is very offended, which can cause great rivalries and disputes. In Hitler's case one of the scapegoats were the Jewish people. And that propaganda act caused a chain reaction of events.

One of the scariest dangers, is the appeal to your emotions without you even realizing it. The propagandist make his audience get all worked up about things they know little about. When someone can make you get all worked up over something you know little about that is scary.

The famous one-sided story is how the propagandist gets to our unconscious mind. If both sides of the story was given, the audience could then rationalize.

Now it should be clear that propaganda could be dangerous and everyone should be concerned about it. When a new idea is given to you, make sure there are no propaganda dangers to you or anyone.

Douna's essay is focused: it has a clear thesis and several supporting ideas. It is not, however, very well developed.

For example, the fourth paragraph begins with the statement: "The famous one-sided story is how the propagandist gets to our unconscious mind." Douna does not explain what this means. What does she mean by a one-sided story? Why would a "one-sided story" affect our subconscious mind more than a story that tells "both sides"? When an essay is as poorly developed as Douna's, it is difficult for the reader to understand.

If you were giving Douna advice on how to develop her essay, what would you tell her?

Monique: The Inclusive Writer

If she wanted to, Monique could describe her writing process in one word—BIG. She tends to select very broad topics that allow her to research and think about a broad range of ideas, and she sometimes has trouble narrowing the topic, even when her deadline is approaching and the essay is not yet written.

Of course, Monique takes her big topics and researches them in a big way. She works hard on her writing assignments and believes that she should not start to write until she has thoroughly researched the topic. She will check a number of books out of the library—sometimes it seems as if she checks out hundreds. Her friends can tell when she is working on a term paper, because her dorm room is cluttered with books, photocopies of journal articles, notecards, and ideas jotted down on little slips of paper. The more she reads, the more she feels that there is to read. There is always one more article to read, one more book to read, one more fact to track down, or one more statistic to locate. Her research just seems to go on and on, without her thinking much at all about her deadline.

She usually does not start to write her rough draft until the eleventh hour, which means that she usually writes late into the night. For some reason, she seems to do her best writing at the last minute; indeed, she prides herself on her ability to write under pressure. The only problem with this approach is that she rarely has a chance to revise her essays; her first draft is often her last and final draft. Sometimes, she believes that she could earn higher grades on her essays if she began early enough to write two or three drafts.

One of her major difficulties with writing is that she feels she has to say everything about her topic that she could possibly say. She sometimes struggles to include all of the important facts or all of her great ideas, which can make her rough drafts very long. Her writing also has a tendency to ramble on as she continues to include one more key point or fact.

Once, she began to write an essay and had written six pages before she even finished her introduction. She realized that the essay was getting a bit too long and her time was running out, so she wrote another paragraph and turned it in.

Since she has been in college, she has learned to start a little earlier and allow more time for revision, but she has also learned that she needs to cut excess information, ideas, and data from her first draft. She has begun to accept that she doesn't need to say everything there is to say: There will be other essays to write, and she can save some of her ideas and facts for those essays. Besides, she believes that writing is a continuing dialogue. In a sense, a writing assignment is never finished. She may turn it in but she will continue to revise it (if only in her mind as she thinks about how the essay could have been better), for she believes that it is good to keep rethinking her ideas, changing her decisions, and re-evaluating her assumptions. It is good to be flexible. And, as long as there is life, there are changes and new ideas and new ways to think about old problems.

_____ **The Text of an "Inclusive" Writer**

Writers like Monique have a natural tendency to be thorough. Such writers feel that they must extensively research a topic before beginning to write. Once they begin to write—usually at the last moment—they want to include everything in their essay that is even remotely related to the topic. In the following rough draft, Monique attempts to include everything that she has learned about propaganda:

Monique's Essay

Jacque Ellul believes that propaganda was around as early as WWI. He also says the "the modern techniques of propaganda developed in advertising." As you know today's advertisements play a big role in our society. T.V., radio, billboards, etc. . . . We look listen and observe without even knowing that we're taking in ideas and knowledge. Propaganda can have an innocent but deadly approach.

In the era of Nazism we find a very organized form of propaganda and how it erupted in one man's mind. Hatred for anyone but the perfect person. The person that Adolph Hitler wanted to be. Instead he was one of the majority, a member of the mixed race. He was not the special individual that he thought made up this other pure race. So one man waged a war on an idea that turned into a massacre of innocent people. Yet Hitler never got his hands dirty with blood. He never committed a direct murder. Ellul says, "An organized massacre is seldom ordered by the authorities."

Adolph Hitler did not wake up one day and say lets make up the perfect race and kill everyone else. Nor did the people go out and start a rampage of murders. This system took time and effective planning. A form of hypnosis or even brainwashing over a long period of time. Strong effective brainwashing. (ex. The leader of the Arian race [Blond hair, blue eyes] *Hitler* was not Arian).

In todays society our world has developed with its different forms of technology. Where there used to be a handful of geniuses there are now multitudes of overachievers. Hitler was not a genius or overachiever but had every well thought out plan, determination to bring about what he thought was total Utopia and patience to take his idea from a crawl to a marathon runner.

Propaganda works best when it is not consciously noticed. Advertisements reaches our society in one way or another.

In the opening I used the quote from Ellul's "Modern techniques of propaganda developed in advertising." Here we have hand in hand the destruction of our society if taken in by another 20th century Adolph Hitler.

If you don't think that propaganda is dangerous, then we are all lost. Everyday we listen, look or acknowledge some form of advertising.

Although this rough draft needs to be reworked in many ways, its most glaring weakness is its poor organization. Because Monique includes every available idea or fact that is even remotely related to the topic, the point that she wishes to make (that propaganda is dangerous) is lost amidst a confusing and chaotic list.

If we accept that Monique's thesis is that propaganda is dangerous, what ideas or facts should be cut? Reread the essay and cross out the information that does not seem to belong.

Of the remaining information, what do you feel should be expanded? Reread the essay and write "expand" next to important ideas that need to be developed.

How do you think that the remaining facts and ideas should be reorganized?

_____ **WRITING ASSIGNMENT**

Now that you have read a series of opposing approaches to writing, you will have a chance to write a story about your own writing process. The following steps will help you to collect information for the story of your writing process.

1. Reread each of the stories and decide which of the pair of opposites best describes the way that you prefer to write. Are you an active writer like Victor or a reflective writer like Darrel? Are you a factual writer like

Sean or a theoretical writer like Scott? Are you an objective writer like Mitzie or a personal writer like Maria? Are you a focused writer like Douna or an inclusive writer like Monique? Remember that all of these processes are okay. There are no good or bad processes. There are only processes that work for you or do not work for you.

After you have decided which of each set of opposites best describes how you go about writing, reread that story; circle the points that seem true of your writing process and cross out the points that do not seem true of your writing process.

2. In small groups, talk about the following questions and any other questions that your instructor wishes to add to the list:

What kinds of topics do you like to write on?
What kinds of topics do you find it difficult to write on?
What do you do before you begin to write?
Do you use an outline?
How long do you think about a topic before you begin to write?
How do you organize your ideas or data?
What kind of difficulties do you tend to get into?
What kind of writer's blocks do you experience?
Do you like to write?
What kind of environment do you prefer to write in, that is, at a desk, lying in bed, and so forth?
What kind of writing rituals do you follow: Do you have to sharpen pencils before you begin, listen to music, take a bath, wear a certain kind of clothes, and so on?
What are your rough drafts like?
How many drafts do you like to write?
Do you develop your best ideas when alone or when talking to someone?
Are your ideas clear before you start to write, or do they become clear as you write?
What kind of feedback helps you to revise better?
When you revise your essays, what do you tend to change?
What kind of comments do your writing instructors tend to make about your essays?
When you revise, do you tend to expand or cut your rough draft?
What are your strengths as a writer?
What are your weaknesses as a writer?
How do you think that you need to improve as a writer?
What are some of your best experiences as a writer?
What are some of your worst experiences as a writer?

After you have discussed these questions, write a story that describes your writing process, but do not feel that you have to answer each of the questions above. As you describe your writing process, include comments about how you will write in the future after you have matured as a writer.

Appendix C

Exploring Texts

Four Approaches to Writing Narratives

In this section, you will read and discuss four essays that exemplify how individual differences influence texts. Each of the four essays that follow was written on the same topic. After discussing Tuchman's "History by the Ounce," the students spent an hour in Woodruff Park, Atlanta, carefully taking notes on what they observed. Their professor then asked them to play the role of historians: they had to take the data that they had collected (by witnessing events, interviewing people, and experiencing the environment) and shape this "historical record" into a story or narrative.

Even though the students collected their data at the same place and time, and they had the opportunity to observe the same reality, their essays varied in both form and content. The writers processed their experience and shaped their texts in distinctively different ways.

The four essays presented here will be discussed as being typical of four basic approaches to narrative: the scientific, the theoretical, the mythic, and the phenomenological. Most of the students' essays on this topic, to some degree or another, fell into these four basic categories.

As you read and discuss these four essays, think of which approach to writing narratives is most like your writing.

_____ **The Scientific**

Although the term _science_ covers a wide range of meanings, it is used here in its most common and restricted sense: science as the accurate observation of a concrete reality. As you read Linda's essay, pay attention to how she tries to describe the "things" of the park, the buildings, sidewalks, benches, and so forth, with great precision.

Linda's Essay

Today at 10:30 A.M. on October 20, 1988, I decided to spend about forty-five minutes at the Robert W. Woodruff Park. The temperature is about 62° F, with partly sunny skies and very strong breezy winds.

As I sit down on a bench, I notice immediately how the small park is shaped almost in a figure eight. Around this figure eight there are two different types of lamps. Inside the figure eight there are lamps with circular objects on top, and outside the figure eight there are regular streetlamps; on one of these, a pigeon sits. Speaking of pigeons, two students who are eating food from the local fast food restaurant, Mc-Donalds, are surrounded by hungry pigeons begging for food. I cannot help but laugh along with the other people around me.

Next I admire some more of the scenery within the park. I notice that flowers are still blooming and the trees also seem to have all their leaves, even though it is late in the season. The bushes also seem to be cut evenly to produce some shade, while the sprinkler systems seem to [be] watering them.

As I admire what is going on outside the park. I notice all the buildings surrounding me to my right. I see the "time" sign above the Fulton Federal Bank, which shows me it is now 10:54 A.M. Next to that is the 7 to 7 News stand, Hardees, Blimpie, GNC, The Foot Locker, Kentucky Fried Chicken, and Hardy Shoes Store. To my left I see a Pearl Vision Center, Muses, and the C&S Bank and clock. Straight in front of me I notice a Chick-Fil-A building with a Canadian flag flying above it, a building that looks like a piece of cardboard which is the Georgia Pacific building, the black Equitable building, and the Company of Georgia building with the United States and Georgia flags flying on it.

The streets that surround me are Edgewood, Park Place, and Peachtree Street. Some of the street signs include "One Way," "Do Not Enter," and "Walk" and "Don't Walk," which is right in front of Mc-Donalds. Parked in the street is an ambulance, a police car and a Wells Fargo truck. I can hear sirens and horns off in the distance.

Then to turn my attention back to the people in the park, I notice a crippled man making his way slowly from one end to the other, a few business men, probably going to lunch, and a couple of students out here who appear to be shivering. I also notice a man walking his little child around the park, a policeman sitting on his motorcycle, and a student making conversation with the policeman.

Over to my left, I notice members of a "lower society" gathering on a bench. They appear to be friendly; they are speaking to a child of about 6 years of age, who is not responding. A female friend walks up to the men on the bench, and I cannot help but notice her hair. It appears to be a wig, but I knew for sure it was when her friend had to put it on correctly for her. They all then begin to drink some sort of beverage wrapped up in a paper bag; I am assuming it is alcohol.

Finally it is now 11:14 A.M. and I decide it is about time to head on down to Five Points to watch the construction of Underground Atlanta; then I'll be on my way home.

_____ **Questions**

1. In what ways does Linda attempt to be accurate in her description? What phrases or words indicate that she is concerned about accuracy?

2. Does she spend more words describing "things" or "people"?

3. Does Linda focus on "details" or "ideas"?

4. How would you describe the organization of Linda's essay? Does she in any way use her description of the layout of the park to organize her essay?

5. Do you feel that Linda tells a story? Does she develop a clear narrative?

6. What are your reactions to Linda's essay?

_____ **The Theoretical**

Some writers, like Linda, are more concerned about accurately describing concrete reality; others, like Jeremy, are more interested in developing ideas or theories that will explain what reality is and what it means. As you read Jeremy's essay, pay attention to his efforts to understand and describe "history."

Jeremy's Essay

History, or what we define as history, isn't merely a past occurrence, not simply a set of events that happened in a previous time period. History, rather, is a constant, a continual happening that affects each individual separately and differently. History as a tangible concept, therefore, is how a certain moment in time affected an individual, group or specific object. History encompasses every one and every thing whether sentient comprehension is possible or not. History is 'physical' study, residing in all, affecting all, resulting in some sort of outcome, whether it be grand in scale or minute by comparison. Our assignment is to view the events we encounter from spending an hour in the park. Remember, if the event happens and whether it is retained as a factual happening or not, the event is still history. Whether it be a second, a minute or longer, something that happened in that day's present will be history when that 'happening' is over. Entropy, for instance, is a direct counterplay to history. For example: it, an event, happens, is completed and remembered, then entropy or change is what follows. Thereby giving the individual the ability of hindsight—reflections on the past events.

————a day in the Park————

11:00   The first thing I do is look around, get acquainted with my
surroundings—get a feel for the rythmn of things—then I look. I see
an assortment of street dwellers—history they will remember of themselves, but hardly recountable on a more all-encompassing view. I see
pigeons, the grass—still wet from the sprinklers being on. I look up—
buildings—definitely history that can be related to by a more general
audience, from the people who built them, to the people who owned
or own them, to the employees working in them (the buildings). I see
the flag, another definitive historical landmark that a general audience
can appreciate, whether they be foreign, naturalized, or native. An ambulance races by, everyone stops to look—(the human penchant towards
crises). History to us in the sense that we remember that there was an
ambulance that passed on this day, but even more historically significant to those *in* the ambulance. I see business men and women. I see
students, all this will be history to them, to us. History is a relation
between man, woman—(animal?) and any other sentience able to comprehend the past, in his/her/its memory. History is memory, but memory is not history, the two are often confused leading way to human
interpretation where instead factual documentation is needed.

_____ **Questions**

   1. Does Jeremy emphasize ideas or examples? Does he seem to think
that examples are important? Does he describe the examples in detail?
Does he relate his examples to his ideas?
   2. Compared with Linda's essay, is Jeremy's essay concrete or abstract?
   3. How would you describe the organization of Jeremy's essay? Why
do you feel that he separates the essay into two parts?
   4. Does Jeremy's tell a story? Does his essay have a clear narrative?
   5. What are your reactions to Jeremy's essay?

_____ **The Mythic**

Although myths may carry many symbolic meanings and may serve a
number of cultural functions, they are, at their very core, stories about
people. It is that sense of a myth that is the focus of this approach to
writing history. As you read Robin's essay, pay attention to how she emphasizes the people of the park and how she fashions the random events
that she observed into a story with a beginning, middle, and end.

Robin's Essay

It all started at 10:25 one morning in Robert Woodruff Park. It was
rather cool that morning. Your typical fall day. It was like a picture on a
Thanksgiving greeting card. The Park was rather empty this time of

morning. There were a few people seated at different places in the park, as if they were in their own little worlds. The pigeons were up and about, they walked anxiously about, as if they were expected to do what ever pigeons do. This was to be a morning I would never forget.

As I was observing what was going on in the park, a man walked up to me and started talking to me and the others that were with me. At first I thought he was some homeless person who had nothing better to do but bug us that morning. To my surprise, he was the parks maintenance man. His name was George. George was very interesting. He knew everything about the park, like the sprinkler system, because he turned them on while we were seated near them. George could tell you all about the people who visited the park and the ones who made it home. After all, he has been working there for over 20 years. He told us all about the park, the people that were there that morning, his life and even tried to give us advice on how to live our lives. George was just one of the people I saw that morning. There were many others.

As time went on and it was nearing the lunch hour; more people were passing through and stopping in the park. There were lots of business men, who I noticed wearing the same styled shoe. It must be the in thing to wear for business men. There were homeless seated or sleeping on benches as if the benches were their personal domains, and dared anyone to try and enter. Some people were in the park talking to others, to themselves, reading, eating, or just enjoying being outside. Like the man I saw seated under a tree. He was so happy he was talking to himself. One person I noticed that was not to happy was a man pushing a grocery cart. He pushed the cart into another man and greeted him with profanity, now that was not a gesture of happiness.

As my morning in the park came to an end there was one more thing that I had noticed earlier about the people passing through the park; especially the women, that was more apparent now, sense more people were passing through. They all seemed to look down at the ground, as if they were scared to look up, frightened of what they might see. Things really aren't that bad there. You might find things a bit interesting. Like I did.

When my time had ended in the park, I told my new found friends, George, and the other people, and the park, farewell, and went on my way.

_____ **Questions**

1. Does Robin emphasize people or things?
2. Is Robin's essay concrete or abstract? Do Robin's ideas seem to come before her examples or description of events, or do they seem to develop from her examples or descriptions? How are her ideas different than Jeremy's?

3. How is Robin's essay organized?
4. Does Robin tell a story? Does she create a narrative?
5. What are your reactions to Robin's essay?

_____ **The Phenomenological**

Phenomenology is a school of philosophy that holds, in brief, that we cannot know concrete reality with any certainty; what we can know, however, and what philosophers should investigate, is our reactions to concrete reality. As you read Susan's essay, pay attention to how she emphasizes her reactions to what happened in the park without describing, at least in detail, what actually happened.

Susan's Essay

That day in the park two main ideas kept repeating in my mind. How our lives are so self-centered and our right to individualism. Most of the people that I observed were either too absorbed in themselves to pay attention to their surroundings or they just didn't care what people thought of them.

For example, there was one little old man sitting on a park bench, dressed in his Sunday suit and hat. I doubt that he even noticed us observing him. He was just sitting there enjoying the day and feeding the pigeons. It's amazing how so many of us become so involved in our own lives and become so blind to the simple things in life.

Businessmen walked by several times, they seem to be the worst at ignoring their surroundings. They walked by seemingly unaware of the football game with the pigeons that was going on, the man playing guitar, the window cleaner scaling the building, or the man preaching about the end of the world. Maybe if we took the time to look around at other people or our surroundings our lives wouldn't seem so complicated or troubled.

Individualism, the right to be ourself, but not to become so self-involved that we begin to ignore others. Many of the people I saw were exercising their right to be themself. The man preaching was the most obvious, he wanted to preach, he felt what he had to say was important. He wanted to share his thoughts and beliefs with the public. I find it odd that in a country that professes freedom of speech a man is stopped by an officer of the law for speaking openly.

Another man was simply spending his day with himself absorbed in his own thoughts. He carried on many a conversation and song with himself. I really don't think he cared what anyone thought of him or what he was saying. He was happy doing what he wanted to do regardless of anyone else.

I guess that everyone's perceptions are different but, I don't understand how people can ignore life around them. Those people in the park like the man preaching and the little old man, in a way I envy because they're doing what they want regardless. They don't seem to be as imparied by society's regulations.

_____ **Questions**

1. Is Susan's essay concrete or abstract?
2. How does it differ from Linda's essay? Jeremy's essay? Robin's essay?
3. How is Susan's essay organized? Does she seem to follow an organizational pattern or follow the flow of her thoughts?
4. Does Susan tell a story? Is her essay a narrative?
5. What are your reactions to Susan's essay?

_____ **Synthesis**

1. In small groups, discuss the strengths and weaknesses of each essay. What do you like about each essay? How can each essay be improved? Which approach to writing history is similar to your approach to writing? What do you feel are your strengths and weaknesses as a writer?
2. In small groups, discuss what kind of profession the writer of each of these four essays would be well suited for or excel in. In other words, what kind of professions or disciplines would require people to write like Linda, Jeremy, Robin, and Susan?
3. In small groups, discuss whether one of your rough drafts fits into one of the four categories: the scientific, the theoretical, the mythic, and the phenomenological. What does this tell you about how you need to revise your rough draft?

Gender Differences

In recent years, scholars have devoted more attention to the influence of gender differences on discourse. Although this work is still developing, several researchers agree that

1. The writing of women is more likely to focus on the writer's network of relationships with the people in her environment or in the literary work being analyzed, while the writing of men is more likely to focus on the things of their environment or the topics of the literary work being analyzed.
2. The writing of women is more likely to value cooperation as a means of solving problems, while the writing of men is more likely to value force or violence as a means of solving problems.
3. The writing of women is more likely to empathize with the people that they are writing about, while the writing of men is more likely to remain objective and distant from the people that they are writing about.

4. The writing of women is more likely to establish a close and personal bond with the reader, while the writing of men is more likely to establish an argumentative or agonistic stance in opposition to the reader.

The two essays below, both film reviews of *A Dry White Season*, can be used to explore gender differences as reflected in written texts. In order to get a sense of how the essays differ, you may want to read and reread them. Once you have a sense of how Carole wrote her essay, you will be better able to detect the distinctive features of Nick's text. After you have read Nick's text, you will be better able to detect the distinctive features of Carole's text.

Carole's Essay

The subject of this film is apartheid. It is a powerful and thought provoking depiction of the destruction of two families in South Africa, one white and one black. On one hand, there is Ben de Tout, a history teacher, and his family, happy and secure in their sheltered little world, seemingly unaware of the strife outside. On the other hand, there is Gordon, de Tout's gardener, and his family, struggling to exist amidst the turmoil and violence that make up their world. When incidents occur, which cause these worlds to collide, the results are devastating to both families. First, Gordon's son, Jonathan, is beaten, then killed by the police. Then Gordon is arrested, and mysteriously dies while in police custody. These violent events cause de Tout to open his eyes, and the walls of security to crumble. He begins, despite objections from his wife, to fight against the injustice. He hires a lawyer, played by Marlon Brando, to discover the truth behind Gordon's death, but all that he learns is that justice is truly blind when applied to the black people in South Africa. He continues his fight for justice, but it costs him the love of his wife, the trust of his daughter, and in the end, his life.

The performances in this film were superb. I was especially impressed by Donald Sutherland, his protrayal of Ben de Tout was very moving. I read a quote once by Spencer Tracy. When asked about his acting technique, he said, "The trick is to never let anyone catch you doing it." I never caught Donald Sutherland acting in this film. I could see on his face every emotion that I was feeling inside. He has been a long time favorite of mine in films such as, "M.A.S.H.", "Klute", and "Ordinary People". This is another fine performance to add to the list.

I thought the writing was good, and the characters were well developed. The only flaw, for me, was the reporter, Melanie. The scenes involving this character seemed disjointed, interrupting the natural flow of the story. This character was portrayed by Susan Sarandon, an actress who has starred in some recent box office hits. It seemed as if this character was added, especially for her, in an attempt to attract a larger audience. One area where I liked the development, was the relationship

between de Tout and his son, Johan. As de Tout's beliefs about apartheid changed, he shared his views with his son, never shutting him
out. It was clear that de Tout was determined that his son would not
grow up blind to the truth, as he had been. One thing that did disturb
me about this relationship was the amount of danger de Tout allowed
Johan to be exposed to. At one point in the film the de Tout house was
shot at; at another time a bomb exploded in the garage. I am not a parent, but if I were I would not subject my son to this danger.

As I was leaving the theatre, after seeing this film, I noticed there
was none of the usual discussion going on among the small crowd of
people in attendance. As I walked to my car, a rush of thoughts and
emotions were going through my head. Disbelief that the South African
government can allow these atrocities to happen, a mixture of anger
and sadness at the lives being lost, the children being shot down in the
streets. When I went to see this film I didn't know very much about
apartheid, and as I was leaving I was wishing I still didn't, but this is
an issue that everyone should be made more aware of. I would recom-
mend this film to everyone.

Nick's Essay

This movie harshly attacks South Africa's apartheid system of racial
segregation. But the attack is unlike what is seen in the American media. Instead of black activists being simply imprisoned, as seen in the
media, innocent blacks are killed in this movie. In short this movie presents a much more harsh view of South Africa's apartheid system than
does America's television and print media.

The story begins with a black child being whipped without reason by
the South African police. His father, Gordon, seeking justice for the police brutality seeks one of his white employers, Ben de Tout. While initially, de Tout believes that the boy did something wrong to deserve the
punishment, his opinion changes after the boy's father, Gordon, is
killed by the police. The police claiming that Gordon committed suicide, will not admit to murdering Gordon. Seeking justice, he hires a
famous civil rights barrister (or trial lawyer) named McKinney to try to
prove that Gordon was in fact murdered by the police. The trial begins
with McKinney's main witness, an Indian doctor, being prevented from
coming to the trial. So without any strong evidence to prove the murder, McKinney loses the case. After this the movie continues on a spi-
raling path of destruction; de Tout privately collects evidence proving
that Gordon was murdered, while the police become more and more
suspicious of de Tout's faith in the South African government. An interesting pattern evolves at this point with de Tout and the police becoming more involved in their causes. De Tout fights against apartheid
more actively, while the police fight to stop de Tout's investigation more
actively.

The concept of de Tout becoming more involved in the fight against apartheid is central to the plot of the film. De Tout initially believed the system but slowly becomes more and more enveloped in the fight to stop it. He becomes more and more willing to risk his own well being in order to stop apartheid. It is this involvement that makes the movies exciting, because as de Tout becomes more and more involved, more and more people are killed. The effect on the viewer is to feel much of what the characters feel; the hate and fear of apartheid, the total emotion of the movement, the grief, etc. The movie is successful in presenting the sheer drama of fighting the system, but in other ways the movie is flawed.

While the main plot was well presented, the subplots of the movie were confusing and hard to follow. Too often these subplots were lost or edited out of recognition. While watching the movie, I often had difficulty understanding what was happening in the background, because the subplots were either dropped or introduced too fast. An example of this is demonstrated near the end of the film, when Ben de Tout decides out of thin air to become a decoy for the South African police. He does this without planning or even expecting the circumstances which led up to this event (namely whether or not his daughter told the police where the affidavits for his murder case were hidden). The film seems to be tainted by extreme editing.

My other complaint was with the film's poor cinematography. Put simply, the quality of sound and picture presented in this movie is below par with what is expected of modern times. The sound tract was filled with background noise and was often too soft to hear, and it seemed as if the film was shot with the camera out of focus. The picture would often blur for no apparent reason in the middle of the film.

But even with its flaws, I liked *A Dry White Season*. Even with its annoying subplots and poor cinematography, its emotion makes it a good film to watch.

_____ **Discussion**

1. Make a list of all of the differences that you can detect between Carole's and Nick's essays.

2. Discuss which of these differences seems to be related to gender differences in writing. In other words, which of the distinctive features of Carole's approach are more typical of women's writing? Which of the distinctive features in Nick's approach are more typical of men's writing? As you discuss these issues, you may want to consider that, since we are living in a society that is still, to a large extent, structured around male values, many women may not feel free to write in a way that feels natural to them.

3. The two essays that you read were film reviews. What other kinds of gender differences might you expect to find in other types of writing? For example, what kinds of gender differences might you expect to find in persuasive essays.

4. Do you feel that it is important to discuss such differences so that we can better appreciate them, or do you feel that such discussions lead to the development of counterproductive stereotypes?

5. As our society changes and women have more opportunities, do you feel that these differences will continue to enter into texts, or do you feel that these differences will slowly vanish?

One of the more frequently employed methods of developing academic essays is the incorporation of quotations. The following essay, an interpretation written by Curt of Chris van Wyk's "The Ballot and the Bullet," illustrates how you can incorporate quotations into your essays. As you read this essay, notice the basic pattern of how Curt includes quotations in his text: (1) he prepares the reader for the quotation by giving background information or by suggesting what to look for while reading the quotation, (2) he introduces the quotation by using a phrase such as "she said," (3) he gives the quotation, and (4) he explains or interprets the quotation. This pattern does not need to be followed exactly, but it can provide you with some basic guidelines for the effective use of quotations.

The Ballot and the Bullet

Since the creation of the written word, authors have tried to express their inner-most feelings on paper. Writers have chronicled the hopes and fears of generations of people to show the strife of everyday life. Where these writings could incur the wrath of the government in control, authors have resorted to hiding the true meaning of their work behind sarcasm, double entendre and veiled threats. A good example of this style of writing can be seen in the poem "The Ballot and the Bullet" by Chris van Wyk.

Van Wyk is extremely critical of the white controlled government of South Africa. On the surface this poem seems to be harmless enough. But on closer examination the reader begins to see the subtle way that van Wyk expresses his dissatisfaction with the Afrikaners. The poem is clearly about a black speaker conversing with a white person. Van Wyk sets the tone for the entire poem in the first four lines:

The ballot.
This means voting.
There is this big box.
It has a slot.

The attack is pointed and immediate. To begin his assault van Wyk
takes the tone of an adult speaking to a child. This shows a total lack of
respect to the whites of South Africa. For a black to openly treat a
white this way under apartheid would bring swift retribution. The
simple sentences he uses in explaining the voting process seems to imply that the whites are stupid. These lines could also be an attempt to
tell the whites that they do not use the right to vote often enough and
must therefore be told what is involved in voting.

After the black explains the basic equipment involved in voting, the
white finally begins to understand. Or does he? The black man continues, "*Ja,* like a money box." Van Wyk implies that the ignorant white
man still doesn't comprehend, so the black speaker compares it to an
object that the white man can understand. In South Africa, the whites
constitute a mere 10% of the population and yet they control 95% of the
economy so money and money boxes are objects with which most Afrikaners are familiar.

At this point van Wyk shifts gears and steps up his attack. In doing
so he gets to the crux of apartheid's unfairness:

You're given options.
Do you want a cruel government
or a kind one?
A lazy one
or one that works?

You are given choices. Van Wyk is saying that the whites can choose
but the blacks have no say. *You* can even choose a government that is
cruel and lazy if that is what you desire but at least you have choices.
The black South African has very few freedoms let alone the right to
vote. In the next few lines, the black man reminds the white listener
that he has the right to vote:

You have to make an X
on a square sheet of paper
to decide who is to be
the custodian of the people.

Van Wyk bitterly points out that one of the double indignities of the
apartheid system. The black is not allowed to vote, and then the white,
with a simple X, can decide who will govern the actions of the blacks.
Van Wyk's use of the word "custodian" is interesting because the definition of the word is "guardian or caretaker." These two terms are usu-

ally not associated with a government that tortures and murders its subjects into submission.

Again van Wyk changes his direction by attacking a long standing policy of South Africa: the passbook. The poem continues:

> But first you have to identify yourself.
> This is easy.
> All you need is an I.D.
> This looks like a passbook;
> It has your photo and signature.
> Only difference is
> you can leave it at home
> and not get caught.

The blacks must carry their passbook, which is like a passport, at all times. This book gets them past checkpoints and proves that individual has clearance to be in that area. If a black is caught without a passbook, he or she is arrested and imprisoned. This is the same tactic that was used by the Nazis during World War II to control the movement of citizens.

The closing lines of the poem can be interpreted in two ways:

> That's a ballot.
> Not a bullet.
> *Ag* now, surely you know
> what a bullet is.

Initially, the reader could see this as just another sarcastic statement. But on closer examination the closing line implies a common understanding between the black man and the white man: "Yes, we both know what a bullet is." The shooting of innocent blacks serves as a reminder of just what that bullet is and who controls it. But you can also look at that last line and read it as a veiled threat. Van Wyk seems to be saying, "If you whites don't vote for people that back reform, then we have ways of removing your vote." That way is the bullet.

Chris van Wyk must be an extremely brave person. To openly attack the Afrikaner government the way he does is at best a very dangerous thing to do. But then, he does have one thing working to his advantage. He has the bullet.

_____ **Guidelines for Incorporating Quotations**

1. Use either a comma or a colon to introduce a quotation. Commas are more frequently used after such expressions as "he said," "she explained," "Chris van Wyk writes," and so on.

EXAMPLE: The black man continues, "*Ja*, like a money box."

Colons are more frequently used to introduce offset quotations (those quotations that are indented in the text) and after statements that introduce quotations.

> EXAMPLE: Van Wyk sets the tone for the entire poem in the first four lines:
>> The ballot.
>> This means voting.
>> There is this big box.
>> It has a slot.

2. When you are quoting only one line of poetry or less than about four lines of prose, include the quotation within the text; that is, do not offset the quotation. If you are quoting more than one line of poetry, dialogue, or about four or more lines of prose, then the quotation should be offset, or indented about a half an inch. When you offset a quotation, you do not need quotation marks.

3. When you have a quotation within a quotation, change the double quotation marks to single quotation marks.

> EXAMPLE: In his essay, Curt wrote: "Van Wyk's use of the word custodian is interesting because the definition of the word is 'guardian or caretaker.' "

4. If you need to add a words within a quotation to enable it to make sense, put your words within brackets [ ].

5. Use ellipsis marks (. . .) to indicate that you have left some of the author's words out of the middle of a quotation.

Appendix E

Reading Like an Editor

Editing Techniques

Editing your work to improve clarity, rework sentences, and correct typographical errors, misspelled words, punctuation, and grammar is an important part of the writing process, but it is not a task that need consume all phases of writing. Although mature writers tend to edit a bit at every stage of writing, they tend to delay most of intense editorial work until their writing is almost finished. Thus, they can focus their attention on more important writing tasks—generating ideas, constructing sentences, refining organization—early in their writing process and concentrate on editing toward the end of their writing process.

But even then editing is difficult. By the time writers finish a text, they may find it difficult to shift from generating a text to reading a text. Because they know what they want to say, they may not realize that their text is difficult to understand.

Editing for spelling and grammar is equally difficult. Because language is complex, it is possible to make thousands of errors in a short essay. Writers must check for all of these, which fragments their attention. To compound the problem, writers often have difficulty "seeing" the errors in their own texts. As writers attempt to edit their own texts, they are naturally drawn into the flow of their thoughts. They begin to read as a reader instead of reading as an editor. Reading as a reader means reading quickly to concentrate on the content of the text. Reading as an editor means reading the text over and over again, each time with a different purpose.

For example, an editor may read a text in a slow, relaxed tempo to see if awkward sentences, cumbersome phrases, or errors "pop up." For some reason, particular weaknesses of a text tend to leap into our awareness when we are not consciously looking for them. Then, the editor might read the text aloud to hear what he or she needs to revise.

Editing is, as you can already see, quite different from reading for enjoyment. It is hard work, but it is the kind of hard work that all writers must do. The following techniques will help you to improve your editing skills.

_____ **Suggestions**

1. Read your essay out loud or have someone else read it to you. Listen for sentences that seem to be awkward or phrases that are unclear.

2. Read your essay once in a relaxed state without consciously focusing on finding any errors. Before you begin, breathe in slowly through your nose and exhale slowly through your mouth a few times. This will relax you. Then slowly read your essay to see if any errors "pop up."

3. Read your essay one line at a time. Place a ruler or a sheet of paper under the first line of your essay. Check this line for errors, then move the ruler or sheet of paper down to the next line and check it for errors. This procedure will force you to read more slowly and allow you to check systematically for errors.

4. Ask yourself questions as you proofread, such as these: Is this clear? Is this word spelled correctly? What is the subject of this verb? Do this subject and verb agree? Do I need a comma here? Is this a complete sentence? By asking yourself questions, you will force your mind to concentrate on a specific feature of your text.

5. Read your essay backwards looking for misspelled words.

6. Look for the types of errors that you tend to make. You may want to sit down with your instructor or someone in a writing lab and categorize the types of errors that you tend to make. If you tend to have a problem with subject-verb agreement, possessives, and comma splices, then proofread your text once for each type of error. Read it once looking for subject-verb agreement errors, once for possessive errors, and once for comma splices. Your instructor may also suggest some textual features that can act as "signals" of the types of errors that you tend to make. For example, if you tend to leave the apostrophe off possessives (e.g., "it is Jims car"), then read the text once looking for words that end in "s." When you find a word that ends in "s," ask yourself whether this word is a possessive.

7. Exchange essays with a classmate and edit each other's text. Your instructor may even provide class time for peer editing before you turn in your essay. If so, your instructor will ask you to write "approved by" and sign your name to the essays that you edited. Also, be sure to ask the student who edits your text to explain why he or she made certain changes.

Editing Sentences

In speech, we are more likely to add ideas to the end of the sentence than to construct a sentence that is built from the inside out. For example, the following sentence, although part of a written text, is more typical of speech than writing:

> Merchants also have celebrities and famous people on their commercials to help the product sell because a lot of viewers will purchase the product because their idol was on the commercial and the viewer truly believes they actually use the product they're advertising.

It is quite natural for some writers to produce sentences like this in early drafts, for then they are trying to quickly put words onto paper. If, however, you tend to write sentences like this in an early draft, you should try to isolate them as you edit and then break them up into several sentences as you revise. For example, the sentence above could be improved, if only slightly, by simply dividing it into two sentences:

> Merchants also have celebrities and famous people on their commercials to help the product sell. A lot of viewers will purchase the product because their idol was on the commercial and the viewer truly believes they actually use the product they're advertising.

Although improved, these sentences are still difficult to read, partially because they are too wordy. If the excess words were cut, the sentences would sound even better:

> Merchants also have celebrities on their commercials to sell their products. Many viewers will buy the product because they believe that their idol actually uses it.

We have improved the sentences again, but an essay of sentences like this might make for rather monotonous reading. We can create some variety by switching the order of the clauses in the second sentence:

> Merchants also have celebrities on their commercials to sell their products. If viewers believe that their idol actually uses the product, they will buy it.

These sentences can be further improved if we make better use of the subject and verb positions. Effective sentences usually draw attention to the most important noun of the sentence by placing it in the subject position. Both of these sentences have important nouns ("merchants," "viewers") in the subject positions, but they make poor use of the verb position. The verbs in these sentences ("have," "sell," "believe," "use," and "buy") are generic and nondescript. Notice how the sentence improves once we substitute more descriptive verbs:

> Merchants also hire celebrities to endorse their products. If viewers are convinced that their idol actually trusts the product, they will purchase it.

Thus far, we have been improving these sentences by making them more economical, by cutting words, or by replacing generic words with more descriptive and meaningful words. But sentences can also be effectively revised by adding examples, adjectives, adverbs, or qualifications:

Merchants also hire celebrities, such as Chris Evert, Michael J. Fox, and Bill Cosby, to endorse their products. If naive viewers are convinced that their idol, whom they believe to be beyond fault, actually trusts the product, they will probably purchase it.

Here, we added examples ("Chris Evert, Michael J. Fox, and Bill Cosby"), an adjective ("naive"), a parenthetical element ("whom they believe to be beyond fault"), and a qualification ("probably"). The two sentences, although much improved, are still not clearly connected to each other. As an additional step of revision, we can add a clause to the end of the first sentence that will draw the reader into the second sentence:

Merchants also hire celebrities, such as Chris Evert, Michael J. Fox, and Bill Cosby, to endorse their products, which can be extremely effective. If naive viewers are convinced that their idol, whom they believe to be beyond fault, actually trusts the product, they will probably purchase it.

You will not have to work this hard to revise all of your sentences, nor will you have to go through all these steps in this order. However, what we have just done does illustrate some techniques for editing sentences.

Editing for Clarity

When we speak to each other, what we say and how these statements are interpreted depend to a great extent on context. If I make the statement "It is warm in here" when we are both in a hot room, you might interpret this statement to mean: "It is too hot in here; please open the window." If I make the same statement after coming into the room during sub-zero weather, you might interpret the statement to mean: "It is terribly cold outside, but it is pleasant in here." Because you know the context of the latter statement (that it is below zero out there), you know that the last thing I want you to do is open the window.

When we write, the context of our statements may not always be clear, and so we need to strive to be more specific and provide more context for our reader. The following paragraph, which was written by Bettye, is the introduction from a film review of *Cry Freedom*. As you read the paragraph, think about which of her statements would be clearer if she provided more context:

In this film we are brought face to face with the realism of the South African conflict. Taken from the pages of the actual lives of these brave individuals, *Cry Freedom* reveals both the racial and political injustices of this country. The two main characters are Steven Biko and Donald Woods, whose lives were vividly portrayed by two outstanding actors. This film has the ability to hold one in check, only to release you drained of any trivial or frivolous thought of life's problems.

Bettye's text is unclear in places because she has not provided sufficient context: she refers to "this film" before she even mentions the title and without saying anything about the movie's plot; she mentions the conflict in South Africa without in any way describing it; she mentions the names of the major characters without explaining who they are, or the roles that they play in the South African conflict or in the plot of the movie; and she makes a vague reference to the film's emotional impact in the last sentence without mentioning what caused her to feel "drained" or what she means by feeling "drained."

Below is a revised version of Bettye's introduction. As you read this version, pay attention to how the text now provides more context:

Many of us have seen the violence of South Africa on the evening news. We have seen the white police beat and shoot at the black protesters, many of whom are children, but such scenes cannot provide an accurate picture of the political struggle of blacks to gain equality. Too much of their struggle takes place behind closed doors. In *Cry Freedom*, a film produced and directed by Richard Attenborough, we learn about the violence that cannot be recorded by television cameras. The film presents the story of Steve Biko, one of the great martyrs of the South African protest movement, who was beaten to death while in police custody, and Donald Woods, a white reporter who investigated Biko's mysterious death. As we follow Biko's story from his resistance to the oppression of his people to the disclosure of the events of his tragic death, we are left feeling drained: we feel both angry about the mistreatment of blacks in South Africa and frustrated that we cannot do more to stop it.

In what ways does the revised paragraph provide the reader with more context? How does the addition of more specific context help to clarify what the author is trying to say?

Editing for Formality

One of the ways that writing is limited is that it does not always allow us to transcribe the sound of our voice (and all of the meaning that it conveys) onto the page. Writers will often compensate for this limitation by adding some visual clues to indicate how they would like to have their text read. Some of these clues are

1. Underlining or capitalizing words or phrases to indicate emphasis.
2. Repeating words or phrases for emphasis.
3. Putting words or phrases within quotation marks to indicate an ironic tone.
4. Using dashes to indicate a dramatic pause.
5. Using exclamation points to indicate excitement.

These visual clues, which can infuse a sense of the writer's voice into the written text, are usually considered acceptable for some types of writing (such as personal narratives), but other characteristics of oral language are less appropriate for academic writing:

1. Using "well," "so," or "then" excessively.
2. Using too many intensifiers, especially "really" (as in a "really good time") and "pretty" (as in "pretty big").
3. Using slang, for example, using "cop" for "police officer."
4. Using parentheses to add extra information, for example, "he was a police officer (very big and tall)." The information "very big and tall" is added almost as an afterthought. It is more appropriate in writing to revise your sentences so that such afterthoughts are incorporated into the basic structure of the sentence, for example, "he was a tall and muscular police officer."
5. Leaving "that" out of sentences—for example, "this is a song I know" instead of "this is a song that I know."
6. Using general, vague words—for example, "something," "this," "someone," "get," and "put."
7. Using abbreviations.

As you read the following essay (a description of a ritual), pay attention to the characteristics of oral language that are present in it:

There are many types of initiations in our society. Bar mitzvahs, weddings, club initiations, funerals, and Baptisms are some examples. The one most people can relate to is club initiations. Many clubs have simple though embarrassing initiations such as running butt naked down a street, panty raids, dancing with the ugliest girl in the house (house meaning party). But few college students have been initiated into a club the way I was.

I was sixteen, and some friends and I wanted to join the biggest, coolest club there was. So I asked a friend who was in this club what we had to do to get in. He told us in order to get in you had to commit a crime such as robbing a store, car theft, or selling drugs. Then after you did this, you had to be initiated. So my friends and I stole a car. The initiation was pretty wild and stupid and could be called a riot by police because this club was big. Unfortunately my initiation was rough. First I had to punch a policeman and get away without getting caught & I had to beat up someone to prove I was a man. After I accomplished this, I was a member but now it was time to be initiated.

What I had to do was pick a "profession" (really a crime) out of several choices; car theft, robbery, drug trafficking, and marksman or ghostman.[1] I chose car theft. I was put in a group away from other members of the club and was taught how to steal open door cars (a common mistake among people). We then were taught how to steal a certain make car, the Volkswagen. Only a few people were Volkswagen specialists, and I was one. After learning the tricks of the trade, we became watchdogs for our comrades, making sure they were not busted or hurt. We then rejoined the rest of the club and became a unit.

While reading "The Growth and Initiation of an Arapesh Boy," a forgotten path had come back to haunt me. The way the article explains an initiation ritual was to an Arapesh boy I saw how it related to my initiation.

Like them I too was separated from the club because I was fresh meat, new, unclean. And I too learned secret knowledge that I share with no one now. I was not ground down but restructured and showed that what I already knew was a sure way to get caught. And upon completing the task of learning, I was allowed to return to be a part of the club and be a club member.

Although I have gotten older and joined many better and more productive clubs, they all have the basic initiation ritual. Like the ones in the article, I don't believe that the rituals are wrong, but they do show that initiations have not changed much in all these years. Most fraternities and sororities have these rituals in their initiations, and they do not harm or distract from a person's morals. Instead it shows a person how to lead a more productive life, how to help others in the club. Initiation rituals will always be a part of life, for all men and women young and old. This is the way most people are accepted in society. They need to belong to a group or club. Without it life would be dull.

[1] A marksman or ghostman is the expert with a gun or rifle. He often is unseen when a drug deal takes place. That is why he is a ghostman.

Given the topic of the essay, how formal do you feel that this writer should attempt to make his essay? Should it be extremely formal? Somewhat informal? Or extremely informal?

In what ways could this essay be revised and edited to add a sense of voice to the text? In other words, in what ways could the text be edited to add a sense of how the essay should be read aloud?

In what ways is the essay too informal? How should it be revised and edited to make it more formal?

Editing for Punctuation

The six punctuation rules explained here will serve as starting points for your mastery of punctuation, for they can guide you through most of the decisions that you have to make about punctuation. If you are trying to punctuate an unusually complex sentence, you may need to consult a grammar handbook.

1. Place a comma before *and, but, or, nor, for, yet,* or *so* (coordinating conjunctions) when they join two complete sentences (or independent clauses).

commas. If you have trouble deciding whether or not a clause is "added information," use your pencil to cross it out. If the sentence still makes sense, then the clause probably needs to be separated with a pair of commas.

Editing for Agreement

Agreement is a grammatical term that refers to both the agreement between subjects and verbs and the agreement between pronouns and the nouns that they modify (their antecedents).

When you have a singular subject, you must have a singular verb (for example, *he wins, she fights, I am,* etc.). When you have a plural subject, you must have a plural verb (for example, *they win, they fight, they are,* etc.).

The same basic principle holds true for pronouns and their antecedents. When you have a singular antecedent, you must have a singular pronoun (for example, "If John goes to the store, he will buy some food.") When you have a plural antecedent, you must have a plural pronoun (for example, "The women felt that they were well prepared for the examination.")

There are, however, a few special situations that will require your attention as you proofread:

1. If two or more nouns are joined with *and*, use a plural verb and pronoun.

> EXAMPLES: John and Bill write almost every day.
>
> Susan and Martha talk about their topic before they begin to write.

2. If two or more nouns are joined with *or*, make any verbs or pronouns agree with the closest noun.

> EXAMPLES: Either the two men or Susan is writing on that topic.
>
> Neither the two men nor Susan will read her essay aloud.

3. When *here* and *there* is the subject of a sentence, its verb will agree with the noun that follows it.

> EXAMPLES: Here are your writing assignments.
>
> There is only one writing assignment for this week.

4. *Who, which,* and *that* (relative pronouns) can be either singular or plural. If they modify a singular noun, they are singular. If they modify a plural noun, they are plural.

> EXAMPLES: John and Nancy, who are excellent writers, offer each other advice.
>
> John, who is an excellent writer, prefers to work alone.

5. *Anyone, anybody, anything, something, somebody, everyone, everybody, everything, nobody,* and *nothing* are singular.

EXAMPLES: Everyone is going to write on the same topic.

Everyone has finished his or her first draft.

PROOFREADING TIP FOR SUBJECT-VERB AGREEMENT: If you tend to make errors of subject-verb agreement, you should proofread your essay searching for verbs. When you find a verb, locate the subject. Then ask yourself whether the subject and verb agree.

PROOFREADING TIP FOR AGREEMENT BETWEEN PRONOUNS AND ANTECEDENTS: If you tend to make errors of pronoun agreement, you should proofread your essay searching for pronouns. When you find a pronoun, locate its antecedent. Then ask yourself whether the pronoun and its antecedent agree.

Index

"Abortion, The" (Walker), 328
"Ann" (Haley), 182
Anxious Pleasures (Gregor), 60
"Aphorisms Concerning the Interpretation of Nature and the Kingdom of Man" (Bacon), 95
Approaches to the Poem (Ong), 283
Archetypes and the Collective Unconscious, The (Jung), 130
Aristotle
  Physics, 94
  Poetics, 318, 319
  The Rhetoric of Aristotle, 229
Aristotle and His Philosophy (Edel), 325
Aristotle's Theory of Poetry and Fine Art (Gassner), 324
Augustine, Saint
  On Christian Doctrine, 231

Bacon, Francis
  De Dignitate et Augmentis Scientiarum, 104
  Novum Organum, 94
Bakhtin, M. M.
  The Dialogic Imagination, 337
"Ballot and the Bullet, The" (van Wyk), 348
Bandler, Richard
  Patterns of the Hypnotic Techniques of Milton H. Erickson, M.D., 186
  The Structure of Magic II, 217
Bearer, 343
Belenky, Mary Field
  Women's Ways of Knowing: The Development of Self, Voice, and Mind, 153

Benedict, Ruth
  The Chrysanthemum and the Sword, 394
  Patterns of Culture, 21, 438
"Body Is a Country of Joy and of Pain, The" (Skinner), 355
Book of Rings, A (Musashi), 390
Borom, Bettye J.
  "Literacy within My Family," 11
Breuer, Josef
  Five Lectures on Psycho-Analysis, 158–159
  Studies on Hysteria, 19
Brown, J. A. C.
  Techniques of Persuasion: From Propaganda to Brainwashing, 263
Bunn, D.
  From South Africa, 339
Burckhardt, Jacob
  Reflections on History, 361
Burke, Kenneth
  A Grammar of Motives, 336
  Permanence and Change, 199
  Rhetoric of Motives, 186

"Case of Anna O., The" (Gay), 159
Cassirer, Ernst
  The Myth of the State, 264
Chagnon, Napoleon A.
  Yąnomamö: The Fierce People, 24, 32
Childhood and Society (Erikson), 263
Chrysanthemum and the Sword, The (Benedict), 394
Classical Rhetoric and Its Christian and Secular Tradition from Ancient to Modern Times (Kennedy), 220, 227

Coetzee, J. M.
Dusklands, 265
Colakovic, Nick
"Is Literacy a Tool of Learning for
Everyone or a Tool of Domination
by the Powerful?" 11
Combs, James E.
*Subliminal Politics: Myths and Myth-
making in America,* 240
*Comparative Studies in Society and His-
tory* (Ingham)
"Human Sacrifice at Tenochtitlán,"
22
*Conversations with Milton J. Erickson,
M.D.* (Haley), 186
Copleston, Frederick
A History of Philosophy, 105
Corrigan, Robert W.
Theater in Search of a Fix, 326
"Cowardice" (Kunene), 354
Crania Americana (Morton), 110
Criticism and Social Change (Lentric-
chia), 358

"Dark Dreams About the White Man"
(Gregor), 53
Davis, Philip J.
The Rhetoric of Human Sciences, 126
Davy, Humphry
Elements of Chemical Philosophy, 87
De Dignitate et Augmentis Scientiarum
(Bacon), 104
de Kok, Ingrid
"Small Passing," 349
Dialogic Imagination, The (Bakhtin), 337
"Doing Fieldwork Among the
Yąnomamö" (Chagnon), 22, 24, 32
Dramas, Fields, and Metaphors (Turner),
51
Dusklands (Coetzee), 265

*Economic and Philosophical Manuscripts
of 1844* (Engels), 254
Edel, Abraham
Aristotle and His Philosophy, 325
Edel, Leon
Literary Biography, 166
Elements of Chemical Philosophy (Davy),
87
Ellis, Albert
Reason and Emotion in Psychotherapy,
188
Ellul, Jacques
"The Technological Society," 264, 273

Elms, Alan C.
Social Psychology and Social Relevance,
239
Engels, Friedrich
*Economic and Philosophical Manuscripts
of 1844,* 254
Erikson, Erik H.
Childhood and Society, 263
Euripides
Medea, 285
Euripides and His Age (Murray), 316
Evans, H. W.
"Where Do We Go From Here?"
431
"Exit Visa" (Nortje), 351

Family Myths: Psychotherapy Implications
(Wamboldt and Wolin), 199
"Feminism and Science" (Keller), 106
Feyerabend, Paul
Against Method, 421
" 'Fictio,' or the Purposes of Historical
Statements" (Lukacs), 417
Five Lectures on Psycho-Analysis
(Breuer), 158–159
For a woman whose baby died still-
born, and who was told by a
man, 349
Foucault, Michel
Madness and Civilization, 157
Francis Bacon: A Selection of His Works
(Bacon)
"Aphorisms Concerning the Inter-
pretation of Nature and the King-
dom of Man," 95
Frazer, Sir James George
The Golden Bough, 16
Freud: A Life for Our Times (Gay)
"The Case of Anna O.," 159
Freud, Sigmund
"The Case of Anna O.," 159
*Introductory Lectures on Psychoanaly-
sis,* 168
On the Aphasias, 14
*Some Elementary Lessons in Psycho-
Analysis,* 178
Studies on Hysteria, 17, 159, 164, 166,
168
From South Africa (Bunn and Taylor)
"The Ballot and the Bullet," 348
"The Body Is a Country of Joy and
of Pain," 355
"Cowardice," 354
"Exit Visa," 351

"*Kodwa Nkosana . . .* (And Yet Master)," 348
"Small Passing," 349
"Steve Biko's Anthem," 353
"The Tyrant," 354
"To Whom It May Concern," 343

Gassner, John
Aristotle's Theory of Poetry and Fine Art, 324
Gay, Peter
Freud: A Life for Our Time, 158, 177, 179
Geertz, Clifford
The Interpretation of Culture, 32, 283
Gilligan, Carol
In a Different Voice, 154
Giving Up the Gun (Perrin), 375, 379
Golden Bough, The (Frazer), 16
Goodfield, June
"An Imagined World," 154
Gorgias (Plato), 220, 221, 229
Gould, Stephen Jay
The Mismeasure of Man, 107
Grammar of Motives, A (Burke), 336
Greek Way, The (Hamilton), 317
Gregor, Thomas
Anxious Pleasures, 60
"Dark Dreams About the White Man," 53
Grinder, John
Patterns of the Hypnotic Techniques of Milton H. Erickson, M.D., 186
The Structure of Magic II, 217
"Growth and Initiation of an Arapesh Boy, The" (Mead), 38
Growth through Reason (Ellis)
"Martha," 189

Haley, Jay
Conversations with Milton J. Erickson, M.D., 186
Uncommon Therapy, 181
Hamilton, Edith
The Greek Way, 317
Hersch, Reuben
The Rhetoric of Human Sciences, 126
Hesiod
Theogomy, 136
Hidden Persuaders, The (Packard), 231
Historical Consciousness (Lukacs)
" 'Fictio,' or the Purposes of Historical Statements," 417

"History by the Ounce" (Tuchman), 364
History of Philosophy, A (Copleston), 105
Hitler, Adolf
Mein Kampf, 255
Hobson, John
"The Social and Economic Context of Advertising," 242
How to Lie with Statistics (Huff), 127
Huff, Darrell
How to Lie with Statistics, 127
"Human Sacrifice at Tenochtitlán" (Ingham), 22

If this was a dream, then it was dreamed each week, 355
"Imagined World, An" (Goodfield), 154
In a Different Voice (Gilligan), 154
In Search of Our Mother's Gardens (Walker), 327, 337
Interpretation of Culture, The (Geertz), 32, 283
"Thick Description," 32
Introductory Lectures on Psychoanalysis (Freud), 168
I overcame her who was my enemy, 354
"Is Literacy a Tool of Learning for Everyone or a Tool of Domination by the Powerful?" (Colakovic), 11
Isocrates
"Nicoles or the Cyrians," 230

Jacques Lacan: The Death of an Intellectual Hero (Schneiderman), 167
Journal of Learning Behavior, 423
Jung, Carl
The Archetypes and the Collective Unconscious, 130

"Katharina" (Freud and Breuer), 19
Keller, Evelyn Fox, 137
"Feminism and Science," 106
Reflections on Gender and Science, 138
Kennedy, George A.
Classical Rhetoric and Its Christian and Secular Tradition from Ancient to Modern Times, 220, 227
Knox, Bernard
Word and Action: Essays on the Ancient Theater, 318

"*Kodwa Nkosana* . . . (And Yet, Master)" (Mazibuko), 348

Kunene, Mazisi
"Cowardice," 354
"Steve Biko's Anthem," 353
"The Tyrant," 354
Zulu Poems, 358

Langer, Susanne K.
Philosophy in a New Key, 219
Lentricchia, Frank
Criticism and Social Change, 358
Lévi-Strauss, Claude
Myth and Meaning, 9
Structural Anthropology, 131
Tristes Tropiques, 1, 2, 9
Levy-Bruhl, Lucien
The Notebooks on Primitive Mentalities, 436
"Literacy Within My Family" (Borom), 11
Literary Biography (Edel), 166
Lives of a Cell, The (Lewis), 131, 136
"Some Biomythology," 131
Lukacs, John
Historical Consciousness, 416
Lyotard, Jean-François
The Postmodern Condition: A Report on Knowledge, 91

McCloskey, Donald N.
The Rhetoric of Economics, 155
Madness and Civilization (Foucault), 157
Mahony, Patrick J.
On Defining Freud's Discourse, 178
"Martha" (Ellis), 189
Mazibuko, M. T.
"*Kodwa Nkosana* . . . (And Yet, Master)," 348
Mead, Margaret
Sex and Temperament in Three Primitive Societies, 3
Medea (Euripides), 285
Mein Kampf (Hitler)
"War Propaganda," 255
"Men and Women" (Shostak) 71
Mismeasure of Man, The (Gould)
"Samuel George Morton—Empiricist of Polygeny," 108
Morton, Samuel George
Crania Americana, 110
Murphy, James J.
A Synoptic History of Classical Rhetoric, 428

Murray, Gilbert
Euripides and His Age, 316
Musashi, Miyamoto
A Book of Rings, 390
Myth and Meaning (Lévi-Strauss), 9
Myth of the State, The (Cassirer), 264

Native American Legends, 61
"Nicoles or the Cyrians" (Isocrates), 230
Nimmo, Dan
Subliminal Politics: Myths and Mythmaking in America, 240
Nisa: The Life and Words of a !Kung Woman (Shostak), 63
"Men and Women," 71
"Women and Men," 63
Nortje, Arthur
"Exit Visa," 351
Notebooks on Primitive Mentalities, The (Levy-Bruhl)
"True Myth Histories, In What Sense?" 436
Novum Organum (Bacon), 94

Objective Knowledge: An Evolutionary Approach (Popper), 88
"The Origin of Science," 89
On Christian Doctrine (Saint Augustine), 231
On Defining Freud's Discourse (Mahony), 178
Ong, Walter J.
Approaches to the Poem, 283
On Literacy (Pattison), 9
On the Aphasias (Freud), 14
"Origin of Science, The" (Popper), 89
Oxford Readings in Greek Tragedy (Schlesinger), 317

"Pacific Seacoast Indians, The" (Benedict), 438
Packard, Vance
The Hidden Persuaders, 231
"Patterns of Communication" (Satir), 202
Patterns of Culture (Benedict), 21
"The Pacific Seacoast Indians," 438
Patterns of the Hypnotic Techniques of Milton H. Erickson, M.D. (Bandler and Grinder), 186
Pattison, Robert
On Literacy, 9

Peoplemaking (Satir)
  "Patterns of Communication," 202
Permanence and Change (Burke), 199
Perrin, Noel
  Giving Up the Gun, 375, 379
Philosophy in a New Key (Langer), 219
Physics (Aristotle), 94
Plato
  Gorgias, 220, 221, 229
Poetics (Aristotle), 318, 319
Popper, Karl
  *Objective Knowledge: An Evolutionary
    Approach*, 88
*Postmodern Condition: A Report on
    Knowledge, The* (Lyotard), 91
Practicing History (Tuchman)
  "History by the Ounce," 364
Primal Myths: Creating the World
    (Sproul), 92

Race, Language, and Culture (Boas)
  "The Writing Lesson," 2
Reason and Emotion in Psychotherapy
    (Ellis), 188
Reflections on Gender and Science
    (Keller), 138
  "A World of Difference," 138
Reflections on History (Burckhardt), 361
Rhetoric of Aristotle, The (Aristotle), 229
Rhetoric of Economics, The (McCloskey),
    155
Rhetoric of Human Sciences, The (Davis),
    126
Rhetoric of Motives (Burke), 186

"Samuel George Morton—Empiricist
    of Polygeny" (Gould) 108
Satir, Virginia
  Peoplemaking, 201
Schlesinger, Eilhard
  Oxford Readings in Greek Tragedy,
    317
Schneiderman, Stuart
  *Jacques Lacan: The Death of an Intellec-
    tual Hero*, 167
Sempamla, Sipho
  "To Whom It May Concern," 343
*Sex and Temperament in Three Primitive
    Societies* (Mead), 36
  "The Growth and Initiation of an
    Arapesh Boy," 38
Shostak, Marjorie
  *Nisa: The Life and Words of a !Kung
    Woman*, 63

Skinner, Douglas Reid
  "The Body Is a Country of Joy and
    of Pain," 355
"Small Passing" (de Kok), 349
"Social and Economic Context of Ad-
    vertising, The" (Hobson), 242
Social Psychology and Social Relevance
    (Elms), 239
"Some Biomythology" (Lewis), 131
*Some Elementary Lessons in Psycho-
    Analysis* (Freud), 178
"Sophists, The" (Murphy), 428
Sproul, Barbara C.
  Primal Myths: Creating the World, 92
"Steve Biko's Anthem" (Kunene), 353
Structural Anthropology (Lévi-Strauss),
    131
Structure of Magic II, The (Grinder and
    Bandler), 217
Studies on Hysteria (Freud and Breuer)
  "Katharina," 19
Study of History, A (Toynbee), 407
*Subliminal Politics: Myths and Myth-
    making in America* (Nimmo and
    Combs), 240
Synoptic History of Classical Rhetoric, A
    (Murphy)
  "The Sophists," 428

Taylor, Jane
  From South Africa, 339
*Teaching Seminar with Milton H. Erick-
    son, A* (Zeig), 187
*Techniques of Persuasion: From Propa-
    ganda to Brainwashing* (Brown), 263
"Technological Society, The" (Ellul),
    264, 273
Theater in Search of a Fix (Corrigan),
    326
The ballot, 348
Theogomy (Hesiod), 136
Theory and Practice of History, The (von
    Ranke), 361
There were evils in the road, 351
"Thick Description" (Geertz), 32
Thomas, Lewis
  The Lives of a Cell, 131, 136
Thompson, William Irwin
  The Time Falling Bodies Take to Light,
    135
Through uncertainty the tyrant im-
    poses his power, 354
Time Falling Bodies Take to Light, The
    (Thompson), 135

"To Whom It May Concern" (Sem-
    pamla), 343
Toynbee, Arnold J.
    A Study of History, 407
Tristes Tropiques (Lévi-Strauss), 1
*Tropics of Discourse: Essays in Cultural
    Criticism* (White), 374
"True Myth Histories, In What
    Sense?" (Levy-Bruhl), 436
Tsunetomo, Yamamoto
    Hagakwe: The Book of the Samurai, 394
Tuchman, Barbara W.
    Practicing History, 362
Turner, Victor
    Dramas, Fields, and Metaphors, 51
"Tyrant, The" (Kunene), 354

Uncommon Therapy (Haley)
    "Ann," 182

van Wyk, Chris
    "The Ballot and the Bullet," 348
von Ranke, Leopold
    The Theory and Practice of History, 361

Walker, Alice
    In Search of Our Mother's Gardens,
    327, 337
Wamboldt, Frederick A.
    *Family Myths: Psychotherapy Implica-
    tions*, 199

"War Propaganda" (Hitler), 255
"Where Do We Go From Here?"
    (Evans), 431
Whether the season be dry or wet or
    cold, 348
White, Hayden
    *Tropics of Discourse: Essays in Cultural
    Criticism*, 374
Wolin, Steven J.
    *Family Myths: Psychotherapy Implica-
    tions*, 199
"Women and Men" (Shostak) 63
*Women's Ways of Knowing: The Develop-
    ment of Self, Voice, and Mind* (Be-
    lenky), 153
*Word and Action: Essays on the Ancient
    Theater* (Knox), 318
"World of Difference, A" (Keller), 138
"Writing Lesson, The" (Boas), 2

Yąnomamö: The Fierce People (Chagnon),
    24, 32
    "Doing Fieldwork Among the
    Yąnomamö," 22, 24, 32
You Can't Keep a Good Woman Down
    (Walker)
    "The Abortion," 328

Zeig, Jeffrey K.
    *A Teaching Seminar with Milton H.
    Erickson*, 187
Zulu Poems (Kunene), 358